THE COOK'S SCRAPBOOK

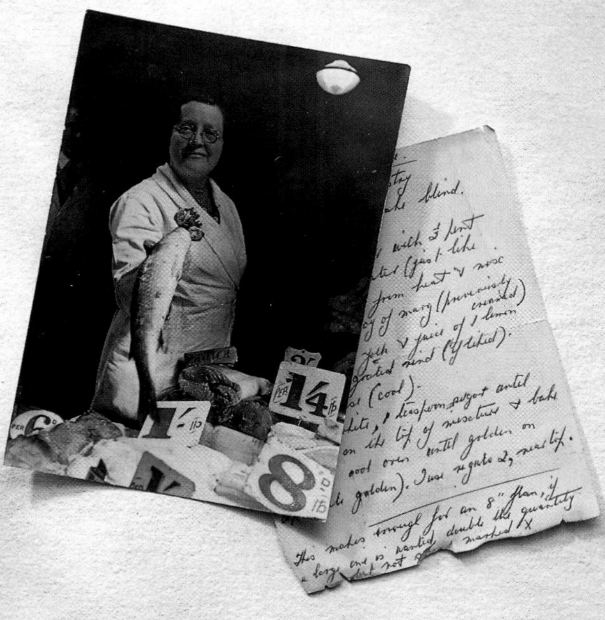

Spare ribs
Temperature : E. 400F, Gas No. 6
Number of portions : 4
Cuts to use : Spare ribs cut in fairly thick chops.
Ingredients : 4 thick chops
½ oz. butter or oil
1 small onion
1 stalk celery
1 level Tbs. brown sugar
2 level tsp. dry mustard
1 level tsp. paprika pepper
2 tsp. tomato paste
2 tsp. Worcester sauce
1 Tbs. Worcester sauce
¼ pt. water, 2 Tbs. lemon
1 Tbs. Vinegar
Preparation : Peel and chop the onion. Wash and chop celery. Squeeze lemon juice. Mix sugar, mustard, salt and pepper with tomato paste and the liquids.
butter or oil with
ingredients and pour over
and continue baking for
Welsh Rabbit—1
This should not be the thick cheese sauce which is generally spread on pieces of toast and then browned under the grill. This is the right way to make it.
Melt half an ounce of butter in a saucepan, add a quarter of a pound of grated cheese and stir until it is melted; then add gradually two tablespoonfuls of milk or beer (in this case beer is definitely best), a teaspoonful of made mustard (or more or less) and a seasoning of salt and pepper. When well mixed, pour over pieces of Buttered toast, and serve at once, handing cayenne pepper.
STORK MARGARINE
COOKERY NOTES
SPONGE and FANCY CA
ICED GINGERBREAD
4 ozs Flour
4 " Sugar
4 " Butter
2 Eggs
Cream Butter & Sugar
Add Eggs
Then Flour
Bake
CREAM.
Cream together 2 ozs. Margarine
2 Dessertspoons Sugar.
Add 1 " Milk
Then stir in a few drops vanilla es
2 Dessertspoons Dried
and whip all well toget
CHARLBURY FETE. 10.

READER'S DIGEST

THE COOK'S SCRAPBOOK

Published by The Reader's Digest Association Limited
LONDON · NEW YORK · SYDNEY · CAPE TOWN · MONTREAL

EDITOR
John Palmer

ART EDITOR
Neal Martin

CONTRIBUTORS

CONSULTANT EDITOR
Pat Albury

RECIPE RESEARCHERS AND TESTERS
Pat Albury Valerie Barrett
Jackie Burrow Maxine Clark
Petra Jackson Angela Kingsbury
Neal Martin John Palmer
Brenda Ratcliffe Jennie Reekie
Jeni Wright

PHOTOGRAPHERS
Martin Brigdale
Laurie Evans
Pia Tryde
Peter Williams

HOME ECONOMISTS
Maxine Clark
Jane Suthering
Carla Tomasi
Berit Vinegrad

STYLISTS
Róisin Neild
Georgina Rhodes
Lesley Richardson
Helen Trent

CALLIGRAPHY
Kate Ridyard

HAND LETTERING
Carol Kemp

DRAWINGS
Rodney Shackell

The publishers would also like to thank the following for their contributions to the book:

Heinrich Boreniok, Executive Chef de Cuisine at the Naval and Military Club (The In and Out), London, for his creation of the Dinner for Two menu.
The Buckden Wine and Beermakers group and its chairman Tony Malvaney for the invaluable help with the chapters Good Cheer and Foods from the Wild.

THE COOK'S SCRAPBOOK
was edited and designed by
The Reader's Digest Association
Limited, London.

First Edition

Printed in Italy

ISBN 0 276 42188 4

The typefaces used in this book are
Caslon Regular and Copperplate.

Contents

Sometimes it is good to return to old cookery values, to meals of deceptive simplicity that depend on skills handed down and good, old-fashioned ingredients. This is the kind of cookery you make time for, the kind that is a joy to create and a shared pleasure to serve.

As **The Cook's Scrapbook** grew, so too did the surprise and delight that so many great recipes remained to be culled from notes and snippings treasured down the years. There was *Bara Brith* and *Onion Cake* from Wales, *Collops* and creamy *Whim Wham* from Scotland, as well as *Wensleydale Soup, Yorkshire Tea Cakes,* an authentic *Irish Stew* and a *Tipsy Trifle* from Kent. There was even a *Cherry Ratafia* that the Victorians loved, and an entire Edwardian breakfast. Altogether there were more than 400 recipes that, gathered together, became a delightful glimpse of the past and an excitingly new cook book for today. It has about it something of the flavour that Alice found in the 'Drink Me' bottle in Wonderland—a flavour reminiscent of 'cherry tart, custard, pineapple, roast turkey, toffee and hot buttered toast' all at once.

Soups and Broths

The Dairy

Vegetables and Salads

Sea and River

Meat

Poultry and Game

Puddings and Desserts

Special Occasions

Afternoon Tea

Good Cheer

Jams, Pickles and Preserves

Foods from the Wild

Techniques and Skills

Foods in Season

Features

Index and Acknowledgments

Soups and Broths

As swallows gather and the first touch of autumn gilds the air and the landscape, the thoughts of British cooks turn towards soups. Many of these evolved out of the warming, one-pot meals of our ancestors: *Cock-a-Leekie, Cornish Fish, Cullen Skink*, that made use of whatever meat, vegetables or fish were to hand. Others, like *Rabbit and Sorrel* and *Grouse and Juniper*, profit from the richness of autumnal game, while *Garden Soup* celebrates the joys of the late vegetable crop.

Crumbled cheese, walnuts and sliced spring onion tops make a colourful and tasty garnish.

Wensleydale Soup

Potatoes give body to this Yorkshire soup, while the flavours of the onions and cider blend perfectly with the Wensleydale cheese

INGREDIENTS

8 SPRING ONIONS, TRIMMED AND WASHED
60 G (2 OZ) BUTTER
225 G (8 OZ) POTATOES, PEELED AND DICED
850 ML (1½ PINTS) CHICKEN OR VEGETABLE STOCK (SEE PP.433, 434)
175 G (6 OZ) WENSLEYDALE CHEESE, CRUMBLED
200 ML (7 FL OZ) MEDIUM-DRY CIDER
½ LEVEL TEASPOON SALT
FRESHLY GROUND BLACK PEPPER
30 G (1 OZ) WALNUTS, CHOPPED
PREPARATION TIME: 20 MINUTES
COOKING TIME: 30 MINUTES
SERVES FOUR

CUT off and reserve the green tops from four of the spring onions, then roughly chop the remainder. Melt the butter in a saucepan and sauté the chopped spring onions until just beginning to soften. Add the potatoes and stock and bring to the boil. Reduce the heat, cover and simmer for 15–20 minutes or until the potatoes are cooked.

Stir two-thirds of the cheese into the soup, remove from the heat, cool for 5 minutes, then blend in a food processor or blender until the soup is just puréed.

Return the soup to the saucepan and stir in the cider. Add salt and pepper to taste, cover and simmer for 10 minutes, stirring occasionally.

Finely slice the reserved spring onion tops. Pour the soup into heated soup bowls and scatter the sliced spring onion tops, walnuts and the remaining crumbled cheese on the surface—if liked, with the sliced spring onion tops in a circle around the cheese and walnuts. Serve the soup accompanied by wedges of warm granary bread.

Tomato Soup

This simple concoction of 'love apples', as tomatoes were known, has a cheerful flavour that matches its sunny, terracotta colour

Melt the butter in a large saucepan, add the bacon, onion, carrot and celery and sauté over a low heat for 5 minutes without browning. Add the fresh tomatoes, tinned tomatoes with their juice and the stock and bring to the boil, stirring occasionally.

Put the mace, herbs, celery seeds and peppercorns in the centre of a small square of muslin, tie the opposite corners together to enclose the spices, then add to the soup. Reduce the heat, cover and simmer gently for about an hour or until the vegetables are soft.

Remove the bag of spices and pass the soup through a nylon sieve into a bowl. Alternatively, first cool the soup, then purée it in a food processor or liquidiser before passing it through a sieve into a clean saucepan.

Just before serving, reheat the soup and pour it into a warmed tureen or bowls. Swirl in the cream and garnish with the sprigs of rosemary.

Sprigs of rosemary add the lightest of herbal touches to this splendid soup.

INGREDIENTS

- 30G (1 OZ) BUTTER
- 2 RASHERS STREAKY BACON, RINDS REMOVED, CHOPPED
- 1 LARGE ONION, PEELED AND CHOPPED
- 1 LARGE CARROT, SCRUBBED AND CHOPPED
- 1 MEDIUM CELERY STICK, TRIMMED AND CHOPPED
- 450G (1 LB) TOMATOES, ROUGHLY CHOPPED
- 400G (14 OZ) TINNED TOMATOES
- 850ML (1½ PINTS) CHICKEN OR VEGETABLE STOCK (SEE PP.433, 434)
- 1 MACE BLADE
- 1 SPRIG EACH FRESH THYME, PARSLEY AND ROSEMARY
- ½ LEVEL TEASPOON CELERY SEEDS
- 10 BLACK PEPPERCORNS
- 150ML (¼ PINT) SINGLE CREAM
- SMALL FRESH ROSEMARY SPRIGS TO GARNISH

PREPARATION TIME: 30 MINUTES
COOKING TIME: 1 HOUR
SERVES FOUR

ISLAND GOODNESS
In the 1930s, advertisements like these extolled the virtues of vegetables from the Channel Isles, which had become the nation's greengrocers. Wartime shortages therefore, especially of onions, became all the more acute when the islands were invaded in 1940.

When cutting grouse carcasses in half, tapping the back of the knife with a heavy weight will make the job easier.

Crushed juniper berries impart a fragrant hint of the pine forest to this Scottish game soup.

Grouse Soup with Juniper Berries

Young grouse are too good for anything but roasting; however their elderly relatives can be turned into a rich, warming soup

INGREDIENTS

- 2 OVEN-READY GROUSE
- 1.15 LITRES (2 PINTS) GAME OR CHICKEN STOCK (SEE P.433)
- 1 LEVEL TEASPOON SALT
- 12 BLACK PEPPERCORNS
- 6 JUNIPER BERRIES, CRUSHED
- 1 MEDIUM ONION, PEELED AND ROUGHLY CHOPPED
- 2 LARGE CARROTS, WASHED AND ROUGHLY CHOPPED, NOT SCRAPED
- 3 CELERY STICKS, TRIMMED AND ROUGHLY CHOPPED
- 30 G (1 OZ) BUTTER
- 60 G (2 OZ) MEDIUM OATMEAL
- 4–6 TABLESPOONS RED WINE
- 2 TABLESPOONS SCOTCH WHISKY
- 150 ML (¼ PINT) SINGLE CREAM
- 1 TABLESPOON SNIPPED FRESH CHIVES TO GARNISH

PREPARATION TIME: 35 MINUTES
COOKING TIME: 2 ¾ HOURS
SERVES FOUR

CUT the breast from the grouse and remove the skin, then refrigerate the breasts until needed. Cut the carcasses in half and put into a large saucepan with the skin. Add the stock, salt, peppercorns, juniper berries, onion, carrots and celery and bring to the boil. Reduce the heat, skim the scum from the surface, then cover and simmer gently for 2 hours. Strain through a large sieve into a bowl. Discard the spices and vegetables and remove any fat from the surface of the stock.

Melt the butter in a clean saucepan, add the grouse breasts and cook over a moderate heat for 4–5 minutes, turning once, until they are only just cooked—do not overcook as they will become dry. Remove from the pan and put on a plate.

Stir the oatmeal into the butter left in the pan, and cook over a moderate heat for 2–3 minutes until lightly toasted. Gradually add the stock and red wine and bring to the boil. Reduce the heat, cover and simmer gently, stirring occasionally, for 30 minutes or until the oatmeal is just cooked and the soup has thickened.

Cut the cooked breast meat into small dice, add to the soup and simmer gently for 2–3 minutes. Stir in the whisky and cream and heat gently for 2–3 minutes without allowing the soup to boil. Season to taste, sprinkle with the chives and serve with hot toast.

Cullen Skink

The dish originates from the Moray Firth on Scotland's east coast—the word 'skink' signifies a stew-like soup

Place the haddock in a shallow pan with the onion, milk and water and bring to the boil. Reduce the heat, cover the pan and poach gently for about 10 minutes. Strain the fish liquid through a large sieve into a saucepan and reserve, discarding the onion. Remove the skin and bones from the haddock, flake the flesh and set aside.

Meanwhile, boil the potatoes in salted water for 10–15 minutes or until tender, then drain and mash well. Whisk the mashed potatoes into the fish liquid, stir in the leeks and bring to the boil. Reduce the heat, cover the pan and simmer for 10–15 minutes until the leeks are tender.

Whisk the cream and egg yolk together and stir into the soup. Reheat gently, stirring until slightly thickened—do not boil as the soup will curdle. Stir in the flaked haddock and season to taste with pepper only. Stir in the chopped parsley and heat through for 2–3 minutes.

Serve piping hot dotted with knobs of butter, which will melt and run over the surface of the soup.

INGREDIENTS

- 900 g (2 lb) finnan haddock, preferably from the Moray Firth, or any other undyed smoked haddock
- 1 medium onion, peeled and sliced
- 425 ml (3/4 pint) milk
- 425 ml (3/4 pint) water
- 450 g (1 lb) floury potatoes, peeled and diced
- Salt
- 225 g (8 oz) leeks, trimmed, sliced and washed
- 285 ml (1/2 pint) single cream
- 1 egg yolk, size 2
- Freshly ground black pepper
- 2 tablespoons chopped fresh parsley
- 60 g (2 oz) butter (optional)

Preparation time: 30 minutes
Cooking time: 35 minutes
Serves four

Beware of imitations: this soup can be made only from undyed finnan haddie.

Smoke signal
Every week the boats return to Seatown on the Moray Firth laden with haddock for the Aberdeen fish market. Some of them still find their way to the town smokeries, but recent imports of the inferior, artificially coloured haddock are beginning to threaten the local finnan haddie with extinction.

The potato ring garnish for this creamy soup can be used in other soups too.

Turkey & Hazelnut Soup

Determine a better fate for leftover turkey than just filling sandwiches

INGREDIENTS

- 1 small, leftover cooked turkey carcass with 225g (8oz) of meat
- 1.15 litres (2 pints) water
- 1 large carrot, peeled and sliced
- 1 large onion, peeled and sliced
- 1 medium leek, trimmed, sliced and washed
- 340g (12oz) potatoes, peeled and diced
- 45g (1½oz) butter
- 115g (4oz) hazelnuts, finely chopped
- 1 shallot, peeled and finely chopped
- 1 small carrot, peeled and finely chopped
- 2 tablespoons sherry
- 2 teaspoons wholegrain mustard
- Salt and freshly ground black pepper
- 2 tablespoons chopped fresh mixed herbs (parsley, oregano and marjoram)
- 150ml (¼ pint) single cream
- 1 egg yolk, size 2

Preparation time: 35 minutes
Cooking time: 1¾ hours
Serves four

Remove the meat from the carcass, cut it into small dice and refrigerate until needed. Break the carcass into pieces and put them into a large saucepan with the water, sliced carrot, onion and leek. Bring to the boil, then reduce the heat, cover and simmer for 1½ hours. Strain the stock through a sieve into a bowl or measuring jug. There should be about 850ml (1½ pints).

Meanwhile, boil the potatoes until soft, then drain and mash well with 15g (½oz) of the butter, beating until smooth. Put the potato mixture into a piping bag fitted with a small star nozzle and pipe 12 circles onto a greased or nonstick baking tray. Sprinkle with 15g (½ oz) of the hazelnuts, and set aside.

Preheat the oven to 220°c (425°f, gas mark 7). Heat the remaining butter in a saucepan, add the chopped shallot and carrot and cook gently for 3–4 minutes. Pour in the sherry, cook for a few minutes until it is reduced by half then stir in the turkey stock, the diced cooked turkey, remaining hazelnuts, mustard, salt and pepper to taste and the herbs. Cover and cook gently for 10 minutes.

Meanwhile, cook the potato rings in the centre of the oven for 8–10 minutes until golden brown. Remove and allow to cool slightly. Whisk together the cream and egg yolk, quickly stir the mixture into the soup and heat gently for 1–2 minutes, stirring continuously. Do not allow to boil as the soup will curdle. Pour into heated soup bowls, garnish each with two potato rings and serve.

A leftover chicken carcass can be used instead of turkey if preferred.

Split Pea Soup with Bacon and Mint

So much a part of the capital's cookery, this soup shares the name of London Particular with the dense fogs of yesteryear

Melt the butter in a large saucepan, add the bacon, onion, carrot and leek and cook gently for 5 minutes, then add the peas, herbs and stock or water.

Bring to the boil and boil rapidly for 10 minutes. Reduce the heat, cover and simmer gently for about 50 minutes or until the peas are tender. Remove the pan from the heat and discard the bay leaf and thyme. Leave to cool, then purée in a food processor or blender.

Return the purée to the pan and stir in the milk. Bring to the boil, reduce the heat and cook gently for 1–2 minutes. Season to taste, then pour into a heated tureen or soup bowls and top with the clotted cream, a sprinkling of fresh chopped mint and some croutons.

A mint and crouton garnish enhances this soup's appearance as well as its taste.

Ingredients

- 30 g (1 oz) butter
- 3 thick rashers smoked back bacon, rinds removed, chopped
- 1 large onion, peeled and chopped
- 1 large carrot, peeled and sliced
- 1 medium leek, trimmed, sliced and washed
- 225 g (8 oz) dried split green peas, rinsed and drained
- 15 g (½ oz) fresh mint leaves
- 1 bay leaf
- 1 fresh thyme sprig
- 1.4 litres (2½ pints) chicken stock (see p.433) or water
- 285 ml (½ pint) milk
- Salt and freshly ground black pepper
- 4–6 tablespoons clotted cream
- 2 tablespoons chopped fresh mint to garnish
- Croutons for serving

Preparation time: 20 minutes
Cooking time: 1 hour
Serves six

Pea-souper
The London fogs beloved of Hollywood directors were composed largely of coal smoke and called 'pea-soupers' from their dense texture and deep, yellowish hue.

Mulligatawny Soup

The name of this soup is derived from the Tamil 'milagu tanni', pepper water, an indication of both its spicy flavour and its Madras origins

INGREDIENTS

- 675G (1½LB) SHIN OF BEEF, TRIMMED OF FAT AND CUT INTO SMALL CUBES
- 1 LEFTOVER COOKED CHICKEN CARCASS OR 4 CHICKEN DRUMSTICKS, COOKED AND SKINNED
- 60G (2OZ) DRIED MANGO
- 2 LITRES (3½ PINTS) CHICKEN OR BEEF STOCK (SEE P.432)
- 1 LEVEL TABLESPOON EACH CORIANDER SEEDS AND CARDAMOM PODS
- 2 LEVEL TEASPOONS CUMIN SEEDS
- 2 LEVEL TEASPOONS FENUGREEK SEEDS
- 1 TABLESPOON BLACK PEPPERCORNS
- 1 LEVEL TABLESPOON DESICCATED COCONUT
- THINLY PARED RIND 1 LEMON
- 2 GARLIC CLOVES, PEELED AND BRUISED
- 1 SMALL FRESH GREEN CHILLI OR 2 SMALL DRIED CHILLIES
- 1 FRESH BAY LEAF
- 2 EGG WHITES
- 2 EGG SHELLS, WASHED AND CRUSHED
- 2 TABLESPOONS MADEIRA
- SALT AND FRESHLY GROUND BLACK PEPPER

PREPARATION TIME: 30 MINUTES
COOKING TIME: 1 HOUR 20 MINUTES
SERVES FOUR

Use the remaining egg yolks for making pastry, beating into mashed potato or enriching custard.

Put the beef into a large saucepan with the chicken carcass or cooked drumsticks, dried mango and stock. Put all the spices, the coconut, lemon rind, garlic, chilli and bay leaf in a square of muslin, tie the opposite corners together to form a bag, then lightly bruise the contents with a rolling pin. Add to the saucepan and bring to the boil. Reduce the heat, skim the scum from the surface, partly cover and simmer for 1 hour.

Strain the stock through a large sieve into a large clean saucepan and discard the contents of the sieve. In a separate bowl, whisk up the egg whites and shells until just foamy and add to the stock, then whisk over a moderate heat for about 10 minutes, without allowing the liquid to boil, until a thick, grey-white crust is formed. Once this crust is formed, stop whisking and allow the stock to come up to the boil and the crust to rise up the sides of the pan—do not let the soup boil over the crust.

Remove the pan from the heat and allow the contents to subside for 10 minutes. Carefully strain the soup through a large sieve, lined with double muslin or kitchen paper, into a clean saucepan, holding back the crust till last. The strained soup should look clear. Stir in the Madeira, season to taste with salt and pepper, reheat and serve.

British in concept, Indian in content, this meat soup speaks of a 300-year association.

Marigold petals lend both a touch of colour and a subtlety of flavour to eel soup.

Conger reel
Jetties are good spots for conger fishing, since the creatures often lurk among the underpinnings. There is much competition to catch the largest eels, which can be as much as 9ft long with a weight of over 90lb.

Jersey Conger Eel Soup

In the Channel Islands farmhouses this would be made with rich Jersey milk in place of the cream

Cut the eel into six steaks and put them into a very large saucepan with the water, chopped onion, sliced carrot, the bunch of herbs and the salt and pepper. Bring to the boil, then reduce the heat, cover and simmer gently for 45 minutes.

Strain the stock from the eel into a clean saucepan, discarding the onion, carrot and herbs. Remove and discard the skin and bones from the eel, flake the flesh and add it to the strained stock. Bring the soup to the boil and add the sliced leek. Reduce the heat and simmer for about 10 minutes, until the leeks are tender but still green.

Stir the cream and chopped parsley into the soup and heat for 1–2 minutes, without boiling. Transfer to a heated tureen or individual soup bowls. Garnish with the marigold petals, if using, and serve with warm, crusty bread.

INGREDIENTS

- 1.5 kg (3¼ lb) piece conger eel
- 1.7 litres (3 pints) water
- 1 large onion, peeled and coarsely chopped
- 1 medium carrot, scrubbed and sliced
- Bunch of herbs (large thyme, bay, parsley and basil sprigs)
- 1 level teaspoon salt
- ¼ level teaspoon freshly ground black pepper
- 1 large leek, trimmed, thinly sliced and washed
- 150 ml (¼ pint) single cream
- 3 tablespoons chopped parsley
- Marigold petals (optional) to garnish

Preparation time: 30 minutes
Cooking time: 1 hour
Serves six

Mussel bound
The mussel beds of the Firth of Forth used to provide a living for many local people. Pollution in recent years in many British inshore areas has led to imports from the French Atlantic coast.

Mussels cooked in cider is one of Scotland's classic gifts to Britain's cookery.

Mussel Brose

For a creamy, smooth brose, thicken with flour or use oatmeal for a textured and more traditional flavour

INGREDIENTS

- 1.8 KG (4 LB) LIVE MUSSELS, SCRUBBED AND DEBEARDED (SEE P.436)
- 340 G (12 OZ) LEEKS, TRIMMED, FINELY SLICED AND WASHED
- 4 MEDIUM CELERY STICKS, TRIMMED AND FINELY SLICED
- 1 MEDIUM ONION, PEELED AND FINELY CHOPPED
- A FEW PARSLEY STALKS
- 570 ML (1 PINT) DRY CIDER OR DRY WHITE WINE
- 60 G (2 OZ) BUTTER
- 30 G (1 OZ) PLAIN FLOUR OR 60 G (2 OZ) MEDIUM OATMEAL
- 570 ML (1 PINT) MILK
- 285 ML (½ PINT) DOUBLE CREAM
- SALT AND FRESHLY GROUND BLACK PEPPER
- FRESHLY GRATED NUTMEG
- 3 TABLESPOONS CHOPPED FRESH PARSLEY

Preparation time: 45 MINUTES
Cooking time: 30 MINUTES
Serves four

Put the mussels into a large saucepan with the leeks, celery, onion, parsley stalks and cider or wine. Cover, bring to the boil and boil for about 10 minutes, shaking the pan occasionally, until the mussels have fully opened. Discard any that do not open. Strain the liquid through a sieve lined with kitchen paper into a jug and set aside.

Remove all but 12 mussels from their shells. Set all the mussels aside.

Melt the butter in a saucepan, stir in the flour or oatmeal and cook gently for 1–2 minutes. Gradually stir in the mussel liquid and milk and bring to the boil. Reduce the heat and simmer for 30 minutes, stirring frequently.

Stir in the cream and all the mussels and heat gently for 2–3 minutes. Season with salt, pepper and nutmeg. Ladle into soup plates, garnish with the chopped parsley and serve with wholemeal bread.

Duck & Orange Soup

Duck and orange together make perfect culinary harmony as this soup proves

Thinly pare the rind from one of the oranges and cut it into fine shreds. Put into a bowl, cover with cold water and set aside. Finely grate the rind from another orange and set aside. Squeeze the juice from all four oranges—you should have about 285 ml (½ pint)—and set aside.

Put the duck carcass into a large saucepan with the onion, leeks, green pepper and gherkins. Add the stock and bring to the boil, then reduce the heat and skim any scum from the surface. Cover and simmer for 1 hour. Season well with salt and pepper and stir in the orange rind and juice, sherry, thyme and parsley. Cook for a further 30 minutes.

Melt the butter in a frying pan, add the duck strips and sauté them until they are well browned all over.

Remove and discard the duck carcass from the soup. Stir the sautéed duck strips, chopped tomatoes and the rice into the soup. Cover the pan and simmer for 15 minutes or until the duck strips are tender and the rice is cooked.

Serve the soup in a heated tureen or individual bowls. Garnish with the soaked shreds of orange rind.

Some breast meat and a leftover carcass are the basic ingredients for this light duck soup.

INGREDIENTS

- 4 large oranges
- Leftover carcass from a roasted duck
- 1 small onion, peeled and chopped
- 2 medium leeks, trimmed, sliced and washed
- 1 green pepper, deseeded and chopped
- 2 small gherkins, sliced
- 1.7 litres (3 pints) chicken stock (see p.433)
- Salt and freshly ground black pepper
- 200 ml (7 fl oz) dry sherry
- 1 level tablespoon chopped fresh thyme
- 1 tablespoon chopped fresh parsley
- 30 g (1 oz) butter
- 2 boneless duck breasts, each approx 175 g (6 oz), skinned and cut into thin strips
- 340 g (12 oz) ripe tomatoes, skinned, deseeded and chopped
- 115 g (4 oz) long-grain white rice

Preparation time: 50 minutes
Cooking time: 1¾ hours
Serves six

Use a stainless steel potato peeler to make an easy job of removing thin strips of rind from the orange.

INGREDIENTS

450g (1 lb) stewing venison, cut into large cubes
675g (1½ lb) shin of beef, cut into large cubes
1 oven-ready grouse or partridge
1 oven-ready wood pigeon
1 oven-ready pheasant
3 medium celery sticks, trimmed and chopped
225g (8 oz) carrots, peeled and chopped
340g (12 oz) swede, peeled and chopped
450g (1 lb) onions, peeled and chopped
Small bunch of parsley
2½ level teaspoons whole black peppercorns
2.8 litres (5 pints) water
425 ml (¾ pint) full-bodied red wine
12 button onions, peeled
675g (1½ lb) potatoes, peeled and quartered
675g (1½ lb) Dutch white cabbage, trimmed and thickly sliced
3 medium celery sticks, trimmed and finely sliced
6 allspice berries
3 juniper berries, crushed
Salt and freshly ground black pepper
800g (1¾ lb) rabbit or hare portions, boned and diced
3 level tablespoons plain flour, seasoned with salt and pepper
60g (2 oz) butter
150 ml (¼ pint) port

Preparation time: 1½ hours
Cooking time: 4 hours (including making stock)
Serves six

Poacher's Soup

It would take an active poacher indeed to assemble all the ingredients for this soup; so buy frozen joints and portions from a game dealer instead

Put the venison and beef into a large saucepan. Remove the legs from the grouse or partridge and the pigeon and pheasant, and add to the saucepan. Carefully remove the breast meat from the birds, pull off the skin and add it with the carcasses to the pan. Dice the breast meat, put it onto a plate, cover and refrigerate until needed.

Add the chopped celery, carrots, swede, onions, parsley, peppercorns, water and red wine to the pan and bring slowly to the boil. Reduce the heat, skim the scum from the surface, partly cover and simmer for 3 hours, skimming occasionally. Strain the stock through a large sieve into a bowl and reserve. Discard the meat and vegetables.

Pour the stock into a large saucepan and add the button onions, potatoes, cabbage, celery, allspice and juniper berries. Season to taste with salt and pepper, bring to the boil, then reduce the heat, cover and simmer for 30 minutes.

Meanwhile, mix the reserved, diced game-bird meat with the diced rabbit or hare and toss in the seasoned flour, shaking off any excess. Melt the butter in a large frying pan, lightly brown the meat, then add it to the soup. Pour the port into the frying pan and bring to the boil, stirring and scraping the sediment from the bottom with a wooden spoon. Pour the port into the soup and simmer for a further 30 minutes. Serve the soup accompanied by glasses of port.

Grouse, hare and red wine make a very rich and gamy version of this soup.

The finest offerings of field and woodland are magnificently united in this rich autumnal soup.

Add the hare's liver for a stronger flavour. For a less gamey taste, use a large rabbit instead of a hare.

Hare & Mushroom Soup

Only the hare's legs are used; the saddle can be saved for another day

Coat the hare joints in the seasoned flour. Heat two-thirds of the butter in a large saucepan, add the hare and fry for 5 minutes until browned, then remove from the pan and set aside. Add the onion, carrots, swedes and celery to the pan and fry for 5 minutes, then add the mushrooms and cook for 1 minute. Return the hare to the pan.

Stir in the water, add the bouquet garni and the black peppercorns and bring to the boil. Reduce the heat, cover and simmer gently for 1½–2 hours or until the meat is very tender and comes away easily from the bone.

Remove the hare joints from the pan and strip the meat from the bones. Shred half of the meat and reserve for garnish. Remove the bouquet garni from the soup and discard. Put the remaining meat and the soup into the bowl of a food processor or blender, and purée. Pour the soup back into the saucepan, add the shredded meat and reheat. Stir in the port and season with salt.

Melt the remaining butter in a small frying pan and sauté the sliced mushrooms until lightly browned.

Serve the soup garnished with the sautéed mushrooms and chopped parsley.

INGREDIENTS

- 900G (2LB) HARE JOINTS ON THE BONE
- 2 LEVEL TABLESPOONS PLAIN FLOUR, SEASONED WITH SALT AND PEPPER
- 45G (1½OZ) BUTTER
- 1 LARGE ONION, PEELED AND CHOPPED
- 115G (4OZ) CARROTS, PEELED AND CHOPPED
- 115G (4OZ) SWEDES, PEELED AND CHOPPED
- 1 MEDIUM CELERY STICK, TRIMMED AND CHOPPED
- 175G (6OZ) FLAT MUSHROOMS, WIPED AND CHOPPED
- 1.15 LITRES (2 PINTS) WATER
- BOUQUET GARNI (SEE P.440)
- ¼ TEASPOON BLACK PEPPERCORNS
- 2 TABLESPOONS PORT
- SALT
- 175G (6OZ) OPEN CUP MUSHROOMS, WIPED AND SLICED
- 1 TABLESPOON CHOPPED FRESH PARSLEY

PREPARATION TIME: 30 MINUTES
COOKING TIME: 1½–2 HOURS
SERVES SIX

Chestnut Soup

An old-time winter warmer that 'doo nourysshe the bodye strongely'

INGREDIENTS

- 850 ML (1½ PINTS) BEEF, CHICKEN OR VEGETABLE STOCK (SEE PP.433, 434)
- 550 G (1¼ LB) FRESH CHESTNUTS, PEELED (SEE P.440), OR 450 G (1 LB) FROZEN PEELED CHESTNUTS
- 150 ML (¼ PINT) MILK
- SALT AND FRESHLY GROUND BLACK PEPPER
- 1–2 TABLESPOONS LEMON JUICE
- 4 TABLESPOONS SINGLE CREAM
- 1 TABLESPOON FINELY CHOPPED FRESH PARSLEY
- 15 G (½ OZ) BLANCHED ALMONDS, LIGHTLY TOASTED AND CHOPPED

Preparation time: 15 MINUTES
Cooking time: 35 MINUTES
Serves four

When chestnuts are at their cheapest, make extra soup and freeze it for use later.

Pour the stock into a saucepan and bring to the boil, add the chestnuts and bring back to the boil. Reduce the heat, cover and simmer for 30 minutes or until the chestnuts are very soft.

Remove from the heat and allow to cool slightly, then purée the chestnuts and stock together in a food processor or blender or pass through a food mill. Pour back into the saucepan and stir in the milk. Season well with salt and pepper and reheat, stirring constantly. Stir in just enough lemon juice to take off the very sweet edge of the soup and sharpen it.

Pour the soup into a heated tureen or individual bowls and swirl in the cream. Sprinkle the parsley and toasted almonds on top and serve. This is a filling soup which does not need bread as an accompaniment if served as a starter. As a light lunch or supper snack, serve it with pumpkin seed bread.

A food mill is a quick way of puréeing the chestnuts which form the basis of this soup.

Partridges and vegetables combine in this rich, country soup.

Romany folk
Among the treasures of the gypsy carts that used to wander the country were fine porcelain and a fragrant, bubbling cauldron whose contents were assembled with little reference to the Game Laws.

Meg Merrilies' Soup

In Sir Walter Scott's 'Guy Mannering', Gypsy Meg made a stew which, in homage to the author, the Duke of Buccleuch's chef translated into this soup

Carefully remove the breast meat from the partridges, put onto a plate, cover and refrigerate.

Put the carcasses into a large saucepan with the cabbage, carrots, onion, cloves, peppercorns, bay leaf and water and bring to the boil. Reduce the heat, skim the scum from the surface, partially cover and simmer for 2 hours, skimming occasionally. Discard the carcasses and vegetables and strain the stock through a large sieve into a clean saucepan.

Cut the reserved breast meat into neat strips and toss in the seasoned flour. Melt the butter in a frying pan until foaming, add the strips of meat and fry until golden brown.

Add the meat to the stock with the sliced celery and broad beans. Season well with salt, black pepper and cayenne. Bring to the boil, reduce the heat, cover and simmer for 15 minutes, or until the meat is tender and the vegetables are cooked. Serve immediately.

INGREDIENTS

- 2 oven-ready partridges (a brace)
- 450g (1 lb) Dutch white cabbage, quartered
- 2 medium carrots, peeled and chopped
- 1 medium onion, peeled and quartered
- 2 cloves
- 8 black peppercorns
- 1 bay leaf
- 1.7 litres (3 pints) water
- 1 level tablespoon flour, seasoned with salt and pepper
- 30g (1 oz) butter
- 6 medium celery sticks, trimmed and finely sliced
- 340g (12 oz) frozen broad beans, thawed, removed from their skins
- Salt and freshly ground black pepper
- Pinch of cayenne pepper

Preparation time: 20 minutes
Cooking time: 2½ hours
Serves four

Pea-Pod Soup

Here is the colour, the scent and the good, strong taste of the early summer vegetable garden

INGREDIENTS

- 60G (2OZ) BUTTER
- 115G (4OZ) SPRING ONIONS, TRIMMED AND CHOPPED
- 3 MEDIUM CELERY STICKS, TRIMMED AND CHOPPED
- 450G (1LB) EMPTY PEA PODS OR SUGAR SNAP PEAS, WASHED
- 115G (4OZ) GREEN SPLIT PEAS, RINSED AND DRAINED
- 1.15 LITRES (2 PINTS) CHICKEN OR VEGETABLE STOCK (SEE PP.433, 434)
- 4 RASHERS STREAKY BACON, RINDS REMOVED
- 15G (½OZ) FRESH MINT LEAVES
- SALT AND FRESHLY GROUND BLACK PEPPER
- FRESHLY GRATED NUTMEG
- 150ML (¼ PINT) SINGLE CREAM

PREPARATION TIME: 25 MINUTES
COOKING TIME: 35 MINUTES
SERVES FOUR

MELT the butter in a large saucepan, add the spring onions, celery, pea pods or sugar snap peas and the split peas and cook for 3–4 minutes until beginning to soften. Add the chicken or vegetable stock, bring to the boil, reduce the heat, cover and simmer for 15–20 minutes or until the split peas and the pea pods or sugar snap peas are very tender.

Meanwhile, grill the bacon until crisp, then drain on kitchen paper. Chop each rasher roughly and reserve for garnish.

Remove the pan from the heat, allow to cool a little then pour the soup into an electric blender or food processor. Add the mint, seasoning to taste and a pinch of grated nutmeg and blend until smooth. Pass through a sieve into a clean saucepan and stir in the cream. Reheat without boiling, adding seasoning if necessary.

Pour the soup into a heated tureen or individual bowls, crumble the grilled bacon over the top and serve accompanied by warm crusty bread.

FIRST TASKS
A trade card of 1920 recalls the days before freezers when almost every child's earliest employment was to sit in the sun shelling peas for mother—and nibbling more than a few of them before the job was done.

Waste not, want not ... shell the peas and turn the pods into a soup that is full of flavour.

As its name suggests, the chief ingredients of this fine Scottish soup are chicken and leeks.

To rid leeks of grit after chopping and slicing, rinse them in a colander under running water and drain well.

Cock-a-Leekie

By hallowed custom, cock-a-leekie should precede the haggis at a Burns supper

Put the beef and bouquet garni into a large saucepan, cover with the water and bring to the boil. Reduce the heat and skim the scum from the surface. Partly cover the pan and simmer for 1 hour.

Add the chicken, the giblets (excluding the liver) and the prunes to the pan and simmer for a further hour or until the chicken is thoroughly cooked. Remove it from the broth, put onto a plate and leave to cool. Strain the broth through a large sieve into a bowl. Reserve the prunes, but discard the beef and bouquet garni. Skim the fat from the stock, reserving 2 tablespoons for cooking the onions and leeks.

Remove the skin from the chicken, then pull the flesh from the bones and tear it into strips. Heat the reserved fat in a large saucepan, add the chopped onion and cook over a moderate heat until soft and translucent.

Finely slice two leeks and finely chop the rest. Stir the leeks into the onions, cover and cook gently for about 5 minutes until soft. Add the reserved stock, the shredded chicken and the prunes. Bring to the boil, then reduce the heat and simmer, uncovered for 10 minutes. Remove from the heat and allow to cool, then refrigerate overnight.

Remove the fat from the top of the soup, reheat and season to taste with salt and pepper. Serve piping hot with good, crusty bread and country butter.

Ingredients

- 900 g (2 lb) shin of beef, trimmed of fat and cubed
- Bouquet garni (see p.440)
- 3.4 litres (6 pints) water
- 1.8 kg (4 lb) boiling fowl or chicken, with giblets, rinsed under cold water and drained
- 12 dried prunes
- 340 g (12 oz) onions, peeled and finely chopped
- 1.1 kg (2½ lb) leeks, trimmed to leave 7.5 cm (3 in) of green, washed
- Salt and freshly ground black pepper

Preparation time: 30 minutes
Cooking time: 2¼ hours
Chilling time: Overnight
Serves six as a main meal

Adapt the soup according to the vegetables available. Turnips, courgettes, green beans and cabbage can all be used instead or in addition.

Favourite country garden vegetables are strengthened with the nourishment of pulses and cheese.

English Garden Soup

There can be nothing so rewarding, after a morning's digging, than to enjoy the fruits of your labours in this soup

INGREDIENTS

- 115G (4OZ) DRIED BUTTER BEANS, SOAKED OVERNIGHT IN COLD WATER
- 30G (1OZ) BUTTER
- 3 MEDIUM CARROTS, PEELED, HALVED LENGTHWAYS AND THINLY SLICED
- 2 MEDIUM ONIONS, PEELED AND FINELY CHOPPED
- 2 MEDIUM LEEKS, TRIMMED, HALVED LENGTHWAYS, THINLY SLICED AND WASHED
- 3 MEDIUM CELERY STICKS, TRIMMED AND THINLY SLICED
- 2.3 LITRES (4 PINTS) GOOD CHICKEN OR VEGETABLE STOCK (SEE PP.433, 434)
- 115G (4OZ) SPLIT RED LENTILS, CLEANED OF GRIT AND RINSED
- BOUQUET GARNI (SEE P.440)
- 115G (4OZ) PEAS, FRESHLY SHELLED OR FROZEN PEAS
- 4 MEDIUM TOMATOES, SKINNED, DESEEDED AND FINELY DICED
- SALT AND FRESHLY GROUND BLACK PEPPER
- 115G (4OZ) CHEDDAR CHEESE, FINELY GRATED

SOAKING TIME: OVERNIGHT
PREPARATION TIME: 30 MINUTES
COOKING TIME: 2½ HOURS
SERVES EIGHT AS A STARTER OR FOUR AS A MAIN COURSE

Drain and rinse the butter beans, then cover with fresh cold water in a saucepan. Bring to the boil and boil rapidly for 10 minutes, then drain.

Melt the butter in a large saucepan and add the carrots, onions, leeks and celery. Cover and cook over a low heat for 10 minutes, stirring frequently. Add the stock, butter beans, lentils and bouquet garni and bring to the boil. Reduce the heat, cover and simmer gently for 2 hours or until the beans are very tender.

Add the peas and tomatoes and cook for a further 10 minutes. Remove and discard the bouquet garni, then season to taste with the salt and pepper.

Ladle the soup into heated soup bowls, sprinkle generously with the Cheddar cheese and serve with warmed crusty farmhouse bread.

Scotch Broth

Broth used to be the inseparable companion of the kitchen range and the focal point in all Scottish households

Put the pearl barley and split peas into a bowl, cover with cold water and leave to soak overnight.

Next day put the lamb into a large saucepan, cover with the water and bring to the boil. Reduce the heat and skim the scum from the surface. Drain the barley and split peas and add them to the saucepan with the bouquet garni and salt and pepper to taste. Cover and simmer for 1 hour, skimming occasionally. Stir in the carrots and swede and simmer for 15 minutes. Add the white parts of the leeks and simmer for a further 15 minutes. Remove the pan from the heat, cool the broth and refrigerate overnight.

Next day, remove the solidified fat from the surface of the soup. Discard the bouquet garni. Lift out the lamb, remove the meat from the bones, cut it into small pieces and return to the soup.

Finely slice the reserved green parts of the leeks and stir them into the soup with the parsley. Reheat until boiling. Season well with salt and black pepper and serve piping hot.

The broth contains plenty of penny-wise protein to go with the vegetables.

Ingredients

- 30 g (1 oz) pearl barley
- 15 g (½ oz) yellow split peas
- 900 g (2 lb) neck or shoulder of lamb, cut into pieces
- 2.3 litres (4 pints) water
- Bouquet garni (see p.440)
- Salt and freshly ground black pepper
- 340 g (12 oz) carrots, peeled and diced
- 225 g (8 oz) swede, peeled and diced
- 225 g (8 oz) leeks, trimmed and washed, white part finely chopped, green part reserved
- 2 tablespoons chopped fresh parsley to garnish

Preparation time: Day 1, overnight soaking; Day 2, 40 minutes
Cooking time: 1½ hours
Chilling time: Overnight
Serves four

Cornish Fish Soup

The culinary use of saffron has lingered longer in Cornwall than anywhere else in Britain

INGREDIENTS

900 g (2 lb) whiting, cod or haddock fillets
2 bay leaves
Thinly peeled rind and juice of ½ lemon
6 black peppercorns
½ level teaspoon salt
1.15 litres (2 pints) water
60 g (2 oz) butter
1 medium onion, peeled and chopped
45 g (1½ oz) plain flour
285 ml (½ pint) milk
¼ level teaspoon saffron strands
Chopped fresh parsley and fine strips of lemon rind to garnish

Preparation time: 30 minutes
Cooking time: 50 minutes
Serves four

Remove the skin from the fish fillets and put it into a saucepan with a quarter of the fish, the bay leaves, lemon rind and juice, peppercorns, salt and the water and bring to the boil. Reduce the heat, cover and simmer for 20 minutes. Strain the stock through a large sieve into a bowl and reserve. Remove the fish from the sieve, take out any bones, then mash with a fork and set aside. Discard the bay leaves, lemon rind and peppercorns.

Melt the butter in a clean saucepan, add the onion and sauté over a moderate heat until soft but not browned. Stir in the flour and cook for 1 minute more. Gradually blend in the strained stock and the milk, and bring to the boil, stirring.

Cut the remaining fish into wide strips and add them to the soup with the saffron strands. Reduce the heat, cover and simmer for 10 minutes until the fish is almost cooked. Stir in the reserved mashed fish and continue to cook for a further 5 minutes. Season with pepper and a little more salt, if necessary.

Pour into a heated tureen or soup plates and garnish with the chopped parsley and strips of lemon rind.

The delicate blending of saffron with white fish makes a delicious, light soup.

Faraway places
With such posters as these, the Great Western Railway enticed Britons to the Cornish Riviera, which was about the closest thing to 'abroad' that many people were able to achieve between the wars.

The basic ingredients of this soup, chicken and leeks, are similar to those for cock-a-leekie, but with a good, rich thickening of eggs and cream.

Refrigerate the cooked chicken legs left over after preparing this dish. Serve them the next day with salad or make them into croquettes or a small pie.

Friar Tuck Soup

As its name suggests, this soup is hearty, honest and robust

Put the stock, chicken, parsley, chervil and two-thirds of the leeks into a large saucepan and bring to the boil. Reduce the heat, skim any scum from the surface, then cover and simmer gently for 1 hour, or until the chicken is tender.

Put the cooked chicken onto a plate and set aside. Skim the fat from the surface of the soup. Carve the legs off the chicken and reserve—they are not needed for the soup. Remove the skin from the breast, then take the meat off the carcass and cut it into thin strips. Return the meat to the soup and heat gently.

In a bowl, whisk the egg yolks with the cream, then gradually stir in 3 ladlefuls of the soup. Stir the egg and cream mixture into the soup, season to taste with the salt and black pepper or ground allspice and heat gently, stirring until the soup thickens slightly—do not let it boil as it will curdle.

Cook the remaining strips of leek in boiling water for 1 minute, then drain well. Pour the soup into a heated tureen and strew generously with the leeks and the finely chopped parsley and chervil. Serve with Melba toast (see p.440).

INGREDIENTS

2 LITRES (3½ PINTS) GOOD CHICKEN STOCK (SEE P.433)
1.4 KG (3 LB) OVEN-READY CHICKEN, RINSED AND DRIED WITH KITCHEN PAPER
60 G (2 OZ) PARSLEY, INCLUDING STALKS, ROUGHLY CHOPPED
60 G (2 OZ) CHERVIL, INCLUDING STALKS, ROUGHLY CHOPPED
3 MEDIUM LEEKS, TRIMMED, CUT INTO FINE STRIPS AND WASHED
4 EGG YOLKS, SIZE 2
150 ML (¼ PINT) SINGLE CREAM
SALT AND FRESHLY GROUND BLACK PEPPER OR GROUND ALLSPICE
2 TABLESPOONS EACH FINELY CHOPPED FRESH PARSLEY AND CHERVIL TO GARNISH

PREPARATION TIME: 45 MINUTES
COOKING TIME: 1½ HOURS
SERVES SIX AS A STARTER OR FOUR AS A MAIN COURSE

Bolted Lettuce Soup

Starve the compost heap and use the run-to-seed lettuces from your garden for this delicately flavoured soup

INGREDIENTS

450G (1 LB) FRESH, BOLTED HOMEGROWN LETTUCE, WASHED
60G (2 OZ) BUTTER
70G (2½ OZ) TRIMMED WATERCRESS, WASHED AND DRIED ON KITCHEN PAPER
175G (6 OZ) POTATOES, PEELED AND DICED
1.15 LITRES (2 PINTS) CHICKEN OR VEGETABLE STOCK (SEE PP.433, 434)
1 EGG YOLK, SIZE 2
150ML (¼ PINT) SINGLE CREAM
SALT AND FRESHLY GROUND BLACK PEPPER
FRESHLY GRATED NUTMEG

PREPARATION TIME: 20 MINUTES
COOKING TIME: 25 MINUTES
SERVES FOUR

FINELY shred a quarter of the lettuce and set it aside to be used as a garnish. Roughly shred the remaining lettuce, including the stalks.

Melt the butter in a large saucepan, add the roughly shredded lettuce and the watercress and cook for 1 minute until wilted. Stir in the diced potato and the chicken or vegetable stock and bring to the boil. Reduce the heat and simmer for 20 minutes until the potato is cooked.

Remove from the heat, allow to cool a little, purée in a food processor or electric blender, then pass through a sieve into a saucepan. Whisk the egg yolk and cream, pour into the soup and reheat, stirring, without boiling, until slightly thickened. Season with salt, pepper and nutmeg, ladle into bowls and serve garnished with the reserved shredded lettuce leaves.

Bought cos lettuce can be used instead of bolted lettuce from the garden.

Lettuce soup makes good sense as a well-earned break from gardening chores.

THE ALLOTMENT
Far more than a supplementary food source, the allotment was for many city dwellers an escape and an all-absorbing hobby. Nationwide clubs were founded between which there was fierce competition to grow the largest marrow or onion, or even the weightiest gooseberry.

Sorrel was highly prized as a vegetable in Tudor kitchens, including Henry VIII's.

Rabbit & Sorrel Soup

Every kitchen garden once had its patch of sorrel whose agreeable acidity is the perfect foil for meat as bland as rabbit

Cut the legs and hindquarters from the rabbit, carefully remove the fillets from each side of the saddle, put on a plate, cover and refrigerate until needed.

Heat the oil in a frying pan and fry the legs, hindquarters and carcass until browned, then transfer to a large saucepan. Add the shin of beef and bacon to the fat remaining in the frying pan and cook until well browned. Add these to the saucepan with the clove-studded onion, peppercorns, mace, chopped carrots and half the sorrel leaves. Pour in the stock or water and bring to the boil, then reduce the heat and skim any scum from the surface. Cover and simmer for 2½ hours, until the rabbit is very tender.

Strain the stock through a fine sieve into a large bowl. Remove the rabbit meat from the bones, chop roughly and set aside. Remove the beef and bacon and set aside with the rabbit. Discard the rabbit bones and the vegetables.

Melt the butter in a large saucepan, add the reserved rabbit fillets and brown on both sides. Remove from the pan, cut into strips and set aside.

Add the chopped onion to the saucepan and sauté until soft. Stir in the flour and cook for 1 minute, then gradually blend in the strained stock. Add the rabbit strips, the reserved cooked rabbit, the beef, bacon, lemon juice and parsley. Stirring continuously, bring the soup to the boil, then reduce the heat, cover and cook for 20 minutes.

Cut the remaining sorrel into shreds, add it to the saucepan and cook for a further 3 minutes. Season well with salt and pepper, and serve immediately.

INGREDIENTS

- 1 whole skinned rabbit, approx 800g (1¾ lb)
- 2 tablespoons olive oil
- 225g (8oz) shin of beef, trimmed of fat and cut into small cubes
- 115g (4oz) streaky bacon, rinds removed, chopped
- 1 medium onion, peeled and studded with 4 cloves
- 10 black peppercorns
- 2 mace blades
- 2 carrots, peeled and chopped
- 60g (2oz) fresh sorrel
- 2.3 litres (4 pints) chicken stock (see p.433) or water
- 30g (1oz) butter
- 1 medium onion, peeled and chopped
- 45g (1½oz) plain flour
- 2 tablespoons lemon juice
- 2 tablespoons chopped fresh parsley
- Salt and freshly ground black pepper

Preparation time: 1 hour
Cooking time: 3¼ hours
Serves six

INGREDIENTS

85 G (3 OZ) BUTTER
900 G (2 LB) PARSNIPS, PEELED AND SLICED
1.4 LITRES (2½ PINTS) BEEF OR VEGETABLE STOCK (SEE PP.432,434)
½ LEVEL TEASPOON SALT
FRESHLY GROUND WHITE PEPPER
1 LEVEL TABLESPOON FRESHLY GRATED HORSERADISH OR 1 LEVEL TABLESPOON HOT HORSERADISH SAUCE
150 ML (¼ PINT) SINGLE CREAM
FRESHLY GRATED NUTMEG AND PARSLEY SPRIGS TO GARNISH

PREPARATION TIME: 20 MINUTES
COOKING TIME: 45 MINUTES
SERVES FOUR

Parsnip Soup

The versatile parsnip here makes a smooth, creamy soup

MELT the butter in a large saucepan, add the parsnips and sauté over a moderate heat for 10 minutes, without browning. Add the stock, salt, pepper and grated horseradish, if using, and bring to the boil. Reduce the heat and simmer for 20 minutes, or until the parsnips are tender.

Remove the parsnips from the heat and leave to cool for 5 minutes, then purée with the stock, in batches, in a food processor or electric blender. Return the soup to the saucepan and, if using, stir in the horseradish sauce. Stir in the cream and reheat the soup for 5–10 minutes, stirring occasionally.

Ladle the soup into heated soup bowls or mugs and garnish with a little grated nutmeg and the sprigs of parsley. Serve with toasted granary bread.

The sweet flavour of parsnips is complemented by peppery horseradish in this warming winter soup.

If fresh horseradish is not available, use a tablespoon of hot horseradish sauce to add that extra something.

To appreciate fully the rich and diverse flavours of this soup, eat it with warm soda bread.

A crab caught
Inshore giants like this, plentiful once, are rare nowadays, but still worth seeking out, particularly around Britain's wilder, western coasts.

Crab Soup with Shrimps

This chunky soup is first cousin to the ocean bouillabaisse of the French Atlantic coast

Put the crab shell and claws and the shrimp shells into a saucepan, cover with the water and bring to the boil. Reduce the heat and simmer for 30 minutes, then strain off and reserve the stock. Discard the shells.

Meanwhile, heat the butter in a large saucepan, add the onion and celery and sauté over a low heat for 5 minutes, without browning. Stir in the rice, then add the milk, salt and pepper. Bring to the boil, reduce the heat, partially cover and simmer for 15 minutes, stirring occasionally, until the rice is completely cooked.

Reserve some of the white crabmeat for garnish, then stir all the rest into the rice and milk. Let it cool a little, then purée in a food processor or liquidiser.

Rinse the saucepan, return the purée to the pan and stir in 570 ml (1 pint) of the reserved crab stock—add a little more if necessary to bring the soup to the right consistency. Bring to the boil, stirring occasionally, then remove the pan from the heat.

Reserve a few of the shrimps for garnish, then stir the remainder into the soup with the Madeira or sherry and the double cream. Return the pan to the heat and heat through gently for 2 minutes.

Pour the soup into a heated tureen or individual soup bowls or mugs and garnish with the reserved crabmeat and shrimps. Sprinkle with the paprika just before serving and serve accompanied by warm soda bread.

Ingredients

- 550 g (1¼ lb) freshly cooked crab, dressed (see p.436), shell and claws reserved for stock
- 450 g (1 lb) fresh shrimps, peeled (see p.436)
- 1.15 litres (2 pints) water
- 30 g (1 oz) butter
- 1 medium onion, peeled and chopped
- 1 medium celery stick, trimmed and chopped
- 85 g (3 oz) long-grain white rice
- 570 ml (1 pint) milk
- ½ level teaspoon salt
- ¼ level teaspoon freshly ground black pepper
- 1 tablespoon Madeira or sherry
- 4 tablespoons double cream
- Paprika to garnish

Preparation time: 1½–2 hours, or 30 minutes with ready prepared crab and prawns

Cooking time: 30 minutes

Serves four

Auntie Gwyneth's Welsh Soup

On a cold winter's day, this filling soup makes a warming meal

INGREDIENTS

900G (2LB) SCRAG END OR MIDDLE NECK OF LAMB, CUT INTO PIECES
15G (½OZ) LARD OR 1 TABLESPOON OLIVE OIL
225G (8OZ) ONIONS, PEELED AND THINLY SLICED
225G (8OZ) TURNIPS, PEELED AND CUT INTO SMALL CUBES
225G (8OZ) CARROTS, PEELED AND THINLY SLICED
225G (8OZ) POTATOES, PEELED AND CUT INTO SMALL CUBES
1.7 LITRES (3 PINTS) WATER
BOUQUET GARNI MADE WITH 1 PARSLEY SPRIG, 1 BAY LEAF AND 1 THYME SPRIG, TIED TOGETHER
SALT AND FRESHLY GROUND BLACK PEPPER
550G (1¼LB) LEEKS, HALVED LENGTHWAYS, THICKLY SLICED AND WASHED
4 LEVEL TABLESPOONS CHOPPED FRESH PARSLEY

PREPARATION TIME: 40 MINUTES
COOKING TIME: 2¼ HOURS
SERVES SIX

REMOVE any excess fat and gristle from the lamb. Heat the lard or oil in a large saucepan, add the meat and cook over a high heat until evenly browned. Remove from the pan with a slotted spoon and drain on kitchen paper.

Add the onions, turnips, carrots and potatoes to the pan and cook gently for 10 minutes, stirring two or three times. Return the lamb to the pan and add the water and bouquet garni. Increase the heat and bring to the boil, then immediately reduce the heat to low and skim any scum from the surface. Cover and simmer gently for 1½ hours or until tender.

Using a slotted spoon, lift the meat from the saucepan and put it onto a plate. Season the soup with the salt and black pepper, increase the heat and add the sliced leeks. When the soup is gently boiling again, cover the saucepan, reduce the heat and leave to simmer gently for a further 30 minutes.

Meanwhile, remove all the meat from the bones, cut it into small cubes and put it back into the soup for the last 10 minutes of cooking time. Skim any excess fat from the surface and remove the bouquet garni. Taste the soup and adjust the seasoning, if necessary.

Pour the soup into a large, heated tureen and sprinkle with the chopped parsley. Serve with wholemeal bread and Caerphilly cheese.

Making the soup in advance will allow the full flavours of the lamb and vegetables to develop.

Savoy cabbage gives the soup its unusually mellow flavour.

Ask the butcher to chop the marrowbones into pieces. You will not have the equipment in the kitchen to do it yourself.

Grandma Bowe's Beef Broth with Marrowfat Peas

This simple soup of fresh vegetables, marrowfat peas and pearl barley is cooked in a beef stock enriched with a nourishing marrowbone

PUT the marrowbone, shin of beef and the water into a large saucepan. Bring to the boil, then immediately reduce the heat and skim any scum from the surface. Partially cover the pan and simmer for 3 hours.

Strain the stock through a large colander, lined with muslin or kitchen paper, into a large bowl. Discard the bones and meat (from which all the goodness will have been extracted).

Pour the stock into a clean saucepan. If there is less than 2 litres (3½ pints), make up the amount with water. Add all the remaining ingredients except the salt and pepper (the addition of salt at this stage would toughen the marrowfat peas). Bring the broth to the boil, then reduce the heat, cover the saucepan and cook gently for 25–30 minutes or until all the vegetables are tender.

Skim any excess fat from the surface of the broth, then season with the salt and a generous amount of pepper. Serve with warm wholemeal bread, or with bread and mature Cheddar cheese.

INGREDIENTS

- 1 BEEF MARROWBONE, CUT INTO PIECES AND RINSED UNDER COLD WATER
- 450G (1 LB) SHIN OF BEEF, CUT INTO SMALL CUBES
- 2.8 LITRES (5 PINTS) WATER
- 225G (8OZ) MARROWFAT PEAS, SOAKED OVERNIGHT IN COLD WATER, RINSED AND DRAINED
- 225G (8OZ) ONIONS, PEELED AND CHOPPED
- 225G (8OZ) CARROTS, PEELED AND SLICED
- 225G (8OZ) SWEDE, PEELED AND CUT INTO SMALL CUBES
- 225G (8OZ) SAVOY CABBAGE, SHREDDED AND WASHED
- 60G (2OZ) PEARL BARLEY
- 3 TABLESPOONS CHOPPED FRESH PARSLEY
- 1½ LEVEL TEASPOONS SALT
- FRESHLY GROUND BLACK PEPPER

PREPARATION TIME: 30 MINUTES
COOKING TIME: 3½ HOURS
SERVES SIX

The Dairy

It is Britain's great fortune to possess an abundance of green meadows and a goodly number of breeds of dairy cattle. To combine them is not only picturesque, but the source of *Soufflés, Stilton Savoury, Welsh Rabbit, Glamorgan Sausage* and *Potted Cheese.* Treasured too in the national larder are richly brown eggs. Up and down the country these are *Mumbled, Devilled, Curried, Poached,* or mingled with *Cheshire Cheese* and *Tomato Butter* to create a highly professional *Omelette.*

Rice and lentils can be used for baking the pastry case 'Blind', instead of dried beans or ceramic baking beans.

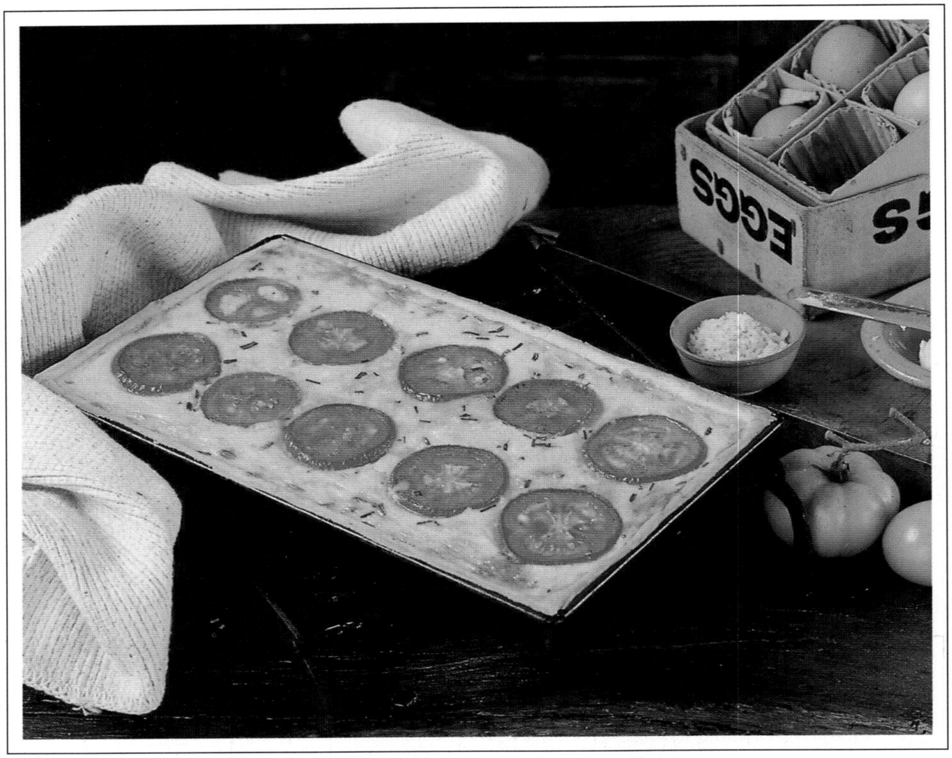

Flans take their name from the blank metal discs, called flans, from which coins are stamped, but they cook as well and taste as good baked in rectangular tins instead of circular ones !

Egg and Cheese Flan

This onion-flavoured flan combines a quartet of cheeses—two from England, one from Switzerland and one from Italy

INGREDIENTS

- 225 G (8 OZ) PLAIN FLOUR
- SALT AND FRESHLY GROUND BLACK PEPPER
- 115 G (4 OZ) BUTTER
- APPROX 3 TABLESPOONS COLD WATER
- 1 TABLESPOON VEGETABLE OIL
- 175 G (6 OZ) ONIONS, PEELED AND COARSELY CHOPPED
- 85 G (3 OZ) LANCASHIRE CHEESE, CRUMBLED OR COARSELY GRATED
- 85 G (3 OZ) RED LEICESTER CHEESE, COARSELY GRATED
- 60 G (2 OZ) GRUYERE CHEESE, COARSELY GRATED
- 60 G (2 OZ) FRESH PARMESAN CHEESE, FINELY GRATED
- 2 TABLESPOONS COARSELY SNIPPED CHIVES
- 4 EGGS, SIZE 2, BEATEN
- 285 ML (½ PINT) MILK
- 2–3 MEDIUM FIRM TOMATOES, SLICED

PREPARATION TIME: 40 MINUTES
COOKING TIME: 50–60 MINUTES
SERVES SIX

PREHEAT the oven to 220°C (425°F, gas mark 7). Sift the flour and a pinch of salt into a bowl, rub in the butter until the mixture resembles fine breadcrumbs, then add enough water to make a firm dough. Roll out the dough, on a lightly floured surface, to an oblong a little larger than a 28 × 18 × 3.8 cm (11 × 7 × 1½ in) tin. Line the tin with the dough and trim the edges, leaving about 1.3 cm (½ in) above the top of the tin. Fold over the excess dough to make a rim and pinch decoratively. Line the pastry case with crumpled greaseproof paper, fill with baking beans and bake 'blind' for 10 minutes.

Meanwhile, heat the oil in a small pan and cook the chopped onions slowly for about 10 minutes, until soft and golden brown. Take the flan case from the oven, remove the paper and the baking beans and reduce the oven temperature to 180°C (350°F, gas mark 4).

Spread the onions evenly over the bottom of the flan case. Mix together all the cheeses and the snipped chives and spread over the onions. Beat together the eggs and milk and season with salt and pepper. Pour the liquid over the cheese and chive mixture and decorate the top attractively with the tomato slices.

Bake in the centre of the oven for 35–40 minutes or until the pastry is golden brown and the filling is lightly set. Serve the flan warm.

Eggs Mornay

Vegetarians will find this makes an excellent main course

PUT the milk, parsley sprig, peppercorns, nutmeg, onion and bay leaf into a saucepan and bring to the boil. Remove from the heat, cover and leave to stand for 30 minutes. Strain the milk into a jug, discarding the herbs and onion.

Arrange the eggs, cut sides down, in single layers in four heatproof dishes. Melt the butter in a saucepan, stir in the flour and cook for 1 minute over a low heat. Gradually stir in the milk and bring to the boil, stirring continuously, until the sauce thickens. Reduce the heat and cook for 2–3 minutes.

Remove from the heat and stir in the Gruyère and Parmesan cheeses and the cream. Season the sauce well, then pour evenly over the eggs. Cook under a moderately hot grill until golden brown and bubbling hot.

Garnish with a sprinkling of paprika and the parsley sprigs. Serve with hot buttered toast as a snack, or with cooked rice and green beans as a main course.

The piquancy of this dish is created by balancing the flavours of Gruyère and Parmesan cheeses with those of the herbs and spices.

INGREDIENTS

- 425ML (3/4 PINT) MILK
- 1 FRESH PARSLEY SPRIG
- 4 BLACK PEPPERCORNS
- 1/4 LEVEL TEASPOON GROUND NUTMEG
- 1/2 SMALL ONION, PEELED AND CHOPPED
- 1 BAY LEAF
- 8 EGGS, SIZE 2, HARD-BOILED, SHELLED AND HALVED
- 30G (1 OZ) BUTTER
- 30G (1 OZ) PLAIN FLOUR
- 30G (1 OZ) GRUYERE CHEESE, GRATED
- 30G (1 OZ) PARMESAN CHEESE, GRATED
- 4 TABLESPOONS SINGLE CREAM
- SALT AND FRESHLY GROUND BLACK PEPPER
- PAPRIKA AND PARSLEY SPRIGS TO GARNISH

PREPARATION TIME: 25 MINUTES
COOKING TIME: 10 MINUTES
SERVES FOUR

THROUGH A GLASS CLEARLY
A significant kitchen revolution was the invention of attractive, heatproof kitchenware that could be brought from oven to table. Much of the credit goes to the German Otto Schott who mixed boron oxide with silica to make a glass that could resist rapid changes in temperature. However, it was Corning, a US company, that first marketed it and called it Pyrex.

Mushroom Pancakes

Served with a green salad, these make a fine lunch or supper dish

INGREDIENTS

For the pancakes
115g (4oz) plain flour
Pinch of salt
1 egg, size 2
285ml (½ pint) milk
3 tablespoons vegetable oil for frying

For the sauce
Bouquet garni (see p.440)
2 cloves
570ml (1 pint) milk
45g (1½oz) butter
45g (1½oz) plain flour
¼ teaspoon ground coriander
3 tablespoons chopped fresh chervil or parsley

For the filling
60g (2oz) unsalted butter
1 large onion, peeled and chopped
675g (1½lb) mixed mushrooms—chanterelles (stalks removed), ceps and field; wiped and chopped
2 tablespoons dry sherry
Salt and freshly ground black pepper
60g (2oz) Cheddar cheese, grated

Preparation time: 1¼ hours
Standing time: 1 hour
Cooking time: 40 minutes
Serves four

To prepare the pancakes, sift the flour and salt into a bowl. Make a well in the centre, add the egg and gradually whisk in the milk until the batter is smooth. Pour into a measuring jug and set aside.

To prepare the sauce, add the bouquet garni and cloves to the milk and bring to the boil. Remove from the heat, cover and infuse for 30 minutes.

Meanwhile, prepare the filling. Melt the butter in a medium saucepan, add the onion and cook until soft. Add the mushrooms and sherry, cover and cook for 30 minutes, stirring occasionally. Uncover and cook for a further 15 minutes or until most of the liquid has evaporated. Remove the pan from the heat, season the filling, cover and set aside.

To cook the pancakes, heat 1 teaspoon of the oil in an 18cm (7in) nonstick frying pan until a faint haze is given off. Stir the batter and pour in one-eighth. Tilt the pan so that it coats the base evenly, then cook over a moderate heat for 1–2 minutes or until the underside is golden. Turn the pancake over and cook for a minute more, then tip it onto a plate and cover with a greaseproof sheet. Make seven more pancakes in this way, interleaving them with greaseproof sheets.

Preheat the oven to 200°C, (400°F, gas mark 6). To make the sauce, strain the infused milk into a jug. Melt the butter in a medium saucepan, stir in the flour and cook over a moderate heat for 1 minute. Gradually stir in the milk and bring to the boil, stirring continuously until the sauce thickens. Reduce the heat and cook for 2–3 minutes. Remove from the heat, season with salt, pepper and coriander and stir in the chopped chervil or parsley.

Lightly oil a shallow ovenproof dish. Spoon some mixture onto the centre of each pancake, roll up and place, folded side down, in the dish. Pour over the sauce, sprinkle with the cheese and cook in the centre of the oven for 35–40 minutes or until golden brown and bubbling.

These country pancakes are filled with field mushrooms, ceps and chanterelles.

As a timesaver, make the pancakes the day before eating. Store them in a polythene bag in the refrigerator.

Cheese sausages were a cheap and healthy alternative for country folk who could not afford meat.

Glamorgan Sausages

This versatile vegetarian sausage is equally at home with bacon and eggs on the breakfast table or with a salad on the picnic table

PUT the cheese, fresh breadcrumbs, leek or spring onion, parsley, thyme and mustard powder into a bowl with some salt and pepper and mix together. Mix in the egg yolks and, if necessary, a little of the white to make a stiff paste. Do not make the mixture too soft as it will be difficult to roll into shapes.

Divide the mixture into eight equal pieces and, using your hands, roll each piece into a sausage shape or a ball. Pour the egg whites onto a plate and whisk them lightly with a fork until they break up. Spread the dried breadcrumbs or raspings on another plate. Put the cheese sausages or balls into the egg white and brush with a pastry brush until well coated. Using a fork, lift one at a time from the egg white, draining off any excess, and roll in the breadcrumbs until evenly covered.

Deep or shallow fry the sausages or balls in the hot vegetable oil or lard for about 4 minutes until crisp and golden brown. Drain well on kitchen paper and serve, piping hot, with a salad.

INGREDIENTS

175G (6OZ) CAERPHILLY CHEESE, FINELY GRATED
115G (4OZ) FRESH WHITE BREADCRUMBS
2 LEVEL TABLESPOONS VERY FINELY CHOPPED LEEK OR SPRING ONION
2 ROUNDED TABLESPOONS FINELY CHOPPED FRESH PARSLEY
½ LEVEL TEASPOON FINELY CHOPPED FRESH THYME OR ¼ LEVEL TEASPOON DRIED THYME
¼ LEVEL TEASPOON ENGLISH MUSTARD POWDER
SALT AND FRESHLY GROUND BLACK PEPPER
2 EGGS, SIZE 2, SEPARATED
45G (1½OZ) DRIED WHITE BREADCRUMBS OR RASPINGS (SEE P.440)
VEGETABLE OIL OR LARD FOR DEEP OR SHALLOW FRYING

PREPARATION TIME: 15 MINUTES
COOKING TIME: 4–6 MINUTES
SERVES FOUR

Home Service

When home deliveries were a commonplace of shopping, an army of carriers brought colour and vitality to the streets

OF ALL THE SPIRITS of the past that may flit about the highways and byways of Britain, the most persistent must surely be those of the generations of entrepreneurs who in their earthly state made a living by bringing goods to the customer. Farthest wandering were the pedlars and packmen who hawked ribbons and pins, needles, bootlaces and gossip to remote Highland crofts and other lonely places. In less harsh latitudes, these were replaced by carriers who with horse and cart, transported village produce to market and returned with parcels, cloth and other goods from town.

On Fridays, a fishmonger's van would call round the villages. Saturday might bring a muffin man, with clanging handbell and tray balanced on his head, and perhaps a pieman with a fragrant basket. There were local specialists too, like the West Country fishermen who used to strike inland hawking herrings and pilchards to be salted down ready for winter. Such men brought colour and a glimpse of the outside world to secluded communities. But street vendors in towns and cities also cultivated dash and style—like the costermongers with their velveteen jackets and impenetrable slang and the pretty fisher girls of Edinburgh who attracted custom with bright, traditional costumes and cries of 'Caller herrin'!'

However, these freelancers did not have the streets to themselves. With refrigeration far from universal, deliveries had to be prompt. And so swelling the host of kerbside purveyors of apples and flowers, pea soup and saveloys, coffee and hot pies that thronged the city streets, was an army of specialist carriers, each with his own dress and traditions. Milk came in churns mounted on three-wheeled handcarts and was measured out from brass-labelled jugs. Butchers' boys wore long, white aprons kilted up at one side and carried the meat on wooden stretchers on their shoulders, while grocers' and greengrocers' lads pedalled massive bicycles with large iron baskets before and the shop's name on a plate beneath the crossbar. Bakers' roundsmen often carried ribboned whips and drove horses and carts of shiny smartness.

THE GREENGROCER'S FLYING SQUAD TAKES A BREAK

Then, as the century advanced, the army of vendors and carriers began to retreat from both countryside and town. Public and private transport improved, enabling people to visit shops more frequently, and food hygiene regulations began to exercise their grip on street traders. Errand boys have almost vanished, as have the itinerant food vendors, taking a touch of spontaneity out of life with them. Now it is only beneath the bright awnings and naphtha flares of street markets and country town squares that some of the old zest can still be savoured.

City types

Day began early for the men and boys who delivered the city's breakfasts. There were the milkmen with odd little three-wheeled carts, who filled jugs from churns at the doorstep. There was the grocer's boy and the baker's roundsman who accepted tokens for bread in lieu of cash.

Country cousins

Deliveries or mobile shops were an essential part of country life. Apart from fish and chipperies, there were grocers, butchers and fishmongers on wheels too.

The entrepreneurs

One of the joys of a city stroll was to pick up snacks along the way—a bag of hot chestnuts straight from the coals, an ice cream in the park, some whelks from a stall, or a meat pie advertised by the pieman's bell.

An Excellent Cheese Soufflé

Cheese soufflé is an excellent standby when time and ingredients are in short supply, and it will never fail to impress family or guests

INGREDIENTS

30G (1 OZ) BUTTER
30G (1 OZ) PLAIN FLOUR
150ML (¼ PINT) MILK
85G (3 OZ) MATURE CHEDDAR CHEESE, GRATED
¼ LEVEL TEASPOON SALT
¼ LEVEL TEASPOON FRESHLY GROUND BLACK PEPPER
¼ LEVEL TEASPOON ENGLISH MUSTARD POWDER OR GROUND NUTMEG
4 EGGS, SIZE 1 OR 2, SEPARATED
15G (½ OZ) PARMESAN CHEESE, GRATED

PREPARATION TIME: 20 MINUTES
COOKING TIME: 30 MINUTES
SERVES FOUR AS A STARTER, TWO AS A LIGHT MEAL

PREHEAT the oven to 190°C (375°F, gas mark 5). Melt the butter in a medium saucepan over moderate heat, stir in the flour and cook gently for 1 minute. Gradually add the milk and bring to the boil, stirring all the time until very thick and smooth.

Remove the pan from the heat and stir in the grated Cheddar cheese, salt and pepper and the mustard or nutmeg. Leave to cool slightly, then beat in the egg yolks, one at a time.

Whisk the egg whites in a clean, grease-free bowl until they are stiff and glossy, but not dry. Add 2–3 tablespoons of the whisked whites to the cheese sauce and stir in so as to thin the sauce to a consistency similar to that of the whisked egg whites. Gently fold the remaining whisked egg whites into the sauce.

Pour into a 1.4 litre (2½ pint) buttered soufflé dish. Sprinkle with the Parmesan cheese and bake in the centre of the oven for about 30 minutes until it is well risen, golden and just set.

Serve immediately either as a starter or accompanied by a salad for a light lunch or supper.

This light soufflé rises so well that the traditional straight-sided dish should be filled no more than three-quarters full with the mixture.

To prevent a disastrous deflation, keep the oven door closed while the soufflé is cooking.

Garnish the eggs with herbs, paprika, finely chopped fried onion or crushed peppercorns.

EGG SELLING
'Go to work on an egg' belongs to much the same era as the Beatles' hit, 'Yesterday'. Yet the slogan, like the song, has much lasting wisdom to recommend it.

Eggs Baked with Cream

Baked eggs make a delicious breakfast, brunch or supper dish—in fact, they are excellent any time you want a quick, simple meal

PREHEAT the oven to 180°C (350°F, gas mark 4). Spread the softened butter over the bases and round the sides of four individual cocotte or ramekin dishes to coat them. Season the insides of the dishes well with the salt and freshly ground black pepper.

Crack an egg into each dish, then spoon 2 tablespoons of the cream over each. Place on a baking tray and bake for 8–10 minutes until the whites are set but the yolks are still quite soft.

Serve at once with slices of crusty bread or hot, buttered toast.

INGREDIENTS

15G (½OZ) BUTTER, SOFTENED
SALT AND FRESHLY GROUND BLACK PEPPER
4 EGGS, SIZE 1 OR 2
8 TABLESPOONS DOUBLE CREAM

PREPARATION TIME: 5 MINUTES
COOKING TIME: 10 MINUTES
SERVES FOUR AS A STARTER

These neatly cut cheese and leek sandwiches are about to be transformed into a substantial dish.

This cheese pudding is a good way of using up stale bread. It can also be made with thinly sliced onions instead of leeks.

Aunt Ida's Welsh Cheese Pudding

There are many recipes for this hearty dish—this version has stood the test of time and remains a family favourite

INGREDIENTS

3 MEDIUM SLICES WHITE BREAD
3 MEDIUM SLICES WHOLEMEAL BREAD
60G (2OZ) BUTTER, SOFTENED
1 MEDIUM LEEK, TRIMMED, THINLY SLICED AND WASHED
225G (8OZ) CAERPHILLY CHEESE, CRUMBLED
2 EGGS, SIZE 2
¼ LEVEL TEASPOON ENGLISH MUSTARD POWDER
SALT AND FRESHLY GROUND BLACK PEPPER
570ML (1 PINT) MILK
30G (1OZ) WALNUT HALVES, CHOPPED
FINELY CHOPPED SPRING ONIONS TO GARNISH

PREPARATION TIME: 20 MINUTES
STANDING TIME: 30 MINUTES
COOKING TIME: 1 HOUR
SERVES FOUR TO SIX

SPREAD each slice of bread thickly with the butter. Using one white slice and one wholemeal slice of bread for each, make sandwiches with the sliced leek and 175g (6oz) of the crumbled cheese. Press firmly together, then cut each sandwich into four triangles and arrange, with the points standing up, in a 2 litre (3½ pint), shallow ovenproof dish.

Beat the eggs, mustard, seasoning and milk together, strain over the sandwiches and leave to stand for 30 minutes.

Preheat the oven to 160°C (325°F), gas mark 3). Scatter the remaining cheese and the walnuts over the pudding and cook in the oven for 45 minutes to 1 hour or until set with a crisp topping. Sprinkle with the spring onions and serve.

Fried Eggs with Anchovy Butter Sauce

These eggs can also be used as a sandwich filling if eight slices of bread are substituted for the toast

Drain the anchovies, reserving the oil. Cut two large anchovy fillets into long, thin strips and reserve for the garnish. Mash the remaining anchovies well with a fork, then mash or beat in 60 g (2 oz) of the butter. Alternatively, for a smoother texture, purée the anchovies and the butter in a small liquidiser or food processor. Toast the bread, spread with the anchovy butter and keep warm.

Put 30 g (1 oz) butter into a large frying pan and heat until bubbling. Break four of the eggs into the butter, spacing evenly in the pan. Fry the eggs over a moderate heat until the whites are set but the yolks are still runny.

Remove from the heat, drain well and transfer to the toast, arranging two eggs on each slice. Keep warm. Add the remaining butter to the pan and prepare the other four eggs in the same way. Keep warm while making the sauce.

Add the reserved anchovy oil to the butter in the pan and cook, over a moderately high heat, until the butter begins to brown. Remove from the heat, carefully add the vinegar (which will sizzle hard), then stir in the chopped parsley. Spoon a little over each egg to glaze. Garnish with the strips of anchovy.

Serve at once on a large, warm platter or on individual plates.

Ingredients

- 50 g (1¾ oz) tinned anchovies
- 115 g (4 oz) butter at room temperature
- 4 large slices of bread, toasted
- 8 eggs, size 1 or 2
- 2 tablespoons red wine vinegar
- 2 tablespoons chopped fresh parsley

Preparation time: 15 minutes

Cooking time: 5 minutes

Serves four

With very little effort, everyday fried eggs, served on slices of hot, buttered toast, are transformed into a delicious weekend breakfast, brunch or light supper.

Relished by gentlemen
Filleted, brined and preserved in oil, the anchovy has been welcomed by British cooks since the 16th century. It has proved its versatility over and over again, not only as a 'whet' or appetiser but as an after-dinner savoury, a pizza topping and, not least, as Patum Peperium, a fish paste.

Take attractively presented, homemade potted cheese with you when visiting friends at Christmas.

Instead of mace and pepper, try some other seasonings—for instance, use curry powder.

Potted Cheese

Here's how to turn workaday cheese—Cheshire, in this case, but any hard cheese will do—into a spirited, celebratory snack

INGREDIENTS

- 225G (8OZ) CHESHIRE CHEESE, FINELY GRATED
- 115G (4OZ) BUTTER, SOFTENED
- ½ LEVEL TEASPOON PAPRIKA
- ½ LEVEL TEASPOON GROUND MACE
- FEW DROPS TABASCO SAUCE
- FRESHLY GROUND BLACK PEPPER
- 2 TABLESPOONS DRY MADEIRA OR SHERRY
- 115G (4OZ) CLARIFIED BUTTER (SEE P.440)

PREPARATION TIME: 15 MINUTES

SERVES EIGHT AS A STARTER OR CHEESE COURSE, FOUR AS A LIGHT LUNCH OR SUPPER

BEAT together the grated cheese, butter, paprika, mace and Tabasco sauce and add black pepper to taste. Finally, beat in the dry Madeira or sherry and press into four 150 ml (¼ pint) ramekins or small pots, and then smooth the surface. Melt the clarified butter and carefully spoon it over the potted cheese to cover completely. Chill in the refrigerator for at least 1 hour.

The potted cheese will keep in the refrigerator for at least a week. Serve with crusty bread, oatcakes and celery.

Macaroni Cheese

This dish, of Italian origin, has been enjoyed in England since the 14th century

PREHEAT the oven to 200°C (400°F, gas mark 6). Bring a large pan of lightly salted water to the boil. Add the macaroni to the pan and cook, uncovered, at a rolling boil for 12 minutes, or as directed on the packet.

In the meantime, melt the butter in a saucepan, stir in the flour and cook gently for 1 minute. Gradually stir in the milk, or the milk and cream. Bring to the boil over a moderate heat, stirring continuously until the mixture thickens. Remove the pan from the heat and season the sauce well with the mustard, salt and nutmeg. Add the Cheddar and Stilton cheeses and stir until melted.

Drain the macaroni well, then mix into the sauce and pour into a large, shallow ovenproof dish. Sprinkle over the Lancashire cheese and cook in the centre of the oven for 35 minutes or until the top is golden and bubbling.

Arrange the tomato slices on top and return to the oven for 5 minutes. Garnish with the celery leaves and serve with a celery, walnut and watercress salad.

Nations united—here Italian pasta has been married to three of the best English cheeses to create a supper dish that is second to none.

INGREDIENTS

275G (10OZ) MACARONI
60G (2OZ) BUTTER
60G (2OZ) PLAIN FLOUR
850 ML (1½ PINTS) MILK OR 725 ML (1¼ PINTS) MILK AND 150ML (¼ PINT) DOUBLE CREAM
¼ LEVEL TEASPOON ENGLISH MUSTARD POWDER
SALT
PINCH OF GRATED NUTMEG
115G (4OZ) MATURE ENGLISH CHEDDAR CHEESE, GRATED
115G (4OZ) BLUE STILTON CHEESE, CRUMBLED
60G (2OZ) LANCASHIRE CHEESE, GRATED
2 TOMATOES, SLICED
CELERY LEAVES TO GARNISH
PREPARATION TIME: 25 MINUTES
COOKING TIME: 40 MINUTES
SERVES SIX

MACARONI IN MIND
Nowadays the trend for pasta enthusiasts is to buy their favourite from a specialist shop where they can watch it being freshly made in front of them. Earlier in the century, however, it was available only in tins and packets, and often in forms that would have seemed strange in its Italian birthplace. This wholesome version, for instance, enjoyed considerable popularity in Britain in the interwar years.

Stand the cooked flan on an upturned bowl to allow the side of the flan tin to drop and the flan to be removed easily.

The flan's Cheddar filling is crowned by a golden, soufflé-style topping.

Melting Cheese Flan

This rather unusual recipe was inspired by Agnes Marshall, who taught it to pupils at her London cookery school in the last century

INGREDIENTS

FOR THE PASTRY CASE
175G (6OZ) PLAIN FLOUR
PINCH OF SALT
PINCH OF ENGLISH MUSTARD POWDER
85G (3OZ) BUTTER
45G (1½OZ) MATURE CHEDDAR CHEESE, FINELY GRATED
1 EGG YOLK, SIZE 2
APPROX 1 TABLESPOON COLD WATER

FOR THE FILLING
30G (1OZ) BUTTER
30G (1OZ) PLAIN FLOUR
150ML (¼ PINT) MILK
175G (6OZ) MATURE CHEDDAR CHEESE, FINELY GRATED
2 EGG YOLKS, SIZE 2
3 TABLESPOONS DOUBLE CREAM
FRESHLY GROUND BLACK PEPPER

FOR THE TOPPING
3 EGG WHITES, SIZE 2
PINCH OF SALT
PINCH OF CAYENNE PEPPER
30G (1OZ) MATURE CHEDDAR CHEESE, FINELY GRATED
1 TABLESPOON FINE FRESH BROWN BREADCRUMBS

PREPARATION TIME: 30 MINUTES
CHILLING TIME: 30 MINUTES
COOKING TIME: 45 MINUTES
SERVES FOUR TO SIX

TO MAKE the pastry case, sift the flour, salt and mustard into a bowl and rub in the butter until the mixture resembles fine breadcrumbs. Mix in the cheese and bind with egg yolk and water to form a stiff dough. Knead the dough on a lightly floured surface until smooth, then roll out and line a 23 cm (9 in) flan tin. Trim the edge, then prick well all over with a fork. Refrigerate for 30 minutes.

Meanwhile, heat the oven to 220°C (425°F, gas mark 7). Bake the chilled pastry case in the centre of the oven for 20–25 minutes until lightly browned.

When the pastry case has been cooking for 15 minutes, start to make the filling. Melt the butter in a saucepan, stir in the flour and cook over a low heat for 1 minute. Gradually stir in the milk and bring to the boil, stirring continuously until the sauce becomes extremely thick. Add the finely grated Cheddar cheese and stir over a moderate heat until the cheese melts and the mixture becomes smooth, but take care not to overheat. Remove the pan from the heat, beat in the egg yolks, one at a time, then stir in the cream. Season well with pepper.

When the pastry case is cooked, remove it from the oven and fill it with the cheese sauce. Whisk the egg whites for the topping with the salt and cayenne pepper until very stiff, then quickly spoon the mixture over the cheese filling to cover it completely. Sprinkle the top of the flan first with the cheese, then with the breadcrumbs, and return it to the oven. Bake for 15 minutes or until golden brown on top. Serve hot, accompanied by a tossed green salad.

Summer Potato Nests

Children will love the flavour and colour of this attractive dish

BOIL the potatoes in lightly salted water for 20 minutes until just cooked, adding the peas for the last 3 minutes of cooking time. Pour into a colander and drain thoroughly. Return to the saucepan and cook over a high heat for a few seconds to evaporate the excess moisture.

Preheat the oven to 200°C (400°F, gas mark 6). Pass the potatoes and peas through a potato ricer or sieve into a bowl, then beat in the butter and season well with salt, pepper and the grated nutmeg. Beat until smooth.

Spread about a quarter of the potato mixture in the bottom of a well-buttered, shallow, 30 × 23 cm (12 × 9 in) ovenproof dish. Put the rest of the mixture into a large piping bag fitted with a large star nozzle and pipe eight potato nests on top of the potato mixture, each nest large enough to hold an egg. Bake in the centre of the oven for 15 minutes, or until lightly browned and piping hot, then remove from the oven.

Break an egg into a cup, then carefully pour it into one of the potato nests. Fill the other nests in the same way. Season lightly with salt and pepper. Mix the chives with the cream and spoon some over each egg. Return the dish to the oven and bake for a further 12 minutes or until the egg whites are just set.

Garnish with long chives and serve immediately with a tomato salad.

INGREDIENTS

- 1.1 KG (2½ LB) BOILING POTATOES, SUCH AS DESIREE, PEELED AND QUARTERED
- 340 G (12 OZ) FROZEN PEAS
- 60 G (2 OZ) BUTTER, CUBED
- SALT AND FRESHLY GROUND BLACK PEPPER
- ¼ LEVEL TEASPOON FRESHLY GRATED NUTMEG
- 8 EGGS, SIZE 3
- 2 TABLESPOONS SNIPPED FRESH CHIVES,
- 150 ML (¼ PINT) DOUBLE CREAM
- A FEW LONG CHIVES TO GARNISH

PREPARATION TIME: 30 MINUTES
COOKING TIME: 50 MINUTES
SERVES FOUR

The delicate pale green of the nests is achieved by mashing peas with the potatoes.

THE ICEMAN COMETH
On trips to arctic Labrador, biologist Clarence Birdseye observed that fish that froze as they were caught remained fresh for months. The speed of freezing was obviously the crucial factor and, after lengthy experiments, he opened his first frozen food plant in 1924.

The addition of tomato butter with Worcestershire sauce gives that extra savour to this omelette.

Cook quickly over a high heat to ensure that the omelette is light and succulent.

Cheshire Cheese Omelette with Tomato Butter

You can swap tomato butter for anchovy butter in this versatile recipe

INGREDIENTS

- 45g (1½oz) butter
- 1 small shallot, peeled and finely chopped
- 4 eggs, size 2
- 2 tablespoons water
- 1 tablespoon finely chopped fresh parsley
- Generous pinch of fresh or dried thyme
- Salt and cayenne pepper
- 1 medium tomato, skinned, deseeded and chopped
- ¼ teaspoon Worcestershire sauce
- 85g (3oz) white Cheshire cheese, finely grated
- Parsley sprigs to garnish

Preparation time: 20 minutes
Cooking time: 10 minutes
Serves two

Set 30g (1oz) of the butter aside, then divide the remainder into three equal pieces. Melt one piece in a small frying pan, add the shallot and sauté gently until softened. Put the shallot into a bowl with the eggs, water, chopped parsley, thyme and some salt and cayenne pepper. Whisk well together and set aside.

Melt the reserved 30g (1oz) of butter in the same small frying pan and, when foaming, add the chopped tomato and Worcestershire sauce. Reduce the heat to very low and keep warm.

In a well seasoned, small omelette pan, melt another of the small pieces of butter until it begins to sizzle, then quickly pour in half of the egg mixture and stir with a fork, over a high heat, until all the butter is absorbed by the egg. Stop stirring and cook for about 30 seconds until the egg is almost set, but still very moist on top. Sprinkle half the cheese over the omelette, fold into three, turn out onto a hot plate and keep hot while making another omelette in the same way.

Spoon the hot tomato butter over each omelette, garnish with the parsley and serve at once with crusty bread and a salad, if wished.

The tomato butter can be replaced with anchovy butter by the addition to the butter of either two finely chopped anchovy fillets, or ¼ teaspoon anchovy essence in place of the tomato.

Alternatively, the amount of cheese can be reduced to 60g (2oz) and 30g (1oz) of finely chopped ham can be added to the omelette.

Mumbled Eggs

Include mumbled eggs in your menu when a leisurely breakfast is the order of the day

MELT 30 g (1 oz) of the butter over a low heat in a nonstick frying pan. Add the mushrooms to the pan, cover and cook gently for 10 minutes or until they are just softened. Steam the asparagus spears for 5–8 minutes until tender.

Meanwhile, in a mixing bowl, beat the eggs and cream together and season with the salt and freshly ground white pepper. Melt the remaining butter in a heavy-based saucepan. Add the egg and cream mixture and stir over a low heat until the eggs are just beginning to set. Remove from the heat and keep warm while toasting the bread. Cut the toast into triangles and arrange in a toast rack.

Spoon the mumbled eggs onto individual, warmed serving plates. Arrange the mushrooms and asparagus spears alongside the eggs. Sprinkle with the chives and serve immediately with the triangles of toast and a dish of butter.

INGREDIENTS

45 G (1½ OZ) BUTTER
4 LARGE FIELD OR FLAT MUSHROOMS, WIPED
225 G (8 OZ) ASPARAGUS SPEARS, TRIMMED
8 EGGS, SIZE 2
150 ML (¼ PINT) SINGLE CREAM
SALT AND FRESHLY GROUND WHITE PEPPER
4 MEDIUM SLICES WHITE BREAD
1 TABLESPOON SNIPPED FRESH CHIVES

PREPARATION TIME: 15 MINUTES
COOKING TIME: 10 MINUTES
SERVES FOUR

This luscious version of scrambled eggs is accompanied by asparagus and mushrooms.

FAST-TRACK FOOD
Breakfast, whether in a railway company hotel or dining car, was considered the star meal by many passengers. This 1930s LNER advertisement emphasised the aim of the railway's chefs—perfection and nothing less.

Tudor Pye with Goat's Cheese

This 'pye' from the past, with its unusual cheese and herb filling is, in fact, an ancestor of the quiche

INGREDIENTS

- 225 g (8 oz) firm goat's cheese
- 1 tablespoon chopped fresh young thyme leaves
- 2 tablespoons extra virgin olive oil
- 275 g (10 oz) wholemeal flour
- Salt and freshly ground black pepper
- 175 g (6 oz) unsalted butter
- Approx 3 tablespoons chilled water
- 2 spring onions, trimmed and finely chopped
- 4 eggs, size 2, beaten
- 425 ml (¾ pint) single cream
- Fresh young thyme sprigs and fresh flowers such as nasturtiums, marigolds or pansies to garnish (optional)

Preparation time: 35 minutes
Marinating time: 1–3 hours
Cooking time: 50 minutes
Serves six to eight

If you don't like goat's cheese, use Lancashire, Stilton or Cheddar instead.

Cut the goat's cheese into small cubes and put them into a bowl. Mix the thyme with the oil, pour over the cheese and toss together very gently. Cover the mixture and set aside to marinate for at least an hour at room temperature or for 2–3 hours in the refrigerator.

Preheat the oven to 220°C (425°F, gas mark 7). Meanwhile, to make the pastry, sift the flour and ¼ level teaspoon of the salt into a mixing bowl, rub in the butter until the mixture resembles coarse breadcrumbs, then mix with enough water to make a moist, but not sticky, dough. Knead the dough lightly on a floured surface for a few seconds until smooth, then roll out a round about 32 cm (12½ in) in diameter. Line a 24 × 3.8 cm (9½ × 1½ in) straight-sided, loose-based flan tin or ring with the dough and trim the edge.

Line the pastry case with crumpled greaseproof paper and fill with ceramic baking beans, then bake 'blind' for 10 minutes. Remove the beans and bake it for 10 minutes more until the pastry is cooked but still pale in colour.

Meanwhile, roll out the trimmings and cut out shapes such as the fleurs-de-lis, crosses, stars, or leaves and flowers. Place the shapes on a baking tray and bake for 5–10 minutes until crisp and lightly browned. Remove the flan and the shapes from the oven and place the shapes on a wire rack to cool. Spoon the cheese mixture into the pastry case and sprinkle with the chopped spring onions. Lightly whisk the eggs with the cream and some salt and pepper and strain the mixture into the pastry case over the cheese and spring onions.

Reduce the oven temperature to 180°C (350°F, gas mark 4) and bake for 20–30 minutes or until the custard is lightly set. Allow to cool slightly, then remove from the tin or ring. Put the pie onto a serving dish and decorate with the pastry trimmings, thyme and the fresh flowers, if using. Serve with a salad.

Small, precooked pastry shapes and fresh flower petals make novel decorations that add an unusual finishing touch much loved by our Elizabethan ancestors.

These little 'devils', filled with anchovy-flavoured cream cheese, make a tasty summer lunch.

Red devil
In the 18th century, the use of hot, spicy sauces, containing ingredients such as cayenne pepper, was a popular means of seasoning meat, poultry, game and leftovers, but by the 19th century, the practice had spread to embrace breakfast dishes, for example kidneys and poached or fried eggs.

Devilled Egg Salad

The old English term 'devilled' implies a dish that is highly seasoned, often through the inclusion of mustard or cayenne pepper

Cut one-third from the top of each egg and set aside, then cut a thin sliver from the bottom of each to expose the yolk. Carefully scoop out the yolks and set the whites aside in pairs. Press the yolks through a nylon sieve into a bowl, add the butter, anchovy essence, a little cayenne pepper and the cream cheese and beat together until smooth.

Spoon the mixture into a piping bag fitted with a small star nozzle. Place a little salad cress in each egg white, then pipe a swirl of the egg yolk mixture on top. Replace the reserved tops, setting them at an angle on top of the yolk mixture, and sprinkle the tops with a little cayenne pepper.

Mix together the watercress, shredded lettuce, sliced radishes and the remaining salad cress. Arrange on a serving dish and nestle the eggs among the leaves. Whisk together the olive oil, lemon juice and mustard for the dressing. Spoon over the salad and serve.

Ingredients

- 8 eggs, size 2, hard boiled and shelled
- 45 g (1½ oz) butter, melted
- 1 teaspoon anchovy essence
- Cayenne pepper
- 175 g (6 oz) cream cheese
- 1 standard punnet salad cress
- 60 g (2 oz) trimmed watercress leaves, washed and drained
- 6 cos lettuce leaves, finely shredded
- 6 radishes, trimmed and thinly sliced

For the dressing

- 3 tablespoons olive oil
- 2 teaspoons lemon juice
- ½–1 level teaspoon whole-grain mustard

Preparation time: 40 minutes
Cooking time: 10 minutes
Serves four

Stilton Savoury

Pears complement this noble cheese which loses not a whit of its flavour in cooking

INGREDIENTS

- 4 THICK SLICES WHOLEMEAL BREAD
- 30G (1 OZ) BUTTER, SOFTENED
- 60G (2 OZ) TRIMMED WATERCRESS LEAVES, WASHED AND DRAINED
- 2 RIPE BUT FIRM PEARS, PEELED, HALVED, CORED AND THICKLY SLICED LENGTHWAYS
- 225G (8 OZ) BLUE STILTON CHEESE, THINLY SLICED

PREPARATION TIME: 15 MINUTES
COOKING TIME: 8 MINUTES
SERVES FOUR

PREHEAT the oven to 220°C (425°F, gas mark 7). Toast the slices of bread on both sides, butter them evenly and place the watercress leaves on top. Arrange the pear slices over the watercress leaves and cover them with the slices of Stilton cheese. Place the savouries, spaced apart, in a shallow ovenproof dish or on a nonstick baking sheet.

Cook in the centre of the oven for about 5 minutes, until the pears begin to turn golden and the cheese has melted.

The king of English cheeses sits magnificently enthroned on pear slices and watercress.

To prevent the peeled pears from turning brown before cooking, put them into a bowl of cold water with some lemon juice added to it.

The eggs and leeks lie ready to be topped with a cheese sauce and popped into the oven.

VICTORY EGG
In 1941, the Ministry of Food began to import dried eggs, with 'nothing taken away but moisture and the shell', from the USA. Consumers were, at first, hostile but as they learned to turn the yellow powder into omelettes and scrambled eggs, they grew more enthusiastic and when the Ministry ended the supply in 1946, it was forced, by housewives' protest, to reinstate it.

Anglesey Eggs

This substantial dish with a crunchy golden topping is perfect on its own or with a crisp green salad

PREHEAT the oven to 200°C (400°F, gas mark 6). Cut off the green parts from the leeks and chop them coarsely. Cut the white parts into 2.5 cm (1 in) pieces. Put the green parts into a saucepan with the potatoes, cover with cold water and bring to the boil. Reduce the heat, partially cover and simmer until the potatoes are cooked. At the same time, cook the white parts of the leeks, in a separate pan of boiling water, for 5–10 minutes, or until just tender. Drain well and set aside.

Drain the leeks and potatoes and mash them well with the cream and half the butter. Season with the salt and pepper and beat until fluffy. Spoon the mixture around the edge of an ovenproof dish and arrange the white leeks and the hard-boiled eggs in the centre.

Melt the remaining butter in a saucepan, stir in the flour and cook over a low heat for 1 minute. Gradually stir in the milk and bring to the boil, stirring continuously. Reduce the heat and cook for 2–3 minutes. Remove the pan from the heat, add the cheese and stir until melted. Season the sauce well, then pour over the eggs and leeks.

Bake in the centre of the oven for 20–30 minutes until heated through and golden brown on top. Sprinkle with a little paprika and serve.

INGREDIENTS

450 G (1 LB) BABY LEEKS, TRIMMED AND WASHED
675 G (1½ LB) POTATOES, PEELED AND QUARTERED
2 TABLESPOONS DOUBLE CREAM
60 G (2 OZ) BUTTER
SALT AND FRESHLY GROUND BLACK PEPPER
8 EGGS, SIZE 2, HARD-BOILED, SHELLED AND QUARTERED
30 G (1 OZ) PLAIN FLOUR
285 ML (½ PINT) MILK
85 G (3 OZ) MATURE CHEDDAR CHEESE, GRATED
PAPRIKA TO GARNISH

PREPARATION TIME: 40 MINUTES
COOKING TIME: 30 MINUTES
SERVES FOUR

Cauliflower Cheese with Tomato

Smooth, rich and velvety cauliflower cheese, a perennial favourite, is enlivened here by additional flavour and colour

INGREDIENTS

- 1 MEDIUM CAULIFLOWER
- 30G (1 OZ) BUTTER
- 30G (1 OZ) PLAIN FLOUR
- 285 ML (½ PINT) MILK
- 115G (4 OZ) RED LEICESTER CHEESE, COARSELY GRATED
- SALT AND FRESHLY GROUND BLACK PEPPER
- 175G (6 OZ) TOMATOES, SKINNED, DESEEDED AND ROUGHLY CHOPPED

PREPARATION TIME: 15 MINUTES

COOKING TIME: 15 MINUTES

SERVES FOUR AS AN ACCOMPANIMENT, OR TWO AS A LUNCH OR SUPPER DISH

TRIM the cauliflower and steam or boil whole for 10–15 minutes or until the floret stems are only just tender.

In the meantime, melt the butter in a saucepan over a low heat, stir in the flour and cook for 1 minute. Gradually stir in the milk and bring to the boil, stirring continuously. Reduce the heat and cook for 2–3 minutes more. Add 85 g (3 oz) of the cheese, some salt and pepper and all but 1 tablespoon of the tomatoes and stir until the cheese melts. Remove the pan from the heat and keep hot.

When the cauliflower is just tender, drain well and put into a warm, heatproof serving dish, pour over the hot sauce, sprinkle with the remaining cheese and tomato and serve at once. If liked, the top can be lightly browned by placing the dish under a hot grill for a few minutes.

Chopped ripe tomatoes and Red Leicester cheese guarantee a well-flavoured dish.

CURDS AND WHEY
After rennet has been added to the warmed milk in the tub, the whey separates from the solidified curds, here being cut by hand. Care must be taken in using the cutter, as rough treatment can fracture the fat globules and lose fat in the whey.

With a few extra ingredients, basic cheese on toast becomes a special treat, and a crunchy garnish of gherkin, celery leaves and tomato slices adds further to the enjoyment.

For instant snacks, keep a supply of the melted cheese mixture in the refrigerator ready to spread on toast.

Welsh Rabbit

Welsh rabbit is perfect for a quick snack or light lunch; for a delicious change, the bread can be fried in bacon fat instead of toasted

Melt the butter in a small saucepan and add the mustard, Worcestershire sauce, pepper, white breadcrumbs, egg yolks and cheese. Stir continuously over a gentle heat until the cheese has just melted. Do not allow the mixture to bubble as it will become stringy. Stir in the ale, remove from the heat and cool for 15 minutes.

Toast the bread on both sides, under a hot grill, until golden brown. Spread the cheese mixture onto one side of each slice of toast and grill for 1–2 minutes until bubbling and lightly browned. Garnish with gherkins, celery leaves and tomato.

To make buck rabbit, poach the eggs and place on top of the toasted cheese.

INGREDIENTS

- 60G (2OZ) BUTTER
- 1 LEVEL TEASPOON ENGLISH MUSTARD POWDER
- 1 TEASPOON WORCESTERSHIRE SAUCE
- FRESHLY GROUND BLACK PEPPER
- 30G (1OZ) FRESH WHITE BREADCRUMBS
- 2 EGG YOLKS, SIZE 2
- 225G (8OZ) MATURE CHEDDAR CHEESE, GRATED
- 5 TABLESPOONS LIGHT ALE
- 4 LARGE THICK SLICES GRANARY OR WHITE BREAD
- SLICED GHERKINS, CELERY LEAVES AND SLICED TOMATO TO GARNISH

To make buck rabbit
You will need 4 eggs, size 2, for poaching

Preparation time: 30 minutes
Cooking time: 5 minutes
Serves four

Adding sugar to the poaching water helps to set the egg white neatly. The fresher the eggs, the better they will keep their shape while they are being poached.

High tea with poached eggs evokes childhood memories of seaside holidays— fresh from the beach and ravenous!

Poached Eggs on Toast

Here is an idea for a quick, simple but colourful way of serving poached eggs

INGREDIENTS

- 8 THICK SLICES WHITE BREAD FROM A SMALL LOAF
- 115G (4OZ) BUTTER
- 4 TOMATOES, QUARTERED
- 30G (1OZ) PLAIN FLOUR
- 285ML (½ PINT) MILK
- SALT AND FRESHLY GROUND BLACK PEPPER
- 60G (2OZ) MATURE CHEDDAR CHEESE, FINELY GRATED
- 1 TABLESPOON WHITE WINE VINEGAR
- 8 VERY FRESH EGGS, SIZE 2, FREE RANGE IF POSSIBLE
- 1 TABLESPOON SNIPPED FRESH CHIVES TO GARNISH

PREPARATION TIME: 20 MINUTES
COOKING TIME: 15 MINUTES
SERVES FOUR

USING a large plain round pastry cutter, stamp out a round from the centre of each slice of bread. Toast the rounds on both sides, then spread them on one side with 30g (1oz) of the butter. Divide the tomatoes equally between four heatproof plates, placing them on the side of each, and dot with 60g (2oz) of the butter. Place two rounds of toast on each plate.

Melt the remaining butter in a small saucepan, stir in the flour and cook over a low heat for 1 minute. Gradually stir in the milk, season well and bring to the boil, stirring until thick. Reduce the heat and cook for 2–3 minutes. Add the cheese and stir until melted. Remove from the heat and keep warm.

Fill a large frying pan with water, add the vinegar and ½ level teaspoon of salt and bring to the boil. Break two eggs, each into a separate cup. Stir the water, then carefully drop in the eggs, one at a time. Cover and cook gently for 2–3 minutes until the whites are set. Lift the eggs out of the water using a slotted spoon, drain them on kitchen paper and place one on each piece of toast.

Cook the remaining eggs quickly in the same way and put them on the remaining rounds of toast. Spoon a little cheese sauce over each egg and grill, in two batches if necessary, for 2 minutes until lightly browned. Sprinkle the chives over the tomatoes and serve immediately.

Curried Eggs with Rice

Apple, spices and mango chutney combine to produce a curry sauce that is reminiscent of the days of the Raj

MELT the butter in a saucepan, add the onion and garlic and cook for 5 minutes, until softened but not browned. Mix in the apple, chutney, spices and curry powder and cook for 1 minute. Stir in the sieved tomatoes and bring to the boil, stirring. Reduce the heat, cover and simmer for 40 minutes. Meanwhile, bring the stock or water to the boil in a saucepan and stir in the rice. Lower the heat, cover tightly and cook gently for 20–25 minutes until the rice is cooked and all the liquid absorbed.

Preheat the oven to 190°C (375°F gas mark 5). Meanwhile, hard-boil the eggs for 10 minutes, immerse in cold water until cool, then remove the shells. Cut the eggs in half lengthways and remove the yolks. Pass the yolks through a nylon sieve into a bowl, add the chopped prawns, 3 tablespoons of the cream and the salt and pepper and mix well. Spoon into the egg whites and garnish with the reserved prawns.

Mix the parsley into the cooked rice and spoon it diagonally across a large, heatproof serving platter. Arrange the eggs on either side of the rice, then cover the platter loosely with foil and put it into the oven for 10 minutes.

Stir the lemon juice and remaining cream into the curry sauce, season to taste and heat for 2–3 minutes—but do not boil, as it will curdle. Pour some sauce into the spaces left at either end of the serving platter, and the rest into a heated serving bowl or sauceboat. Serve immediately, with a simple green salad, if liked.

Alternatively, the eggs and rice can be arranged on individual serving plates, heated through as above and served surrounded by the curry sauce.

Whole spices keep for up to six months in airtight containers and can be freshly ground as required.

INGREDIENTS

30G (1OZ) BUTTER
1 SMALL ONION, PEELED AND FINELY CHOPPED
1 GARLIC CLOVE, PEELED AND CRUSHED
1 DESSERT APPLE, PEELED, CORED AND FINELY CHOPPED
1 TABLESPOON MANGO CHUTNEY
½ LEVEL TEASPOON CHILLI POWDER
½ LEVEL TEASPOON GROUND CORIANDER
½ LEVEL TEASPOON GROUND CUMIN
PINCH OF GROUND GINGER
PINCH OF GROUND CINNAMON
1 LEVEL TEASPOON CURRY POWDER
400G (14OZ) TINNED TOMATOES, SIEVED
570ML (1 PINT) CHICKEN STOCK (SEE P.433) OR WATER
225G (8OZ) LONG-GRAIN WHITE RICE
8 EGGS, SIZE 2
225G (8OZ) FRESH COOKED PEELED PRAWNS OR FROZEN PRAWNS, THAWED AND DRAINED—16 RESERVED FOR GARNISH, THE REST CHOPPED
150ML (¼ PINT) SINGLE CREAM
SALT AND FRESHLY GROUND BLACK PEPPER
2 TABLESPOONS CHOPPED FRESH PARSLEY
2 TEASPOONS LEMON JUICE

PREPARATION TIME: 20 MINUTES
COOKING TIME: 45 MINUTES
SERVES FOUR

Vegetables and Salads

One sign that vegetables are being regarded as fun and not merely Good for You is the trend towards growing them decoratively, as in monastery gardens of old. Another is the gathering of recipes that present vegetables today as intriguing dishes in their own right rather than adjuncts to meat. There are *Parsnips and Walnuts* for instance; sturdy *Potato Baskets with Carrot and Oatmeal, Vegetable Loaf, Onion Cake, Mushrooms in Batter* for cocktail bites; and lastly the sharply refreshing *Dandelion and Nasturtium Salad.*

Cucumbers Braised with Baby Onions

Continental holidays have introduced the British to the taste of cooked cucumbers. Here, though, is a native recipe, and an old one at that

INGREDIENTS

285 ML (½ PINT) VEGETABLE STOCK (SEE P.434)
SALT
225 G (8 OZ) SPRING OR BUTTON ONIONS, PEELED
2 LARGE OR 4–5 SMALL CUCUMBERS
2 LARGE BASIL SPRIGS, FINELY SHREDDED
30 G (1 OZ) BUTTER
1 FRESH BASIL SPRIG TO GARNISH

PREPARATION TIME: 30 MINUTES
COOKING TIME: 35–50 MINUTES
SERVES FOUR

POUR the vegetable stock into a saucepan and season lightly with the salt, taking care not to add too much as the stock will later be boiled and reduced. Bring to the boil, add the spring or button onions and cook for 15–20 minutes, or until they are just tender.

Meanwhile, peel the cucumbers, cut them in half lengthways, remove the seeds with a teaspoon then cut them into thick slices. Add the cucumbers and shredded basil to the onions and cook for 10 minutes or until the cucumbers are just cooked through. Do not overcook.

Drain the cucumbers and onions, reserve the stock and put the vegetables into a serving dish and keep warm. Boil the reserved stock rapidly until it is reduced to about 3 tablespoons. Stir in the butter and heat gently, then spoon over the cucumbers and onions. Garnish with the sprig of basil and serve.

The joy of this dish lies in the blending of the flavours of the onions, cucumbers and basil.

If using small pickling onions, they will require 20-30 minutes cooking to tenderise them. But large bulbs from spring onions or small pearl onions require only 5-10 minutes cooking.

Beaten egg whites provide a crisp, golden cushion for the asparagus tips that top this elegant bake.

'SPARRERGRASS'
Asparagus has been grown in Britain since Roman times and has always been a luxury vegetable due to its fine flavour, brief season and problems of cultivation. Nowadays it is chiefly grown in the Vale of Evesham and East Anglia.

Asparagus à la Princesse

A royal approach to asparagus, the recipe includes a sauce enriched with egg yolks, cream and Parmesan cheese

PREHEAT the oven to 200°C (400°F, gas mark 6). Steam the asparagus for 12 minutes, or until just tender, then rinse under a cold running tap to stop the cooking and preserve the colour. Drain and dry well on kitchen paper. Cut into 3.8 cm (1½ in) pieces, and set the tips aside.

Melt the butter in a saucepan, add the shallots, and cook for 5 minutes over a moderate heat until softened but not coloured. Stir in the flour and cayenne pepper and cook for 1 minute. Whisk in the double cream or milk and stir over a moderate heat until the sauce thickens, then stir in the egg yolks, a squeeze of lemon juice, and 60 g (2 oz) of the Parmesan cheese. Season with the salt and pepper and fold in the asparagus stems. Pour the asparagus mixture into a shallow, ovenproof dish.

Whisk the egg whites with a pinch of salt and a squeeze of lemon juice until very stiff but not dry, then spoon evenly over the asparagus, to cover completely.

Arrange the reserved asparagus tips on top of the beaten egg whites and sprinkle with the remaining Parmesan cheese. Stand the dish in a roasting tin and fill the tin with hot water to halfway up the sides of the dish. Bake in the centre of the oven for 15 minutes until the egg is golden and crisp.

INGREDIENTS

- 450 G (1 LB) FRESH ASPARAGUS, TRIMMED
- 60 G (2 OZ) BUTTER
- 2 SHALLOTS, PEELED AND FINELY CHOPPED
- 30 G (1 OZ) PLAIN FLOUR
- ¼ LEVEL TEASPOON CAYENNE PEPPER
- 285 ML (½ PINT) DOUBLE CREAM, OR MILK
- 3 EGG YOLKS, SIZE 2
- ½ SMALL LEMON
- 85 G (3 OZ) PARMESAN CHEESE, GRATED
- SALT AND FRESHLY GROUND BLACK PEPPER
- 6 EGG WHITES, SIZE 2

PREPARATION TIME: 20 MINUTES
COOKING TIME: 15 MINUTES
SERVES SIX

The gallic touch
Natives of London's suburbia have long been convinced that the popular Breton onion sellers have pedalled from the coast with their wares on their handlebars. Alas, the onions are brought over in trucks and, from August to December, the vendors lodge in Lambeth whence they cycle out each day.

Chopped sage gives a special flavour to this cheese, walnut and raisin stuffing.

Stuffed Onions

These nutty, fruity onions are particularly good served with roast pork

INGREDIENTS

- 4 large onions, each 225–275g (8–10oz), peeled
- 175g (6oz) Brie cheese, cubed
- 60g (2oz) walnuts, almonds or hazelnuts, coarsely chopped
- 2 level tablespoons raisins
- 1 level tablespoon chopped fresh sage
- Salt and freshly ground black pepper
- 150ml (¼ pint) vegetable stock (see p.434)
- 30g (1oz) butter, melted
- 2 level teaspoons soft light brown sugar

Preparation time: 25 minutes
Cooking time: 45 minutes
Serves four

Preheat the oven to 180°c (350°f, gas mark 4). Cook the onions in boiling water for 10 minutes, then drain well and rinse under cold water until cool enough to handle. Using a sharp knife, cut a thin slice from the top and remove the centre from each onion, making a hollow about 4cm (1½in) deep and 5cm (2in) wide. Chop the centres and the tops finely.

In a bowl, mix together the chopped onion, cheese, nuts, raisins and sage and season well. Pack the mixture into the centre of each onion, pressing it down firmly. Pile any leftover filling on top.

Put the stuffed onions into a shallow, heatproof dish, large enough to hold them comfortably, and pour over the vegetable stock. Brush the onions with the melted butter and sprinkle the brown sugar over the top.

Cover the dish with foil, but do not let the foil touch the onions. Bake in the oven for 15 minutes, then remove the foil and bake for a further 20–30 minutes or until the onions are lightly browned and tender. Remove the dish from the oven, baste the onions with the cooking juices and serve.

Potato Basket filled with Carrot & Oat Mixture

This is a novel and attractive way to serve vegetables, and the oatmeal adds extra goodness too

Preheat the oven to 180°C (350°F, gas mark 4). Boil the potatoes in salted water for 15 minutes until cooked. Drain and rinse under cold water until cool enough to handle. Peel and discard the skins. Mash the potatoes with the egg and season well with the salt and pepper.

Using your fingers, spread half the butter over the base and sides of an 18 cm (7 in) diameter deep, loose-based cake tin. Shake the breadcrumbs gently in the tin to coat the inside evenly. Spoon the potato over the base and up the sides of the tin to make a case 2.5 cm (1 in) thick.

Put the tin into the centre of the oven and bake for 30 minutes or until the potato is very lightly browned.

Meanwhile, to make the filling, heat the remaining butter in a saucepan, add the carrots, cover and sauté for 10 minutes. Stir in the oatmeal and cook, stirring, for 2 minutes. Blend in the Worcestershire sauce and stock and cook gently for 30 minutes until the mixture has thickened and the liquid is absorbed, stirring frequently towards the end of cooking to prevent it from sticking. Mix in the parsley and season well. Spoon the carrot mixture into the potato basket and return to the oven for 5 minutes.

Remove from the oven and leave to stand for 2 minutes then carefully remove the basket from the tin and transfer to a heated serving plate.

INGREDIENTS

- 900 G (2 LB) POTATOES, WELL SCRUBBED AND HALVED IF LARGE
- 1 EGG, SIZE 2, BEATEN
- SALT AND FRESHLY GROUND BLACK PEPPER
- 60 G (2 OZ) BUTTER, SOFTENED
- 60 G (2 OZ) FRESH WHITE BREADCRUMBS, TOASTED UNTIL GOLDEN
- 550 G (1¼ LB) CARROTS, PEELED AND DICED
- 30 G (1 OZ) MEDIUM OATMEAL
- 1 TABLESPOON WORCESTERSHIRE SAUCE
- 285 ML (½ PINT) VEGETABLE STOCK (SEE P.434)
- 1 TABLESPOON CHOPPED FRESH PARSLEY
- FRESH PARSLEY SPRIGS TO GARNISH

PREPARATION TIME: 25 MINUTES
COOKING TIME: 40 MINUTES
SERVES SIX

Oatmeal and carrots make a colourful filling for the potato shell with its breadcrumb coating.

Spreading the mashed potatoes round the side of the greased tin will be easier to do if you lay the tin on its side.

Parsnips with Walnuts and Madeira

This recipe would work well with most root vegetables

INGREDIENTS

900G (2LB) PARSNIPS, TRIMMED AND PEELED
45G (1½OZ) BUTTER
150ML (¼ PINT) DOUBLE CREAM
4 TABLESPOONS DRY MADEIRA
SALT AND FRESHLY GROUND BLACK PEPPER
FRESHLY GRATED NUTMEG
60G (2OZ) WALNUT HALVES
PREPARATION TIME: 10 MINUTES
COOKING TIME: 30 MINUTES
SERVES SIX

Preheat the oven to 200°c (400°f, gas mark 6). If using young parsnips, keep them whole, but cut older, longer ones into quarters lengthways.

Steam the parsnips for 8–10 minutes, depending on their size, until they are just tender.

Melt the butter in a saucepan, stir in the cream and Madeira and season well with the salt, pepper and nutmeg. Bring to the boil and stir in the parsnips. Transfer to a shallow, ovenproof dish and scatter over the walnuts. Bake in the centre of the oven for 15 minutes, or until beginning to brown.

The parsnips should absorb most of the cream and Madeira, leaving a little at the bottom of the dish to serve as a sauce. Parsnips cooked in this way are excellent served with beef and game dishes.

Madeira
The wines from the island of the same name were once very popular in Britain. Their youthful acidity is corrected by long heating and the addition of brandy, resulting in the liquors of deceptive strength that were such a boon to the villains of Edwardian melodrama.

The lavish cream sauce makes these parsnips a fitting accompaniment to beef or game.

Use wild field mushrooms for an extra-tasty filling

Mushrooms and onions flavoured with sage and nutmeg make a pleasant, savoury pudding.

Mushroom Pudding

This pudding is ideal for vegetarians or for meat eaters seeking an alternative to the traditional steak and kidney filling

Put the flour, breadcrumbs and some salt into a bowl and mix together, then rub in the butter until the mixture resembles breadcrumbs. Add enough of the cold water to form a soft but not sticky dough.

On a lightly floured surface, roll out two-thirds of the dough to a large round and use to line a 1.4 litre (2½ pint) greased pudding basin, leaving a little dough overhanging the edge of the basin.

Mix together the mushrooms, onion, sage, plain flour and nutmeg and season with the salt and pepper. Pack into the basin, press down well and dot with the butter. Roll out the remaining dough to a round large enough to make a 'lid' for the top of the basin. Brush the edges of the dough with a little cold water and put on the 'lid', pressing the edges together to seal and folding in any excess dough.

Place a circle of greased greaseproof paper on top of the pudding. Cover the top of the basin with a sheet of foil, pleated in the centre to allow for expansion, and make sure it is tucked well under the rim. Steam for 2 hours.

Uncover the pudding and turn it out onto a heated serving dish. Sprinkle with the parsley, if using, and serve immediately with a tossed green salad.

INGREDIENTS

For the pastry

- 225 g (8 oz) self-raising flour
- 60 g (2 oz) fresh white breadcrumbs
- Salt and freshly ground black pepper
- 85 g (3 oz) butter
- Approx 150 ml (¼ pint) cold water

For the filling

- 450 g (1 lb) flat mushrooms, peeled and roughly chopped
- 1 medium onion, peeled and finely chopped
- 1 level teaspoon dried sage
- 2 level tablespoons plain flour
- Large pinch freshly grated nutmeg
- 30 g (1 oz) butter
- Chopped fresh parsley to garnish (optional)

Preparation time: 30 minutes
Cooking time: 2 hours
Serves four

Halloween Baked Pumpkin

Celebrate All Saints' Eve in style with this traditional dish

INGREDIENTS

- 2 TABLESPOONS OLIVE OIL
- 60G (2OZ) BUTTER
- 1 MEDIUM ONION, PEELED AND THINLY SLICED
- 1KG (2LB 3OZ) PIECE PUMPKIN, PEELED, SEEDS REMOVED, FLESH CUT INTO SMALL CUBES
- 1 LEVEL TABLESPOON PLAIN FLOUR
- ½ LEVEL TEASPOON SALT
- ¼ LEVEL TEASPOON FRESHLY GROUND BLACK PEPPER
- ¼ LEVEL TEASPOON FRESHLY GRATED NUTMEG
- 60G (2OZ) FRESH WHITE BREADCRUMBS
- 1 TABLESPOON CHOPPED FRESH PARSLEY
- 1 TABLESPOON CHOPPED FRESH BASIL OR MARJORAM

PREPARATION TIME: 45 MINUTES
COOKING TIME: 45 MINUTES
SERVES FOUR

PREHEAT the oven to 180°C (350°F, gas mark 4). Heat the oil and half the butter in a large frying pan and sauté the onion over a moderate heat for 3 minutes. Add the pumpkin and sprinkle with the flour, salt, pepper and nutmeg. Continue to cook for a further 3 minutes, stirring until golden, then transfer to a lightly oiled 1.4 litre (2½ pint) ovenproof dish.

Combine the breadcrumbs with the chopped parsley and basil or marjoram and spoon evenly over the pumpkin. Dot the top of the breadcrumbs with the remaining butter.

Bake in the centre of the oven for about 45 minutes until the pumpkin is tender and the breadcrumbs are golden brown. Serve hot.

The pumpkin, flavoured with herbs and nutmeg, is excellent alone or with baked or roast ham.

Buttered crumbs can be frozen and used to top other steamed vegetables such as green beans or broccoli.

Crisp suet crust pastry encases an onion shell stuffed with a creamy courgette filling.

Baked Onion Dumplings

These big, chunky dumplings will satisfy the heartiest appetite

Cut a thin slice from the top of each onion, then remove the outer skin and roots. Using a small, sharp knife, cut a large cone-shaped piece from the centre of each. Chop the centres and set aside.

Cook the onions gently in lightly salted boiling water for 15 minutes, then pour into a colander and rinse under cold water. Drain well and set aside.

Meanwhile, melt the butter in a frying pan, add the reserved chopped onion and the grated courgettes and cook gently for 5–10 minutes until softened. Transfer to a bowl and allow to cool, then add the curd or cream cheese, breadcrumbs, tomatoes, Parmesan cheese and dried mixed herbs. Season well with salt and pepper, add the nutmeg and mix together.

Using a fork, carefully remove the centres from the cooled onions, leaving three or four of the outer layers intact. (Reserve the centre layers for another use.)

Fill the prepared onion shells with the courgette and onion mixture, press it in well, then set aside.

Preheat the oven to 220°c (425°f, gas mark 7). To make the pastry, sift the flour and salt into a bowl, mix in the suet and enough chilled water to make a soft but not sticky dough.

Divide the dough into four equal pieces and roll out each to about 28 cm (11 in) in diameter. Place a filled onion upside-down in the centre of each round, lightly brush the edges of the dough with a little beaten egg and mould it round the onion. Trim off the excess and press the joins firmly together. Stand the onions, join sides down, on a greased baking tray and brush with a little beaten egg.

Knead the trimmings together, roll them out to an oblong about 28 x 10 cm (11 x 4 in) and cut the oblong into eight long strips. Tie two strips round each onion, like string round a parcel. Brush the dumplings once more with the beaten egg and bake them in the centre of the oven for 35–40 minutes or until the pastry is crisp and light golden. Serve the onions with a tossed mixed salad.

Ingredients

- 4 large onions, each approx 275–340 g (10–12 oz)
- 30 g (1 oz) butter
- 225 g (8 oz) courgettes, trimmed, washed and coarsely grated
- 115 g (4 oz) curd or cream cheese
- 60 g (2 oz) fresh white breadcrumbs
- 115 g (4 oz) tomatoes, skinned, deseeded and chopped
- 85 g (3 oz) freshly grated Parmesan cheese
- 1–2 level teaspoons dried mixed herbs
- Salt and freshly ground black pepper
- ¼ level teaspoon freshly grated nutmeg

For the pastry

- 340 g (12 oz) self-raising flour
- ½ level teaspoon salt
- 175 g (6 oz) shredded vegetable suet
- 225 g (8 fl oz) chilled water
- 1 egg, size 2, beaten

Preparation time: 1¼ hours
Cooking time: 35–40 minutes
Serves four

Pride of the pit
Giant leek competitions were as much a part of life in the Durham coalfields as racing pigeons. Monsters such as these were raised with utmost care by their growers, the secret of whose success lay in jealously guarded fertiliser recipes.

Ripe tomatoes and a cheese sauce over whole leeks make a light, bright lunch dish.

INGREDIENTS

- 425 ml (3/4 pint) vegetable stock (see p.434)
- 2 fresh marjoram sprigs
- 1 fresh thyme sprig
- Few parsley sprigs
- 8 medium leeks, trimmed and washed
- 45 g (1½ oz) butter
- 45 g (1½ oz) flour
- 150 ml (¼ pint) single cream or milk
- 150 g (5 oz) mature Cheddar cheese, grated
- Salt and freshly ground black pepper
- 4 tomatoes, sliced

Preparation time: 20 minutes
Cooking time: 1 hour
Serves four as a main course or eight as a vegetable accompaniment

Leeks with Cheese Sauce and Tomatoes

This is a simple dish that nevertheless manages to make some sophisticated contrasts of colour, flavour and texture

Pour the stock into a large saucepan, add the herbs and bring to the boil. Put the leeks into the stock, cover and cook gently for 20–25 minutes, or until tender, but not overcooked. Place a colander over a bowl and pour in the leeks. Reserve the stock and discard the herbs.

Preheat the oven to 220°C (425°F, gas mark 7). When the leeks are thoroughly drained, arrange them in a large ovenproof dish.

Melt the butter in a saucepan, stir in the flour and cook for 1 minute, then gradually stir in the reserved stock and bring to the boil, stirring all the time until the sauce thickens. Remove from the heat and stir in the cream or milk, then beat in 85 g (3 oz) of the cheese. Season the sauce to taste with salt and pepper and pour it over the leeks.

Arrange the tomato slices in an attractive pattern on top and sprinkle with the remaining cheese. Bake in the centre of the oven for 25–30 minutes or until bubbling hot and golden brown. Serve with creamy mashed potatoes.

Cauliflower Polonaise

The Polish-style cauliflower is easy to prepare as a snack or to accompany a dish such as Newcastle baked haddock

STEAM the cauliflower florets for 8–10 minutes or until just tender.

Meanwhile, melt the butter in a frying pan. Add the breadcrumbs and fry over a moderate heat, stirring constantly until golden, taking care not to let them burn. Remove the pan from the heat, season the crumbs with the salt and white pepper and keep hot.

Remove the yolk from the egg and pass it through a small sieve. Finely chop the white. Arrange the cauliflower florets in a heated, shallow dish and quickly spoon alternate lines of buttered crumbs, egg white and yolk and parsley on top.

Alternatively, pour the crumbs all over the cauliflower, then sprinkle on the egg white, yolk and parsley.

INGREDIENTS

- 1 MEDIUM CAULIFLOWER, TRIMMED AND CUT INTO FLORETS
- 85 G (3 OZ) BUTTER
- 30 G (1 OZ) DRY WHITE BREADCRUMBS
- SALT AND FRESHLY GROUND WHITE PEPPER
- 1 EGG, SIZE 2, HARD BOILED, SHELLED AND HALVED
- 3 TABLESPOONS CHOPPED FRESH PARSLEY

PREPARATION TIME: 15 MINUTES
COOKING TIME: 8–10 MINUTES
SERVES TWO AS A SNACK OR FOUR AS AN ACCOMPANIMENT

Buttered breadcrumbs give cauliflower a nutty flavour, egg and parsley a colourful garnish.

Cut a small cross in the bottom of each stalk of each floret to help them cook quickly and evenly.

Beetrootability
Wartime ingenuity discovered several hitherto unexplored uses for the beetroot. It became a colour rinse for auburn hair, a tint on marzipan, a nourishing sandwich filling and, being sweet, a colourful ingredient in buns and cakes.

Freshly picked beetroot has the finest flavour. Here it is complemented by fresh herbs and cream.

INGREDIENTS

- 8 small beetroots
- 60 g (2 oz) butter
- 4 spring onions, trimmed, washed and finely sliced
- 1 tablespoon snipped fresh chives
- 2 teaspoons chopped fresh parsley
- 115 ml (4 fl oz) double cream
- 2 baby gherkins, cut into very fine strips

Preparation time: 20 minutes
Cooking time: 3 ¾ hours
Serves four as an accompaniment

Baked Beetroot

For perfect tenderness, bake the beetroot very slowly at a low temperature

Preheat the oven to 150°c (300°f, gas mark 2). Carefully wash the beetroots, taking care not to pierce or bruise the skins, then wrap each one in a square of buttered foil and put into a roasting tin. Bake in the oven for 3–3½ hours or until the skins come away easily when rubbed gently. Remove from the oven and, when cool enough to handle, peel carefully and cut into quarters.

Melt the butter in a large frying pan, add the beetroot, spring onions and herbs and toss gently until coated in the butter. Remove the beetroot and put into a heated serving dish. Add the cream to the pan, bring to the boil, boil for a minute then pour over the beetroot.

Sprinkle with the gherkins and serve with roast pork, grilled loin chops or crispy roast duckling.

Dandelion & Nasturtium Salad

All the leaves and petals for this summer salad can be grown in the garden

Put the lettuce leaves into a salad bowl with the dandelion leaves, watercress and the hard-boiled eggs. Arrange the nasturtium flowers on the top and sprinkle with the parsley, chervil and chives.

To make the dressing, put all the ingredients into a bowl, whisk together and pour into a small jug. At the table, immediately before serving, pour the dressing over the salad and toss gently, or serve the dressing separately and allow everyone to add their own.

If served as a starter, the salad may be arranged on individual plates.

Lettuce, dandelion and watercress leaves make a refreshing salad, while the nasturtium flowers add a subtle, peppery flavour and lend colour to the dish.

INGREDIENTS

- 115G (4OZ) LETTUCE LEAVES, WASHED AND DRIED, TORN INTO SMALL PIECES IF LARGE
- 30G (1OZ) YOUNG DANDELION LEAVES, WASHED AND DRIED (ROCKET COULD BE USED INSTEAD)
- 30G (1OZ) WATERCRESS LEAVES, WASHED AND DRIED
- 6 EGGS, SIZE 2, HARD BOILED, SHELLED AND QUARTERED
- 12 NASTURTIUM FLOWERS
- 3 LARGE FRESH PARSLEY SPRAYS, SEPARATED INTO SMALL SPRIGS
- 12 CHERVIL SPRIGS
- 12 CHIVES, CUT INTO 2 OR 3 PIECES, DEPENDING ON SIZE

FOR THE DRESSING

- 6 TABLESPOONS LIGHT OLIVE OIL
- 2 TABLESPOONS RASPBERRY VINEGAR, HOMEMADE (SEE P.380) OR BOUGHT
- SALT AND FRESHLY GROUND BLACK PEPPER

PREPARATION TIME: 20 MINUTES

SERVES FOUR AS A MAIN COURSE, SIX AS A STARTER

Pick only delicate young dandelion leaves for this salad – the others will be too bitter.

Braised Farmhouse Celery

All the flavour and aroma of the celery hearts is retained by gentle simmering

INGREDIENTS

60G (2OZ) BUTTER
1 MEDIUM ONION, PEELED AND SLICED
225G (8OZ) CARROTS, PEELED AND SLICED
6 CELERY HEARTS, EACH APPROX 225G (8OZ), TRIMMED
725ML (1¼PINTS) BEEF OR VEGETABLE STOCK (SEE P.434)
3 BAY LEAVES
1 TABLESPOON CHOPPED FRESH PARSLEY
SALT AND FRESHLY GROUND BLACK PEPPER
FRESH BAY LEAVES TO GARNISH (OPTIONAL)

PREPARATION TIME: 20 MINUTES
COOKING TIME: 25 MINUTES
SERVES SIX

MELT the butter in a large frying pan or shallow, flameproof casserole. Add the onion and sauté until just soft. Arrange the carrots in a layer over the onion then place the celery hearts on top. Pour over the stock and add the bay leaves and chopped parsley. Season well.

Bring to the boil, reduce the heat, cover and simmer for 20 minutes or until the celery hearts are just tender, basting frequently with the stock. Remove the celery hearts and vegetables from the pan with a slotted spoon and arrange in a warm serving dish or on individual plates. Cover and keep warm.

Bring the pan juices to the boil and cook rapidly until reduced by half. Discard the bay leaves, then pour the juices over the celery. Garnish with the fresh bay leaves, if using, and serve.

Celery hearts, here braised with carrots and onions, are an excellent vegetable to serve with roast or casseroled game birds.

If the celery hearts are not tightly compact, tie them with fine string to retain their shape. Remove the string before serving.

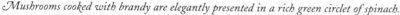

Mushrooms cooked with brandy are elegantly presented in a rich green circlet of spinach.

'I YAM WHAT I YAM'
As befits a figure of US folklore, Popeye's origins are mysterious. Some say he was created to sell tinned spinach, others to encourage farmers to grow spinach and the public to eat it during the Depression. Whatever the case, he remains the spirit of spinach.

Baked Spinach Ring with Brandied Mushrooms

Reinforced by crusty bread, this would be an attractive lunch or supper dish; equally, it would make a glamorous companion for fish or poultry

PREHEAT the oven to 180°C (350°F, gas mark 4). Put the spinach into a large saucepan with only the water that clings to the leaves after washing. Cover and cook over a high heat for 1–2 minutes, turning occasionally until the spinach is wilted but still bright green. Drain well, squeeze dry and chop coarsely.

To make the sauce, melt 45 g (1½ oz) of the butter in a saucepan. Stir in the flour, cook for 1 minute then gradually add the milk. Bring to the boil, stirring constantly until the sauce is very thick and smooth. Stir in the cream, add the salt, pepper and nutmeg and leave to cool for 2–3 minutes, then gradually beat in the eggs until smooth. Stir the chopped spinach into the sauce.

Lightly grease a 1.15 litre (2 pint) ring mould and arrange the sliced tomatoes, overlapping, on the bottom. Carefully pour the spinach mixture on top of the tomatoes and level the surface. Bake in the centre of the oven for 40–50 minutes, or until set right through.

Meanwhile, melt the remaining butter in a frying pan, add the shallot and sauté for 2 minutes. Add the mushrooms and sauté for 2 minutes more, then stir in the brandy and lemon juice and cook for a further minute. Remove the spinach ring from the oven, run a knife round the edges and centre to loosen it, then turn it out onto a warm serving plate. Fill the centre with the mushrooms and garnish with the parsley leaves.

INGREDIENTS

675 G (1½ LB) SPINACH, TRIMMED AND WASHED
70 G (2½ OZ) BUTTER
45 G (1½ OZ) PLAIN FLOUR
200 ML (7 FL OZ) MILK
4 TABLESPOONS SINGLE CREAM
¼ LEVEL TEASPOON SALT
¼ LEVEL TEASPOON FRESHLY GROUND BLACK PEPPER
¼ LEVEL TEASPOON FRESHLY GRATED NUTMEG
2 EGGS, SIZE 2, BEATEN
225 G (8 OZ) TOMATOES, SLICED
1 SHALLOT, PEELED AND FINELY CHOPPED
250 G (9 OZ) CLOSED CUP OR BUTTON MUSHROOMS, TRIMMED AND WIPED
1 TABLESPOON BRANDY
1 TEASPOON LEMON JUICE
FLAT PARSLEY LEAVES TO GARNISH

PREPARATION TIME: 30 MINUTES
COOKING TIME: 50 MINUTES
SERVES FOUR AS LIGHT MAIN COURSE, SIX AS A STARTER OR ACCOMPANIMENT

Tabasco sauce adds a little bite to the mayonnaise dressing for the crisp cauliflower florets.

Cauliflower Salad

The pyramid shape of this salad makes it a fine centrepiece for a buffet table

INGREDIENTS

1 medium cauliflower, trimmed and cut into florets
115 ml (4 fl oz) olive oil
1 small garlic clove, peeled and crushed
1 teaspoon white wine vinegar
2 tablespoons chopped fresh parsley
¼ small shallot, finely chopped
Pinch each salt and sugar
3 tomatoes, skinned, deseeded and finely chopped
4 tablespoons mayonnaise, homemade (see p.436) or bought
1 teaspoon tomato purée
¼ teaspoon Tabasco sauce
1 teaspoon lemon juice
Salt and freshly ground black pepper
1 soft, round lettuce, washed
3.8 cm (1½ in) piece cucumber and ½ small red pepper, deseeded, cut into very fine strips
18 large capers
Preparation time: 40 minutes
Cooking time: 7 minutes
Serves six

Steam the cauliflower florets for 7 minutes or until almost cooked but still slightly crisp. Meanwhile, whisk together the olive oil, garlic, vinegar, parsley, shallot, salt and sugar. Put the cauliflower into a bowl, then pour over the oil dressing, while the cauliflower is still hot, gently turning the florets until they are evenly coated. Leave to cool.

Mix together the chopped tomatoes, mayonnaise, tomato pureé, Tabasco sauce, lemon juice and seasoning. Arrange a layer of lettuce leaves on a flat serving plate, put a layer of cauliflower on top and spoon over a little of the tomato mayonnaise. Continue in this way, alternating layers of lettuce, cauliflower and mayonnaise in a pyramid shape and ending with a layer of cauliflower. Spoon over any remaining mayonnaise then sprinkle with the shreds of cucumber and pepper and the capers.

Serve at once. It goes well with whole prawns and crusty wholemeal bread.

Victorian Vegetable Salad

The formality of the Victorian dining room is echoed in this elaborate creation

Steam separately the cauliflower florets, potatoes and carrots until just cooked, then allow to cool.

Meanwhile, to make the dressing, mix all the ingredients together in a bowl and set aside. Thoroughly oil a 1.4 litre (2½ pint) pudding basin.

Cut the potatoes and carrots lengthways into 6 mm (¼ in) thick slices. Using aspic cutters, cut a heart shape from each potato slice and petal shapes from the carrot slices. Set the shapes aside, then roughly chop the remaining pieces of potato and carrot. Mix the chopped potatoes with 2 tablespoons of the dressing.

Arrange some of the tomato slices decoratively in the bottom of the oiled pudding basin. Having done so, continue the pattern with a few cucumber slices radiating outwards from the tomatoes and up the sides of the basin. Put half the cauliflower florets carefully into the basin and arrange the chopped carrot round the edge. Next, spread the diced beetroot in an even layer and cover with 2 tablespoons of the dressing.

Place the remaining cauliflower on top, spread evenly with the potato mixture and cover with the remaining cucumber slices. Press the vegetables down gently but with sufficient firmness to pack them well together, then leave them to stand for 10 minutes.

Put a very large and decorative plate or cake stand on top of the basin, then swiftly invert both basin and plate. Keeping a tight hold, shake gently to free the salad, then carefully remove the basin and tidy up any loose pieces of salad.

Arrange the lettuce round the salad and garnish with the potato and carrot shapes and the chopped parsley. Pour the remaining dressing into a serving bowl and serve separately.

Potato hearts, carrot petals and an array of other colourful vegetables are skilfully assembled to produce this Victorian period piece.

Ingredients

- 275 g (10 oz) cauliflower florets
- 450 g (1 lb) waxy potatoes, peeled
- 2 large, fat carrots, peeled
- 2 small tomatoes, sliced
- 7.5 cm (3 in) piece cucumber, halved lengthways and thinly sliced
- 150 g (5 oz) cooked beetroot, peeled and cut into small dice
- ½ small crisp lettuce, washed and finely shredded
- 2 tablespoons chopped fresh parsley to garnish

For the dressing

- 150 ml (¼ pint) soured cream
- 150 ml (¼ pint) mayonnaise, homemade (see p.436) or bought
- 1 tablespoon tarragon or wine vinegar
- Salt and freshly ground white pepper
- 15 g (½ oz) chopped fresh parsley
- 15 g (½ oz) snipped fresh chives

Preparation time: 1 hour
Cooking time: 20–25 minutes
Cooling time: 30 minutes
Serves six

The faint-hearted can arrange this salad in layers in a deep glass dish, if preferred.

Stuffed Cabbage Leaves

The cabbage-leaf 'parcels' can be served alone, with meat, or as part of a buffet

INGREDIENTS

- 115G (4OZ) BUTTER
- 4 TABLESPOONS OLIVE OIL
- 2 LARGE ONIONS, PEELED AND FINELY DICED
- 800G (1¾LB) TINNED CHOPPED TOMATOES
- 285ML (½ PINT) RED WINE, VEGETABLE STOCK (SEE P.434) OR WATER
- 1 LARGE SAVOY CABBAGE
- 2 GARLIC CLOVES, PEELED AND CRUSHED
- 4 CELERY STICKS, TRIMMED AND FINELY CHOPPED
- 275G (10OZ) LARGE OPEN-CUP MUSHROOMS, WIPED AND FINELY CHOPPED
- 60G (2OZ) BLANCHED ALMONDS OR PINE NUTS, LIGHTLY TOASTED
- 2 TABLESPOONS EACH CHOPPED FRESH THYME, OREGANO AND SAGE OR 2 LEVEL TEASPOONS EACH, DRIED
- 85G (3OZ) LONG-GRAIN BROWN OR MIXED-GRAIN RICE, COOKED AND DRAINED
- 175G (6OZ) CHEDDAR CHEESE OR PARMESAN CHEESE, GRATED
- 2 TABLESPOONS WORCESTERSHIRE SAUCE
- SALT AND FRESHLY GROUND BLACK PEPPER

PREPARATION TIME: 1 HOUR
COOKING TIME: 30 MINUTES
SERVES FOUR AS A LIGHT SUPPER OR EIGHT AS A VEGETABLE ACCOMPANIMENT

HEAT half the butter with half the oil in a large saucepan, add half the onions and cook for 5 minutes over a moderate heat or until the onions are soft and starting to brown. Stir in the chopped tomatoes and wine, stock or water and bring to the boil. Reduce the heat, partly cover the saucepan and simmer for 1 hour.

Meanwhile, pull eight large leaves from the cabbage and cook them in a large saucepan of boiling, salted water for 1 minute. Pour into a colander and rinse under a cold running tap. Dry well with kitchen paper and set aside.

Preheat the oven to 180°C (350°F, gas mark 4). Heat the remaining butter and oil in a saucepan, add the remaining onion and the crushed garlic and cook gently for 5 minutes or until soft but not coloured. Add the celery and mushrooms and cook, stirring, for 5 minutes until soft. Stir in the almonds or pine nuts and the herbs, followed by the rice, 150g (5oz) of cheese, and 2 tablespoons of Worcestershire sauce.

Season well, then divide the mixture into eight portions. Spoon a portion onto each cabbage leaf. Tuck the edges of the leaf round the filling, then roll it up to enclose completely. Place in an ovenproof dish with the joins underneath.

Purée the tomato sauce in a blender or food processor and pour it over the cabbage rolls. Sprinkle with the remaining cheese and bake for 30 minutes or until brown and bubbling hot.

As an accompaniment for four or six, reduce the quantities by half or a quarter.

Almonds enhance the stuffing and the dish is given a further dimension by rich tomato sauce.

The combination of the creamy with the crunchy is an appetising adventure in texture and taste.

Patriotic Pete
Through the war, Potato Pete, a creature of the Ministry of Food, exhorted the British to stretch the rations by growing and eating more potatoes. They should, he said, eat them at least twice a day in sandwiches, pies and even steamed puddings.

Crisp and Creamy Potatoes

Thrifty cooks will approve this flavoursome use for leftover potato

Mash the cooked potatoes with the parsley and season well. Divide and shape into 12 small balls. Dip each ball in the beaten egg, then roll in the breadcrumbs until evenly coated—reshaping the balls after coating if necessary. Put onto a plate, cover and chill until required.

Boil the raw potatoes in salted water until cooked. Drain well, then mash with the butter and soured cream until smooth. Season with the salt and pepper and mix in the snipped chives. Spoon the mashed potato into a mound in the centre of a heatproof serving dish and swirl it attractively with a palette knife, leaving a 2.5 cm (1 in) border round the edge. Cover the dish loosely with foil and keep warm.

Deep fry the chilled potato balls in hot oil for 3–4 minutes until lightly golden and drain well on kitchen paper. Arrange the croquettes round the edge of the mashed potato mound and serve. If liked, garnish with chives or sprigs of mint.

INGREDIENTS

- 600 g (1 lb 5 oz) potatoes, peeled and cooked
- 1 tablespoon chopped fresh parsley
- Salt and freshly ground black pepper
- 1 egg, size 3, beaten
- 85 g (3 oz) fresh white breadcrumbs
- 1.1 kg (2½ lb) potatoes, peeled and cut into quarters
- 30 g (1 oz) butter
- 4 tablespoons soured cream
- 2 tablespoons snipped fresh chives
- Oil for deep frying
- Chives or fresh mint sprigs to garnish (optional)

Preparation time: 1 hour
Cooking time: 20 minutes
Serves six

Cheese, Potato and Onion Pie

Vegetarians and omnivores alike will enjoy this wholesome dish

INGREDIENTS

- 900G (2LB) POTATOES, PEELED AND QUARTERED
- SALT AND FRESHLY GROUND BLACK PEPPER
- 85G (3OZ) BUTTER
- 2–3 TABLESPOONS MILK
- 175G (6OZ) MATURE CHEDDAR CHEESE, DICED OR GRATED
- 340G (12OZ) ONIONS, PEELED AND SLICED
- ½–1 LEVEL TEASPOON DRIED THYME
- 1 LEVEL TABLESPOON CASTER SUGAR
- 4 TOMATOES, SLICED
- 15G (½OZ) DRY WHITE BREADCRUMBS
- 15G (½OZ) PARMESAN CHEESE, GRATED

PREPARATION TIME: 30 MINUTES
COOKING TIME: 30 MINUTES
SERVES FOUR

BOIL the potatoes in lightly salted water until cooked, drain well and mash with 60g (2oz) of the butter and the milk. Season and mix in the Cheddar cheese.

Preheat the oven to 200°C (400°F, gas mark 6). Melt the remaining butter in a frying pan, add the onions and cook over a moderate heat for 10 minutes. Stir in the thyme and sugar and continue cooking until golden brown and caramelised.

Spread half the mashed potato in the bottom of a pie dish or ovenproof dish. Spread the onions on top, then cover with the remaining potato. Arrange the tomato slices on top and sprinkle with the breadcrumbs and Parmesan cheese.

Bake in the centre of the oven for 30 minutes until golden brown and piping hot. Serve with a crisp green salad or cooked green vegetables.

With its potato crust and onion filling, the pie will keep the winter chill at bay.

A PINCH OF SALT
Potato crisps had been enjoyed in the US for years before London grocer Frank Smith began making them in 1910. He hawked them around pubs, but it was the inspired inclusion of a paper twist of salt in each pack that made them best sellers.

The summery contents of the salad—lettuce, artichoke hearts, tomatoes, spring onions and a hint of honey—make it an English treat indeed.

For really crisp radishes, prepare them 1–2 hours in advance and keep them in iced water in the refrigerator.

A Very English Salad

This collation, served with cold meats, sardines or cheeses, would make a fine traditional curtain raiser for high tea

To prepare the radishes, cut thin slices across each, cutting only three-quarters of the way through so that the radish stays intact. Leave in a bowl of iced water for 30 minutes, during which time they will open in a fan shape. If necessary, squeeze gently to help them open. Drain well.

Meanwhile, to make the dressing, put the honey into a mixing bowl with some salt and pepper to taste and the white wine vinegar, then, adding a little at a time, gradually whisk in the oil to make a slightly thick dressing.

Cover a serving platter with the lettuce leaves, then arrange the artichoke hearts, tomatoes and drained radishes on top. Sprinkle with the spring onion slices and garnish with small bunches of the salad cress. Just before serving, whisk the dressing again and spoon over the salad.

INGREDIENTS

115G (4OZ) RADISHES, TRIMMED AND WASHED
1 TEASPOON CLEAR HONEY
SALT AND FRESHLY GROUND BLACK PEPPER
1 TABLESPOON WHITE WINE VINEGAR
3 TABLESPOONS OLIVE OIL
1 SMALL OR ½ LARGE CRISP LETTUCE, WASHED AND DRIED
225G (8OZ) FRESHLY COOKED ARTICHOKE HEARTS, OR BOTTLED ARTICHOKE HEARTS WELL DRAINED
225G (8OZ) TOMATOES, SLICED
2 SPRING ONIONS, TRIMMED AND SLICED
1 PUNNET SALAD CRESS

PREPARATION TIME: 30 MINUTES
SERVES FOUR AS A MAIN COURSE WITH COLD MEATS OR SIX AS A STARTER ON ITS OWN

Cheese, Sage & Onion Bake

This quick and easy recipe would be equally at home with sausages or chops, or served as a vegetarian supper dish

INGREDIENTS

900G (2LB) ONIONS, PEELED AND SLICED
115G (4OZ) SAGE DERBY CHEESE
115G (4OZ) MATURE CHEDDAR CHEESE
15G (½OZ) BUTTER
FRESH SAGE TO GARNISH
PREPARATION TIME: 10 MINUTES
COOKING TIME: 30–40 MINUTES
SERVES FOUR

PREHEAT the oven to 200°C (400°F, gas mark 6). Butter a deep baking dish, about 1.7 litres (3 pints), and arrange the onion slices in layers on the bottom.

Cut the cheeses into large, thin slices and arrange them, overlapping, on top of the onions to cover them completely. Cut the butter into small pieces and dot them on top of the cheese.

Bake in the top of the oven for 30–40 minutes until the cheese has melted and lightly browned and the onions are cooked. (As the onions cook, the level will drop slightly.)

Garnish with the fresh sage leaves and serve hot as an accompaniment to sausages, roasts or chops, or as a supper dish with a salad and granary bread.

Sage Derby and Cheddar cheese form a crisp topping for this dish, to be garnished later with sage.

Leaving the root end on onions when peeling them is said to prevent tears while slicing!

Orange juice, demerara sugar and whisky can bring about the elevation of the humblest carrot.

CARROTS
keep you healthy and help you
to see in the blackout

Visionaries

There was some truth in the Ministry of Food's claim that the Vitamin A content of carrots improved eyesight, though not to the extent that they enabled nightfighters to see enemy aircraft in the dark. Actually the claim was a cover for radar, then on the secret list.

Glazed Carrots with Orange & Whisky

This is a richly different way of preparing and serving the highly adaptable carrot

Trim the carrots and cut them into finger-sized sticks if large. If using baby carrots, leave them whole. Put them into a saucepan and add just enough water to cover. Add the demerara sugar, butter, orange rind and juice and bring to the boil. Boil rapidly for 12–15 minutes until the carrots are cooked and glazed with the juices which should have reduced and become syrupy.

Stir in the whisky and season well with the salt and pepper. Serve the carrots immediately, garnished with the chopped chervil or parsley.

Ingredients

- 340g (12oz) young carrots, scraped and washed
- 30g (1oz) demerara sugar
- 30g (1oz) butter
- Finely grated rind and strained juice 1 orange
- 1 tablespoon whisky
- Salt and freshly ground black pepper
- Chopped fresh chervil or parsley to garnish

Preparation time: 5–10 minutes
Cooking time: 15 minutes
Serves four

Runner Beans with Turnips

Here is a novel and exciting way to serve familiar garden vegetables

INGREDIENTS

- 450 G (1 LB) TURNIPS, PEELED AND CUT INTO CUBES
- 45 G (1½ OZ) BUTTER, SOFTENED
- SALT AND FRESHLY GROUND BLACK PEPPER
- 250 G (9 OZ) RUNNER BEANS, TRIMMED AND SLICED
- 1 LEVEL TABLESPOON CHOPPED FRESH MIXED HERBS (PARSLEY, BASIL, OREGANO, MARJORAM AND CHERVIL)
- 2 TABLESPOONS LEMON JUICE

PREPARATION TIME: 15 MINUTES
COOKING TIME: 25 MINUTES
SERVES FOUR AS AN ACCOMPANIMENT

STEAM the turnips for 15–20 minutes or until soft. Put them into a bowl with 15 g (½ oz) of the butter, season to taste with the salt and pepper and mash well.

Spread the turnip in the bottom of a warm gratin dish, making a slight hollow in the centre. Cover and keep warm.

Boil the runner beans in salted water for 4–5 minutes or until just cooked. Meanwhile, mix the chopped herbs with the remaining butter.

Drain the beans well, return to the pan, add the lemon juice and toss well. Spoon the beans into the hollow of mashed turnip in the gratin dish and dot the top with the herb butter.

If preferred, mashed swede can be used instead of turnip.

ALLOTMENT'S PRIDE
Runner beans have always been a firm favourite with city and country gardeners. Easily grown, they are a confirmation of summer in the kitchen, while their scarlet flowers, especially when supported on a wigwam frame, lend the vegetable patch a festive air.

This presentation of beans, turnips and garden herbs is fitting tribute to both cook and gardener.

When preparing the celery, leave as much of the root end as possible. This helps to hold the stalks together when the plant is halved.

The halved celery hearts make perfect receptacles for the cream cheese, prune and apple topping.

Celery, Prune & Cheese Salad

The celery hearts in this salad are cooked—an old-fashioned idea that adds an unusual savour to the dish

Cut 2.5 cm (1 in) from the top of each celery heart and reserve.

Pour the stock or water into a large, shallow pan, add ½ level teaspoon of salt and bring to the boil. Add the celery hearts, cover the pan and cook gently for 10–15 minutes or until slightly softened, taking care not to overcook. Remove from the heat, drain and allow to cool.

Cut the cold celery hearts in half and arrange them on a serving dish, cut sides uppermost. Chop the reserved raw celery finely. Core the apple, cut it into small dice and toss in the lemon juice to prevent the pieces from discolouring.

Beat the cream cheese and mayonnaise together, then mix in the chopped celery, apple and prunes. Season to taste with salt and pepper. Spoon the cheese mixture on top of the celery hearts. Cover and chill for at least 1 hour.

Stir the parsley into the vinaigrette dressing and drizzle it all over the celery hearts. Serve immediately.

INGREDIENTS

- 4 CELERY HEARTS, WASHED
- 570 ML (1 PINT) VEGETABLE STOCK (SEE P.434), OR WATER
- SALT
- 1 CRISP RED DESSERT APPLE
- 1 TABLESPOON LEMON JUICE
- 200 G (7 OZ) CREAM CHEESE
- 2 LEVEL TABLESPOONS MAYONNAISE, HOMEMADE (SEE P.436) OR BOUGHT
- 6 READY-TO-USE PITTED PRUNES, FINELY CHOPPED
- FRESHLY GROUND BLACK PEPPER
- 2 LEVEL TABLESPOONS FINELY CHOPPED FRESH PARSLEY
- 5 TABLESPOONS VINAIGRETTE DRESSING (SEE P.435)

PREPARATION TIME: 40 MINUTES
CHILLING TIME: 1 HOUR
COOKING TIME: 10–15 MINUTES
SERVES FOUR AS A MAIN COURSE, EIGHT AS A SIDE SALAD

Red Cabbage with Orange

Red cabbage, cooked slowly until tender, improves with keeping and any that is left over can be retained for another meal

INGREDIENTS

- 1.4 KG (3 LB) RED CABBAGE, FINELY SHREDDED
- 2 MEDIUM ORANGES
- 1 SMALL ONION, PEELED AND FINELY CHOPPED
- 1 GARLIC CLOVE, CRUSHED
- 30 G (1 OZ) CASTER SUGAR
- 3 TABLESPOONS RED WINE VINEGAR
- SALT AND FRESHLY GROUND BLACK PEPPER
- 1 BAY LEAF
- 1 TABLESPOON BLACK TREACLE
- 30 G (1 OZ) BUTTER

PREPARATION TIME: 25 MINUTES
STANDING TIME: OVERNIGHT
COOKING TIME: 2 HOURS
SERVES EIGHT

PUT the cabbage into a large bowl. Finely grate the rind from 1 orange and squeeze the juice. Stir the rind and juice into the cabbage with the onion, garlic, sugar, vinegar, salt and pepper and the bay leaf. Cover and leave to stand overnight.

Melt the black treacle and butter in a large, heavy-based, stainless steel or enamel saucepan. Stir in the cabbage mixture and slowly bring to the boil, stirring occasionally. Reduce the heat, cover and simmer for 2 hours or until the juices have almost evaporated and the cabbage is tender. Stir every 30 minutes. Remove and discard the bay leaf.

Thinly pare the rind from the remaining orange and cut it into very fine shreds. Stir half the shreds into the cabbage, then spoon into a serving dish and sprinkle with the remaining shreds.

Serve with Cumberland sausages or grilled meats and mashed potatoes.

Overnight marinating of the vegetables in orange juice and vinegar is the key to success.

Before shredding the cabbage, divide into quarters with a large, sharp knife and cut away the hard core.

Fresh garden vegetables are combined under golden pastry to make a sturdy, warming meal.

Leek and Parsnip Plate Pie

The pastry here is given a special touch by the addition of hazelnuts and cheese

To MAKE the pastry, sift the flour and salt into a mixing bowl and rub in the butter until the mixture resembles fine breadcrumbs. Stir in the chopped hazelnuts and the cheese, then mix with the egg and water to a firm dough. Wrap in cling film and chill for 30 minutes.

To make the filling, cut the leeks into 2.5 cm (1 in) pieces. Heat the butter in a saucepan, add the leeks and onion and cook gently for 5–10 minutes until softened but not browned. At the same time, cook the parsnips in boiling, salted water for 10 minutes until tender. Drain well, cut into small cubes and add to the leeks. Remove from the heat, stir in the lemon rind, cream and mustard, season with the salt and pepper and allow to cool.

On a lightly floured surface, roll out half the dough thinly into a round a little larger than a 24 cm (9½ in) pie plate. Line the plate with the dough and fill with the leek mixture to within 1.3 cm (½ in) of the edge.

Roll out the remaining dough to a round large enough to cover the pie. Dampen the edges of the dough on the plate with water and cover the pie with the 'lid', pressing the edges together well to seal. Trim and decorate the edge of the pie and use the trimmings to make leaves to decorate the top. Make a small hole in the centre of the pie to allow the steam to escape, then chill for 30 minutes. While the pie is chilling, heat the oven to 200°C (400°F, gas mark 6).

Brush the top of the pie with the milk and put it onto a baking sheet. Bake in the oven for 35–40 minutes or until the pastry is crisp and golden. Remove from the oven and serve, while still warm, with a green salad.

INGREDIENTS

For the pastry
- 275 g (10 oz) plain flour
- Pinch of salt
- 150 g (5 oz) butter or polyunsaturated margarine
- 45 g (1½ oz) hazelnuts, skinned and finely chopped
- 85 g (3 oz) mature Cheddar cheese, finely grated
- 1 egg, size 2, beaten
- 1–2 tablespoons cold water
- Milk to glaze

For the filling
- 675 g (1½ lb) leeks, trimmed and washed, to give 340 g (12 oz) prepared weight
- 60 g (2 oz) butter
- 1 medium onion, peeled and sliced
- 225 g (8 oz) parsnips, peeled and cut into quarters lengthways
- Finely grated rind 1 lemon
- 6 tablespoons single cream
- 1–2 level tablespoons whole-grain mustard
- Salt and freshly ground black pepper

Preparation time: 50 minutes
Chilling time: 1 hour
Cooking time: 35–40 minutes
Serves six

For a shorter textured pastry, substitute 60g (2 oz) of lard or white vegetable fat for half the butter or margarine.

The pie's pastry envelope is brimful of apple and onion and laced with cream.

Onion, Apple & Sage Pie with Clotted Cream

Served cold, this pie is perfect company for cold picnic meats

INGREDIENTS

For the pastry
- 225g (8oz) plain flour
- Pinch of salt
- 115g (4oz) butter or polyunsaturated margarine
- 3 tablespoons cold water
- 1 small egg, beaten or milk to glaze

For the filling
- 340g (12oz) onions, peeled, halved and thinly sliced
- 340g (12oz) cooking apples, peeled, cored and thinly sliced
- 2 teaspoons finely chopped fresh sage, or 1 level teaspoon dried sage
- ¼ level teaspoon salt
- ¼ level teaspoon ground pepper
- 4 tablespoons clotted or soured cream
- Sage leaves to garnish

Preparation time: 1 hour
Cooking time: 40 minutes
Serves four

To make the pastry, sift the flour and salt into a mixing bowl. Rub in the butter or margarine until the mixture resembles fine breadcrumbs. Add the water and mix to a dough. Knead gently on a lightly floured surface for a few seconds until smooth, then wrap in cling film and chill.

On a lightly floured surface, roll out the chilled dough to a square a little larger than 30 cm (12 in), trim the edges to that size and place on a large baking sheet. Put half the sliced onions, followed by half the apples, in the centre of the dough square and sprinkle with half the sage, salt and pepper. Add the remaining onion, apple and seasonings and spread the clotted or soured cream on top.

Brush some beaten egg or milk round the edges of the dough and fold two opposite corners over the filling so that they meet and overlap slightly in the centre. Repeat with the other two corners to make an envelope shape, pressing the joins together gently to seal. Use the trimmings to decorate the pie. Chill for 30 minutes. Meanwhile, preheat the oven to 220°C (425°F, gas mark 7).

Brush the chilled pie all over with the remaining beaten egg or milk, then bake in the centre of the oven for 40 minutes, or until the pastry is crisp and golden brown. If the pastry begins to brown too much, cover the pie loosely with greaseproof paper or foil.

Carefully transfer to a serving plate or board and garnish with the sage leaves. Serve hot or cold, on its own or with cold meats, sausages and cheese.

Roasted Root Vegetables

Thyme, marjoram, rosemary and sage season this delicious dish

Preheat the oven to 200°c (400°f, gas mark 6). Put the prepared swedes, carrots, parsnips and turnips into a large saucepan. Sprinkle with the salt and pour over enough boiling water to cover the vegetables completely. Bring them back to the boil and cook for 5 minutes. Pour the vegetables into a large colander and leave to drain thoroughly.

Put the dripping or olive oil into a large roasting tin and heat in the oven for 10 minutes. Take the tin out of the oven and carefully add the drained vegetables to the hot fat. Sprinkle with the herbs and baste well until evenly coated.

Roast the vegetables in the centre of the oven for 40–45 minutes, turning once, until tender and browned. Serve hot.

Harvest home—the season's crop of root vegetables are cooked to golden perfection.

Ingredients

- 450 g (1 lb) swedes, peeled and cut into 2.5 cm (1 in) cubes
- 340 g (12 oz) carrots, peeled and halved lengthways
- 340 g (12 oz) parsnips, peeled and quartered lengthways
- 225 g (8 oz) turnips, peeled and cut into wedges
- 1 level teaspoon salt
- 60 g (2 oz) beef dripping or 4 tablespoons olive oil
- 1 level tablespoon fresh thyme leaves
- 1 level tablespoon fresh marjoram leaves
- 1 level tablespoon fresh rosemary leaves
- 1 level tablespoon shredded fresh sage leaves

Preparation time: 20 minutes

Cooking time: 45 minutes

Serves four

Digging for Victory
Vegetables were not rationed in the war, but with the Channel Islands occupied and shipping at a premium, there were often shortages. Every inch of spare earth from road verges to bombed sites was called into service to redress the balance.

Vegetable Loaf

Here is a dish of substance and flavour that would make an impressive centrepiece for a dinner table, and in which meat plays no part

Ingredients

225 g (8 oz) mixed dried beans
285 ml (½ pint) milk
2 cloves
Bouquet garni (see p.440)
340 ml (12 fl oz) vegetable stock (see p.434)
115 g (4 oz) long-grain brown rice
1 large carrot, peeled
¼ large red pepper, and ¼ large green pepper, deseeded
60 g (2 oz) very large fresh spinach leaves, washed and trimmed
60 g (2 oz) watercress, trimmed, washed and chopped
6 spring onions, trimmed and chopped
3 tablespoons chopped fresh parsley
60 g (2 oz) blanched almonds, halved and toasted
45 g (1½ oz) butter
45 g (1½ oz) plain flour
Freshly grated nutmeg
2 eggs, size 2, beaten
Beetroot slices and salad leaves to garnish (optional)

Soaking time: 5 hours or overnight
Preparation time: 1 hour
Chilling time: Overnight
Cooking time: 2½–3 hours
Serves eight

THE BEANS

Spread the beans on a plate and remove any grit or discoloured beans. Transfer to a colander and rinse thoroughly under cold, running water until the water runs clear, then put the beans into a large bowl and cover with cold water. The water should come at least 10 cm (4 in) above the beans. Cover and leave to soak for at least 5 hours or, if preferred, overnight.

Drain and rinse the soaked beans and put them into a large saucepan. Cover with cold water, bring to the boil and boil for 10 minutes. Pour into a colander, rinse under cold water and return to the saucepan. Cover with fresh cold water, bring to the boil, then reduce the heat, cover and cook gently for 1–1½ hours until tender. Pour into a colander and drain well. Meanwhile, put the milk, cloves and bouquet garni into a saucepan and bring to the boil. Remove from the heat, cover, and leave the liquid to infuse until it is required.

THE RICE AND VEGETABLES

Pour the stock into a saucepan and bring to the boil. Stir in the brown rice, reduce the heat, cover and cook gently for 25–30 minutes or until the rice is cooked and all the stock has been absorbed.

Cut the carrot lengthways into slices about 6 mm (¼ in) thick, then cut the slices in half lengthways. Cut the red and green peppers into long strips. Boil the strips of carrot and pepper for 2 minutes, then pour into a colander, rinse under cold water and drain on kitchen paper.

PREPARING THE LOAF TIN

Butter a 23 × 12.5 × 6 cm (9 × 5 × 2½ in) nonstick loaf tin. Line the bottom with baking paper and butter it. Blanch the spinach leaves for 20 seconds in a large saucepan of boiling water, then pour them carefully into a colander and rinse well under cold water. Drain and pat dry with kitchen paper. Line the base and sides of the prepared loaf tin with all but three of the leaves. Arrange the carrot and pepper strips attractively on top of the leaves in the bottom of the tin.

THE LOAF

Preheat the oven to 180°C (350°F, gas mark 4). In a large bowl, mix the beans with the rice, watercress, spring onions, parsley and almonds and season well.

Strain the infused milk into a jug. Melt the butter in a saucepan, stir in the flour and cook for 1 minute. Gradually stir in the milk and bring to the boil, stirring constantly until the mixture is thick and smooth. Remove from the heat, season to taste with the nutmeg and beat in the eggs. Pour over the beans and other ingredients and mix well.

Carefully spoon the mixture into the tin, level the top and cover it completely with the remaining spinach leaves. Cover the tin with buttered foil and stand it in a roasting tin filled with boiling water to halfway up the sides of the loaf tin. Cook in the centre of the oven for 1½ hours or until firmly set. Remove from the oven and allow to cool a little.

WEIGHTING

Remove the foil and cover the tin with cling film. Put a small board on top and place some heavy weights on the board. Cool and refrigerate overnight.

The next day, remove the loaf from the refrigerator and remove the weights, board and cling film. With your hand, gently loosen the loaf by easing it away from the sides of the tin. Place a flat serving plate on top of the tin and, holding the tin and plate firmly together, invert them. Remove the tin from the loaf.

Cut the loaf into slices and serve with a mixed salad and crusty bread. The loaf may also be garnished with beetroot slices and salad leaves before serving if liked.

Blanched spinach leaves encase the beans, brown rice and vegetables that make the well-flavoured loaf.

Sheltered garden
Wartime city dwellers had great faith in the Anderson shelter, not only as an air raid refuge but as an extra patch for growing vegetables, especially marrow, which was used as a substitute for an array of foods.

Pine nuts and garlic add a distinctive flavour to the rice stuffing for the marrow.

Savoury Stuffed Marrow

Stuffed marrow is an easily prepared and filling family meal

INGREDIENTS

- 285 ML (½ PINT) VEGETABLE STOCK (SEE P.434)
- 85 G (3 OZ) LONG-GRAIN WHITE RICE
- 1 KG (2 LB 3 OZ) MARROW
- 60 G (2 OZ) PINE NUTS
- 60 G (2 OZ) BUTTER, SOFTENED
- 1 TABLESPOON OLIVE OIL
- 1 MEDIUM ONION, PEELED AND CHOPPED
- 1 CELERY STICK, TRIMMED AND CHOPPED
- 1 GARLIC CLOVE, PEELED AND CRUSHED
- 4 TEASPOONS CHOPPED FRESH MINT
- 2 TOMATOES, SKINNED, DESEEDED AND CHOPPED
- ½ LEVEL TEASPOON SALT
- FRESHLY GROUND BLACK PEPPER
- FRESH MINT LEAVES TO GARNISH
- 285 ML (½ PINT) TOMATO SAUCE (SEE P.435) FOR SERVING (OPTIONAL)

PREPARATION TIME: 25 MINUTES
COOKING TIME: 1¾ HOURS
SERVES FOUR AS A SIDE DISH OR TWO AS A MAIN MEAL

Bring the stock to the boil and stir in the rice, reduce the heat, cover and cook gently for 20–25 minutes until the rice is cooked and the stock is absorbed.

Meanwhile, preheat the oven to 200°C (400°F, gas mark 6). Cut a slice about 2.5 cm (1 in) thick from each end of the marrow and, with a dessertspoon, remove all the seeds to leave a hollow along its entire length. Set aside.

Put the pine nuts into a dry, heavy-based frying pan and heat gently until the nuts are lightly browned, then remove from the pan and set aside. Melt half the butter with the oil in the frying pan, add the onion and sauté until just soft. Stir in the celery and garlic and cook for 5 minutes. Remove from the heat and add the cooked rice, pine nuts, half the mint and the chopped tomatoes, season well and mix together. Spoon this rice filling into the marrow pressing it in well.

Spread the remaining butter over a piece of foil large enough to wrap round the marrow. Sprinkle it evenly with the remaining mint, then season it well. Place the marrow in the centre of the foil, wrap it up tightly, place in a roasting tin and bake in the oven for 1–1¼ hours or until the marrow is tender.

Remove from the oven, unwrap and leave to stand for 5 minutes. Cut into 12 even slices and arrange on a serving dish or on individual plates. Garnish with fresh mint leaves and serve, accompanied by the tomato sauce, if using.

Wild Mushrooms in Sherry

This versatile dish can be made with any variety or mixture of mushrooms you like

Soak the dried mushrooms in the boiling water for 20 minutes, then pour into a sieve lined with kitchen paper to drain. Reserve the liquid.

Melt the butter in a frying pan, add the shallots and sauté gently until just tender, then stir in the garlic and cook for 1 minute. Add all the mushrooms to the pan, followed by the thyme and rosemary. Season with the salt and pepper, add the sherry and then stir in 2 tablespoons of the reserved mushroom liquid. Cover the pan and simmer for 10 minutes or until the mushrooms are just cooked.

Spoon the mushrooms into four heated individual serving dishes, garnish with the sprigs of thyme and rosemary and serve with french bread.

The assorted mushrooms are flavoured with garlic and herbs and cooked in a sherry sauce.

INGREDIENTS

30G (1OZ) DRIED WILD MUSHROOMS
150ML (¼ PINT) BOILING WATER
30G (1OZ) BUTTER
115G (4OZ) SHALLOTS, PEELED AND HALVED OR QUARTERED IF LARGE
2 GARLIC CLOVES, PEELED AND THINLY SLICED
175G (6OZ) CHESTNUT MUSHROOMS, WIPED AND HALVED
225G (8OZ) FIELD MUSHROOMS, WIPED AND THICKLY SLICED
175G (6OZ) FRESH CEPS, CLEANED, LARGER STALKS TRIMMED AND SLICED
60G (2OZ) FRESH CHANTERELLES, CLEANED
1 TABLESPOON CHOPPED FRESH THYME
2 FRESH ROSEMARY SPRIGS
SALT AND FRESHLY GROUND BLACK PEPPER
3 TABLESPOONS DRY SHERRY
FRESH THYME AND ROSEMARY SPRIGS TO GARNISH
FRENCH BREAD FOR SERVING

PREPARATION TIME: 35 MINUTES

COOKING TIME: 20 MINUTES

SERVES FOUR AS A STARTER OR SIX AS AN ACCOMPANIMENT

The Kitchen Front

Despite a tightening of belts, wartime rationing, with 'extras' for children, built the healthiest generation for centuries

SUITING ITS mood to the occasion, Monday, January 8, 1940, dawned grey and chill. Rationing had at last come into force, and this was the first day on which the housewife gathered up the family's ration books and took them to the shops. At the grocer's she discovered that each individual was entitled to buy 4 oz each of butter and bacon a week and 12 oz of sugar. These purchases made, the assistant snipped the appropriate coupons from the books and the housewife completed her weekly shop with the many goods still unrationed.

These rapidly grew fewer. In March, the meat ration was set at one shilling and tenpence worth a week—roughly two small chops or a modest piece of stewing steak—while in July margarine and cooking fats were fixed at 4 oz. Then, too, the unkindest cut to a tea-drinking nation was the rationing of its favourite beverage to 2 oz a week. Spring 1941 saw jam fixed at about 1 lb per month and cheese at 2 oz a week. This was a serious matter for people who depended on the midday cheese sandwich, though later on manual workers at least were awarded a much larger ration. Chocolate and sweets, the last foods to join the list during the war, were rationed in July 1942, but by this time a new and supplementary scheme had been introduced. This was the personal points system, which entitled the holder of each ration book to 20 points—actually a different kind of coupon—a month. These entitled the holder to purchase a number of specified foods, mostly tinned, in any preferred shop.

A HARD-PRESSED FIGHTER ON THE KITCHEN FRONT

No one went hungry. But no one could pretend either that wartime fare was anything other than dull and monotonous. Aware of this, the Ministry of Food, under the dynamic leadership of Lord Woolton, undertook to inject a little joy into it. Bulletins and leaflets of robust cheerfulness were issued informing citizens how they might make the best of what was available. Cinemagoers were bombarded with Food Facts, and newspaper readers with the exhortations of the cartoon characters Dr Carrot and Potato Pete.

Recipes ranged from the ingenious, like mock marzipan made from haricot beans and ground rice, to the bizarre. Vegetable and oatmeal goulash roused little enthusiasm; nor did such intriguing dishes as Carrot Christmas Pudding and Poor Man's Goose, the principal ingredients of which were pig's fry, potatoes and sage. Despite these lapses, the nation was very aware of the efforts the Minister of Food and his department had made on its behalf. One small girl, saying her prayers and coming to the line, 'Give us this day our daily bread', broke off to ask: 'Mummy, why do we have to have both God *and* Lord Woolton?'

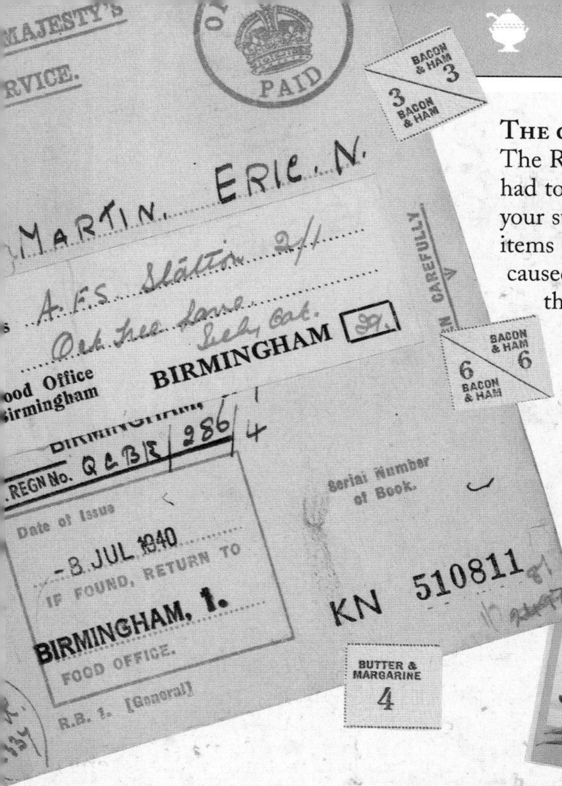

The good book

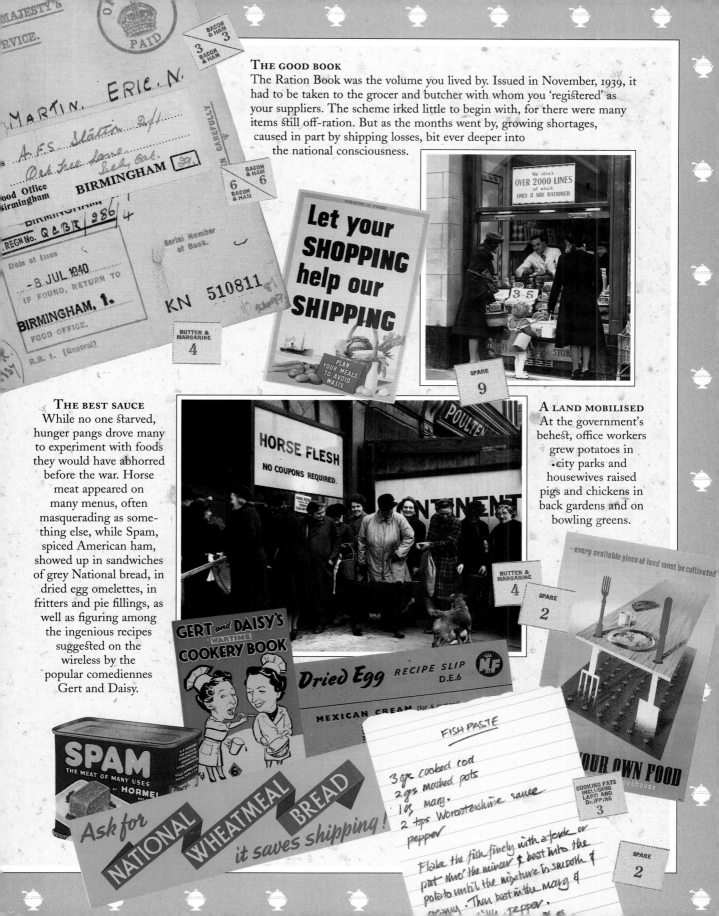

The Ration Book was the volume you lived by. Issued in November, 1939, it had to be taken to the grocer and butcher with whom you 'registered' as your suppliers. The scheme irked little to begin with, for there were many items still off-ration. But as the months went by, growing shortages, caused in part by shipping losses, bit ever deeper into the national consciousness.

The best sauce

While no one starved, hunger pangs drove many to experiment with foods they would have abhorred before the war. Horse meat appeared on many menus, often masquerading as something else, while Spam, spiced American ham, showed up in sandwiches of grey National bread, in dried egg omelettes, in fritters and pie fillings, as well as figuring among the ingenious recipes suggested on the wireless by the popular comediennes Gert and Daisy.

A land mobilised

At the government's behest, office workers grew potatoes in city parks and housewives raised pigs and chickens in back gardens and on bowling greens.

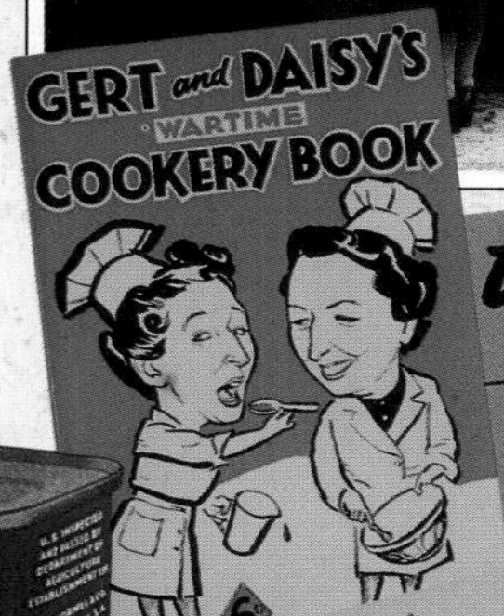

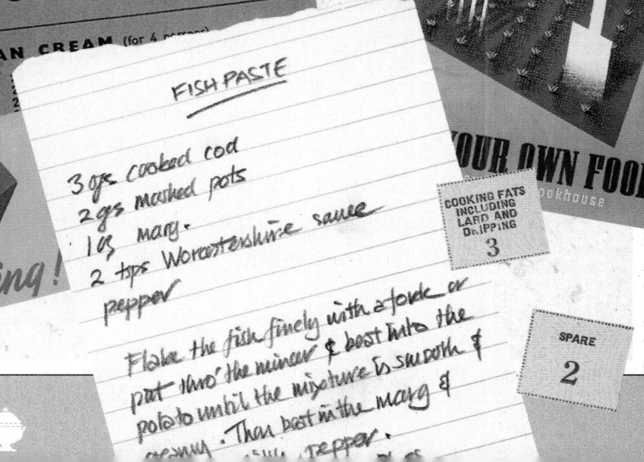

Vegetable Saucer Pies

These pies can be frozen before baking and taken straight from freezer to oven to provide a substantial, healthy snack for hungry children

INGREDIENTS

For the filling

- 60 g (2 oz) butter
- 225 g (8 oz) leeks, trimmed, thinly sliced and washed
- 225 g (8 oz) carrots, peeled and diced
- 3 small peppers, 1 red, 1 green and 1 yellow, deseeded and diced
- 115 g (4 oz) field, flat or open cup mushrooms, wiped and sliced
- 60 g (2 oz) frozen peas
- 60 g (2 oz) walnut pieces (optional)
- 60 g (2 oz) plain flour
- 1 level teaspoon ground coriander
- 150 ml (¼ pint) single cream
- 150 ml (¼ pint) milk
- 4 tablespoons chopped fresh dill
- Salt and freshly ground black pepper

For the pastry

- 450 g (1 lb) plain flour
- 225 g (8 oz) butter
- 115 g (4 oz) mature Cheddar cheese, grated
- ½ level teaspoon English mustard powder
- ¼ level teaspoon salt
- 175 ml (6 fl oz) milk
- 1 egg, size 2, beaten

Preparation time: 1¼ hours
Chilling time: 30 minutes
Cooking time: 40 minutes

To make the filling, melt the butter in a large frying pan, add the leeks and carrots and cook gently for 5 minutes. Mix in the peppers, mushrooms and peas and cook for a further 5 minutes, then add the walnuts, if using. Stir in the flour and coriander and cook, stirring, for 2 minutes. Gradually add the cream and the milk and cook over a moderate heat for 5 minutes or until the mixture comes to the boil and thickens. Remove from the heat, stir in the dill, season well with salt and pepper and leave to cool.

To make the pastry, sift the flour into a mixing bowl and rub in the butter. Stir in 85 g (3 oz) of the Cheddar cheese, the mustard powder and the salt. Add the milk and mix to make a soft but not sticky dough. Knead lightly on a floured surface until smooth.

Lightly grease six ovenproof saucers, 15 cm (6 in) in diameter, cut the dough in half, roll out one half thinly and, using a saucer as a guide, cut out six rounds, each a little larger than the saucer. Line the saucers with the rounds and divide the filling equally among them, spreading it to within 1.3 cm (½ in) of the edges.

Roll out the remaining dough thinly and, using a 16 cm (6½ in) teaplate as a guide, cut out six more rounds. Brush the edges of the dough on the saucers with cold water, cover with the 'lids' and press the edges together well. Trim and decorate the edges. Make a small hole in the centre of each pie to allow the steam to escape, then chill for 30 minutes.

Preheat the oven to 200°C (400°F, gas mark 6). Put the pies on two baking sheets, brush with the beaten egg and sprinkle with the remaining Cheddar cheese. Bake for 30 minutes, then reverse the position of the trays and cook for a further 10 minutes or until golden brown.

Grated cheese and mustard powder lend piquancy to the pastry for these small but filling pies.

Parmesan cheese and chives flavour the floury potato base of this soufflé that tastes as light as it looks.

Collapse of stout party
Cartoonist Fougasse of *Punch* feelingly depicts the loss of morale that attends the deflation of a soufflé. Before the advent of oven thermometers earlier in the century, this must have been a regular occurrence indeed.

Potato Soufflé

This light and delicious soufflé will rise to any occasion

Preheat the oven to 220°c (425°f, gas mark 7), and butter a 1.7 litre (3 pint) soufflé dish.

Steam the potatoes until soft, then put into a bowl with the butter and egg yolks and mash well together. Beat in enough milk to make a slightly soft, dropping consistency, then add the chives and all but 1 tablespoon of the grated cheese. Season liberally with the salt, pepper and freshly grated nutmeg.

Whisk the egg whites until stiff, but not dry. Fold a third of the whites into the potato mixture to loosen it, then very gently and carefully fold in the remainder.

Pour the mixture into the buttered soufflé dish, sprinkle the remaining cheese over the top and bake in the centre of the oven for 25 minutes until well risen, golden brown and soft but firm to the touch.

Serve immediately, as a main course with a tossed salad, or as a vegetable accompaniment to other cooked dishes, such as roast poultry, grilled meat or fish, casseroles or cold cooked meats.

INGREDIENTS

450g (1 lb) floury potatoes, peeled and quartered
30g (1 oz) butter
4 eggs, size 2, separated
4–6 tablespoons milk
2 tablespoons snipped fresh chives
70g (2½ oz) Parmesan cheese, grated
Salt and freshly ground black pepper
Freshly grated nutmeg
Preparation time: 30 minutes
Cooking time: 25 minutes
Serves two as a main course, four as an accompaniment

Cooked samphire can also be added to salads. It should be treated like any other vegetable, such as asparagus or green beans.

Samphire, lettuce and a garnish of fried almonds produce a salad with a delightfully crunchy texture.

Brancaster Salad

Long an East Anglian delicacy, the bright green stems of samphire give a pleasant, salty tang to any salad

INGREDIENTS

225g (8oz) samphire
1 medium crisp lettuce, such as Webb's, washed, dried and shredded
3 tablespoons light olive oil
45g (1½oz) blanched almonds, roughly chopped
1 tablespoon walnut or hazelnut oil
2 tablespoons cider vinegar
Freshly ground black pepper
Pinch of mustard powder
Preparation time: 15 minutes
Cooking time: 2 minutes
Serves four

Snip the tender young shoots off the samphire and cut the main stalk roughly in half. Reserve the lower half—it is too tough to eat raw, but it can be cooked on another occasion. Wash the samphire well in cold water and dry it thoroughly on a tea towel.

Mix the lettuce and samphire together in a large salad bowl. Heat 2 tablespoons of the olive oil in a frying pan and quickly fry the almonds until lightly browned. Remove the pan from the heat and drain the oil into a small bowl. Add the remaining olive oil, the walnut or hazelnut oil, vinegar, pepper and mustard and whisk together with a fork. Do not add salt, as there is sufficient in the samphire.

Pour the dressing over the salad and scatter the browned almonds on top. Toss the salad immediately before serving.

Brussels Sprouts Gratinée

This dish is substantial enough to be served on its own, or as an accompaniment to liver or lamb cutlets

STEAM the brussels sprouts until just cooked. Meanwhile, cook the bacon in a frying pan, without any fat, until crisp and brown, then remove from the pan and keep warm. Melt the butter in the same pan and cook the almonds and chestnuts until golden brown. Add the bacon and grapes, cook for a few minutes until heated through then season well.

Transfer the bacon and grape mixture to a warm, flameproof dish. Add the steamed brussels sprouts to the dish and mix well. Mix the breadcrumbs with the Parmesan cheese and sprinkle evenly over the sprouts.

Place the dish under a hot grill and cook for 2–3 minutes until crisp and golden brown. Serve at once.

An imaginative combination of sprouts, chestnuts, grapes, almonds and bacon produces a vivid array of textures, flavours and colours.

INGREDIENTS

- 675G (1½LB) BUTTON BRUSSELS SPROUTS, TRIMMED
- 4 THICK RASHERS BACK BACON, RINDS REMOVED, COARSELY CHOPPED
- 60G (2OZ) BUTTER
- 60G (2OZ) WHOLE BLANCHED ALMONDS
- 225G (8OZ) COOKED CHESTNUTS, FRESH OR FROZEN
- 175G (6OZ) SEEDLESS RED GRAPES
- SALT AND FRESHLY GROUND BLACK PEPPER
- 60G (2OZ) FRESH WHITE BREADCRUMBS
- 60G (2OZ) PARMESAN CHEESE FRESHLY GRATED

PREPARATION TIME: 15 MINUTES
COOKING TIME: 25 MINUTES
SERVES FOUR AS A LIGHT LUNCH OR SUPPER DISH, SIX AS A SIDE DISH

SOLDIERS OF THE PLOUGH
During the last war some 65,000 women served in the Women's Land Army, releasing men to the Forces and gradually taking over even the toughest and most skilled jobs, from ploughing and harvesting to animal husbandry, horse management and forestry.

Hallowe'en Colcannon

Colcannon, Ireland's equivalent of Scotland's rumbledethumps and England's bubble and squeak, is traditionally eaten at Hallowe'en

INGREDIENTS

- 900 g (2 lb) potatoes, peeled and quartered
- 450 g (1 lb) green cabbage or curly kale, washed and shredded
- 4 tablespoons milk
- ¼ level teaspoon salt
- ⅛ level teaspoon freshly ground black pepper
- ⅛ level teaspoon ground mace
- 3 spring onions, trimmed and thinly sliced
- 60 g (2 oz) butter

Preparation time: 10 minutes
Cooking time: 25 minutes
Serves four

Preheat the oven to 160°C (325°F, gas mark 3). Boil the quartered potatoes gently in salted water for 15 minutes, or until cooked. Drain well.

Meanwhile, put the shredded cabbage or kale into another saucepan, cover with boiling water and simmer for 5 minutes until tender, then drain well.

Put a deep serving dish into the oven to warm. Mash the potatoes in the saucepan until smooth, add the milk, salt, pepper and mace and mash again.

Reserve 1 tablespoon of the green part of the sliced spring onions for garnish, then add the rest to the potatoes with the drained cabbage. Place the saucepan over a low heat and continue to mash for 5 minutes until fluffy and heated through.

Spoon the colcannon into the heated serving dish, make a well in the centre, add the butter and return to the oven for 5 minutes or until the butter has melted. Sprinkle with the reserved spring onion and serve piping hot.

Potatoes, cabbage and spring onions, mashed and flavoured with mace, make this Gaelic treat.

The music makers
Whether the Irish Hallowe'en celebrates All Saints' Eve or more ancient beliefs in the Sun God and Samhain, Lord of Death, does not really matter. It is still a great time for a *ceilidh*, with fiddle and squeezebox to set feet dancing until morning.

Sliced radishes bring a peppery undertone to the broad beans which are served in a smooth herb sauce.

For a better colour, texture and flavour, skin the beans. Make a slit with your thumbnail at one end and then the bean can be squeezed out easily.

Broad Beans & Radishes in a Herb Sauce

This delicate vegetable dish can be served as an unusual starter or as an accompaniment to fish, chicken or boiled bacon

POUR the milk into a small saucepan and add the thyme, parsley, bay leaf and onion. Bring to the boil, then remove from the heat, cover and leave to infuse for 1 hour.

Put the shelled beans into a saucepan, pour over boiling water to cover, bring back to the boil then reduce the heat and simmer for 1 minute. Drain and reserve the water. Rinse the beans under cold water, until cool enough to handle, then remove and discard their white skins.

Steam the beans and radishes together over boiling water for 5 minutes, or until they are just cooked.

Meanwhile, to make the sauce, strain the infused milk into a jug and make up to 340 ml (12 fl oz) with the reserved bean water. Melt the butter in a saucepan, stir in the flour and cook for 1 minute, then gradually stir in the milk and water mixture. Bring to the boil, stirring constantly until the sauce becomes thick and smooth. Add the salt, pepper and ground mace and simmer for 2 minutes, then stir in the parsley.

Transfer the beans and radishes to a warm serving dish and pour over the sauce. Garnish with the sprigs of thyme and serve hot.

INGREDIENTS

285 ML (½ PINT) MILK
2 SPRIGS EACH THYME AND PARSLEY
1 BAY LEAF
1 SMALL ONION, PEELED AND QUARTERED
675 G (1½ LB) SHELLED FRESH BROAD BEANS
175 G (6 OZ) RADISHES, TRIMMED AND SLICED
30 G (1 OZ) BUTTER
30 G (1 OZ) PLAIN FLOUR
¼ LEVEL TEASPOON SALT
⅛ LEVEL TEASPOON FRESHLY GROUND BLACK PEPPER
⅛ LEVEL TEASPOON GROUND MACE
1 TABLESPOON CHOPPED FRESH PARSLEY
FRESH THYME SPRIGS TO GARNISH

PREPARATION TIME: 35 MINUTES
STANDING TIME: 1 HOUR
COOKING TIME: 10 MINUTES
SERVES FOUR

A brief spell in the oven brings out the full flavour of onion and herb-stuffed mushrooms.

Stuffed Mushrooms in Crisp Batter

The caper sauce for the mushrooms is made in a moment and tastes superb

INGREDIENTS

For the batter

- 115g (4oz) plain flour
- ½ level teaspoon salt
- 1 tablespoon corn or vegetable oil
- 150ml (¼ pint) water
- 1 egg white, size 2

For the mushrooms

- 1 onion
- 30g (1oz) butter
- 115g (4oz) fresh white breadcrumbs
- 3 tablespoons chopped fresh parsley
- 2–3 teaspoons chopped fresh tarragon
- 12 open cup or flat mushrooms, each approx 30g (1oz), wiped, stalks removed and chopped
- Salt and freshly ground black pepper
- 1 egg yolk, size 2
- 2 level tablespoons plain flour, seasoned well with salt and pepper
- Groundnut oil for frying

For the sauce

- 2 tablespoons capers, finely chopped
- 150ml (¼ pint) mayonnaise, homemade (see p.436) or bought

Preparation time: 30 minutes
Standing time: 1 hour
Cooking time: 25 minutes
Serves four as a starter, six as an accompaniment or three as a main course

To make the batter, sift the flour and salt into a bowl. Make a well in the centre, add the oil and water and whisk until smooth. Cover and set aside for 1 hour.

Preheat the oven to 200°c (400°f, gas mark 6). Meanwhile, peel and finely chop the onion. Melt the butter in a small saucepan and fry gently for 5 minutes or until transparent. Transfer the onion, and any butter that remains in the pan, to a bowl. Add the breadcrumbs, herbs, mushroom stalks, and some salt and pepper and bind with the egg yolk.

Spoon an equal amount of stuffing into each mushroom and press into place. Bake on a lightly greased baking tray for 10 minutes until slightly softened, then remove from the oven and leave to cool.

Meanwhile, make the sauce. Mix the capers with the mayonnaise and spoon the mixture into a small dish or bowl.

Coat the cooled mushrooms very lightly with the seasoned flour, then pour about 2.5cm (1in) of oil into a wide frying pan. Heat to 190°c (375°f), or until a cube of bread dropped into the oil browns in 5–6 seconds. Whisk the egg white until stiff, then fold it into the batter. Using two forks, lift the prepared mushrooms, one at a time, stuffing uppermost, and dip them into the batter. Allow any excess batter to drip back into the bowl, then immediately lower the mushrooms into the oil. Fry for 3–4 minutes, turning them over halfway through cooking, until they are crisp and golden brown—you should be able to fry about six mushrooms at a time.

Remove from the oil with a slotted spoon and drain well on kitchen paper. Keep warm while frying the remainder. Serve with the caper sauce.

Welsh Onion Cake

The onion cake is delicious on its own, or as a bed for lean, luscious Welsh lamb

Preheat the oven to 220°c (425°f, gas mark 7), and line the base and sides of a greased 18 cm (7 in) solid-base round cake tin with nonstick baking paper. Arrange a layer of overlapping potato slices in the bottom of the tin and sprinkle with a few of the chopped shallots. Season well with the salt and pepper and pour over a little of the melted butter.

Continue to make layers of potatoes and shallots until all the potatoes are used up and the tin is full. Pour any remaining butter over the top and bake in the centre of the oven for 1 hour, or until the potatoes are cooked.

Remove the cake from the oven and turn it out carefully onto an ovenproof dish, then return it to the oven for 10 more minutes or until it is golden brown.

Cut the cake into wedges and serve as an accompaniment to casseroles, roast meats, cold meats or savoury pies.

INGREDIENTS

1.4 kg (3 lb) baking potatoes, peeled and thinly sliced
115 g (4 oz) shallots or onions, peeled and finely chopped
Salt and freshly ground black pepper
175 g (6 oz) butter, melted

Preparation time: 30 minutes
Cooking time: 1 hour 10 minutes
Serves six

Layers of potatoes and shallots, drenched in butter, are baked to a golden crispness.

Wales forever!
A quartet of Welsh ladies taking tea in the 1930s. Their dress is based upon countrywomen's clothes of the 1820s, while the hats are like those worn by men at that period. The ensemble was popularised as Welsh national costume by print makers and photographers.

JUBILEE ~ QUEEN
WY174
SOREL
ELIZABETH MICHELLE

Sea and River

With tidal water no more than 75 miles away from any of us, and tumbling streams or sleek rivers even closer, it is hardly surprising that fish made such a mark on Britain's cookery. Northern seaports contributed *Cod*, *Herring* and *Flatfish* too, from the drowned, sandy plain between Scotland and Norway. From Cornwall's granite coast came *Lobsters* and *Shrimps*, while misty North Sea creeks supplied *Crab* and *Shellfish*. Tweed and Severn presented us with *Salmon* and *Eels*, and swift streams from the Scottish Highlands to the Cotswolds offered *Trout*. Ingenuity did the rest, using local produce to create a vast spectrum of *Sauces* and other *Accompaniments*.

Herrings in Oatmeal

The legendary dish that nourished the brain and muscle of many a Scottish empire-builder in his hard-up student days

INGREDIENTS

2 TABLESPOONS OLIVE OIL
115 G (4 OZ) STREAKY BACON, CHOPPED
4 HERRINGS, GUTTED, CLEANED AND BONED
SALT AND FRESHLY GROUND BLACK PEPPER
85 G (3 OZ) COARSE OATMEAL
1 TABLESPOON FINELY CHOPPED FRESH PARSLEY
1 LEMON, CUT INTO 4 WEDGES
PREPARATION TIME: 15 MINUTES
COOKING TIME: 10–12 MINUTES
SERVES FOUR

Heat the oil in a large, nonstick frying pan, add the bacon and cook over a moderate heat until the bacon is crisp and all the fat has been extracted.

Meanwhile, season the herrings well with salt and pepper. Spread the oatmeal on a plate, then open the herrings out flat and press them one at a time in the oatmeal, coating both sides evenly.

Remove the bacon from the frying pan and discard, then fry the herrings, one or two at a time, for 3–4 minutes on each side until golden brown and crisp. Drain on kitchen paper.

Arrange on a hot serving dish, sprinkle with the parsley and garnish with the lemon wedges. Serve with warm granary bread and a tomato salad.

Wood smoke, fried bacon and herring produce an unforgettable aroma.

Caller herrin'
In days gone by one of the colourful sights of Edinburgh was the fisher girls who, in their striped petticoats, sold herring in the streets. Their wares they called 'lives o' men' in recognition of the dangers of the East Coast herring fisheries.

If any mussels are open before cooking, tap them lightly. If they remain open, discard them, as they are dead and poisonous. Likewise, throw away any that stay closed after cooking.

Chestnut mushrooms blend beautifully with mussels in an aromatic sauce.

Mussel Ragout

Mussels are widespread around Britain's rocky coasts and estuaries and can often be found attached to rocks in tightly packed clumps

Put about 150 ml (¼ pint) of water into a large saucepan and add a double layer of mussels. Cover and cook over a high heat for about 3 minutes, shaking occasionally.

Remove the saucepan from the heat and leave, with the lid on, for 3–5 minutes. With a slotted spoon remove the mussels from the saucepan and put them onto a plate, discarding any that have remained closed. Repeat the process with the remaining mussels, adding them to the liquid in the saucepan.

Take the mussels from their shells. Strain the mussel liquid through a sieve lined with kitchen paper into a clean saucepan. Bring to the boil and boil rapidly until the liquid is reduced to about 2 tablespoons. Remove the pan from the heat and set aside.

Melt the butter in a saucepan, add the mushrooms and cook for about 5 minutes until soft. Stir in the flour and cook for a further minute. Remove from the heat and gradually stir in the cream and the reserved mussel liquid. Return to the heat and bring to the boil, stirring. Add the mussels, seasoning, nutmeg and parsley and heat through gently for about 5 minutes. Stir in the lemon juice and pour the ragout into a heated serving dish. If liked, sprinkle with chopped parsley. Serve with wholemeal bread.

INGREDIENTS

- 900 G (2 LB) FRESH MUSSELS, CLEANED AND DEBEARDED (SEE P.436)
- 60 G (2 OZ) BUTTER
- 115 G (4 OZ) CHESTNUT MUSHROOMS, WIPED AND ROUGHLY CHOPPED
- 1 LEVEL TABLESPOON PLAIN FLOUR
- 150 ML (¼ PINT) SINGLE CREAM
- SALT AND FRESHLY GROUND BLACK PEPPER
- LARGE PINCH FRESHLY GRATED NUTMEG
- 1 LEVEL TABLESPOON CHOPPED FRESH PARSLEY
- 1 TABLESPOON LEMON JUICE

PREPARATION TIME: 20 MINUTES
COOKING TIME: 20 MINUTES
SERVES TWO AS A MAIN COURSE, FOUR AS A STARTER

Plain fare
One of mankind's earliest foods, cockles are still at their best when served most simply—at a wayside stall, for instance, accompanied by no more than vinegar, pepper and salt.

A serving of two of these rich, fishy rings apiece should satisfy the most voracious of your guests.

Plaice Fillets Stuffed with Cockles

The addition of an astringent shellfish and a creamy sauce adds a new dimension to the smooth flavour of plaice

INGREDIENTS

- 8 plaice fillets, each approx 115g (4oz), skinned
- 225g (8oz) cockles
- 60g (2oz) butter
- ½ level teaspoon celery seeds
- 1 medium onion, peeled and finely chopped
- 6 medium celery sticks, thinly sliced
- 200ml (7fl oz) dry white wine
- 150ml (¼ pint) double cream
- 1 tablespoon chopped fresh parsley
- Salt and freshly ground black pepper
- Chopped fresh parsley sprigs and lemon halves or wedges to garnish

Preparation time: 25 minutes
Cooking time: 35 minutes
Serves four

Preheat the oven to 180°c (350°f, gas mark 4). Take a single plaice fillet and cut it in half lengthways. Lay the halves end to end, with the skin uppermost and the head end of one half overlapping the tail of the other. Wrap the fish, with the skin inside, round the base of a straight-sided glass tumbler to shape it into a ring. Remove the tumbler and put the fish ring into a greased, ovenproof dish.

Make seven more rings in the same way with the remaining fillets and put them into the greased dish. Fill the plaice rings with the cockles and set aside.

To make the sauce, melt the butter in a frying pan, add the celery seeds and cook for 1 minute, stirring. Add the chopped onion and sliced celery and sauté gently until they are just soft. Reserve 2 tablespoons of the wine and pour the rest over the onion and celery. Simmer for 5 minutes. Remove from the heat, stir in the cream and chopped parsley, and season well.

Pour the celery sauce carefully round the plaice rings and drizzle the reserved wine over the fish. Cover the dish with foil and bake in the oven for 20 minutes or until the plaice is cooked. Stir the sauce in the cooking dish, to blend it with the juices from the fish, then spoon some of it over the plaice and cockles.

Garnish with the parsley sprigs and serve with the lemon halves or wedges. New potatoes, broccoli or fine green beans go well with this dish.

Trout Cooked in Newspaper

Wet newspaper conserves moisture and succulence by effectively steaming these fish, particularly when they are cooked over an open fire

INGREDIENTS

- 4 TROUT, EACH APPROX 275–340 G (10–12 OZ), GUTTED AND WASHED
- SALT AND FRESHLY GROUND BLACK PEPPER
- 1 LARGE LEMON, CUT INTO 8 SLICES
- 4 FENNEL OR TARRAGON SPRIGS (OPTIONAL)
- 12–16 SHEETS NEWSPAPER

PREPARATION TIME: 10 MINUTES
COOKING TIME: 25–30 MINUTES
SERVES FOUR

TROUT IN NEWSPAPER

Preheat the oven to 200°C (400°F, gas mark 6) or light the barbecue. Season the trout well with salt and pepper and put two slices of lemon and a sprig of fennel or tarragon, if using, inside each one.

Lay each fish on three layers of newspaper and wrap, tucking in the ends of the paper carefully. Soak the wrapped fish in cold water until thoroughly wet. Place the 'parcels' in the oven or on the barbecue and cook for 25–30 minutes or until the paper is dry, turning once halfway through cooking.

Serve the trout in the paper and cut it open with scissors at the table. The skin will peel off with the paper, leaving a perfectly cooked, moist and succulent fish.

To cook larger fish, such as salmon or bass weighing about 1.4 kg (3 lb), in the same way increase the amount of paper and the cooking time in proportion to the size of the fish.

VARIATIONS

Trout, or other fish such as mackerel, can be cooked in hay, either on the barbecue or in the oven.

Take some sweet-smelling hay and soak thoroughly for about 30 minutes in a large bucket of cold water. Take a double handful of the soaked hay and put one or two of the fish into the centre, making sure they are completely covered by a 5 cm (2 in) layer of hay. Cook the 'parcels' on the barbecue, or in the oven, for about 30 minutes or until just cooked through, turning once halfway through cooking.

Bass and other larger fish can be wrapped in seaweed and cooked on a barbecue or open fire. Depending on the type of seaweed, either bury the fish inside a mound of seaweed, as if cooking in hay, or wrap about eight layers of seaweed all round the fish and, depending on the size, cook for about an hour or until the fish is just cooked through.

The skin peels away with the newspaper when the 'parcels' are opened.

If cooking the trout in hay, make sure you use good quality, sweet smelling hay. Any mustiness will spoil the flavour.

Scallop shells, filled with a lobster, cream and brandy sauce, bring grace and flavour to the table.

Scallops with Lobster Sauce

These shellfish make an elegant starter for a stylish occasion

INGREDIENTS

12 FRESH MEDIUM SCALLOPS WITH CORALS, CLEANED (SEE P.436)
60 G (2 OZ) PLAIN FLOUR, SEASONED WELL WITH SALT AND PEPPER
2 EGGS, SIZE 2, BEATEN
85 G (3 OZ) FRESH WHITE BREADCRUMBS
2 TABLESPOONS OLIVE OIL
115 G (4 OZ) UNSALTED BUTTER
1 TABLESPOON FINELY CHOPPED FRESH PARSLEY
LEMON WEDGES TO GARNISH
COARSE SEA SALT FOR SERVING

FOR THE SAUCE
450 G (1 LB) COOKED FEMALE LOBSTER, PREPARED BY FISHMONGER (OR SEE P.437), CORAL RESERVED
1 TABLESPOON FRESH LEMON JUICE
30 G (1 OZ) BUTTER
PINCH EACH CAYENNE PEPPER AND GROUND MACE
285 ML (½ PINT) DOUBLE CREAM
1 TABLESPOON BRANDY
SALT AND FRESHLY GROUND WHITE PEPPER

PREPARATION TIME: 1 HOUR
COOKING TIME: 15 MINUTES
SERVES SIX

SEPARATE the corals from the scallops, then slice the white muscles in half horizontally. Coat the slices and the corals first in the seasoned flour, then in the beaten egg and next in the breadcrumbs. Put onto a plate, cover and refrigerate.

To make the sauce, chop the lobster meat finely. Mash the coral with the lemon juice and set aside. Melt the butter in a saucepan, add the lobster meat and sauté for 2 minutes. Add the cayenne pepper, mace, cream and brandy. Bring to the boil, remove from the heat and stir in the coral. Season with the salt and pepper and keep warm.

To cook the scallops, heat 1 tablespoon of the oil with half the unsalted butter, in a large frying pan, until sizzling. Add half the coated scallops and cook over a moderate heat for 1–2 minutes on each side or until the coating is crisp and golden. Remove from the pan and drain on kitchen paper. Heat the remaining oil and butter and fry the remaining scallops in the same way.

Pour the sauce into six clean scallop shells, arrange the scallops on top and sprinkle with the parsley. Arrange on a bed of sea salt on a platter, garnish with the lemon wedges and serve immediately.

Baked Carp with Spicy Orange & Raisin Sauce

Farmed, imported carp is available, but for flavour cannot touch that of its wild cousins fished from lakes and slow rivers

Preheat the oven to 200°c (400°f, gas mark 6). Fill a bowl with cold water, add the vinegar and wash the carp thoroughly. Drain and dry on kitchen paper. On each side of the fish, make three diagonal cuts down to, but not through, the bone.

Spread all but 15 g (½ oz) of the butter into the cuts, then season well. With the remaining butter, grease an ovenproof dish just large enough to hold the fish, and a sheet of foil to cover the dish. Lay the carp in the dish and set aside.

To make the sauce, heat the olive oil in a saucepan and cook the onion over a moderate heat for 5–10 minutes until softened but not browned. Stir in the spices, orange juice, wine and raisins and pour the sauce over the carp. Cover with the foil and cook in the centre of the oven for 30 minutes.

Uncover the dish and bake for a further 10–15 minutes or until the fish is cooked. Using two large fish slices, transfer the carp to a heated ovenproof serving dish. Strain the cooking juices into a saucepan. Spoon the remaining onion and raisins round the carp, cover loosely with foil and keep warm.

Season the cooking juices with salt and pepper to taste, stir in the lemon juice and sweeten with the honey, if necessary. Blend the arrowroot with 1 tablespoon of water until smooth. Stir into the sauce and bring to the boil, stirring until it clears and thickens slightly. Glaze the carp with some of the sauce and pour the remainder into a heated jug.

Garnish with celery leaves and lemon and orange wedges, and serve with new potatoes tossed in butter and chives.

Ingredients

- 6 tablespoons malt vinegar
- 1·4 kg (3 lb) carp, scaled and gutted
- 115 g (4 oz) butter, softened
- Salt and freshly ground black pepper

For the sauce

- 1 tablespoon olive oil
- 1 large onion, peeled and thinly sliced
- Pinch each ground mace, cinnamon and cumin
- Strained juice 1 large orange
- 175 ml (6 fl oz) dry white wine
- 60 g (2 oz) stoned raisins, washed and dried
- 2 teaspoons lemon juice
- ½ teaspoon honey (optional)
- 1 level teaspoon arrowroot
- 1 tablespoon water
- Celery leaves and lemon and orange wedges to garnish

Preparation time: 30 minutes
Cooking time: 50–55 minutes
Serves six

This noble fish requires company no more imposing than new potatoes and crusty bread.

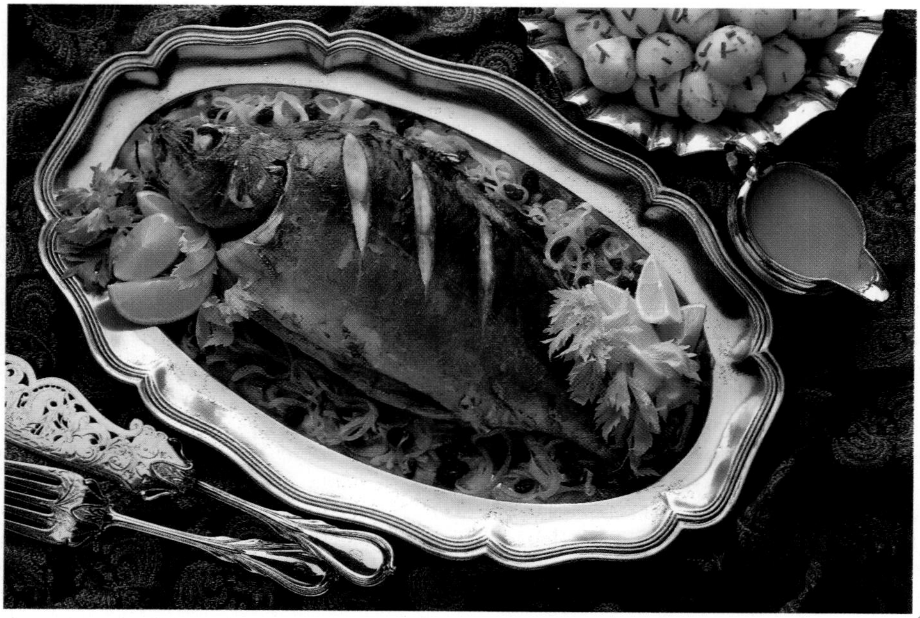

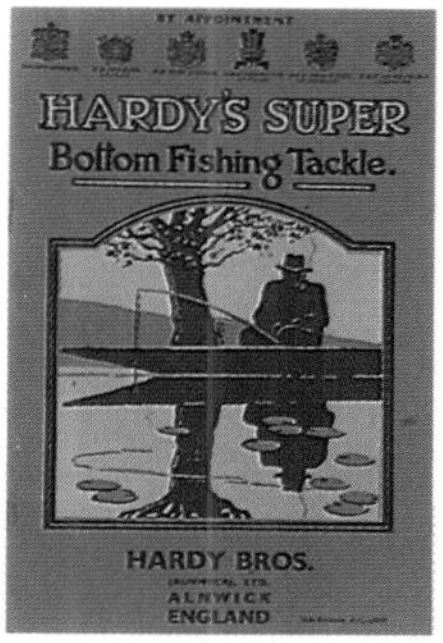

Patience rewarded
With their suspicious natures, fondness for still waters, thick reedbeds and lilypads, big carp are not easy to catch. But expert anglers agree that the fishes' fighting qualities make a long wait well worth while.

Mussels in Murphies

Originally these were hot, portable, midday meals for Irish farmhands

INGREDIENTS

- 4 LARGE BAKING POTATOES, EACH APPROX 250G (9OZ), SCRUBBED, DRIED AND PRICKED ALL OVER
- 1 TABLESPOON OLIVE OIL
- ½ TEASPOON COARSE SEA SALT
- 2 KG (4½ LB) FRESH, LIVE MUSSELS, CLEANED (SEE P.436), OR 340 G (12OZ) FROZEN SHELLED MUSSELS, THAWED
- 6 TABLESPOONS WATER
- 1 SPRIG EACH PARSLEY AND THYME
- 1 SMALL ONION, PEELED AND CHOPPED
- 60G (2OZ) BUTTER
- 2 SHALLOTS, PEELED AND FINELY CHOPPED
- ½ TEASPOON SAFFRON STRANDS
- 4 TABLESPOONS DRY WHITE WINE OR WHITE WINE VINEGAR
- 150ML (¼ PINT) DOUBLE CREAM
- 1 TABLESPOON CHOPPED FRESH PARSLEY

PREPARATION TIME: 15 MINUTES
COOKING TIME: 1 HOUR
SERVES FOUR

Preheat the oven to 200°c (400°f, gas mark 6). Rub the potatoes all over with the olive oil, sprinkle them with the coarse salt and bake on the oven shelf for about an hour.

Meanwhile, if using fresh mussels, put them into a large saucepan with the water, herbs and onion. Cover and cook over a high heat for 3–4 minutes until the mussels have opened, shaking the pan frequently. Remove the pan from the heat and remove the mussels from their shells, discarding any which have not opened.

When the potatoes are cooked, reduce the oven temperature to low.

Melt the butter in a saucepan and sauté the shallots gently for 3 minutes. Stir in the saffron and the wine or vinegar and simmer for 1–2 minutes until the liquid is reduced by half.

Add the cream, simmer for 1 minute, add the mussels and simmer, uncovered, for about 3 minutes, stirring occasionally, until the sauce has thickened and the mussels are hot. Cut each potato in half and fill with the mussel sauce.

The mussel-filled potato was an early form of takeaway, carried to the fields in a cloth.

Hot bread rolls can be used instead of potatoes. Scoop out the insides of the rolls and fill the crusts with the shellfish.

Marsh samphire and shrimps can often be found on the same slab in East Anglian fishmongers.

HERB OF ST PETER
Rock samphire, which grows in the south and west of Britain, shares similarities of flavour and texture with the marsh species, but tends to anchor itself in crevices in dizzying cliff-faces. Both samphires derive their name from Saint Pierre, or St Peter, the 'rock' of the Christian Church.

Samphire with Shrimps

The salt-sea tang of samphire is just right with fish: prawns, mussels, oysters, clams, cockles or dabs can all be recruited in place of shrimps

PICK off only the very tender side shoots and about 3.8 cm (1½ in) from the main stalk of the samphire.

Put the finely chopped shallots and carrot into a saucepan with the dry cider. Bring to the boil and continue to boil rapidly until the cider has reduced to about 60 ml (2 fl oz). Put the cream into a separate saucepan, bring to the boil and boil until it has reduced by about a third. Strain the cider into the cream and stir well. Remove the pan from the heat and set aside until required.

Boil the samphire in a large pan of unsalted water for about 4 minutes or until just tender then drain well.

Stir the shrimps into the sauce and heat gently for a few minutes until piping hot, but do not allow the sauce to boil as this will toughen the shrimps. Taste and adjust the seasoning, but take care not to add too much salt.

Arrange the samphire on heated plates, spoon the sauce over the top and serve with the lemon halves and crusty brown bread.

INGREDIENTS

- 675 G (1½ LB) SAMPHIRE, WASHED
- 2 SHALLOTS, PEELED AND FINELY CHOPPED
- 1 SMALL CARROT, PEELED AND FINELY CHOPPED
- 285 ML (½ PINT) DRY CIDER
- 285 ML (½ PINT) DOUBLE CREAM
- 450 G (1 LB) BROWN OR PINK SHRIMPS, PEELED (SEE P.436), OR 225 G (8 OZ) READY-PEELED SHRIMPS
- SALT AND FRESHLY GROUND BLACK PEPPER
- LEMON HALVES FOR SERVING

PREPARATION TIME: 30 MINUTES, LONGER IF PEELING SHRIMPS
COOKING TIME: 10 MINUTES
SERVES FOUR AS A MAIN COURSE OR SIX AS A STARTER

Salmon in Pastry with Watercress Sauce

Here is pomp and circumstance for a great occasion—a dish that complements both your table and your skills as a cook

Ingredients

For the sauce

285 ML (½ PINT) MILK
285 ML (½ PINT) SINGLE CREAM
BOUQUET GARNI (SEE P.440)
2 CLOVES
1 MACE BLADE
30 G (1 OZ) BUTTER
30 G (1 OZ) PLAIN FLOUR
1 BUNCH WATERCRESS, TRIMMED, WASHED AND DRIED
SALT AND FRESHLY GROUND BLACK PEPPER

For the pastry

450 G (1 LB) PLAIN FLOUR
1 LEVEL TEASPOON GROUND GINGER
½ LEVEL TEASPOON SALT
275 G (10 OZ) BUTTER
60 G (2 OZ) LARD
2 EGGS, SIZE 2
5 TABLESPOONS CHILLED WATER
30 G (1 OZ) BLANCHED ALMONDS, LIGHTLY TOASTED AND CHOPPED
15 G (½ OZ) PRESERVED STEM GINGER, FINELY CHOPPED
4 TABLESPOONS CHOPPED FRESH PARSLEY
SALT AND FRESHLY GROUND BLACK PEPPER

For the fish

20 THIN ASPARAGUS SPEARS, TRIMMED TO EQUAL LENGTHS, WASHED
2.3 KG (5 LB) WHOLE SALMON, FILLETS REMOVED IN ONE PIECE FROM EACH SIDE AND SKINNED
STRAINED JUICE 1 LEMON
FRESH WATERCRESS TO GARNISH

Preparation time: 1¾ HOURS
Chilling time: 30 MINUTES
Cooking time: 40 MINUTES
Serves eight

PUT the milk, cream, bouquet garni, cloves and mace into a saucepan, and heat until almost boiling. Remove from the heat, cover and leave to infuse until required for the sauce.

THE PASTRY AND THE ALMOND BUTTER

Sift the flour, ground ginger and salt into a mixing bowl. Rub in 175 g (6 oz) of the butter and all of the lard until the mixture resembles fine breadcrumbs. Lightly beat together one of the eggs and the chilled water, add to the rubbed-in mixture and mix to form a soft but not sticky dough. Turn the dough out onto a lightly floured surface and knead gently. Wrap the dough in cling film and chill in the refrigerator for 30 minutes.

Beat the remaining butter in a bowl until fluffy. Stir in the toasted chopped almonds, stem ginger, chopped parsley and plenty of salt and freshly ground black pepper. Cover the bowl and leave to stand at room temperature.

THE SALMON AND THE ASPARAGUS

Preheat the oven to 200°C (400°F, gas mark 6). Put the asparagus spears into a saucepan of boiling water, cook for 5 minutes, then rinse under cold water and drain well in a colander.

Cut the chilled dough in half, roll out one half on a floured surface and trim to a rectangle a little larger than the salmon fillets. Place one of the salmon fillets, skinned side down, on the rectangle and spread with the almond butter to cover completely. Sprinkle the butter with half the lemon juice, then arrange the asparagus spears, pointing towards the head, on top. Place the second fillet, skinned side up, on top of the asparagus, sprinkle with the remaining lemon juice and season well with the black pepper.

Roll out the remaining dough to an oblong large enough to cover the salmon completely. Brush the edges of the dough round the salmon with a little water then cover with the rolled out dough and press the edges together well to seal. Trim the dough into a neat fish shape and tuck the edges underneath to make it slightly rounded, then put onto a large baking tray. Reknead and roll out the trimmings thinly and stamp out rounds with a 1.9 cm (¾ in) plain, round cutter. Beat the remaining egg and brush it over the dough. Arrange the rounds of dough on top, overlapping them slightly, to represent fish scales. Use the remaining trimmings to decorate the head and tail. Glaze well all over with the remaining beaten egg. Put the salmon into the centre of the oven and bake for 35 minutes, or until the pastry is golden and completely cooked. Turn the baking tray round halfway through the cooking time.

THE SAUCE

Meanwhile, complete the sauce. Strain the infused milk and cream into a jug and discard the bouquet garni and the cloves and mace. Melt the butter in a saucepan, stir in the flour and cook for 1 minute. Gradually stir in the milk and cream over a moderate heat, then bring to the boil, stirring continuously until the sauce thickens slightly. Season well with the salt and pepper, reduce the heat and simmer for 2–3 minutes. Roughly chop the watercress leaves and stir them into the sauce, heat through for 1 minute then pour into a sauceboat.

Carefully transfer the salmon from the baking tray to a flat serving platter or board and garnish with the watercress. Cut into slices and serve accompanied by the watercress sauce and a green salad.

Despite its grandeur, this salmon, baked with almond butter and asparagus in a rich, ginger-spiced pastry, is relatively straightforward.

Soused Herrings

This is a highly popular dish in northern Europe, though in some countries the herrings are fried before being soused

INGREDIENTS

- 6 herrings, each approx 225g (8oz), heads removed, gutted, boned and washed
- Freshly ground black pepper
- 285ml (½ pint) cider vinegar
- 285ml (½ pint) water
- 1 level teaspoon salt
- 10 black peppercorns
- 2 bay leaves
- 2 fresh marjoram sprigs
- 3–4 fresh parsley sprigs
- 1 large onion, peeled and thinly sliced
- 1 large carrot, peeled and thinly sliced

Preparation time: 30 minutes
Cooking time: 25 minutes
Serves six

Preheat the oven to 180°c (350°f, gas mark 4). Lay the herrings out flat with the flesh sides uppermost. Season well with the pepper, then roll up each one from the head end and secure by inserting the small piece of bone on the tail into the flesh. Put the herrings into an ovenproof glass, enamel or ceramic dish.

Put the vinegar, water and all the remaining ingredients into a stainless steel or enamel saucepan and bring to the boil, then reduce the heat, cover and simmer gently for 10 minutes. Pour the hot liquid, herbs and vegetables over the herrings, cover and bake in the oven for 15 minutes. Remove from the oven and allow to cool in the cooking liquid, then refrigerate for 1–2 hours before serving.

Serve cold with potato salad and a tossed green salad.

Drenched in cider vinegar and herbs, these herrings are sweeter and less sharp than the more familiar rollmops.

Sea harvest
With the big trawl net winched in, the bosun releases the knot at the bottom, allowing the catch to spill onto the deck. The trawl is then returned to the sea while the crew gut the catch, a task that will continue until the net is again hauled in.

Covering with foil retains the full, rich flavour of this plump fish.

Baked Char with Buttered Almonds

Our native Lake District char is elusive both in shops and in its habitat, but the Arctic variety is available and delicious

Preheat the oven to 160°c (325°f, gas mark 3). Put the almonds into a small saucepan, cover with cold water and bring to the boil. Drain and cool slightly then remove the skins. Using a small, sharp knife, split the almonds in half and cut into long slivers.

Wipe the char with kitchen paper then season lightly inside with the salt and pepper. Place the fish side-by-side in a large ovenproof dish.

In a small saucepan, heat half the butter with the slivered almonds. Remove from the heat and pour over the char, then dot the fish with the remaining butter. Cover the dish with foil and cook in the centre of the oven for 30 minutes. Remove the foil from the dish, baste the char with the butter and continue cooking for another 15–20 minutes or until the char is cooked and flakes easily when tested with a knife, and the almonds are browned. The fish should come away easily from the bone and the flesh should be opaque. Cooking times may vary, so check after 40 minutes. Remove the cooked fish from the oven and leave to rest for 5 minutes.

Using two fish slices, carefully transfer the cooked char to a heated serving plate and pour over the juices. Garnish with the sprigs of dill and the lemon wedges. Serve with new potatoes, spinach or salad and warm, crusty bread.

INGREDIENTS

115g (4oz) whole almonds, unskinned
2 Lakeland or Arctic char, each approx 450g (1lb), gutted and cleaned
Salt and freshly ground black pepper
115g (4oz) butter, softened
Fresh dill sprigs to garnish
2 lemons, cut into wedges
Preparation time: 30 minutes
Cooking time: 45–50 minutes
Serves four

Halibut Steaks Baked in Cider

The use of herbs and cider gives a rich, flavoursome sauce that keeps the halibut moist and succulent

INGREDIENTS

85 g (3 oz) butter
450 g (1 lb) leeks, trimmed, sliced and washed
4 halibut steaks, each approx 225 g (8 oz)
3 bay leaves
6 black peppercorns
1 mace blade
1 rosemary sprig
425 ml (3/4 pint) strong dry cider
6 tablespoons double cream
Salt and freshly ground black pepper
Fresh rosemary sprigs to garnish

Preparation time: 20 minutes
Cooking time: 40 minutes
Serves four

Preheat the oven to 180°c (350°f, gas mark 4). Melt 60 g (2 oz) of the butter in a frying pan and add the sliced leeks. Sauté gently for 5–10 minutes, or until the leeks are just beginning to soften, then spread them over the bottom of a large, ovenproof dish.

Place the halibut steaks on top and add the bay leaves, peppercorns, mace and rosemary. Pour the cider over the fish and dot with the remaining butter.

Cover the dish with foil and bake in the centre of the oven for 20–25 minutes or until the fish is cooked.

Remove the dish from the oven and, using a fish slice or slotted spoon, transfer the halibut steaks and leeks to a heated serving dish or individual plates and keep warm while making the sauce.

Strain the cooking juices from the dish into a saucepan and boil rapidly until reduced by half. Stir in the cream, season well with the salt and pepper and heat through, stirring for 1 minute.

Spoon the sauce over the halibut steaks, then garnish with the sprigs of rosemary. Serve with creamy mashed potatoes, and strong dry cider.

A cream sauce topped with fresh rosemary sprigs creates both visual and culinary appeal.

Homeward bound
Trailing black smoke and shrieking gulls over her wake, an Aberdeen scratcher—a deep-sea trawler—heads fully laden for home. Such vessels spent long periods in the cold, distant seas that are the dwelling-place of cod and halibut.

The 'pudding' is a delicious fruity prawn stuffing with sage and onion.

Small haddock and salmon, large trout and char, can all be cooked in this way.

Grey Mullet with a Pudding in its Belly

Grey mullet is common in Britain's coastal waters and estuaries

Preheat the oven to 200°c (400°f, gas mark 6). Melt 60 g (2 oz) of the butter in a saucepan, then add the onion and sauté gently until just softened. Remove from the heat and stir in the orange rind and juice, parsley, sage, 115 g (4 oz) of the breadcrumbs and the shrimps or prawns. Season well, then mix with half the beaten eggs to make a soft stuffing.

Fill both mullet with the stuffing, then sew up the belly flaps with fine, clean string or secure with cocktail sticks. Brush the remaining egg over both sides of the stuffed fish then press them in the remaining breadcrumbs, coating them evenly on both sides. Put them into an oiled roasting tin, melt the remaining butter and drizzle it over them.

Bake the stuffed mullet, uncovered, for 35–40 minutes in the centre of the oven until they are cooked and the coating is golden brown, basting frequently with the melted butter.

Carefully transfer the mullet to heated serving plates and serve with coarsely shredded savoy cabbage, and chunks of warm brown bread.

If liked, the mullet can be garnished with orange and lemon wedges and sprigs of fresh parsley and sage.

Ingredients

- 175 g (6 oz) butter
- 1 large onion, peeled and finely chopped
- Finely grated rind and strained juice 1 orange
- 3 tablespoons chopped fresh parsley
- 1 tablespoon chopped fresh sage
- 275 g (10 oz) fresh white breadcrumbs
- 175 g (6 oz) peeled cooked shrimps or prawns, chopped
- 3 eggs, size 2, beaten
- Salt and freshly ground black pepper
- 2 grey mullet, each approx 800 g (1¾ lb), descaled, heads removed, gutted, cleaned and boned

Preparation time: 40 minutes

Cooking time: 45 minutes

Serves four

Potted Shrimps

Lancashire gave the world Gracie Fields—and also potted shrimps

INGREDIENTS

225 g (8 oz) unsalted butter
450 g (1 lb) shrimps, peeled (see p.436) or 225 g (8 oz) ready peeled shrimps
Pinch of cayenne pepper
Pinch of grated nutmeg
1 teaspoon fresh lemon juice
Preparation time: 10 minutes, longer if peeling shrimps
Cooking time: 5 minutes
Chilling time: 1 hour
Serves four

To ring the changes in this recipe, replace the shrimps with poached fresh salmon, trout or peeled prawns.

Melt 175 g (6 oz) of the butter in a frying pan over a low heat. Stir in the shrimps, cayenne, nutmeg and lemon juice and heat gently for 1–2 minutes. Take care not to overcook. Divide the mixture between four 150 ml (¼ pint) ramekins and chill for 30 minutes.

Melt the remaining butter over a very low heat, leave to stand until cooled, then pour through a small sieve lined with muslin, taking care not to pour in the white 'solids' from the bottom of the pan. Spoon the butter over each dish of potted shrimps to cover completely. Return to the fridge and chill for a further 30 minutes, or until the butter has set.

Serve with warm, crusty bread or with fingers of hot toast.

As variations, prawns and other fish can be potted by following this method. Especially good are hot, smoked fish such as mackerel, trout, salmon or char. Keep to the same quantity—225 g (8 oz) prepared fish to 225 g (8 oz) butter. Flake the fish fairly coarsely and remove any bones. You may like to increase the amount of lemon juice when using oily fish such as mackerel or salmon.

Potting is a simple way to preserve fish as the butter forms a seal and, providing the pots are kept in a refrigerator, the contents should last at least a fortnight.

Stuff and wrap the fish 2–3 hours in advance and refrigerate it before baking.

Lettuce-wrapped Sea Trout with a Regalia of Cucumber

A combination of spinach and sorrel makes a stuffing for the trout that is both unusual and delicious

Preheat the oven to 220°c (425°f, gas mark 7). To prepare the stuffing, squeeze the spinach dry, chop finely and put into a bowl with the breadcrumbs, sorrel, parsley, tarragon, melted butter and egg. Season with the salt and pepper and mix well. Fill the trout with the stuffing, fold the belly flaps together to bring the fish back to its former shape then set aside.

Soften the lettuce leaves in gently boiling water, two or three at a time, for a few seconds until just beginning to wilt. Taking care not to damage the leaves, transfer them to a colander, using a slotted spoon. Rinse gently under cold water, then lay them out flat on kitchen paper to drain. Keeping the head and tail exposed, wrap the trout in the leaves, smoothing and overlapping them neatly.

Sprinkle the shallots into the bottom of a very large, buttered, ovenproof dish and place the trout on top. Pour over the wine and dot with half the butter. Add the reserved bones to the dish, cover with buttered foil and bake in the oven for 30 minutes, basting occasionally. Carefully transfer the trout to a warmed serving plate, cover and keep warm.

Discard the bones and strain the juices through a fine sieve into a saucepan. Boil to reduce by half, stir in the cream and again reduce by half to a light, strongly flavoured sauce. Keep warm.

Sauté the spring onions, garlic and cucumber in the remaining butter in a small frying pan for 3 minutes until they are slightly softened, but not coloured. Remove from the heat, stir in the parsley and tarragon, season to taste, then spoon around the trout. Pour the sauce into a sauceboat and serve separately. Serve with cooked asparagus.

INGREDIENTS

For the stuffing

- 225g (8oz) spinach, blanched in boiling water and drained
- 60g (2oz) fresh white breadcrumbs
- 60g (2oz) sorrel leaves, finely shredded
- 30g (1oz) finely chopped fresh parsley
- 1 level teaspoon finely chopped fresh tarragon
- 30g (1oz) butter, melted
- 1 egg, size 3, beaten
- Salt and freshly ground black pepper

For the fish

- 1.4kg (3lb) sea trout, gills removed, boned and bones reserved
- Approx 40 lettuce leaves from 2 large, soft, round lettuces
- 2 shallots, finely chopped
- 150ml (¼ pint) dry white wine
- 60g (2oz) butter
- 150ml (¼ pint) double cream
- 4 spring onions, trimmed and finely chopped
- 1 garlic clove, peeled and finely chopped
- 1 large cucumber, peeled, halved lengthways, deseeded and cut into 6mm (¼ in) slices
- 2 level tablespoons chopped fresh parsley
- 2 level tablespoons finely shredded fresh tarragon

Preparation time: 40 minutes, plus 30 minutes if boning the fish

Cooking time: 45 minutes

Serves six

If you don't want the bother of making the sauce on the barbecue, you can prepare it at home, up to a day in advance.

The mackerel are stuffed with apple, then basted with honey as they grill over an open fire.

Barbecued Mackerel & Gooseberry Sauce

Happily for this dish, gooseberries ripen in May at just about the time when mackerel are cheapest and most readily available

INGREDIENTS

- 450G (1 LB) GOOSEBERRIES, TOPPED, TAILED AND WASHED
- 60G (2 OZ) CASTER SUGAR
- 4 TABLESPOONS WATER
- 4 SMALL-TO-MEDIUM MACKEREL, HEADS REMOVED, GUTTED AND WASHED
- SALT AND FRESHLY GROUND BLACK PEPPER
- 1–2 SWEET DESSERT APPLES, CORED, HALVED AND THICKLY SLICED
- 60G (2 OZ) BUTTER, SOFTENED
- 2 TABLESPOONS CLEAR HONEY

PREPARATION TIME: 20 MINUTES
COOKING TIME: 20 MINUTES
SERVES FOUR

Put the gooseberries, sugar and water into a saucepan on the barbecue or over a campfire and bring to the boil. Move the pan to a cooler part of the fire and cook gently, uncovered, until the gooseberries have split open and become mushy. Remove from the heat and allow to cool.

Slit each mackerel open along the belly right up to the tail, season well with the salt and pepper and arrange about six slices of apple inside each fish. Rub the softened butter over the skin.

Put all the prepared mackerel into a wire fish grill and trickle half of the honey over the top of the fish. Cook over the barbecue or campfire for about 5 minutes. Turn the fish over, still inside the wire grill, trickle on the remaining honey and cook for another 5 minutes or until cooked through. Alternatively, the mackerel can be wrapped in foil and cooked on the barbecue or in the hot embers of a campfire. Serve immediately with the gooseberry sauce.

Devilled Whitebait

Once a speciality of London, whitebait is at its best when accompanied by a squeeze of lemon and brown bread and butter

Dry the whitebait very thoroughly with a clean tea towel or kitchen paper. If they are not properly dried, they will not become crisp when fried.

Heat the oil in a deep-fat fryer to 190°C (375°F), or until a cube of stale bread dropped into it turns golden and crisp in 20–30 seconds.

Meanwhile, put the flour, the curry powder, cayenne pepper and the salt into a polythene bag and shake well. Add the whitebait and toss until thoroughly and evenly coated with the seasoned flour. Transfer to a large sieve and shake to remove excess flour.

When the oil is hot enough, carefully lower about a third of the whitebait, in a basket, into the pan and deep fry until crisp—the time taken will vary according to the size of the fish. Lift out, drain on kitchen paper and keep warm. Repeat with the remaining whitebait.

As soon as it is cooked, serve the whitebait on warmed, individual plates garnished with the parsley sprigs. Serve the lemon wedges separately.

INGREDIENTS

450G (1 LB) FRESH WHITEBAIT, RINSED AND DRAINED OR FROZEN WHITEBAIT, DEFROSTED
APPROX 1 LITRE (1¾ PINTS) VEGETABLE OIL, FOR DEEP FRYING
4 LEVEL TABLESPOONS PLAIN FLOUR
2 LEVEL TABLESPOONS HOT CURRY POWDER
½ LEVEL TEASPOON CAYENNE PEPPER
¼ LEVEL TEASPOON SALT
PARSLEY SPRIGS TO GARNISH
2 LEMONS, CUT INTO 8 WEDGES

PREPARATION TIME: 10 MINUTES
COOKING TIME: 10 MINUTES
SERVES FOUR

Whitebait, with curry powder and cayenne, can be served as a first course or for high tea.

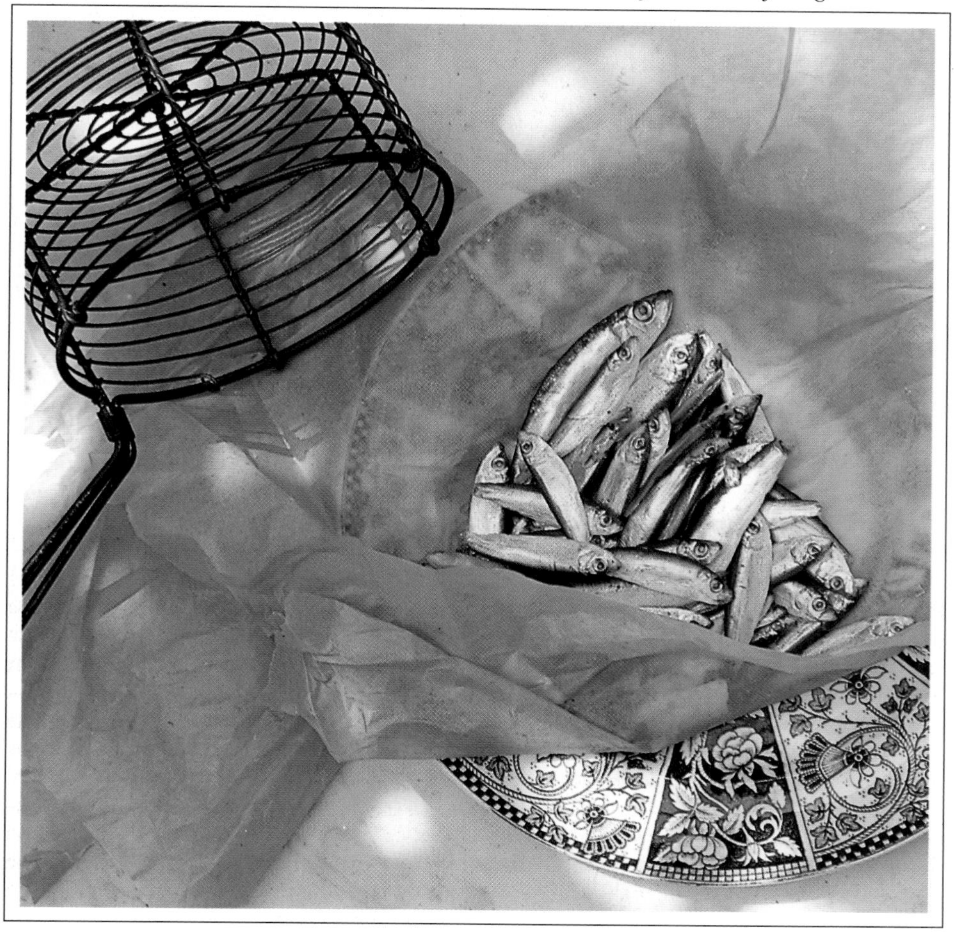

Politically correct Whitebait used to occur in vast shoals in the Thames estuary. Until the turn of the century, senior politicians would hasten to Greenwich, there to partake of whitebait dinners at The Trafalgar Tavern or The Old Ship. The custom has been recently revived.

To give yourself more time with your guests or for other jobs, prepare the pie 2-3 hours before serving and refrigerate until ready to bake.

Golden, crunchy potato topping rounds off a pie filled with cod, salmon and smoked haddock.

Mixed Fish Pie

Each flavour interweaves with the others in this beautifully orchestrated seafood medley

INGREDIENTS

- 1 small onion, peeled and thinly sliced
- 8 black peppercorns
- 2 bay leaves
- 2 parsley sprigs
- 340 g (12 oz) cod fillet
- 225 g (8 oz) smoked haddock fillet
- 425 ml (3/4 pint) milk
- 340 g (12 oz) tail end of salmon
- 2 slices lemon
- 1.1 kg (2½ lb) potatoes, peeled and quartered
- 85 g (3 oz) butter
- 30 g (1 oz) plain flour
- Salt and freshly ground black pepper
- 2 tablespoons chopped fresh parsley
- 2 tablespoons lemon juice
- 200 g (7 oz) fresh cooked peeled prawns (see p.436), or frozen prawns, thawed and drained
- 6–8 tablespoons milk
- 1 egg, size 3, beaten

Preparation time: 1 hour
Cooking time: 35 minutes
Serves six

Put half the onion slices, four peppercorns, one bay leaf and one parsley sprig into a large frying pan, and the same into a saucepan. Add the cod and haddock to the frying pan and pour in the milk. Put the salmon into the saucepan, barely cover with water and add the lemon slices. Bring both pans to the boil, remove from the heat, cover and leave to stand for 10 minutes.

Cook the potatoes in boiling water for 20–25 minutes. Preheat the oven to 190°c (375°f, gas mark 5).

Meanwhile, using a nylon sieve, strain the milk from the cod and haddock into a measuring jug. There should be about 425 ml (¾ pint). If there is less, make up the difference with a little extra milk. Remove the salmon from the saucepan and discard the cooking water and the flavourings from both pans. Remove the skins and bones from all the fish then flake the flesh and set it aside.

Melt 30 g (1 oz) of the butter in a large saucepan, stir in the flour, cook over a low heat for 1 minute then gradually stir in the strained milk. Stirring continuously, bring to the boil then reduce the heat and simmer for 2 minutes. Remove from the heat and season with freshly ground black pepper. Stir in the parsley and lemon juice and gently mix in the flaked fish and the prawns. Pour into a large, shallow ovenproof dish and set aside.

Drain the cooked potatoes well and pass them through a potato ricer or sieve, or mash them well. Beat in the remaining butter and add enough milk to make a smooth, creamy, but fairly firm mixture. Season with salt and pepper and spread or pipe over the fish mixture, covering it evenly. Brush the top of the potatoes with the egg and cook in the oven for 35 minutes, or until golden brown and heated through. Serve with broccoli and cauliflower, or with a green salad.

Skate Wings with Capers

This easily prepared version parallels a classic French dish

Preheat the oven to 200°c (400°f, gas mark 6). Oil a large baking tray or shallow baking dish. Arrange the skate wings on it, making sure they do not overlap.

Put one slice of butter on each skate wing and sprinkle with the capers, the caper vinegar and the chopped parsley.

Bake near the top of the oven for 20–30 minutes (depending on the thickness of the skate) until lightly browned and cooked through. Serve hot, accompanied by new potatoes and a green salad.

The wing is the only part of the skate that is eaten— here, it is baked with butter and capers.

Ingredients

- 4 skate wings, each approx 250–300g (9–11oz), well washed
- 60g (2oz) butter, cut into 4 equal slices
- 2 tablespoons drained capers
- 2 tablespoons vinegar from jar of capers
- 2 tablespoons chopped fresh parsley

Preparation time: 5 minutes
Cooking time: 30 minutes
Serves four

Flower power
Utilised only in their pickled form, capers are the unopened flower buds of a Mediterranean shrub. At one time in Britain pickled broom buds were also used but nowadays you are more likely to encounter the pickled nasturtium seeds marketed as 'English' capers.

For a lighter version of this dish, drizzle the coated whiting with melted butter and bake them in a hot oven.

Each whiting is curled into a circle and secured with a skewer before being coated in the crumbs.

Fried Whiting with Tartare Sauce

Homemade tartare sauce has a zest lacking in the bought version. Here, it adds its sprightliness to whiting cooked whole

INGREDIENTS

For the tartare sauce
- 150 ml (¼ pint) mayonnaise, homemade (see p.436) or bought
- 1 teaspoon vinegar
- ½ teaspoon made English mustard
- 1 tablespoon finely chopped gherkins
- 1 tablespoon finely chopped capers
- 1 large spring onion, trimmed and finely chopped

For the fish
- 4 whiting, each approx 340 g (12 oz), gutted and cleaned, heads and tails left on
- 2 level tablespoons plain flour
- ½ level teaspoon salt
- ¼ level teaspoon freshly ground black pepper
- 1 egg, size 2, beaten
- 60 g (2 oz) fine fresh white breadcrumbs
- Oil for deep frying
- Lemon wedges and parsley to garnish

Preparation time: 30 minutes
Cooking time: 10–20 minutes
Serves four

To make the tartare sauce, put all the ingredients into a bowl and mix together. Spoon the mixture into a serving dish, cover and refrigerate until required.

To prepare the whiting, curl each fish round and secure it by pushing a fine skewer through the head and tail.

On a large plate, mix the flour with the salt and black pepper. Coat the whiting in the seasoned flour, then in the beaten egg and finally in the breadcrumbs, ensuring that each fish is completely and evenly covered.

Half fill a deep frying pan with the oil and heat to 190°C (375°F) or until a cube of bread will brown in a few seconds. Fry the whiting, one or two at a time, for about 5 minutes until golden brown. Remove from the pan with a slotted spoon, drain on kitchen paper and keep warm while frying the remaining fish.

Arrange the whiting on a heated serving dish, garnish with the lemon wedges and parsley and serve with the tartare sauce. New potatoes and salad make a good accompaniment.

Aunt Daisy's De Luxe Fish Cakes

You can ring the changes by substituting any firm white fish for the salmon and replacing the crabmeat with chopped, cooked prawns

Steam the potatoes until they are soft. Meanwhile, put the salmon into a frying pan and barely cover with cold water. Season with the salt and pepper and add the lemon slices. Bring to the boil, then remove from the heat, cover and leave to stand until the potatoes are cooked.

Drain the potatoes, put them into a bowl with the butter and, if necessary, a little milk, and mash well. The mixture should be firm enough to hold its shape. Drain the salmon, remove and discard the skin and bones, and flake the flesh.

Add the salmon, crab and parsley to the potatoes, season well and mix together. Allow to cool, then cover and refrigerate for 1–2 hours.

Divide the salmon mixture into 12 equal portions and, with lightly floured hands, shape each portion into a flat cake. Mix the breadcrumbs with the almonds and put into a shallow dish or onto a baking tray. Pour the beaten egg into a shallow dish.

Dip the fish cakes in the beaten egg, then in the breadcrumb mixture, making sure they are evenly coated all over. Reshape the fish cakes, put them onto a plate and chill well.

Heat a little of the oil in a frying pan and cook the fish cakes, in batches, over a moderate heat for 4 minutes on each side or until crisp, golden and heated through. Drain on kitchen paper, then arrange on a heated serving plate.

Garnish the fish cakes with the lemon wedges and serve with tartare sauce and a tossed green salad.

INGREDIENTS

- 675G (1½LB) POTATOES, PEELED AND QUARTERED
- 225G (8OZ) FRESH SALMON STEAKS
- SALT AND FRESHLY GROUND BLACK PEPPER
- 2 SLICES LEMON
- 30G (1OZ) BUTTER
- 1 TABLESPOON MILK, IF NECESSARY
- 115G (4OZ) FRESH WHITE CRABMEAT OR FROZEN, THAWED
- 30G (1OZ) FINELY CHOPPED FRESH PARSLEY
- 115G (4OZ) FINE DRY WHITE BREADCRUMBS OR RASPINGS (SEE P.440)
- 60G (2OZ) GROUND ALMONDS
- 2 EGGS, SIZE 2, BEATEN
- VEGETABLE OIL FOR FRYING
- LEMON WEDGES TO GARNISH

PREPARATION TIME: 40 MINUTES
CHILLING TIME: 1½ HOURS
COOKING TIME: 24 MINUTES
SERVES SIX

Fish cakes are given a touch of glamour with the addition of crabmeat and salmon.

The sinister snoek
Snoek—barracuda—was imported from South Africa by the wartime government who promoted it as not only tasty but cheap. Housewives were not impressed, however, and many still recall it as one of the minor horrors of war.

Sole Puddings in a Shrimp Sauce

Light and delicate, this is a perfect starter to precede a heavy main course

Ingredients

For the sole puddings
- 340g (12oz) sole fillets, skinned and cut into cubes
- 2 eggs, size 2, beaten
- 285ml (½ pint) double cream, chilled

For the shrimp sauce
- 45g (1½ oz) butter
- 2 shallots, peeled and chopped
- 2 level teaspoons plain flour
- ½ teaspoon paprika
- ½ garlic clove, peeled and bruised
- 285ml (½ pint) fish stock (see p.433) or water
- 175g (6oz) fresh cooked shrimps, peeled, heads and shells reserved (see p.436)
- 150ml (¼ pint) double cream
- Lemon juice
- Salt and freshly ground white pepper

Preparation time: 45 minutes
Cooking time: 35–40 minutes
Serves six as a starter

Butter six small ramekins or teacups and stand them in a roasting tin. Blend the fish to a fine purée in a food processor. With the machine still running, pour in the beaten eggs. Turn off immediately the eggs are blended in. Put the bowl into the refrigerator and chill for 20 minutes.

Meanwhile, to make the sauce, melt the butter in a saucepan and cook the shallots over a moderate heat until soft, then stir in the flour, paprika and garlic. Gradually stir in the stock or water, add the shrimp heads and shells and bring to the boil, stirring continuously. Stir in the cream and bring back to the boil. Reduce the heat, cover and simmer for 20 minutes, stirring occasionally.

Strain into a clean saucepan, add the lemon juice and season to taste. Cover closely with cling film and set aside.

Preheat the oven to 200°c (400°f, gas mark 6). Return the bowl of fish purée to the food processor and, with the machine running, pour in the chilled cream. Do not overprocess as it will curdle—the mixture should be of a dropping consistency. Season well, then fill each ramekin or teacup two-thirds full with the mixture and level the surface. Pour boiling water into the roasting tin to come halfway up the sides of the ramekins or teacups. Bake in the centre of the oven for 15–20 minutes or until set, risen and golden brown on top.

About 5 minutes before the end of the cooking time, reheat the sauce without allowing it to boil. Stir in the shrimps and keep warm. Turn the puddings onto warmed individual plates, spoon over the shrimp sauce and serve at once.

The fleet's in! One of the joys of living near a fishing port was the chance to buy fish straight from the boats. None of the customers in this 1947 picture seem at all perturbed by the catch being cleaned onto the cobbles of St Ives' quay.

These little sole puddings are cooked gently in a roasting tin part-filled with hot water.

Pink prawns in the sauce bring flavour and an attractive blush to the turbot's pale flesh.

Turbot with a Prawn Sauce

A whole turbot is impressive, but steaks will cook in half the time

Reserve a few prawns for garnish, then peel the remainder (see p.436) and refrigerate until required.

Put the prawn shells into a saucepan with the onion, lemon, bay leaf, parsley, thyme and water, bring to the boil, reduce the heat, cover the pan and simmer for 20 minutes. Strain off and reserve the stock, discarding the shells and herbs. There should be about 425 ml (¾ pint) of stock.

Preheat the oven to 180°c (350°f, gas mark 4). Put the turbot, with the white skin side uppermost, into a lightly oiled, large, shallow roasting tin. Add the stock, cover with foil and cook for 30–40 minutes or until just cooked through.

Remove the turbot from the oven and strain off and reserve the stock. Turn the oven off, cover the turbot and return it to the oven to keep warm.

To make the sauce, melt the butter in a saucepan, stir in the flour and cook for a minute. Gradually pour in the stock and bring to the boil, stirring constantly until the sauce is thickened. Add the lemon juice, ground mace, cayenne pepper and salt and simmer for 3–4 minutes, stirring frequently. Add the peeled prawns and cream and simmer gently for 1 minute, then pour into a heated sauceboat.

Lift the turbot carefully onto a large, heated serving platter and cut down the centre from the head to the tail, cutting through to the bone. Peel off the skin and, using a long fish slice, lift off the two fillets from the top. Turn the fish over and remove the remaining fillets in the same way.

Garnish the turbot with the reserved whole prawns and the parsley and serve with the hot prawn sauce.

INGREDIENTS

- 450 g (1 lb) cooked shell-on prawns
- 1 small onion, peeled and quartered
- 1 slice lemon
- 1 bay leaf
- Parsley and thyme sprigs
- 570 ml (1 pint) water
- 1 small 'chicken' turbot, approx 1.6–1.8 kg (3½–4 lb), cleaned, gills removed

For the sauce

- 30 g (1 oz) butter
- 30 g (1 oz) flour
- ½ teaspoon lemon juice
- Pinch of ground mace
- ¼ level teaspoon salt
- Small pinch of cayenne pepper
- 2–3 tablespoons double cream
- Fresh parsley to garnish

Preparation time: 40 minutes
Cooking time: 50 minutes
Serves four

Newcastle Baked Haddock

Humble haddock is elevated to a superior dish by a rich prawn sauce

INGREDIENTS

60G (2OZ) BUTTER, MELTED
285ML (½ PINT) BEEF STOCK (SEE P.432)
150ML (¼ PINT) MILK
150ML (¼ PINT) DRY WHITE WINE, SUCH AS RIESLING
1.4KG (3LB) HADDOCK, HEAD, TAIL AND FINS REMOVED, WASHED UNDER COLD WATER AND DRIED ON KITCHEN PAPER
1 MEDIUM ONION, PEELED AND FINELY CHOPPED
3 BAY LEAVES
1 LEVEL TEASPOON DRIED MIXED HERBS
2 TEASPOONS WORCESTERSHIRE SAUCE
½ LEVEL TEASPOON FRESHLY GROUND BLACK PEPPER
12 WHOLE PRAWNS AND FRESH PARSLEY TO GARNISH

FOR THE SAUCE
30G (1OZ) BUTTER
30G (1OZ) FLOUR
6 TABLESPOONS DOUBLE CREAM
175G (6OZ) PEELED FRESH PRAWNS, OR FROZEN PRAWNS, THAWED AND DRAINED

PREPARATION TIME: 20 MINUTES
COOKING TIME: 1 HOUR
SERVES FOUR

PREHEAT the oven to 180°C (350°F, gas mark 4). Pour the butter, stock, milk and wine into a roasting tin just large enough to hold the haddock. Place the fish in the tin, add the onion, bay leaves, herbs, Worcestershire sauce and pepper and bake for 45 minutes, basting frequently.

Remove the roasting tin from the oven, transfer the haddock carefully to a heated serving dish and keep hot while making the sauce. Reserve the basting juices, but discard the bay leaves.

To make the sauce, melt the butter in a saucepan, stir in the flour, cook over a low heat for 1 minute, then gradually stir in the cooking juices and the onion. Bring to the boil, stirring until thickened slightly, reduce the heat and simmer gently for 5 minutes. Add the cream and peeled prawns and heat for 2 minutes.

Garnish the fish with the unpeeled prawns and parsley and serve with the sauce, mashed potatoes, spinach and baked parsnips.

The haddock is baked in an unusual blend of dry white wine, beef stock and milk.

To be sure of getting a whole fish, order it in advance from your fishmonger.

Famed round the world are Scotland's salmon, whisky and honey...all combined in this recipe.

Bright deceivers
Fly-tying and fly-fishing were practised in Macedonia in 200 BC, but were not widely known in Britain before Izaak Walton and Charles Cotton wrote *The Compleat Angler* in the 1670s.

Salmon Steaks with Whisky Cream Sauce

The salmon and the sauce make an opulent combination—one steak per person should satisfy even the most ravenous appetite

Preheat the oven to 110°c (225°f, gas mark ¼). Season the salmon steaks well on both sides with the salt and black pepper. Melt the butter in a large frying pan, add the salmon and fry over a moderate heat for 5 minutes on each side, turning once.

Using a fish slice, transfer the steaks from the frying pan to a heated serving dish, cover loosely with foil and keep warm in the oven. Add the sliced mushrooms to the butter remaining in the pan and cook for 5 minutes.

Meanwhile, combine the whisky with the honey, lemon juice and cream and pour the mixture over the mushrooms. Bring the sauce to the boil and simmer for 2–3 minutes or until it has reduced and thickened slightly.

Spoon the mushrooms onto the fish, then pour the sauce over and around it. Sprinkle with the parsley and garnish with the lemon. Serve with new potatoes and fine green beans or broad beans.

Trout fillets or haddock steaks can also be cooked in this way.

Ingredients

- 4 salmon steaks, each approx 225 g (8 oz), rinsed and dried
- Salt and freshly ground black pepper
- 60 g (2 oz) butter
- 225 g (8 oz) button mushrooms, wiped and sliced
- 4 tablespoons Scotch whisky
- 1½ tablespoons clear honey, preferably heather honey
- 4 tablespoons lemon juice
- 150 ml (¼ pint) double cream
- 2 tablespoons chopped fresh parsley
- Slices or wedges of lemon to garnish

Preparation time: 10 minutes
Cooking time: 20 minutes
Serves four

Fish 'n' Chips

Despite the capital's claims, the curtain probably first rose on this celebrated duo in Bradford or Oldham in the 1860s

INGREDIENTS

FOR THE BATTER
- 175 ML (6 FL OZ) TEPID MILK
- ½ LEVEL TEASPOON CASTER SUGAR
- 1 LEVEL TEASPOON DRIED YEAST
- 115 G (4 OZ) PLAIN FLOUR
- ½ LEVEL TEASPOON SALT
- 900 G (2 LB) POTATOES, PEELED AND WASHED
- VEGETABLE OIL FOR DEEP FRYING
- 900 G (2 LB) COD OR HADDOCK FILLET, SKINNED AND CUT INTO 4 EQUAL PIECES
- 2 TABLESPOONS FLOUR, SEASONED WITH SALT AND PEPPER
- LEMON WEDGES TO GARNISH

PREPARATION TIME: 40 MINUTES
COOKING TIME: 25 MINUTES
SERVES FOUR

To MAKE the batter, pour the tepid milk into a small bowl. Add the sugar and stir until dissolved, then whisk in the yeast. Leave to stand for 5 minutes in a warm place until frothy.

Sift the flour and salt into a bowl. Make a well in the centre and pour in the yeast liquid, then beat with a balloon whisk or wooden spoon to a smooth batter. Cover and leave to rise in a warm place for 30 minutes.

Meanwhile, cut the potatoes into chips, about 6 mm (¼ in) thick. Put them into cold water for 5 minutes, to remove excess starch, then drain well and dry on a clean tea towel. Half fill a deep frying pan with oil and heat to 196°C (385°F). Blanch the chips in the hot oil, in two batches, for 4–5 minutes until very pale golden. Remove from the oil, drain well and set aside.

Allow the temperature of the oil to drop to 190°C (375°F). Then coat the fish lightly in the seasoned flour. Stir the batter vigorously and dip two pieces of fish into it. Lift out the fish and allow the excess batter to drip back into the bowl. Carefully lower the fish into the hot oil (do not use a frying basket as the yeast will cause the batter to expand and stick to the basket), and cook for 4–5 minutes until crisp and golden, turning once. Using a large wire skimmer or slotted spoon, lift the fish out of the pan and drain on kitchen paper. Keep warm while dipping and frying the remaining fish.

Increase the oil temperature to 202°C (395°F) and fry the chips for 2–3 minutes more until crisp and golden. Drain on kitchen paper, arrange on heated plates, garnish with the lemon wedges and serve with pickled onions and cucumbers.

Accompanied by vinegar and pickled onions, the pair put on a great extempore performance.

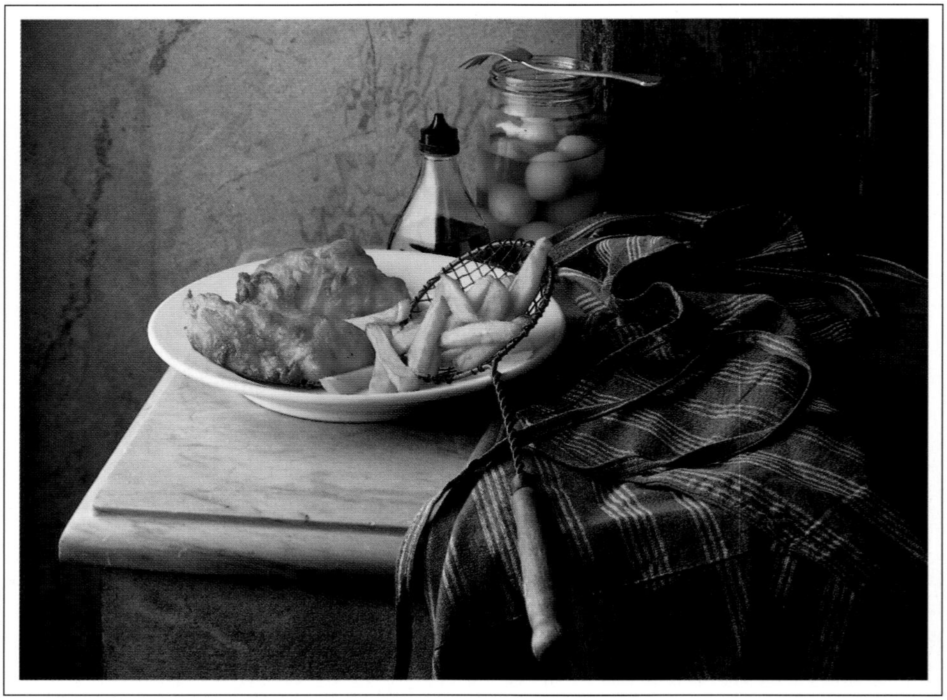

THE CHIPPIE
Though deeply enshrined in British folklore, fish and chip shops are fairly recently descended from the fried fish and baked potatoes sold by street vendors in Charles Dickens' day.

Diced salmon, prawns and mushrooms are simmered gently in white wine—serve hot or cold.

Tweed Kettle

Also known as salmon hash, this recipe had its origins as a staple of Edinburgh's backstreet eating houses

Remove and discard the skin and bones from the salmon. Cut the flesh into small chunks and weigh it. There should be about 800 g (1¾ lb).

Put the fish into a flameproof casserole. Add the shallots, mushrooms, chives, fish stock and the wine and bring to the boil, then reduce the heat and simmer very gently, uncovered, for about 15 minutes, stirring occasionally.

Add the prawns, anchovy essence and parsley to the casserole, season well and heat through gently for 5 minutes.

Serve the salmon hot with fresh potato scones or creamy mashed potato, or cold with cucumber and watercress.

INGREDIENTS

- 1.1 KG (2½ LB) SALMON, PREFERABLY TAIL ENDS
- 2 LARGE SHALLOTS, PEELED AND CHOPPED
- 115 G (4 OZ) CHESTNUT MUSHROOMS, WIPED AND QUARTERED
- 1 TABLESPOON SNIPPED FRESH CHIVES
- 150 ML (¼ PINT) FISH STOCK (SEE P.433)
- 60 ML (2 FL OZ) DRY WHITE WINE
- 200 G (7 OZ) FRESH PEELED COOKED PRAWNS OR FROZEN PRAWNS, THAWED AND DRAINED
- 2 TEASPOONS ANCHOVY ESSENCE
- 1 TABLESPOON CHOPPED FRESH PARSLEY
- SALT AND FRESHLY GROUND BLACK PEPPER

PREPARATION TIME: 20 MINUTES
COOKING TIME: 20 MINUTES
SERVES FOUR

Cod with Parsley Sauce

Cod, a fish of the Arctic seas, is much improved by a salt and vinegar marinade

INGREDIENTS

4 cod steaks, each approx 200g (7oz), rinsed
1½ level teaspoons salt
1.15 litres (2 pints) water
2 teaspoons distilled malt vinegar
285ml (½ pint) milk
2 cloves
1 mace blade
Bouquet garni (see p.440)
1 spring onion, trimmed and chopped
Freshly ground black pepper
1 bay leaf
1 parsley sprig
60g (2oz) butter
45g (1½oz) plain flour
6 tablespoons chopped fresh parsley
Pinch of grated nutmeg
Juice ½ lemon
Lemon slices to garnish
Preparation time: 40 minutes
Soaking time: 3 hours
Cooking time: 15 minutes
Serves four

Put the cod steaks into a shallow dish. Dissolve the salt in the water, stir in half the vinegar and pour over the fish. Cover and refrigerate for 3 hours.

Meanwhile, pour the milk into a saucepan and add the cloves, mace blade, bouquet garni and chopped spring onion. Bring to the boil, then remove the pan from the heat, cover and stand aside to infuse until needed.

Drain the cod steaks and place them in a large frying pan. Strain the infused milk over the fish and add the bay leaf and the sprig of parsley. Simmer gently, uncovered, for 15 minutes. Strain off and reserve the milk. Discard the bay leaf and parsley, cover the cod steaks and keep them warm while making the sauce.

Melt 45g (1½oz) of the butter in a saucepan and stir in the flour. Cook for a minute, then gradually stir in the reserved milk. Bring to the boil over a moderate heat, stirring constantly, until thickened and smooth. Stir in the parsley, nutmeg and remaining vinegar and season to taste. Cook over a low heat for 3–4 minutes, stirring frequently.

Put the cod steaks onto heated serving plates, dot with the remaining butter and spoon a little lemon juice over each. Season with freshly ground black pepper and pour over a little of the parsley sauce. Serve the remaining sauce separately.

Garnish with the lemon slices and serve with fresh croquette potatoes, baby carrots and broccoli florets.

Milk, infused with herbs and spices, is used first to cook the cod and then as a base for the sauce.

The smaller, inshore cod are best for this recipe, and the best steaks are those cut from the tail ends of the fish.

A simple crust of breadcrumbs, lemon and parsley complements the flavour of red mullet.

Holiday fare
In the great hotels along the Promenade des Anglais, few dishes are more popular than cold red mullet Niçoise, served with olives, tomatoes and slices of orange.

Baked Red Mullet

Though mainly Mediterranean, red mullet is caught in the English Channel

Preheat the oven to 180°c (350°f, gas mark 4). Pour half the butter into a large roasting tin or ovenproof dish and sprinkle with half the parsley and half the breadcrumbs. Place the mullet on top, pour the lemon juice over them and scatter the lemon rind on top. Season the fish well. Sprinkle the remaining parsley and breadcrumbs over the mullet and drizzle over the remaining butter. Bake, uncovered, in the centre of the oven for 20–25 minutes or until the fish is cooked.

Serve the red mullet with a beetroot, rocket and cucumber salad.

Ingredients

- 115g (4oz) butter, melted
- 4 tablespoons chopped fresh parsley
- 175g (6oz) fresh white breadcrumbs
- 6 red mullet, each approx 225g (8oz) scaled, gutted and washed
- Thinly pared rind and strained juice 1 lemon, rind coarsely chopped
- Salt and freshly ground black pepper

Preparation time: 25 minutes
Cooking time: 35 minutes
Serves four

You can almost smell the sea as you eat this assembly of shellfish.

Seaside Platter

Fresh ingredients are essential for this maritime salad

INGREDIENTS

For the dressing
150 ml (¼ pint) olive oil
1 tablespoon cider vinegar
1 tablespoon lemon juice
1 level teaspoon Dijon mustard
½ teaspoon honey
1 level tablespoon chopped fresh dill
Salt and freshly ground black pepper

For the platter
Crushed ice
Fresh Seaweed (obtainable from fishmonger), or fresh dill or parsley
Small lettuce leaves
175 g (6 oz) large, fresh cooked peeled prawns
4 fresh oysters
8–12 shell-on, cooked king prawns or small crevettes
115 g (4 oz) shell-on, cooked prawns
115 g (4 oz) shrimps
285 ml (½ pint) whelks
115 g (4 oz) cockles, washed and drained
285 ml (½ pint) winkles
24 cooked mussels in their shells
Lemon wedges and fresh dill sprigs to garnish

Preparation time: 25 minutes
Serves four

Put all the dressing ingredients into a bowl and whisk together, then transfer to a small bowl.

Make a mound of crushed ice on a very large serving platter and cover it with fresh seaweed, dill or parsley. Place the bowl of dressing, slightly off-centre, on top of the ice. Arrange the lettuce leaves round the bowl and sprinkle the peeled prawns on top.

Using an oyster knife, carefully open the fresh oysters (see p.436) and place them on the platter. Arrange the shell-on prawns and shrimps around the oysters, then add the whelks, cockles, winkles and mussels. Garnish the seafood with the lemon wedges and the dressing with dill.

Serve the platter with hot, buttered soda bread, a crisp green salad and chilled, dry white wine.

Dressed Crab and Lobster Salad with Ginger and Prawn Cream

This seafood salad has a positively Edwardian opulence about it

To make the sauce, pour the double cream into a bowl and whisk until it will hold a soft peak, then gently fold in the mayonnaise, chopped prawns, ginger, lemon juice and the salt and pepper. Spoon the mixture into a serving dish, sprinkle with the chives, cover and refrigerate until required.

To make the salad, put the brown crabmeat into a bowl—there should be about 115 g (4 oz)—add the breadcrumbs, mustard, salt, cayenne pepper and 1 tablespoon of the chopped parsley and mix well together.

Put the white crabmeat into a bowl, taking care to remove any particles of shell. Stir in the vinegar and pile the mixture into each side of the shell, leaving a space in the centre. Fill the space in the centre with the brown crabmeat. Garnish the crab with rows of chopped parsley, egg yolk and chopped egg white arranged on each side of the brown meat.

Make a bed of lettuce leaves on a serving platter, put the crab in the centre with the lobsters round it. Cover and refrigerate for 1 hour before serving with the sauce, and brown bread and butter.

Freshly cooked dressed crab and lobster taste best simply served and eaten on the beach, with a dressing made at home.

INGREDIENTS

For the sauce

- 150 ML (¼ PINT) DOUBLE CREAM
- 150 ML (¼ PINT) MAYONNAISE, HOMEMADE (SEE P.436) OR BOUGHT
- 115 G (4 OZ) FRESH COOKED PEELED PRAWNS, CHOPPED
- 15 G (½ OZ) PIECE ROOT GINGER, PEELED AND FINELY GRATED OR CHOPPED
- 1 TABLESPOON LEMON JUICE
- PINCH OF SALT AND PEPPER
- 1 TABLESPOON SNIPPED FRESH CHIVES

For the salad

- 1 LARGE COOKED CRAB, APPROX 900 G (2 LB), DRESSED BY FISHMONGER (OR SEE P.436)
- 4 TABLESPOONS FRESH WHITE BREADCRUMBS
- ¼ LEVEL TEASPOON ENGLISH MUSTARD POWDER
- PINCH OF SALT
- PINCH OF CAYENNE PEPPER
- 2 TABLESPOONS CHOPPED FRESH PARSLEY
- 1 TABLESPOON WHITE WINE VINEGAR
- 1 HARD-BOILED EGG, SIZE 2, SHELLED, YOLK SIEVED, WHITE FINELY CHOPPED
- 2 SMALL LOBSTERS, EACH APPROX 450 G (1 LB), PREPARED BY FISHMONGER (OR SEE P.437)
- 1 LETTUCE, LEAVES SEPARATED, WASHED AND DRIED

Preparation time: 1 HOUR
Chilling time: 1 HOUR
Serves four

Quayside craftsmanship
These wicker and twine crabpots, weighted by stones, are made and repaired by the fishermen who use them. Their design has not changed for a thousand years and more.

The flaky pastry that encases the crab and prawn mixture can be made the day before.

Cornish Crab and Prawn Patties

These savoury patties would make a welcome treat after a brisk morning's walk

Ingredients

For the flaky pastry
- 225 g (8 oz) strong plain white flour
- Good pinch of salt
- 115 g (4 oz) butter and 60 g (2 oz) lard, at room temperature, blended together and divided into quarters
- 8 tablespoons chilled water
- 1 teaspoon lemon juice

For the filling
- 15 g (½ oz) unsalted butter
- 15 g (½ oz) plain flour
- 150 ml (¼ pint) fish stock (see p.433)
- 2–3 tablespoons cider or dry white wine
- Freshly ground black pepper
- 60 g (2 oz) fresh white crabmeat or frozen crabmeat, thawed
- 85 g (3 oz) fresh cooked peeled prawns or frozen cooked peeled prawns
- Beaten egg to glaze

Preparation time: 1½ hours
Chilling time: 30 minutes
Cooking time: 25–30 minutes
Makes eight patties

To make the pastry, sift the flour and salt into a bowl, rub in a single portion of the fat and mix with the water and lemon juice. Knead it on a lightly floured surface for 5 minutes until smooth, then roll out to about 38 × 12.5 cm (15 × 5 in). Take a second portion of the fat and dot evenly over the top two-thirds of the dough. Fold the bottom third of the dough up and over the centre to cover the fat, then bring the top third down to cover the bottom third. Seal the open ends with the rolling pin.

Give the dough a quarter turn, roll out and fold as above, twice more, using up the remaining portions of fat. Wrap in cling film and chill for 30 minutes.

To make the filling, heat the butter in a small saucepan, stir in the flour and cook for 1 minute. Gradually stir in the fish stock and the cider or white wine. Bring to the boil, stirring continuously. Remove from the heat, season with pepper, leave until cool, then mix in the crab and prawns.

Roll out the dough until a little less than 5 mm (¼ in) thick. Using a 10 cm (4 in) plain round cutter, stamp out rounds and set aside. Lay the trimmings neatly on top of each other, reroll and cut more rounds to make 16 in all. Lay eight rounds on a baking sheet, spoon some filling onto the centre of each, brush the edges with cold water and cover with the remaining rounds. Flake the edges and chill for 30 minutes while heating the oven to 220°C (425°F, gas mark 7).

Glaze the patties with beaten egg, make two small slits in the tops and bake for 25 minutes or until golden brown.

Finnan Haddie

The Scottish fishing village of Findon gave us this spirited lunch or supper dish

PUT the water, onion, carrot, bay leaf, parsley stalks, peppercorns and lemon rind into a saucepan. Cover and bring to the boil, then reduce the heat and simmer gently for 30 minutes. Strain the water into a large frying pan, discarding the vegetables, and bring to the boil. Add the haddock, skin side up, and cook it gently for 3 minutes or until the flesh flakes easily, taking care not to overcook. Lift the haddock out of the pan with a fish slice and place, skin side down, in a shallow roasting tin. Cover with foil and put in a very low oven, 110°C (225°F, gas mark ¼), to keep hot. Repeat for the other fish.

Poach the eggs in the stock remaining in the frying pan, lift them out with a fish slice and place one on top of each haddock. Cover again with foil.

Boil the stock remaining in the pan until reduced to about 150 ml (¼ pint). Meanwhile, in a separate saucepan, bring the cream to boiling point and stir in two-thirds of the chopped parsley. Strain the reduced stock through a fine sieve into the cream and continue to boil it gently for 2–3 minutes. Strain the juices from the roasting tin into the sauce, taste and add salt if necessary.

Carefully lift the haddock onto heated individual plates, spoon the sauce over them and sprinkle with the remaining chopped parsley. Serve the haddock with stoneground wholemeal bread.

INGREDIENTS

- 570 ML (1 PINT) WATER
- 1 ONION, PEELED AND HALVED
- 1 CARROT, PEELED AND ROUGHLY CHOPPED
- 1 LARGE BAY LEAF
- FEW FRESH PARSLEY STALKS
- 1 TEASPOON BLACK PEPPERCORNS
- FINELY PARED RIND 1 LEMON
- 4 FINNAN HADDIE, OR SIMILAR SMALL, SPLIT SMOKED HADDOCK, EACH APPROX 175–225 G (6–8 OZ), FINS REMOVED
- 4 VERY FRESH EGGS
- 150 ML (¼ PINT) DOUBLE CREAM
- 3 TABLESPOONS CHOPPED FRESH PARSLEY
- SALT, IF NECESSARY, AND FRESHLY GROUND BLACK PEPPER

PREPARATION TIME: 20 MINUTES
COOKING TIME: 45 MINUTES
SERVES FOUR

These gilded, palely smoked treasures are admirably set off by spicy poached eggs.

If you find finnan haddie, or even small whole smoked haddock, difficult to obtain, you can use large fillets of smoked haddock cut into 175g (6oz) pieces instead.

JESSE SMIT
HOME MADE
SAUSAGES.
PORK BUTCHER

MEAT

You can still find them in old-fashioned high streets, the butchers' shops whose sausages have been famous for generations and whose walls bear ceramic portraits of surprisingly cheerful beasts. There you will discover true craftsmanship, in the skilled preparation of *Crown of Lamb*, or in the sweetness of their *Gammon* and the succulence of their *Beef Forerib*. They are profoundly knowledgeable, too, about the best cuts for *Lancashire Hot Pot, Loin of Pork* or *Guard of Honour*. Not even an enquiry for the ingredients of a *Mittoon* will perplex them.

Baked Gammon with Broad Beans & Parsley Sauce

Parsley's mildly spicy flavour adds piquancy to gammon and beans

INGREDIENTS

1.6–1.8 KG (3½–4 LB) PIECE TOP END OR MIDDLE SMOKED GAMMON, SOAKED IN COLD WATER OVERNIGHT
2 LEVEL TABLESPOONS DIJON MUSTARD
3–4 LEVEL TABLESPOONS DEMERARA SUGAR
20 CLOVES
70 G (2½ OZ) BUTTER
45 G (1½ OZ) PLAIN FLOUR
450 ML (16 FL OZ) MILK
SALT AND FRESHLY GROUND BLACK PEPPER
3 TABLESPOONS FINELY CHOPPED FRESH PARSLEY
3 TABLESPOONS SINGLE CREAM
340 G (12 OZ) SHELLED FRESH OR FROZEN BROAD BEANS
340 G (12 OZ) RUNNER BEANS, CUT INTO 2.5 CM (1 IN) PIECES

SOAKING TIME: OVERNIGHT
PREPARATION TIME: 30 MINUTES
COOKING TIME: 1 HOUR 40 MINUTES
SERVES SIX

REMOVE the gammon from the water and drain well. Preheat the oven to 180°C (350°F, gas mark 4).

Put a large piece of foil into a roasting tin, place the gammon in the middle and loosely wrap the foil round it, folding the edges securely together. Bake it in the centre of the oven allowing 20 minutes per 450 g (1 lb) of gammon. Remove the roasting tin and increase the oven temperature to 220°C (425°F, gas mark 7).

Remove the foil from the gammon, then use a sharp knife to cut away the brown skin. Score the fat in a diamond pattern and spread the mustard evenly all over the surface. Sprinkle the sugar over the mustard, pressing it firmly into place with your hand. Stud the gammon with the cloves and return it to the oven for 20 minutes or until glazed and golden.

Meanwhile, make the parsley sauce. Melt 45 g (1½ oz) of the butter in a pan, stir in the flour and cook for 1 minute. Gradually add the milk, bring to the boil, then stir over a gentle heat for 2–3 minutes. Season well, stir in the parsley and cream and simmer for 2–3 minutes.

Steam or boil the broad beans and runner beans until tender. Drain well, melt the remaining butter and mix in the beans. Place the gammon on a serving dish and surround it with the beans.

BUTCHER'S BLUFF
Handsome coloured tiles depicting contented, and even cheerful, animals were part of the furnishing of every butcher's shop. Presumably they were intended to divert the customers from the reality of the carcasses around them.

Golden gammon is served on a succulent bed of broad and runner beans.

Glazed baby turnips, carrots, courgettes and button onions make a colourful throne for the crown.

Crown Roast of Lamb

A butcher will prepare a crown roast for you, if you order it in advance, and will often supply cutlet frills too

PREHEAT the oven to 180°C (350°F, gas mark 4). Put the veal or pork, the shallots, parsley, thyme and garlic into a bowl, season well and mix. Fill the crown with the stuffing, then weigh it and calculate the cooking time, allowing 25 minutes per 450 g (1 lb), plus 30 minutes.

Put the lamb into a roasting tin, rub all over with the oil, sprinkle with the rosemary and season well. Cover the top half with foil and roast in the centre of the oven for the time calculated, basting occasionally. Remove the foil for the last 20 minutes to brown the top.

When the crown is uncovered, put all the vegetables into a wide frying pan with the butter, demerara sugar and the chicken stock or water. Season with salt and bring to the boil, then reduce the heat and cook gently, partially covered, until the vegetables are tender and the liquid has almost evaporated, shaking the pan often towards the end of cooking to prevent the vegetables from sticking to it. Remove from the heat, cover and keep hot while making the gravy.

Carefully lift the crown out of the roasting tin and put it onto a heated serving plate. Cover and keep warm. Skim all but 2 tablespoons of fat from the roasting tin, then stir in the flour and the veal or chicken stock and bring to the boil, stirring and scraping the browned residue from the bottom of the tin. Strain the gravy through a sieve into a saucepan and simmer for 5 minutes. Season well.

Trim the crown roast with cutlet frills and surround with the glazed vegetables. Serve with the hot gravy and buttered new potatoes.

INGREDIENTS

- 250 G (9 OZ) MINCED BRITISH VEAL OR PORK
- 3 SHALLOTS, PEELED AND FINELY CHOPPED
- 2 TABLESPOONS CHOPPED FRESH PARSLEY
- 1 TABLESPOON CHOPPED FRESH THYME
- 1 GARLIC CLOVE, PEELED AND CRUSHED
- SALT AND FRESHLY GROUND BLACK PEPPER
- 2 RACKS BEST END NECK OF LAMB, 6 BONES EACH, CHINED AND PREPARED INTO A CROWN
- 2 TABLESPOONS OLIVE OIL
- 2 LEVEL TEASPOONS DRIED ROSEMARY
- 2 LEVEL TABLESPOONS PLAIN FLOUR
- 425 ML (3/4 PINT) VEAL OR CHICKEN STOCK (SEE P.433)

FOR THE VEGETABLES

- 225 G (8 OZ) BABY TURNIPS, TRIMMED AND WASHED
- 225 G (8 OZ) BUTTON ONIONS, PEELED
- 225 G (8 OZ) BABY CARROTS, TRIMMED AND WASHED
- 225 G (8 OZ) BABY COURGETTES, WASHED AND HALVED LENGTHWAYS
- 60 G (2 OZ) BUTTER
- 2 LEVEL TABLESPOONS DEMERARA SUGAR
- 285 ML (1/2 PINT) CHICKEN STOCK (SEE P.433) OR WATER

PREPARATION TIME: 45 MINUTES
COOKING TIME: 1 3/4 HOURS
SERVES SIX

Beef Stew with Parsley Dumplings

The deliciously different dumplings give added savour to an old favourite

INGREDIENTS

45 G (1½ OZ) PLAIN FLOUR
¼ LEVEL TEASPOON SALT
¼ LEVEL TEASPOON FRESHLY GROUND BLACK PEPPER
900 G (2 LB) CHUCK STEAK, TRIMMED OF FAT AND CUT INTO 2.5 CM (1 IN) CUBES
60 G (2 OZ) BEEF DRIPPING OR 4 TABLESPOONS OLIVE OIL
450 G (1 LB) CARROTS, PEELED, HALVED WIDTHWAYS AND QUARTERED
450 G (1 LB) ONIONS, PEELED AND QUARTERED
225 G (8 OZ) TURNIP, PEELED AND DICED
725 ML (1¼ PINTS) BEEF STOCK (SEE P.432)
1 BAY LEAF
4 FRESH THYME SPRIGS

FOR THE DUMPLINGS
175 G (6 OZ) SELF-RAISING FLOUR
60 G (2 OZ) FRESH BEEF SUET, GRATED, OR SHREDDED SUET
115 G (4 OZ) PORK AND BEEF SAUSAGE MEAT, ROUGHLY CHOPPED
3 TABLESPOONS CHOPPED FRESH PARSLEY
SALT AND FRESHLY GROUND BLACK PEPPER
6 TABLESPOONS COLD WATER

PREPARATION TIME: 30 MINUTES
COOKING TIME: 2½ HOURS
SERVES FOUR

SIFT the flour, salt and pepper onto a plate, add the beef in two batches and toss it well to coat it thoroughly.

Heat half the dripping or olive oil in a large saucepan until sizzling, add half the beef cubes and cook over a moderate heat, turning frequently until evenly browned. Remove the meat from the saucepan with a slotted spoon and put onto a plate. Fry the rest of the meat in the dripping or oil remaining in the saucepan, then add to the first batch.

Heat the remaining dripping or oil in the saucepan, add the quartered carrots and onions and the diced turnip and cook, stirring frequently, until the onions have softened. Return the browned meat to the saucepan with any remaining flour and cook for 1 minute.

Gradually stir in the beef stock, add the bay leaf and thyme and bring to the boil, stirring continuously. Then reduce the heat to very low, cover and simmer the stew for 2 hours, stirring occasionally.

To make the dumplings, sift the flour into a bowl and mix in the suet, sausage meat and chopped parsley. Season lightly with the salt and black pepper, then add the cold water to the mixture to make a soft, slightly sticky dough.

With floured hands, divide the dough into eight equal portions and roll each lightly into a ball. Add the dumplings to the gently simmering stew, spacing them well apart. Cover and cook the stew for a further 30 minutes or until the dumplings have puffed up and are cooked through. Remove the bay leaf and thyme.

Carrots, onions and turnips form a tasty base for this traditional stew.

For light, fluffy dumplings, simmer the stew gently and keep it covered throughout the cooking time.

The succulent steak 'pocket' is doused with brandy and served on a bed of spinach.

Fillet Steaks of Beef Stuffed with Mushrooms

Shallots and a touch of lemon enliven the mushroom filling for the steaks

To MAKE the maître d'hôtel butter, blend the butter with the parsley, salt, lemon rind and juice, then shape into a roll about 3.8 cm (1½ in) in diameter. Wrap in greaseproof paper and roll gently until smooth and even. Chill until required.

To prepare the filling, melt the butter in a frying pan and sauté the shallots gently until just beginning to soften. Add the mushrooms, lemon rind and juice and cook, uncovered, until the mushrooms are tender and the liquid has almost evaporated. Season well and set aside.

To prepare the steaks, using a sharp knife carefully cut a horizontal pocket in the side of each steak to within 1.3 cm (½ in) of the edge. Fill generously with the mushroom mixture and season well with salt and black pepper.

Heat the oil and half the butter in a heavy-based frying pan until sizzling hot, add the steaks and cook for 4–6 minutes on each side for medium-rare, or until done to your liking.

Meanwhile, blanch the spinach in boiling water for 1 minute and drain well. Melt the remaining butter in a saucepan, add the nutmeg and spinach and cook for 1–2 minutes until tender and hot. Spoon the spinach onto a large, heated serving plate, or individual plates, and arrange the steaks on top. Cover and keep hot.

Add the brandy to the frying pan and boil rapidly for 30 seconds, stirring and scraping the browned residue from the bottom of the pan. Cut the maître d'hôtel butter into eight slices. Pour the brandy over the steaks and top with the maître d'hôtel butter. Garnish with the grilled tomatoes and lemon wedges, then serve.

Sautéed or new potatoes make a good accompaniment to this dish.

INGREDIENTS

FOR THE MAITRE D'HOTEL BUTTER
- 115 G (4 OZ) BUTTER, SOFTENED
- 1 TABLESPOON FINELY CHOPPED FRESH PARSLEY
- ¼ LEVEL TEASPOON SALT
- 1 LEVEL TEASPOON FINELY GRATED LEMON RIND
- 1 TEASPOON LEMON JUICE

FOR THE MUSHROOM FILLING
- 60 G (2 OZ) BUTTER
- 85 G (3 OZ) SHALLOTS, PEELED AND FINELY CHOPPED
- 175 G (6 OZ) MUSHROOMS, WIPED AND FINELY CHOPPED
- FINELY GRATED RIND AND JUICE ½ LEMON
- SALT AND FRESHLY GROUND BLACK PEPPER

FOR THE STEAKS
- 4 BEEF FILLET STEAKS, EACH APPROX 175–225 G (6–8 OZ)
- SALT AND COARSELY GROUND BLACK PEPPER
- 2 TABLESPOONS OLIVE OIL
- 115 G (4 OZ) BUTTER
- 900 G (2 LB) FRESH SPINACH, STALKS REMOVED, WASHED
- ¼ LEVEL TEASPOON FRESHLY GRATED NUTMEG
- 4 TABLESPOONS BRANDY
- GRILLED TOMATO HALVES AND LEMON WEDGES TO GARNISH

PREPARATION TIME: 30 MINUTES
COOKING TIME: 20 MINUTES
SERVES FOUR

Boiled Beef & Carrots with Pease Pudding

Order the meat at least a fortnight in advance to give the butcher time to salt it for you, though salted brisket can be used instead of silverside if preferred

Ingredients

2 kg (4½ lb) salted silverside
Large bouquet garni (see p.440)
1 large onion, peeled and studded with 4 cloves
1 level teaspoon black peppercorns
675 g (1½ lb) carrots, peeled
1 celery head, trimmed
4 large leeks, green parts removed, washed
450 g (1 lb) small turnips, peeled
8 medium onions, peeled

For the pease pudding
340 g (12 oz) green or yellow split peas
2.3 litres (4 pints) water
60 g (2 oz) butter
2 eggs, size 2, beaten
2 tablespoons chopped fresh mint
2 tablespoons chopped fresh parsley
Salt and freshly ground black pepper

For the dumplings
225 g (8 oz) plain flour
1 level teaspoon baking powder
¼ level teaspoon salt
Freshly ground black pepper
115 g (4 oz) shredded beef suet
225 ml (8 fl oz) cold water

For the sauce
30 g (1 oz) butter
30 g (1 oz) plain flour
2 tablespoons fresh horseradish, grated
Freshly ground black pepper
1 tablespoon lemon juice
3–4 tablespoons single cream

Preparation time: 45 minutes
Cooking time: 2 hours
Serves eight

Half fill a very large saucepan with water and heat until lukewarm. Rinse the beef under cold water, drain, put into the pan and bring slowly to the boil. Immediately the water boils, lower the heat and skim the surface. Add the bouquet garni, the onion and peppercorns. Partially cover and simmer gently for 1 hour.

The pease pudding and vegetables

While the beef is simmering, rinse and drain the peas, put them into a saucepan, cover with water and bring to the boil. Boil for 10 minutes, skimming off the scum as it rises to the surface. Reduce the heat, partially cover the pan and cook gently for 45–50 minutes until tender.

While the peas are cooking, prepare the vegetables. Leave small carrots whole, cut medium ones in half widthways and large ones into 2.5 cm (1 in) pieces. Cut the celery into quarters lengthways, then across into pieces about 5–7.5 cm (2–3 in) long. Cut the leeks into 7.5 cm (3 in) pieces. Halve or quarter the turnips and leave the onions whole.

When the peas are cooked, drain well and put them into a food processor with the butter, eggs, mint and parsley. Season well and blend until smooth. Alternatively, mash with a potato masher and beat in the butter, eggs, herbs and seasoning. Spoon the pease pudding into a buttered 1.15 litre (2 pint) pudding basin and press down evenly. Cover with buttered foil, tucking it tightly under the rim, and set aside. When the beef has simmered for 1 hour, add the vegetables and continue cooking for 40–50 minutes, until they are tender.

Meanwhile, cook the pease pudding for 45 minutes in a steamer or a saucepan filled with boiling water to halfway up the sides of the basin, and prepare the dumplings and sauce.

Sift the flour, baking powder and salt and pepper for the dumplings into a bowl, stir in the suet and set aside. For the sauce, melt the butter in a saucepan, remove from the heat, stir in the flour and horseradish and set aside.

When all the vegetables are tender, transfer the beef to a heated serving platter. Remove the vegetables with a slotted spoon and arrange them round the meat. Cover the platter loosely with foil and keep hot while cooking the dumplings and completing the sauce. Remove the pease pudding from the heat.

The dumplings

Reserve 725 ml (1¼ pints) of the beef stock, and bring the remainder to a gentle boil. Combine the cold water with the dumpling mixture to form a soft, slightly sticky dough. Divide the dough into eight pieces and, with floured hands, shape each piece into a ball. Drop the balls into the stock, cover and cook gently for 10–15 minutes or until well risen, light and fluffy—do not boil too hard as the dumplings will break up.

The horseradish sauce

While the dumplings are cooking, complete the sauce. Stir the reserved stock gradually into the horseradish mixture and bring to the boil, stirring continuously. Reduce the heat, season the sauce well with pepper, stir in the lemon juice and simmer for 10 minutes, stirring frequently. Stir in the cream, pour the sauce into a heated sauceboat and keep hot.

Turn out the pease pudding into a heated serving dish and mash with a fork. Transfer the dumplings to a heated dish. Serve the beef and vegetables immediately with the pease pudding, dumplings, horseradish sauce and with hot English mustard if wished.

Dumplings, pease pudding and horseradish sauce provide the traditional support for succulent boiled beef and carrots.

Lucky find
Worcestershire sauce has been marketed since 1837 when chemists John Wheeley Lea and William Perrins discovered that a recipe made up by them two years before had matured from an unpleasant concoction into a delightfully piquant sauce.

Dashes of sauces and chutney add an exotic flavour to the lamb in this traditional dish.

Shepherd's Pie

A favourite standby transforms the Sunday roast leftovers into a satisfying meal for all the family

INGREDIENTS

- 900G (2LB) BOILING POTATOES, PEELED AND QUARTERED
- 150ML (¼ PINT) DOUBLE CREAM OR CREAMY MILK
- 60G (2OZ) BUTTER
- SALT AND FRESHLY GROUND BLACK PEPPER
- FRESHLY GRATED NUTMEG
- 2 TABLESPOONS VEGETABLE OIL
- 1 MEDIUM ONION, PEELED AND CHOPPED
- 1 GARLIC CLOVE, PEELED AND CRUSHED
- 1 TABLESPOON WORCESTERSHIRE SAUCE
- 1 TABLESPOON TOMATO PURÉE
- 1 TABLESPOON CHILLI AND GARLIC SAUCE
- 1 TABLESPOON MANGO CHUTNEY
- 1 LEVEL TABLESPOON DRIED MIXED HERBS
- 450G (1LB) COOKED LAMB, TRIMMED OF FAT AND MINCED
- 150ML (¼ PINT) LAMB GRAVY OR BEEF STOCK (SEE P.432)

PREPARATION TIME: 40 MINUTES
COOKING TIME: 45 MINUTES
SERVES FOUR

Preheat the oven to 180°C (350°F, gas mark 4). Boil or steam the potatoes until tender, then drain and mash well. Heat the cream or milk and half the butter in a saucepan and beat into the mashed potatoes. Season well with the salt, pepper and nutmeg. Cover and keep warm.

Heat the oil in a saucepan, add the onion and garlic and cook over a moderate heat for 5 minutes, or until soft and golden. Stir in the Worcestershire sauce, tomato purée, chilli and garlic sauce, mango chutney and herbs. Stir in the meat followed by the gravy or stock.

Transfer to an ovenproof dish and spoon the potatoes carefully over the surface. Smooth the potatoes, then fork the surface decoratively.

Dot with the remaining butter and bake in the centre of the oven for 45 minutes, until golden brown and thoroughly heated through.

Steak & Kidney Pudding

Here is a classic version of the noble dish that holds pride of place from country tavern to London club

INGREDIENTS

For the suet crust pastry
- 225 g (8 oz) self-raising flour
- ¼ level teaspoon freshly grated nutmeg
- ½ level teaspoon salt
- 115 g (4 oz) shredded beef suet
- Approx 150 ml (¼ pint) chilled water

For the filling
- 2 level tablespoons plain flour
- ½ level teaspoon salt
- Freshly ground black pepper
- 1 level teaspoon chopped fresh thyme
- 450 g (1 lb) rump steak or beef skirt, trimmed of fat and cut into 2.5 cm (1 in) cubes
- 115 g (4 oz) lamb's kidney, skin and white core removed, washed, dried and cut into 1.3 cm (½ in) pieces
- 1 small onion, peeled and finely chopped
- 60 ml (2 fl oz) beef stock (see p.432), or water
- 1 tablespoon tomato purée
- 2 teaspoons Worcestershire sauce

Preparation time: 30 minutes
Cooking time: 3 hours
Serves four

To make the pastry, sift the flour, nutmeg and salt into a bowl. Mix in the suet and sufficient chilled water to make a soft dough. Cover and set aside.

To make the filling, mix the flour, salt, pepper and thyme together in a bowl, add the steak and kidney and stir well until the meat is evenly coated with the flour mixture, then mix in the onion.

On a lightly floured surface, roll out the dough to a round of about 30 cm (12 in) in diameter. Cut out a quarter and reserve. Fold the remaining dough loosely and place in a 1.15 litre (2 pint) lightly buttered pudding basin. Unfold and press into the shape of the basin, sealing the join firmly. Allow the excess dough to overhang the rim of the basin.

Spoon the meat into the basin. Mix the stock or water with the tomato purée and Worcestershire sauce and pour over the meat. Roll out the reserved dough to a round the size of the top of the basin and place it on the meat. Lightly brush the overhanging dough with cold water, then fold in and press well to seal.

Cover the pudding with a round of buttered greaseproof paper, folded in a pleat in the centre to allow for expansion. Cover the top of the basin with a sheet of pleated foil and secure with string. Cook for 3 hours in a steamer or large saucepan filled with boiling water to halfway up the sides of the basin and fitted with a tightly fitting lid, replenishing frequently with more boiling water until cooked.

Anticipate the pleasure of eating the succulent pudding by serving it with a touch of ceremony.

You can buy saltpetre from any well-stocked independent chemist.

Sugar, spice, ground black pepper and saltpetre will all work their magic on the raw meat.

Spiced Beef

Though the meat takes over ten days to marinate, the end result will more than justify the lengthy preparation time

INGREDIENTS

- 115G (4OZ) MUSCOVADO SUGAR
- 15G (½OZ) SALTPETRE
- 30G (1OZ) ALLSPICE BERRIES, COARSELY GROUND
- 15G (½OZ) BLACK PEPPERCORNS, FRESHLY GROUND
- 115G (4OZ) SALT
- 2.3–2.7KG (5–6LB) JOINT BEEF, LEAN BRISKET BONED AND ROLLED, TOP RUMP OR THICK FLANK
- WATERCRESS AND TOMATOES TO GARNISH

PREPARATION TIME: 30 MINUTES PLUS 5 MINUTES EVERY DAY FOR 10 DAYS

COOKING TIME: 4 HOURS (DEPENDING ON SIZE)

SERVES EIGHT

IN A small bowl, mix the sugar with the saltpetre, allspice, pepper and salt. With clean hands, rub the spice mixture evenly all over the meat. Put the beef into a large stainless steel or glass casserole or deep glass dish that will hold it comfortably.

Cover the casserole with a lid or, if using a deep dish, cover it with a large plate. Do not use foil as it will react with the salt. Put the beef into the lower part of the refrigerator and leave to marinate for ten days, turning daily and rubbing the spices well into the meat. Gradually, the spice mixture will become more liquid and can then be basted over the meat.

Preheat the oven to 150°C (300°F, gas mark 2). Before cooking, take the beef from the casserole or dish and rinse off the spicy marinade. Put the rinsed beef into a casserole in which it will fit snugly and pour over 285ml (½ pint) water. Cover the casserole with two layers of foil and then with the lid to make a tight seal and to prevent evaporation.

Cook the beef in the centre of the oven for 3–4 hours, calculating the cooking time at 40 minutes per 450g (1lb). Remove from the oven and leave to cool.

The beef may be stored in a cool larder for two to three days or in the refrigerator for one week. Remove from the refrigerator 2 hours before serving to let the meat come to room temperature and to bring out the full spicy flavour.

To serve, remove the strings from the meat, carve it into thin slices and arrange them on a platter. Garnish with the watercress and tomatoes.

Pig in a Blanket

Rural wit supplied the quaint name for this economical and filling old recipe

PREHEAT the oven to 190°C (375°F, gas mark 5). Sift the flour into a bowl and stir in the suet, dried herbs, parsley, bacon, onion and some salt and pepper. Make a well in the centre and gradually stir in the egg mixture to form a soft but not sticky dough. Knead the dough lightly on a floured surface for a few seconds until smooth, then shape into a roll about 30 cm (12 in) long.

Cut a sheet of greaseproof paper, large enough to enclose the bacon roll, and grease it well. Place the roll in the centre of the paper, then wrap it loosely, leaving room for expansion. Twist the ends of the paper and tie securely with clean string. Overwrap the roll with foil, folding the join two or three times and twisting the ends tightly to seal. Place the foil parcel seam side up in a roasting tin, allowing at least 2.5 cm (1 in) between the parcel and the sides of the tin. Pour in enough boiling water to come halfway up the side of the tin. Put the tin into the oven and cook for 1½ hours or until the point of a skewer inserted into the centre of the bacon roll comes out clean.

Carefully lift the foil parcel out of the roasting tin onto a board and remove the foil and greaseproof paper. Slice the roll thickly and arrange it on a heated serving dish. Garnish with the celery leaves and fresh parsley and serve with baked tomatoes and braised celery.

INGREDIENTS

- 450G (1 LB) SELF-RAISING FLOUR
- 225G (8 OZ) SHREDDED BEEF SUET
- 1 LEVEL TEASPOON DRIED MIXED HERBS
- 3 TABLESPOONS CHOPPED FRESH PARSLEY
- 225G (8 OZ) BACON SCRAPS, RINDS REMOVED, CUT INTO SMALL PIECES
- 1 LARGE ONION, PEELED AND VERY FINELY CHOPPED
- SALT AND FRESHLY GROUND BLACK PEPPER
- 1 EGG, SIZE 2, BEATEN WITH 150ML (¼ PINT) WATER
- CELERY LEAVES AND FRESH PARSLEY SPRIGS TO GARNISH

PREPARATION TIME: 40 MINUTES
COOKING TIME: 1½ HOURS
SERVES SIX

Bacon, herbs and onions join the mixture for a delicious and aromatic suet roll.

A PIG OF ONE'S OWN
In 1940 the Small Pig Keepers' Council campaigned for town dwellers to be allowed to keep pigs in their back yards. This led to the establishment of 'pig clubs' whose members benefited from such perks as cut-price feed and insurance cover for their animals.

INGREDIENTS

For the stuffing
- 175g (6oz) minced pork
- 30g (1oz) fresh white breadcrumbs
- Finely grated rind ½ lemon
- 1 shallot or spring onion, trimmed and finely chopped
- 1 tablespoon chopped fresh parsley
- 1 tablespoon fresh thyme leaves, or 1 level teaspoon dried thyme
- ¼ level teaspoon ground nutmeg
- ¼ level teaspoon salt
- ¼ level teaspoon freshly ground black pepper

- 4 British veal escalopes, each approx 115g (4oz), beaten thin
- 4 rashers smoked back bacon, rinds removed
- 1 level tablespoon plain flour
- 1 tablespoon olive oil
- 15g (½oz) butter
- 150ml (¼ pint) dry white wine
- 150ml (¼ pint) chicken stock (see p.433)
- Salt and freshly ground black pepper
- Bouquet garni made with bay leaf, parsley and thyme sprigs (see p.440)
- Fresh thyme sprigs to garnish

Preparation time: 30 minutes
Cooking time: 45–60 minutes
Serves four

Veal Olives

Popular for centuries, veal olives offer textures and flavours to tempt any appetite

PREHEAT the oven to 180°c (350°F, gas mark 4). To make the stuffing, put all the ingredients into a bowl and mix well.

Lay the escalopes on a board and place a bacon rasher on top of each, then spread a quarter of the stuffing on top of the bacon rasher. Roll up the escalopes and tie securely with clean, fine string or strong cotton. Roll them in the flour until evenly coated, then shake off the excess.

Heat the olive oil and butter in a frying pan and fry the veal olives until brown all over. Remove from the pan and put them into an ovenproof dish.

Add any remaining flour to the frying pan and stir over a gentle heat until slightly browned. Add the wine, stock, salt and pepper, and bring to the boil, stirring continuously. Pour the sauce over the veal olives and add the bouquet garni.

Cover and cook in the centre of the oven for 45 minutes to 1 hour until the meat is tender. Discard the bouquet garni, then, using a slotted spoon, transfer the veal olives to a plate. Remove the string or cotton, return the olives to the sauce and reheat if necessary.

Garnish with the thyme and serve hot with peas tossed in butter, chopped mint and ground black pepper.

The olives can be made with escalopes of pork if preferred.

The veal parcels, enclosing bacon, pork and herbs, are further flavoured by wine and stock.

A profusion of spices, herbs and fruit cooked with pork in wine gives the dish a festive accent.

Elizabethan Pork

Only the very best recipes survive the centuries—this one has been enjoyed by successive generations since it first graced the board at Tudor banquets

PREHEAT the oven to 160°C (325°F, gas mark 3). Heat the oil in a large, flameproof casserole, add the pork in batches and fry until well browned. Remove each batch from the casserole with a slotted spoon, put onto a plate and set aside.

Add the onion to the fat remaining in the casserole and sauté until just softened. Sprinkle the flour over the onions and cook, stirring, for 1 minute. Gradually stir in the wine, scraping the browned bits from the bottom of the casserole. Add the garlic, mace, curry powder, cayenne pepper, celery seeds and salt and pepper. Tie the fresh herbs together with fine string and add them to the casserole with the apricots, raisins, dates, lemon rind and juice. Using a vegetable peeler, peel the orange; put the rind into cold water and set aside. Squeeze the juice from the orange and stir into the casserole with the apple slices and sugar.

Return the pork to the casserole, cover and cook on the centre shelf of the oven for 2 hours or until the meat is very tender, stirring occasionally.

Before serving, garnish with the reserved strips of orange rind, walnut halves and fresh marjoram sprigs. Serve the pork with hot rice.

INGREDIENTS

- 4 TABLESPOONS OLIVE OIL
- 1.1 KG (2½ LB) LEG OF PORK, BONED AND TRIMMED OF EXCESS FAT, CUT INTO CUBES
- 225 G (8 OZ) ONIONS, PEELED, HALVED AND SLICED
- 3 LEVEL TABLESPOONS PLAIN FLOUR
- 425 ML (¾ PINT) RED WINE
- 3 GARLIC CLOVES, PEELED AND CRUSHED
- 1 LEVEL TEASPOON GROUND MACE
- 1–2 LEVEL TEASPOONS MEDIUM-HOT CURRY POWDER
- ¼ LEVEL TEASPOON CAYENNE PEPPER
- 1 LEVEL TEASPOON CELERY SEEDS
- ½ LEVEL TEASPOON SALT
- FRESHLY GROUND BLACK PEPPER
- 1 SPRIG EACH FRESH MARJORAM, THYME, SAGE AND ROSEMARY
- 225 G (8 OZ) STONED FRESH APRICOTS OR 115 G (4 OZ) READY-TO-USE DRIED APRICOTS
- 115 G (4 OZ) LARGE STONED RAISINS
- 175 G (6 OZ) LARGE STONED FRESH OR SEMI-DRIED DATES
- FINELY GRATED RIND AND STRAINED JUICE 1 LEMON
- 1 LARGE ORANGE
- 3 SMALL DESSERT APPLES, COX OR RUSSET, PEELED, CORED, HALVED AND THICKLY SLICED
- 2 LEVEL TEASPOONS SOFT LIGHT BROWN SUGAR
- 30 G (1 OZ) WALNUT HALVES AND FRESH MARJORAM SPRIGS TO GARNISH

PREPARATION TIME: 40 MINUTES
COOKING TIME: 2¼ HOURS
SERVES FOUR

Downstairs Remembered

Behind every successful Edwardian dinner party was a minor miracle of organisation, expertise and sheer hard work

By the beginning of Edward VII's reign, the meal known as 'dinner'—which down the centuries had migrated through every hour from ten in the morning to ten at night—was firmly established in the late evening and had just about reached its gourmandising peak. Even in houses of the upper middling sort, there was served thick soup and clear soup, a huge boiled turbot lolling over a shield-like dish, two brown entrées, mutton and venison, as well as a joint of beef, and also two white entrées, perhaps rabbit, sweetbreads or chicken. Then there was duck or game birds, followed by, say, trifles and iced puddings. These were often succeeded by Stilton cheese, creamy pastries and ingenious desserts. Course would follow course with a precision that was almost magical.

Yet magic had little to do with it. Such vast meals were achieved only through anxious planning and almost unending drudgery. The huge kitchen of the early 20th century was highly labour-intensive and was almost exclusively a female domain. In most big houses, the kitchen was run by a professed cook, so called from having reached the peak of her profession; her underlings and, not infrequently, the mistress of the house, held her in considerable awe.

Cook Harriet Rogers in her 58th year of service

She was aided by kitchen maids, aspiring cooks themselves, and by one or more scullery maids who tackled the endless washing up. The scullery maid also served the closed range or kitchener, a black, iron, coal-guzzling tyrant that had to be cleaned, polished and coaxed into flame before even the first early morning tea could be made.

From dawn onwards there were mountains of vegetables to peel, birds to be plucked and animals to skin. Baking, boiling, roasting and basting continued daylong. There were servants' and nursery meals to prepare and cook, and dishes that had to be carried up one or more floors to the dining room and somehow arrive hot. There was bread to be baked for the morrow, and when dinner was long over and the kitchen scrubbed and tidied up, there might easily be a call from upstairs for a light supper of an omelette or devilled bones.

Cooks had time-honoured perquisites, most hallowed of which was beef dripping, which they sold to local tradesmen. It is difficult to blame the cook, for there were few enough perks in a servant's life. Before the First World War, a professed cook was paid about £70 a year and a first kitchen maid about £28. Though the calling offered security, personal freedom was curtailed and class distinctions were rigidly maintained, even within the servants' hall.

For many, the war was a heaven-sent opportunity to escape, and few of the women who spent its years as ambulance drivers, bus conductresses or lathe operators showed much enthusiasm to return to service at its end.

FULL HOUSE
Keeping a middle-class family fed and in comfort at the turn of the century called for teamwork. The gardeners grew the vegetables, the butler maintained the silver, the parlour maid served tea and the footmen, dinner. The housekeeper guarded the stores, the cook prepared the meals and the kitchen maids washed up.

MAIDS & DOMESTICS (2s. per line)
SITUATIONS VACANT.

COOK'S DOMAIN
By 1900, the cook had a few useful inventions to call upon, like baking powder, self-raising flour and patent polish. She also bought the latest cookery book. But the coal-fired stove still scorched clothes and boot leather, and the only way to judge its temperature was to throw a sheet of paper into the oven. If it burst into flame, the stove was too hot. Brown charring was just right for pastry.

COOKERY FOR EVERY HOUSEHOLD
1333. Eggs with Vegetable Marrow
1334. Eggs à la Clifton
1335. Egg Croquettes
1336. Egg Cutlets
1337. Egg Dormers
1338. Egg Patties
1339. Curried Egg Rissoles
1341. Scotch Eggs
1342. Stuffed Eggs with Cheese (Œufs au Fromage)
Scotch Eggs

Lemon wedges, more often served with fish, add sharpness to these breadcrumbed lamb morsels.

Lamb Scrumpets with Tartare Sauce

Deep-fried lamb receives a special touch from homemade tartare sauce

INGREDIENTS

2 LEAN BREASTS OF LAMB, TOTAL WEIGHT APPROX 1.1 KG (2½ LB), BONED
1 ONION, PEELED AND QUARTERED
2 CARROTS, PEELED AND HALVED
2 CELERY STICKS, TRIMMED AND ROUGHLY CHOPPED
1 BAY LEAF
8 BLACK PEPPERCORNS
WATER OR CHICKEN STOCK (SEE P.433)
2 LEVEL TABLESPOONS WHOLE-GRAIN MUSTARD
2 EGGS, SIZE 2, BEATEN
175 G (6 OZ) DRY WHITE BREADCRUMBS
VEGETABLE OIL FOR DEEP FRYING
CHOPPED FRESH PARSLEY AND LEMON WEDGES TO GARNISH

FOR THE TARTARE SAUCE
285 ML (½ PINT) MAYONNAISE, HOMEMADE (SEE P.436) OR BOUGHT
1 TABLESPOON CHOPPED FRESH PARSLEY
1 TEASPOON CHOPPED FRESH TARRAGON
1 TABLESPOON CAPERS, CHOPPED
2 TABLESPOONS CHOPPED GHERKINS
1 TABLESPOON STUFFED OLIVES, CHOPPED

PREPARATION TIME: 30 MINUTES
COOKING TIME: 1¼ HOURS
CHILLING TIME: OVERNIGHT
SERVES FOUR

PUT the lamb breasts into a saucepan with the onion, carrots, celery, bay leaf and peppercorns. Cover with the water or stock and bring to the boil, reduce the heat, cover and simmer gently for 1 hour or until tender. Remove the lamb from the saucepan, drain well, then lay out flat on a baking tray lined with cling film. Cover and refrigerate overnight.

To make the tartare sauce, mix all the ingredients in a bowl then transfer to a serving dish, cover and chill.

Put the chilled lamb breasts onto a board and trim off any excess fat. Spread the mustard all over one side of each. Cut the breasts diagonally into thin strips, then dip the strips in the beaten egg and coat well with the breadcrumbs. Deep fry in hot oil for 4–5 minutes until the breadcrumbs are crisp and golden.

Drain on kitchen paper, arrange on a heated serving dish, sprinkle with the parsley and serve with the lemon wedges and tartare sauce.

Pork Guard of Honour with Mustard Sauce

English mustard, with its peppery tang, is the ideal partner for pork

Trim the pork loins, exposing 3.8 cm (1½ in) of bone at the top. Remove the skin and score the fat in a diamond pattern. Put the meat, fat side up, into a shallow dish and add the gin. Mix the juniper berries, peppercorns, herbs and grated rinds and rub the mixture over the fat. Cover the dish with foil and refrigerate overnight.

Preheat the oven to 190°c (375°f, gas mark 5). Stand the loins upright, with the fat outside and bones interlocking, in a roasting tin. Tie the joints securely with string between each pair of bones. Put the roasting tin into the oven and roast the pork for 2½ hours, basting occasionally. If the meat browns too quickly, cover it with foil. The pork is done if the juices run clear when a skewer is inserted into the centre of the joint.

Meanwhile, bring the bouquet garni and milk to the boil in a saucepan. Cover and stand aside for 1 hour, then remove the bouquet garni.

Transfer the cooked pork to a heated dish, cover and leave for 30 minutes.

Meanwhile, make the sauce. Melt the butter in a saucepan, stir in the flour and cook over a moderate heat for 1 minute, then gradually stir in the milk. Bring to the boil, stirring, until thickened and smooth, then simmer for 2–3 minutes. Stir in the mustard and the cream, season to taste and continue to cook gently for 3–4 minutes. Pour into a heated sauceboat and keep warm.

Remove the string from the guard of honour, then garnish with the slices of lemon and lime and the parsley sprigs. Carve by cutting between the bones.

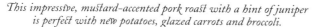

This impressive, mustard-accented pork roast with a hint of juniper is perfect with new potatoes, glazed carrots and broccoli.

INGREDIENTS

- 2 rib end loins of pork, each with 6 bones and weighing approx 1.1 kg (2½ lb), chined
- 4 tablespoons gin
- 1 tablespoon juniper berries, coarsely crushed
- 1 tablespoon black peppercorns, coarsely crushed
- 2 tablespoons chopped fresh parsley
- 1 tablespoon chopped fresh sage
- Finely grated rind 1 small lemon
- Finely grated rind 1 small lime
- Bouquet garni (see p.440)
- 570 ml (1 pint) milk
- 45 g (1½ oz) butter
- 45 g (1½ oz) plain flour
- 1–2 tablespoons English mustard powder blended with 1 tablespoon cold water
- 285 ml (½ pint) single cream
- Slices of lemon and lime and parsley sprigs to garnish

Preparation time: 1¾ hours
Marinating time: Overnight
Cooking time: 2¾ hours
Serves eight

Shrewd switch
The bull's head trademark of Colman's mustard was created in 1855 by Edward Colman, nephew of Jeremiah, the founder of the company. It was originally registered for a 'Starch for Laundry and Manufacturing Purposes'.

The light stuffing of herbs, leeks and redcurrants is perfect for the roast lamb.

Stuffed Leg of Lamb with Lavender

Lavender, a delicate reminder of summer-scented country gardens, lends a tantalising fragrance to roast leg of lamb

INGREDIENTS

- 2.3 KG (5 LB) LEG OF LAMB, TUNNEL BONED
- 225 G (8 OZ) FRESH WHITE BREADCRUMBS
- 3 TABLESPOONS CHOPPED FRESH PARSLEY
- 2 TABLESPOONS CHOPPED FRESH MINT
- 2 SMALL LEEKS, TRIMMED, WASHED AND FINELY CHOPPED
- 85 G (3 OZ) FRESH REDCURRANTS, STALKS REMOVED, WASHED OR FROZEN REDCURRANTS, THAWED
- 1 GARLIC CLOVE, PEELED AND CRUSHED
- FINELY GRATED RIND ½ LEMON
- ¼ LEVEL TEASPOON GRATED NUTMEG
- 30 G (1 OZ) BUTTER, MELTED
- 2 EGGS, SIZE 2, BEATEN
- SALT AND FRESHLY GROUND BLACK PEPPER
- 2 LARGE ONIONS, PEELED AND ROUGHLY CHOPPED
- 4 FRESH LAVENDER SPRIGS
- 570 ML (1 PINT) VEAL OR CHICKEN STOCK (SEE P.433)
- 150 ML (¼ PINT) RED WINE
- 1 TABLESPOON REDCURRANT JELLY, HOMEMADE (SEE P.401) OR BOUGHT
- 30 G (1 OZ) BUTTER, SOFTENED
- 30 G (1 OZ) PLAIN FLOUR
- FRESH LAVENDER FOR SERVING (OPTIONAL)

PREPARATION TIME: 1¼ HOURS
COOKING TIME: 2½ HOURS
SERVES EIGHT

PREHEAT the oven to 190°C (375°F, gas mark 5). To make the stuffing, mix the breadcrumbs, parsley, mint, leeks, redcurrants, garlic, lemon rind, nutmeg, butter, eggs and seasoning in a bowl.

Stuff the lamb with one-third of the mixture, tuck in the ends and tie with string. Put the onions into a roasting tin, place the lamb on top, sprinkle with the lavender flowers and roast in the centre of the oven for 2 hours, basting frequently.

Meanwhile, with wet hands, shape the remaining stuffing into eight balls and place in a small, greased dish.

Remove the tin from the oven, lift the lamb onto a heated dish, cover loosely with foil and leave it for 30 minutes. Meanwhile, increase the oven temperature to 200°C (400°F, gas mark 6) and bake the stuffing balls for 30 minutes, or until golden and cooked through.

Skim the fat from the roasting tin. In a food processor, purée the onions with the juices from the tin and half the stock until smooth. Strain through a sieve into a saucepan and stir in the remaining stock, the wine, redcurrant jelly and any juices from round the lamb.

Blend the butter with the flour to form a smooth paste. Bring the gravy to the boil and gradually whisk in the paste until the gravy is smooth, glossy and slightly thickened. Reduce the heat, season to taste and simmer for 5 minutes.

Place the lamb, with string removed, on a bed of lavender on a heated serving dish. Garnish with the stuffing balls and serve with the onion gravy and vegetables.

A Very Satisfying Irish Stew

Any additions to the few ingredients in the dish would detract from the pure flavour and turn it into just another stew

ARRANGE half the meat in the bottom of a medium, flameproof casserole and cover with half the onions followed by half the potatoes, seasoning each layer well with salt and pepper and adding a little of the thyme. Repeat the layers, seasoning as before and finishing with a layer of potatoes. Pour over enough water to just cover the top layer of potatoes.

Bring to the boil, reduce the heat, cover and cook very gently for 1½ hours or until the meat and potatoes are tender. Check frequently to make sure that the water has not evaporated and add a little more if necessary. The cooked dish may be browned under the grill, if wished. Serve with the traditional accompaniment of red cabbage.

INGREDIENTS

900 G (2 LB) SCRAG END OR MIDDLE NECK OF LAMB, TRIMMED OF FAT
450 G (1 LB) ONIONS, PEELED AND SLICED
1.1 KG (2½ LB) POTATOES, PEELED AND SLICED
½ LEVEL TEASPOON SALT
FRESHLY GROUND BLACK PEPPER
1 TABLESPOON CHOPPED FRESH THYME
425 ML (¾ PINT) WATER
FRESH THYME SPRIGS TO GARNISH

PREPARATION TIME: 20 MINUTES
COOKING TIME: 1½–2 HOURS
SERVES FOUR

Tenderness and excellent flavour characterise lamb layered with onions, potatoes and thyme.

IRELAND'S OFFERING
It was Irish immigrants and seamen who brought Irish stew to Liverpool, where it rapidly became as popular as in the old country. In Ireland, it was made with kid because no one would dream of killing a valuable sheep. Liverpudlians, however, firmly preferred mutton.

Lancashire Hot Pot

Sealed with golden-brown potatoes, this is among the most English of stews

INGREDIENTS

- 8 BEST END NECK OF LAMB CUTLETS, TRIMMED OF EXCESS FAT
- 450 G (1 LB) ONIONS, PEELED AND SLICED
- 450 G (1 LB) CARROTS, PEELED AND SLICED
- SALT AND FRESHLY GROUND BLACK PEPPER
- 4 TABLESPOONS CHOPPED FRESH PARSLEY
- 12 FRESH OYSTERS, SHUCKED (SEE P.436)
- 900 G (2 LB) POTATOES, PEELED AND THINLY SLICED
- 425 ML (¾ PINT) CHICKEN STOCK (SEE P.433)
- 1 TABLESPOON FRESH THYME LEAVES
- 30 G (1 OZ) BUTTER

PREPARATION TIME: 30 MINUTES
COOKING TIME: 2½ HOURS
SERVES FOUR

PREHEAT the oven to 180°C (350°F, gas mark 4). Layer the lamb cutlets, onions and carrots in a large casserole, sprinkling each layer with some salt, pepper and chopped parsley. Put the oysters on top and spoon over their juices. Arrange the potatoes, overlapping in a double layer, on top of the oysters. Pour over the chicken stock and sprinkle with more salt and pepper and the thyme leaves.

Cover the casserole and cook the hot pot in the centre of the oven for 2 hours, then increase the oven temperature to 230°C (450°F, gas mark 8). Remove the lid from the casserole, dot the potatoes with the butter and continue cooking, uncovered, for a further 30 minutes or until the potatoes are golden.

Serve the hot pot accompanied by spring cabbage or curly kale.

OUR GRACIE
Born in Rochdale, Gracie Fields made Lancashire wit and grit world famous. Her repertoire ranged from *Ave Maria* to *The Biggest Aspidistra*, and she could make audiences laugh or cry at will. She died in 1979.

Reverting to tradition, this hot pot contains oysters as well as lamb and vegetables.

Flaky puff pastry conceals mouth-watering beef, kidneys, oysters and mushrooms.

Steak, Kidney & Oyster Pie

The addition of oysters adds a special savour to the pie, while Guinness gives body to the sauce

Heat 1 tablespoon of the oil in a heavy-based saucepan, add the onion and fry gently until softened, but not browned, then remove and put onto a plate.

Heat the remaining oil in the pan and fry the steak and kidney in batches until evenly browned. Remove the meat as it browns and put it with the onion.

Stir the flour into the pan, then gradually stir in the stock and Guinness. Bring to the boil, stirring and scraping any brown residue from the bottom of the pan. Return the meat and onion to the pan, adding any juices left on the plate. Bring to the boil, add the bouquet garni, then reduce the heat, cover and simmer very gently for 2 hours or until the meat is tender. Add the mushrooms and cook for 10 more minutes. Remove from the heat, cool, then chill overnight.

The next day, open the oysters and add them, with their juice, to the meat. Remove the bouquet garni, then season the meat and oysters and transfer them to a 1.2 litre (2¼ pint) pie dish. Add enough sauce to cover and reserve the remainder.

Roll out the pastry, on a floured surface, to 5 cm (2 in) larger than the top of the pie dish, then cut off a 2.5 cm (1 in) strip from round the edge.

Brush the edge of the pie dish with water, press the pastry strip onto it, then brush the strip with water. Cover the pie with the remaining pastry, pressing the edges together to seal. Trim and decorate the edge. Glaze with the beaten egg and make a small hole in the centre of the pastry. Chill while heating the oven to 230°C (450°F, gas mark 8).

Bake for 25–30 minutes, then cover the pie loosely with foil to prevent further browning. Reduce the oven temperature to 160°C (325°F, gas mark 3) and cook for a further 20–25 minutes until the pastry is cooked. Reheat the reserved sauce and serve separately with the pie.

INGREDIENTS

- 3 TABLESPOONS OLIVE OIL
- 1 ONION, PEELED AND CHOPPED
- 900 G (2 LB) BEEF SKIRT (BRAISING STEAK), TRIMMED AND CUT INTO 3.8 CM (1½ IN) CUBES
- 225 G (8 OZ) OX KIDNEY, SKINNED, CORED AND SLICED
- 3 LEVEL TABLESPOONS PLAIN FLOUR, SEASONED WITH SALT AND FRESHLY GROUND BLACK PEPPER
- 570 ML (1 PINT) BEEF STOCK (SEE P.432)
- 425 ML (¾ PINT) GUINNESS
- BOUQUET GARNI (SEE P.440)
- 115 G (4 OZ) FIELD, FLAT OR OPEN CUP MUSHROOMS, WIPED AND QUARTERED
- 6 OYSTERS
- 600 G (1 LB 5 OZ) PUFF PASTRY, HOMEMADE (SEE P.441) OR BOUGHT
- 1 EGG, SIZE 3, BEATEN

PREPARATION TIME:
DAY 1: 25 MINUTES, OR 4 HOURS IF MAKING PASTRY
DAY 2: 30 MINUTES

COOKING TIME:
DAY 1: APPROX 3 HOURS
DAY 2: 1 HOUR

SERVES SIX

Lobscouse

Having wandered the world, this seafaring stew has come home to Merseyside

INGREDIENTS

2 TABLESPOONS OLIVE OIL
900G (2LB) NECK OF LAMB FILLET, TRIMMED OF FAT, CUT INTO CUBES
12 SHALLOTS, PEELED AND ROUGHLY CHOPPED
340G (12OZ) CARROTS, PEELED AND DICED
340G (12OZ) SWEDE, PEELED AND DICED
2 LARGE CELERY STICKS, TRIMMED AND CHOPPED
1 LARGE LEEK, TRIMMED, WASHED AND CHOPPED
570ML (1 PINT) CHICKEN STOCK (SEE P.433)
SALT AND FRESHLY GROUND BLACK PEPPER
½ LEVEL TEASPOON DRIED SAGE
½ LEVEL TEASPOON DRIED ROSEMARY
900G (2LB) POTATOES, PEELED AND CUT INTO LARGE DICE

PREPARATION TIME: 45 MINUTES
COOKING TIME: 1 HOUR 50 MINUTES
SERVES FOUR

HEAT 1 tablespoon of the olive oil in a large heavy-based saucepan or flameproof casserole, add the lamb and fry it until evenly browned all over.

Meanwhile, heat the remaining oil in a frying pan, add the shallots, carrots, swede, celery and leek and fry gently for 2–3 minutes, then add to the lamb. Stir in the stock, season well with salt and pepper and add the dried herbs. Bring to the boil, then reduce the heat and cover. Simmer gently for an hour, or until the meat is almost tender.

Add the diced potatoes to the saucepan or casserole and continue cooking for 30–40 minutes until they are soft, and most of the stock has been absorbed—stir gently from time to time to ensure that the lobscouse does not stick to the pan. Serve at once, accompanied by crusty bread and pickled red cabbage, which counteracts the richness of the dish.

A mingling of juicy lamb, winter vegetables and herbs makes a cheery antidote to a chilly evening.

FERRY ACROSS THE MERSEY
'Scouse', minted from 'Lobscouse', has come to signify all things Liverpudlian and, not least, the kind of '60s sound that emanated from Gerry and the Pacemakers at The Cavern. The stew originated as a naval dish consumed on ships sailing to and from the port of Liverpool.

A novel and piquant sauce brings new life to an old way of using up leftovers.

Bubble and Squeak with Wow Wow Sauce

The many versions of bubble and squeak take their name from the murmurings and hissings of the ingredients in the frying pan

FIRST, make the sauce. Melt the butter in a saucepan and stir in the flour, then gradually stir in the stock or water and the vinegar. Bring to the boil, stirring continuously, then reduce the heat and simmer for 2 minutes. Stir in the mustard, parsley, walnuts, capers and chives and simmer for 2 minutes more. Remove the pan from the heat, cover and keep hot while cooking the bubble and squeak.

To make the bubble and squeak, season the slices of meat on both sides with salt, pepper and the ground allspice, then heat one tablespoon of the olive oil in a frying pan and fry the meat, a few slices at a time, for a few seconds on each side until golden brown—do not overcook as the meat will become tough. Transfer to a plate, cover and keep hot.

Heat the remaining oil and all the butter in the frying pan, add the chopped onion and cook gently for 3–4 minutes until softened. Mix in the cabbage and potatoes and stir, over a high heat, until heated through, scraping up any crispy bits from the bottom of the pan. Arrange the meat on top of the vegetables and serve directly from the pan with the sauce. If preferred, the vegetables can be transferred to a heated dish.

INGREDIENTS

FOR THE WOW WOW SAUCE

- 60 G (2 OZ) BUTTER
- 1 LEVEL TABLESPOON PLAIN FLOUR
- 285 ML (½ PINT) BEEF STOCK (SEE P.432) OR COOKING WATER FROM BOILED BEEF
- 1 TABLESPOON WHITE WINE VINEGAR
- 1 LEVEL TEASPOON DIJON MUSTARD, OR MADE ENGLISH MUSTARD
- 2 TABLESPOONS CHOPPED FRESH PARSLEY
- 5 LARGE PICKLED WALNUTS, ROUGHLY CHOPPED
- 2 TEASPOONS CAPERS, CHOPPED
- 1 TABLESPOON SNIPPED FRESH CHIVES

FOR THE BUBBLE AND SQUEAK

- 550 G (1¼ LB) LEFTOVER COLD BOILED SALT BEEF, ROAST BEEF, LAMB OR PORK—CUT INTO SLICES OR WIDE STRIPS
- SALT AND FRESHLY GROUND BLACK PEPPER
- ¼ LEVEL TEASPOON GROUND ALLSPICE
- 3 TABLESPOONS OLIVE OIL
- 30 G (1 OZ) BUTTER
- 1 LARGE ONION, PEELED AND FINELY CHOPPED
- 340 G (12 OZ) LEFTOVER COLD COOKED GREEN CABBAGE, CHOPPED
- 550 G (1¼ LB) LEFTOVER COLD BOILED POTATOES, CHOPPED

PREPARATION TIME: 25 MINUTES
COOKING TIME: 20 MINUTES
SERVES FOUR

Roast Leg of Pork with Apple Sauce

The apple sauce accompanying the familiar roast is just that little bit different with its spicy, herby background

Ingredients

- 2.7–3 kg (6–6½ lb) leg of pork
- 2–3 tablespoons olive oil
- 2 level teaspoons salt
- 2 fresh rosemary sprigs, broken into small pieces

For the potatoes

- 1.8 kg (4 lb) potatoes, peeled and halved or quartered, depending on size, scored deeply all over with a fork
- 1 level teaspoon salt
- 175 g (6 oz) lard

For the apple sauce

- 340 g (12 oz) cooking apples, peeled, cored and sliced
- 1 tablespoon water
- ¼ level teaspoon ground allspice
- 2 level teaspoons soft brown sugar
- 4 dessert apples, Cox or russet
- 2 tablespoons lemon juice
- 85 g (3 oz) butter
- 2 tablespoons chopped fresh sage

For the gravy

- 2 tablespoons plain flour
- 425 ml (¾ pint) chicken stock (see p.433)
- 1 tablespoon redcurrant or rowan jelly, homemade (see pp.401, 411) or bought
- 2 tablespoons dry sherry
- Fresh sage sprigs to garnish

Preparation time: 30 minutes
Cooking time: 3 hours
Serves eight

The Pork

Preheat the oven to 200°c (400°f, gas mark 6). Weigh the joint and calculate the cooking time allowing 25 minutes per 450 g (1 lb) plus 25 minutes.

Wipe the meat with kitchen paper then, using a very sharp knife, make scores in the skin diagonally across or vertically down 6–13 mm (¼–½ in) apart and about 3 mm (⅛ in) deep. Tie the joint securely with clean, thin string.

Put the meat into a roasting tin and, to encourage the skin to 'crackle', rub it all over with the olive oil, then rub in the salt and scatter with the rosemary.

Roast the pork in the centre of the oven for 30 minutes to start the skin crisping, then reduce the oven temperature to 180°c (350°f, gas mark 4). Baste every 30 minutes with the fat from the bottom of the tin, until well done.

The Potatoes

About 1 hour before the pork is due to come out of the oven, put the potatoes into a large saucepan, cover with cold water, add the salt and bring to the boil. Drain well, return to the pan and shake over a high heat for 1–2 minutes until dry.

In a roasting tin on the shelf above the pork, heat the lard until it sizzles, then add the potatoes, baste well and roast for 1¼ hours, until crisp and golden. When the pork is cooked, increase the oven temperature to 220°c (425°f, gas mark 7) and leave the potatoes to finish cooking while making the gravy.

The Apple Sauce

About 30 minutes before the end of the calculated cooking time, put the cooking apples into a small saucepan with the water, allspice and sugar. Cover and cook gently until soft and pulpy. Remove from the heat and mash with a fork. Peel and core the dessert apples, cut in half horizontally and brush each half all over with the lemon juice.

Melt the butter in a large frying pan, add the sage, then place the apple halves in the pan, cut sides up. Fill each half with the apple sauce and baste well with the sage butter. Cover the pan and cook gently for 10 minutes or until the apples are just softened, basting occasionally. Remove from the heat and keep warm.

The Gravy

At the end of the calculated cooking time, pierce the pork with a skewer at the thickest part. The juices should run clear with no trace of pink. If necessary, continue roasting until done.

Lift the cooked pork from the roasting tin onto a large, heated serving plate, cover loosely with foil and allow to stand while making the gravy.

Skim off all but 2 tablespoons of the fat from the roasting tin, then stir the flour into the fat and juices remaining in the tin. Cook over a moderate heat until well browned but not burnt. Gradually add the chicken stock and bring to the boil stirring continuously and scraping the browned residue from the bottom of the tin. Strain the gravy through a fine sieve into a saucepan, then blend in the redcurrant or rowan jelly and the dry sherry, simmer for 5 minutes and season with salt and pepper to taste.

Remove the string from the pork and arrange the apple halves round the joint. Garnish with the sprigs of sage and serve with the roast potatoes, buttered cabbage or spring greens, and the gravy.

Smaller or larger joints of pork, such as loin, hand and spring, shoulder or neck can be cooked in the same way.

Apples and sage combine perfectly with the flavour of the succulent roast pork to make it both aromatic and appetising.

Saddle of Lamb Stuffed with Crab

A saddle of lamb is traditionally both loins joined together in a single piece. Here, unusually, it is wrapped round crabmeat

INGREDIENTS

1 SADDLE OF LAMB APPROX 1.8 KG (4 LB), SKINNED AND BONED
1 TABLESPOON OLIVE OIL
285 ML (½ PINT) DRY WHITE WINE OR CHICKEN STOCK (SEE P.433)

FOR THE STUFFING
225 G (8 OZ) FRESH WHITE CRABMEAT OR FROZEN CRABMEAT, THAWED
60 G (2 OZ) FRESH WHITE BREADCRUMBS
50 G (1¾ OZ) TINNED ANCHOVY FILLETS, DRAINED AND CHOPPED, OIL RESERVED
1 TABLESPOON CAPERS
2 TABLESPOONS CHOPPED FRESH PARSLEY OR MARJORAM
1 EGG YOLK, SIZE 2
FRESHLY GROUND BLACK PEPPER

FOR THE GARNISH (OPTIONAL)
50 G (1¾ OZ) TINNED ANCHOVY FILLETS, DRAINED
1 TABLESPOON CAPERS
FRESH MARJORAM OR PARSLEY SPRIGS

PREPARATION TIME: 20 MINUTES
COOKING TIME: 1½ HOURS
SERVES SIX TO EIGHT

The stuffing will have a much better flavour if meat picked from a fresh crab is used.

PREHEAT the oven to 200°C (400°F, gas mark 6). To make the stuffing, put all the ingredients, including the anchovy oil, into a bowl and mix well. Lay the meat out flat, fat side down, on a work surface and spread the stuffing over the middle section. Fold the side flaps of lamb over the stuffing to enclose it completely, trimming off the sides if there is surplus. Using fine string, tie the saddle at 2.5 cm (1 in) intervals along its length.

Weigh the lamb, put it into a roasting tin and rub all over with the olive oil. Roast near the top of the oven for about 1½ hours, basting frequently. (Calculate 20 minutes per 450 g (1 lb) stuffed weight for slightly pink lamb or 25–30 minutes for well done.) Halfway through cooking, pour over the wine or stock.

When the lamb is cooked, remove from the oven and transfer to a serving platter. Cover loosely with foil and allow to stand for 20 minutes. Meanwhile, skim off any excess fat from the roasting tin, then strain the juices through a fine sieve into a saucepan.

Garnish the lamb—simply with a bunch of marjoram or, if preferred, more decoratively with a lattice of anchovy fillets, the capers and fresh marjoram or parsley. Reheat the juices, pour round the lamb and serve. The Welsh onion and potato cake on p.107 and fine green beans make good accompaniments.

Lamb with a shellfish and anchovy stuffing forms a successful combination of textures and flavours.

A clove-studded golden glaze makes juicy gammon look especially appetising.

Home range
Even after the advent of gas and electricity, many cooks still clung loyally to their coal-fired ranges. Despite the chores of lighting and cleaning, there is no doubt that the later models at least bestowed great benefits both in versatility and in evenness of heat.

Gammon in a Huff Crust

Cooking in a huff crust is the forerunner of cooking in foil—it keeps in the flavour and prevents the meat from drying out

Preheat the oven to 180°C (350°F, gas mark 4). Press the peppercorns or herbs, if using, over the cut sides of the gammon to add extra flavour.

Gradually mix the flour with just enough cold water to form a stiff dough—if it is too soft it will split and tear. Roll out the dough to about 6 mm (¼ in) thick, and large enough to completely wrap round the gammon.

Place the gammon in the centre of the dough, then bring the sides up and over it. Brush the joins with cold water and pinch together to seal securely. Put the gammon into a roasting tin and bake in the centre of the oven for 3 hours. For a smaller or larger joint, allow 30 minutes per 450 g (1 lb) plus 30 minutes extra.

Remove from the oven and leave to cool. Then, with a knife, carefully break open the crust and discard it—the skin should come away with the crust.

Serve hot or cold. Alternatively, to glaze the gammon, turn the oven up to 230°C (450°F, gas mark 8). While the gammon is still hot, score the fat in a diamond pattern and coat with the brown sugar mixed with the mustard. Press the cloves into the diamonds and bake in the oven for 5–10 minutes until well glazed.

INGREDIENTS

- 2.3 KG (5 LB) SMOKED OR UNSMOKED MIDDLE GAMMON JOINT
- 2 TABLESPOONS MIXED PEPPERCORNS, CRUSHED OR MIXED HERBS, CHOPPED (OPTIONAL)
- 450 G (1 LB) PLAIN WHITE FLOUR

For the glaze (optional)
- 60 G (2 OZ) SOFT DARK BROWN SUGAR
- 1 LEVEL TABLESPOON MUSTARD POWDER
- APPROX 20 CLOVES

Preparation time: 30 MINUTES
Cooking time: 3 HOURS PLUS 5–10 MINUTES GLAZING (OPTIONAL)
Serves ten to twelve

Collared Pork with Pickled Walnuts

This old method of preserving cooked meat in a flavoursome wet pickle was so called because it was tied up in the shape of a collar

INGREDIENTS

FOR THE STUFFING

- 85G (3OZ) FRESH WHITE BREADCRUMBS
- FINELY GRATED RIND 1 LEMON
- 100G (3½OZ) PICKLED WALNUTS, CHOPPED
- 3 TABLESPOONS CHOPPED FRESH PARSLEY
- 3 TABLESPOONS CHOPPED FRESH MARJORAM
- 3 TABLESPOONS SNIPPED FRESH CHIVES
- ½ LEVEL TEASPOON FRESHLY GRATED NUTMEG OR GROUND NUTMEG
- ½ LEVEL TEASPOON GROUND GINGER
- ½ LEVEL TEASPOON SALT
- ½ LEVEL TEASPOON FRESHLY GROUND BLACK PEPPER
- 1 EGG, SIZE 4

FOR THE COLLARED PORK

- 1 HAND OF PORK, APPROX 2.3KG (5LB), BONED, BONES RESERVED
- 2 LITRES (3½ PINTS) COLD WATER
- 1 CARROT, SCRUBBED AND SLICED
- 1 ONION, PEELED AND SLICED
- 1 CELERY STICK, TRIMMED AND SLICED
- 2 BAY LEAVES
- ¼ TEASPOON BLACK PEPPERCORNS
- 285ML (½ PINT) MALT VINEGAR
- 6 TABLESPOONS CHOPPED FRESH PARSLEY
- 2 TABLESPOONS CHOPPED FRESH MARJORAM
- LETTUCE LEAVES, PICKLED WALNUTS AND RADISHES TO GARNISH

PREPARATION TIME: 30 MINUTES
COOKING TIME: 2 HOURS
MARINATING TIME: 3 DAYS
SERVES SIX

TO MAKE the stuffing, combine all the ingredients in a bowl. Lay the pork, skin side down, on a work surface and put the stuffing into the space formerly occupied by the bone. Fold the pork over the stuffing and shape into a roll. Tie with string at 3.8cm (1½in) intervals, keeping a neat shape.

Put the stuffed, rolled joint into a large saucepan or flameproof casserole with the reserved bones. Pour over enough cold water to just cover the meat, bring to the boil, then reduce the heat and skim off any scum from the surface.

Add the carrot, onion, celery, bay leaves and peppercorns and cover the saucepan or casserole. Simmer gently for 2 hours or until the meat feels tender when pierced with a skewer.

When the pork is cooked, remove from the stock and let it cool. Strain the stock into a bowl through a sieve lined with kitchen paper and leave to cool.

Put the pork into a deep (preferably oval) dish, just large enough to hold it comfortably. Measure 850ml (1½ pints) of the stock and stir in the vinegar. Pour over the pork. (If not completely covered, add more liquid in the ratio of one part vinegar to three parts stock.) Cover and leave for three days in the refrigerator.

To serve, remove the pork from the marinade, pat dry with kitchen paper and remove the string and the skin. Mix the parsley and marjoram, then coat the pork completely with the mixture. Slice the roll and garnish with the lettuce leaves, pickled walnuts and radishes.

Hand of pork is stuffed with a spicy concoction of pickled walnuts, herbs and ginger.

Cooks in the know add the luxury of Madeira to the old supper favourite, liver and bacon, so making it even more tempting.

Keeping the rules
Rule's restaurant has stood in London's Maiden Lane since 1798, and is as famous for its theatrical memorabilia as for its traditional English fare. Among its patrons were the future Edward VII and Lillie Langtry who had their own private entrance built for them.

Liver, Bacon & Onions with Sage & Madeira Sauce

This is not only a mouth-watering dish—it is also very easy to prepare and cook when you want to rustle up a meal quickly

Heat 1 tablespoon of the oil in a large frying pan, fry the bacon rashers until lightly browned on both sides, drain on kitchen paper and keep warm.

Add the remaining oil to the pan and fry the onions until lightly browned, then push them to the side of the pan.

Meanwhile, on a plate, mix the flour with the salt and pepper. Dip the liver, a slice at a time, in the seasoned flour until evenly coated, shaking off the excess.

Add the butter to the pan and heat over a moderate heat until sizzling. Add the liver, sprinkle with half the sage leaves and fry for 2 minutes until lightly browned then cook the other side, sprinkling with the remaining sage. Remove the liver from the pan and set aside.

Stir any remaining flour into the pan, pour over the Madeira and stir well to deglaze. Add the stock and bring to the boil, stirring occasionally. Return the liver to the pan, reduce the heat and simmer gently for 4–5 minutes or until the liver is tender but still slightly pink.

Return the bacon to the pan and serve immediately with rice or mashed potatoes and a green vegetable.

INGREDIENTS

- 2 TABLESPOONS OLIVE OIL
- 4 RASHERS BACK BACON, RINDS REMOVED
- 2 MEDIUM ONIONS, PEELED AND THINLY SLICED
- 2 LEVEL TABLESPOONS PLAIN FLOUR
- ½ LEVEL TEASPOON SALT
- ¼ LEVEL TEASPOON FRESHLY GROUND BLACK PEPPER
- 450G (1 LB) LAMB'S LIVER, CUT INTO 4 THIN SLICES
- 30G (1 OZ) BUTTER
- 16 LARGE SAGE LEAVES
- 6 TABLESPOONS MADEIRA
- 285ML (½ PINT) CHICKEN STOCK (SEE P.433)

PREPARATION TIME: 10 MINUTES
COOKING TIME: 15 MINUTES
SERVES FOUR

Unglazed and thinly sliced, the roll makes an excellent sandwich filling with salad and chutney.

Mrs Biggs' Beef & Bacon Roll

The rich, meaty flavour is augmented by spices and black pepper

INGREDIENTS

- 450 G (1 LB) BEEF SKIRT, MINCED
- 340 G (12 OZ) SMOKED STREAKY BACON, RINDS REMOVED, MINCED
- 225 G (8 OZ) FRESH WHITE BREADCRUMBS
- 1½ LEVEL TEASPOONS SALT
- ½ LEVEL TEASPOON FRESHLY GROUND BLACK PEPPER
- ½ LEVEL TEASPOON FRESHLY GRATED NUTMEG
- ½–1 LEVEL TEASPOON GROUND MIXED SPICE
- 2 EGGS, SIZE 2, BEATEN
- 150 ML (¼ PINT) ASPIC JELLY (SEE P.434)
- FRESH THYME AND PARSLEY SPRIGS TO GARNISH

PREPARATION TIME: 45 MINUTES
COOKING TIME: 2 HOURS
CHILLING TIME: OVERNIGHT
SERVES SIX

PUT all the ingredients, except the aspic jelly and herbs, into a bowl and mix well. Spoon onto a large sheet of double-thickness greaseproof paper and mould to a sausage shape, about 23 cm (9 in) long. Roll up in the greaseproof, then wrap in double-thickness foil, twisting the ends tightly to seal.

Immerse the roll in boiling water and cook gently for 2 hours, turning every 30 minutes. Remove from the water, allow to cool, then put into the refrigerator to chill overnight, still wrapped.

The next day, unwrap the roll and put it onto a wire rack set over a tray. Chill the aspic jelly until it becomes syrupy, then brush it evenly all over the roll. Chill until set, then brush once more with the aspic jelly.

Garnish with the thyme and parsley and serve, sliced, with creamed potatoes, beetroot salad and tomato pickle.

Veal Loaf with Mushroom Sauce

A profusion of textures and flavours is completed by mushroom sauce

PREHEAT the oven to 180°C (350°F, gas mark 4). Line a loaf tin 21.5 × 11.5 × 6 cm (8½ × 4½ × 2½ in) with nonstick baking paper, then arrange the carrot and courgette sticks in an attractive pattern in the bottom of the tin.

Put the minced veal into a large bowl and add the bacon, breadcrumbs, mushrooms, lemon rind, mace, cayenne, salt to taste and the egg. Mix well together and then spoon the mixture carefully on top of the layer of vegetables in the loaf tin. Press down gently and smooth the top.

Bake in the centre of the oven for 50 minutes to 1 hour or until the point of a skewer inserted into the centre of the loaf is hot enough when removed to sting the back of your hand. Remove the tin from the oven, pour the juices carefully into a measuring jug and make up to 285 ml (½ pint) with milk. Turn out the loaf onto a serving dish and keep warm by covering with the tin.

Melt the butter in a saucepan and cook the mushrooms for 2–3 minutes. Stir in the flour, cook for 1 minute, then gradually add the milk and cooking juice mixture. Bring to the boil, stirring continuously until thickened. Season the sauce with salt and pepper, then simmer gently for 5 minutes.

Remove the tin from the loaf and garnish with the sage leaves. Serve the sauce from a heated sauceboat.

The loaf can be made with lean, minced pork if preferred.

INGREDIENTS

- 115G (4OZ) BABY CARROTS, HALVED LENGTHWAYS
- 2–3 BABY COURGETTES, HALVED WIDTHWAYS, THEN QUARTERED
- 800G (1¾ LB) BRITISH VEAL, MINCED
- 225G (8OZ) BACON, RINDS REMOVED, CHOPPED
- 60G (2OZ) FRESH WHITE BREADCRUMBS
- 60G (2OZ) BUTTON MUSHROOMS, WIPED AND CHOPPED
- FINELY GRATED RIND ½ LEMON
- ½ LEVEL TEASPOON GROUND MACE
- ¼ LEVEL TEASPOON CAYENNE PEPPER
- SALT
- 1 EGG, SIZE 2, BEATEN
- 175–225ML (6–8FL OZ) MILK
- 30G (1OZ) BUTTER
- 60G (2OZ) BUTTON MUSHROOMS, WIPED AND SLICED
- 1 LEVEL TABLESPOON PLAIN FLOUR
- FRESH SAGE LEAVES TO GARNISH

PREPARATION TIME: 30 MINUTES
COOKING TIME: 1 HOUR
SERVES SIX

A topping of sliced carrots and courgettes adds colour to this substantial dish.

If you don't have a mincer, then chop the meat finely in a food processor.

Loin of Pork with Sage & Onion Stuffing

Sultanas and apples enrich the sage and onion stuffing

INGREDIENTS

- 30G (1OZ) BUTTER
- 275G (10OZ) ONIONS, PEELED AND CHOPPED
- 2 GREEN CELERY STICKS, TRIMMED AND CHOPPED
- 1 TABLESPOON CHOPPED FRESH SAGE
- 225G (8OZ) COOKING APPLES, PEELED, CORED AND CHOPPED
- 175G (6OZ) FRESH WHITE BREADCRUMBS
- 60G (2OZ) SULTANAS OR READY-TO-USE PRUNES, CHOPPED
- SALT AND FRESHLY GROUND BLACK PEPPER
- 1 EGG, SIZE 2, BEATEN
- 1.6–1.8KG (3½–4LB) RIB END LOIN OF PORK, BONED, SKIN REMOVED AND RESERVED
- 2 LEVEL TABLESPOONS PLAIN FLOUR
- 285ML (½ PINT) BEEF OR VEGETABLE STOCK (SEE PP.432, 434)
- 85ML (3FL OZ) RED WINE
- 1 TABLESPOON REDCURRANT OR ROWAN JELLY, HOMEMADE (SEE PP.401, 411) OR BOUGHT
- FRESH SAGE AND PARSLEY SPRIGS TO GARNISH

PREPARATION TIME: 30 MINUTES
COOKING TIME: 2 HOURS
SERVES SIX

PREHEAT the oven to 190°C (375°F, gas mark 5). Melt the butter in a frying pan, add the onions and cook gently until soft and golden. Put the onions into a bowl and add the celery, sage, chopped apple, breadcrumbs and the sultanas or prunes. Season well, then mix in just sufficient beaten egg to bind the mixture together.

Make a deep horizontal cut the whole length of the thickest part of the loin, open out flat and season well with salt and pepper. Spread the stuffing evenly over the meat, then roll up and tie securely with fine string at 2.5cm (1in) intervals along its entire length. Put into a roasting tin, cover with the reserved skin and cook in the centre of the oven, allowing 30 minutes per 450g (1lb) of meat. Remove the pork skin for the last 30 minutes of cooking time and baste frequently with the pan juices until the pork is cooked and browned and the juices run clear when the meat is tested with a skewer. Transfer from the roasting tin to a heated serving plate and keep hot.

Skim all but 1 tablespoon of the fat from the juices remaining in the roasting tin. Stir the flour into the juices and gradually stir in the stock and red wine. Bring to the boil, stirring continuously, then reduce the heat, stir in the redcurrant or rowan jelly, season well and cook for 5 minutes. Strain the gravy through a sieve into a heated gravy boat.

Remove the string from the pork, garnish with the fresh sage and parsley and serve with the gravy, creamed potatoes and buttered red or green cabbage.

The pork skin, after removal, can be basted with the meat to make delicious crackling.

Make any leftover stuffing into balls and cook alongside the loin for the last 20 minutes.

The rich, sweet, herby flavour of hay is absorbed by the lamb and permeates the dark, succulent juices left in the casserole.

TOMMY COOKER
Hay boxes proved their efficiency as makeshift ovens in the First World War. They were constructed from packing cases that were lined with newspapers and packed with hay. The hot dixie containing the food was placed inside and more hay piled on top.

Lamb Baked in Hay with Herbs

A dough-sealed casserole captures the authentic taste of country cooking

PREHEAT the oven to 180°C (350°F, gas mark 4). Take a large, heavy casserole that will accommodate the lamb fairly easily and place a thick layer of hay in the bottom. Season the lamb joint well with salt and pepper. (If necessary, remove some fat from the lamb.) Lay half the fresh herbs over the hay, place the lamb on top, add the remaining herbs and enough hay to cover thickly. Place the lid on the casserole.

Mix the flour with the water to make a smooth, pliable dough and roll into a long sausage. Wet the edges of the casserole and lid and press the dough round the join to seal. If necessary, make a little more dough to seal the lid. Bake in the centre of the oven for 2 hours. If cooking a smaller or larger leg of lamb, allow 20 minutes per 450 g (1 lb) plus 20 minutes.

Remove the casserole from the oven and allow to rest for 10 minutes. Break the dough seal and remove the lid. Remove and discard the top layer of hay and lift the lamb onto a warm serving dish. Strain the juices from the casserole, skim off any fat and serve the juices with the lamb. This dish is usually accompanied by puréed vegetables and plainly cooked potatoes.

INGREDIENTS

- A FEW HANDFULS OF FRESH, CLEAN HAY (AVAILABLE FROM PET SHOPS)
- 2.3 KG (5 LB) LEG OF LAMB
- SALT AND FRESHLY GROUND BLACK PEPPER
- 3 LARGE FRESH ROSEMARY SPRIGS
- 4 LARGE FRESH THYME SPRIGS
- 225 G (8 OZ) PLAIN FLOUR
- 285 ML (½ PINT) WATER

PREPARATION TIME: 15 MINUTES
COOKING TIME: 2 HOURS
SERVES SIX

Lamb Cutlets Reform

Chef Alexis Soyer created this classic dish at the Reform Club in Pall Mall

INGREDIENTS

FOR THE SAUCE REFORM
- 2 TABLESPOONS VEGETABLE OIL
- 250G (9OZ) MILD ONIONS, PEELED AND FINELY CHOPPED
- 150G (5OZ) CARROTS, PEELED AND FINELY DICED
- 1 CELERY STICK, TRIMMED AND DICED
- 2 LEVEL TABLESPOONS PLAIN FLOUR
- 2 TABLESPOONS RED WINE VINEGAR
- 150ML (1/4 PINT) PORT
- 425ML (3/4 PINT) WHITE WINE
- 4 JUNIPER BERRIES, CRUSHED
- BOUQUET GARNI (SEE P.440)
- 10 BLACK PEPPERCORNS, CRUSHED
- 2 LITRES (3½ PINTS) GOOD BEEF STOCK (SEE P.432)
- SALT
- 1 TABLESPOON REDCURRANT JELLY

FOR THE CUTLETS
- 15G (½ OZ) HAM, CHOPPED
- 15G (½ OZ) TONGUE, CHOPPED
- 1 TABLESPOON CHOPPED FRESH PARSLEY
- 225G (8OZ) FRESH WHITE BREADCRUMBS
- 18 BEST END NECK OF LAMB CUTLETS WITH LONG BONES, CHINED
- 60G (2OZ) PLAIN FLOUR, WELL SEASONED WITH SALT AND PEPPER
- 1–2 EGGS, SIZE 2, BEATEN
- 150ML (1/4 PINT) VEGETABLE OIL

FOR THE GARNISH
- 30G (1OZ) EACH COOKED HAM, TONGUE, GHERKINS, HARD-BOILED EGG WHITE, BEETROOT AND TRUFFLES, ALL CUT INTO FINE SHREDS (ALTHOUGH PART OF THE CLASSIC GARNISH, TRUFFLES MAY BE OMITTED)
- REDCURRANT JELLY TO SERVE

COOKING TIME: 2½ HOURS FOR SAUCE (MOSTLY UNATTENDED), 6 MINUTES FOR CUTLETS

SERVES SIX

TO MAKE the sauce, heat the oil in a large saucepan, add the onions, carrots and celery and cook over a moderate heat for 10 minutes or until very brown, but not burnt, stirring frequently. Stir in the flour and cook for 1 minute. Add the vinegar, port, wine, juniper berries, bouquet garni, peppercorns and stock. Bring to the boil, reduce the heat and simmer, uncovered, for 2 hours, stirring occasionally.

Strain through a fine sieve or muslin into a clean saucepan, pressing the vegetables to squeeze out the juice. You will have about 1.15 litres (2 pints). Reduce to 570 ml (1 pint) by boiling fast, then taste and season. Stir in the redcurrant jelly and keep warm.

Mix the chopped ham, tongue and parsley with the breadcrumbs. Using a small sharp knife, ruthlessly trim the cutlets of any fat or gristle and scrape the bones clean to look very elegant with just the 'eye' of the meat clinging to the bone. Coat the cutlets with the seasoned flour, then brush with the beaten egg and coat with the breadcrumb mixture, pressing it neatly over each cutlet. Put onto a plate and chill for 15 minutes.

Meanwhile, heat the oil in a frying pan and fry the cutlets gently for about 3 minutes on each side until golden brown on the outside, but still slightly pink in the middle. Drain on kitchen paper, then arrange on a heated serving platter. Arrange the garnish ingredients round the cutlets and spoon over a little of the sauce. Serve the remaining sauce in a warm sauceboat.

Lamb cutlets coated in an unusual breadcrumb mixture are served with a rich wine sauce.

A marinade of wine, herbs and honey makes this casseroled lamb an aristocrat among stews.

Alnwick Stew

The recipe originated in Alnwick Castle, for centuries the home of the earls and dukes of Northumberland

Lay the steaks in a large, shallow dish. Put all the ingredients for the marinade, except the clove-studded onion, into a saucepan and bring to the boil. Reduce the heat and simmer gently for 5 minutes. Pour the marinade over the meat, add the clove-studded onion and leave to cool, then cover and put into the refrigerator or a cold larder to marinate overnight.

The following day, preheat the oven to 150°C (300°F, gas mark 2). Lift the meat out of the marinade and pat it dry with kitchen paper. Reserve the marinade.

Heat the butter in a flameproof casserole, add the meat and fry for 2–3 minutes on each side. Remove from the casserole, put onto a plate and set aside. Add the chopped onion to the casserole and cook for a few minutes until softened, then add the split peas. Strain the marinade into the casserole, put in the clove-studded onion and bring to the boil. Discard the remaining marinade ingredients.

Return the lamb, and any juices, to the casserole, cover and cook in the oven for 2½ hours, adding the potatoes 50 minutes before the end of the cooking time and, if necessary, a little more water or wine. Remove and discard the clove-studded onion, then taste and adjust the seasoning. Serve from the casserole or transfer to a serving dish. Serve with spinach.

INGREDIENTS

6 LEG OF LAMB (GIGOT) STEAKS, EACH APPROX 225G (8OZ), TRIMMED OF FAT

FOR THE MARINADE

- 2 CELERY STICKS, TRIMMED AND CHOPPED
- 1 FRESH ROSEMARY SPRIG
- 2 FRESH THYME SPRIGS
- 4 BAY LEAVES
- 1 TEASPOON BLACK PEPPERCORNS
- 1 LEVEL TEASPOON SALT
- 425ML (¾ PINT) FULL BODIED RED WINE
- 285ML (½ PINT) WATER
- 2 TABLESPOONS HONEY
- 1 ONION, PEELED AND STUDDED WITH 5 CLOVES

FOR THE STEW

- 30G (1OZ) BUTTER
- 1 LARGE ONION, PEELED AND CHOPPED
- 115G (4OZ) DRIED SPLIT GREEN PEAS, WELL RINSED AND DRAINED
- 675G (1½LB) NEW POTATOES OR SMALL WHOLE POTATOES, PEELED
- SALT AND FRESHLY GROUND BLACK PEPPER

PREPARATION TIME: 45 MINUTES PLUS OVERNIGHT MARINATING OF THE MEAT

COOKING TIME: 2½ HOURS

SERVES SIX

The rich oxtail sits expansively on a bed of succulent root vegetables.

Oxtail Braised with Red Wine

Cooked slowly in red wine, the meat becomes so tender that it falls off the bone

INGREDIENTS

2 LEVEL TABLESPOONS PLAIN FLOUR
1/4 LEVEL TEASPOON SALT
1/4 LEVEL TEASPOON GROUND BLACK PEPPER
1 OXTAIL, APPROX 1.1 KG (2 1/2 LB), CUT INTO 8–10 PIECES
30 G (1 OZ) DRIPPING OR 2 TABLESPOONS OLIVE OIL
2 LARGE ONIONS, PEELED AND SLICED
200 G (7 OZ) CARROTS, PEELED AND SLICED
200 G (7 OZ) SWEDE, PEELED AND DICED
200 G (7 OZ) PARSNIPS, PEELED AND DICED
2 CELERY STICKS, TRIMMED AND SLICED
1 LARGE LEEK, TRIMMED, SLICED AND WASHED
150 ML (1/4 PINT) RED WINE
285 ML (1/2 PINT) WATER
BOUQUET GARNI MADE WITH BAY LEAVES, PARSLEY, THYME AND MARJORAM (SEE P.440)

FOR THE GARNISH
60 G (2 OZ) EACH CARROT, PARSNIP, SWEDE AND CELERY, CUT INTO VERY FINE STRIPS
2 TABLESPOONS CHOPPED FRESH PARSLEY

PREPARATION TIME: 30 MINUTES
COOKING TIME: 2 1/2–3 HOURS
SERVES FOUR

Preheat the oven to 150°C (300°F, gas mark 2). Mix the flour, salt and pepper together on a plate, add the oxtail and coat well with the seasoned flour. Heat the dripping or oil in a large, flameproof casserole and fry the oxtail until browned all over, then remove from the pan.

Add the vegetables and sauté over a moderate heat for 10 minutes, stirring occasionally. Increase the heat and fry for a couple of minutes to brown lightly. Add the wine, stir to deglaze the casserole, then add the water. Bring to the boil, stirring, then remove from the heat.

Place the oxtail on top of the vegetables, tuck in the bouquet garni and cover the top with a butter wrapper (butter side down) or a piece of buttered greaseproof paper. Cook in the centre of the oven for 2½–3 hours until the oxtail is tender.

To serve, transfer the oxtail to a heated plate and keep warm. Using a slotted spoon, lift the vegetables out of the casserole and arrange them on a heated serving platter. Arrange the oxtail on top of the vegetables. Pour the red wine sauce over the meat and vegetables, cover the platter and keep warm.

Bring a small saucepan of water to the boil, add the vegetable strips for the garnish and boil for 1–2 minutes. Drain through a sieve and sprinkle over the meat. Garnish with the chopped parsley and serve immediately.

Beef Braised with Stout

The use of a flour-and-water paste to seal the casserole is an old cooking technique that ensures no flavour or moisture is lost

PREHEAT the oven to 150°C (300°F, gas mark 2). Bring the stout to the boil in a pan and boil vigorously until reduced to 225 ml (8 fl oz). Cover the bottom of a heavy casserole with the sliced onions, then place the carrots on top, followed by the beef, button onions and the pork. Tie the herbs and allspice in a small square of muslin and bury this in the casserole with the garlic. Bring the reduced stout to the boil and pour into the casserole, then season with a little salt and lots of pepper. Little liquid will be visible at this stage.

Put the flour into a bowl and mix with the water to make a smooth, pliable dough. Roll the dough into a long sausage. Place the lid on the casserole, wet the edges with a little water and seal the join with the dough. Cook in the centre of the oven for 3 hours.

Remove the casserole from the oven and break the dough seal. Remove and discard the muslin bag of herbs, stir the meat and vegetables together carefully and serve immediately with potatoes and a green vegetable—brussels sprouts, say.

Rich and mellow, the casserole is flavoured with stout, vegetables, herbs and spices.

INGREDIENTS

- 850 ML (1½ PINTS) STOUT
- 2 MEDIUM ONIONS, PEELED AND SLICED
- 340 G (12 OZ) YOUNG CARROTS, SCRAPED AND SLICED, OR LARGE CARROTS, PEELED AND CUT INTO LARGE CHUNKS
- 1.4 KG (3 LB) THICK-CUT SHIN OF BEEF OR BEEF SKIRT, TRIMMED OF FAT AND CUT INTO CUBES
- 225 G (8 OZ) BUTTON ONIONS, SKINNED
- 115 G (4 OZ) BELLY OF PORK, THICKLY SLICED
- A FEW THYME SPRIGS
- 6 PARSLEY STALKS
- 1 BAY LEAF
- 6 ALLSPICE BERRIES, CRUSHED
- 1 GARLIC CLOVE, PEELED AND BRUISED
- SALT AND FRESHLY GROUND BLACK PEPPER
- 225 G (8 OZ) PLAIN FLOUR
- 150 ML (¼ PINT) WATER

PREPARATION TIME: 40 MINUTES
COOKING TIME: 3 HOURS
SERVES SIX

STOUT PARTY
Hall's Oxford Brewery's 'Oxford Eight', was one of a number of English stouts that were popular between the wars. Gradually, however, dominated by Guinness and others, this type of ale became very largely an Irish speciality.

Personalise the meat-filled pasties by initialling them with leftover scraps of dough.

INGREDIENTS

Cornish Pasties
For the Pastry
340 g (12 oz) plain flour
Pinch of salt
85 g (3 oz) butter
85 g (3 oz) lard or white vegetable fat
Approx 4 tablespoons chilled water to mix
Milk for brushing

For the Filling
340 g (12 oz) lean braising steak, trimmed of fat and cut into small dice
225 g (8 oz) potatoes, peeled and cut into small dice
115 g (4 oz) turnip, peeled and cut into small dice
115 g (4 oz) onion, peeled and finely chopped
1 level teaspoon salt
Freshly ground black pepper
60 g (2 oz) butter, cut into small dice
2 tablespoons water

Bridies
For the Pastry
As for Cornish pasties above

For the Filling
550 g (1¼ lb) lean braising steak, trimmed of fat and cut into small dice
225 g (8 oz) onions, peeled and finely chopped
85 g (3 oz) fresh beef suet, finely grated or shredded beef suet
1 level teaspoon salt
¼ level teaspoon mustard powder
Freshly ground black pepper
1 egg, size 3, beaten, to glaze

Preparation time: 1 hour
Cooking time: 1¼ hours
Makes six of each pasty

Pasties

These hearty meals in pastry cases, one originating in the Highlands of Scotland and the other in England's South-west, are universal favourites

To make the pastry, sift the flour and salt into a mixing bowl, rub in the fats until the mixture resembles fine breadcrumbs then mix with the chilled water to make a firm dough. Wrap and chill the dough and prepare the filling while preheating the oven to 220°c (425°f, gas mark 7).

CORNISH PASTIES

To make Cornish pasties, mix the filling ingredients in a bowl. Roll out the dough to about 3 mm (⅛ in) thick and cut out as many 18–20 cm (7–8 in) rounds as possible, using a saucer or teaplate as a guide. Reknead and reroll the trimmings until you have cut six rounds.

Divide the filling into six and spoon a portion onto the centre of each round. Brush the edges of the dough with milk, bring the two opposite sides together to meet over the centre of the filling and press well to seal, then crimp with your fingers to make the traditional Cornish pasty shape.

Brush with milk and bake, on a greased baking sheet, for 15 minutes. Reduce the oven temperature to 180°c (350°f, gas mark 4) and bake for 1 hour more. If the pasties brown too quickly, cover loosely with foil. Serve hot with cooked vegetables, or cold with salad.

BRIDIES

To make bridies, mix the filling ingredients, then roll and cut out the dough as for pasties above. Spoon some filling onto one half of each round, brush the edges with water and fold in half to enclose the filling. Press the edges together to seal and decorate by marking with a teaspoon or fork handle. Glaze with the beaten egg and bake as for the Cornish pasties.

Mittoon of Pork

The mittoon was served to Charles II, yet closely resembles the modern terrine

PREHEAT the oven to 160°C (325°F, gas mark 3). Melt the butter in a saucepan, add the onion and cook gently until softened. Stir in the mushrooms, cook for a further 4 minutes, then remove the pan from the heat.

Finely mince the pork and liver, or chop them finely in a food processor. Put them into a bowl, add the onion and mushroom mixture, breadcrumbs, herbs, seasoning, sherry and the beaten eggs and mix thoroughly.

Lay the bacon rashers on a board, stretch them with the back of a knife and use them to line a 2.3 litre (4 pint) terrine or nonstick loaf tin.

Cutting horizontally lengthways, cut each tenderloin almost in half. Open out and place each one between two sheets of cling film. Flatten with a mallet or rolling pin until it is the same shape and size as the terrine or tin.

Place one piece of tenderloin in the bottom of the lined terrine or loaf tin. Spread the minced pork mixture evenly on top, then cover with the second piece.

Wrap the terrine or loaf tin completely in at least two layers of foil and stand it in a roasting tin containing 2.5 cm (1 in) of water. Cook in the centre of the oven for 3 hours, or until the point of a skewer inserted into the centre of the meat becomes very hot to the touch.

Remove from the oven and take the terrine or loaf tin out of the roasting tin. Place a small, flat board on top and put weights on top of the board. Stand aside to cool for at least 2 hours, then chill overnight in the refrigerator.

The next day, turn the mittoon out onto a serving platter or board, cut a few slices and arrange them neatly about the remaining portion. Serve the mittoon with pickled onions or a green salad.

Bacon-wrapped tenderloin encloses pork and liver forcemeat, flavoured with mushrooms and herbs.

INGREDIENTS

- 30 G (1 OZ) BUTTER
- 1 MEDIUM ONION, PEELED AND FINELY CHOPPED
- 225 G (8 OZ) MUSHROOMS, WIPED AND FINELY CHOPPED
- 340 G (12 OZ) PORK BELLY, WEIGHED WITHOUT SKIN AND BONE
- 340 G (12 OZ) PIG'S LIVER
- 175 G (6 OZ) FRESH WHITE BREADCRUMBS
- 3 TABLESPOONS CHOPPED FRESH PARSLEY
- 2 TEASPOONS CHOPPED FRESH THYME
- 1 TEASPOON CHOPPED FRESH SAGE
- 1 LEVEL TEASPOON SALT
- FRESHLY GROUND BLACK PEPPER
- 4 TABLESPOONS DRY SHERRY
- 2 EGGS, SIZE 3, BEATEN
- 225 G (8 OZ) SMOKED STREAKY BACON RASHERS, RINDS REMOVED
- 2 PORK TENDERLOINS, APPROX 340 G (12 OZ) EACH

PREPARATION TIME: 1¼ HOURS
COOKING TIME: 3 HOURS
CHILLING TIME: OVERNIGHT
SERVES TEN

Suffolk Sausages

Making your own sausages means that you can flavour them to your taste

INGREDIENTS

- 200G (7OZ) WHITE BREAD, WEIGHED WITHOUT CRUSTS
- NATURAL SAUSAGE CASINGS (FROM YOUR BUTCHER) OR A LITTLE FLOUR
- 900G (2LB) LEAN PORK, BLADE, COLLAR OR LEG
- 225G (8OZ) PORK BACK FAT
- 1 TABLESPOON CHOPPED FRESH SAGE OR ¾ LEVEL TEASPOON DRIED SAGE
- 1 TEASPOON CHOPPED FRESH THYME OR ¼ LEVEL TEASPOON DRIED THYME
- ¼ TEASPOON GROUND MACE, (FRESHLY GROUND IN A MORTAR, IF POSSIBLE)
- ¼ TEASPOON FRESHLY GRATED NUTMEG
- ¼ TEASPOON FRESHLY GROUND WHITE PEPPER
- 2 LEVEL TEASPOONS SALT

PREPARATION TIME: 1 HOUR
MATURING TIME: OVERNIGHT
COOKING TIME: 12–15 MINUTES
MAKES 1.4KG (3LB)

SOAK the bread in cold water for 10 minutes, then squeeze dry. Meanwhile, rinse the casings thoroughly in cold water by attaching one end to the cold tap and letting the water run through. Alternatively, attach one end to a funnel and flush through with water.

Mince the lean pork and the pork fat. For coarse sausages, mince it once, for slightly finer ones, mince twice. Do not use a food processor, as the action of the blades breaks down the fibres of the meat. Put the meat into a bowl with the bread, add all the herbs and seasonings and mix well with your hands.

If you have a sausage-making attachment for a mixer or a sausage-making machine, then follow the manufacturer's instructions. Otherwise, fill a large piping bag fitted with a 1.3cm (½in) plain nozzle and dampen with water the ends of the nozzle and the bag. Take the casing and push as much of it as possible carefully onto the end of the nozzle, gathering it up slowly. Do not try to pipe the mixture straight into the casing as the pressure will cause the casing to split.

Using gentle pressure, squeeze the mixture into the casing. Cut off any surplus casing and twist so that you make sausages the size and shape you want.

If you are unable to obtain sausage casings, or if you prefer sausages skinless, simply form the mixture into 'sausage' shapes and roll lightly in flour.

Put the sausages onto a shallow dish or large plate and refrigerate for 24 hours before cooking to allow the seasonings to become properly infused into the meat and to reduce the risk of the casings breaking and splitting as they cook.

To cook, either fry or grill the sausages for 12–15 minutes until they are browned and cooked through.

CLOWNING MOMENT
For some reason, clowns and sausages have always gone together, perhaps influenced by the string that always appears in Punch and Judy shows. This figure is part of a children's game, in which quoits are thrown over the sausages and the clown's hat.

Sage, thyme, mace and nutmeg add a wonderful aroma to plump pork sausages.

Spices and herbs, red wine and vegetables combine to make this tender pot roast really special.

Pot Roasted Beef with Salsify

Salsify, also known as 'vegetable oyster' or 'oyster plant', imparts a distinctive flavour to the pot roast

PREHEAT the oven to 160°C (325°F, gas mark 3). Mix the flour with the mustard powder, allspice and a generous amount of salt and pepper, then coat the beef in the mixture. Heat the oil in a large flameproof casserole and brown the beef well all over. Transfer to a plate and set aside.

Put the onions, carrots, turnips and celery into the casserole and cook gently for 10 minutes, stirring occasionally. Add the marjoram, cloves, mace, 1 tablespoon of the parsley, the bay leaf, red wine and stock. Place the beef on top of the vegetables, cover the casserole with a tightly fitting lid and cook in the centre of the oven for about 2 hours or until tender.

Boil the salsify in water, to which 1 tablespoon of the lemon juice has been added, until just cooked, then drain well. Melt the butter in a saucepan, add the salsify and sauté gently until lightly browned. Add the remaining lemon juice and parsley, stir well, then transfer to a heated serving dish. Cover and keep hot.

Transfer the beef to a serving dish. Using a slotted spoon, arrange the vegetables round the beef, discarding the bay leaf. Cover and keep hot.

Stir the horseradish sauce and the cornflour into the juices remaining in the casserole and bring to the boil, stirring constantly. Reduce the heat, simmer for 2–3 minutes, then pour into a heated gravy boat or jug.

Serve the beef and vegetables with the gravy and the salsify.

Parsnips can be used instead of salsify if preferred.

INGREDIENTS

- 1 LEVEL TABLESPOON PLAIN FLOUR
- 1/4 LEVEL TEASPOON MUSTARD POWDER
- 1/2 LEVEL TEASPOON GROUND ALLSPICE
- SALT AND FRESHLY GROUND BLACK PEPPER
- 1.1–1.4 KG (2 1/2–3 LB) PIECE TOP RUMP OF BEEF
- 4 TABLESPOONS OLIVE OIL
- 2 MEDIUM ONIONS, PEELED AND ROUGHLY CHOPPED
- 2 LARGE CARROTS, PEELED AND THICKLY SLICED
- 225 G (8 OZ) TURNIPS, PEELED AND DICED
- 3 CELERY STICKS, TRIMMED AND THICKLY SLICED
- 2 LEVEL TEASPOONS DRIED MARJORAM
- LARGE PINCH OF GROUND CLOVES
- 1/4 LEVEL TEASPOON GROUND MACE
- 2 TABLESPOONS CHOPPED FRESH PARSLEY
- 1 BAY LEAF
- 200 ML (7 FL OZ) RED WINE OR DRY SHERRY
- 200 ML (7 FL OZ) BEEF STOCK (SEE P.432)
- 675 G (1 1/2 LB) SALSIFY, PEELED AND CUT INTO STICKS
- 3 TABLESPOONS LEMON JUICE
- 60 G (2 OZ) BUTTER
- 1 TABLESPOON HORSERADISH SAUCE
- 1 LEVEL TABLESPOON CORNFLOUR BLENDED WITH 1 TABLESPOON WATER

PREPARATION TIME: 40 MINUTES
COOKING TIME: 2 1/4 HOURS
SERVES SIX

Ingredients

For the beef
- 3.6 kg (8 lb) forerib of beef, chined
- 3 tablespoons olive oil
- 1 level teaspoon salt
- ¼ level teaspoon freshly ground black pepper
- 1 level teaspoon mustard powder

For the roast potatoes
- 1.6 kg (3½ lb) baking potatoes, peeled and washed
- 1 level teaspoon salt

For the Yorkshire pudding
- 175 g (6 oz) plain flour
- ½ level teaspoon salt
- 2 eggs, size 2
- 285 ml (½ pint) milk

For the horseradish sauce
- 1 tablespoon white wine vinegar
- ¾ level teaspoon mustard powder
- Salt and freshly ground white pepper
- 3 tablespoons finely grated peeled horseradish
- 225 ml (8 fl oz) double cream

For the gravy
- 3 level tablespoons plain flour
- 725 ml (1¼ pints) beef stock (see p.432)
- 150 ml (¼ pint) red wine

Preparation time: 45 minutes
Cooking time: 2 hours
Serves eight to ten

Roast Beef with Yorkshire Pudding

Rich gravy, piquant sauce and roast potatoes join this superlative combination

Preheat the oven to 220°c (425°f, gas mark 7). Calculate the cooking time for the meat: for rare meat, allow 10–12 minutes per 450 g (1 lb), for medium rare, allow 15 minutes per 450 g (1 lb), and for well done, 20 minutes, all plus an extra 10–12 minutes.

Put the beef, fat side uppermost, into a large roasting tin and rub it all over with the oil. Mix the salt, pepper and mustard and rub evenly over the meat. Roast the meat in the centre of the oven for 20 minutes, reduce the temperature to 190°c (375°f, gas mark 5) and continue to cook for the remaining calculated time.

When the temperature has reduced, halve or quarter the potatoes, depending on their size, and put them into a large saucepan. Cover with cold water, add the salt and bring to the boil. Drain well, return to the pan and shake over a high heat for 1–2 minutes.

Remove the meat tin from the oven, spoon the fat from the bottom into a second tin and return the beef to the oven. If necessary, add extra lard or vegetable oil to the second tin to make a depth of 6 mm (¼ in). Heat on the shelf above the meat until the fat sizzles. Carefully add the potatoes, basting until well coated. Roast for about 1¼ hours, turning and basting every 20 minutes, until crisp and golden.

The batter

While the meat is roasting, make the Yorkshire pudding batter. Sift the flour and salt into a bowl, make a well in the centre and put the eggs and a third of the milk into the well. Stir with a wire whisk, gradually incorporating the flour from the sides to make a thick batter, then beat until very smooth. Gradually whisk in the rest of the milk. Cover the bowl and leave to stand for 1 hour.

The horseradish sauce

While the batter is standing, make the horseradish sauce. Put the wine vinegar, mustard, some salt and pepper and the horseradish into a small bowl and mix well. Whisk the cream until it will hold a soft peak, then fold in the horseradish mixture, taking care not to overmix. Cover and refrigerate until required.

When the beef is cooked transfer it to a heated serving dish, cover loosely with foil and allow it to rest while cooking the Yorkshire pudding.

If the potatoes are cooked, remove them from the oven and put them onto a heated serving dish, cover and keep hot. Otherwise, leave them to roast for a little longer while the oven heats up for the Yorkshire pudding.

The pudding and the gravy

Increase the oven temperature to 220°c (425°f, gas mark 7). Transfer 3 tablespoons of fat from the meat tin to a roasting tin or baking tin 25 × 18 × 3.8 cm (10 × 7 × 1½ in). Heat in the centre of the oven until the fat sizzles. Stir the batter, pour it into the tin and cook for 20 minutes until puffed up and golden.

Meanwhile, make the gravy. Skim all but 2 tablespoons of fat from the meat tin. Stir the flour into the tin and gradually add the stock and wine. Bring to the boil, stirring and scraping the residue from the bottom of the tin. Strain into a saucepan and simmer for 5–10 minutes until slightly thickened, skimming off any fat that rises to the surface. Season and pour into a heated gravy boat.

Serve the beef with portions of the Yorkshire pudding, the gravy, roast potatoes and the horseradish sauce, thinned with a little single cream or milk, if necessary. Also provide freshly made English mustard and green vegetables.

The roast beef of Old England stars with Yorkshire pudding among other traditional accompaniments.

Raised Pork Pie

Time spent on this project will result in a pork pie equal to the best you can buy anywhere

INGREDIENTS

FOR THE FILLING
675G (1½LB) SHOULDER OF PORK, TRIMMED OF FAT AND CUT INTO SMALL CUBES
½ LEVEL TEASPOON SALT
FRESHLY GROUND BLACK PEPPER
1 TEASPOON ANCHOVY ESSENCE
1 LEVEL TEASPOON DRIED RUBBED SAGE
¼ LEVEL TEASPOON GROUND OR FRESHLY GRATED NUTMEG

FOR THE HOT-WATER CRUST
250G (9OZ) PLAIN FLOUR
1 LEVEL TEASPOON SALT
85G (3OZ) LARD OR POLYUNSATURATED MARGARINE
150ML (¼ PINT) WATER
1 EGG, SIZE 4, BEATEN

FOR THE JELLY
285ML (½ PINT) VEAL OR CHICKEN STOCK (SEE P.433)
2 LEVEL TEASPOONS GELATINE

PREPARATION TIME: 1 HOUR
COOKING TIME: 1 HOUR 50 MINUTES
SETTING TIME: 4–5 HOURS
SERVES FOUR

PREHEAT the oven to 200°C (400°F, gas mark 6). Thoroughly grease a spring-clip tin, 18 cm (7 in) in diameter and 6 cm (2½ in) deep. Mix the ingredients for the filling in a bowl, cover and set aside.

To make the pastry, sift the flour and salt into a bowl and make a well in the centre. Put the lard or margarine and the water into a saucepan, heat gently until the fat melts, then bring slowly to the boil. Remove from the heat immediately and mix into the flour with a wooden spoon. Cover and set aside until cool enough to handle.

Cut off a third of the dough, cover and set aside. On a lightly floured surface, roll out the remainder to about 30 cm (12 in) in diameter. Fit the dough into the tin, pressing it evenly over the base and sides.

Spoon the filling into the tin, pressing it down well. Roll out the remaining dough, brush the edges of the dough in the tin with cold water, cover with the 'lid' and press the edges together to seal. Trim off the excess dough and make a hole in the centre of the pie.

Bake the pie, on a baking tray, in the centre of the oven for 30 minutes, then reduce the temperature to 180°C (350°F, gas mark 4) and bake for 1 hour more. Cover with foil if overbrowning.

Take the pie from the oven, leave it to stand for 5 minutes, then carefully remove the side of the tin. Brush the side of the pie with the beaten egg and return it to the oven for 20 minutes until golden brown. Then put it, still on the base of the tin, on a rack until completely cold.

Put 3 tablespoons of the stock into a small saucepan and sprinkle the gelatine on top. Leave to stand for 2-3 minutes, heat until the gelatine has dissolved then stir into the remaining stock. Cool until slightly syrupy, then pour into the pie through the hole in the centre. Chill the pie overnight before serving.

Pork is sealed in savoury jelly in a pie that can be decorated with the pastry trimmings.

To make the job of filling the pie with jellied stock easier, pour it in through a small funnel.

A wine and lemon-flavoured cream sauce complements tender veal escalopes.

Scotch Collops

In many parts of the North, Collop Monday figured as the last day on which meat could be eaten before the Lenten fast

Trim the escalopes and, using a meat mallet or rolling pin, beat or roll them out thinly between sheets of cling film, then coat them with the seasoned flour.

Heat the butter in a large frying pan and brown the escalopes well on both sides, two at a time if necessary. Add the grated lemon rind, mace and white wine, then simmer, uncovered, for about 5 minutes until the meat is tender.

Remove the escalopes from the frying pan, put onto a heated serving dish, cover and keep warm.

Boil the sauce until slightly reduced. Mix the egg yolk with the cream and stir into the sauce. Reheat the sauce without allowing it to boil. Taste and season well, then strain, through a small sieve, over the collops. Garnish with the parsley sprigs and the lemon slices.

INGREDIENTS

4 British veal escalopes, each approx 175 g (6 oz)
2 tablespoons flour, seasoned well with salt and pepper
60 g (2 oz) butter
Finely grated rind ½ lemon
Pinch ground mace
150 ml (¼ pint) dry white wine
1 egg yolk, size 3
3 tablespoons double cream
Salt and freshly ground black pepper
Fresh chopped parsley and lemon wedges to garnish

Preparation time: 10 minutes
Cooking time: 15–20 minutes
Serves four

INGREDIENTS

175 G (6 OZ) PLAIN FLOUR
¼ LEVEL TEASPOON SALT
2 EGGS, SIZE 2
200 ML (7 FL OZ) MILK
200 ML (7 FL OZ) WATER
30 G (1 OZ) DRIPPING OR LARD
12 PORK SAUSAGES, WEIGHING APPROX 675 G (1½ LB), HOMEMADE (SEE P.184) OR BOUGHT

PREPARATION TIME: 5 MINUTES
STANDING TIME: 1 HOUR
COOKING TIME: 50–60 MINUTES
SERVES FOUR

Toad-in-the-Hole

A batter similar to that served with roast beef transforms the everyday sausage into a festive yet economical dish for the whole family

TO MAKE the batter, sift the flour and salt into a mixing bowl and make a well in the centre. Add the eggs and pour the milk into the well. Beat the eggs and milk together with a wooden spoon, gradually drawing in the flour from the sides of the bowl, until the batter is thick and smooth. Add the water gradually, stirring all the time, then beat the batter well for 1 minute. Cover the bowl and leave to stand for 1 hour.

Preheat the oven to 200°C (400°F, gas mark 6). Put the sausages and dripping or lard into a large, shallow roasting tin. Cook near the top of the oven for 15 minutes until the fat is sizzling and the sausages are beginning to brown.

Remove the roasting tin from the oven and pour in the batter. Return to the oven and cook for a further 35–45 minutes until the batter is well risen and crisp and the sausages are cooked. Serve at once.

BANGERS OF BRITAIN
The best sausage, like the best football team, is defined by local patriotism. Cambridge, Oxford, Wiltshire, Cumberland, Glasgow and Newmarket all make claims, and all quote their champion's superior succulence in Toad-in-the-Hole.

Juicy sausages nestle in golden batter to create a mouth-watering treat.

The dish is a feast of lamb and vegetables, topped with black pudding and potatoes.

Cumberland Tatie Pot

This Cumbrian dish is quick and easy to prepare, and for most of its long, slow cooking time will look after itself

The day before, make the stock. Put the lamb breasts into a large, stainless steel or enamel saucepan, cover with the cold water and bring to the boil. Reduce the heat and skim the scum from the surface. Add the leek, carrot, onion, peppercorns and herbs, partially cover and simmer gently for 3 hours. Remove from the heat, allow to cool, then chill overnight.

The next day, remove the solidified fat from the top and strain the stock, then discard the meat and vegetables.

Preheat the oven to 160°C (325°F, gas mark 3). Put the flour into a bowl and season it well with salt and pepper. Toss the pieces of lamb in the flour until evenly coated, then remove and shake off the excess flour.

Heat the oil in a frying pan and fry the lamb until lightly browned, then transfer to a shallow ovenproof dish or roasting tin of about 4.5 litres (1 gallon) capacity. Do not use a deep dish.

Arrange the onions, swede and carrots round the lamb and pour in enough stock to just cover the meat and vegetables—if necessary, top up with water. Cover the dish or roasting tin with foil and cook in the centre of the oven for 3½ hours. After 2½ hours, drain and rinse the peas and add them to the lamb.

Cut the potatoes into quarters and put them into a large saucepan. Cover with water, bring to the boil, then drain well.

Remove the dish or roasting tin from the oven. Increase the oven temperature to 220°C (425°F, gas mark 7). Uncover the lamb, add the black pudding, arrange the potatoes on top and spoon over some of the juices to moisten them. At this point there may seem to be too much liquid, but this will reduce as the potatoes cook. Return to the oven and cook for 45 minutes to 1 hour or until the potatoes are cooked and golden brown. Serve with savoy or red cabbage.

Ingredients

For the stock

- 2 breasts of lamb, cut into strips
- 2.3 litres (4 pints) water
- 1 leek, trimmed, sliced and washed
- 1 large carrot, peeled and sliced
- 1 onion, peeled and sliced
- 1 teaspoon black peppercorns
- 1 large parsley sprig
- 1 thyme sprig

Preparation time: 15 minutes
Cooking time: 3 hours
Cooling time: Overnight

For the tatie pot

- 30g (1oz) plain flour
- Salt and freshly ground black pepper
- 1.4kg (3lb) middle neck of lamb, trimmed of excess fat, cut into 12 pieces
- 2 tablespoons olive oil
- 450g (1lb) large onions, peeled and cut into thick wedges
- 450g (1lb) swede, peeled and thickly sliced
- 225g (8oz) carrots, peeled and thickly sliced
- 1.15 litres (2 pints) lamb stock (see above)
- 115g (4oz) marrowfat peas, soaked overnight in cold water
- 1.8kg (4lb) baking potatoes, peeled and covered with cold water until needed
- 340g (12oz) black pudding, thickly sliced

Preparation time: 30 minutes
Cooking time: 4½ hours, mostly unattended
Serves six

Poultry and Game

As moorland is to grouse and stubble and woods are to partridge and pheasant, so the farmyard is to poultry. Such an upbringing enables dishes like *Chicken with Fennel*, or with *Orange* or *Coronation Sauce*, to rank almost alongside *Spiced Partridges* or *Salmi of Duck* in the great repertoire of game and poultry recipes. This also embraces within it traditional dishes such as *Michaelmas Goose*, *Harvest Rabbit Pie*, *Casseroled Pigeons* and *Braised Venison with Claret* that help to illuminate the culinary calendar.

Chicken with Orange and Lemon Sauce

Rosewater adds an unusual and delicate bouquet to this casserole

INGREDIENTS

- 2.7 KG (6 LB) OVEN-READY CHICKEN, RINSED AND DRIED
- 285 ML (½ PINT) CHICKEN STOCK (SEE P.433)
- 1 SMALL ONION, PEELED
- 2 BAY LEAVES
- THINLY PARED RIND ½ LEMON
- 12 BLACK PEPPERCORNS

FOR THE SAUCE

- 60 G (2 OZ) CURRANTS
- 115 G (4 OZ) FRESH DATES, STONED AND CHOPPED
- 1 LARGE ORANGE, PEEL AND PITH REMOVED, FLESH SEGMENTED AND ROUGHLY CHOPPED
- 60 G (2 OZ) READY-TO-USE DRIED APRICOTS, CHOPPED
- 150 ML (¼ PINT) RED WINE
- 1 TABLESPOON ROSEWATER
- 2 LEVEL TABLESPOONS CASTER SUGAR
- 1 TABLESPOON LEMON JUICE
- 1 LEVEL TABLESPOON ARROWROOT BLENDED WITH 1 TABLESPOON WATER
- SALT AND FRESHLY GROUND BLACK PEPPER

PREPARATION TIME: 40 MINUTES
COOKING TIME: 2¼ HOURS
SERVES SIX

PREHEAT the oven to 190°C (375°F, gas mark 5). Put the chicken into a large casserole, pour in the stock and add the onion, bay leaves, lemon rind and peppercorns. Cover and cook in the oven for 1½–2 hours or until the chicken is tender, basting frequently.

Take the chicken out of the casserole and remove the skin and bones. Cut the meat into small pieces, arrange them on a heated dish, cover and keep warm.

To make the orange and lemon sauce, skim all the fat from the chicken stock, then strain and measure the stock—there should be about 425 ml (¾ pint). Put the measured stock into a saucepan. (If there is too much, boil rapidly to reduce to the right amount. Add water if there is too little.) Add the currants, dates, chopped orange segments and apricots to the stock and simmer gently for 5 minutes. Stir in the wine, rosewater, sugar and lemon juice and simmer for another 5 minutes. Stir in the blended arrowroot and cook, stirring, until the sauce has thickened.

Season to taste, then pour the sauce over the chicken and serve with hot rice and a tossed green salad.

The flavours of citrus fruits, apricots, dates and currants combine to give the sauce a distinctive tang.

The pincushion-shaped poussins are garnished with lemon wedges, thyme and sliced pickled walnuts.

Surprised Fowls

The surprise in this recipe is the unusual sauce which is based on anchovies and oysters

To MAKE the stuffing, melt the butter in a frying pan and sauté the shallots gently until soft. Remove from the heat and stir in the remaining ingredients. Shape half the mixture into four balls, and the rest into eight smaller balls, and set aside.

Open out each boned poussin, cutting open the leg, and arrange the flesh evenly over the skin. Put one large ball of stuffing in the centre and wrap the poussin neatly round it. Place the bird, breast side down, on a work surface and slip a length of string underneath it. Bring the ends up to meet in the centre and tie. Give the poussin a quarter turn and tie as before. Repeat twice more, between the quarters, to form a neat ball. Trim excess string.

Heat 60g (2oz) of the butter in a large frying pan and brown the poussins evenly all over. Pour the excess fat from the pan, add the stock and wine, cover and simmer for 40 minutes.

Meanwhile, fry the small stuffing balls in the oil over a moderate heat for 10–15 minutes until lightly browned. Drain on kitchen paper, cover and keep warm.

Remove the poussins from the pan and keep warm. Strain the juices through a sieve into a measuring jug and make up to 285ml (½ pint) with wine, stock or water. Wipe the pan with kitchen paper.

Melt the remaining butter in the pan and sauté the onion until soft. Add the flour and cook for 1 minute. Blend in the chicken juices, nutmeg, mushrooms, anchovies and lemon juice, season with pepper and cook gently for 5 minutes.

Remove from the heat, stir in the oysters and their juice and pour the sauce onto a heated serving plate. Remove the strings and place the poussins in the sauce. Garnish with the stuffing balls and walnut slices and the oyster shells filled with lemon wedges and thyme sprigs.

INGREDIENTS

FOR THE STUFFING

- 30G (1OZ) BUTTER
- 60G (2OZ) SHALLOTS, PEELED AND FINELY CHOPPED
- 60G (2OZ) FRESH WHITE BREADCRUMBS
- 1 TABLESPOON CHOPPED FRESH THYME
- 1 LEVEL TABLESPOON TOMATO PURÉE
- 340G (12OZ) PORK SAUSAGE MEAT
- SALT AND FRESHLY GROUND BLACK PEPPER

FOR THE FOWLS

- 4 POUSSINS, EACH APPROX 400G (14OZ), BONED BY BUTCHER OR SEE P.437
- 85G (3OZ) BUTTER
- 150ML (¼ PINT) GOOD CHICKEN STOCK (SEE P.433)
- 150ML (¼ PINT) DRY WHITE WINE
- 3 TABLESPOONS OLIVE OIL
- 1 SMALL ONION, PEELED AND CHOPPED
- 2 LEVEL TABLESPOONS PLAIN FLOUR
- ¼ LEVEL TEASPOON FRESHLY GRATED NUTMEG
- 15G (½OZ) DRIED MORELS OR CEPS, RECONSTITUTED IN BOILING WATER, THEN DRAINED
- 30G (1OZ) TINNED ANCHOVY FILLETS, DRAINED AND HALVED LENGTHWAYS
- 1 TEASPOON LEMON JUICE
- 4 FRESH OYSTERS, SHUCKED (SEE P.436), SHELLS RESERVED FOR GARNISH
- LEMON WEDGES, FRESH THYME SPRIGS, 4 PICKLED WALNUTS, SLICED, TO GARNISH

PREPARATION TIME: 1 HOUR, PLUS 1 HOUR IF BONING POUSSINS YOURSELF

COOKING TIME: 1 HOUR

SERVES FOUR

CORONATION DAY
On June 2, 1953, many Britons caught their first glimpse of TV. Some 20 million people watched the Coronation on 2.5 million tiny, flickering sets, of which 500 000 had been bought in the previous few weeks.

The chicken breasts are coated with a creamy curry sauce, flavoured with fruit and wine.

Coronation Chicken

This recipe was created to mark the coronation of HM Queen Elizabeth II in 1953

INGREDIENTS

- 6 BONELESS CHICKEN BREASTS, EACH APPROX 175 G (6 OZ), SKINNED
- 285 ML (½ PINT) CHICKEN STOCK (SEE P.433)
- 1 BAY LEAF
- 6 BLACK PEPPERCORNS
- 2 PARSLEY STALKS
- 2 FRESH THYME SPRIGS
- 1 LEMON SLICE

FOR THE SAUCE

- 1 TABLESPOON OLIVE OIL
- 1 SMALL ONION, PEELED AND CHOPPED
- 1 LEVEL TABLESPOON MEDIUM-HOT CURRY POWDER
- 1 TEASPOON TOMATO PURÉE
- 3 TABLESPOONS WATER
- 4 TABLESPOONS RED WINE
- SALT AND FRESHLY GROUND BLACK PEPPER
- 1 TABLESPOON APRICOT JAM
- 1 LEMON SLICE
- 2 TEASPOONS LEMON JUICE
- 150 ML (¼ PINT) MAYONNAISE, HOMEMADE (SEE P.436) OR BOUGHT
- 200 ML (7 FL OZ) DOUBLE CREAM
- FRESH CORIANDER SPRIGS OR WATERCRESS TO GARNISH

PREPARATION TIME: 30 MINUTES
COOKING TIME: 40–50 MINUTES
SERVES SIX

PUT the chicken into a large, shallow saucepan and add the stock, bay leaf, peppercorns, parsley stalks, thyme and the lemon slice. Bring to the boil, reduce the heat, cover and simmer gently for about 20 minutes or until tender. Remove the saucepan from the heat and allow the chicken to cool in the stock.

Meanwhile, to make the sauce, heat the oil in a saucepan, add the onion and cook gently for 7–10 minutes until softened, but not browned. Mix in the curry powder and cook for 1 minute. Stir in the tomato purée, water, wine, some salt and pepper, the jam and the lemon slice and juice and simmer for 8 minutes. Remove from the heat and discard the lemon slice. Pass the sauce through a nylon sieve into a bowl, pushing through as much as possible with a wooden spoon. Cover and leave to cool.

Lightly whip the cream. Stir it and the mayonnaise into the cold curry sauce to make a thin, coating sauce. Drain the cold chicken breasts and slice them thickly. Add the chicken to the curried mayonnaise and mix lightly together. Spoon the mixture into a serving dish, garnish with the coriander or watercress and serve with a rice salad.

Salmi of Duck

A salmi is a dish of game served in a spicy red wine sauce

Preheat the oven to 230°c (450°f, gas mark 8). Rinse the ducks under cold water and pat dry with kitchen paper. Rinse and drain the giblets and set aside. Prick the ducks all over with a fork and place them on a grid in a large roasting tin. Roast on the top shelf of the oven for 30 minutes until well browned, but still rare. Remove from the oven and carve off all the meat as neatly as possible, keeping the breast and leg meat separate. Put onto a plate, cover and chill in the refrigerator until required.

Put the duck bones and giblets into a large saucepan, add sufficient water to cover and bring to the boil. Reduce the heat, partially cover the saucepan and cook gently for 1 hour. Strain off and measure the duck stock—there should be about 570 ml (1 pint). If there is more, boil until reduced; if less, make up with chicken stock or water.

Melt the butter in a large saucepan, add the onion and sauté gently for 5 minutes. Stir in the flour, then gradually add the duck stock and bring to the boil, stirring until slightly thickened. Add the herbs, orange rind, redcurrant jelly, nutmeg, salt and pepper and simmer, uncovered, for 20 minutes, stirring occasionally until reduced by a quarter.

Pass the sauce through a sieve into a clean saucepan, pressing the chopped onion through the mesh. Stir in the red wine, brandy and lemon juice and simmer for 5 minutes. Add the reserved leg meat and simmer for another 5 minutes, then add the breast slices and mushrooms and simmer very gently for a further 10 minutes until heated through.

Transfer the duck and sauce to a deep, heated serving dish. Garnish with halved kumquats or orange wedges and redcurrants. Serve with rice and green beans.

The richly flavoured sauce for the duck is fortified with a little brandy.

INGREDIENTS

- 2 oven-ready ducks, each approx 2 kg (4½ lb), with giblets
- 45 g (1½ oz) butter
- 1 medium onion, peeled and finely chopped
- 30 g (1 oz) flour
- A few fresh thyme and parsley sprigs
- 2 bay leaves
- Finely grated rind 1 orange
- 2 teaspoons redcurrant jelly, homemade (see p.401) or bought
- ¼ level teaspoon freshly grated nutmeg
- ¼ level teaspoon salt
- ¼ level teaspoon freshly ground black pepper
- 150 ml (¼ pint) red wine
- 1 tablespoon brandy
- 2 teaspoons lemon juice
- 115 g (4 oz) flat or field mushrooms, wiped, sliced, and sautéed in 15 g (½ oz) butter
- Kumquat halves or orange wedges and fresh redcurrants to garnish

Preparation time: 2½ hours
Cooking time: 45 minutes
Serves four

This is a perfect dish for entertaining. All can be done in advance. Just reheat the salmi before serving.

Chicken Casserole with Cheese Dumplings

Cheese dumplings raise a simple chicken casserole into a class on its own

INGREDIENTS

1.6 KG (3½ LB) OVEN-READY CHICKEN CUT INTO 8 PORTIONS AND SKINNED (SEE P.437)
30 G (1 OZ) BUTTER
2 TABLESPOONS OLIVE OIL
2 MEDIUM ONIONS, PEELED AND SLICED
4 CELERY STICKS, TRIMMED AND SLICED
450 G (1 LB) CARROTS, PEELED, CUT INTO SHORT PIECES AND TRIMMED INTO BARREL SHAPES
2 LEVEL TABLESPOONS PLAIN FLOUR
450 G (1 LB) TOMATOES, SKINNED AND CHOPPED
570 ML (1 PINT) CHICKEN STOCK (SEE P.433)
2 BAY LEAVES
SALT AND FRESHLY GROUND BLACK PEPPER

For the dumplings
115 G (4 OZ) SELF-RAISING FLOUR
60 G (2 OZ) FINELY GRATED FRESH BEEF SUET OR SHREDDED SUET
60 G (2 OZ) MATURE CHEDDAR CHEESE, GRATED
1 LEVEL TEASPOON ENGLISH MUSTARD POWDER
PINCH OF SALT
3 TABLESPOONS MILK
3 TABLESPOONS WATER
1 TABLESPOON CHOPPED FRESH PARSLEY
CELERY LEAVES TO GARNISH (OPTIONAL)

Preparation time: 1¼ HOURS
Cooking time: 1½ HOURS
Serves four

Preheat the oven to 180°C (350°F, gas mark 4). Wipe the chicken joints with kitchen paper. Melt the butter with the oil in a large, flameproof casserole, add the chicken pieces, four at a time, and fry over a moderate heat for 10 minutes, or until golden, then transfer to a plate. Add the onions, celery and carrots to the pan and cook over a moderate heat, stirring frequently, for 10 minutes or until all the vegetables have softened.

Add the flour to the casserole and stir for 1 minute, then add the tomatoes and the stock and bring to the boil, stirring. Add the bay leaves and season well. Return the chicken pieces to the casserole, coating them well with the sauce. Cover and cook in the centre of the oven for 1½ hours.

When the casserole has been cooking for 55 minutes, make the dumplings. Sift the flour into a bowl. Stir in the suet, 45 g (1½ oz) of the cheese, the mustard and a pinch of salt. Make a well in the centre, pour in the milk and water and mix to a smooth, soft, but not sticky dough.

Now increase the oven temperature to 200°C (400°F, gas mark 6) and uncover the casserole. Divide the dumpling mixture into eight equal portions and place, spaced a little apart, on top of the chicken mixture. Cover and cook for 30 minutes or until the dumplings have risen and are cooked through. Uncover the casserole, sprinkle with the remaining cheese and cook for a further 5 minutes or until lightly browned. Alternatively, if you have a grill element inside your oven, switch it on to brown the top of the dumplings.

Sprinkle with the chopped parsley and garnish with the fresh celery leaves. Serve with steamed broccoli and green beans.

The rich juices of the chicken casserole lend succulence to the savoury dumplings.

The sweet, aniseed flavour of fennel adds a mellow touch to chicken and gammon.

Because the gammon is salty, it is best not to season the dish with salt until cooking is completed.

Beryl's Chicken with Fennel

Florence, or bulb fennel, is the inspiration behind this dish

Preheat the oven to 190°C (375°F, gas mark 5). Heat the oil in a large, ovenproof frying pan or flameproof casserole and cook the chicken and gammon over a moderate heat until richly browned. Set the meat aside, add the onion, garlic and fennel to the pan or casserole and cook gently for 5 minutes, or until softened, then stir in the mushrooms and cook for a further 2–3 minutes. Add the tomatoes, Worcestershire sauce, wine and basil. Season with pepper and stir well. Return the meat to the pan or casserole, cover and cook in the oven for 1½ hours or until tender.

Taste and adjust the seasoning and cut the gammon into six serving pieces, discarding the rind. Garnish with the basil leaves and serve accompanied by jacket potatoes and spinach.

INGREDIENTS

2 tablespoons olive oil
6 large chicken thigh joints, each approx 175g (6oz), skinned
340g (12oz) thick gammon steak
1 large onion, peeled and thinly sliced
2 garlic cloves, peeled and crushed
225g (8oz) Florence fennel, trimmed and sliced
225g (8oz) mushrooms, wiped and sliced
400g (14oz) tinned tomatoes, drained and chopped (juice will not be needed)
1 teaspoon Worcestershire sauce
150ml (¼ pint) red wine
2–3 tablespoons finely shredded fresh basil
Salt and freshly ground black pepper
Finely shredded basil and whole basil leaves to garnish

Preparation time: 30 minutes
Cooking time: 1½ hours
Serves six

Roast Michaelmas Goose with Plum Sauce

Roast goose has long been a traditional dish for Michaelmas because it is then that geese are in prime condition

INGREDIENTS

- 4.5–5 kg (10–11 lb) oven-ready goose, with giblets
- 850 ml (1½ pints) chicken stock (see p.433) or water
- 1 medium onion, peeled and quartered
- 1 medium carrot, peeled and sliced
- 1 celery stick, trimmed and sliced
- 1 thyme sprig
- 1 parsley sprig
- 1 bay leaf
- 1 mace blade
- 6 black peppercorns
- Salt and freshly ground black pepper
- 450 g (1 lb) purple plums, halved, stoned and sliced
- 45 g (1½ oz) demerara sugar

For the stuffing

- 60 g (2 oz) butter
- 275 g (10 oz) onions, peeled and chopped
- 175 g (6 oz) smoked back bacon, rinds removed, chopped
- 1 goose liver, chopped
- 450 g (1 lb) fresh white breadcrumbs
- 3 tablespoons chopped fresh parsley
- 2 tablespoons chopped fresh sage
- Finely grated rind 1 lemon
- ¼ level teaspoon freshly grated nutmeg
- ½ level teaspoon salt
- Freshly ground black pepper
- 340 g (12 oz) plums, same variety as above, halved, stoned and sliced

For the sauce

- 30 g (1 oz) plain flour
- 200 ml (7 fl oz) port
- Salt and freshly ground black pepper
- Fresh sage leaves to garnish

Preparation time: 1¾ hours
Cooking time: 3–3½ hours
Serves six to eight

Remove the giblets from inside the goose, separate the liver and set it aside for the stuffing. Take off, and discard, any white fat that surrounds the gizzard. Rinse the gizzard, heart and neck under cold water and put into a saucepan. Add the chicken stock or water and bring to the boil, then reduce the heat and skim any scum from the surface. Add the prepared onion, carrot and celery, the thyme, parsley, bay leaf, mace blade, peppercorns and ½ level teaspoon of salt. Partially cover the saucepan and simmer for 1 hour, then strain off and reserve the stock—you will need 570 ml (1 pint).

THE STUFFING

To make the stuffing, melt the butter in a large frying pan, add the onions and bacon and sauté gently until just cooked. Chop and add the goose liver and sauté for 1 minute. Stir in the breadcrumbs and cook for 2 minutes. Remove from the heat and mix in the parsley, sage, lemon rind, nutmeg, salt, some pepper and the sliced plums. Set aside to cool.

THE GOOSE

Preheat the oven to 220°C (425°F, gas mark 7). Rinse the goose cavity under a cold running tap, then pat dry with kitchen paper. Season the inside of the goose with some salt and pepper, then spoon the stuffing into the goose and secure the vent with clean string or skewers. Put the bird into a roasting tin with 150 ml (¼ pint) of the stock. Cover with foil, tucking it under the rim of the roasting tin, and cook in the centre of the oven for 45 minutes.

Reduce the oven temperature to 180°C (350°F, gas mark 4) and cook for a further 1¾ hours, then remove the foil, place the plums around the goose and sprinkle them with the demerara sugar. Continue cooking for another 20–30 minutes or until the plums are soft and pulpy and the goose is cooked—test by piercing the thickest part of the thigh with a skewer. When the goose is cooked, the juices will run clear. If the juices are pink, continue cooking until done, then carefully transfer to a heated serving plate, cover with foil and keep warm.

THE SAUCE

To make the sauce, skim all but 3 tablespoons of the fat from the roasting tin, leaving the cooking juices and plums in the tin. Blend in the flour and cook for 1–2 minutes. Stir in the remaining stock and bring to a gentle boil, stirring and scraping the browned residue from the bottom of the tin. Remove from the heat and strain the sauce through a nylon sieve into a saucepan, pressing the plum flesh through the sieve with the back of a spoon. Stir in the port and simmer the sauce for 5 minutes. Season to taste and, if necessary, sweeten with a little sugar.

Garnish the goose with the fresh sage leaves and serve with the hot plum sauce.

CARVING

Use a sharp, heavy knife to cut through the joints which are somewhat tougher to deal with than those of other birds.

Working on one side first, remove the wing by cutting firmly through the joint. Next, cut through the skin around the leg, then cut down between the thigh and the body. The leg will come away from the body, but will still be attached by the joint. Cut firmly through the joint to completely separate the leg and thigh, then cut into two pieces where the drumstick joins the thigh. Working from the front of the bird, carve the breast into long slices with the blade of the knife held almost, but not quite, horizontally.

Purple plums are the juicy main ingredient in both the stuffing and the sauce for this festive roast goose.

INGREDIENTS

- 115g (4oz) fine green beans, trimmed and cut into short pieces
- 200g (7oz) fresh white cocktail or button onions, peeled
- 1.4kg (3lb) oven-ready chicken, roasted or poached until tender, then cooled
- 10 tinned anchovy fillets, drained
- 1 level tablespoon chopped fresh parsley
- 1–2 tablespoons lemon juice
- 45g (1½oz) large, seeded raisins, halved
- Salt and freshly ground black pepper
- 1 Webb's lettuce, washed and finely shredded
- 30g (1oz) flaked almonds, toasted
- 175g (6oz) white grapes, peeled, pips removed
- 1 large Granny Smith apple, peeled, cored and roughly chopped
- 4 hard-boiled eggs, shelled and cut into wedges

For the dressing

- ½ level teaspoon salt
- Freshly ground black pepper
- 2 level teaspoons Dijon mustard
- 1 garlic clove, peeled and crushed
- 4 tablespoons red wine vinegar
- 9 tablespoons olive oil
- 1 level tablespoon tomato purée
- 1 tablespoon each chopped fresh parsley, chives, basil and marjoram

Preparation time: 1 hour

Serves four to six

Cooked and raw ingredients are mixed in this elaborate assembly of colours, textures and flavours.

Salmagundi

Salmagundi is as ornamental as it is delicious and was frequently the centrepiece of the Victorian supper table

Steam the green beans and the peeled onions separately for 4–5 minutes or until tender, then rinse quickly under cold water to preserve their colour. Drain well.

Remove the skin from the chicken, carve the breast meat into thin slices and set aside. Chop all the dark meat into small dice. Chop four of the anchovy fillets and put them into a bowl with the diced meat, parsley, lemon juice and raisins. Season to taste and mix well.

Arrange the shredded lettuce on a large platter. Shape the chicken mixture into a neat mound, place it in the centre of the dish and garnish with the remaining anchovy fillets.

Place the slices of chicken breast on the platter, add the beans and sprinkle with the almonds. Mix the grapes with the chopped apple and arrange on the platter in attractive groups with the eggs and onions

To make the dressing, put all the ingredients into a bowl and whisk together. Pour the dressing over the salad and serve.

Chicken Kromeskies

The recipe for these delectable mouthfuls was brought to Britain by immigrants from eastern Europe

Melt the butter in a saucepan, stir in the flour and cook gently over a low heat for 1 minute. Gradually pour in the milk and bring to the boil, stirring until the sauce becomes smooth and very thick. Season with the salt, pepper and nutmeg and remove from the heat.

Mix the chopped chicken, mushrooms and parsley into the sauce, allow to cool, then chill for 1 hour.

Meanwhile, to make the batter, sift the flour and salt into a bowl and make a well in the centre. Add the egg yolk and water and beat with a wire whisk until smooth. Cover and leave to stand.

Divide the chicken and sauce mixture into 12 then, on a floured board, shape into cork shapes. Wrap half a bacon rasher round each one, secure with a cocktail stick and chill for 30 minutes.

Half fill a deep frying pan with the vegetable oil and heat until 190°C (375°F) is reached on a frying thermometer or until a small piece of bread will brown in the oil in a few seconds. Whisk the egg white until it will hold a soft peak and fold it into the batter.

Dip the kromeskies, one at a time, into the batter to coat completely, then fry, three or four at a time, in the hot oil for 3–5 minutes until golden brown and crisp. Lift out of the oil with a slotted spoon, drain on kitchen paper and keep warm while frying the others.

Remove the cocktail sticks from the kromeskies and arrange them on a heated serving dish. Garnish with the lemon wedges and watercress.

Serve with a curry or tomato sauce (see p.435) and a salad.

Ingredients

- 30 g (1 oz) butter
- 30 g (1 oz) flour
- 150 ml (¼ pint) milk
- ¼ level teaspoon salt
- ¼ level teaspoon ground black pepper
- ¼ level teaspoon ground nutmeg
- 250 g (9 oz) cooked chicken, finely chopped
- 85 g (3 oz) field or flat mushrooms, wiped, finely chopped and sautéed in 20 g (¾ oz) butter
- 2 tablespoons chopped fresh parsley
- 6 thin rashers back bacon, rinds removed, halved lengthways

For the batter

- 115 g (4 oz) plain flour
- Pinch of salt
- 1 egg, size 2, separated
- 150 ml (¼ pint) water
- Vegetable oil for deep frying
- Lemon wedges and watercress to garnish

Preparation time: 30 minutes
Chilling time: 1½ hours
Cooking time: 3–5 minutes for each batch
Serves four

Nuggets of chicken, mushroom and parsley are wrapped in bacon, dipped in light batter, then deep-fried until golden, crisp and irresistible.

Fricassee of Guinea Fowl

Herbs and vegetables enhance the firm, creamy-white flesh of the guinea fowl in this fricassee

INGREDIENTS

- 1.6 KG (3½ LB) OVEN-READY GUINEA FOWL, RINSED AND DRIED WITH KITCHEN PAPER
- 425 ML (¾ PINT) WATER
- 2 MEDIUM ONIONS, PEELED AND QUARTERED
- 4 CELERY STICKS, TRIMMED AND CHOPPED
- 2 BAY LEAVES
- 2 CLOVES
- SMALL BUNCH FRESH THYME
- SMALL BUNCH FRESH PARSLEY
- 1 LEVEL TEASPOON SALT
- FRESHLY GROUND BLACK PEPPER
- 85 G (3 OZ) BUTTER
- 1 BUNCH SPRING ONIONS, TRIMMED AND CHOPPED
- 175 G (6 OZ) MUSHROOMS, WIPED AND SLICED
- 60 G (2 OZ) PLAIN FLOUR
- 115 G (4 OZ) PUFF PASTRY, HOMEMADE (SEE P.441) OR BOUGHT
- 1 EGG YOLK MIXED WITH 1 TABLESPOON MILK
- 2 TABLESPOONS LEMON JUICE
- 3 TABLESPOONS DOUBLE CREAM
- 15 G (½ OZ) FLAKED ALMONDS, LIGHTLY TOASTED
- FRESH CHOPPED PARSLEY TO GARNISH

PREPARATION TIME: 1 HOUR
COOKING TIME: APPROX 1½ HOURS
COOLING TIME: 1 HOUR
SERVES FOUR

PUT the guinea fowl into a saucepan in which it will fit snugly. Pour in the water and add the onions, celery, bay leaves, cloves, thyme, parsley, salt and pepper. Bring to the boil, reduce the heat, cover and simmer for 1 hour, or until the guinea fowl is cooked.

Remove from the heat and leave the fowl to cool in the stock for 1 hour then carefully transfer it from the saucepan to a plate. Strain the stock into a measuring jug to reach the 570 ml (1 pint) mark. Reserve the onions and celery. Remove and discard the skin from the guinea fowl. Remove the meat from the bones and cut it into neat pieces.

Preheat the oven to 220°C (425°F, gas mark 7). To make the sauce, melt 30 g (1 oz) of the butter in a saucepan, add the spring onions and mushrooms and sauté for 5 minutes, then remove with a slotted spoon and reserve. Add the remaining butter to the pan and melt over a low heat. Stir in the flour, cook over a moderate heat for 2–3 minutes, then gradually stir in the measured stock. Bring to the boil, stirring continuously until the sauce is thick and smooth, then gently mix in the guinea fowl meat and the reserved onions and celery and the spring onions and mushrooms. Simmer, stirring occasionally, for 20 minutes.

Meanwhile, roll out the puff pastry on a lightly floured surface and cut out 16 croutons, using a small, crescent-shaped biscuit cutter. Place on a baking sheet, spaced apart, and brush with the egg and milk. Bake for 10–15 minutes or until puffed up and pale golden.

Stir the lemon juice and cream into the fricassee and pour into a heated serving dish. Arrange the croutons round the edge. Garnish with the almonds and parsley and serve with rice.

For something different, dine on guinea fowl garnished with almonds and puff pastry crescents.

The British warm to a curry that cools the fiery spices while retaining the fruity flavour.

English Chicken Curry

Fine Indian food has been enjoyed in Britain since it was introduced in the 17th century by merchants of the East India Company

HEAT the butter and oil in a large saucepan, add the chicken pieces and brown them all over. Remove from the saucepan and drain well on kitchen paper.

Add the shallots and onions to the saucepan and cook over a moderate heat for 5 minutes, or until soft. Mix in the curry powder and cook for 1 minute, then add the curry paste and flour and cook for 1 minute. Gradually pour in the stock and bring to the boil, stirring until thickened. Add the mango chutney, lemon juice and apples and mix well. Return the chicken to the saucepan, reduce the heat, cover and simmer gently for 30–40 minutes or until the chicken is tender. Using a slotted spoon, remove the chicken pieces from the sauce and arrange them on a serving dish.

Pour the curry sauce into a food processor and blend until smooth. Return it to the saucepan, stir in the sultanas and cream and season to taste. Reheat the sauce gently, but do not boil as it will curdle. Pour over the chicken pieces and serve with long-grain rice.

EMPIRE PREFERENCE
British merchants and soldiers, and their wives, took many Western institutions to India, from pale ale to cricket. But India subtly retaliated, and when the sahibs and the mems went home, they brought an insatiable appetite for tiffin, with curries and hot chutneys.

INGREDIENTS

- 30 G (1 OZ) BUTTER
- 2 TABLESPOONS VEGETABLE OIL
- 1.4 KG (3 LB) CHICKEN, CUT INTO SMALL JOINTS
- 2 SHALLOTS, PEELED AND CHOPPED
- 4 SMALL ONIONS, PEELED, HALVED AND SLICED
- 1 LEVEL TABLESPOON MEDIUM-HOT CURRY POWDER
- 1 LEVEL TABLESPOON CURRY PASTE
- 1 LEVEL TABLESPOON PLAIN FLOUR
- 425 ML (3/4 PINT) CHICKEN STOCK (SEE P.433)
- 2 TABLESPOONS MANGO CHUTNEY
- STRAINED JUICE 1 LEMON
- 225–275 G (8–10 OZ) COOKING APPLES, PEELED, CORED AND CHOPPED
- 60 G (2 OZ) SULTANAS
- 150 ML (1/4 PINT) SINGLE CREAM
- SALT AND FRESHLY GROUND BLACK PEPPER

PREPARATION TIME: 30 MINUTES
COOKING TIME: 50–60 MINUTES
SERVES FOUR

Guinea Fowl with Asparagus

Rolled, stuffed breasts, sliced and served with a mouth-watering sauce and buttered vegetables make this a dish for a special occasion

INGREDIENTS

2 oven-ready guinea fowls, each approx 1.4 kg (3 lb)
285 ml (½ pint) double cream
1 egg white, size 2
Good pinch freshly grated nutmeg
Salt and freshly ground black pepper
12 spears of sprue asparagus or thin asparagus spears
8 g (¼ oz) dried wild mushrooms
150 ml (¼ pint) boiling water
30 g (1 oz) butter
225 g (8 oz) button mushrooms, wiped and sliced
115 ml (4 fl oz) dry sherry
Fresh chervil to garnish

For the vegetables
900 g (2 lb) small, new potatoes, well scrubbed and scraped
450 g (1 lb) fine green beans, topped and tailed
450 g (1 lb) carrots, peeled and cut into fine strips
Salt
60 g (2 oz) butter
2 tablespoons chopped fresh parsley

Preparation time: 1½ hours
Cooking time: 45 minutes
Serves four

THE FILLING

Using a sharp knife, cut the leg and thigh joints from the guinea fowls, then remove the wings. Remove the skin from the legs and wings and discard it. Take the meat off the bones and mince it finely or chop finely in a food processor. Put the minced or chopped meat into a bowl and mix in 3 tablespoons of the cream, followed by the egg white, nutmeg, and salt and black pepper to taste. Cover and chill in the refrigerator for 1 hour.

Meanwhile, trim the asparagus spears to equal lengths, then steam for 4 minutes until just tender. Rinse under cold water to arrest cooking and drain well.

THE GUINEA FOWL

Carefully remove the breasts from the guinea fowls and discard the skins. (Freeze all the bones for making stock later.) Place each breast between two pieces of cling film and beat out to 3 mm (⅛ in) thick with a rolling pin. Cut four pieces of foil, each 30 cm (12 in) square, and grease one side of each lightly.

Put the dried mushrooms into a bowl with the boiling water and leave to soak.

Lay the guinea fowl breasts on a board, narrow ends pointing towards you, and spread a quarter of the chilled filling over each, leaving a 1.3 cm (½ in) border. Place three asparagus spears across the centre of each breast. Starting at the narrow end, roll up to enclose the filling. Place each breast on a sheet of greased foil, then roll up in the foil and twist the ends tightly to seal. Put the prepared parcels into a baking dish and chill for 30 minutes. Meanwhile, preheat the oven to 190°C (375°F, gas mark 5).

Put the baking dish into the centre of the oven and cook for 45 minutes or until the meat is cooked through.

In the meantime, drain the mushrooms through a sieve lined with kitchen paper, chop them finely and reserve the liquid. Melt the butter in a frying pan, add the soaked mushrooms and button mushrooms and cook over a moderate heat for 5 minutes, stirring frequently until softened. Add the sherry and the mushroom liquid, bring to the boil and keep it boiling until the liquid is reduced to about 1 tablespoon. Set aside until the guinea fowl is cooked.

THE VEGETABLES

When the bird has cooked for 20 minutes, cook the potatoes in lightly salted boiling water for 15–20 minutes.

When the potatoes have been cooking for 15 minutes, cook the beans and carrots, in separate saucepans, in lightly salted boiling water for 5–6 minutes until tender. Drain all the vegetables well.

Melt 30 g (1 oz) of the butter in the potato saucepan, and 15 g (½ oz) in each of the other two saucepans. Stir the chopped parsley into the carrot saucepan. Return the vegetables to their respective pans and toss gently in the hot butter, then transfer to separate heated serving dishes and keep hot while finishing the guinea fowl.

When the guinea fowl is ready, stir the remaining cream into the mushrooms, season well and heat for 3–4 minutes.

Unwrap the foil parcels, cut each roll into thick slices, arrange on heated, individual serving dishes and spoon over a little of the mushroom sauce. Pour the remaining hot sauce into a sauceboat. Garnish the guinea fowl with the fresh chervil and serve with the mushroom sauce and potatoes, beans and glazed carrot strips. Alternatively, serve with cooked rice and a tossed green salad.

Guinea fowl is displayed with principal ingredients that include delicate asparagus and cream for the stuffing and mushrooms for the sauce.

Mixed Game Pie

The lengthy preparation time is amply justified by a richly filled pie

INGREDIENTS

For the rough puff pastry

- 225 g (8 oz) plain flour
- ½ level teaspoon salt
- 175 g (6 oz) butter, cut into walnut-sized pieces
- 1 tablespoon lemon juice
- A little less than 150 ml (¼ pint) chilled water

For the filling

- 2 tablespoons olive oil
- 1 large onion, peeled and chopped
- 900 g (2 lb) oven-ready pheasant, skinned and quartered
- 450 g (1 lb) chicken quarters, skinned
- 2 oven-ready quails
- 340 g (12 oz) venison, diced
- 1 level tablespoon chopped fresh thyme
- 2 level teaspoons chopped fresh rosemary
- 425 ml (¾ pint) red wine
- 425 ml (¾ pint) chicken or game stock (see p.433)
- ½ level teaspoon salt
- Freshly ground black pepper
- 45 g (1½ oz) butter
- 115 g (4 oz) field or closed cup mushrooms, wiped and halved
- 45 g (1½ oz) plain flour
- 1 egg, size 4, beaten

Preparation time: 3 hours
Cooking time: 40–45 minutes
Serves six

To make the rough puff pastry, sift the flour and salt into a bowl and mix in the butter. Do not overmix—the butter must remain in lumps. Add the lemon juice and enough chilled water to bind into a soft dough. Turn onto a floured surface and, without kneading, roll out to about 30 × 18 cm (12 × 7 in). Fold the bottom third up over the centre then bring the top third down over the bottom third. Repeat three times more, wrap and chill.

In the meantime, make the filling. Heat the oil in a saucepan and cook the onion, pheasant and chicken until lightly browned. Add the quails, venison, herbs, wine, stock and seasoning and bring to the boil. Reduce the heat, cover the pan and simmer for 1½ hours or until tender.

Remove the meat from the pan and boil the juices until reduced to 725 ml (1¼ pints). Cut the meat from the bones, cut up large pieces, and discard the bones.

Melt the butter in a saucepan, add the mushrooms and cook gently for 5 minutes. Stir in the flour and cook, stirring, for 1 minute then gradually blend in the reduced cooking juices and boil gently for 5 minutes. Add the meat to the sauce, spoon into a 2 litre (3½ pint), 25 × 20 cm (10 × 8 in) pie dish, place a pie funnel in the centre, and allow to cool.

Preheat the oven to 220°C (425°F, gas mark 7). Roll out the dough to about 5 cm (2 in) larger than the dish. Cut a 2.5 cm (1 in) strip from the edge, brush the edge of the dish with water, press the strip onto it, then brush the strip with water. Cut a small cross in the centre of the remaining dough for the funnel, then cover the pie and press the edges of the dough together. Trim and decorate the edge of the pie, brush the top with the beaten egg and bake for 40–45 minutes until crisp and golden brown.

Pheasant and chicken, quail and venison mingle temptingly beneath a rough puff pastry lid.

The chicken and gammon filling is enriched with cream just before serving.

An elevating story
To Newcastle manufacturer Thomas Bell must go the credit for self-raising flour. In 1901, he mixed his Royal baking powder, so called from its Royal warrant, with plain flour and called it BeRo. His firm was later acquired by Rank Hovis McDougall.

Cornish Chicken & Gammon Pie

Pies like this have always been delightfully decorated either with shapes such as pastry leaves, or with patterns cut into the pastry

To make the pastry, sift the flour and salt into a mixing bowl and rub in the butter and the lard or vegetable fat until the mixture resembles fine breadcrumbs. Add the beaten egg and water and mix to form a firm dough. Wrap the dough in cling film and chill while preheating the oven to 220°c (425°f, gas mark 7).

Roll out just over half the dough into a round large enough to line the base and sides of a deep, 20 cm (8 in) pie plate. Line the plate with the dough, place a pie funnel in the centre and arrange the chicken round the funnel. Season well with the pepper and sprinkle with the parsley and onion. Arrange the gammon on top and sprinkle with the mace and more black pepper. Brush the edges of the dough with cold water.

Roll out the remaining dough into a round large enough to cover the pie and place it in position, cutting a cross in the centre to accommodate the pie funnel. Press the edges of the dough together well to seal, then trim and decorate the edge. Decorate the top of the pie with leaves made from the trimmings.

Brush the pie all over with milk and bake in the centre of the oven for 15 minutes. Reduce the temperature to 190°c (375°f, gas mark 5) and continue cooking for 1 hour. If the pastry begins to brown too much, cover it loosely with foil.

Remove the pie from the oven. Pour the cream into a saucepan, bring it almost to the boil and pour it carefully through the pie funnel. Serve immediately the cream has been added.

Ingredients

For the pastry
- 225 g (8 oz) plain flour
- Pinch of salt
- 60 g (2 oz) butter
- 60 g (2 oz) lard or white vegetable fat
- 1 egg, size 3, beaten
- 1 tablespoon cold water
- Milk for brushing

For the filling
- 450 g (1 lb) boneless chicken, skinned and cut into large cubes
- Freshly ground black pepper
- 60 g (2 oz) fresh parsley, chopped
- 85 g (3 oz) onion, peeled and chopped
- 225 g (8 oz) gammon steak, rind removed, cut into large cubes the same size as the chicken cubes
- ¼ level teaspoon ground mace
- 150 ml (¼ pint) double cream

Preparation time: 30 minutes
Cooking time: 1¼ hours
Serves four to six

Casseroled Pigeons with Red Wine

The one-pot meal needs no attention once it is in the oven, so you can go out and have a hot meal ready on your return

INGREDIENTS

- 30G (1OZ) LARD OR 2 TABLESPOONS OLIVE OIL
- 4 OVEN-READY WOOD PIGEONS
- 2 MEDIUM ONIONS, PEELED AND CHOPPED
- 550G (1¼ LB) RED CABBAGE, FINELY SHREDDED
- 425ML (¾ PINT) RED WINE
- 3 TABLESPOONS REDCURRANT OR ROWAN JELLY, HOMEMADE (SEE PP.401, 411) OR BOUGHT
- 225G (8OZ) PEELED FRESH CHESTNUTS (SEE P.440) OR FROZEN PEELED CHESTNUTS
- SALT AND FRESHLY GROUND BLACK PEPPER

PREPARATION TIME: 40 MINUTES
COOKING TIME: 2½ HOURS
SERVES FOUR

Preheat the oven to 160°C (325°F, gas mark 3). Heat the lard or oil in a large, flameproof casserole, add the pigeons and fry them over a high heat until well browned all over. Using a slotted spoon, transfer them to a plate. Reduce the heat, add the onions to the casserole and cook gently for 5 minutes. Add the cabbage and toss lightly in the fat, then add the wine and the redcurrant or rowan jelly and bring to the boil. Remove from the heat and mix in the chestnuts.

Using a large, sharp knife or poultry shears, cut away the backbone from each pigeon, cutting from the tail end down to the neck end and leaving the breast with the wings and legs still attached. This makes it easier to eat the pigeons, as they will sit more steadily on the plate.

Return the pigeons to the casserole, season well and bury them in the cabbage, making sure they are well covered. Cover the casserole, put it in the centre of the oven and cook for 2½ hours, or until the pigeons are tender.

Serve the pigeons, straight from the casserole, accompanied by either jacket or creamed potatoes.

Farmer's enemy
The reason for the wood pigeon's plumpness is its voracious appetite which, when multiplied by flocks, can lay waste to acres of root crops, clover, kale or peas.

Red wine, chestnuts, and rowan or redcurrant jelly enrich this warming casserole of wood pigeons.

The partridges are poached in a rich, red wine sauce, then served with mushrooms stuffed with veal.

Brighouse Spiced Partridges

This is a Yorkshire version of a favourite old recipe

Remove and finely chop the stalks from the mushrooms and put them into a large bowl with the veal or pork and the breadcrumbs, parsley, thyme, lemon rind and some salt and pepper. Add the egg and mix well, then cover the bowl and chill until required.

Heat the butter and 1 tablespoon of the oil in a large, heavy-based saucepan. Add the partridges and cook over a moderate heat, turning them frequently until golden, then transfer to a plate. Add the onions to the saucepan and cook gently for 5 minutes until just softened.

Put the cloves, mace, cayenne pepper, flour and 1 level teaspoon of the pepper into a small bowl and mix well. Return the birds to the pan and sprinkle with the seasoned flour. Pour in the wine and stock and bring to the boil, stirring occasionally. Reduce the heat, cover and simmer very gently for 1 hour or until the birds are tender. Meanwhile, preheat the oven to 200°C (400°F, gas mark 6).

Put the mushrooms, stalk sides up, onto a lightly greased baking tray. Divide the chilled veal mixture equally among the mushrooms and drizzle with the remaining olive oil. Cook in the centre of the oven for 30 minutes or until the mushrooms are tender and the stuffing is cooked through.

Transfer the cooked partridges to a chopping board and, using poultry shears or a large knife, cut each one in half through the breast. Using a slotted spoon, remove the onions from the pan and arrange them on a heated serving dish. Place the partridges on top of the onions, cover and keep hot. Bring the cooking juices to the boil and strain into a heated gravy boat. If the juices are thin, boil rapidly to reduce and thicken.

Arrange the stuffed mushrooms round the partridges and serve with the sauce. Savoy cabbage, steamed with fennel seeds and walnut pieces, and creamed potatoes make good accompaniments.

INGREDIENTS

- 8 medium field, flat or open cup mushrooms, approx 400g (14oz) in weight
- 225g (8oz) British veal, minced, or pork, minced
- 115g (4oz) fresh white breadcrumbs
- 4 tablespoons chopped fresh parsley
- 2 level teaspoons chopped fresh thyme
- Finely grated rind 1 small lemon
- Salt and freshly ground black pepper
- 1 egg, size 3, beaten
- 30g (1oz) butter
- 2 tablespoons olive oil
- 2 oven-ready partridges, rinsed and dried
- 2 large onions, peeled and cut into eighths
- 1 level teaspoon ground cloves
- ½ level teaspoon ground mace
- Pinch of cayenne pepper
- 30g (1oz) plain flour
- 285ml (½ pint) red wine
- 150ml (¼ pint) chicken stock (see p.433)

Preparation time: 1 hour
Cooking time: 1¼ hours
Serves four

The pork back fat and the red wine keep the venison moist and succulent during cooking.

Braised Venison with Claret

The rich, dark meat combines with everyday carrots and onions to create a winner for you to put before family and friends

INGREDIENTS

- 175 g (6 oz) pork back fat, chilled and cut into wide strips
- 1.1–1.4 kg (2½–3 lb) piece venison cut from the top of the haunch, skin removed
- 2 tablespoons olive oil
- 2 medium onions, peeled and quartered
- 1 garlic clove, peeled and crushed
- 2 medium carrots, peeled and roughly chopped
- Bouquet garni made with a thyme sprig, parsley, bay leaf and celery leaves (see p.440)
- 285 ml (½ pint) claret
- 150 ml (¼ pint) beef stock (see p.432)
- 1 tablespoon red wine vinegar
- 1 tablespoon brown sugar
- 2 level tablespoons plain flour
- 15 g (½ oz) butter, softened
- Salt and freshly ground black pepper
- Pinch of cayenne pepper

Preparation time: 40 minutes
Cooking time: Approx 2 hours
Serves four

Preheat the oven to 180°c (350°f, gas mark 4). Lay the strips of pork fat over the venison and tie at intervals with clean, thin string.

Heat the oil in a flameproof casserole just big enough to hold the venison and vegetables. Brown the venison well all over, remove from the casserole and set aside. Add the onions, garlic, carrots and bouquet garni to the oil remaining in the casserole and stir well until the vegetables glisten. Put the venison on top and pour in the claret, stock, vinegar and brown sugar. Cover and cook in the centre of the oven for 1½–2 hours until tender.

Carefully transfer the venison to a heated serving dish, cover and keep hot. Skim the fat from the cooking liquid and strain the liquid into a measuring jug. There should be 425 ml (¾ pint). If there is more, boil rapidly until reduced to the right amount. If less, make up with stock or water and bring to the boil.

Blend the flour with the softened butter and gradually whisk it into the hot liquid, stirring over a moderate heat until the sauce has thickened slightly. Reduce the heat, season with the salt, black pepper and cayenne pepper and simmer for 2–3 minutes. Pour into a gravy boat and serve with the venison.

Boiled potatoes, hot chestnut purée and braised celery make excellent accompaniments to the venison.

Fillets of Fowl with Cucumbers

The Victorians were fond of cucumber as a hot vegetable—here it complements the flavour of the chicken very well

Heat the oil and butter in a large frying pan until foaming. Add the chicken and brown well all over, then remove from the pan and put onto a plate.

Add the cucumber sticks and fry gently for 2 minutes or until they are just beginning to change colour. Return the chicken to the pan, pour over the vermouth and season well. Bring to the boil, reduce the heat, cover and simmer gently for 20 minutes, or until cooked through.

Using a slotted spoon, transfer the chicken and cucumber to a warm serving dish. Cover and keep warm.

Stir the cream into the juices remaining in the pan, bring to the boil and boil for 1 minute or until the sauce thickens slightly. Taste and adjust the seasoning.

Pour the sauce over the chicken and cucumbers and garnish with the parsley. Serve immediately, accompanied by new potatoes cooked with mint.

Ingredients

- 2 tablespoons olive oil
- 60 g (2 oz) butter
- 4 boneless chicken breasts, each approx 175–225 g (6–8 oz), skinned
- 1 medium cucumber, well washed and cut into 5 cm (2 in) sticks
- 150 ml (¼ pint) dry vermouth or dry white wine
- Salt and freshly ground black pepper
- 285 ml (½ pint) double cream
- Fresh parsley sprigs to garnish

Preparation time: 15 minutes
Cooking time: 25 minutes
Serves four

Dry vermouth and double cream give the tender chicken and cucumber a taste of luxury.

Church flock
A member of the WVS and the vicar—an ARP warden—feed chickens in a churchyard in East London. During the war, with eggs rationed at one per person per fortnight, those who could keep a hen or two ate a little better whilst helping the war effort.

Roast Duck with Orange Sauce

Rosemary sprigs and orange in the stuffing, with red wine, redcurrant jelly and orange in the sauce, give piquancy to this dish

Ingredients

- 2.3–2.7 kg (5–6 lb) oven-ready duck, with giblets
- 850 ml (1½ pints) water
- Bouquet garni (see p.440)
- 1 small onion, peeled and halved
- 6 black peppercorns
- 4 allspice berries
- 1 small carrot, peeled and sliced
- 2 fresh rosemary sprigs
- 1 medium onion, peeled
- 1 orange, halved
- 30 g (1 oz) butter
- Salt and freshly ground black pepper

For the sauce

- 2 tablespoons olive oil
- 1 small onion, peeled and chopped
- 1 medium carrot, peeled and chopped
- 1 level tablespoon plain flour
- Salt and freshly ground black pepper
- 1 large orange, washed
- Strained juice 2 oranges
- 200 ml (7 fl oz) red wine
- 2 tablespoons redcurrant jelly, homemade (see p.401) or bought
- Fresh rosemary sprigs to garnish

For the vegetables

- 900 g (2 lb) potatoes
- 30 g (1 oz) butter
- 1–2 tablespoons cream or milk
- 450 g (1 lb) shelled peas
- 1–2 tablespoons mint jelly, homemade (see p.388) or bought

Preparation time: 35 minutes
Cooking time: 2½ hours
Serves four

The Giblet Stock

Rinse the giblets under cold water and put them into a saucepan with the water, bouquet garni, small onion, peppercorns, allspice berries and sliced carrot. Bring to the boil then immediately reduce the heat and skim off any scum which has risen to the surface. Partially cover and simmer gently for 1 hour. Meanwhile, preheat the oven to 220°C (425°F, gas mark 7).

Strain the giblet stock through a fine sieve and reserve for the sauce. There should be 570 ml (1 pint). If necessary, boil gently until reduced or make up with cold water or chicken stock (see p.433).

Rinse the inside of the duck under cold running water, drain well and pat dry with kitchen paper. Put the rosemary sprigs, the medium onion and one orange half inside the duck and truss the legs together. Prick the skin all over with a fork or skewer, put the duck onto a rack in a roasting tin and squeeze over the juice from the other orange half. Dot the bird with the butter and season well with the salt and pepper. Put into the centre of the oven and roast for 30 minutes, then reduce the oven temperature to 180°C (350°F, gas mark 4) and continue to cook for a further 1–1½ hours or until the duck is well done. Baste twice during cooking and cover with foil if the skin begins to brown too much.

The Sauce and the Potatoes

Twenty minutes before the end of the cooking time, start to make the sauce. Heat the oil in a saucepan and sauté the chopped onion and carrot gently until the onion is light golden brown. Stir in the flour and cook for 1 minute then blend in the strained giblet stock and season well. Bring to the boil, stirring, then boil gently until the sauce is reduced to 425 ml (¾ pint). Remove from the heat, strain into a clean saucepan and set aside.

While the sauce is reducing, boil the potatoes until tender, drain well and mash with the butter, cream or milk and some salt and pepper. Transfer to a serving dish, cover and keep hot.

Using a stainless steel vegetable peeler, thinly pare the rind from the orange and cut it into fine shreds with a sharp knife. Remove and discard the pith. Holding the orange over a bowl to catch the juice, cut out each segment by slicing down between the segment and the membrane on either side, cutting as close to the membrane as possible. Squeeze the remaining tissue to extract the juice and set the segments and juice aside. Put the shredded peel into a saucepan with barely enough water to cover and boil for 2 minutes. Remove from the heat and set aside.

Carefully transfer the cooked duck to a heated serving plate, cover with foil and keep warm. Skim all the fat from the roasting tin. Heat the rich juices that are left behind, then pour in the red wine and bring to the boil, stirring and scraping the browned residue from the bottom of the tin. Strain through a sieve into the sauce. Stir in the orange juice, half the blanched orange rind and the redcurrant jelly. Simmer for 5 minutes, stirring frequently, then stir in the orange segments with their juice, and heat for 1 minute. Season to taste with salt and pepper.

The Minted Peas

While completing the sauce, cook the peas until tender, drain well and return to the pan. Add the mint jelly and toss over a moderate heat until the peas are evenly coated. Transfer to a heated serving dish, cover and keep hot.

Spoon a little of the sauce over and around the duck as a glaze. Pour the remainder into a heated sauceboat and garnish with the remaining orange rind and the fresh rosemary.

Using a sharp carving knife, cut off the duck's legs, then carve the breast meat into long, medium-thick slices. Serve accompanied by the sauce and vegetables.

Mashed potatoes and minted peas accompany the duck, which is glazed with the orange sauce.

Roast Chicken Blistered with Raspings & Cheese

In this traditional recipe, chicken takes the place of capon, which was a mainstay of British cooking for hundreds of years

INGREDIENTS

For the stuffing

- 175g (6oz) fresh white breadcrumbs
- 115g (4oz) shredded beef or vegetable suet
- 85g (3oz) lean back bacon, rinds removed, finely diced
- 2 heaped tablespoons finely chopped fresh parsley
- Finely grated rind 1 lemon
- 1 small onion, peeled and grated
- 2 eggs, size 4, beaten
- ¼ level teaspoon each ground nutmeg, salt and freshly ground black pepper

For the chicken

- Small bunch fresh thyme or 1 level tablespoon dried thyme
- 85g (3oz) butter, softened
- 2.3–2.7 kg (5–6lb) oven-ready chicken
- Salt and freshly ground black pepper
- 200ml (7fl oz) hot water
- 85g (3oz) raspings (see p.440)
- 30g (1oz) Lancashire or Cheddar cheese, finely grated
- 285ml (½ pint) chicken stock (see p.433)

Preparation time: 30 minutes
Cooking time: 2 hours
Serves eight

Preheat the oven to 180°c (350°f, gas mark 4). Mix all the ingredients for the stuffing in a bowl with a fork. Stuff the neck end of the bird loosely with half the mixture, then shape the remainder into balls and set aside.

Put the thyme and 30g (1oz) of the butter inside the chicken, season well and truss neatly. Place in a roasting tin, spread the remaining butter over the skin and season. Cover the breast with foil and roast for 1 hour, basting frequently.

Remove the bird from the oven and stir the hot water into the pan juices, then baste again. Arrange the stuffing balls round the bird and return to the oven for 40 minutes, basting occasionally. Meanwhile, mix the raspings and cheese together and set aside.

Take the bird out of the oven and increase the oven temperature to 200°c (400°f, gas mark 6). Baste the bird once more, then press the raspings mixture all over the breast and legs. Return to the oven for 20 minutes, or until golden brown and cooked through.

Transfer the chicken and the stuffing balls to a serving dish, cover and keep warm. Stir the stock into the pan juices and bring to the boil, stirring frequently. Reduce the heat and simmer for 2–3 minutes, then strain the gravy into a heated gravy boat.

Serve the chicken surrounded by roast potatoes and bacon rolls and accompanied by the gravy and buttered cabbage or spring greens, brussels sprouts or green beans and carrots.

Raspings mixed with cheese give a crisp golden finish to the lavishly stuffed roast bird.

The casserole has a robust flavour because the venison has been marinated in stout and ruby port.

Press a plate on top of the venison pieces to ensure that they are all covered completely by the marinade.

Civet of Venison

Glazed button onions and bacon strips embellish this very special dish

Put the venison, stout, bouquet garni and port into a large bowl. Cover the bowl and refrigerate overnight.

To cook the venison, preheat the oven to 140°c (275°f, gas mark 1). Using a slotted spoon, lift the meat from the marinade and pat dry with kitchen paper. Reserve the marinade. Heat the butter and 2 tablespoons of the oil in a large, flameproof casserole, brown the cubes in batches and transfer them to a plate.

Heat the remaining oil in the casserole, add the onion and garlic and cook for 2–3 minutes. Add the meat and any juices remaining on the plate, stir in the flour and cook for 2 minutes. Pour in the marinade with the bouquet garni and bring to simmering point, stirring. Cover the casserole and cook in the centre of the oven for 3 hours or until the venison is tender. Season to taste.

To prepare the garnish, about 30 minutes before the end of the cooking time put the button onions into a saucepan, large enough to contain them in a single layer, and barely cover them with cold water. Add the butter, a little salt and the sugar. Bring to the boil and continue boiling until the liquid has been reduced to a syrup. Reduce the heat to low. Shake the pan and swirl the onions until they are evenly coated in the caramel glaze, taking care not to let them burn. Remove from the heat, cover and keep warm.

Heat 1 tablespoon of the oil in a frying pan and fry the bacon strips until just crisp. Drain on kitchen paper and keep warm. Heat the remaining oil and fry the bread on each side until golden. Drain on kitchen paper and keep warm.

To serve the venison, remove the bouquet garni from the casserole, then scatter the onions and bacon on top. Dip the edges of the fried bread in the parsley and arrange the slices around the rim of the casserole. Alternatively, the fried bread can be arranged round the casserole and the parsley scattered on top.

Ingredients

- 1.4 kg (3 lb) shoulder of venison, cut into large cubes
- 570 ml (1 pint) stout
- Bouquet garni of thyme, parsley and bay leaf (see p.440)
- 150 ml (¼ pint) ruby port
- 30 g (1 oz) butter
- 3 tablespoons olive oil
- 1 medium onion, peeled and chopped
- 1 garlic clove, peeled and chopped
- 2 level tablespoons plain flour
- Salt and freshly ground black pepper

For the garnish

- 12 button onions, peeled
- 15 g (½ oz) butter
- Salt
- 1 level tablespoon demerara sugar
- 5–6 tablespoons olive oil
- 115 g (4 oz) thickly sliced streaky bacon, rinds removed, cut into strips
- 6 thin slices stale white bread, crusts removed, each slice cut into 4 triangles
- 3 tablespoons very finely chopped fresh parsley

Preparation time: 45 minutes
Marinating time: overnight
Cooking time: 3 hours
Serves six

Straw potatoes and rowan jelly add the final touch to the roast grouse.

Heather Roast Grouse

Roasting the grouse with heather gives a subtle savour to the meat

INGREDIENTS

175 G (6 OZ) BUTTER, SOFTENED
2 TEASPOONS LEMON JUICE
SALT AND FRESHLY GROUND BLACK PEPPER
4 THICK SLICES DESSERT APPLE
4 OVEN-READY GROUSE, LIVERS RESERVED
FEW FRESH HEATHER SPRIGS
16 LARGE RASHERS STREAKY BACON, RINDS REMOVED
4 SLICES DAY-OLD WHITE BREAD, 1.3 CM (½ IN) THICK, CRUSTS REMOVED
VEGETABLE OIL FOR FRYING
FRESH HEATHER SPRIGS TO GARNISH

PREPARATION TIME: 45 MINUTES
COOKING TIME: APPROX 45 MINUTES
SERVES FOUR

PREHEAT the oven to 180°C (350°F, gas mark 4). Mix 60 g (2 oz) of the butter with the lemon juice and salt and pepper to taste. Put half the seasoned butter and one slice of apple inside each grouse.

Place a few sprigs of heather on the breast of each bird and cover and secure them with the bacon rashers.

Put the grouse into a roasting tin and cover lightly with buttered foil or greaseproof paper. Roast in the centre of the oven for 30–45 minutes or until just cooked, removing the foil or greaseproof paper for the last 10 minutes to allow the bacon to brown.

Meanwhile, melt 60 g (2 oz) of the remaining butter in a small frying pan, add the grouse livers and sauté them for 2–3 minutes until just cooked through. Mash the cooked livers in a mortar with a pestle or in a bowl with a wooden spoon. Mix the remaining butter into the livers and season to taste.

Heat a little vegetable oil in a frying pan, add the slices of bread and fry until crisp and golden brown on both sides. Drain well on kitchen paper, then spread the liver paste over each slice and place on a serving dish.

Remove the heather and bacon from the grouse and discard the heather. Place one bird on each slice of fried bread and garnish with the crisp bacon and fresh sprigs of heather. Serve with straw potatoes (see p.441), watercress and rowan or redcurrant jelly.

Winchester Pheasant Casserole

This method of cooking pheasant is ideal for adding succulence to older birds

PREHEAT the oven to 180°c (350°F, gas mark 4). Put the two pheasants into a roasting tin, cover the tin tightly with foil, put into the centre of the oven and cook for 1 hour or until the meat is tender and the juices run clear. Remove from the oven, transfer the pheasants to a plate and cover with foil. Leave the oven on.

Next, make the sauce. Pour the liquid from the roasting tin into a measuring jug, then spoon 2 tablespoons of fat from the top back into the tin. Skim off and discard the remainder of the fat. Make the juices up to 725 ml (1¼ pints) with chicken stock.

Add the sliced onion to the fat in the roasting tin and cook over a moderate heat for 10 minutes or until dark golden but not browned, scraping the sediment from the base of the tin. Mix in the flour and cook for 2–3 minutes, stirring continuously, then gradually blend in the stock and the sherry. Bring to the boil, stirring continuously, and boil until the sauce is smooth and has thickened. Reduce the heat, stir in the redcurrant jelly and season with salt and pepper, then simmer gently for 5 minutes.

Meanwhile, using a sharp knife or poultry shears, cut each pheasant into quarters and cut away the backbone of each. If the legs or wings contain shot, carefully remove as much as possible of the surrounding bruised meat. Put the pheasant quarters into a large casserole and pour over the sauce. Cover the casserole and cook in the centre of the oven for 1¼ hours.

Thirty minutes before the end of the cooking time, melt the butter in a frying pan, add the mushrooms and sauté gently for 5 minutes, then add to the casserole and continue cooking.

Serve garnished with the grapes and accompanied by brussels sprouts, braised celery and sautéed potatoes.

INGREDIENTS

1 BRACE OVEN-READY PHEASANTS,
APPROX 285 ML (½ PINT) CHICKEN STOCK (SEE P.433)
1 LARGE ONION, PEELED AND FINELY SLICED
60 G (2 OZ) PLAIN FLOUR
150 ML (¼ PINT) DRY SHERRY
2 TEASPOONS REDCURRANT JELLY, HOMEMADE (SEE P.401) OR BOUGHT
SALT AND FRESHLY GROUND BLACK PEPPER
30 G (1 OZ) UNSALTED BUTTER
225 G (8 OZ) SMALL, CLOSED CAP MUSHROOMS, WIPED
SEEDLESS WHITE GRAPES TO GARNISH

PREPARATION TIME: 45 MINUTES
COOKING TIME: 2¼ HOURS
SERVES FOUR

Sherry and redcurrant jelly blend beautifully with the pheasant juices in a rich sauce.

PICKING UP
The springer spaniel is greatly valued on pheasant shoots for its keen nose, soft mouth and sheer muscle power which make it ideal for picking up dead birds in cover. It is perhaps a little too exuberant to make an ideal household pet.

Shops & Supershops

'Pile it high and sell it cheap' was the swashbuckling slogan of Jack (later Sir John) Cohen, founder of Tesco Stores

BY THE 1930s most of the Olympians of High Street food retailing were firmly in place. Some indeed had been there for a considerable time already, owing their beginnings to the outward sprawl of the industrial cities.

John James Sainsbury opened his first shop in London's Drury Lane in 1869, and two years later Thomas Lipton launched his grocery business in Glasgow. In 1872, John Budgen founded a chain of stores in the Thames Valley and by the 1880s firms like Home & Colonial and David Greig were making their mark in other parts of the country. Two young shop assistants named Waite and Rose amalgamated names and futures in their Acton premises in 1904. Appearing still later on the scene was ex-Royal Flying Corps mechanic and costermonger Jack Cohen, who quit the markets to open his first Tesco store in 1930.

A STARCHED AND STACKED MAYPOLE DAIRY OF THE 1920S

All in fact had realised that, to entice customers with an ever-expanding range of cheap provisions, market stalls were inadequate and even fixed shops must constantly grow in size and numbers. Profits depended on fast turnover and low margins. All started small and spread rapidly, and all sold much the same commodities—butter, tea and sugar, bacon and ham, and a growing range of preserves and tinned foods. But their styles of doing so, in the earlier years of the century, were very different. Waitrose favoured a restrained approach, with mahogany shelves and counters inlaid with satinwood and backed by mirrors. Sainsbury, however, preferred long, cool interiors with small window areas in relation to the depth of the room. The decor was in the firm's highly individual style—white marble counters faced with floral tiles. It was the backdrop for a sumptuous display of cheeses, bacon, eggs in straw baskets and York hams on china stands.

Though late in the field, Tesco overhauled fast during the 1930s. Its early methods owed much to the street market techniques of its founder, who was not known as Slasher Jack for nothing. The shops were small, and fronted on the pavement by tables and benches stacked with mountains of tinned fruit and meat. A barker stood beside them extolling their virtues to passers-by and shaving halfpence off the prices to attract wavering customers.

Whatever their methods, the multiple stores kept long hours and employed many assistants. The Second World War brought acute staff shortages and, in reply, the Romford Co-operative Society opened the first British self-service store in 1942. Other stores followed suit, no doubt intending to return to normal when hostilities ceased. But busy shoppers felt no yearning for the old, leisurely counter service, and the seeds of the future supermarkets were already firmly planted.

First in the field
Born in Rochdale in 1844, the Co-operative Movement's shops won early success by paying a dividend to customers.

Cutting it fine
A prewar Sainsbury manager shows his skills on the hand-operated bacon slicer which could swiftly dispense rashers in any one of 20 thicknesses.

Packers' pride
At the century's beginning, most groceries were weighed from anonymous sacks and cases into unmarked paper bags. In a few decades, however, high-street chain stores were concentrating on prepacked goods bearing either their own names or those of manufacturers, some of whose labels brought them nationwide fame.

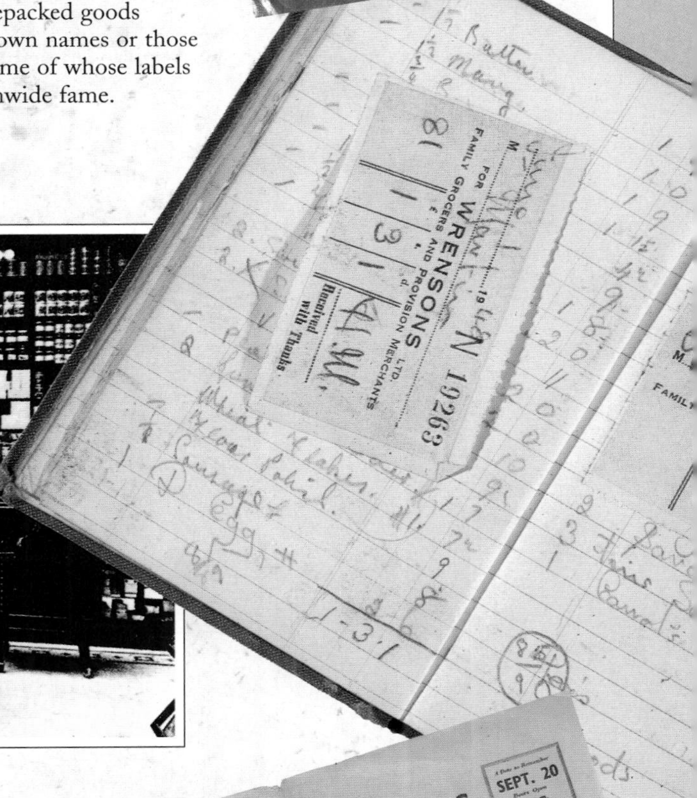

Purveyors' progress
Since the 1920s, shopping has seen many changes, from the customer's order book with its comfort of weekly credit, to the discreetly opulent manner of a high-street Waitrose. The postwar years saw the onset of self-service, paving the way for the modern supermarket.

Pigeon Pie

Wood pigeons, considered choice meat, were often made into pies both in great houses and country cottages

INGREDIENTS

For the pastry
- 225 g (8 oz) plain flour
- Pinch of salt
- 60 g (2 oz) butter or polyunsaturated margarine
- 60 g (2 oz) lard
- 3 tablespoons cold water
- 1 egg, beaten or milk to glaze

For the filling
- 450 g (1 lb) pigeon meat (taken from breasts and legs of 4 pigeons), skinned
- 225 g (8 oz) rump steak, trimmed of fat, diced
- 1 level tablespoon plain flour seasoned well with salt and pepper
- 115 g (4 oz) bacon, rinds removed, diced
- 115 g (4 oz) field, flat or open cup mushrooms, wiped and sliced
- 200 ml (7 fl oz) chicken or game stock (see p.433)
- 2 bay leaves

Preparation time: 1½ hours
Cooking time: 1½ hours
Serves four

To make the pastry, sift the flour and salt into a bowl and rub in the fats until the mixture resembles fine breadcrumbs. Add the water and mix to form a dough. Knead gently on a lightly floured surface for a few seconds until smooth, then wrap in cling film and chill while preparing the filling.

Put the pigeon meat into an 850 ml (1½ pint) pie dish or a casserole with a rim. Toss the steak in the seasoned flour and add it to the dish with the bacon, mushrooms, stock and bay leaves.

Roll out the dough on a floured surface to about 2.5 cm (1 in) larger than the top of the pie dish or casserole. Cut a 1.3 cm (½ in) wide strip from round the edge of the dough, and press it onto the dampened rim. Brush with water and cover the pie with the remaining piece of dough, pressing the edges together well to seal. Make a small hole in the centre of the pie to allow the steam to escape. Trim the excess dough from round the edge and use to decorate the pie top. Chill for 30 minutes or until required for baking.

Preheat the oven to 220°C (425°F, gas mark 7). Brush the top of the pie with the beaten egg or milk and put it onto a baking tray. Bake in the centre of the oven for 30 minutes or until golden brown, then reduce the oven temperature to 180°C (350°F, gas mark 4) and continue cooking for 1 hour more or until the meat is tender. Cover with foil if the pastry starts to overbrown. To test if it is tender, insert a skewer into the meat through the hole in the centre of the pastry.

Under its pastry crust, the pie is brimful with pigeon meat, steak, bacon and mushrooms.

It is usual to serve the birds slightly underdone and accompanied by a piquant sauce.

Mallard
This, the best known of British ducks, has learned to live in close proximity to humankind in city parks and even depends upon it to supplement its food. In the country, however, the bird is extremely wary and will reconnoitre a pond for some time before landing.

Spit-Roasted Wild Duck

Originally roasted by rotating over an open fire, wild duck can easily be cooked in the oven even if there is no spit

Preheat the oven to 200°c (400°f, gas mark 6). Wipe the mallards inside and out with a damp cloth. Slice the bread in half, lay it in a dish and pour over the port. Leave to soak for 2–3 minutes, then put two pieces of bread inside each duck, together with a sprig of thyme.

Dust the birds all over with the seasoned flour and either spit roast them for 50–60 minutes, basting regularly with melted butter, or place them on a rack in a roasting tin. Dot the breasts with the butter and roast in the oven for 50–60 minutes, basting three or four times.

While the birds are roasting, make the sauce. Put the port into a small saucepan, add the shallot and simmer gently for 10 minutes. Stir in the thyme jelly and, when it has melted, add the vinegar. Taste and add a little more vinegar if wished—the sauce should be sweet with just a hint of sharpness. Pour into a heated sauceboat and keep warm.

Remove the ducks from the spit or roasting tin and place them on a heated serving dish. Skim all the fat from the roasting tin, or from the drip pan beneath the spit, leaving the juices behind. Spoon the juices over the birds and serve with small, crisp, roast potatoes, roast parsnips, lightly boiled leeks and brussels sprouts. Serve the sauce separately.

Ingredients

- 2 oven-ready mallards, each approx 550g (1¼lb)
- 2 thick slices white bread, crusts removed
- 4 tablespoons port
- 2 fresh thyme sprigs
- 2 tablespoons plain flour seasoned well with salt and pepper
- 30g (1 oz) butter (melted if spit roasting)

For the sauce

- 115ml (4fl oz) port
- 1 shallot, peeled and very finely chopped
- 2 tablespoons thyme jelly, homemade (see p.388) or bought
- 2 teaspoons red wine vinegar

Preparation time: 25 minutes
Cooking time: 50–60 minutes
Serves four

Mrs Bond and the ducks
According to an old folk song, Mrs Bond was an innkeeper who went to the pond with plenty of onions and sage, calling to her ducks 'Dilly, dilly, dilly, come and be killed, For you must be stuffed and my customers filled!'

The duck in its spicy sauce is delicious with new potatoes and runner beans.

Ragout of Duck with Allspice

In France, a ragout is a plain stew but in Britain it is a dish that is braised slowly in a highly seasoned sauce

INGREDIENTS

- 2 oven-ready ducks, each approx 1.4 kg (3 lb), quartered
- 1 large onion, peeled and studded with 6 cloves
- 12 allspice berries
- 2.5 cm (1 in) piece fresh root ginger, peeled and sliced
- 1 level teaspoon ground allspice
- 425 ml (¾ pint) chicken stock (see p.433)
- 30 g (1 oz) butter
- 30 g (1 oz) plain flour
- 1–2 tablespoons lemon juice
- 1 tablespoon mushroom ketchup
- Salt and freshly ground black pepper

Preparation time: 20 minutes
Cooking time: 1¾ hours
Serves four

Dry fry the duck in a flameproof casserole until well browned. Strain off the fat, add the onion, spices and stock and bring to the boil. Cover and simmer for 1–1½ hours until the duck is tender, then transfer to a heated dish and keep warm.

Skim the fat from the casserole and strain the stock into a measuring jug; there should be about 425 ml (¾ pint). Boil to reduce, or add water if required.

Melt the butter in a saucepan, stir in the flour and cook for 1 minute, then gradually add the stock. Bring to the boil, stirring, then simmer for 2 minutes. Stir in the lemon juice and ketchup, season to taste, then pour over the duck and serve.

Duck Braised with Green Peas

Cooking the peas in the roasting tin with the duck ensures that each absorbs a little of the other's complementary flavour

Preheat the oven to 180°C (350°F, gas mark 4). Remove the giblets from the duck, rinse it well under cold water and pat dry with kitchen paper. Rinse and drain the giblets. Prick the duck's skin all over with a fork.

Heat the oil and 30g (1oz) of the butter in a large, flameproof casserole or deep roasting tin. Add the duck, breast side down, and fry for 3–4 minutes until the breast is well browned, then fry the underside. Remove the duck, add the giblets to the pan and fry for 2–3 minutes until lightly browned. Remove from the pan and put with the duck. Pour away all the fat from the casserole or roasting tin and wipe it with kitchen paper.

Return the duck and giblets to the casserole or roasting tin, add the stock and bring to the boil. Remove from the heat, cover with a lid or foil and cook near the top of the oven for 30 minutes. Take the casserole or roasting tin out of the oven, remove the giblets and add the peas, herbs and seasonings. Cover and return to the oven for 1 hour or until the duck is cooked.

Remove the duck from the casserole or roasting tin and place on a heated serving dish. Using a slotted spoon, lift the peas out of the stock, place them round the duck, cover and keep warm.

Soften the remaining butter and mix in the flour. Gradually add the mixture to the duck stock and, with a wire whisk, stir over a gentle heat until slightly thickened. Strain into a heated sauceboat.

Garnish the duck with the mint or marjoram sprigs and serve with the sauce and sliced, minted new potatoes.

INGREDIENTS

- 2.5KG (5½LB) OVEN-READY DUCK
- 1 TABLESPOON OLIVE OIL
- 60G (2OZ) BUTTER
- 570ML (1 PINT) CHICKEN STOCK, (SEE P.433)
- 450G (1LB) FRESHLY SHELLED PEAS FROM APPROX 1KG (2LB 3OZ) PEAS IN PODS, OR FROZEN PEAS
- 1 TABLESPOON CHOPPED FRESH MINT
- 1 TABLESPOON CHOPPED FRESH MARJORAM
- ¼ LEVEL TEASPOON GROUND MACE
- ¼ LEVEL TEASPOON SALT
- ¼ LEVEL TEASPOON FRESHLY GROUND BLACK PEPPER
- 20G (¾OZ) PLAIN FLOUR
- MINT OR MARJORAM SPRIGS TO GARNISH

PREPARATION TIME: 20 MINUTES
COOKING TIME: 1½ HOURS
SERVES FOUR

Duck braised in stock with peas, mint and marjoram makes a tender, springtime dish.

Raised Game Pie

This creation of high culinary art is quite easy to make if you follow these straightforward instructions

INGREDIENTS

675g (1½lb) duck breasts
2 oven-ready pheasants
4 tablespoons brandy
1 tablespoon olive oil
A few fresh thyme sprigs
Salt and freshly ground black pepper
1 carrot, peeled and halved
1 onion, peeled and halved
Bouquet garni, made with parsley sprig, thyme sprig and a bay leaf (see p.440)
115g (4oz) minced pork
115g (4oz) lean bacon, rinds removed, minced or finely chopped
30g (1oz) fresh white breadcrumbs
1 level teaspoon dried sage
60g (2oz) shelled pistachio nuts

For the pastry
450g (1lb) plain flour
¼ level teaspoon salt
150g (5oz) unsalted butter or polyunsaturated margarine, cut into small pieces
150ml (¼ pint) water
1 egg, size 3, beaten
2 level teaspoons powdered gelatine
1 teaspoon very finely chopped fresh parsley

Preparation time: 1½ hours
Marinating time: 2 hours or overnight
Cooking time: Approx 2 hours
Cooling time: 3 hours
Chilling time: Overnight
Serves eight to ten

Pull off and discard the skin from the duck breasts. Cut the breasts lengthways into thin strips and put them into a bowl.

Pull off and discard the skin from the pheasants and, using a sharp knife, cut the flesh away from the bones—make an incision down to the bone along the centre of the breast and, keeping the knife close to the bone, gradually cut away the flesh. Do the same to the legs and thighs. Reserve the carcasses, cut the flesh into small cubes and add them to the bowl. Add the brandy, olive oil, thyme and some salt and pepper. Toss well together, cover and leave to marinate in a cool place for at least 2 hours or, if preferred, in the refrigerator overnight.

THE STOCK AND STUFFING

Meanwhile, put the reserved pheasant carcasses into a saucepan and add just enough cold water to cover them. Add the carrot and onion halves and bouquet garni and bring to the boil. Reduce the heat, partially cover the pan and then simmer for 40 minutes. Strain the stock into a clean saucepan and boil gently until it is reduced to 285ml (½ pint). Allow to cool, then chill until required.

Mix the minced pork with the bacon, breadcrumbs and sage and shape into 1.3cm (½in) balls. Put these on a plate, cover and refrigerate until required.

Barely cover the pistachio nuts with water in a saucepan and bring to the boil. Remove from the heat and, using a slotted spoon, remove the nuts, a few at a time, and peel. Set aside until required.

THE PASTRY

Preheat the oven to 190°C (375°F, gas mark 5). Sift the flour and salt into a mixing bowl. Put the butter or margarine into a saucepan with the water and heat gently until the fat melts. Bring the water to boiling point, pour into the flour and mix to form a dough. Knead on a lightly floured surface until smooth and pliable. Cut off a quarter of the dough and set aside, covered with a basin. Quickly roll out the rest to a round 36cm (14in) in diameter. Ease it into a lightly greased raised pie mould, about 21.5 × 14.5cm (8½ × 5¾in), and press it well over the base and up the sides. Allow the excess to overhang the edge.

FILLING THE PIE

Drain the duck and pheasant meat and discard the thyme. Arrange the meat and the pork balls in the tin and sprinkle in the pistachio nuts. Press the mixture in well and mound it slightly in the centre. Roll out the remaining dough to an oval large enough to cover the top of the tin. Brush the edge of the dough in the tin with the beaten egg, cover with the lid and press the edges together well to seal. Trim off the excess and make leaves to decorate the top. Brush the pie with the beaten egg, arrange the leaves on top, make a hole in the centre and brush again with the egg. Put onto a baking tray and bake for 1½ hours, covering loosely with foil after 45 minutes.

Take the pie from the oven and carefully remove the sides of the tin, leaving the pie on the base. Brush the sides with beaten egg and return to the oven for a further 30 minutes, until the sides are brown and crisp.

THE FINISHING TOUCH

Remove the pie from the oven and allow to cool for about 3 hours then replace the sides of the tin. Put 3 tablespoons of the stock into a small saucepan, sprinkle over the gelatine and leave to stand for 2 minutes, then heat gently until dissolved. Stir in the rest of the stock and the parsley and leave to stand for about 30 minutes until slightly syrupy. Carefully pour the stock through the hole in the top of the pie. Refrigerate overnight before slicing.

The magnificent pie is crammed with marinated duck and pheasant mixed with pork, bacon and pistachios.

The chicken, cloaked with a lemon sauce, sits on top of hard-boiled eggs on a 'nest' of rice.

INGREDIENTS

- 2.3–2.7 KG (5–6 LB) BOILING FOWL
- 225 G (8 OZ) CARROTS, SCRUBBED AND QUARTERED LENGTHWAYS
- 225 G (8 OZ) ONIONS, PEELED AND CUT INTO WEDGES
- 15 G (½ OZ) PIECE ROOT GINGER, PEELED AND SLICED
- THINLY PARED STRIP LEMON RIND
- BOUQUET GARNI MADE WITH BAY LEAVES, THYME AND PARSLEY (SEE P.440)
- 1 LEVEL TEASPOON SALT
- ¼ TEASPOON BLACK PEPPERCORNS
- 2 LITRES (3½ PINTS) WATER
- 115 G (4 OZ) BUTTER
- 340 G (12 OZ) BROWN, LONG-GRAIN RICE
- 6 EGGS, SIZE 1
- 60 G (2 OZ) PLAIN FLOUR
- 150 ML (¼ PINT) DOUBLE CREAM
- 2 TEASPOONS LEMON JUICE
- ¼ LEVEL TEASPOON GROUND NUTMEG
- FRESH TARRAGON LEAVES TO GARNISH

PREPARATION TIME: 40 MINUTES
COOKING TIME: 2 HOURS
SERVES SIX TO EIGHT

Hen on her Nest

Originating in the farmhouse, this tangy chicken dish has kept its popularity

PREHEAT the oven to 180°C (350°F, gas mark 4). Rinse the chicken under cold water and pat dry with kitchen paper. Tie the legs neatly together with string and put it into a large, flameproof casserole. Add the carrots, onions, ginger, lemon rind, bouquet garni, salt, peppercorns and water. Bring to the boil, reduce the heat and skim any scum from the surface. Cover and cook in the oven for 1¾ hours or until the chicken is tender.

Remove the casserole from the oven, carefully lift the chicken out of the stock, drain on kitchen paper and place in a roasting tin. Spread half the butter over the chicken and return it to the oven for a further 15 minutes to brown, then turn the oven off but leave the chicken inside to keep warm.

Meanwhile, strain the stock from the chicken into a measuring jug—there should be about 1.6 litres (2¾ pints). If necessary, make up the quantity with cold water or stock. Pour 1 litre (1¾ pints) of the stock into a saucepan and bring to the boil. Add the rice and eggs and simmer for 10 minutes. Transfer the eggs to a bowl of cold water, then cook the rice for a further 10–15 minutes or until cooked. Shell the eggs, cover and keep warm.

To make the sauce, melt the remaining butter in a saucepan, stir in the flour and cook for 1 minute. Gradually add the rest of the chicken stock and bring the sauce to the boil, stirring until thickened and smooth. Simmer for 2 minutes, then stir in the cream, lemon juice and nutmeg and heat through for 1 minute.

Drain the rice and arrange it, on a large serving platter, to resemble a nest. Place the shelled, hard-boiled eggs on top and put the chicken on top of the 'nest'. Pour over half the hot sauce and pour the remainder into a heated sauceboat. Garnish the chicken with the tarragon leaves and serve.

Tudor Smothered Rabbit

Currants, onions and vinegar give this juicy rabbit dish a sweet-and-sour flavour

Put half the onions and currants into a very large saucepan. Season the rabbit well with salt and pepper and add to the pan. Cover with the remaining onions and currants, pour over the stock and vinegar and add the butter. Bring to the boil, reduce the heat, cover and simmer gently for 2–2½ hours or until the rabbit is cooked and the onions are soft.

Cut the crusts off the bread and cut each slice in half diagonally. Arrange the slices of bread in a large, shallow serving dish. Lift the pieces of rabbit out of the pan and place them on top of the bread 'sops', then ladle over the onions, currants and the stock. Alternatively, the meat can be removed from the bones and reheated before being placed on top of the bread and covered with the sauce.

Serve garnished with fruits in season and accompanied by hot, buttered, crisp green cabbage.

Ingredients

- 1.4 kg (3 lb) onions, peeled and quartered
- 175 g (6 oz) currants
- 6 rabbit leg joints, each approx 225 g (8 oz)
- Salt and freshly ground black pepper
- 425 ml (¾ pint) chicken or vegetable stock (see pp.433, 434)
- 5 tablespoons red wine vinegar
- 60 g (2 oz) butter, cut into small pieces
- 6 thick slices of bread from a sandwich or bloomer loaf
- Fresh redcurrants, raspberries, cranberries or other fruit in season to garnish

Preparation time: 30 minutes
Cooking time: 2–2½ hours
Serves six

In old recipes like this savoury rabbit stew, it was customary to garnish the dish with fresh fruit.

Currant events
The name 'currants' is derived from the Anglo-French *raisins de corauntz*, 'grapes of Corinth', from where they have been imported since the Middle Ages. In the 17th century, the English crammed them into meat pies, of which they consumed an enormous amount daily.

Martinmas Steaks with Cumberland Sauce

Piquant Cumberland sauce, made with oranges, lemon, redcurrant jelly and port, offsets the rich Martinmas steaks

INGREDIENTS

340G (12OZ) VENISON
225G (8OZ) PORK BELLY, WEIGHT WITHOUT RIND OR BONE
1 SMALL ONION, PEELED AND GRATED
1 TABLESPOON CHOPPED FRESH THYME OR 1 TEASPOON DRIED THYME
4 JUNIPER BERRIES, CRUSHED
1 TABLESPOON WHISKY, PREFERABLY MALT
SALT AND FRESHLY GROUND BLACK PEPPER
2 TABLESPOONS FLOUR, SEASONED WELL WITH SALT AND PEPPER
1 EGG, SIZE 3, BEATEN WITH 1 TABLESPOON WATER
85G (3OZ) DRY FRESH WHITE BREADCRUMBS
LARD OR OIL FOR SHALLOW FRYING

FOR THE CUMBERLAND SAUCE
2 ORANGES, WASHED
1 LEMON, WASHED
1 LEVEL TEASPOON MADE ENGLISH MUSTARD
4 TABLESPOONS REDCURRANT JELLY, HOMEMADE (SEE P.401) OR BOUGHT
4 TABLESPOONS PORT
PREPARATION TIME: 30 MINUTES
COOKING TIME: 25 MINUTES
SERVES FOUR

MINCE the venison and pork finely, or chop finely in a food processor. Put the meat into a bowl and add the onion, thyme, crushed juniper berries and the whisky. Season well with the salt and pepper and mix thoroughly.

Divide the venison mixture into four equal portions and shape into neat steaks, each about 1.3 cm (½ in) thick. Coat each steak in the seasoned flour, then dip in the egg and, finally, coat evenly with the breadcrumbs. Put the steaks onto a plate and refrigerate while making the sauce.

To make the sauce, remove the rinds from the oranges and lemon with a zester or peel thinly with a potato peeler, taking care not to remove any of the white pith, and cut into fine shreds. Blanch the shreds in boiling water for 30 seconds, drain well and set aside.

Squeeze the oranges and lemon and strain the juice into a jug. Put the mustard into a saucepan and gradually blend in the juice, the redcurrant jelly and the port. Stir over a moderate heat until the jelly has melted, then bring to the boil and boil rapidly until the mixture has reduced by a quarter. Stir in the blanched orange and lemon shreds, cover the saucepan and keep the sauce warm while frying the steaks.

Heat some lard or oil in a frying pan, add the Martinmas steaks and fry them gently for 7–8 minutes on each side until golden brown and cooked through. Drain on kitchen paper, then arrange on a heated serving dish. Serve the steaks with the Cumberland sauce (served separately in a sauceboat), creamed potatoes and mashed turnips.

Very lean venison is mixed with pork belly, juniper berries and whisky, then shaped into succulent steaks and served with a fruity sauce.

Tail feathers flaunt the attractions of roast pheasant with traditional bread sauce and game chips.

Roast Pheasant with Game Chips

Plump young pheasants taste best simply roasted in the time-honoured style

To make the bread sauce, put the milk, onion, bay leaf, mace and salt and pepper into a small saucepan. Bring to the boil, remove from the heat, cover and leave to infuse for at least 15 minutes. Stir in the bread and butter and set aside.

Preheat the oven to 200°c (400°F, gas mark 6). Put the pheasants into a roasting tin, cover the breasts with the bacon and dot with the butter. Roast in the top of the oven for 45 minutes, basting occasionally. Beat the bread sauce and cook it, in a covered dish, in the bottom of the oven, stirring twice.

To make the game chips, use a mandolin cutter with a serrated blade to cut the potatoes into a lattice pattern or slice them with a knife or a wide cutting blade on a grater. Soak in cold, salted water, drain and dry thoroughly. Heat the oil in a deep frying pan, then fry in batches for 3–5 minutes until crisp and golden. Drain well on kitchen paper and keep warm.

Remove and reserve the bacon from the pheasants. Sprinkle the breasts with the flour, baste, then roast for another 10–15 minutes until browned. Transfer to a heated dish and keep warm.

To make the gravy, add the stock, lemon juice, salt and pepper to the roasting tin and bring to the boil, stirring. Reduce the heat, simmer for 2 minutes, then strain into a heated sauceboat. Put the bread sauce into a heated dish, discarding the onion and bay leaf.

Garnish the birds with the reserved bacon, some game chips, the watercress, and the tail feathers, if using. Serve with the gravy, bread sauce and the remaining game chips.

Ingredients

For the bread sauce
- 285 ml (½ pint) milk
- 1 small onion, peeled and studded with 4 cloves
- 1 bay leaf
- Pinch of ground mace or nutmeg
- Pinch of salt and pepper
- 60 g (2 oz) stale, crustless white bread, cubed
- 15 g (½ oz) butter

For the pheasants
- 1 brace oven-ready pheasants, each approx 675–900 g (1½–2 lb)
- 4 rashers streaky bacon
- 30 g (1 oz) butter
- 1 level tablespoon plain flour
- Watercress and tail feathers to garnish (optional)

For the game chips
- 675 g (1½ lb) medium-large potatoes, washed and peeled
- 1 litre (1¾ pints) vegetable oil for frying

For the gravy
- 285 ml (½ pint) chicken stock (see p.433)
- 1 teaspoon lemon juice
- Pinch of salt and pepper

Preparation time: 20 minutes
Cooking time: 1 hour
Serves four

Turkey with Celery Stuffing & Celery Sauce

The turkey is only part-boned, leaving the wings and legs attached, so that when the bird is remoulded it closely resembles its original shape

INGREDIENTS

3.2 KG (7 LB) OVEN-READY TURKEY, GIBLETS RESERVED FOR STOCK
225 G (8 OZ) SMOKED STREAKY BACON, RINDS REMOVED

For the stuffing
85 G (3 OZ) BUTTER, SOFTENED
275 G (10 OZ) ONIONS, PEELED AND CHOPPED
225 G (8 OZ) CELERY, TRIMMED AND CHOPPED
275 G (10 OZ) GRANARY BREAD, CRUSTS REMOVED, MADE INTO CRUMBS
85 G (3 OZ) WALNUTS, COARSELY CHOPPED
2 TABLESPOONS CHOPPED FRESH MARJORAM
4 TABLESPOONS CHOPPED FRESH PARSLEY
FINELY GRATED RIND AND STRAINED JUICE ½ ORANGE
½ LEVEL TEASPOON SALT
FRESHLY GROUND BLACK PEPPER
1 EGG, SIZE 2, BEATEN

For the sauce
30 G (1 OZ) BUTTER
3 SMALL CELERY STICKS, TRIMMED AND CUT INTO VERY FINE STRIPS
½ LEVEL TEASPOON CELERY SEEDS
30 G (1 OZ) PLAIN FLOUR
425 ML (¾ PINT) STOCK, MADE FROM THE GIBLETS (SEE P.434)
3 TABLESPOONS DRY SHERRY
CELERY LEAVES AND WALNUT HALVES TO GARNISH

Preparation time: 1 HOUR
Cooking time: 3¼ HOURS
Serves six to eight

To prepare the turkey, place it breast-side down on a board and, using a very sharp knife, make a deep incision along the centre of the backbone, cutting right down to the bone. Starting at one side, insert the knife under the skin and flesh and, with small cutting strokes, gradually cut the flesh away from the carcass, keeping the knife close to the bone at all times and working from the backbone down to the tip of the breastbone.

When the knife comes into contact with the thigh, work around the ball and socket joint and gently pull it free from the main carcass. Do the same with the wing joint. On reaching the tip of the breastbone, turn the turkey round and repeat along the other side. Finally, work the knife carefully along the tip of the breastbone to free it completely, taking care not to cut through the skin, which is very thin at this point.

THE STUFFING

To prepare the stuffing, melt half the butter in a large frying pan and sauté the chopped onions and celery gently until just softened. Stir in the breadcrumbs and cook for 5 minutes, taking care not to let them burn. Remove from the heat, add the chopped walnuts, marjoram, parsley and the orange rind and juice. Season well with salt and pepper, stir in the beaten egg and leave to cool.

Preheat the oven to 220°C (425°F, gas mark 7). Place the turkey breast-side down on the work surface and open it out flat. Spoon the stuffing along the centre then bring the sides and neck flap neatly back over the stuffing. Using a trussing needle and fine string, sew the turkey together to enclose the stuffing. Turn the bird over and mould it back into its original shape. Tuck the wings underneath and tie the legs together.

Put the prepared turkey into a roasting tin, rub it all over with the remaining butter, then cover it with the streaky bacon. Cover the roasting tin with foil, tucking it securely under the rim of the tin. Place the tin in the centre of the oven and roast for 50 minutes.

Reduce the oven temperature to 180°C (350°F, gas mark 4) and continue to roast, basting frequently, for a further 1½–2 hours or until cooked through, removing the foil and bacon for the last 30 minutes to allow the bird to brown. Crumble the bacon into small pieces and set aside in a warm place.

At the end of the cooking time, to test if the turkey is cooked, pierce the thigh at the thickest part with a skewer. The turkey is ready when the juices run clear. If necessary, return to the oven and continue roasting until done.

THE SAUCE

To make the sauce, melt the butter in a saucepan, add the celery and seeds and sauté gently until the celery has softened. Remove from the heat and set aside.

Carefully lift the turkey from the roasting tin and put it onto a heated serving plate. Cover with foil and keep warm while finishing the sauce.

Skim all but 2 tablespoons of the turkey fat from the roasting tin. Add the flour, stir it into the remaining juices in the tin and cook for 1–2 minutes, then add the giblet stock and bring to the boil, stirring and scraping any bits from the bottom of the tin. Strain the sauce into the celery mixture and add the sherry. Season well with salt and pepper and simmer gently for 5 minutes.

Garnish the turkey generously with the fresh celery leaves and the walnut halves. Scatter over the reserved crispy bacon and serve.

The moist turkey is bursting with celery, walnut and herb stuffing and, because the rib cage is removed, it is easy to carve.

A slice out of the crisp pastry reveals tender rabbit and plump prunes cooked in cider.

Harvest Rabbit Pie

The pie has a special mellowness that marries well with late summer and the grain harvest

INGREDIENTS

60 g (2 oz) butter
1 tablespoon olive oil
675–900 g (1½–2 lb) rabbit, cut into 6 portions or 6 ready-jointed portions
150 g (5 oz) streaky bacon, rinds removed, diced
1 large onion, peeled and chopped
3 level tablespoons plain flour
725 ml (1¼ pints) dry cider
225 g (8 oz) dried prunes (not ready-to-eat variety)
Bouquet garni (see p.440)
Salt and freshly ground black pepper

For the pastry
225 g (8 oz) self-raising flour
85 g (3 oz) shredded beef or vegetable suet
60 g (2 oz) butter, chilled and coarsely grated
1 teaspoon finely grated lemon rind
2 tablespoons chopped fresh parsley
Strained juice ½ lemon
1 egg, size 2, beaten
2 tablespoons milk to glaze

Preparation time: 1½ hours
Chilling time: overnight
Cooking time: 45 minutes
Serves six

Heat the butter and oil in a flameproof casserole or a saucepan and fry the rabbit portions until golden brown, then move them to a plate. Add the bacon to the casserole or pan and fry gently until it begins to release its fat. Then stir in the onion and cook for 5 minutes or until it softens and begins to brown. Stir in the flour and cook for 1 minute, then gradually stir in the cider.

Return the rabbit portions to the pan, add the prunes and bouquet garni and season well with the salt and pepper. Bring to the boil, then reduce the heat, cover and simmer for 1 hour or until the rabbit is very tender. Remove the pan from the heat and allow to cool, then chill overnight in the refrigerator.

Next day, preheat the oven to 200°c (400°f, gas mark 6). To make the pastry, mix the flour with the suet, grated butter, lemon rind and parsley and form a well in the centre. Make the lemon juice up to 175 ml (6 fl oz) with cold water and stir in the beaten egg. Pour into the well in the centre of the flour and mix together to make a soft dough. Knead the dough on a lightly floured surface for 1 minute, until smooth.

Transfer the cold rabbit stew to a large, deep pie dish. Roll out the dough to an oval 5 cm (2 in) larger than the dish and cut off a 2.5 cm (1 in) strip from round the edge. Wet the edge of the pie dish and press the strip firmly onto it. Brush the strip with milk, then cover the pie with the remaining dough. Press the edges together well to seal, then trim off the excess dough and decorate the edge.

Make a hole in the centre of the pie to let the steam escape. Brush with the milk to glaze, then bake in the centre of the oven for 45 minutes until the pastry is risen and golden brown. Should the pie begin to brown too much, cover it loosely with a piece of foil.

Turkey Croquettes

Here is a very acceptable way to use up turkey left over after Christmas

Pour the milk into a saucepan, add the herbs, cloves and onion and bring to the boil. Remove from the heat, cover and leave to infuse for 1 hour.

Meanwhile, steam the potatoes until soft, then pass them through a sieve into a bowl. Add the chopped turkey, ham and mushrooms, chives and nutmeg. Season well and mix together.

Strain the infused milk through a sieve into a jug. Discard the herbs, cloves and onion. Melt the butter in a saucepan, stir in half the flour and cook over a moderate heat for 1 minute. Gradually stir in the infused milk, then bring the mixture to the boil, stirring continuously until the sauce thickens and leaves the side of the pan. Stir the sauce into the turkey mixture, cover and chill for 1 hour.

Put the remaining flour onto a plate and season lightly with salt and ground black pepper. Using a fork, whisk the egg and milk together lightly on a second plate and put the breadcrumbs onto a third. With slightly dampened hands, take about 3 tablespoons of turkey mixture and roll into an oval. Make another 17 croquettes in the same way. Coat each in the seasoned flour, then dip into the egg and roll in the breadcrumbs. Reshape the croquettes by rolling them in your hands. Put onto a baking tray, cover and chill for 30 minutes, or until required.

Heat the oil in a deep frying pan until the temperature reaches 190°C (375°F) on a cooking thermometer, or until a cube of bread dropped in the oil browns and rises within 30 seconds. Fry the croquettes, in four batches, for 8–10 minutes, turning frequently until evenly golden. Drain on kitchen paper, keeping each batch hot.

Serve with jacket potatoes, cranberry relish and winter cabbage salad or a tossed green salad.

Even those who thought they were tired of turkey will devour these crunchy croquettes with gusto.

INGREDIENTS

- 285 ML (½ PINT) MILK
- 4 FRESH THYME SPRIGS OR ¼ LEVEL TEASPOON DRIED THYME
- 2 LARGE FRESH PARSLEY SPRIGS
- 1 BAY LEAF
- 2 CLOVES
- 1 SMALL ONION, PEELED AND HALVED
- 225 G (8 OZ) POTATOES, PEELED AND QUARTERED
- 550 G (1¼ LB) COOKED TURKEY, FINELY CHOPPED
- 60 G (2 OZ) COOKED HAM, FINELY CHOPPED
- 115 G (4 OZ) BUTTON MUSHROOMS, WIPED AND FINELY CHOPPED
- 4 TABLESPOONS SNIPPED FRESH CHIVES
- ½ LEVEL TEASPOON FRESHLY GRATED NUTMEG
- SALT AND FRESHLY GROUND BLACK PEPPER
- 45 G (1½ OZ) BUTTER
- 85 G (3 OZ) PLAIN FLOUR
- 1 EGG, SIZE 2, BEATEN
- 1 TABLESPOON MILK
- 85 G (3 OZ) FRESH WHITE BREADCRUMBS
- VEGETABLE OIL FOR DEEP FRYING

PREPARATION TIME: 1½ HOURS
CHILLING TIME: 1½ HOURS
COOKING TIME: 40 MINUTES
SERVES SIX

Puddings and Desserts

Among the sun-washed apples of an elderly orchard, tits and finches sing, celebrating, perhaps, the recurrence of summer's bounty. Here is a harvest that all cooks have welcomed over the centuries, translating it into *Fruit Fools, Gooseberry and Rosemary Pie, Elderflower Fritters* and *Wardens in Comfort*. Soft fruits are gathered in *Sorbets, Trifles, Eton Mess* and *Knickerbocker Glories* while apples are given warm welcome in massive *Pies* or as a *Fluffy Cider Sauce* for *Bread and Butter Pudding*.

Few things can be nicer than apples, spices and cider brimming beneath golden pastry.

To make a quick and attractive decoration round the pie, simply pinch the edge between your thumb and forefinger.

Mrs Marshall's Very Conservative Apple Pie

Here conservatism lies in the thrifty use of the apple peelings and in the rich traditional flavour they impart

INGREDIENTS

- Finely grated rind and strained juice 1 lemon
- 1.1 kg (2½ lb) dessert apples, Cox, russet or Granny Smith, peeled, quartered, cored and sliced, peel reserved
- 225 g (8 oz) plain flour
- ¼ level teaspoon salt
- 60 g (2 oz) chilled butter, cut into small cubes
- 60 g (2 oz) chilled lard or white vegetable fat, cut into small cubes
- 2–2½ tablespoons cold water
- 2 cloves
- 7.5 cm (3 in) cinnamon stick broken into 3 pieces
- 225 ml (8 fl oz) medium-sweet cider
- 60 g (2 oz) butter, melted
- 115 g (4 oz) sultanas or raisins
- 2 tablespoons milk
- 1 tablespoon granulated sugar

Preparation time: 1 hour
Cooking time: 1½ hours
Serves four to six

Half fill a bowl with cold water, add the lemon juice and apples and set aside.

Sift the flour and salt into a bowl, rub in the butter and the lard or vegetable fat, then mix with the water to form a firm dough. Wrap and chill for 30 minutes.

Preheat the oven to 200°C (400°F, gas mark 6). Simmer the apple peel in a covered saucepan with the cloves, cinnamon and cider for 20 minutes. Uncover and cook gently for 10 minutes until the liquid is reduced to 5 tablespoons.

Strain the peel through a sieve, pressing down well with a spoon to extract all the juices. Discard the peel and spices. Stir the melted butter into the apple juice with the lemon rind and sultanas or raisins. Drain the apples, mix into the butter mixture and spoon into a 1.15 litre (2 pint) round or oval pie dish.

Roll out the dough to 5 cm (2 in) larger than the pie dish, then cut a 2.5 cm (1 in) strip from round the edge. Brush the edge of the dish with cold water, press the strip onto it and brush with water. Roll the remaining dough round the rolling pin, then ease it into place over the pie. Press the edges together to seal, then trim and decorate the edge.

Make a small hole in the centre of the pie, then brush with the milk and sprinkle with the sugar. Bake in the centre of the oven for 20 minutes, then reduce the heat to 180°C (350°F, gas mark 4) and bake for a further 30–40 minutes or until the pastry is golden and the apples are tender. Test for tenderness by inserting a skewer into the pie through the hole in the centre. If the pie starts to brown too quickly, cover it loosely with foil.

Oaty Crumble

The crisp topping probably has its roots in the North, where for centuries the use of oats in cookery far exceeded that of wheaten flour

To MAKE the crumble topping, sift the flour into a mixing bowl and rub in the butter until the mixture resembles fine breadcrumbs. Stir in the oats, ground almonds and sugar.

Preheat the oven to 190°C (375°F, gas mark 5). Put the apples into a saucepan with the sugar and water. Cover and cook gently for 10 minutes or until they begin to soften, then remove from the heat.

Peel and slice the banana and stir it into the apples, stir in the blackberries, then transfer to a 1.15 litre (2 pint) ovenproof dish and stand the dish on a baking tray. Spoon the crumble mixture evenly over the fruit and press it down very lightly. Bake in the centre of the oven for 30–35 minutes or until the crumble is golden brown and the juices from the filling begin to bubble up.

The flavour of banana enhances the blissful marriage of apples and blackberries in the filling.

INGREDIENTS

FOR THE TOPPING

115G (4OZ) PLAIN FLOUR
85G (3OZ) BUTTER
60G (2OZ) ROLLED OATS
30G (1OZ) GROUND ALMONDS
45G (1½OZ) CASTER SUGAR

FOR THE FILLING

675G (1½LB) COOKING APPLES, PEELED, CORED AND SLICED
85G (3OZ) CASTER SUGAR
4 TABLESPOONS WATER
1 LARGE BANANA
175G (6OZ) BLACKBERRIES, DEFROSTED IF FROZEN

PREPARATION TIME: 35 MINUTES
COOKING TIME: 40–45 MINUTES
SERVES SIX

BANANA SKID
The fall induced by a banana skin is one of the cornerstones of British humour—except, that is, during the war years when the near-total absence of the fruit would have brought an awe-struck crowd to gaze at its remains.

Bakewell Pudding

This rich, sweet pudding reflects country folks' fondness for a filling dessert after a sometimes frugal main course

INGREDIENTS

- 215g (7½oz) unsalted butter
- 175g (6oz) plain flour
- Pinch of salt
- Approx 3 tablespoons chilled water
- 115g (4oz) raspberry jam, homemade (see p.389) or bought
- 2 eggs, size 2
- 115g (4oz) caster sugar
- ½ teaspoon natural almond extract or essence
- 115g (4oz) ground almonds
- Icing sugar for dusting

Preparation time: 45 minutes
Cooking time: 1 hour
Serves six to eight

Grease well a spring-clip cake tin, 18 cm (7 in) in diameter and (2½ in) deep, with 15 g (½ oz) of the butter. Sift the flour and salt into a bowl and rub in 85 g (3 oz) of the remaining butter until the mixture resembles fine crumbs. Make a well in the centre, add the water and mix to form a soft but not sticky dough.

Knead lightly on a floured surface then roll out to a round about 30 cm (12 in) in diameter. Ease the dough into the tin and smooth it over the base and up the sides. Prick lightly with a fork, then trim the excess dough from the edge. Spread the jam evenly over the bottom and chill while making the filling.

Preheat the oven to 200°c (400°f, gas mark 6). Meanwhile, heat the remaining butter until just melted, then cool it slightly. Using an electric whisk, beat the eggs and sugar until the mixture is thick and mousse-like and will hold a ribbon trail for at least 5 seconds. Gradually whisk in the melted butter and almond extract or essence, and then fold in the ground almonds.

Stand the cake tin on a baking sheet and pour in the mixture. Cook in the centre of the oven for 15 minutes, then reduce the heat to 180°c (350°f, gas mark 4) and cook for 45–50 minutes more or until the filling is set and golden brown.

Cool in the tin for 15 minutes before carefully transferring to a serving plate. Sift icing sugar over the pudding just before serving. Serve warm with cream.

A pastry shell and a raspberry jam and almond filling provide a pudding of surprising textures.

Divine error
In 1859, the cook at the Rutland Arms, Bakewell, inadvertently poured an eggy mixture over the jam in a jam tart and popped the dish into the oven. The result met with such acclaim that it brought fame not only to the inn, but to the Olde Original Bakewell Pudding Shop nearby that still dispenses large quantities of it to visitors.

Fragrant rosemary adds distinction to the filling and a crunchy glaze completes the pie.

Make sure your hands are cool for making this rich butter pastry; put them under a cold running tap before starting.

Gooseberry and Rosemary Plate Pie with Nellie's Butter Pastry

One of the first fruit crops of the year stars in this pie, made with pastry that melts on the tongue

MIX the gooseberries, semolina and demerara sugar together in a mixing bowl and set aside. Put a heavy baking tray into the oven and preheat the oven to 200°C (400°F, gas mark 6).

To make the pastry, sift the flour, cornflour and icing sugar into a bowl, then rub in the butter until the mixture resembles breadcrumbs. Add the lemon rind and just enough of the egg yolk and water mixture to make a firm dough that will not stick to the side of the bowl.

Turn the dough onto a lightly floured surface and knead lightly into a smooth ball. Roll out half of the dough to about 5 cm (2 in) larger than a 24 cm (9½ in) enamel pie plate. Line the plate with the dough and carefully trim off the excess. Brush the edge of the dough on the plate with any remaining egg and water mixture or just with water, then gently press the trimmed strip round it.

Spoon the gooseberry mixture onto the lined plate and push the rosemary sprig into the centre. Roll out the remaining piece of dough into a round large enough to cover the pie. Brush the edge of the lining dough with water, then cover the pie with the 'lid', pressing the edges firmly together to seal. Trim and decorate, then make a small hole in the centre to allow the steam to escape.

Brush the pie with the milk and sprinkle with the crushed sugar cubes. Place on the heated tray and bake for 30 minutes, then reduce the oven temperature to 180°C (350°F, gas mark 4). Loosely cover the pie with foil and continue baking for another 30 minutes, or until the pastry is lightly browned and the gooseberries are tender—test them with a skewer inserted through the steam hole.

Serve the pie warm with chilled custard sauce (see p.435) or cream.

INGREDIENTS

- 550 G (1¼ LB) COOKING GOOSEBERRIES, TOPPED AND TAILED, WASHED AND DRAINED
- 1 LEVEL TABLESPOON FINE SEMOLINA
- 85 G (3 OZ) DEMERARA SUGAR
- 7.5 CM (3 IN) FRESH ROSEMARY SPRIG

FOR THE PASTRY

- 250 G (9 OZ) PLAIN FLOUR
- 30 G (1 OZ) CORNFLOUR
- 2½ LEVEL TABLESPOONS ICING SUGAR
- 175 G (6 OZ) CHILLED BUTTER, CUT INTO CUBES
- FINELY GRATED RIND 1 LEMON
- 2 EGG YOLKS, SIZE 3, MIXED WITH 3 TABLESPOONS COLD WATER
- 2 TABLESPOONS MILK FOR BRUSHING
- 12 SUGAR CUBES, COARSELY CRUSHED

PREPARATION TIME: 30 MINUTES
COOKING TIME: 1 HOUR
SERVES SIX

Keep the left-over egg whites from this pudding for making meringues, meringue topping and royal icing.

Cider sauce brings a bite to fruit-loaf slices, baked in creamy vanilla custard.

Bread & Butter Pudding with Fluffy Cider Sauce

Using fruit loaf rather than stale white bread makes the pudding a little more adventurous; raisin and cinnamon bread would be positively daring!

INGREDIENTS

FOR THE PUDDING
- 425 ML (3/4 PINT) FULL CREAM MILK
- 285 ML (1/2 PINT) DOUBLE CREAM
- 1 VANILLA POD, SPLIT LENGTHWAYS
- 1 DAY-OLD LIGHT FRUIT LOAF, CUT INTO 1.3 CM (1/2 IN) THICK SLICES
- 85 G (3 OZ) UNSALTED BUTTER, SOFTENED
- 60 G (2 OZ) SULTANAS
- 6 EGG YOLKS, SIZE 2
- 115 G (4 OZ) CASTER SUGAR
- 1 TABLESPOON FRESHLY GRATED NUTMEG
- 85 G (3 OZ) DEMERARA SUGAR

FOR THE SAUCE
- 200 G (7 OZ) CASTER SUGAR
- 6 EGG YOLKS, SIZE 2
- 285 ML (1/2 PINT) DRY CIDER

PREPARATION TIME: 50 MINUTES
COOKING TIME: 45 MINUTES
SERVES SIX

PUT the milk and cream into a saucepan with the vanilla pod and heat gently until almost boiling. Remove from the heat, cover and leave to infuse for 30 minutes.

Meanwhile, spread each slice of bread liberally with butter and cut it in half diagonally. Overlap the slices attractively in a buttered, shallow, ovenproof dish, scattering sultanas over them as you go.

Put the egg yolks and caster sugar into a large bowl and whisk together until pale and creamy. Strain the infused milk and cream onto the eggs and whisk well, then pour evenly over the buttered fruit bread. Leave to soak for 20 minutes.

Meanwhile, heat the oven to 180°C (350°F, gas mark 4). Sprinkle the nutmeg and demerara sugar evenly over the pudding, then set the dish in a roasting tin and pour in enough boiling water to come halfway up the sides of the dish. Bake in the centre of the oven for 45 minutes or until the custard is just set and the top is golden and crisp.

Start to make the sauce 15 minutes before the pudding is due to come out of the oven. Put the sugar and egg yolks into a heatproof bowl and place snugly over a pan of barely simmering water, making sure that the bottom of the bowl does not touch the water. Whisk until the egg and sugar mixture is pale and creamy and the sugar has dissolved. Still whisking, slowly pour in the cider and continue to whisk for 5 minutes, or until the mixture froths up to a creamy mousse, then whisk for another 5–10 minutes until the sauce is light and foamy.

Pour into a jug and serve immediately with the pudding.

Baked Jam Roly-Poly

Orange-flavoured pastry filled with jam and raspberries is a favourite treat

INGREDIENTS

- 250G (9OZ) SELF-RAISING FLOUR
- 3 LEVEL TABLESPOONS CASTER SUGAR
- ½ LEVEL TEASPOON SALT
- ¾ LEVEL TEASPOON GROUND CINNAMON
- 130G (4½OZ) SHREDDED BEEF OR VEGETABLE SUET
- FINELY GRATED RIND AND JUICE 1 LARGE ORANGE
- 115G (4OZ) RASPBERRY JAM, HOMEMADE (SEE P.389) OR BOUGHT
- 225G (8OZ) RASPBERRIES, DEFROSTED IF FROZEN
- 30G (1OZ) SLIVERED ALMONDS, LIGHTLY TOASTED

PREPARATION TIME: 20 MINUTES
COOKING TIME: 55 MINUTES
SERVES FOUR

PREHEAT the oven to 200°C (400°F, gas mark 6). Sift the flour into a bowl and stir in 1 tablespoon of the sugar. Add the salt, cinnamon, suet and orange rind and make a well in the centre. If necessary, add water to make the orange juice up to 175 ml (6 fl oz), then pour it into the flour and mix to make a soft dough.

Turn onto a lightly floured surface and roll out to about 36 × 25 cm (14 × 10 in). Spread evenly with the jam to within 1.3 cm (½ in) of the edge. Reserve about 30 g (1 oz) of the best raspberries for decoration and scatter the rest over the jam. Brush the edges of the dough with a little cold water, roll up from a narrow end and press the join firmly to seal.

Wrap the roll in a sheet of nonstick baking paper, pleating the paper along the length of the roll to allow for expansion, then wrap in a sheet of pleated foil.

Put the wrapped roll onto a baking sheet and bake in the centre of the oven for 40 minutes. Remove from the oven, open out the foil and baking paper and return the roll to the oven for a further 15 minutes or until lightly browned.

Remove the roly-poly from the oven and leave to stand for 5 minutes, then carefully lift it onto a heated serving plate. Sprinkle with the remaining caster sugar, the toasted almonds and the reserved raspberries. Serve with homemade custard (see p.435) or single cream.

A sprinkling of sugar, juicy raspberries and toasted slivered almonds adds the finishing textures.

What cheer?
Good cheer,
Xmas here!
The best Christmas Pudding tastes better with Bird's Custard HOT. When cold and set, Bird's goes like clotted cream with Mince Pies and all Fruits.
BIRD'S CUSTARD
"Something to sing about."

HOUSEHOLD BIRD
It was his wife's indigestion that led Birmingham chemist Alfred Bird to invent baking and custard powders in the 1840s. Some 90 years later the firm was advocating hot custard with Christmas pudding and cold with mince pies.

INGREDIENTS

9 EGG YOLKS, SIZE 2
85G (3OZ) CASTER SUGAR
1 LEVEL TEASPOON CORNFLOUR
570ML (1 PINT) DOUBLE CREAM
1 VANILLA POD OR 1/4 TEASPOON NATURAL VANILLA EXTRACT OR ESSENCE

PREPARATION TIME: 20 MINUTES
COOKING TIME: 30–40 MINUTES
STANDING TIME: OVERNIGHT CHILLING, THEN 2 HOURS AFTER CARAMELISING THE TOP
SERVES SIX

Crème Brûlée

This is a simple but elegant little pudding of rich vanilla custard beneath a sugary crust

Put the egg yolks into a mixing bowl with 30g (1oz) of the sugar. Add the cornflour and whisk very lightly together.

Pour the cream into a saucepan, add the vanilla pod, if using, and heat gently until almost boiling, then whisk it into the egg yolk mixture.

Place the bowl over a saucepan of gently simmering water, making sure that the bottom of the bowl does not touch the water, and cook, stirring, until the custard thickens enough to coat the back of the spoon. If using vanilla extract or essence, stir it in now. As soon as the custard thickens, strain it through a nylon sieve into a shallow, flameproof serving dish about 20cm (8in) in diameter and 2.5cm (1in) deep. Stand the custard aside until completely cold, then cover the dish and refrigerate overnight.

About 2 hours before serving, take the custard out of the refrigerator and sprinkle the remaining sugar evenly over the surface to form a thin, even layer, adding a little extra sugar if necessary. Leave to stand for 10 minutes.

Meanwhile, heat the grill to high. Cook the custard under the hot grill until the sugar melts and turns a golden caramel colour. To ensure even browning, carefully turn the dish round as the sugar melts. Remove the dish from the grill and set it aside to cool, then chill in the refrigerator until ready to serve.

Crack crème brûlée's surface and spoon out a combination of smooth custard and crunchy caramel.

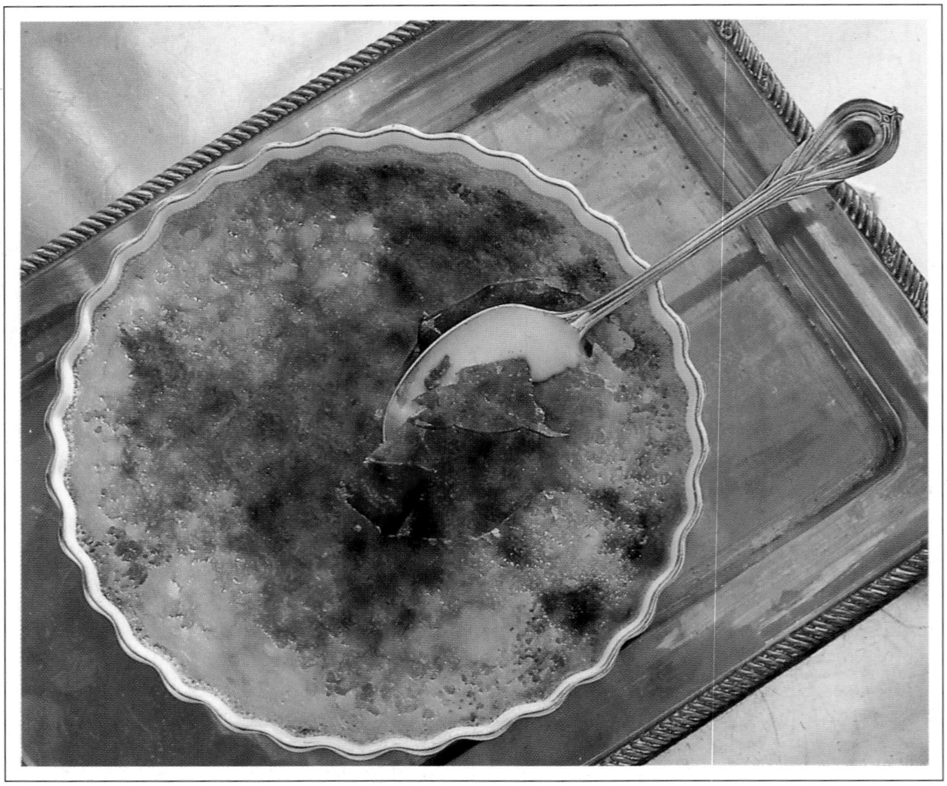

Good fellowship
Consumed in vast quantities at Cambridge May Week Balls, this recipe was introduced to the University about 100 years ago by a Fellow of Trinity, who brought it with him from his native Aberdeen. Despite this, it is firmly identified in the colleges as Cambridge Cream.

Jellies are more shapely and turn out more readily when set in a metal mould.

Freshly squeezed lemon juice flavoured with cinnamon results in a truly memorable jelly.

Real Lemon Jelly

A clear and sparkling moulded jelly always evokes oohs of appreciation

Pour 150 ml (¼ pint) of the water into a small bowl, sprinkle in the gelatine and set aside for 10 minutes, or until the gelatine is swollen and opaque.

Meanwhile, scald a large saucepan and a balloon whisk with boiling water. Line a large nylon sieve with a double thickness of muslin or a clean tea towel, place over a large bowl and scald to remove all traces of grease.

Put the remaining water into the saucepan, add the gelatine and all the remaining ingredients. Whisk over a moderate heat until the mixture forms a thick, heavy, white froth on the surface. Stop whisking, increase the heat and allow the froth to rise almost to the top of the pan, then immediately remove from the heat and allow the froth to settle back down. Repeat twice more and leave to stand for 5 minutes.

Taking care not to break up the froth, pour the jelly through the lined sieve into a 1–1.15 litre (1¾–2 pint) wetted jelly mould and refrigerate for 3–4 hours, or overnight until firmly set.

To turn the jelly out, dip the mould up to the rim in very hot water for 5 seconds. Put a flat plate on top of the mould and, holding both together tightly, invert and give a good sharp shake to free the jelly, then remove the mould. Repeat the process should the jelly not come out of the mould the first time.

Serve with whipped cream and, if liked, decorate with fresh lemon slices.

INGREDIENTS

- 850 ML (1½ PINTS) WATER
- 45 G (1½ OZ) OR 5 LEVEL TABLESPOONS GELATINE
- FINELY GRATED RIND 2 LEMONS
- 285 ML (½ PINT) FRESHLY SQUEEZED LEMON JUICE, FROM 7 OR 8 LEMONS
- 175 G (6 OZ) GRANULATED SUGAR
- 1 CINNAMON STICK
- 2 EGG WHITES, SIZE 2
- 2 EGG SHELLS, WELL WASHED IN COLD WATER AND CRUSHED

Preparation time: 15 minutes
Cooking time: 10 minutes
Setting time: 3–4 hours or overnight
Serves six

INGREDIENTS

190G (6½OZ) BUTTER
2 LEVEL TABLESPOONS SOFT LIGHT BROWN SUGAR
2 SMALL ORANGES, RIND FINELY GRATED AND RESERVED, PITH REMOVED, FLESH NEATLY SLICED
175G (6OZ) CASTER SUGAR
3 EGGS, SIZE 2
175G (6OZ) SELF-RAISING FLOUR
45G (1½OZ) GROUND ALMONDS
2 TABLESPOONS WARM WATER

FOR THE SAUCE
5 TABLESPOONS MARMALADE, HOMEMADE (SEE P.391) OR BOUGHT
5 TABLESPOONS WATER
1 TABLESPOON STRAINED LEMON JUICE

PREPARATION TIME: 20 MINUTES
COOKING TIME: 1½–2 HOURS
SERVES SIX

THE INCOMER
About 1870, a gift of Perthshire marmalade to Mrs Cooper, an Oxford grocer, led to its being sold in the city for the first time. The undergraduates loved it, calling it 'squish'. Only later, with the addition of molasses, did it gain the true dark hue of Oxford marmalade.

Orange Sponge Pudding with Marmalade Sauce

A snowcap of slow-pouring Devon cream or custard would add a luxurious touch

PUT 15 g (½ oz) of the butter into a well-buttered 1.15–1.4 litre (2–2½ pint) pudding basin, add the brown sugar, then overlap the orange slices on top.

Cream the remaining butter with the caster sugar and orange rind until light and fluffy, beat in the eggs, one at a time, beating well between each addition then fold in the flour, almonds and water.

Spoon the mixture on top of the oranges and smooth the surface. Cover the basin with buttered foil, pleated in the centre to allow for expansion and tucked tightly under the rim of the basin.

Cook in a steamer for 1½–2 hours or stand the basin on a trivet in a saucepan, add boiling water to halfway up the side of the basin, cover and simmer gently for 1½–2 hours, replenishing the water frequently. The pudding is cooked when it is well risen, firm, and when a skewer inserted into the centre comes out clean.

Make the sauce 5 minutes before the pudding is to be turned out. Stir all the ingredients together in a small saucepan over a moderate heat until the marmalade blends with the water and lemon juice. Transfer to a jug and keep hot while turning the pudding onto a heated plate.

The sponge pudding can also be made with 3 tablespoons of golden syrup, jam or marmalade in place of the orange slices and syrup or jam sauce can be made in the same way as the marmalade sauce.

Add 60–85 g (2–3 oz) of dried fruit to the mixture for a fruit pudding. Another variation is to substitute 45 g (1½ oz) of cocoa and ½ level teaspoon of baking powder for 45 g (1½ oz) of flour and serve the pudding with a chocolate sauce.

Steamed orange and almond-flavoured sponge is delectably complemented by a zesty sauce.

An old-fashioned dessert blends a rich bouquet of flavours—the muskiness of elderflower, the sweet tang of apricot and the plumminess of kirsch.

The secret of filigree fritters lies in coating the flowers lightly, and in lowering them headfirst into the hot oil.

Elderflower Fritters with Apricot Sauce

The elder tree flowers from late May to June

INGREDIENTS

FOR THE BATTER
- 115 G (4 OZ) PLAIN FLOUR
- 30 G (1 OZ) CASTER SUGAR
- 225 ML (8 FL OZ) PALE ALE OR STRONG LAGER
- 30 G (1 OZ) UNSALTED BUTTER, MELTED
- 1 EGG WHITE, SIZE 2

FOR THE SAUCE
- 150 ML (¼ PINT) WATER
- 60 G (2 OZ) CASTER SUGAR
- SHORT STRIP THINLY PARED LEMON RIND
- 225 G (8 OZ) FRESH RIPE APRICOTS, HALVED AND STONED OR 115 G (4 OZ) READY-TO-USE DRIED APRICOTS
- 2 TEASPOONS KIRSCH OR APRICOT LIQUEUR

FOR THE FRITTERS
- APPROX 24–30 MEDIUM-SIZE ELDERFLOWER HEADS, WITH 2.5 CM (1 IN) OF STALK ATTACHED
- VEGETABLE OR CORN OIL FOR DEEP FRYING
- CASTER SUGAR FOR SPRINKLING
- ELDERFLOWERS AND THEIR LEAVES TO DECORATE, OPTIONAL

PREPARATION TIME: 1 HOUR
COOKING TIME: 20 MINUTES
SERVES SIX

TO MAKE the batter, sift the flour and sugar into a bowl and make a well in the centre. Add the ale or lager and the butter and beat with a wire whisk to form a smooth batter. Cover the bowl and leave to stand for 1 hour.

Meanwhile, make the sauce. Bring the water, sugar and lemon rind to the boil in a saucepan, stirring occasionally. Boil for 1 minute, then remove the rind. Add the fresh or dried apricots, reduce the heat, cover and cook gently until the apricots are very soft (10–15 minutes for fresh apricots or 25–30 minutes for dried).

Pass the apricots and juice through a nylon sieve into a bowl to make a purée. Stir in the kirsch or apricot liqueur, then pour the sauce into a serving jug and set aside. The sauce should have a pouring consistency. If necessary, add 2–3 tablespoons of water if it is too thick.

To cook the elderflowers, half fill a frying pan with oil and heat to 180°C (350°F) or until a little of the batter, dropped into the oil, turns golden brown in 3–4 seconds.

While the oil is heating, whisk the egg white until it forms soft peaks and fold it carefully into the batter.

Holding them by their stalks, dip the flowers into the batter. Allow the excess to run off, then, frying no more than three at a time, lower them, heads down, into the oil and fry for 1–2 minutes until light golden brown, turning over once. Remove from the pan with a slotted spoon and drain on kitchen paper. Keep warm while frying the remainder.

Pile onto a heated serving dish and dredge heavily with the caster sugar. Decorate with elderflowers and leaves, and serve with the apricot sauce.

INGREDIENTS

Vanilla ice cream
2 vanilla pods
225 g (8 oz) granulated sugar
285 ml (½ pint) milk
3 egg yolks, size 2
570 ml (1 pint) double cream
Makes 1 litre (1¾ pints)

Strawberry ice cream
550 g (1¼ lb) fresh strawberries, hulled
340 g (12 oz) strawberry conserve
285 ml (½ pint) milk
175 g (6 oz) caster sugar
570 ml (1 pint) double cream
Strained juice 2 lemons
Makes 1.15 litres (2 pints)

Brown bread ice cream
4 thick slices white bread, approx 115 g (4 oz), crusts removed
225 g (8 oz) granulated sugar
150 ml (¼ pint) milk
570 ml (1 pint) double cream
6 tablespoons amaretto or maraschino liqueur
Cooking time: 20 minutes
Makes 1 litre (1¾ pints)

Peppermint & chocolate chip ice cream
225 g (8 oz) granulated sugar
285 ml (½ pint) milk
3 egg yolks, size 2
570 ml (1 pint) double cream
1–2 teaspoons peppermint essence
200 g (7 oz) dark chocolate
Few drops green food colouring (optional)
Preparation time: 20–30 minutes for each ice cream
Freezing time: 8–10 hours in the freezer, 25–40 minutes in an ice cream maker
Makes 1 litre (1¾ pints)

Ice Creams

No bought ice cream can compare with the richness and consistency of homemade varieties. Best flavours, however, demand the freshest, juciest ingredients—and the patience to delay the first spoonful until the ice cream begins to soften

VANILLA ICE CREAM

Using a fine, sharp knife, cut the vanilla pods in half lengthways. Scoop out the insides with a teaspoon and put them into a saucepan with the empty pods and the sugar. Lightly whisk together the milk and egg yolks, pour into the saucepan and stir over a gentle heat until the sugar has dissolved, then bring almost to the boil, stirring continuously. Remove from the heat and leave until the custard is completely cold. Strain into a bowl, discard the vanilla pods and stir in the cream. (Note that the custard will be speckled with the vanilla.)

Freeze the custard until it has frozen 2.5 cm (1 in) round the edge. Remove from the freezer, whisk well and return to the freezer. Repeat this process four to six times more, then allow the ice cream to freeze completely. Alternatively, the mixture can be frozen for 25 minutes in an electric ice cream maker.

To give vanilla ice cream a coffee flavour, add 115 g (4 oz) mocha or other richly flavoured coffee beans or 1 level tablespoon of instant coffee granules with, or instead of, the vanilla pods.

STRAWBERRY ICE CREAM

Put the strawberries and the strawberry conserve into a food processor, blend well, then stir in the milk and pass the mixture through a nylon sieve to remove the seeds. Alternatively, mash the strawberries and the conserve together and whisk in the milk, then pass the mixture through a sieve and discard the seeds. Stir the caster sugar, cream and lemon juice into the strawberry mixture and freeze as for vanilla ice cream.

Raspberry or blackberry ice cream can be made in the same way by substituting the conserve and the same quantity of fresh raspberries or blackberries for the strawberries and strawberry conserve.

BROWN BREAD ICE CREAM

Preheat the oven to 180°c (350°f, gas mark 4). Put the slices of bread onto a baking tray and bake in the oven for about 20–30 minutes or until golden brown and dried into rusks. Remove from the oven and set aside until cool, then grind into fine crumbs in a food processor or put into a strong polythene bag and crush finely with a rolling pin.

Put one-third of the crumbs into a saucepan, add the sugar, milk and double cream and bring very slowly to the boil, stirring all the time. As soon as boiling point is reached, remove the pan from the heat and pour the mixture through a nylon sieve into a bowl. Set aside and allow to become completely cold, then stir in the remaining crumbs and the amaretto or the maraschino liqueur. Freeze as for vanilla ice cream.

PEPPERMINT & CHOCOLATE CHIP ICE CREAM

For peppermint and chocolate chip ice cream, put the sugar, milk and egg yolks into a bowl and whisk lightly together, then pour the mixture into a saucepan and stir over a gentle heat until the sugar has dissolved. Stirring continuously, bring the mixture almost to the boil, then remove from the heat and allow to become completely cold.

Stir the cream into the cooled custard mixture and add 1 teaspoon of the peppermint essence or to taste. Chop the chocolate very finely and stir it in. Add a few drops of the green food colouring, if using. Freeze as for vanilla ice cream.

This method can also be used to make rum and raisin ice cream. Omit the peppermint essence, the chocolate and the green colouring. Soak 115 g (4 oz) of seedless raisins in 3–4 tablespoons of dark rum, then stir the raisins into the mixture after adding the cream.

Ice cream has been popular in Britain since the mid-1870s, when the first ice-storage facilities were built.

INGREDIENTS

285 ML (½ PINT) MILK
285 ML (½ PINT) SINGLE CREAM
1 VANILLA POD, HALVED LENGTHWAYS
5 EGGS, SIZE 2
2 LEVEL TEASPOONS CORNFLOUR
60 G (2 OZ) CASTER SUGAR
450 G (1 LB) SMALL, ENGLISH STRAWBERRIES
3–4 TABLESPOONS SWEET SHERRY
5 LEVEL TABLESPOONS ICING SUGAR, SIFTED
300 G (11 OZ) MADEIRA CAKE
175 G (6 OZ) STRAWBERRY JAM, HOMEMADE (SEE P.389) OR BOUGHT
425 ML (¾ PINT) DOUBLE CREAM
½ TEASPOON NATURAL VANILLA EXTRACT OR ESSENCE
15 G (½ OZ) FLAKED ALMONDS, LIGHTLY TOASTED

PREPARATION TIME: 20 MINUTES
COOKING TIME: 20 MINUTES
SERVES EIGHT

Kentish Strawberry Tipsy Trifle

This frivolous confection harks back to the syllabubs of the 16th century

Pour the milk and the single cream into a saucepan, add the vanilla pod and bring slowly to the boil. Whisk the eggs, cornflour and sugar together in a bowl and stir in the hot milk and cream.

Place the bowl over a saucepan of gently simmering water, making sure the bottom of the bowl does not touch the water, and stir until the custard thickens enough to coat the back of the spoon. Strain through a nylon sieve into a clean bowl. Cover the surface of the custard closely with cling film, to prevent a skin from forming, and leave to cool.

Reserve two or three strawberries to decorate the finished trifle. Slice the remainder and put them into a bowl with the sherry and 3 tablespoons of the icing sugar. Mix together and set aside.

Cut the Madeira cake into three layers horizontally and sandwich together with the jam. Cut into thin slices and arrange in the bottom and slightly up the sides of a glass bowl. Cover with the strawberries and their juice. Pour in the custard, cover the bowl and leave in the refrigerator for at least 2 hours or overnight.

Whisk the double cream with the vanilla and the remaining icing sugar until it will hold a soft peak, then spread on top of the trifle. Slice the reserved strawberries and use, with the toasted almonds, to decorate the top. Chill the trifle until required.

The trifle mingles cake with sherry-coated strawberries, vanilla custard and whisked cream.

Chocolate pudding encircles syrup-sweetened clementines, dressed with chocolate sauce.

BADGE OF PROGRESS
The name on the tin recalls the reforms in housing, working conditions and adult education carried out by George Cadbury after he established his Bournville chocolate factory in Birmingham in 1879.

Chocolate Pudding with Clementines and Chocolate Sauce

A rich concoction unites two flavours that were made for each other—chocolate and orange

To MAKE the chocolate sauce, stir all the ingredients over a gentle heat until the sugar has dissolved and the sauce is dark and glossy. Strain into a bowl and cool, stirring from time to time.

To prepare the clementines, remove the peel and pith. Dissolve the sugar in the water over a gentle heat, then simmer the clementines gently for 5–10 minutes until soft and translucent. With a slotted spoon, transfer them to a bowl. Boil the syrup to reduce to 150 ml (¼ pint), remove from the heat, add the Cointreau, if using, and pour over the clementines.

To make the pudding, put the trifle sponge cakes, chocolate and sugar into a bowl. Bring the cream almost to the boil in a saucepan, remove from the heat, add the vanilla and pour into the bowl. Mix well and leave to stand for 10 minutes.

Meanwhile, preheat the oven to 180°C (350°F, gas mark 4). Butter a nonstick 20 cm (8 in) ring mould generously. Beat the egg gradually into the cake mixture and pour into the mould. Stand the mould in a roasting tin and add enough very hot water to come halfway up the side of the mould. Cook for 35 minutes or until set. Remove the mould from the tin and wipe dry. Loosen the pudding round the edge and turn onto a dish. Fill the centre with the clementines and spoon the syrup over them and the pudding. Pour the chocolate sauce into a jug.

INGREDIENTS

FOR THE CHOCOLATE SAUCE
60 G (2 OZ) GOLDEN SYRUP
30 G (1 OZ) COCOA POWDER, SIFTED
285 ML (½ PINT) SINGLE CREAM
1 TEASPOON NATURAL VANILLA EXTRACT OR ESSENCE

FOR THE CLEMENTINES
12 VERY SMALL CLEMENTINES
115 G (4 OZ) GRANULATED SUGAR
285 ML (½ PINT) WATER
1–2 TABLESPOONS COINTREAU (OPTIONAL)

FOR THE CHOCOLATE PUDDING
4 TRIFLE SPONGE CAKES, APPROX 100 G (3½ OZ), CRUMBLED
100 G (3½ OZ) PLAIN CHOCOLATE, FINELY CHOPPED OR GRATED
30 G (1 OZ) CASTER SUGAR
425 ML (¾ PINT) SINGLE CREAM
1 TEASPOON NATURAL VANILLA EXTRACT OR ESSENCE
4 EGGS, SIZE 2, LIGHTLY BEATEN

PREPARATION TIME: 1¼ HOURS
COOKING TIME: 45 MINUTES
SERVES SIX

Eton Mess

Parents and children unite in their praises of this delightful summer pudding

INGREDIENTS

- 60 g (2 oz) caster sugar
- 60 g (2 oz) soft dark brown sugar
- 2 egg whites, size 2
- 450 g (1 lb) small fresh strawberries, hulled and quartered
- 2 tablespoons orange-flavoured liqueur
- 570 ml (1 pint) double cream
- 2 level tablespoons vanilla sugar, or caster sugar and ½ teaspoon natural vanilla extract or essence

Preparation time: 30 minutes

Cooking time: 3–4 hours

Serves six

Preheat the oven to 110°c (225°f, gas mark ¼). Sift the caster sugar and the soft brown sugar together into a bowl to remove any lumps. Put the egg whites into a large mixing bowl and whisk until very stiff but not dry. Adding a spoonful at a time, gradually whisk in the combined sugars, allowing the mixture to become very stiff between each addition.

Line a baking sheet with nonstick baking parchment and pipe or spoon about 12 portions of the mixture onto the parchment, spacing them well apart. Put the baking sheet into the oven and bake for 3–4 hours or until the meringues have thoroughly dried out. Remove the baking sheet from the oven and leave the meringues on the parchment to cool.

Toss the quartered strawberries in the orange-flavoured liqueur, then whip the cream with the vanilla sugar, or the sugar and vanilla extract or essence, until it will hold a soft peak. Break the meringues into smallish chunks. Immediately before serving, put all the ingredients into a large bowl and fold loosely together.

Playing fields' winner
In its original form, plain strawberries and cream mashed together, this pudding is part of the celebrations at Eton's annual prize-giving, when boys and parents picnic on the playing fields. The meringue, however, is a distinct improvement.

Serve this meringue, strawberry and cream concoction in elegant glassware.

Fruit purée, made from fresh gooseberries, rhubarb, apples, plums or greengages, together with custard and whipped cream form a scrumptious union in fruit fool.

Fresh Fruit Fool

The dessert has nothing to do with foolishness: the name is derived from the French 'fouler', to crush

Prepare the fruit according to type—top and tail gooseberries; trim and chop rhubarb; peel, core and slice apples; halve and stone plums or greengages.

Put the prepared fruit into a saucepan with 60 g (2 oz) of the caster sugar and 2 tablespoons of water. Cover and cook over a moderate heat for 20 minutes or until the fruit is very soft.

Meanwhile, to make the custard, bring the single cream almost to the boil. Lightly whisk the egg, egg yolk and the remaining sugar together in a bowl, then stir in the hot cream and the vanilla extract or essence.

Place the bowl over a saucepan of gently boiling water and stir the mixture until it thickens enough to hold a slight trail and thinly coat the back of the spoon. Take care not to overheat it, as it may curdle. Remove the bowl from the saucepan and cover the surface closely with cling film to prevent a skin from forming. Allow the custard to cool, then chill in the refrigerator.

Purée the cooked fruit in a food processor or blender, or pass it through a nylon sieve. Chill the purée. Whisk the double cream in a large bowl until it will hold soft peaks.

Mix the custard and fruit purée together, then fold it gently into the whipped cream. Spoon the fool into glasses and chill for 2 hours. If wished, serve sprinkled with pistachio nuts and, if using shallow dishes, decorated with flowers. Serve with homemade shortbread fingers (see p.347).

To make the fool with soft fruits, use 450 g (1 lb) strawberries, raspberries or blackberries; skinned, stoned and sliced peaches or apricots; or pitted cherries.

Put the prepared fruit into a bowl and, depending on its sweetness, sprinkle with 30–60 g (1–2 oz) of sugar and leave to macerate for 30 minutes, then purée in a food processor or electric blender. Pass strawberry, raspberry or blackberry purée through a fine nylon sieve into a bowl to remove the pips.

INGREDIENTS

- 450 G (1 LB) GOOSEBERRIES, RHUBARB, APPLES, PLUMS OR GREENGAGES
- 70 G (2½ OZ) CASTER SUGAR
- 150 ML (¼ PINT) SINGLE CREAM
- 1 EGG, SIZE 2
- 1 EGG YOLK, SIZE 2
- ½ TEASPOON NATURAL VANILLA EXTRACT OR ESSENCE
- 285 ML (½ PINT) DOUBLE CREAM
- 15 G (½ OZ) CHOPPED PISTACHIO NUTS TO DECORATE (OPTIONAL)
- FRESH OR SUGARED FLOWERS TO DECORATE (OPTIONAL)

Preparation time: 30 minutes
Cooking time: 20 minutes
Chilling time: 2 hours
Serves six

Rich Bread Pudding with Custard Sauce

Here is a most accommodating pudding, since any leftovers will keep for about a week in a refrigerator or in an airtight tin

INGREDIENTS

FOR THE PUDDING

- 225 G (8 OZ) 2–3 DAY-OLD UNSLICED WHITE BREAD FROM A SANDWICH OR TIN LOAF, CRUSTS REMOVED, CUT INTO SMALL CUBES
- 285 ML (½ PINT) MILK
- FINELY GRATED RIND AND JUICE 1 LARGE ORANGE
- 2 TABLESPOONS BRANDY OR RUM (OPTIONAL)
- 3 EGGS, SIZE 2, BEATEN
- 60 G (2 OZ) SOFT DARK BROWN SUGAR
- 225 G (8 OZ) MIXED DRIED FRUIT
- 60 G (2 OZ) CHOPPED MIXED PEEL
- 60 G (2 OZ) BLANCHED ALMONDS, CHOPPED
- 2 LEVEL TEASPOONS GROUND CINNAMON
- ½ LEVEL TEASPOON FRESHLY GRATED NUTMEG
- ½ LEVEL TEASPOON GROUND CLOVES
- ½ LEVEL TEASPOON GROUND ALLSPICE
- 1 TABLESPOON BLACK TREACLE
- 115 G (4 OZ) BUTTER, MELTED
- 1 TABLESPOON GRANULATED SUGAR FOR DREDGING

FOR THE CUSTARD SAUCE

- 4 EGG YOLKS, SIZE 2
- 1 LEVEL TEASPOON CORNFLOUR
- 1½ LEVEL TABLESPOONS CASTER SUGAR
- 425 ML (¾ PINT) MILK
- 1–2 TEASPOONS ANGOSTURA BITTERS OR 3 TABLESPOONS BRANDY OR RUM

PREPARATION TIME: 30 MINUTES PLUS 20 MINUTES SOAKING
COOKING TIME: 1 HOUR
SERVES NINE

PREHEAT the oven to 180°C (350°F, gas mark 4). To make the bread pudding, put the bread into a mixing bowl. Heat the milk to boiling point, pour over the bread and leave to soak for 20 minutes. Mash the bread with a fork, add the orange rind and juice, and the brandy or rum if using, and mash again to remove any remaining lumps of crust. Beat in the egg, then add all the remaining ingredients except the butter and granulated sugar. Mix well and then beat in the butter.

Pour into a well buttered 23 cm (9 in) square tin and bake for 1–1¼ hours or until firm and golden brown.

While the bread pudding is cooking, make the custard. Put the egg yolks, cornflour and sugar into a mixing bowl and whisk well. Pour the milk into a saucepan and heat until it just comes to the boil, then whisk into the egg yolk mixture. Pour the mixture back into the saucepan and stir continuously over a very gentle heat until the sauce is thick enough to coat the back of the spoon—on no account allow the sauce to boil as it will curdle. Alternatively, cook in a double boiler or in a mixing bowl over a saucepan of simmering water. Remove the pan from the heat and either stir in the Angostura bitters for a spicy flavour, or add the brandy or rum.

Remove the pudding from the oven, sprinkle with the granulated sugar and cut into nine squares. Serve hot with the custard or cold as a cake.

Spices, fruit and nuts transform bread and milk into a delicious pudding.

Apricot jam and stem ginger lie encased between sponge and meringue.

Seaside favourites
With its immaculate seafront gardens, Pier Pavilion and rows of decorous bathing huts along the promenade, Felixstowe's Edwardian atmosphere is not even dented by the large container port close by.

Felixstowe Tart

This dish was a firm favourite with the Edwardian holidaymakers who once thronged the promenade

Preheat the oven to 180°c (350°f, gas mark 4). Cream the butter and half the sugar together until light and fluffy. Beat in the egg yolks, one at a time, then mix in the flour.

Press the mixture into a buttered, 20 cm (8 in) loose-based sandwich cake tin or flan tin and bake in the centre of the oven for 20–25 minutes until golden brown and firm to the touch. Remove from the oven and set aside for 10 minutes. Increase the oven temperature to 220°c (425°f, gas mark 7).

Transfer the base to an ovenproof serving dish, spread evenly with the jam to within 1.3 cm (½ in) of the edge, and sprinkle with half the ginger

To make the topping, whisk the egg whites until they are stiff but not dry. Reserve 1 tablespoon of the remaining caster sugar, then gradually whisk the remainder, a tablespoon at a time, into the egg whites, whisking well between each addition. Spread the meringue over the base of the tart, taking care to take it right to the edge. Dredge with the reserved sugar and scatter the remaining chopped ginger over the top.

Return the tart to the oven and bake for 8–10 minutes until lightly browned.

Ingredients

- 85 g (3 oz) butter
- 175 g (6 oz) caster sugar
- 3 eggs, size 2, separated
- 150 g (5 oz) self-raising flour
- 6 tablespoons apricot jam, homemade (see p.395) or bought
- 4 pieces preserved stem ginger in syrup, drained and chopped

Preparation time: 40 minutes
Cooking time: 35 minutes
Serves six to eight

This fantasy of fruit and frothy cream includes sprinkled nuts, sauces and lashings of ice cream.

Knickerbocker Glory

Originally created in America, this dessert bears the nickname of New York's Dutch founders, the 'Knickerbockers'

INGREDIENTS

FOR THE CHOCOLATE SAUCE
100 ML (3½ FL OZ) HOT WATER
30 G (1 OZ) GRANULATED SUGAR
60 G (2 OZ) PLAIN CHOCOLATE
SMALL KNOB UNSALTED BUTTER

FOR THE MELBA SAUCE
225 G (8 OZ) FRESH RASPBERRIES, OR FROZEN RASPBERRIES THAWED AND DRAINED
60 G (2 OZ) ICING SUGAR, SIFTED
1 TEASPOON LEMON JUICE

FOR THE FILLING
450 G (1 LB) MIXED SLICED OR CHOPPED FRESH FRUIT, BANANAS, PEACHES, PINEAPPLE, RASPBERRIES, STRAWBERRIES AND GRAPES OR 800 G (1¾ LB) MIXED CANNED FRUIT IN NATURAL JUICE, DRAINED
500 ML (18 FL OZ) VANILLA ICE CREAM, HOMEMADE (SEE P.248) OR QUALITY BOUGHT ICE CREAM

FOR THE TOPPING
150 ML (¼ PINT) DOUBLE CREAM, WHIPPED
15 G (½ OZ) FLAKED ALMONDS, LIGHTLY TOASTED
4 WALNUT HALVES, CHOPPED
FAN WAFERS AND MARASCHINO CHERRIES TO DECORATE

PREPARATION TIME: 30 MINUTES
SERVES FOUR

To make the chocolate sauce, stir the water, sugar and chocolate in a saucepan over a gentle heat until the chocolate has melted. Bring to the boil, simmer gently for 1 minute, remove from the heat and stir in the butter then leave to cool.

To make the Melba sauce, purée the raspberries through a nylon sieve then stir in the sugar and lemon juice to give a smooth, thick, pouring sauce.

To assemble the knickerbocker glories, just before serving, spoon alternate layers of the fruit, ice cream and Melba sauce into each of four tall, 340 ml (12 fl oz) glasses, filling almost to the top. Pipe or spoon a large swirl of whipped cream on top of each, drizzle with the chocolate sauce and sprinkle with the nuts. Decorate with the fan wafers and cherries and serve immediately.

Raspberry Vinegar Sorbet

Steeping the raspberries for five days produces a vinegar with an intense fruit flavour which forms the base for the sorbet

To make the raspberry vinegar, put the raspberries into a glass or china jug or a glass jar and pour in the vinegar. Cover and leave in a cool place to steep for five days, stirring or shaking occasionally.

Strain the liquid into a measuring jug and discard the raspberries. If there is less than 570 ml (1 pint), add a little extra vinegar to make up the amount. Pour the liquid into a stainless steel or enamel saucepan, add the sugar, bring slowly to the boil, then boil for 2–3 minutes. Pour into warm, sterilised bottles and seal.

To make the sorbet, purée the raspberries in a food processor and pass through a nylon sieve into a bowl, then stir in 225 ml (8 fl oz) of the raspberry vinegar.

Freeze the sorbet in an ice cream maker or in a plastic container in the freezer until about 2.5 cm (1 in) of the mixture is frozen round the edge. Remove from the freezer and whisk well. Repeat twice more, then cover and freeze until softly frozen.

Serve the sorbet immediately or store for up to one month in the freezer.

Ingredients

For the raspberry vinegar
- 450 g (1 lb) fresh raspberries or frozen raspberries, thawed
- 285 ml (½ pint) cider vinegar or white wine vinegar
- 340 g (12 oz) caster sugar

For the sorbet
- 450 g (1 lb) fresh raspberries or frozen raspberries, thawed

Preparation time: 5 minutes
Steeping time: 5 days
Freezing time: 30 minutes or 2 hours, depending on freezing method
Cooking time: 5 minutes
Serves four to six

Show off the sorbet, capturing the essence of raspberries, in elegant glasses.

If the sorbet has been stored in a freezer, take it out at least 15-20 minutes before serving to allow it to become softly frozen – the best way of eating it.

Rose-Scented Rice Pudding

A blending of perfumes and flavours recalls the days of the crinoline

INGREDIENTS

- 45G (1½ OZ) BUTTER
- 85G (3OZ) PUDDING RICE
- 70G (2½OZ) CASTER SUGAR
- 285ML (½ PINT) SINGLE OR DOUBLE CREAM
- 570ML (1 PINT) FULL CREAM MILK
- 2 TABLESPOONS ROSEWATER
- FRESHLY GRATED NUTMEG FOR SPRINKLING

PREPARATION TIME: 5 MINUTES
COOKING TIME: 2–2¼ HOURS
SERVES FOUR

PREHEAT the oven to 160°C (325°F, gas mark 3) and grease a 1.15 litre (2 pint) ovenproof dish lightly with 15g (½oz) of the butter.

Put the rice and caster sugar into the prepared dish and mix together, then stir in the cream, milk and rosewater. Cut the remaining butter into tiny pieces and float them on the surface of the pudding. Grate the nutmeg over the top.

Put the dish into the oven and cook on the centre shelf for 2 hours or until the top is golden brown and the pudding is just set. Take care not to overcook as the pudding will become dry. Remove from the oven and serve while still hot.

A PUZZLE
It was A.A. Milne who anxiously inquired, what could be the matter with Mary Jane, when she was perfectly well and hadn't a pain? And it was lovely rice pudding for dinner again!

Though grand enough to be eaten on its own, the pudding can be topped with jam or stewed fruit.

Use a little of the selected fresh fruit or mint leaves to decorate the water ices.

Water Ices

Sprightly water ices were created to refresh the palate after a rich main course

Put the sugar and water into a heavy-based stainless steel or enamel saucepan and stir over a moderate heat until the sugar has completely dissolved. Bring to the boil, boil for 2 minutes, then remove from the heat and set aside to cool while preparing the chosen fruit.

REDCURRANT OR BLACKCURRANT WATER ICE

Put the redcurrants or blackcurrants into a saucepan with 2 tablespoons of water. Cover and simmer for 5 minutes or until just beginning to soften.

Remove from the heat, cool slightly and purée in a food processor. Pass the purée through a nylon sieve to remove the pips, then allow to cool completely.

Stir the cooled syrup and the lemon and orange juices into the fruit purée. Pour the mixture into a shallow, plastic freezer container and freeze for 4 hours, whisking vigorously every hour to break up the ice crystals. Once frozen, the water ice remains soft and creamy and can be scooped straight from the freezer.

Just before serving, spoon into chilled or frosted glasses. Serve with brandy snaps (see p.341) or light, crisp biscuits.

RASPBERRY OR BLACKBERRY WATER ICE

Substitute 450 g (1 lb) fresh or frozen raspberries or blackberries for the redcurrants or blackcurrants. Process and sieve as for the currants. Precooking the fruit is not necessary.

PINEAPPLE WATER ICE

To make pineapple water ice, use a large pineapple, skinned and cored. Process the flesh—about 550 g (1¼ lb)—and sieve as above. Precooking is not necessary.

INGREDIENTS

225 g (8 oz) granulated sugar
150 ml (¼ pint) water
450 g (1 lb) redcurrants or blackcurrants, stalks removed
OR
450 g (1 lb) fresh raspberries or blackberries, hulled or frozen fruit, thawed
OR
550 g (1¼ lb) prepared fresh pineapple flesh
Strained juice 1 lemon
Strained juice 1 orange

Preparation time: 35 minutes
Cooking time: 7 minutes
Freezing time: 4 hours
Serves four to six

Spotted Dick

Redolent of childhood, this memorable steamed pudding is always welcome on a chill winter's day

INGREDIENTS

225 G (8 OZ) SELF-RAISING FLOUR
½ LEVEL TEASPOON GROUND CINNAMON
115 G (4 OZ) SHREDDED BEEF OR VEGETABLE SUET
60 G (2 OZ) CASTER SUGAR
115 G (4 OZ) CURRANTS
150 ML (¼ PINT) MILK
60 G (2 OZ) SOFT LIGHT BROWN SUGAR
60 G (2 OZ) LARD, AT ROOM TEMPERATURE
60 G (2 OZ) PLAIN FLOUR
CUSTARD FOR SERVING

PREPARATION TIME: 25 MINUTES
COOKING TIME: 2 HOURS
SERVES SIX

HALF fill a large, wide saucepan or flameproof casserole with water and bring to the boil. Sift the self-raising flour and the ground cinnamon into a large mixing bowl, then stir in the shredded suet, caster sugar and currants. Add the milk and mix to a firm dough, kneading lightly to bring together.

On a lightly floured surface, roll out the dough to about 28 cm (11 in) long and 23 cm (9 in) wide, or 2.5 cm (1 in) narrower than your saucepan or casserole. Sprinkle the brown sugar over the dough, roll it up, like a swiss roll, from a short end and press the join firmly to seal.

Fold a large, thick tea towel or cloth, about 76 × 30 cm (30 × 12 in), in half widthways and spread evenly all over with the lard. Sift the plain flour evenly over the fat. Place the suet roll on the prepared tea towel or cloth, about 5 cm (2 in) from one of the short ends, and roll it up loosely, allowing room for the pudding to expand during cooking. Gather each end of the tea towel or cloth and tie securely with string. Make a loop in the string at one end. Put the pudding into the saucepan and boil gently for 2 hours, replenishing the boiling water during cooking as necessary.

When cooked, carefully remove from the pan by inserting a large fork through the string loop. Put onto a board and unwrap immediately. Place the pudding on a heated serving plate, cut into slices and serve with hot custard.

The lard lining the wrapping gives the spotted dick a creamy white coat.

HALLOWED TRADITIONS
Roast beef has been served on silver trolleys at Simpson's in London's Strand since 1848. Diners in the know will often round off the meal with spotted dick and custard.

A golden tart, filled with syrup laced with lemon, never fails to please the palate.

Treacle Tart

This recipe is lighter and sunnier than the old-fashioned, black treacle version

SIFT the flour and salt into a bowl and rub in the butter and the lard or white vegetable fat until the mixture resembles fine breadcrumbs. Mix to a firm dough with the egg. Turn onto a lightly floured surface and knead for a few seconds until smooth. Wrap and chill for 30 minutes.

Preheat the oven to 200°C (400°F, gas mark 6). Put the syrup, lemon rind and juice into a small saucepan and heat gently for 1–2 minutes to thin the syrup. Remove from the heat, stir in the breadcrumbs and leave to cool.

Roll the dough out fairly thinly and line a 23 cm (9 in) pie plate, pressing the dough down gently. Trim off the surplus from round the edge and prick the base lightly with a fork.

Reknead and roll out the trimmings and cut out small shapes (hearts, rounds, etc) with a 1.3 cm (½ in) diameter fancy cutter. Alternatively, cut out 2.5 cm (1 in) rounds with a fluted cutter and cut each round into quarters. Spread the syrup mixture in the lined pie plate, leaving a 1.3 cm (½ in) border round the edge. Brush the shapes with water and arrange them round the edge of the plate. Put the plate onto a baking tray and bake in the centre of the oven for 25–30 minutes until the pastry is cooked. Serve the tart, warm or cold, with cream.

INGREDIENTS

FOR THE PASTRY

175 G (6 OZ) PLAIN FLOUR

PINCH OF SALT

60 G (2 OZ) BUTTER

30 G (1 OZ) LARD OR WHITE VEGETABLE FAT

1 EGG, SIZE 2, BEATEN

FOR THE FILLING

225 G (8 OZ) GOLDEN SYRUP

FINELY GRATED RIND 1 SMALL LEMON

2 TEASPOONS LEMON JUICE

30 G (1 OZ) FRESH WHITE BREADCRUMBS

PREPARATION TIME: 45 MINUTES

COOKING TIME: 25–30 MINUTES

SERVES SIX

Wardens in Comfort

Wardens were an old variety of hard, cooking pear that probably originated in the village of Old Warden in Bedfordshire

INGREDIENTS

725 ML (1¼ PINTS) MEDIUM-DRY, FRUITY RED WINE
4 TABLESPOONS ORANGE FLOWER WATER
175 G (6 OZ) GRANULATED SUGAR
STRAINED JUICE 1 ORANGE AND 1 LEMON
10 CM (4 IN) CINNAMON STICK
4 CLOVES
2.5 CM (1 IN) PIECE FRESH GINGER PEELED AND QUARTERED
6 LARGE, RIPE, FIRM PEARS, WILLIAMS OR COMICE

PREPARATION TIME: 15 MINUTES
COOKING TIME: 45 MINUTES
SERVES SIX

PUT all the ingredients, except the pears, into a large, stainless steel or enamel saucepan and heat gently, stirring occasionally, until the sugar has dissolved. Bring to the boil and boil for 2 minutes.

Peel the pears carefully, without removing their stalks, and add them to the saucepan. Cover and cook slowly for 30–40 minutes or until just softened, turning frequently to ensure that they cook and colour evenly.

Using a slotted spoon, lift the pears from the saucepan and put them onto a serving dish. Strain the juice through a nylon sieve and discard the spices. Return the juice to the pan, bring back to the boil, reduce the heat a little and boil gently until the juice has reduced by half and is heavy and syrupy.

Pour the syrup over the pears and allow to cool. Serve with whipped cream flavoured with kirsch.

The spicy nature of the syrup carries a strong hint of the late medieval ancestry of this pear dish.

For an unusual twist, make this recipe with home-made elderberry and blackberry wine (see p 362)

Thin pancakes, rolled round a sprinkling of lemon juice and sugar, are quite irresistible.

BUCKS FLIP
At Olney in Buckinghamshire a pancake race is held every Shrove Tuesday in a tradition that dates from the 15th century. Today, the race is timed against one held in Liberal in the USA.

Pancakes

The tradition of making pancakes on Shrove Tuesday has its origin in the need to use up perishable foods before the Lenten fast began

SIFT the flour and salt into a large mixing bowl and make a well in the centre. Beat in the egg and a little of the milk until smooth, then gradually beat in the remaining milk and 4 tablespoons of the melted butter. Cover the bowl and leave to stand for 1 hour.

Preheat the oven to 140°C (275°F, gas mark 1). Stir the batter and pour it into a measuring jug. In a small, nonstick or well-proved frying pan, heat about 1 teaspoon of the remaining butter until sizzling, taking care not to let it burn.

Pour one-twelfth of the batter into the pan, turning the pan to coat the base evenly. Cook over a moderate heat until the pancake is light golden brown underneath and appears dry on top. Flip over and cook the other side until golden.

Turn the pancake onto a plate and sprinkle it with a little of the lemon juice and caster or demerara sugar, then roll it up or fold it twice. Transfer to a large, heatproof serving plate and cover with greaseproof paper before putting it into the oven to keep warm. Make 11 more pancakes in the same way.

Sprinkle the finished pancakes with any remaining melted butter, lemon juice and sugar. Decorate with the lemon slices and serve immediately.

Instead of lemon juice and sugar, the pancakes can be served with ice cream topped with maple syrup or orange liqueur, or raspberry or chocolate sauce. Alternatively, the pancakes can be filled with stewed fruits, such as apples or blackberries, and served with cream.

INGREDIENTS

115G (4OZ) PLAIN FLOUR
¼ LEVEL TEASPOON SALT
1 EGG, SIZE 2
285ML (½ PINT) MILK
115G (4OZ) BUTTER, MELTED
STRAINED JUICE 2 LEMONS
60G (2OZ) CASTER OR DEMERARA SUGAR
LEMON SLICES TO DECORATE
PREPARATION TIME: 15 MINUTES
COOKING TIME: 20 MINUTES
STANDING TIME: 1 HOUR
SERVES FOUR

Layers of luscious cream, sponge, wine and redcurrant jelly compose this delightful dessert.

When toasting almonds, watch them all the time to make sure that they don't burn.

Whim Wham

A rich Scottish dessert, 'made on a whim', bridges the culinary gap between syllabub and trifle

INGREDIENTS

- 425ML (3/4 PINT) DOUBLE CREAM
- 45G (1 1/2 OZ) CASTER SUGAR
- FINELY GRATED RIND 1 LEMON
- 150ML (1/4 PINT) MEDIUM-SWEET WHITE WINE OR SHERRY
- 16–20 SPONGE FINGERS (BOUDOIR BISCUITS)
- 225G (1/2LB) REDCURRANT JELLY, HOMEMADE (SEE P.401) OR BOUGHT
- CANDIED CITRON AND ORANGE PEEL AND TOASTED BLANCHED WHOLE ALMONDS TO DECORATE

PREPARATION TIME: 15 MINUTES

SERVES FOUR

WHISK the cream with the sugar, lemon rind and half the wine or sherry until it will hold soft peaks. Break each sponge finger into three pieces.

Divide a third of the cream, followed by half the sponge fingers, half the remaining wine or sherry and half the redcurrant jelly into four glasses or bowls.

Top with half the remaining cream and the remaining sponge fingers and drizzle with the last of the wine, then spoon over the remaining jelly. Swirl the remaining cream on top and decorate with the candied peel and the almonds.

Serve immediately, or chill for no longer than 30 minutes.

Fresh Raspberry Milk Jelly with Macaroons

Here is a magical pudding that separates, as it sets, into two deliciously different jellies

Put the raspberries into a blender or a liquidiser and blend until smooth, then pass through a sieve to remove the seeds. Pour 3 tablespoons of the milk into a small bowl and sprinkle the gelatine over the top. Leave to stand for 2–3 minutes until the gelatine is swollen and softened.

Put the remainder of the milk and the sugar, egg yolks, lemon rind and softened gelatine into a saucepan. Bring to the boil slowly, stirring continuously. The mixture will thicken and curdle slightly. Strain through a nylon sieve into a large bowl and leave to cool for about 30 minutes.

Lightly oil a 1.4 litre (2½ pint) decorative jelly mould with the almond oil. Stir the raspberry purée into the custard. Whisk the egg whites until they are stiff but not dry and fold them carefully into the raspberry mixture. Stir in the lemon juice and immediately pour the jelly mixture into the prepared mould. Put into the refrigerator and chill for 3–4 hours or until firmly set.

To turn out the jelly, dip the mould up to its rim in hot water for 5 seconds, put a plate on top and invert, holding tightly. Give the jelly a firm shake to free it, then remove the mould.

Decorate with the whipped cream and the tiny macaroons. Keep the jelly refrigerated until required.

INGREDIENTS

450 G (1 LB) FRESH RASPBERRIES, HULLED, OR FROZEN RASPBERRIES, THAWED
570 ML (1 PINT) MILK
30 G (1 OZ) GELATINE
225 G (8 OZ) CASTER SUGAR
3 EGGS, SIZE 2, SEPARATED
THINLY PARED RIND AND STRAINED JUICE 2 LEMONS
ALMOND OIL FOR GREASING MOULD
WHIPPED CREAM AND SMALL MACAROONS TO DECORATE

PREPARATION TIME: 25 MINUTES
COOKING TIME: 5 MINUTES
CHILLING TIME: 3–4 HOURS
SERVES SIX

The turned-out dessert reveals an intriguing mixture of clear raspberry jelly and rich mousse.

Feasts of yesteryear
In the world of talking toy animals that inhabited the pages of *Rainbow* and other comics for young children in the first half of the century, no festival was ever celebrated without a battery of jellies.

Special Occasions

Beyond its buildings and its setting, the joy of a village lies in its continuity, the cycle of seasons and festivals that make the present at one with past and future. Such occasions must be properly celebrated, with creamy *Choux Swans* and *Raspberries* for a christening perhaps, or *Baked Trout, Simnel Cake* and *Syllabub* at Easter. A *Champagne Sorbet* would be well suited to Valentine's Day and *Pumpkin Soup* and *Spiced Fruit Turnovers* for Guy Fawkes. At Christmas, *Sack Posset* could pave the way for the *Turkey, Plum Pudding* and *Royal Mince Pies.*

An EDWARDIAN BREAKFAST

At *Country House Parties* in the early years of this century, *Breakfast* was a *Veritable Feast*. Sideboards groaned under the weight of the many different dishes on offer. So forget the quick fix of the modern bowl of cornflakes or muesli and step back in time to enjoy the *Hearty Breakfast Dishes* of a more leisurely era, maybe *Inviting Friends* to share the experience with you one weekend.

Menu

Porridge

Compote of Dried Fruits

Kedgeree

Mixed Grill

Grilled Kippers

Devilled Kidneys

Boxty Potatoes

Bread Rolls and Oatcakes (see pp.338, 354)

Toast and Marmalade

Coffee

Start your day the healthy way with porridge or dried fruits soaked in fruit juice and honey.

—PORRIDGE—

Pour the water into a saucepan and bring to the boil. Put the oatmeal into a clean, dry jug and gradually pour it into the water in a slow, steady stream, stirring constantly. Continue to stir while bringing the porridge to the boil, then reduce the heat, cover and simmer for 20 minutes, stirring only occasionally.

Add the salt and pour the porridge into a large, heated serving dish or individual bowls. Serve with the cream, milk or buttermilk poured over and sprinkled with the demerara sugar.

—DRIED FRUIT COMPOTE—

The day before, put the dried fruits into a stainless steel or enamel saucepan. Using a zester, remove the rinds in thin strips from the orange and lemon and add to the fruits. Alternatively, pare the orange and lemon rinds thinly with a potato peeler and cut into very fine shreds with a knife. Cut the orange and lemon in half, then squeeze out and strain the juice. Pour the fruit juice and water over the fruit, add the honey and heat gently until hot but not boiling. Remove from the heat, cover and leave to stand overnight. Pour the compote into a serving bowl and serve with the single cream if desired.

INGREDIENTS

Porridge

1.7 litres (3 pints) still Highland spring water
275g (10oz) medium oatmeal
½ level teaspoon salt
285ml (½ pint) cream, milk or buttermilk for serving
Demerara sugar for sprinkling

Preparation time: 5 minutes
Cooking time: 20 minutes
Serves eight

Dried fruit compote

115g (4oz) each dried figs and pitted prunes
60g (2oz) dried apple rings
85g (3oz) each dried apricots and peaches
1 orange, washed
1 lemon, washed
850ml (1½ pints) water
1 tablespoon clear honey
Single cream for serving (optional)

Preparation time: 10 minutes
Standing time: Overnight
Serves eight

Kedgeree, a mixture of finnan haddie, rice and lightly curried celery and onions always available at Edwardian breakfasts, is now often served as a light lunch or supper.

INGREDIENTS

- 900 G (2 LB) FINNAN HADDIE FILLET
- 285 ML (½ PINT) MILK
- 1 LITRE (1¾ PINTS) WATER
- 4 CELERY STICKS, TRIMMED AND CHOPPED
- 2 MEDIUM ONIONS, PEELED AND CHOPPED
- 2 MACE BLADES
- A FEW BLACK PEPPERCORNS
- 400 G (14 OZ) BASMATI RICE, RINSED
- SALT
- 30 G (1 OZ) BUTTER
- 4 LEVEL TEASPOONS MILD CURRY POWDER OR GARAM MASALA
- 285 ML (½ PINT) DOUBLE CREAM
- FRESHLY GROUND BLACK PEPPER
- 4 HEAPED TABLESPOONS FINELY CHOPPED FRESH PARSLEY
- 4 EGGS, SIZE 2, HARD BOILED, SHELLED AND QUARTERED LENGTHWAYS
- CHOPPED FRESH PARSLEY TO GARNISH

PREPARATION TIME: 20 MINUTES
COOKING TIME: 30 MINUTES
SERVES EIGHT

—KEDGEREE—

Put the finnan haddie into a wide, shallow pan and pour over the milk and 225 ml (8 fl oz) of the water. Scatter half the chopped celery and onion over the fish, add the mace blades and the peppercorns and bring slowly to the boil. Take immediately from the heat, cover and set aside.

Put the rice into a medium saucepan, cover with the remaining cold water and add a good pinch of salt. Bring to the boil, reduce the heat, cover the pan and simmer for 10 minutes. Remove the pan from the heat and leave to stand without removing the lid.

Melt the butter in a large frying pan, add the remaining celery and onion and fry over a gentle heat, stirring, for about 5 minutes until soft but not coloured. Mix in the curry powder or garam masala and fry, stirring, for 1–2 minutes until fragrant. Remove from the heat.

Take the fish out of the poaching liquid and strain, discarding the flavourings but reserving the liquid. Flake the fish into large pieces, removing and discarding the skin and any bones. Return the frying pan to a moderate heat, add the cooked rice and mix with the curried celery and onion, then add the cream, and pepper to taste. Stir until heated through, then add the flaked fish and toss very gently so that it mixes in but does not break up.

Remove from the heat and fork in the parsley and a little of the reserved poaching liquid to moisten. Season to taste.

Serve the kedgeree in a heated serving dish with the eggs arranged on top and garnished with the chopped parsley.

—MIXED GRILL—

To prepare the meats, brush the kidneys, lamb cutlets and steaks with the olive oil and season well with the salt and pepper. Put the bacon rashers onto a board and stretch them with the back of a knife, cut in half, then roll up and thread onto two skewers.

Preheat the oven to 150°C (300°F, gas mark 2). Put two large, heat-proof serving dishes into the oven to warm.

Heat the grill to high and grill the ingredients in the following order, removing them as they are cooked and putting them onto the serving dishes to keep hot in the oven.

First, grill the sausages and kidneys for 8–10 minutes, turning frequently, then grill the lamb cutlets and bacon rolls for 5–6 minutes. Next grill the steaks and black pudding for 2–3 minutes on each side. Finally, remove the rack from the grill pan, add the tomatoes and mushrooms and brush with the hot fat remaining in the pan. Season well with salt and pepper and grill for 2–3 minutes.

Arrange the tomatoes and mushrooms on the dish with the meats. Skim all the fat from the juices remaining in the grill pan and spoon the juices over the meats.

INGREDIENTS

8 LAMB'S KIDNEYS, SKINNED, HALVED AND CORED, RINSED AND DRIED WITH KITCHEN PAPER
8 LAMB CUTLETS, TRIMMED OF EXCESS FAT
8 FILLET OF BEEF STEAKS, EACH 115G (4OZ) OR 900G (2LB) RUMP STEAK CUT INTO 8 PIECES
4 TABLESPOONS OLIVE OIL
SALT AND FRESHLY GROUND BLACK PEPPER
8 RASHERS STREAKY BACON, RINDS REMOVED
8 PORK SAUSAGES
450G (1LB) BLACK PUDDING, CUT INTO 8 SLICES
8 TOMATOES, HALVED
8 LARGE, FLAT MUSHROOMS, PEELED
PREPARATION TIME: 40 MINUTES
COOKING TIME: 25 MINUTES
SERVES EIGHT

Really hearty appetites are necessary to do full justice to this magnificent mixed grill of steak, kidneys, cutlets, bacon, sausages, black pudding, mushrooms and tomatoes.

Golden treasury
Smoke curing, an ancient way of preserving fish, enabled vast numbers of herring to be transported inland. They were slit, soaked in brine and smoked for some 20 hours when they became kippers. Particularly renowned are those from Loch Fyne, Craster and the Isle of Man.

Overnight marinating makes grilled kippers just that little bit special.

INGREDIENTS

- 8 oak-smoked kippers
- 285 ml (½ pint) milk mixed with 285 ml (½ pint) water
- 150 ml (¼ pint) olive oil
- Freshly ground black pepper
- 1 level teaspoon caster sugar
- 8 tablespoons chopped fresh parsley
- 8 spring onions, trimmed and chopped
- 4 tablespoons snipped fresh chives
- Lemon wedges, granary or rye bread and butter for serving

Preparation time:
1st Day: 15 minutes
2nd Day: 10 minutes
Marinating time: 3 hours plus overnight refrigeration
Cooking time: 5 minutes
Serves eight

—GRILLED KIPPERS—

The day before, put the kippers, flesh side down, into a large, shallow dish and pour over the milk and water to immerse them. Cover the dish and leave to stand in a cool place for 3 hours. (This removes some of the salt from the kippers.)

Drain and rinse the kippers, pat dry with kitchen paper and place, flesh side uppermost, in a shallow dish. Mix the olive oil in a small bowl with some pepper, the sugar, parsley, spring onions and chives and spoon over the kippers. Cover the dish tightly with foil to prevent the odour from escaping, then refrigerate overnight.

Next day place the kippers, skin side uppermost, on a piece of foil on the grill rack. Preheat the grill, then cook the kippers gently for about 5 minutes until the skin is crisp and the fish is hot and cooked through.

Serve, flesh side up, on hot plates with the lemon wedges and oatcakes or thinly sliced brown bread and butter.

— DEVILLED KIDNEYS —

Remove the skins from the kidneys and slice them in half horizontally. Using scissors, snip away the white central cores and surrounding tubes. Rinse the kidneys well under cold water and pat dry with kitchen paper.

Mix the chutney, mustard, Tabasco sauce, oil, sugar, lemon juice and cayenne pepper together in a shallow dish. Add the kidneys and toss gently to coat. Cover and marinate in the refrigerator for 2 hours.

Preheat the grill to medium and line the grill pan with foil. Remove the kidneys from the marinade and arrange in the pan. Grill for 10 minutes, turning frequently and brushing with the marinade as they cook.

Meanwhile, blend the butter with the tomato purée and the chopped parsley. Toast the muffins and spread with the tomato butter.

Serve the kidneys on the hot toasted muffins, sprinkled with the chillies and garnished with the mushrooms or tomatoes and the parsley.

— BOXTY POTATOES —

Put the grated potatoes into a colander and rinse well under cold, running water. Squeeze, then dry thoroughly in a tea towel.

In a large mixing bowl, beat the flour, salt, black pepper and milk together with a wooden spoon until smooth. Add the sage and the potatoes, then mix. Make sure that the grated potatoes are evenly coated with the batter. Divide the mixture into 16 equal portions.

Heat half the butter or oil in a large, nonstick frying pan until sizzling hot. Spoon four portions of the mixture into the pan to form cakes about 7.5 cm (3 in) in diameter. Fry over a moderate heat for 5 minutes until golden and crisp underneath then turn and fry the other side. Drain on kitchen paper and keep hot while cooking the rest.

Finely shredded chilli peppers add the final fiery touch to the hot and spicy kidneys.

INGREDIENTS

Devilled kidneys

16 lamb kidneys
2 tablespoons mango chutney
½ level teaspoon English mustard powder
8 drops Tabasco sauce
2 teaspoons olive oil
2 level teaspoons demerara sugar
2 tablespoons fresh lemon juice
Pinch of cayenne pepper
60 g (2 oz) unsalted butter, softened
2 level teaspoons tomato puree
4 teaspoons chopped fresh parsley
4 muffins, homemade (see p.346) or bought, halved
2 small red chillies, deseeded and cut into fine shreds
Sauteed mushrooms or grilled tomato halves and parsley sprigs to garnish

Preparation time: 40 minutes
Marinating time: 2 hours
Cooking time: 10 minutes
Serves eight

Boxty potatoes

1.4 kg (3 lb) baking potatoes, peeled and coarsely grated
115 g (4 oz) plain flour
1 level teaspoon salt
Freshly ground black pepper
8 tablespoons milk
2 tablespoons chopped fresh sage or 2 level teaspoons dried sage
85 g (3 oz) butter or 4 tablespoons olive oil

Preparation time: 30 minutes
Cooking time: 40 minutes
Serves eight

An EASTER CELEBRATION

EASTER *Recipes* ARE LONG BOUND UP WITH TRADITION. GOOD FRIDAY MARKS THE PEAK OF THE LENTEN FAST, WHEN *Fish* IS SERVED. THEN TOO, KITCHENS ARE FILLED WITH THE WARM AROMA OF *Hot Cross Buns* AND, IN RECENT YEARS, THAT OF *Simnel Cake*. ON EASTER DAY, WHEN THE FAST IS AT AN END, THE FAMILY CAN SIT DOWN TO A JOYFUL *Lunch* OF *Roast Lamb* AND ALL THE TRIMMINGS, FOLLOWED BY A FROTHY CONCOCTION FOR *Dessert*.

MENU

STUFFED
BAKED TROUT
WITH
NEW POTATOES

HOT CROSS BUNS AND
SIMNEL CAKE

ROAST LEG OF LAMB
WITH
MINT SAUCE

SYLLABUB TRIFLE

Serve the trout with zesty wedges of lemon, fresh rolls and the season's new potatoes.

AN EGG AT EASTER
Eggs represent rebirth—the return of spring in pagan times, the Resurrection to Christians. Long before chocolate eggs, it was the custom for children to hard boil and paint 'Pace' Eggs and roll them down hillsides on Easter Sunday.

STUFFED BAKED TROUT

INGREDIENTS

- 60G (2OZ) BUTTER
- 175G (6OZ) SHALLOTS, PEELED AND FINELY CHOPPED
- 2 GARLIC CLOVES, PEELED AND FINELY CHOPPED
- 225G (8OZ) FRESH WHITE BREADCRUMBS
- 2 LEVEL TABLESPOONS CHOPPED FRESH PARSLEY
- 2 LEVEL TABLESPOONS CHOPPED FRESH SAGE
- 4 ANCHOVY FILLETS, CHOPPED
- FINELY GRATED RIND 2 ORANGES
- 2 EGGS, SIZE 3, BEATEN
- SALT AND FRESHLY GROUND BLACK PEPPER
- 8 RAINBOW TROUT, EACH APPROX 225G (8OZ) GUTTED AND CLEANED, HEADS AND TAILS LEFT ON
- BUTTER FOR GREASING
- STRAINED JUICE 2 LEMONS
- 400ML (14FL OZ) DRY WHITE WINE
- LEMON WEDGES AND CHOPPED FRESH PARSLEY TO GARNISH

PREPARATION TIME: 40 MINUTES
COOKING TIME: 35 MINUTES
SERVES EIGHT

Melt the butter in a small saucepan, add the shallots and garlic and cook gently for 5 minutes or until softened but not browned. Remove from the heat and leave to cool.

Preheat the oven to 180°C (350°F, gas mark 4). Put the breadcrumbs into a bowl, add the shallots and garlic, the parsley, sage, anchovy fillets, orange rind, egg and some salt and pepper and mix together. Divide into eight equal portions and fill the cavity of each trout. Sew the openings with fine string or secure with small skewers or cocktail sticks.

Butter two large baking dishes. Arrange the fish in the dishes, sprinkle with salt and pepper, then pour over the lemon juice and wine. Cook, uncovered, in the oven for about 30 minutes, basting with the cooking liquid every 10 minutes.

Remove the trout from the baking dishes, arrange on heated serving dishes, cover and keep warm. Strain the cooking liquid into a saucepan and boil until reduced by half. Pour the sauce over the trout, garnish with the lemon wedges and chopped parsley and serve immediately, accompanied by new potatoes and salad.

Ingredients

Hot cross buns
30 g (1 oz) fresh yeast, or 15 g (½ oz) dried yeast
5 tablespoons lukewarm water
150 ml (¼ pint) lukewarm milk
450 g (1 lb) strong plain flour
85 g (3 oz) caster sugar
1 level teaspoon salt
2 level teaspoons mixed spice
60 g (2 oz) butter, softened
85 g (3 oz) currants
30 g (1 oz) chopped mixed peel
1 egg, size 3, beaten
85 g (3 oz) plain flour
1 teaspoon sunflower oil
2–3 tablespoons water
2 tablespoons each milk and water, to glaze
Preparation time: 45 minutes
Rising time: 1½ hours
Cooking time: 20 minutes
Makes 12 buns

Simnel cake
For the almond paste
115 g (4 oz) icing sugar
115 g (4 oz) caster sugar
225 g (8 oz) ground almonds
1 teaspoon orange flower water
1 egg size 3, beaten
1 teaspoon fresh lemon juice

For the cake
225 g (8 oz) butter, softened
225 g (8 oz) soft light brown sugar
3 eggs, size 3
275 g (10 oz) plain flour
2 level teaspoons mixed spice
175 g (6 oz) glace cherries, washed, dried and halved
600 g (1 lb 5 oz) mixed dried fruit
Finely grated rind 1 lemon
1 egg white, size 3, lightly beaten
Preparation time: 1¼ hours
Cooking time: 3 hours

—HOT CROSS BUNS AND SIMNEL CAKE—

To make the hot cross buns If using fresh yeast, mix the water and milk, add the yeast and stir until dissolved. If using dried yeast, see p.441. Sift 115 g (4 oz) of the strong flour into a bowl, stir in 1 teaspoon of the caster sugar, pour in the yeast liquid and beat until smooth. Cover and leave in a warm place for 15 minutes or until frothy.

Sift the salt, mixed spice and remaining strong flour into a bowl and rub in the butter. Stir in the currants, peel and 60 g (2 oz) of the remaining caster sugar. Make a well in the centre and add the yeast mixture and the egg. Mix to a soft dough, then knead it on a lightly floured surface for 10 minutes until smooth and elastic. Put the dough into a bowl, cover and leave in a warm place for 1 hour or until doubled in size.

Reknead and shape the dough into 12 smooth balls. Place, spaced slightly apart, on greased baking sheets, cover with lightly oiled cling film and leave in a warm place for 30 minutes or until doubled in size.

Meanwhile, preheat the oven to 190°c (375°f, gas mark 5). To make the crosses, sift the plain flour into a bowl then stir in the oil and enough water to make a smooth paste which will hold its shape when piped. Spoon into a small, paper piping bag, cut a small hole in the bottom and pipe a cross on the top of each bun. Bake for 20 minutes or until the buns are golden brown and sound hollow when tapped on the bottom.

Meanwhile, heat the remaining sugar in the milk and water until dissolved. Keep hot, and brush over the buns immediately they are removed from the oven. Cool on wire racks.

To make the simnel cake Grease a 20 cm (8 in) round cake tin, line it with double thickness greaseproof paper then grease the paper. Preheat the oven to 150°c (300°f, gas mark 2). To make the almond paste, sift the icing sugar into a bowl and stir in the caster sugar and almonds. Add the remaining ingredients and mix to a stiff paste. On a surface lightly dusted with icing sugar, knead until smooth, then wrap and set aside.

To make the cake, beat the butter and sugar together until light and fluffy, then beat in the eggs, one at a time, beating well between each addition. Sift the flour and spice into the bowl and fold in with a metal spoon. Gradually mix in the cherries, dried fruit and grated lemon rind. On a surface lightly dusted with icing sugar, roll out half the almond paste to an 18 cm (7 in) round. Spoon half the cake mixture into the prepared tin, level the surface and lay the almond paste on top. Spoon the remaining mixture on top and spread evenly. Bake for 3 hours until a rich brown on top and a skewer, inserted into the centre, comes out clean. If the top browns too quickly, cover with greaseproof paper.

Cool in the tin for 1 hour, then turn out onto a wire rack to cool completely. Roll out half the remaining paste to cover the top of the cake. Brush a little egg white over the cake top and press the paste gently into position with a rolling pin. Pinch the edge between your thumb and forefinger. Using a sharp knife, mark a diamond pattern on top of the paste. Roll the remaining paste into 11 balls, brush the top of the cake with egg white, arrange the balls evenly around the edge and brush them with egg white. Stand the cake on a baking tray and grill until the paste is lightly browned. When cold, store in an airtight tin.

The crosses on the spicy buns and the almond paste balls on the cake are all Lenten symbols.

INGREDIENTS

- 2.7 KG (6 LB) LEG OF LAMB
- SALT AND FRESHLY GROUND BLACK PEPPER
- 2 MEDIUM ONIONS, PEELED AND ROUGHLY CHOPPED OR 2 SMALL LEEKS, TRIMMED, WASHED AND ROUGHLY CHOPPED
- 2 MEDIUM CARROTS, PEELED AND QUARTERED LENGTHWAYS
- 1 SMALL TURNIP, PEELED AND QUARTERED
- SMALL FRESH ROSEMARY SPRIG

FOR THE MINT SAUCE

- 20 G (¾ OZ) FRESH MINT
- 3 TEASPOONS CASTER SUGAR
- 2 TABLESPOONS BOILING WATER
- 85 ML (3 FL OZ) DISTILLED MALT VINEGAR OR WHITE WINE VINEGAR

FOR THE GRAVY

- 2 LEVEL TABLESPOONS PLAIN FLOUR
- 850 ML (1½ PINTS) VEGETABLE STOCK (SEE P.434)

PREPARATION TIME: 40 MINUTES
COOKING TIME: 2¼ HOURS
SERVES EIGHT

—ROAST LEG OF LAMB WITH MINT SAUCE—

Preheat the oven to 200°C (400°F, gas mark 6). Calculate the cooking time for the lamb according to its exact weight and your personal preference: allow 20 minutes per 450 g (1 lb) for well done meat; 15 minutes for medium; or 10 minutes for juicy pink meat.

Wipe the lamb with kitchen paper then season well with salt and pepper. Mix all the vegetables together and arrange in a layer in the bottom of a lightly greased roasting tin. Put the lamb on top, add the rosemary and roast in the centre of the oven for the required time.

To make the mint sauce While the lamb is cooking, put the mint into a bowl and cover with boiling water. Drain immediately and rinse under cold water. Dry on kitchen paper, remove the leaves, chop them finely and put them into a small bowl. Add the sugar and measured boiling water and stir until the sugar has dissolved. Stir in the vinegar, pour into a serving jug and set aside. When the lamb is cooked, remove it from the roasting tin and put it onto a heated serving dish. Cover loosely with foil and leave to stand while making the gravy.

To make the gravy Discard the vegetables from the roasting tin, then skim off all but 2 tablespoons of the fat from the juices in the tin. Mix the flour into the remaining juices and cook over a low heat for 3–4 minutes, stirring constantly. Gradually add the stock and bring to the boil, stirring. Reduce the heat and simmer for 6–7 minutes or until the gravy is slightly thickened and smooth. Strain into a heated gravy boat.

Serve the lamb with the mint sauce and gravy, accompanied by buttered spring cabbage, buttered carrots and peas, and new potatoes.

Roasting the lamb on a bed of root vegetables adds richness to the juices for the gravy.

The lemon syllabub topping for the trifle is a tangy change from the usual whipped cream.

—SYLLABUB TRIFLE—

INGREDIENTS

- 200G (7OZ) FATLESS SPONGE CAKE OR 8 TRIFLE SPONGES
- 175G (6OZ) STRAWBERRY OR RASPBERRY JAM, HOMEMADE (SEE P.389) OR BOUGHT
- 115ML (4FL OZ) MEDIUM-DRY SHERRY, MARSALA OR MADEIRA
- 10 SMALL ALMOND MACAROONS
- 250G (9OZ) FRESH MIXED SOFT FRUITS (RASPBERRIES, STRAWBERRIES, REDCURRANTS AND BLACKBERRIES) OR FROZEN FRUITS, THAWED

FOR THE CUSTARD

- 4 EGGS, SIZE 1
- 2 LEVEL TEASPOONS CORNFLOUR
- 570ML (1 PINT) RICH, CREAMY MILK
- 45G (1½OZ) CASTER SUGAR
- 1 VANILLA POD, HALVED LENGTHWAYS

FOR THE SYLLABUB

- FINELY PARED RIND AND STRAINED JUICE 1 LEMON
- 85ML (3FL OZ) MEDIUM OR SWEET WHITE WINE
- 2 TABLESPOONS BRANDY
- 85G (3OZ) CASTER SUGAR
- 285ML (½ PINT) DOUBLE CREAM
- FRESH VIOLETS OR ROSE PETALS TO DECORATE

PREPARATION TIME: 45–50 MINUTES
COOKING TIME: 15 MINUTES
CHILLING TIME: OVERNIGHT PLUS 2–3 HOURS

Starting the day before the meal, cut the sponge cake or trifle sponges in half horizontally and sandwich back together with the jam. Cut into neat slices and arrange in the bottom of a large, deep, glass serving bowl. Spoon half the chosen fortified wine over the sponge and arrange the macaroons on top. Cover the macaroons with the fruit, pour over the remaining fortified wine and set aside.

To make the custard Put the eggs and cornflour into a mixing bowl and whisk lightly together. Pour the milk into a saucepan, add the sugar and vanilla pod and bring almost to the boil. Stirring with a whisk, gradually add the hot milk to the egg mixture. Pour into a clean saucepan and stir continuously over a low heat for 5–6 minutes or until the custard thickens enough to coat the back of the spoon. Do not allow it to boil as it will curdle. Remove the custard from the heat and pour immediately through a nylon sieve into a clean bowl. Cover the surface of the custard closely with cling film to prevent a skin from forming and leave to cool. Pour the cooled custard evenly over the fruit in the trifle bowl. Cover the bowl and chill overnight.

To make the syllabub Put the pared lemon rind and juice into a bowl, add the wine, brandy and sugar and stir until the sugar dissolves. Cover and leave to stand overnight at room temperature.

Next day, strain the syllabub liquid through a nylon sieve into a mixing bowl and gradually stir in the double cream, pouring it into the bowl in a thin stream. Whisk until the mixture will hold soft peaks when the whisk is lifted from the bowl. Pour the syllabub on top of the trifle and chill for 2–3 hours.

Just before serving, decorate the trifle with the fresh violets or rose petals or, if preferred, with crystallised flowers.

A CHRISTENING TEA

A *Splendid Tea Party* IS PARTICULARLY APPROPRIATE TO WELCOME THE NEW MEMBER OF THE FAMILY. THE MOUTH-WATERING RECIPES ARE *Sufficient For Twenty People* AND CAN BE PREPARED IN ADVANCE SO THAT YOU ARE FREE TO JOIN YOUR GUESTS. BUT BE WARNED: THESE *Tea-time Treats* ARE LIKELY TO BE SUCH A SUCCESS THAT YOU WILL BE ASKED TO PROVIDE THEM AGAIN FOR SIMILAR *Family Celebrations*.

MENU

DAINTY SANDWICHES

A SELECTION OF EASY CANAPES

CHOUX SWANS
FILLED WITH
RASPBERRIES AND CREAM

CHRISTENING CAKE

These little mouthfuls offer a choice of meat, fish or vegetable fillings.

— DAINTY SANDWICHES —

To make salmon pinwheels Prepare them the day before. Mix the cream cheese and watercress together. Using a rolling pin, gently roll each slice of bread to make it thin and flexible. Spread evenly with the cream cheese mixture, then cover with a thin layer of salmon, trimming to fit where necessary. Sprinkle the lemon juice over the salmon and season with the pepper. Starting from a short end, roll up each slice tightly like a swiss roll. Wrap each roll tightly in cling film and refrigerate overnight. Just before serving, unwrap, cut each roll into five slices and arrange on a serving dish.

To make chicken and anchovy triangles Make 3–4 hours ahead. Put the chopped chicken, anchovies, capers, tartare sauce and mayonnaise into a bowl, season with the black pepper and mix well together. Spread the butter thinly over each slice of bread, then spread the chicken mixture evenly over each brown slice. Sprinkle with the shredded lettuce and top with the slices of white bread. Stack the sandwiches together, wrap in cling film and chill. Just before serving, unwrap, remove the crusts, cut the sandwiches into small triangles and arrange on a serving dish.

To make asparagus rolls Make 3–4 hours ahead. Tie the asparagus spears together in two bundles and cook them in gently boiling, salted water for 5–10 minutes or until just tender. Remove the spears carefully from the saucepan, put them into a colander and rinse under cold water, then drain well and allow to cool. Using a rolling pin, lightly roll each slice of bread to make it thinner. Blend the butter, lemon rind and cayenne pepper together and spread the mixture evenly over each slice. Cut each slice, and each asparagus spear, in half widthways. Lay a piece of asparagus lengthways on each piece of bread, trimming to fit if necessary. Roll up tightly, wrap in cling film and chill. Just before serving, unwrap, cut each asparagus roll in half and arrange on a serving dish.

INGREDIENTS

SALMON PINWHEELS
- 340 G (12 OZ) CREAM CHEESE
- 85 G (3 OZ) TRIMMED WATERCRESS, FINELY CHOPPED
- 8 LONG, THIN SLICES WHITE BREAD, CUT LENGTHWAYS FROM A LARGE SANDWICH LOAF, CRUSTS REMOVED
- 450 G (1 LB) SMOKED SALMON, THINLY SLICED
- LEMON JUICE FOR SPRINKLING
- FRESHLY GROUND BLACK PEPPER

PREPARATION TIME: 20 MINUTES
CHILLING TIME: OVERNIGHT

CHICKEN AND ANCHOVY TRIANGLES
- 450 G (1 LB) COOKED CHICKEN, FINELY CHOPPED
- 60 G (2 OZ) TINNED ANCHOVY FILLETS, WELL DRAINED AND FINELY CHOPPED
- 2 TABLESPOONS CAPERS, FINELY CHOPPED
- 6 LEVEL TABLESPOONS TARTARE SAUCE (SEE P.436)
- 4 LEVEL TABLESPOONS MAYONNAISE, HOMEMADE (SEE P.436) OR BOUGHT
- FRESHLY GROUND BLACK PEPPER
- 115 G (4 OZ) BUTTER, SOFTENED
- 10 THIN SLICES BROWN BREAD
- 175 G (6 OZ) CRISP LETTUCE, TRIMMED AND SHREDDED
- 10 THIN SLICES WHITE BREAD

PREPARATION TIME: 25 MINUTES

ASPARAGUS ROLLS
- 450 G (1 LB) FRESH ASPARAGUS, APPROX 10 SPEARS, TRIMMED AND PEELED TO HALFWAY UP EACH SPEAR
- 10 THIN SLICES WHOLEMEAL BREAD, TAKEN FROM A LARGE LOAF, CRUSTS REMOVED
- 115 G (4 OZ) BUTTER, SOFTENED
- 2 LEVEL TEASPOONS FINELY GRATED LEMON RIND
- PINCH OF CAYENNE PEPPER

PREPARATION TIME: 30 MINUTES
COOKING TIME: 10 MINUTES

INGREDIENTS

Egg rolls
7 eggs, size 2, hard boiled
6 tablespoons mayonnaise, homemade (see p.436) or bought
1 teaspoon anchovy essence
Freshly ground black pepper
10 bridge rolls, 7.5 cm (3 in) long
85 g (3 oz) butter, softened
½ punnet salad cress
225 g (8 oz) fresh cooked peeled prawns
Preparation time: 30 minutes

Prawn rolls
10 bridge rolls, 7.5 cm (3 in) long
2 tablespoons olive oil
2 teaspoons raspberry vinegar, homemade (see p.380) or bought
1 tablespoon mayonnaise, homemade (see p.436) or bought
225 g (8 oz) fresh cooked peeled prawns, roughly chopped
60 g (2 oz) cream cheese
115 g (4 oz) crisp lettuce, trimmed, washed and finely shredded
Cayenne pepper
Fresh dill and peeled prawns to garnish
Preparation time: 25 minutes
Cooking time: 2 minutes

Mushroom and ham scones
150 g (5 oz) butter
275 g (10 oz) mushrooms, wiped and chopped
2 tablespoons dry sherry
2 tablespoons chopped fresh parsley
½ level teaspoon salt
Freshly ground black pepper
8 thin slices ham
10 cheese scones (see p.357)
Fresh parsley to garnish
Preparation time: 30 minutes
Cooking time: 10–15 minutes

Bridge rolls and savoury scones support the egg, prawn and ham and mushroom toppings.

—A SELECTION OF EASY CANAPES—

To make egg rolls Shell and finely chop the eggs, put them into a bowl, carefully mix in the mayonnaise and anchovy essence and season well with the pepper. Cut each bridge roll in half horizontally and spread with the butter. Spread the egg mixture on top and garnish the roll with the salad cress.

To make prawn rolls Cut each roll in half horizontally, lightly toast the cut sides, then let them cool. Mix the oil, vinegar and mayonnaise together, add the prawns and stir until evenly coated with the dressing. Spread the cream cheese over the toasted side of each roll, sprinkle the shredded lettuce on top, then spoon on the prawn mixture. Sprinkle with a little cayenne pepper and garnish with prawns and a small sprig of dill.

To make mushroom and ham scones Melt 60 g (2 oz) of the butter in a frying pan. Add the mushrooms, sherry and chopped parsley and cook over a moderate heat for 10–15 minutes or until the mushrooms are soft and all the liquid has evaporated. Remove from the heat, season with the salt and pepper and leave to cool. Using a 5 cm (2 in) plain round cutter, stamp out 20 rounds from the ham and set aside. Finely chop the remaining slices of ham and the trimmings and stir into the mushrooms.

Cut the scones in half horizontally. Spread each half lightly with the remaining butter, place a round of ham on each and spoon on the mushroom mixture. Garnish with the sprigs of parsley and arrange on a serving dish.

— CHOUX SWANS FILLED WITH RASPBERRIES AND CREAM —

Sift the flour and salt onto greaseproof paper. Heat the butter and water gently in a saucepan until the butter melts. Bring to the boil, remove from the heat, add the sifted flour and beat with a wooden spoon. Return to the heat and stir for 1 minute until the mixture forms a stiff ball. Cool slightly, then, using a hand-held electric mixer, add the egg a little at a time, beating vigorously between each addition.

Preheat the oven to 220°C (425°F, gas mark 7) and line two baking sheets with nonstick paper. Spoon an eighth of the choux paste into a piping bag fitted with a 6 mm (¼ in) plain nozzle and pipe 20 'S' shapes, for the heads and necks, 10 cm (4 in) long, spaced well apart, onto the paper. Bake for 10 minutes, turn over and bake for another 5 minutes until golden and crisp. Remove from the paper and cool on a wire rack.

Reline the cooled baking sheets. With a metal spoon, take a slightly rounded tablespoon of the paste for the 'body' and, with a second spoon, ease it onto the baking sheet and shape it into a neat oval. Repeat another 19 times. Bake for 30 minutes, remove from the oven, make a small hole in one end of each 'body' and return to the oven for 5–10 minutes until quite dry. Cool on wire racks. Cutting horizontally, slice the top third off each 'body' and cut in half lengthways for the 'wings'.

Whisk the cream with 85 g (3 oz) of the icing sugar and the chosen liqueur until it will hold a soft peak, then fold in 340 g (12 oz) raspberries.

Fill the bottom part of each 'body' with the cream mixture and place the 'necks' and 'wings' in position. Fill the centres with the remaining raspberries. Dredge the swans heavily with the remaining icing sugar and arrange on a serving dish. Keep refrigerated until serving.

INGREDIENTS

For the choux pastry
- 275 g (10 oz) plain flour
- ¼ level teaspoon salt
- 225 g (8 oz) butter
- 570 ml (1 pint) water
- 8 eggs, size 2, beaten

For the filling
- 1.15 litres (2 pints) double cream
- 150 g (5 oz) icing sugar, sifted
- 4 tablespoons orange liqueur or kirsch
- 675 g (1½ lb) fresh raspberries, hulled

Preparation time: 1 hour
Cooking time: 55 minutes

Filled with cream, raspberries and orange liqueur, these swans are delectable and elegant.

Godmotherly gift
Godparents play an important role at the christening and later. So it was with Cinderella. Her fairy godmother transformed a pumpkin, mice, lizards and a rat into coach, horses and servants and triumphantly despatched her goddaughter to the ball.

INGREDIENTS

FOR THE CAKE
450G (1 LB) BUTTER, AT ROOM TEMPERATURE
225G (8 OZ) CASTER SUGAR
8 EGGS, SIZE 2, SEPARATED
450G (1 LB) PLAIN FLOUR
½ LEVEL TEASPOON GROUND MACE
½ LEVEL TEASPOON GROUND CINNAMON
5 TABLESPOONS BRANDY OR WHISKY
450G (1 LB) SULTANAS, PICKED OVER TO REMOVE ANY STALKS
115G (4 OZ) SLIVERED ALMONDS
340G (12 OZ) CHOPPED MIXED PEEL

FOR THE ALMOND PASTE
450G (1 LB) ICING SUGAR
450G (1 LB) GROUND ALMONDS
8 EGG YOLKS, SIZE 2
1 TEASPOON NATURAL VANILLA EXTRACT OR ESSENCE
2 TEASPOONS TRIPLE STRENGTH ROSE WATER
6 TABLESPOONS APRICOT JAM, HEATED AND SIEVED

FOR THE ICING
6 EGG WHITES, SIZE 2, LIGHTLY WHISKED
1.4 KG (3 LB) ICING SUGAR, SIFTED
1½ TABLESPOONS GLYCERINE

FOR THE DECORATION
A SELECTION OF FRESH FLOWER HEADS, SUCH AS MINIATURE ROSES, FREESIAS, PRIMROSES, VIOLETS OR ROSE PETALS
2 LEVEL TEASPOONS GUM ARABIC (FROM CHEMISTS OR CAKE DECORATING SHOPS), OR 1 SMALL, LIGHTLY BEATEN EGG WHITE
4 TEASPOONS ROSE WATER
APPROX 225G (8 OZ) CASTER SUGAR
RIBBON TO DECORATE

PREPARATION TIME: APPROX 7 HOURS, OVER 7 DAYS
COOKING TIME: 1¼–1½ HOURS

—CHRISTENING CAKE—

To make the cake, preheat the oven to 180°C (350°F, gas mark 4), and grease and line a 23 cm (9 in) square cake tin. Beat the butter until soft and creamy, add the sugar and beat until very light and fluffy.

Whisk the egg whites until they will hold a soft peak then gradually beat them into the creamed mixture. Whisk the egg yolks until they are light, thick and creamy and gradually beat them into the mixture.

Sift the flour and spices into the bowl and, using a large metal spoon, carefully fold them into the mixture. Gently mix in the brandy or whisky, then fold in the sultanas and slivered almonds.

Spoon a third of the mixture into the tin, spread evenly and sprinkle with half the peel. Add half the remaining mixture, sprinkle with the remaining peel then spread the last of the mixture on top.

Bake in the centre of the oven for 1¼–1½ hours, or until a skewer inserted into the centre comes out clean. Remove from the oven, leave in the tin for 1 hour to cool, then transfer to a wire rack to cool completely.

To make the almond paste Sift the icing sugar into a bowl, mix in the almonds, add the egg yolks, vanilla and rose water and mix to a stiff paste. Turn onto a work surface, lightly sifted with icing sugar, and knead for a few seconds until smooth. Roll out to 38 cm (15 in) square.

Put the cake onto a 28 cm (11 in) cake board and brush it all over with boiling hot apricot jam. Lift the almond paste carefully onto the cake and smooth it evenly over the top and down the sides. Trim the excess from around the bottom. Leave overnight in a cool place to dry.

To make the icing Put the egg whites into a bowl and beat in the icing sugar gradually. Beat well until smooth, then beat in the glycerine. Using a palette knife, spread an even layer of icing over the top of the cake, then pull a ruler, preferably a metal one, across the top of the cake to smooth the icing. Trim the excess from the edges. Spread a coat of icing over one side of the cake, then pull a cake scraper along the side to smooth it. Repeat with the other sides. Leave overnight to dry. Meanwhile, put the remaining icing into a clean bowl, cover the surface closely with cling film, cover the bowl and refrigerate.

The next day, using a sharp knife, trim the rough icing from around the top edge and corners of the cake. Beat the chilled icing mixture and coat the cake as before. Repeat twice more, leaving each coat to dry overnight before adding the next. Reserve the remaining icing for piping.

To make the decoration Select about 18 to 24 of the most perfect flower heads and, depending on their size, leave them whole or separate the petals. Blend the gum arabic (or egg white) smoothly with the rose water. Using a clean, fine paintbrush, paint each flower lightly and evenly with the gum arabic (or egg white) mixture, then immediately sift lightly all over with caster sugar. Put the flowers onto a wire rack to dry in a warm place for two to three days. Spoon some of the remaining icing into a paper piping bag fitted with a small star nozzle and pipe a decorative border around the top and bottom edges of the cake. This can be stars or shells or a double shell edge as shown. Leave overnight to dry. Tie the ribbon round the cake and decorate the top with the flowers.

The beautiful floral decoration is surprisingly simple to make with dainty fresh flower heads lightly dusted with caster sugar.

A SUMMER CELEBRATION

IF A SPECIAL OCCASION FALLS IN SUMMERTIME, A *Wedding* OR A *Twenty-first Birthday* PERHAPS, THERE IS NO MORE DELIGHTFUL WAY TO *Celebrate* THAN WITH A *Lunch Party* IN THE GARDEN. *The Menu,* WITH QUANTITIES FOR TWENTY PEOPLE, IS AN ASSEMBLY OF *Classic British Recipes,* ENJOYED FOR GENERATIONS. IT HAS THE *Additional Virtue* OF BEING SIMPLE TO PREPARE AND SERVE, LEAVING YOU FREE TO MINGLE WITH YOUR GUESTS.

MENU

PIMM'S NO.1 PUNCH

ASPARAGUS WITH CHERVIL AND PARSLEY DRESSING

POACHED SALMON GLAZED WITH ASPIC
WITH
MINTED NEW POTATOES

MIXED GREEN SALAD WITH WHITE WINE DRESSING

PINEAPPLE ICE CREAM WITH RASPBERRY SAUCE

STRAWBERRIES IN CLARET

PEAR FLAN

—PIMM'S NO. 1 PUNCH—

Just before your guests arrive put the cucumber skin and all the sliced fruits into a very large punchbowl and add the ice cubes. Alternatively, make the punch in smaller bowls or large jugs, dividing the ingredients equally among them.

Pour the Pimm's into the bowl, then the lemon and lime juice and stir well. Add the tonic, soda water, lemonade or ginger ale and stir again.

Decorate with the sprigs of mint and serve ladled into glasses. If wished, the glasses may be decorated with fruits and mint leaves.

—ASPARAGUS WITH CHERVIL AND PARSLEY DRESSING—

Using a potato peeler, thinly peel the lower three-quarters of each spear of asparagus, and trim off the woody end. Wash and set aside.

For the best flavour, steam the asparagus in a tiered steamer for 10–15 minutes, or until tender, taking care not to overcook.

Alternatively, tie the asparagus in bundles with clean, thin string (about 15 spears per bundle) and cook in batches in large saucepans of boiling water. If serving hot, arrange on heated serving dishes, stir the dressing and pour it over the spears. Serve immediately.

If serving cold, quickly rinse the cooked asparagus under cold water to stop the cooking and to preserve the green colour. Drain well, allow to cool and then arrange on serving dishes. Cover and refrigerate until required. Pour the dressing over just before serving.

To prepare the dressing Put the vinegars into a bowl, add a generous amount of salt and pepper, the mustard and the sugar and stir until the salt has dissolved. Whisk in the olive oil and the herbs, cover and leave to stand while cooking the asparagus.

Sipping Pimm's and nibbling asparagus is the epitome of the summer garden party.

INGREDIENTS

Pimm's No.1 Punch

- Thinly peeled skin from 1 cucumber (reserve the cucumber for the mixed green salad)
- 2 small lemons, sliced
- 1 small orange, sliced
- 2 limes, sliced
- 225g (8oz) strawberries, hulled, washed and sliced
- 2 small red apples, washed, quartered and thinly sliced
- 40 ice cubes
- 1.7 litres (3 pints) Pimm's No.1 Cup, chilled
- Strained juice 2 lemons
- Strained juice 2 limes
- 3.4 litres (6 pints) tonic water, soda water, lemonade or ginger ale, chilled
- Fresh mint sprigs

Preparation time: 20 minutes
Serves twenty

Asparagus with Chervil and Parsley Dressing

- 1.8kg (4lb) fresh asparagus (approx 30 spears to 450g (1lb), allowing 6 spears per person)

For the dressing

- 115ml (4fl oz) red wine vinegar
- 115ml (4fl oz) white wine vinegar
- Salt and freshly ground black pepper
- 4 level teaspoons Dijon mustard
- 1 level teaspoon caster sugar
- 450ml (16fl oz) olive oil
- 2 tablespoons each chopped fresh parsley and chervil

Preparation time: 1¼ hours
Cooking time: 10–15 minutes per batch
Serves twenty

INGREDIENTS

2 FRESH SALMON, EACH APPROX 2.7 KG (6 LB), DESCALED, GUTTED AND CLEANED
4.5 LITRES (1 GALLON) COLD WATER
450 ML (16 FL OZ) DRY WHITE WINE
2 LEMONS, SLICED
6 FRESH PARSLEY SPRIGS
16 BLACK PEPPERCORNS

FOR THE ASPIC JELLY
285 ML (½ PINT) COLD WATER
3 LEVEL TABLESPOONS POWDERED GELATINE
400 ML (14 FL OZ) DRY WHITE WINE
150 ML (¼ PINT) DRY SHERRY
2 TABLESPOONS TARRAGON VINEGAR OR LEMON JUICE
FRESH TARRAGON AND CHERVIL TO GARNISH
PREPARATION TIME: 2½ HOURS
COOKING TIME: 12 MINUTES
COOLING TIME: 5–6 HOURS
CHILLING TIME: OVERNIGHT
SERVES TWENTY

THE GARDEN PARTY
British summers are not noted for their dependability, and that of 1923 was one that lived down to their reputation. Garden parties were among June's social casualties, and *Punch's* comment depicts a stoical hostess making the best of things by offering her guests hot water bottles and bowls of hot soup before their departure.

—POACHED SALMON GLAZED WITH ASPIC—

The day before, put each salmon into a fish kettle (which supermarkets loan free of charge to purchasers of salmon) or a very large roasting tin in which it will fit comfortably. Trim off the tail fin if necessary. If the salmon is still too large to fit in the fish kettle or roasting tin, cut off the tail end and cook it alongside the main body of the fish. When the salmon is cooked, reposition the tail on the serving dish and camouflage the join with decoration before serving.

Adding half to each pan, pour in the water and the dry white wine and add the lemon slices, parsley sprigs and black peppercorns. Cover the fish kettles or roasting tins with lids or foil, bring to the boil, quickly reduce the heat and simmer for 12 minutes only. Remove the pans from the heat immediately and set aside until the salmon are completely cold.

When cold, carefully lift each salmon, still on its rack, from its kettle and drain off the liquid. If using roasting tins, lift the fish from the tins with two very large fish slices onto a wire rack and leave to drain. Put each salmon onto a fish plate, a very large flat serving platter or a long, wooden board. Carefully remove the skin and, with the back of a small knife, scrape away the brown coating from the flesh, wiping the knife clean after each scraping to prevent smears on the pink flesh of the fish. Cover the salmon carefully and put into the refrigerator, or somewhere cool such as a larder or garage, while making the aspic jelly.

To make the aspic jelly Pour the water into a bowl and sprinkle the powdered gelatine evenly over the surface. Leave to stand for 2–3 minutes until the gelatine swells and becomes opaque. Place the bowl over a saucepan of hot water and leave until the gelatine has dissolved completely. Stir in the white wine, dry sherry, and the tarragon vinegar or lemon juice and remove from the heat. Chill the aspic in the refrigerator for about 1 hour or until it becomes syrupy.

To glaze the salmon Start at the head end of the fish. Brush a thin layer of the jelly over the flesh to coat it completely, then return the fish to the refrigerator and chill until set. Repeat this three times more. (If the aspic in the bowl begins to set, soften it by standing the bowl in hot water.)

To decorate the fish Separate the tarragon leaves carefully and select those that are uniform in size. Dip the leaves, one at a time, in the aspic and arrange them along the length of each salmon, spaced apart in a herringbone pattern. Dip some chervil leaves in the aspic and arrange them along the salmon among the tarragon leaves. Arrange more chervil decoratively around the head and at the tail end of each fish. If the tail has been trimmed, cover the cut end by wrapping tarragon leaves around it. Refrigerate the salmon and the remaining aspic jelly until required. If the salmon will not fit in the refrigerator, store in a cool larder or cool room such as a garage or outhouse, standing the dishes on ice in large, deep-sided trays or roasting tins.

Just before serving, turn the set aspic jelly out of the bowl onto a sheet of wet greaseproof paper, chop it finely with a wet knife and arrange it around the salmon.

Serve the salmon with homemade mayonnaise (see p.436), minted new potatoes and a mixed green salad with a white wine dressing.

A pattern of tarragon and chervil leaves beneath a gleaming sheet of aspic turns the salmon into a triumphal centrepiece.

Ingredients

Minted new potatoes

3.6 kg (8 lb) new potatoes, preferably Jersey Royals, well washed
3 large mint sprigs, washed
4½ level teaspoons salt
175 g (6 oz) butter
6 tablespoons chopped fresh parsley
Fresh mint and parsley sprigs to garnish (optional)
Preparation time: 20 minutes
Cooking time: 20–25 minutes
Serves twenty

White wine dressing

285 ml (½ pint) dry white wine
2 teaspoons lemon juice
2 garlic cloves, peeled and thinly sliced
2 shallots, peeled and finely chopped
1 level teaspoon salt
1 level teaspoon caster sugar
Preparation time: 30 minutes
Standing time: Overnight
Serves twenty

Mixed green salad

1½ crisp lettuces, such as Webb's, washed and dried
1½ large cos lettuces, washed and dried
1 large celery head (approx 12 sticks), trimmed and thinly sliced
1 bunch rocket, washed and drained (optional)
3 ripe avocados, halved, stoned, peeled and sliced
2 peeled cucumbers (including the one peeled for Pimm's), halved, deseeded and sliced
10–12 tablespoons olive oil
Freshly ground black pepper
Preparation time: 30 minutes
Serves twenty

—MINTED NEW POTATOES—

Divide the potatoes equally among three large saucepans and add a sprig of mint and 1½ teaspoons of salt to each one. Cover the potatoes with boiling water from a kettle and bring back to the boil. Reduce the heat, partially cover and simmer gently for 20–25 minutes until the potatoes are cooked. Drain well in separate colanders.

Melt 60 g (2 oz) of the butter in each saucepan and stir in the parsley. Return the potatoes to the saucepans and toss them gently in the hot parsley butter. Transfer to heated serving dishes, garnish with the sprigs of mint and parsley, if using, and serve immediately.

—MIXED GREEN SALAD WITH WHITE WINE DRESSING—

Make the dressing the day before eating. Put all the ingredients into a plastic container or clean jam jar, cover with a tightly fitting lid and shake well. Refrigerate until required. Next day, tear the lettuce leaves into small pieces and divide them between two large salad bowls. Add the celery, rocket leaves, avocados and cucumber slices in equal amounts to each bowl. Pour 5–6 tablespoons of the olive oil over each bowl, season well with the pepper and toss well. Shake the dressing before straining half into each bowl, toss once again and serve.

New potatoes doused in parsley butter and a mixed green salad tossed in a white wine dressing make worthy accompaniments for the salmon.

The contrasting flavours of luscious, fresh pineapple and raspberry balance each other perfectly.

—PINEAPPLE ICE CREAM WITH RASPBERRY SAUCE—

Pour half the cream into a small saucepan and add half the sugar. Stir over a low heat until the sugar has dissolved and the cream is hot, but do not let it boil. Remove from the heat, stir in the remaining cream and chill. Meanwhile, purée the pineapple in a food processor or blender and pass it through a nylon sieve into a bowl. Add the remaining sugar and the lemon juice, stir until the sugar dissolves, then chill.

To freeze in an ice-cream maker, pour the chilled cream into the bowl and freeze until softly frozen. With the paddle still turning, gradually pour in the chilled pineapple purée. Continue freezing until firm. Transfer to a rigid plastic container, cover and store in the freezer.

To freeze in the freezer, pour the chilled cream into a bowl and whisk until it becomes slightly thickened. Freeze for 1 hour until about 2.5 cm (1 in) of cream has frozen all round the edge. Remove from the freezer and whisk well. Freeze again until 2.5 cm (1 in) has frozen round the edge. Remove from the freezer and whisk well, gradually adding the pineapple purée. Repeat the freezing and whisking processes twice more, then pour into a plastic container, cover and freeze until solid.

To make the sauce Put the raspberries into a bowl and mix in the sugar. Cover and leave to stand for 1 hour, then purée the raspberries through a nylon sieve. Discard the seeds. Stir in the kirsch if using, pour into a serving jug, cover and chill.

Remove the ice cream from the freezer about 20 minutes before serving. Scoop it into a well-chilled glass bowl, stand the bowl inside a larger one and surround with crushed ice. Serve with the raspberry sauce.

INGREDIENTS

570 ML (1 PINT) DOUBLE CREAM
225 G (8 OZ) CASTER SUGAR
1 LARGE RIPE PINEAPPLE, SKIN, EYES AND WOODY CORE REMOVED, YIELDING 450 G (1 LB) PREPARED PINEAPPLE FLESH
STRAINED JUICE 1 LEMON

FOR THE SAUCE
450 G (1 LB) FRESH RASPBERRIES, HULLED OR FROZEN RASPBERRIES, THAWED
85–115 G (3–4 OZ) CASTER SUGAR
2 TABLESPOONS KIRSCH (OPTIONAL)
PREPARATION TIME: 20 MINUTES
COOKING TIME: 3 MINUTES
FREEZING TIME: 20 MINUTES IN AN ICE-CREAM MAKER OR 4–5 HOURS IN A FREEZER
SERVES EIGHT TO TEN

INGREDIENTS

Strawberries in claret
1.4 kg (3 lb) English strawberries, hulled, cut in half if large
225 g (8 oz) caster sugar
340 ml (12 fl oz) good claret
Rose petals for decoration (optional)
Preparation time: 15 minutes
Serves twelve

Pear flan
For the flan case
275 g (10 oz) plain flour
60 g (2 oz) icing sugar
175 g (6 oz) chilled butter, cut into cubes
4 egg yolks, size 2

For the pear topping
275 g (10 oz) granulated sugar
725 ml (1¼ pints) water
Thinly pared rind and strained juice 1 lemon
7 large ripe, firm pears, peeled and halved, cores removed
Sprigs of fresh redcurrants to decorate (optional)

For the filling
225 g (8 oz) ginger conserve, heated and gently sieved to remove the ginger pieces (reserve the pieces)
250 g (9 oz) curd or cream cheese
Finely grated rind 2 small lemons
200 ml (7 fl oz) double cream
425 ml (¾ pint) very thick cold custard, made with 45 g (1½ oz) custard powder, 45 g (1½ oz) caster sugar and 425 ml (¾ pint) milk
Preparation time:
Day before, 1 hour
On the day, 40 minutes
Chilling time: Overnight
Cooking time: 20 minutes
Serves ten to twelve

Make a choice—strawberries in claret or a pear flan with a gingery, creamy, custard filling.

— STRAWBERRIES IN CLARET —

Put the strawberries into individual glasses or one large bowl, sprinkle with the sugar, then pour over the claret. Allow to macerate in the claret for 20–30 minutes, decorate with the rose petals if using, and serve.

— PEAR FLAN —

Prepare the flan case, the topping and the custard for the filling the day before. For the flan case, sift the flour and icing sugar into a bowl and rub in the butter. Mix in the egg yolks to form a soft but not sticky dough, then knead briefly on a lightly floured surface until smooth. Roll out and line a 29 cm (11½ in) diameter, 2.5 cm (1 in) deep flan tin or ring. Trim and decorate the edge, prick the dough lightly all over with a fork and chill overnight, covering with foil once the dough is firm.

To prepare the topping Put the sugar and water into a large, stainless steel or enamel saucepan and stir over a gentle heat until the sugar has dissolved. Bring to the boil, then boil for 2 minutes. Reduce the heat, stir the lemon rind and juice into the syrup and then submerge the pear halves.

Simmer gently, covered, for 20–25 minutes until the pears are just tender. Carefully transfer to a large bowl, cool, then cover and chill overnight.

Next day, preheat the oven to 220°C (425°F, gas mark 7) and bake the flan case for 15–20 minutes until golden. Remove from the oven and cool. Meanwhile, strain the juice from the pears into a saucepan, heat and boil gently until it has reduced to about 150 ml (¼ pint) and become syrupy. Remove from the heat, stir in the ginger pieces, cool and chill. Drain the pears on kitchen paper and cut each half into six slices lengthways.

To prepare the filling Bring the sieved ginger conserve to the boil. Put the flan case onto a serving plate and brush the inside with the hot conserve. Whisk the curd or cream cheese with the lemon rind until blended. Whisk the cream until thick but not buttery. Whisk the cold custard until smooth, then whisk in the cheese mixture and fold in the cream.

Spread the cream mixture evenly in the flan case and smooth the top. Arrange the pear slices on top, overlapping in concentric circles, then cover with cling film and chill. Just before serving, spoon the pear and ginger syrup evenly over the pears. Decorate with redcurrants, if using.

—PARTY PLANNING—

Whether the asparagus is served hot or cold will depend on the equipment available and if there is anyone else to help. With limited equipment and no extra help, it will be easier to serve it cold.

Cook the centrepiece, the salmon, the day before, glaze them and keep them in the refrigerator. Put the prepared salad leaves, cucumbers and celery into salad bowls, cover and refrigerate until ready to serve, adding the avocado, olive oil and infused wine at the last minute.

For the very best flavour, take the strawberries out of the refrigerator 1–2 hours before macerating them with the claret.

TIMESAVER
Christmas cards were invented in 1843, only three years after the introduction of the penny post. Cards like this, however, designed to match a special occasion, did not appear until some 60 years later. Even then, though attractive and energy-saving, they would have been considered less correct than a letter.

Gleaming china, crisp linen, flowers and fair weather complete the recipe for success.

A DINNER FOR TWO

On Valentine's Day—or indeed, on any evening you fancy—surprise your partner with a *Romantic Dinner* lovingly prepared. This menu has been carefully planned to create a *Sentimental Mood* and *Delight the Senses.* So put the bubbly on ice, light the candles and set the scene for your *Private Delectation.*

Menu

Salad Belle Patricia with Dublin Bay Prawns, Quail's Eggs and Smoked Salmon

Champagne Sorbet

Medallions of Veal in a Young Morel Sauce with Mangetout and Crispy Almond Potatoes

Orange Delight

A mélange of quail's eggs, smoked salmon and prawns make this a salad to be remembered.

INGREDIENTS

FOR THE DRESSING

- 3 TABLESPOONS CREAM SHERRY
- 3 TABLESPOONS FRESH LEMON JUICE
- 3 TABLESPOONS EXTRA VIRGIN OLIVE OIL
- SALT AND FRESHLY GROUND BLACK PEPPER

FOR THE SALAD

- 4 QUAIL'S EGGS
- 8 COOKED DUBLIN BAY PRAWN TAILS
- 80 G ($2\frac{3}{4}$ OZ) MIXED SALAD LEAVES, WASHED AND DRIED
- 50 G ($1\frac{3}{4}$ OZ) SMOKED SALMON, CUT INTO 7.5 CM (3 IN) STRIPS
- FRESH CHERVIL TO GARNISH

PREPARATION TIME: 20 MINUTES
COOKING TIME: $2\frac{1}{4}$ MINUTES

FOR THE CHAMPAGNE SORBET

- 115 ML (4 FL OZ) CHAMPAGNE
- 1 TABLESPOON EACH STRAINED FRESH ORANGE JUICE AND LEMON JUICE
- APPROX 3 LEVEL TABLESPOONS ICING SUGAR

PREPARATION TIME: 10 MINUTES
FREEZING TIME: IN AN ICE-CREAM MAKER, 5 MINUTES. IN THE FREEZER, $1-1\frac{1}{2}$ HOURS

Organisation is the key to success—read the recipes thoroughly before you start and follow the instructions for preparing ahead. Be sure to put the Orange Delight into the oven to cook before cooking the main course—having the ingredients ready and weighed out will ensure a speedy completion.

— SALAD BELLE PATRICIA *followed by* CHAMPAGNE SORBET —

Three hours ahead, prepare the salad. Whisk all the ingredients for the dressing together in a small bowl and set aside. Boil the quail's eggs for 2¼ minutes, then cool immediately in iced water. Shell the quail's eggs and peel the prawns, put onto a plate, cover and refrigerate. Prepare the salad leaves, put into a bowl, cover with cling film and chill.

Just before serving, whisk the dressing and pour half over the salad leaves, add the salmon, season and toss gently together, then arrange on two plates. Cut the quail's eggs in half and arrange, alternately with the prawns, around the salad. Drizzle over the remaining dressing and garnish with the chervil.

To make the champagne sorbet The day before, pour the champagne and the orange and lemon juice into a small bowl and whisk in the sugar until it has dissolved. If the champagne is very dry, add a little extra icing sugar. Put the bowl into the freezer until the sorbet is frozen, whisking every 20 minutes to prevent ice crystals from forming. When frozen, cover and keep in the freezer until serving.

Before serving the sorbet, frost the glasses in which it will be served by dipping them in cold water and freezing them briefly.

CHEEK TO CHEEK
A Valentine card of the late 1920s and a reminder of the days when a successful courtship depended heavily on hair oil and finely tuned skills on the dance floor.

INGREDIENTS

Medallions of veal
8 g (¼ oz) young dried morels, soaked in 150 ml (¼ pint) cold water overnight
4 medallions of British veal, from the tenderloin, trimmed, each approx 85 g (3 oz)
Salt and freshly ground white pepper
30 g (1 oz) unsalted butter
2 medium shallots, peeled and very finely chopped
4 tablespoons dry white wine
2 teaspoons lemon juice
250 ml (9 fl oz) good veal stock (see p.433)
115 ml (4 fl oz) double cream
2 teaspoons snipped chives
Preparation time: 20 minutes
Soaking time: 24 hours
Cooking time: 20 minutes

Mangetout with red pepper hearts
115 g (4 oz) mangetout, topped and tailed
1 red pepper, deseeded and cut into hearts with a heart-shaped aspic cutter
30 g (1 oz) unsalted butter
Salt and freshly ground white pepper
Pinch of caster sugar
Preparation time: 10 minutes
Cooking time: 2 minutes

Crispy almond potatoes
1 egg, size 4
375 g (13 oz) Maris Piper potatoes, peeled, boiled, drained and mashed
Salt and freshly ground white pepper
Freshly grated nutmeg
20 g (¾ oz) plain flour
1 egg, size 2, beaten
50 g (1¾ oz) flaked almonds
Oil for frying
Preparation time: 20 minutes
Cooking time: 30 minutes

Mashed, coated with almonds and deep fried, the humble potato takes on a fascinating air.

—MEDALLIONS OF VEAL IN A YOUNG MOREL SAUCE WITH MANGETOUT AND CRISPY ALMOND POTATOES—

In the morning, prepare the mangetout and the red pepper hearts, cover and refrigerate.

Prepare the crispy almond potatoes. Beat the egg into the mashed potatoes and season well with the salt, pepper and nutmeg. Divide into four, shape each piece into a smooth ball, then roll in the flour and coat with the beaten egg and the almonds. Put onto a plate, cover and chill.

Strain the water from the morels through a sieve lined with kitchen paper and reserve. Rinse the morels and set aside.

When ready to cook and serve, preheat the oven to 200°C (400°F, gas mark 6). When the oven is heated, put in the Orange Delight on the shelf below the centre. Season the medallions well. Heat the butter in a heavy frying pan, add the medallions and seal them on each side, cooking until golden brown. Lift out of the pan onto a small baking tray and cook on the middle shelf in the oven, above the Orange Delight, for 12 minutes, then remove and keep warm.

To make the sauce, pour off the excess fat from the veal frying pan, add the shallots and cook gently until golden brown. Add the wine, lemon juice, morel liquid and stock and bring to the boil, stirring and scraping any browned bits from the bottom of the pan. Continue to boil until the liquid is reduced to a syrupy consistency. Add the morels and cream and cook gently until the sauce thickens slightly. Stir in the chives and season. Remove the pan from the heat and keep the sauce hot.

Half fill a frying pan with oil, heat the oil and fry the potatoes until golden. Drain on kitchen paper and keep hot. At the same time, heat the butter for the mangetout and peppers in a heavy-based frying pan until sizzling, add the mangetout and peppers and stir fry for 1–2 minutes. Season well and add the sugar. Arrange the medallions on heated plates, coat with the sauce, add the vegetables and serve.

—ORANGE DELIGHT—

In the morning, cut the orange segments free from the connective tissue over a small bowl. Squeeze the juice from the tissue into the bowl. Spoon the segments and juice into two, lightly buttered, 285 ml (½ pint), ovenproof dishes. Add the Grand Marnier, cover and refrigerate.

Before cooking the veal, complete the puddings and put into the oven already heated for the veal.

Beat the butter, sugar and lemon rind together until light and fluffy and almost white. Beat in the egg yolks, fold in the flour and gently mix in the milk and lemon juice. Whisk the egg whites until they will hold soft peaks, fold carefully into the mixture, then pour over the oranges.

Stand the dishes in a small roasting tin and add hot tap water to halfway up their sides. Bake on the shelf below the centre for 20–25 minutes or until just firm to the touch and pale golden brown on top.

Remove from the oven and leave to stand while eating the main course. Serve sifted with icing sugar and decorated with the rose petals.

INGREDIENTS

2 medium oranges, peel and white pith removed
2 tablespoons Grand Marnier
30 g (1 oz) unsalted butter, softened
30 g (1 oz) caster sugar
Finely grated rind and strained juice ½ lemon
1 egg, size 2, separated
30 g (1 oz) self-raising flour
6 tablespoons milk
2 teaspoons icing sugar for sifting
Rose petals for decoration

Preparation time: 20 minutes
Cooking time: 15 minutes
Standing time: 15 minutes

Petal-strewn and pretty, the topping conceals a filling of orange and Grand Marnier.

A FORMAL PICNIC

IMAGINE YOURSELF DINING WITH *Family* AND *Friends* ON A PERFECT SUMMER EVENING AT A CHARITY CRICKET MATCH ON THE VILLAGE GREEN, BY THE BANKS OF THE RIVER AT *Henley* OR IN THE GROUNDS OF A STATELY HOME, SUCH AS *Castle Howard* OR *Audley End*. THE PICTURE IS COMPLETED BY THIS *Elegant Picnic—Traditional* AND *Delicious* FOOD WHICH IS EASY TO TRANSPORT AND *Ideally Suited* TO OUTDOOR EATING ON SUCH A *Memorable Occasion*.

MENU

CHILLED FENNEL AND CUCUMBER SOUP

LAMB CUTLETS IN MINTED ASPIC
WITH
POTATO SALAD WITH CRISPY BACON

PEA, BEAN AND ARTICHOKE SALAD

TOMATO AND ONION SALAD

UNIVERSITY CREAMS
WITH
BRANDY SNAPS

CHEESE BOARD

CHAMPAGNE

Chilled soup is a refreshing starter complete with croutons and crusty rolls.

TEDDY BEAR'S PICNIC
In childhood, a meal outdoors is an adventure in itself, as well as a precursor to even greater things. So it was with Christopher Robin as he swallowed a last mouthful and began to tell Pooh and Piglet about his sighting of a Heffalump.

—CHILLED FENNEL AND CUCUMBER SOUP—

INGREDIENTS

- 1 TEASPOON OLIVE OIL
- 60 G (2 OZ) BLANCHED ALMONDS
- SALT AND FRESHLY GROUND WHITE PEPPER
- 30 G (1 OZ) BUTTER
- 1 LARGE ONION, PEELED AND CHOPPED
- 550 G (1¼ LB) FENNEL, TRIMMED AND CHOPPED, GREEN FRONDS RESERVED FOR GARNISH
- 2 LEVEL TEASPOONS FRESHLY GRATED PEELED ROOT GINGER
- 1 LARGE CUCUMBER, PEELED, HALVED, DESEEDED AND CHOPPED
- 850 ML (1½ PINTS) GOOD CHICKEN STOCK (SEE P.433)
- 150 ML (¼ PINT) DRY WHITE WINE
- 3 TABLESPOONS SINGLE CREAM
- 6 MEDIUM SLICES WHOLEMEAL BREAD, CRUSTS REMOVED, CUT INTO SMALL CUBES
- VEGETABLE OIL FOR FRYING

PREPARATION TIME: 30 MINUTES
COOKING TIME: 45 MINUTES
CHILLING TIME: 2–3 HOURS OR OVERNIGHT
SERVES EIGHT

Heat the olive oil in a large saucepan, add the almonds and fry gently until golden brown all over, stirring constantly and taking care not to let them overbrown or burn. Drain the nuts on kitchen paper, sprinkle with a little salt and set aside.

Warm the butter in the saucepan, add the onion, 400 g (14 oz) of the fennel and all the ginger and cook over a gentle heat until the onion and fennel are softened but not browned. Stir in the cucumber and cook for 5 minutes more. Pour in the stock and wine, season with salt and bring to the boil. Reduce the heat, cover with a tightly fitting lid and simmer for 30 minutes. Meanwhile, roughly chop the almonds and finely chop the remaining fennel.

Remove the soup from the heat, stir in the almonds and allow to cool for 10 minutes. Purée in two batches in a food processor. Stir in the cream and finely chopped fennel, season with white pepper, and a little more salt if necessary, cover and chill for 2–3 hours or overnight.

Heat the oil in a frying pan and fry the diced brown bread until lightly browned and crisp. Drain well on kitchen paper, allow to cool, then pack the croutons in an airtight container.

Pour the chilled soup into vacuum flasks for carrying. Serve from a tureen or in individual bowls garnished with some croutons and the chopped fennel fronds. Serve the remaining croutons separately.

Aspic gives the cutlets a minty glaze and frills make them easier to manage on a picnic.

INGREDIENTS

LAMB CUTLETS IN MINTED ASPIC

- 4 RACKS (6 BONES EACH) BEST END NECK OF LAMB CUTLETS, CHINED, BONES SHORTENED BY 5 CM (2 IN), EXCESS FAT REMOVED TO LEAVE JUST EYE OF MEAT ATTACHED TO THE BONE, BONES SCRAPED CLEAN
- SALT AND FRESHLY GROUND BLACK PEPPER
- 2 TABLESPOONS CHOPPED FRESH MINT
- 1–2 TABLESPOONS WHITE WINE VINEGAR
- 570 ML (1 PINT) ASPIC JELLY, HOMEMADE (SEE P.434) OR BOUGHT
- 1 CRISP LETTUCE, FINELY SHREDDED
- 24 CUTLET FRILLS

PREPARATION TIME: 30 MINUTES
COOKING TIME: 25 MINUTES
CHILLING TIME: 4 HOURS MINIMUM FOR LAMB, 1½ HOURS FOR ASPIC OR OVERNIGHT
SERVES EIGHT

—LAMB CUTLETS IN MINTED ASPIC—

Preheat the oven to 220°C (425°F, gas mark 7). Put the racks of lamb into a roasting tin, season well and cook in the oven until done to taste (20 minutes for rare, 25 minutes for medium rare, 30 minutes for well done). Remove from the oven and allow to become completely cold. Cut the racks into cutlets and place on one or two wire racks set over a tray.

Stir the mint and vinegar into the aspic and chill until it starts to become syrupy then quickly spoon it over each lamb cutlet, coating evenly. (If the aspic starts to set, stand the container in a bowl of hot water, stir quickly until melted, then continue.) Chill the cutlets until the aspic is set, then repeat until all the aspic is used.

Arrange the lettuce on two or three serving dishes that will fit into your cool boxes. Put a cutlet frill on each cutlet bone and arrange on the lettuce. Cover the dishes with cling film, making sure it does not touch the cutlets. Keep refrigerated until packing.

—POTATO SALAD WITH CRISPY BACON—

Steam or boil the potatoes until cooked, drain well and allow to cool. Cook the bacon in a frying pan with no extra fat until very crisp and brown. Remove from the pan, drain on kitchen paper and leave to cool.

Put the potatoes into a bowl, add the mayonnaise, chives and seasoning to taste and mix well together. Transfer to a serving dish and sprinkle the bacon over the top. Cover the bowl with cling film and keep refrigerated until packing.

— PEA, BEAN AND ARTICHOKE SALAD —

Steam or boil the peas and beans until tender, drain well and put into a bowl with the artichoke hearts. Pour the dressing over the hot vegetables, add the parsley and mix gently together. Spoon into a serving dish and cover with cling film. Keep refrigerated until packing.

— TOMATO AND ONION SALAD —

Arrange the tomato and onion slices in a serving dish. Sprinkle over the spring onions, basil and black pepper to taste. Drizzle over the olive oil. Cover the dish with cling film and refrigerate until packing.

These salads of varied textures and colours all go very well with the lamb cutlets.

INGREDIENTS

Potato Salad with Crispy Bacon

- 1.4 kg (3 lb) baby new potatoes, washed
- 3 rashers lean back bacon, rinds removed, chopped
- 200 ml (7 fl oz) thick mayonnaise, homemade (see p.436) or bought
- 2 tablespoons snipped fresh chives
- Salt and freshly ground black pepper

Preparation time: 15 minutes
Cooking time: 25 minutes
Serves eight

Pea, Bean and Artichoke Salad

- 225 g (8 oz) shelled fresh peas, or frozen peas
- 225 g (8 oz) fresh fine green beans, cut into short lengths
- 400 g (14 oz) freshly cooked artichoke hearts or bottled artichoke hearts, drained and halved
- 200 ml (7 fl oz) vinaigrette dressing (see p.435)
- 2 tablespoons chopped fresh parsley

Preparation time: 20 minutes
Cooking time: 15 minutes
Serves eight

Tomato and Onion Salad

- 675 g (1½ lb) ripe tomatoes, cores removed, sliced
- 1 red salad onion or small Spanish onion, peeled and thinly sliced
- 6 spring onions, trimmed and finely chopped
- 2 tablespoons shredded fresh basil
- Coarsely ground black pepper
- 8 tablespoons extra virgin olive oil, or to taste

Preparation time: 15 minutes
Serves eight

The creamy layers of strawberry and vanilla look especially pretty in glass goblets.

INGREDIENTS

FOR THE STRAWBERRY CREAM
450G (1 LB) RIPE STRAWBERRIES, WASHED AND DRIED, HULLED AND SLICED
115G (4 OZ) CASTER SUGAR
115ML (4 FL OZ) WATER
15G (½ OZ) GELATINE
285ML (½ PINT) DOUBLE CREAM

FOR THE VANILLA CREAM
150ML (¼ PINT) MILK
115G (4 OZ) SUGAR
15G (½ OZ) GELATINE
85ML (3 FL OZ) WATER
2 TEASPOONS NATURAL VANILLA EXTRACT OR ESSENCE
285ML (½ PINT) DOUBLE CREAM
425ML (¾ PINT) LIQUID LEMON JELLY, HOMEMADE (SEE P.245) OR BOUGHT
60G (2 OZ) PISTACHIO NUTS, SKINNED AND ROUGHLY CHOPPED

FOR THE DECORATION
150ML (¼ PINT) DOUBLE CREAM, WHIPPED
15G (½ OZ) PISTACHIO NUTS, SKINNED AND FINELY CHOPPED
6 SMALL STRAWBERRIES, HULLED AND SLICED
BRANDY SNAPS FOR SERVING (SEE P.341)

PREPARATION TIME: 3 HOURS
SERVES EIGHT

— UNIVERSITY CREAMS —

To make the strawberry cream, put the strawberries into a bowl, sprinkle with the sugar and leave to stand for at least 30 minutes until the juices start to run. Purée in a food processor or blender until smooth. Make space in the refrigerator for eight goblets, each about 225ml (8 fl oz), which should be leant at an angle against the refrigerator wall.

Pour the water into a small bowl and sprinkle the gelatine over the surface, allow to stand for 5 minutes, then place the bowl in a small saucepan of hot water until the gelatine dissolves. Put the strawberry purée into a bowl, stir in the dissolved gelatine and chill until just beginning to set. Whisk the cream until it will hold a soft peak, then whisk in the strawberry mixture until it is thick and mousse-like. Holding each goblet at an angle, quickly pour in the strawberry mixture, dividing it equally among them, and put them in the refrigerator (see above).

To make the vanilla cream Heat the milk and sugar in a saucepan until the sugar has just dissolved. Remove from the heat and leave to cool. Dissolve the gelatine in the water, as above, and stir into the milk together with the vanilla. Chill until just beginning to set. Whisk the cream until it will hold a soft peak, whisk in the vanilla mixture until it is thick and pour the mixture into the goblets. Stand the goblets in an upright position and chill until the vanilla cream is set.

Chill the lemon jelly until syrupy, then stir in the roughly chopped pistachios. Pour the jelly, in an even layer, on top of the set creams and chill until set. Decorate the creams with piped rosettes or spooned whirls of cream sprinkled with the pistachio nuts and sliced strawberries. Cover the goblets with cling film and refrigerate until packing.

— PICNIC PLANNING —

With careful planning and joint effort, a formal picnic for a large group of people can be made and transported quite easily. Simply allocate the making of a dish to everyone involved. A hosted picnic is also easy to prepare, although a little more time-consuming, and may necessitate borrowing extra cool boxes.

The chilled soup will travel easily in vacuum flasks. The salads can be stacked in cool boxes in their covered serving dishes (check first that they will fit!). Keep them separated by covering the dishes with the flat bases from flan or cake tins. The meat dishes can then be placed on top of the salads. Stand the creams upright in a cool box next to the champagne on ice. If using glass goblets, protect them in the cool box by interleaving them with sheets of kitchen paper or thin bubble wrap.

The cheeseboard and champagne complete the perfect picnic. Always take a good selection of both hard and soft cheeses and keep them in a cool bag until ready to eat. An assortment of water biscuits and crackers should satisfy all your guests. You can substitute a good white wine for the champagne—the most important thing is to serve it well chilled. Keep it cool by putting it in a string bag and immersing it in the waters of a nearby stream or lake, but make sure it is well anchored. Once opened, always keep it in the shade.

Fashionable flutter
The scene is the Ascot Gold Cup meeting of 1921, where the gleam of crystal, silver and starched napery in the perfect picnic hampers bids to outdo that of the assembled Rolls Royces.

Prior organisation ensures that the picnic arrives in pristine condition without hassle.

A GUY FAWKES PARTY

'REMEMBER, REMEMBER, THE FIFTH OF NOVEMBER...' FIREWORKS, A BONFIRE AND THESE WARMING DISHES WILL KEEP OUT THE AUTUMN COLD. *Finger Food* CAN BE PREPARED BEFOREHAND AND SERVED WHILE THE FIRE BLAZES AND ROCKETS LIGHT UP THE SKY—STEAMING MUGS OF *Delicious Soup* WILL WARM THE HANDS AND YOUNGER REVELLERS CAN EXPERIENCE THE DELIGHTS OF HOMEMADE *Toffee Apples* AND *Treacle Toffee.*

MENU

PUMPKIN SOUP

HERBY SCOTCH EGGS
WITH
HOT TOMATO RELISH,
BAKED POTATOES AND
CUMBERLAND SAUSAGE
CATHERINE WHEELS

SPICED FRUIT TURNOVERS

YORKSHIRE PARKIN

GINGERBREAD MEN

TREACLE TOFFEE

TOFFEE APPLES

Add a special touch: ladle the soup from a seasonal tureen made from a hollowed-out pumpkin.

—PUMPKIN SOUP—

Using a spoon, carefully remove and discard the seeds from the pumpkin. Cut away the skin then roughly chop up the flesh—there should be about 675 g (1½ lb).

Heat the oil in a large saucepan, add the chopped onions and carrots and cook gently until the onions are softened but not browned. Add the chopped pumpkin, tomatoes, stock, lemon juice, nutmeg, salt and pepper, and the lentils. Bring to the boil, reduce the heat, cover and simmer for 35 minutes, or until all the vegetables and lentils are cooked.

Remove the saucepan from the heat, allow the soup to cool slightly, then purée it, a little at a time, in a food processor or electric blender. Return the puréed soup to the saucepan and stir in the milk. Season to taste with salt and black pepper. Reheat for 5–10 minutes, then pour the soup into mugs and serve with crusty bread.

INGREDIENTS

1.4 KG (3 LB) PUMPKIN
2 TABLESPOONS OLIVE OIL
2 LARGE ONIONS, PEELED AND CHOPPED
225 G (8 OZ) CARROTS, PEELED AND CHOPPED
675 G (1½ LB) TOMATOES, SKINNED, DESEEDED AND CHOPPED
2 LITRES (3½ PINTS) CHICKEN OR VEGETABLE STOCK (SEE PP.433, 434)
STRAINED JUICE OF 1 LEMON
¼ LEVEL TEASPOON FRESHLY GRATED NUTMEG
1 LEVEL TEASPOON SALT
FRESHLY GROUND BLACK PEPPER
115 G (4 OZ) RED LENTILS, RINSED AND DRAINED
285 ML (½ PINT) MILK

PREPARATION TIME: 20 MINUTES
COOKING TIME: 55 MINUTES
SERVES TWELVE

Ingredients

For the tomato relish
- 2 tablespoons olive oil
- 1 red pepper, deseeded and finely chopped
- 1 large onion, peeled and finely chopped
- 1 garlic clove, peeled and crushed
- 225g (8oz) tomatoes, skinned, deseeded and chopped
- 400g (14oz) tinned tomatoes, sieved
- 1 level teaspoon dried marjoram
- 2 tablespoons Worcestershire sauce
- 2 level tablespoons tomato ketchup
- 2 level tablespoons wholegrain mustard
- ¼ teaspoon Tabasco sauce
- 1 level tablespoon soft dark brown sugar
- ½ level teaspoon salt
- Freshly ground black pepper

For the herby Scotch eggs
- 1.1kg (2½lb) pork sausage meat
- Small bunch parsley
- Small bunch sage
- 4 tablespoons tomato purée
- 1 level teaspoon salt
- Freshly ground black pepper
- 12 eggs, size 2, hard-boiled, shelled
- 6 level tablespoons plain flour
- 3 eggs, size 2, beaten
- 115g (4oz) fine white breadcrumbs
- Vegetable oil for deep frying
- Hot tomato relish, made as above (optional)

Preparation time: 45 minutes
Cooking time: 30–45 minutes
Serves twelve

—HERBY SCOTCH EGGS WITH HOT TOMATO RELISH—

To make the tomato relish Heat the oil in a saucepan, add the chopped red pepper, onion and garlic and sauté until soft but not browned. Stir in the chopped fresh tomatoes, sieved tomatoes, marjoram, Worcestershire sauce, tomato ketchup, mustard, Tabasco sauce, sugar and some salt and pepper. Bring to the boil, then reduce the heat and simmer for 30–40 minutes or until thick and pulpy, stirring occasionally.

To make the herby Scotch eggs Put the sausage meat into a bowl. Chop the parsley and sage, add to the bowl with the tomato purée and the salt and pepper and mix well. Divide the mixture into 12 equal pieces. Dry the hard-boiled eggs with kitchen paper, then roll them in a little flour until evenly coated. With floured hands, take a piece of sausage meat and flatten into a round. Place an egg in the centre and wrap the sausage meat around it, pinching the join together. Shape neatly and set aside. Repeat with the remaining eggs. Lightly coat all the eggs with the remaining flour, then with the beaten egg and breadcrumbs.

Half fill a deep frying pan with oil and heat until the temperature reaches 190°C (375°F) on a fat-frying thermometer or until a piece of bread dropped into the oil browns within a few seconds. Fry the eggs in batches for 10–15 minutes until golden brown. Using a slotted spoon, transfer onto kitchen paper. Reheat the oil between batches.

When the eggs are cooked, cover them loosely with foil and keep them warm in the oven. To serve, cut the eggs in half and arrange on a serving dish accompanied by the hot tomato relish.

Serve Scotch eggs with baked potatoes and Cumberland sausages curled like catherine wheels.

The little pies, with their spicy apple, date and prune filling, are just right to hold in the hand.

Pyrotechnics
Of ancient Chinese origin, fireworks have been part of European celebrations since the invention of gunpowder. They have been central to Guy Fawkes Night rites for 250 years at least.

— SPICED FRUIT TURNOVERS —

To make the flaky pastry Sift the flour and salt into a bowl and rub in half the butter. Add the water and mix to make a soft dough. On a lightly floured surface, roll the dough into an oblong about 6 mm (¼ in) thick. Dot half the remaining butter over the top two-thirds of the oblong, then fold the bottom third up and over the centre third and bring the top third down to cover the bottom third. Press the edges firmly together with the rolling pin. Give the dough a quarter turn to the left so that the side joins are to the bottom and top. Roll out again into an oblong 6 mm (¼ in) thick and dot the vegetable fat over the top two-thirds of the pastry, then fold and turn as before. Repeat using the remaining butter. Wrap and chill for 30 minutes or until required.

To make the filling Put the apples, dates, prunes, orange juice, brown sugar and cinnamon into a saucepan, cover and cook gently for 5–8 minutes. Remove from the heat and allow to cool.

Cut the dough in half, roll out one piece to 38 × 25 cm (15 × 10 in), cut in half lengthways and into three widthways to make six pieces each about 12.5 cm (5 in) square. Spoon half the filling onto the squares, dividing it equally and placing it on the centre of each. Brush the edges with a little beaten egg, then fold each square in half diagonally to enclose the filling and form a triangle. Press the edges together well to seal, flake them with a sharp knife and decorate with a fork. Put the turnovers onto a baking sheet and refrigerate while making six more in the same way.

Preheat the oven to 220°C (425°F, gas mark 7). Remove the turnovers from the refrigerator, brush with the remaining beaten egg, sprinkle with the caster sugar and bake in the oven for 20–25 minutes until well risen, crisp and golden brown. Put onto wire racks and allow to cool a little. Serve warm, wrapped in paper napkins.

INGREDIENTS

For the flaky pastry
- 340 g (12 oz) plain flour
- ½ level teaspoon salt
- 150 g (5 oz) butter
- 175 ml (6 fl oz) chilled water
- 115 g (4 oz) white vegetable fat

For the filling
- 800 g (1¾ lb) cooking apples, peeled, cored and sliced
- 115 g (4 oz) ready-to-eat stoned dates, roughly chopped
- 115 g (4 oz) ready-to-eat stoned prunes, roughly chopped
- 1 tablespoon fresh orange juice
- 60 g (2 oz) soft light brown sugar
- ½ level teaspoon ground cinnamon
- 1 egg, size 2, beaten
- 2–3 tablespoons caster sugar

Preparation time: 45 minutes
Cooking time: 20–25 minutes
Makes 12 turnovers

Penny plea
Bonfires and bangs, masks and disguises, feasting and sacrifice, were part of the rites of the autumnal solstice millenia before Guy Fawkes went to his death in 1606.

Children will find these little men, with currants for eyes and buttons, quite irresistible.

INGREDIENTS

For the Yorkshire parkin
225 g (8 oz) plain flour
2 level teaspoons ground ginger
1 level teaspoon bicarbonate of soda
½ level teaspoon salt
225 g (8 oz) medium oatmeal
115 g (4 oz) black treacle
115 g (4 oz) golden syrup
115 g (4 oz) soft light brown sugar
115 g (4 oz) butter
150 ml (¼ pint) milk
1 egg, size 2, beaten
Preparation time: 20 minutes
Cooking time: 30 minutes
Serves twelve

For the gingerbread men
225 g (8 oz) plain flour
2 level teaspoons ground ginger
1 level teaspoon bicarbonate of soda
60 g (2 oz) butter
60 g (2 oz) soft dark brown sugar
3 tablespoons golden syrup
1 egg, size 2, beaten
Few currants for decoration
Preparation time: 25 minutes
Cooking time: 15–20 minutes
Makes 12 gingerbread men

—YORKSHIRE PARKIN AND GINGERBREAD MEN—

To make the Yorkshire parkin Preheat the oven to 180°c (350°f, gas mark 4). Grease and line a 30 × 25 × 5 cm (12 × 10 × 2 in) roasting tin with nonstick baking paper. Sift the flour, ground ginger, bicarbonate of soda and salt into a mixing bowl, stir in the oatmeal and make a well in the centre. Put the treacle, golden syrup, sugar and butter into a saucepan and heat gently until the butter has melted. Remove from the heat, stir in the milk and egg, add to the dry ingredients and beat thoroughly. Pour into the tin and bake in the centre of the oven for 30 minutes until firm and a skewer inserted through the parkin comes out clean.

Leave to cool in the tin. When cold, wrap in greaseproof paper and store in an airtight tin for five to six days. Cut into squares for serving.

To make the gingerbread men Preheat the oven to 180°c (350°f, gas mark 4). Sift the flour, ginger and bicarbonate of soda into a bowl and make a well in the centre. Put the butter, sugar and golden syrup into a small saucepan, heat gently until melted, then pour into the flour. Add the egg and mix to form a soft dough. Knead lightly on a floured surface for a few seconds until smooth, then roll out to 6 mm (¼ in) thick. Using a 10 cm (4 in) specially shaped cutter, stamp out the gingerbread men and place them, spaced apart, on lightly greased baking sheets. Reknead and reroll the trimming. Cut out 12 men in all.

Cut six currants in half and gently press two bits on each man for eyes. Use whole currants for the buttons. Bake the gingerbread men in the oven for 15–20 minutes or until lightly browned.

Leave on the baking sheets for 5 minutes then, using a palette knife, carefully transfer onto a wire cooling rack and cool completely.

—TREACLE TOFFEE AND TOFFEE APPLES—

To make treacle toffee Grease a shallow, 18 cm (7 in) square tin and line the bottom with nonstick baking paper. Put the black treacle, golden syrup, sugar, butter and water into a heavy-based saucepan and stir over a gentle heat until the butter has melted and the sugar has completely dissolved. Bring to the boil and boil rapidly for 5–10 minutes until 130°C (260°F) is reached on a sugar thermometer or until a teaspoon of the mixture becomes hard and brittle when poured into a bowl of cold water. Remove the pan from the heat each time before testing. Pour immediately into the tin and leave until cold.

Remove the cold toffee from the tin and place between two sheets of nonstick baking paper. Using a small hammer, crack the toffee into pieces. Serve in paper cones made from nonstick baking paper.

To make toffee apples Wash the apples and dry with kitchen paper. Remove the stalks and push a wooden stick into the centre of each apple. Line a baking tray with nonstick baking paper. Put half each of the sugar, syrup, butter, lemon juice and water into a heavy-based saucepan and make the toffee in the same way as for treacle toffee above, boiling for about 10 minutes until the correct temperature is reached.

Remove from the heat and stand the saucepan on a wooden board. One at a time, quickly dip six of the apples into the toffee until evenly coated, lift out and let the excess toffee drip back into the pan. Stand the coated apples on the prepared baking tray and leave to set in a cool, dry place until serving—if left in a steamy kitchen, the toffee will become soft and sticky. Make another batch of toffee in the same way with the remaining ingredients and coat the remaining apples—if you try to make all the toffee at once, it will harden before you can coat all 12 apples.

INGREDIENTS

For the treacle toffee
- 225 g (8 oz) black treacle
- 60 g (2 oz) golden syrup
- 225 g (8 oz) soft light brown sugar
- 115 g (4 oz) butter
- 85 ml (3 fl oz) water

Preparation time: 10 minutes
Cooking time: 10–15 minutes
Makes 450 g (1 lb)

For the toffee apples
- 12 small dessert apples, Cox's or Spartan
- 12 wooden sticks, such as lollypop sticks
- 450 g (1 lb) demerara sugar
- 2 tablespoons golden syrup
- 60 g (2 oz) butter
- 4 teaspoons lemon juice
- 4 tablespoons water

Preparation time: 15 minutes
Cooking time: 10–15 minutes
Makes 12 toffee apples

Crunchy treacle toffee and glistening toffee apples will keep the party going with a swing.

A FAMILY CHRISTMAS

TAKE *Holly* AND *Mistletoe*, *Yule Logs* AND *Pine Cones*, TINKLING *Sleigh Bells* AND FLICKERING *Candles*. ADD THE SWEET SOUND OF *Carols*, THE LAUGHTER OF *Children* AND THIS FESTIVE MENU. HERE ARE ALL THE INGREDIENTS FOR A *Celebration* OF CHRISTMAS AS IT USED TO BE—SO COME IN FROM THE COLD, SHARE THE *Christmas Spirit*, AND GOD BLESS US, EVERY ONE!

MENU

MULLED WINE

SACK POSSET

CHAMPAGNE CUP

MRS BEETON'S VERY LUXURIOUS MINCEMEAT

ROYAL MINCE PIES

ROAST TURKEY
WITH
CHESTNUT STUFFING

FORCEMEAT BALLS

BACON ROLLS

GRAVY
OR
CHESTNUT SAUCE

BREAD SAUCE

CRANBERRY SAUCE

BUTTERY ROAST POTATOES

SWEDE AND POTATO GRATIN

BRAISED CARROTS, PEAS AND ONIONS IN CREAM SAUCE

CHRISTMAS PUDDING
WITH
HOT RUM OR BRANDY SAUCE

RUM OR BRANDY BUTTER

FROZEN BRANDY CREAM

CHRISTMAS CAKE

SWEETMEATS

Get into the Christmas spirit with warm, mulled wine, frothy posset or cool champagne cup.

—CHRISTMAS CHEER—

To make mulled wine Pour the water into a large saucepan, add the sugar, the whole lemon and the spices and heat gently until the sugar has dissolved. Bring the mixture to the boil, then reduce the heat and simmer for 1 minute. Pour in the red wine and the brandy or rum and heat gently for a few minutes till hot but not boiling. Strain into a heatproof punch-bowl, float the tangerine and lemon slices on top and serve immediately.

To make sack posset Put the egg yolks, egg whites, sherry and spices into a large mixing bowl and whisk until well blended. Place the bowl over a saucepan of gently boiling water and stir until the mixture is warm. Take care not to let it overheat as it will scramble. Reserve 1 teaspoon of the caster sugar, then heat the remainder and the cream in a saucepan until it rises to the boil. Pour the mixture immediately, in a steady stream from a height, onto the warm egg mixture, whisking as you pour to make it frothy. Leave the posset to stand in a warm place for 5 minutes, then sprinkle the reserved sugar over the surface and serve, with a little nutmeg sprinkled on top, in heatproof glasses. This sweet, warming drink goes well with mince pies and because it is rich, one glass per person should be sufficient.

To make champagne cup Put the prepared fruit into a large, glass jug. Pour in the brandy and Grand Marnier and stir well. Cover and chill for 1 hour. Just before serving, add the ice and pour in the champagne and the soda or mineral water. Decorate with the cucumber slices, add the cherries and serve immediately.

INGREDIENTS

Mulled Wine

425 ml (3/4 pint) water
150 g (5 oz) caster sugar
1 small lemon, washed
6 cloves
1/4 level teaspoon freshly grated nutmeg
2 cinnamon sticks
3 mace blades
2 bottles fruity red wine
225 ml (8 fl oz) brandy or rum
Thin slices tangerine and lemon for decoration

Preparation time: 15 minutes
Cooking time: 10 minutes
Serves twelve

Sack Posset

6 egg yolks, size 2
3 egg whites, size 2
225 ml (8 fl oz) fino sherry
1/4 level teaspoon each ground cinnamon and mace
1/4 level teaspoon freshly grated nutmeg
130 g (4 1/2 oz) caster sugar
850 ml (1 1/2 pints) single cream
Grated nutmeg for sprinkling

Preparation time: 15 minutes
Cooking time: 10 minutes
Makes 12 small glasses

Champagne Cup

60 g (2 oz) each fresh pineapple pieces, seedless grapes, halved, and clementine or orange segments
85 ml (3 fl oz) brandy
115 ml (4 fl oz) Grand Marnier
12 ice cubes
1 bottle champagne, well chilled
285 ml (1/2 pint) soda water or sparkling mineral water, chilled
A few cucumber slices
6 maraschino cherries

Preparation time: 15 minutes
Chilling time: 1 hour
Serves four to six

INGREDIENTS

FINELY GRATED RIND AND STRAINED JUICE 3 LARGE LEMONS, EMPTY SHELLS RESERVED
800G (1¾LB) COOKING APPLES
450G (1LB) SEEDLESS RAISINS
450G (1LB) CURRANTS
450G (1LB) SHREDDED BEEF OR VEGETABLE SUET
900G (2LB) LIGHT OR DARK MUSCOVADO SUGAR
30G (1OZ) CANDIED CITRON PEEL, FINELY DICED
30G (1OZ) CANDIED LEMON PEEL, HOMEMADE (SEE P.392) OR BOUGHT, FINELY DICED
30G (1OZ) CANDIED ORANGE PEEL, HOMEMADE (SEE P.392) OR BOUGHT, FINELY DICED
2 TABLESPOONS ORANGE MARMALADE HOMEMADE (SEE P.391) OR BOUGHT
450ML (16FL OZ) BRANDY
PREPARATION TIME: 1 HOUR
STANDING TIME: 12 HOURS OR OVERNIGHT
COOKING TIME: 3 HOURS
MAKES 3.6–4.1KG (8–9 LB)

Make the mincemeat in early December to allow time for it to mature. Rum, whisky, Calvados or Armagnac can be used instead of brandy.

—MRS BEETON'S VERY LUXURIOUS MINCEMEAT—

Preheat the oven to 180°C (350°F, gas mark 4). Put the reserved lemon shells into a pan, cover with cold water and bring to the boil. Reduce the heat, partially cover and simmer for 45 minutes or until very soft.

Meanwhile, core the apples and make a shallow cut, just through the skin, around the middle of each. Place on a baking tray in the oven for about 45 minutes or until soft. Remove from the oven and cool.

Drain the lemon shells well and chop finely. Halve the apples and scoop out the pulp. Put the chopped lemon, apple pulp, lemon rind and juice into a very large, ovenproof casserole and beat well. Stir in all the remaining ingredients and half the brandy. Cover with the lid and leave in a cool place for 12 hours or overnight to infuse.

Preheat the oven to 110°C (225°F, gas mark ¼). Cook the mincemeat for 3 hours, then remove the casserole from the oven and take off the lid. Allow the mincemeat, which will be swimming in fat, to cool, stirring occasionally. The suet will coat the fruit and be evenly distributed throughout the mincemeat.

When cold, stir in the remaining brandy, spoon into clean jars and pack down to exclude any air. Seal with a little melted suet or in the usual way. Store in a cool, dark place and use within a year.

Marmalade and a generous lacing of brandy raise this mincemeat to the height of luxury.

Each of these luxurious mince pies is enriched with a spoonful of brandy butter.

—ROYAL MINCE PIES—

Sift the flour into a bowl and mix in the ground almonds, orange rind, caster sugar and a pinch of salt. Rub the butter into the flour until the mixture resembles fine breadcrumbs. Add the egg and mix into the flour with a round-bladed knife, until the dough starts to come together, then gently gather it into a ball with your hands. Knead the dough swiftly on a lightly floured surface until smooth. Wrap in cling film and chill for at least 30 minutes.

Preheat the oven to 200°c (400°f, gas mark 6). Roll the dough out as thinly as possible and cut out 20 rounds, 6 cm (2½ in) in diameter, with a fluted biscuit cutter. Gather the trimmings together, roll again and cut out 20 rounds 7.5 cm (3 in) in diameter. Line 20 small bun tins with the larger rounds and spoon in just enough mincemeat to fill each pie. Put a teaspoon of the brandy butter on top of the mincemeat. Brush the pastry edges with a little milk and place a smaller round on top of each pie, pressing the edges to seal. Brush with the milk and make a hole in the top of each pie. Bake in the centre of the oven for 25 minutes until golden brown. Remove from the oven, leave to cool in the tins for 5 minutes, then lift out onto a wire rack to cool for 10 minutes.

Whisk the egg white until frothy then beat in the sifted icing sugar. Spread a little icing over the top of the mince pies and arrange them on a baking sheet. Bake at 200°c (400°f, gas mark 6) for 5–10 minutes or until the icing has browned a little and the pies are heated through. Let them cool for 5 minutes before serving.

INGREDIENTS

200 g (7 oz) plain flour
85 g (3 oz) ground almonds
Finely grated rind 1 orange
30 g (1 oz) caster sugar
Salt
150 g (5 oz) butter, chilled and cut into small cubes
1 egg, size 2, beaten
Approx 550 g (1¼ lb) mincemeat (see opposite)
115 g (4 oz) brandy butter
2 tablespoons milk
1 egg white, size 2
225 g (8 oz) icing sugar, sifted

Preparation time: 40 minutes
Chilling time: 30 minutes
Cooking time: 35 minutes
Makes approx 20 pies

Ingredients

- 8 kg (18 lb) oven-ready turkey with giblets (a traditional fresh, free-range bird, hung for 1–2 weeks, is best)
- 2 medium onions, peeled and quartered
- 2–3 bay leaves
- 1.15 litres (2 pints) water

For the stuffing

- 450 g (1 lb) peeled chestnuts, fresh or frozen (see p.440)
- 60 g (2 oz) butter
- 115 g (4 oz) onion, peeled and finely chopped
- 1 reserved chopped turkey liver
- 115 g (4 oz) fresh white breadcrumbs
- 450 g (1 lb) pork sausage meat
- 4 tablespoons chopped fresh parsley
- 1 tablespoon finely chopped fresh sage
- 1 level teaspoon salt
- ½ level teaspoon freshly ground black pepper
- ½ level teaspoon freshly grated nutmeg
- Finely grated rind and strained juice 1 lemon
- 4 tablespoons dry or medium sherry
- 4 tangerines, washed and quartered
- Small bunch fresh sage
- 60 g (2 oz) butter, softened

For the bacon rolls

- 18 rashers lean back bacon, rinds removed

For the gravy

- 3 level tablespoons plain flour
- 2 tablespoons dry or medium sherry

Preparation time: 1½ hours
Time to bring turkey to room temperature: 2–3 hours
Cooking time: 4 hours
Standing time: 20–30 minutes
Serves twelve

—Roast Turkey with Chestnut Stuffing—

On Christmas Eve, rinse the turkey giblets under cold water and drain well. Chop and reserve the liver for the stuffing. Put the remaining giblets into a saucepan, add half of the quartered onions, the bay leaves and the water. Bring to the boil, reduce the heat, skim any scum from the surface, cover and simmer for 1 hour. Strain the stock into a measuring jug—there should be about 850 ml (1½ pints). If necessary, make up to the required amount with water. Cool, cover and refrigerate.

To make the stuffing Cook the chestnuts in gently boiling water for 10–15 minutes or until tender, drain well and chop. Heat the butter in a frying pan, add the chopped onion and cook gently for 5 minutes. Add the chopped liver and cook for a further 2 minutes. Transfer to a mixing bowl and leave to cool then mix in the chopped chestnuts, breadcrumbs, sausage meat, chopped parsley and sage, salt and pepper, nutmeg, lemon rind and juice and the sherry.

Rinse the turkey cavity under cold water and wipe dry with kitchen paper. Stuff the neck end with half the stuffing, smooth the skin over it and secure with a skewer. Shape the remaining stuffing into 12 forcemeat balls, put onto a plate, cover and refrigerate.

Put the tangerines, remaining onion quarters and some of the sage inside the turkey, reserving a few sage leaves for garnish. Truss the legs together with clean string. Spread the butter over the breast and season well. Wrap the turkey in a large sheet of foil, seal loosely over the breast, put into a roasting tin and refrigerate.

To make the bacon rolls Stretch the bacon rashers with the back of a knife, cut them in half, roll up each piece, thread onto three or four skewers, wrap and refrigerate.

On Christmas Day, bring the turkey to room temperature 2–3 hours before cooking. About 5 hours before the meal, preheat the oven to 220°C (425°F, gas mark 7). Put the turkey into the oven and cook for 1 hour. Remove from the oven, unwrap and baste with the juices. Rewrap and return to the oven. Reduce the temperature to 180°C (350°F, gas mark 4) and cook for another 3 hours, basting every hour.

About 1 hour before the end of the cooking time, put the forcemeat balls and bacon rolls onto a greased baking tray and cook them above the turkey for 30–40 minutes until cooked through and golden brown. Remove from the oven and keep warm.

If necessary, unwrap the turkey for the last 30 minutes of cooking time to allow it to brown. To check if it is cooked, insert a skewer into the thickest part of the thigh. The juices should run clear—if there is any trace of pink, continue to cook, testing every 15 minutes until done.

Carefully lift the turkey onto a serving platter, loosely cover with clean foil and keep warm while making the gravy. Remove and discard the cooking foil from the roasting tin. Skim off all but 3 tablespoons of fat from the juices in the tin. Stir in the flour and the giblet stock, then strain into a saucepan. Bring to the boil, stirring, then simmer for 5 minutes. Season well, add the sherry and pour into a gravy boat.

Arrange the forcemeat balls around the turkey, garnish it with the sage leaves and serve accompanied by the bacon rolls and vegetables.

Dinner is served—the festive menu offers the very best of traditional Christmas fare.

Offer a choice of bread, orange-flavoured cranberry, or chestnut sauces with the turkey.

INGREDIENTS

BREAD SAUCE
570ML (1 PINT) FULL CREAM MILK
1 SMALL ONION, PEELED AND STUDDED WITH 4 CLOVES
1 BAY LEAF
PINCH OF GROUND MACE OR NUTMEG
¼ LEVEL TEASPOON SALT
¼ LEVEL TEASPOON BLACK PEPPERCORNS
30G (1OZ) BUTTER
1 LARGE SHALLOT OR 1 SMALL ONION, PEELED AND FINELY CHOPPED
115G (4OZ) FRESH WHITE BREADCRUMBS
2 TABLESPOONS DOUBLE CREAM
PREPARATION TIME: 30 MINUTES
COOKING TIME: 30 MINUTES PLUS SOAKING
SERVES TWELVE

CRANBERRY SAUCE
GRATED RIND OF 1, JUICE OF 2 MEDIUM ORANGES
225G (8OZ) GRANULATED SUGAR
1 CINNAMON STICK
150ML (¼ PINT) WATER
450G (1LB) CRANBERRIES
PREPARATION TIME: 10 MINUTES
COOKING TIME: 10 MINUTES
SERVES TWELVE

CHESTNUT SAUCE
340G (12OZ) PEELED CHESTNUTS, FRESH OR FROZEN (SEE P.440)
570ML (1 PINT) CHICKEN STOCK (SEE P.433)
PREPARATION TIME: 30 MINUTES
COOKING TIME: 10 MINUTES
SERVES TWELVE

—THE SAUCES—

To make the bread sauce Pour the milk into a small saucepan and add the onion, bay leaf, mace or nutmeg, salt and peppercorns. Bring to the boil slowly, then remove from the heat, cover and leave to infuse for at least 30 minutes. Meanwhile, heat the butter in another saucepan and cook the shallot or onion gently for 5 minutes. Remove from the heat, strain the infused milk into the pan, stir in the breadcrumbs and leave to soak for 30 minutes. Heat gently, stirring frequently, for about 15 minutes until thickened. Stir in the cream and keep warm.

To make the cranberry sauce Put the grated rind and orange juice into a saucepan and add the sugar, cinnamon stick and water. Cook over a low heat until the sugar dissolves, then bring to the boil. Add the cranberries and continue to cook, uncovered, for 10 minutes or until they have burst and the liquid has thickened slightly. Remove the cinnamon stick and serve the sauce warm or cold.

To make the chestnut sauce Put the chestnuts into a saucepan and add the chicken stock. Bring to the boil, reduce the heat, cover and cook gently for 10–15 minutes or until tender. Drain off and reserve the stock. Put the chestnuts into a food processor, add 285 ml (½ pint) of the stock and blend until smooth. Alternatively, pass the chestnuts through a nylon sieve and stir in the measured stock. Make the turkey gravy as directed on p.316, stir in the chestnut mixture and heat through.

— THE VEGETABLES —

To make buttery roast potatoes Put the potatoes into a large saucepan, cover with cold water, add the salt and bring to the boil and drain. Meanwhile, put the butter into a large, shallow, ovenproof dish or roasting tin, take 2–3 tablespoons of the fat from the turkey, add it to the butter and heat in the oven, above the turkey, until it is sizzling hot. Add the potatoes to the hot fat and turn until evenly coated. Cook above the turkey for 1–1½ hours until crisp and golden brown. If you have a double oven, it may be easier to cook the potatoes separately.

To make swede and potato gratin Steam or boil the swedes and potatoes together until tender then drain well and mash. Beat in half of the butter, season with the salt, pepper and nutmeg and spoon into an ovenproof dish. Melt the remainder of the butter in a frying pan, remove from the heat and stir in the breadcrumbs and the chopped parsley. Sprinkle the mixture over the swedes and potatoes and set aside.

When the turkey is removed from the oven, increase the temperature to 220°C (425°F, gas mark 7). While making the gravy, put the gratin into the oven to cook until golden brown on top.

To make braised carrots, peas and onions in cream sauce Put the onions in the bottom of a large saucepan, add the carrots, sprinkle with the sugar, salt and pepper and pour in the stock—it will not cover the carrots, but they will cook in the steam.

Cover the pan and bring to the boil, then reduce the heat and simmer for 5 minutes until the carrots are just tender. Remove the lid from the pan and boil rapidly to reduce the stock by three-quarters. Add the peas and heat through. Stir in the cream and serve hot.

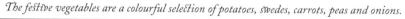

The festive vegetables are a colourful selection of potatoes, swedes, carrots, peas and onions.

INGREDIENTS

BUTTERY ROAST POTATOES

2.3 KG (5 LB) POTATOES, PEELED AND THICKLY SLICED
1 TEASPOON SALT
60 G (2 OZ) BUTTER
2–3 TABLESPOONS TURKEY FAT
PREPARATION TIME: 15 MINUTES
COOKING TIME: 1–1½ HOURS
SERVES TWELVE

SWEDE AND POTATO GRATIN

1 KG (2 LB 3 OZ) SWEDES, PEELED AND ROUGHLY CHOPPED
1 KG (2 LB 3 OZ) POTATOES, PEELED AND ROUGHLY CHOPPED
60 G (2 OZ) BUTTER
½ LEVEL TEASPOON SALT
½ LEVEL TEASPOON FRESHLY GROUND BLACK PEPPER
¼ LEVEL TEASPOON GROUND NUTMEG
60 G (2 OZ) FRESH WHITE BREADCRUMBS
1 TABLESPOON CHOPPED FRESH PARSLEY
PREPARATION TIME: 30 MINUTES
COOKING TIME: 20 MINUTES
SERVES TWELVE

BRAISED CARROTS, PEAS AND ONIONS IN CREAM SAUCE

450 G (1 LB) BUTTON ONIONS, PEELED, HALVED IF LARGE
1 KG (2 LB 3 OZ) CARROTS, PEELED AND CUT INTO LONG, THIN STRIPS
30 G (1 OZ) DEMERARA SUGAR
¼ TEASPOON EACH, SALT AND FRESHLY GROUND BLACK PEPPER
285 ML (½ PINT) CHICKEN STOCK, (SEE P.433)
500 G (1 LB 2 OZ) FROZEN PEAS, THAWED AND DRAINED
4 TABLESPOONS DOUBLE CREAM
PREPARATION TIME: 25 MINUTES
COOKING TIME: 15–20 MINUTES
SERVES TWELVE

Christmas Pudding

Ingredients

- 30g (1oz) butter, melted for greasing
- 225g (8oz) ready-to-use pitted prunes, roughly chopped
- 225g (8oz) currants
- 225g (8oz) sultanas
- 225g (8oz) stoned raisins, roughly chopped
- 115g (4oz) mixed candied peel, homemade (see p.392) or bought, chopped
- 115g (4oz) glace cherries, quartered
- 85g (3oz) ground almonds
- 2 level teaspoons mixed spice
- 250g (9oz) shredded beef or vegetable suet
- 225g (8oz) dark muscovado sugar
- 225g (8oz) fresh white or brown breadcrumbs
- 115g (4oz) plain flour
- Finely grated rind 2 oranges
- Finely grated rind 2 lemons
- 1 large carrot, approx 175g (6oz), peeled and grated
- 1 large potato, approx 175g (6oz), peeled and grated
- 1 cooking apple, approx 175g (6oz), peeled, cored and grated
- 5 eggs, size 2, beaten
- 150ml (¼ pint) strong ale, brandy, whisky or rum
- Sprigs of holly for decoration
- 4–6 tablespoons brandy, whisky or rum for flaming

Preparation time: 1 hour
Standing time: Overnight
Cooking time: 9 hours
Reheating time: 2–3 hours
Serves twelve

With the melted butter, thoroughly grease a 2.3 litre (4 pint) heatproof mixing bowl or pudding basin, line the bottom with a round of nonstick baking paper and grease the paper. Cut a round of nonstick baking paper large enough to cover the top of the bowl or basin and grease it well.

Put all the ingredients into a very large mixing bowl and mix them thoroughly. Spoon the mixture into the prepared mixing bowl or pudding basin and smooth the surface. Cover the mixture with the greased paper, then cover the bowl or basin with heavy-duty cooking foil, pleated in the centre to allow for expansion. Using strong string, tie the foil securely in position under the rim of the bowl or basin and leave the pudding to stand in a cold place overnight.

To cook the pudding Stand it on a trivet or a small block of wood in a large saucepan and fill the saucepan to halfway up the side of the bowl or basin with boiling water. Add some slices of lemon to prevent the saucepan from blackening during cooking, cover and boil very gently for 9 hours. Replenish the water frequently with more boiling water. Do not replenish with cold water as the pudding bowl or basin may crack.

Remove the bowl or basin from the pan and discard the foil. Leave to cool, then cover with fresh nonstick baking paper and foil. Store in a cool, dry, airy cupboard.

On Christmas Day, steam the pudding in the same way for a further 2–3 hours and then remove the bowl or basin from the saucepan. Pour the brandy, whisky or rum into a cup and stand the cup to heat in the water in the saucepan. Meanwhile, remove the foil and paper, loosen the sides of the pudding from the bowl or basin with a palette knife, turn out onto a heated serving plate and decorate with the sprigs of holly.

Take the heated spirit to the table with the pudding. Before serving, remove the sprigs of holly, pour the spirit over the pudding and ignite it. Alternatively, pour the spirit into a long-handled ladle, ignite it and, once flaming, pour it over the pudding. Serve with one or more of the traditional accompaniments.

Accompaniments

To make the hot rum or brandy sauce Melt the butter in a saucepan, stir in the flour and cook for 1 minute over a low heat, without browning. Gradually add the milk and bring to the boil, stirring continuously, until the sauce thickens. Reduce the heat and continue stirring for 1–2 minutes to remove all traces of raw flour. Add sugar to taste, then the cream and rum or brandy. Stir the sauce over the heat for 1–2 minutes until hot but not boiling, pour into a hot serving jug and serve with the pudding. (The sauce can be made the day before. Cover with cling film to prevent a skin from forming, but remove before reheating.)

To make the rum or brandy butter Beat the butter, sugar and orange rind together in a mixing bowl, or with an electric hand-whisk, until light and fluffy. Very gradually add the rum or brandy, a little at a time, beating well between each addition until smooth and creamy. Do not add the spirit too quickly as the mixture will curdle. Spoon the butter into a serving dish, cover and chill until required.

The pudding, rich and moist, is enhanced by a selection of traditional butters and sauces.

To make the frozen brandy cream Whisk all the ingredients together in a mixing bowl until smooth and slightly thickened, taking care not to over whisk as the mixture will curdle. Pour the cream into a 21.5 × 10 × 6 cm (8½ × 4 × 2½ in) nonstick loaf tin lined with nonstick baking paper, cover and freeze. Remove from the freezer just before serving, dip the loaf tin in warm water for 1 second and turn the brandy cream onto a flat serving dish. Cut into slices and serve with the pudding.

INGREDIENTS

Hot Rum or Brandy Sauce
45 g (1½ oz) unsalted butter
45 g (1½ oz) plain flour
570 ml (1 pint) milk
30–45 g (1–1½ oz) caster sugar
285 ml (½ pint) single cream
6 tablespoons rum or brandy
Preparation time: 10 minutes
Serves twelve

Rum or Brandy Butter
115 g (4 oz) unsalted butter
115 g (4 oz) light muscovado sugar
Finely grated rind 1 large orange
6–8 tablespoons rum or brandy
Preparation time: 10 minutes
Chilling time: 2 hours or overnight
Serves twelve

Frozen Brandy Cream
570 ml (1 pint) double cream
150 g (5 oz) icing sugar, sifted
Finely grated rind 1 lemon
3 tablespoons lemon juice, strained
150 ml (¼ pint) brandy
3 tablespoons Amaretto or Maraschino
1 teaspoon natural vanilla extract or essence
Preparation time: 5 minutes
Freezing time: Overnight
Serves twelve

INGREDIENTS

225g (8oz) butter
225g (8oz) dark muscovado sugar
6 eggs, size 2
225g (8oz) plain flour, sifted
450g (1lb) sultanas, picked over to remove any stalks
275g (10oz) currants
450g (1lb) stoned raisins, roughly chopped
275g (10oz) glace cherries, halved
115g (4oz) mixed candied peel, homemade (see p.392) or bought, chopped
85g (3oz) ground almonds
Finely grated rind 1 large orange
Finely grated rind 1 large lemon
3–4 tablespoons whisky, brandy or rum for adding to the cake before icing
Preparation time: 1 hour
Cooking time: 3½–4 hours
Makes a 23cm (9in) cake

For the almond paste
450g (1lb) ground almonds
225g (8oz) icing sugar, sifted
225g (8oz) caster sugar
8 egg yolks, size 2
1 teaspoon natural almond extract or 1 teaspoon natural vanilla extract or essence
3 tablespoons apricot jam, heated and sieved
Preparation and making time: Total time 1 hour
Drying time: 24 hours

For the royal icing
900g (2lb) icing sugar, sifted
4 egg whites, size 2
1 tablespoon glycerine
2 teaspoons lemon juice
Preparation and icing time: Total time 1 hour
Drying time: 24 hours

—CHRISTMAS CAKE—

To make the cake, line the base and sides of a 23cm (9in) round cake tin with a double thickness of greaseproof paper. Preheat the oven to 150°C (300°F, gas mark 2). Put the butter and sugar into a large mixing bowl and beat together until very light and fluffy. Beat in the eggs, one at a time, beating well after each addition—as there is a larger proportion of eggs than normal in this recipe, the mixture will curdle a little, but do not worry. Fold in the flour and mix in the dried fruit, glacé cherries, chopped peel, ground almonds and the orange and lemon rinds.

Spoon the mixture into the prepared tin and smooth the top. Bake in the centre of the oven for 3½–4 hours or until a warmed skewer, inserted into the centre of the cake, comes out clean. Remove the cake from the oven and leave to cool in the tin for 1 hour, then carefully turn it out onto a wire rack and leave to cool completely.

When the cake is cold, without removing the baking paper, wrap it in cling film. Overwrap it in foil, put it into an airtight container and store in a cool, dry, airy cupboard until ready to ice.

To make the almond paste Mix the ground almonds with the sifted icing sugar and the caster sugar, add the egg yolks and the almond or vanilla extract or essence and mix together to form a soft, but not sticky paste. Smooth the paste by kneading it very briefly on a work surface lightly sifted with icing sugar. To cover the cake with the almond paste, remove it from its wrappings and put it, upside-down, in the centre of a 30cm (12in) round, silver or gold cake board, or on a cake stand if preferred. Using a fine, clean skewer, make several holes over the base of the cake, inserting the skewer to about two-thirds of its depth. Carefully spoon the whisky, brandy or rum over the base of the cake and allow it to seep into the holes.

Roll out the almond paste to a neat round about 33cm (13in) in diameter. Brush the cake all over with the warm, sieved apricot jam, then carefully lift the paste onto the cake and smooth it evenly over the top and down the sides, pressing it gently but firmly into position. Trim away any excess paste from around the bottom edge of the cake, finally smoothing it with a palette knife. Leave the cake, uncovered, in a cool, dry place for 24 hours before icing.

To make the royal icing Put the sifted icing sugar and the egg whites into a large mixing bowl and beat together until smooth, white and fluffy, then beat in the glycerine and the lemon juice. Spoon 3 tablespoons of the icing mixture onto the cake and spread it evenly over the top only. Using a clean, metal ruler, smooth the icing by pulling the ruler over the top of the cake. Trim the excess icing from around the edge of the cake and leave to dry overnight.

Put the remaining icing into a clean bowl, cover the surface closely with cling film and refrigerate. The next day, beat the icing up again and give the top of the cake another coat in the same way as before. Spread the remaining icing around the side of the cake, letting a little overflow onto the top (see picture). Pull the icing up into peaks and mark into swirls with a palette knife. Allow the icing to dry then decorate the cake with traditional Christmas ornaments of your choice.

The rich fruit cake and almond paste are iced in a simple style that looks impressive, but is very easy to achieve.

Pass round rum truffles and marzipan-filled dates, and enjoy the after-dinner conversation.

INGREDIENTS

Rum truffles
200g (7oz) plain chocolate, broken into small pieces
2 tablespoons rum
60g (2oz) unsalted butter, at room temperature
2 teaspoons single cream
30g (1oz) ground almonds
30g (1oz) icing sugar, sieved
30g (1oz) cocoa powder for coating, sieved
Preparation time: 25 minutes
Standing time: 10–20 minutes
Cooking time: 5 minutes
Makes approx 24 truffles

Marzipan-filled dates
115g (4oz) ground almonds
60g (2oz) caster sugar
60g (2oz) icing sugar, plus a little extra for rolling out
A few drops natural almond extract or essence
½ egg white, size 2
Natural green food colouring (optional)
115g (4oz) boxed dates, each slit along the top and stoned
115g (4oz) small, soft, ready-to-eat prunes, each slit and stoned
115g (4oz) each small, soft, ready-to eat apricots and figs, each fruit sliced in half horizontally
60g (2oz) granulated sugar
Preparation time: 40 minutes
Makes approx 24 filled dates

— SWEETMEATS —

To make the rum truffles Melt the chocolate in the rum in a heatproof bowl placed over a saucepan of simmering water. Do not allow the water to boil or the chocolate to become hot. Remove the bowl from the heat and beat in the butter a little at a time. Stir in the cream, ground almonds and icing sugar. Let the mixture cool, then chill for about 10 minutes until firm enough to handle.

With dampened fingertips, take teaspoons of the mixture and roll into small balls. Roll in the cocoa powder, spread on a baking tray lined with nonstick baking paper, and return to the refrigerator until firm. Put the truffles into individual paper cases and store in a plastic container in the refrigerator for up to ten days. Serve after dinner with coffee.

Variations:
Orange truffles Add orange juice in place of the rum and ½ level teaspoon finely grated orange rind.
Coffee truffles Replace the spirit with 1–2 tablespoons black coffee.
Hazelnut truffles Replace the ground almonds with 30g (1oz) shelled, ground hazelnuts.

To make the marzipan-filled dates Put the almonds and sugars into a bowl. Add a few drops of almond flavouring and sufficient egg white to make a stiff paste. If using, blend in a few drops of green colouring.

Sprinkle a board or work surface with a little sifted icing sugar and roll the marzipan into a sausage shape, about 25cm (10in) long. Cut the roll into about 48 equal pieces. Shape each piece into a neat oval and insert one into the centre of each fruit, gently moulding the fruits around the marzipan. Roll lightly in granulated sugar and put into individual paper cases. Store in an airtight container for up to four weeks.

To make vanilla fudge Butter an 18 cm (7 in) square, shallow tin. Pour the water into a heavy-based saucepan, add the butter, caster sugar and golden syrup and stir over a low heat until all the sugar has dissolved. Brush down the sides of the pan with hot water from time to time. Add the condensed milk, bring to the boil and cook, stirring continuously, for about 10 minutes until the mixture reaches a temperature of 118°C (240°F) on a sugar thermometer. Alternatively, take the pan off the heat and test by dropping a teaspoon of the mixture into a bowl of cold water—if it does not form a soft ball when taken out, continue to boil for a little longer and retest as before.

When the fudge is ready, remove the pan from the heat and stand aside until the bubbles subside. Stir in the vanilla extract or essence and beat with a wooden spoon until the texture is thick and creamy and a heavy trail is formed when the mixture is allowed to fall from the spoon. Pour the mixture immediately into the prepared tin and allow to cool. When almost set, mark the fudge into squares with an oiled knife. Cut when completely cold and firm. Store in an airtight tin for up to four weeks, interleaved with waxed or nonstick baking paper.

Variations:

Walnut fudge Stir 30 g (1 oz) chopped nuts into the mixture just before the fudge is poured into the tin.

Chocolate fudge Add 15 g (½ oz) sifted cocoa powder with the condensed milk.

Fruit and nut fudge Stir 30 g (1 oz) each of raisins and chopped, toasted hazelnuts into the fudge before pouring into the tin.

INGREDIENTS

Vanilla Fudge

4 tablespoons water

115 g (4 oz) butter

550 g (1¼ lb) caster sugar

2 tablespoons golden syrup

175 ml (6 fl oz) sweetened condensed milk

½ teaspoon natural vanilla extract or essence

Preparation time: 20 minutes plus standing time

Cooking time: 30 minutes

Makes approx 450 g (1 lb)

Butter, caster sugar and condensed milk make this fabulous fudge that will melt in your mouth.

Afternoon Tea

When the smack of leather on willow takes on an evening echo, and the shadows are laid in lengthening lances upon the immaculate turf, the thoughts of both teams naturally turn towards the pavilion. There, wives and girlfriends have laid out a feast. For the hungry, there are *Muffins, Fruit Malt Loaf* and sandwiches of *Homemade Bread*, while traditionalists make inroads upon the *Scones*, the *Bath* and *Chelsea Buns*, and the *Dundee Cake*. One adventurous cook has even brought along spicy *Sally Lunns* and a *Lemon Curd Sponge*.

Crushed sugar lumps and a milk glaze complete these sticky, yeasty, fruity buns.

Bath Buns

Created in Bath, the distinctive dough, rich with sultanas and mixed peel, ensures continuing fame and popularity for the buns

INGREDIENTS

For the batter

- 115G (4OZ) STRONG PLAIN WHITE FLOUR
- 1 LEVEL TEASPOON CASTER SUGAR
- 2 LEVEL TEASPOONS DRIED YEAST OR 15G (½OZ) FRESH YEAST
- 115ML (4FL OZ) WARM MILK
- 115ML (4FL OZ) WARM WATER

For the dough

- 340G (12OZ) STRONG PLAIN WHITE FLOUR
- 1 LEVEL TEASPOON SALT
- 85G (3OZ) CASTER SUGAR
- 60G (2OZ) BUTTER
- 2 EGGS, SIZE 4, BEATEN
- 175G (6OZ) SULTANAS
- 60G (2OZ) CHOPPED MIXED PEEL

For the glaze

- 12 SUGAR LUMPS, COARSELY CRUSHED
- 1 LEVEL TEASPOON CASTER SUGAR
- 2 TABLESPOONS MILK

Preparation time: 30 MINUTES
Rising time: 2½ HOURS
Cooking time: 15 MINUTES
Makes 12 buns

To make the batter, sift the flour into a bowl. Dissolve the sugar and the dried or fresh yeast in the milk and water, add to the flour and beat with a whisk until smooth. Cover with cling film and set aside in a warm place until frothy.

Sift the flour for the dough with the salt and sugar into a separate bowl and rub in the butter with the fingertips until the mixture resembles fine breadcrumbs. Add to the batter with the beaten eggs and dried fruit and mix to a soft dough.

The dough will be too sticky to knead by hand in the normal way—this consistency is characteristic of Bath buns. Beat the dough in the bowl with either a wooden spoon, your hand or the dough hook on an electric mixer. The dough should be worked for about 10 minutes until it develops a very elastic texture. Cover the bowl with cling film and leave the dough to rise in a warm place for about 1½ hours, or until doubled in size.

Grease and flour two baking trays. Beat the risen dough and, using a tablespoon, place six heaps, spaced well apart, on each tray. Slip the trays inside lightly oiled polythene bags (clean pedal-bin liners are ideal) and leave in a warm place for 30 minutes, or until the buns have doubled in size. Meanwhile, heat the oven to 200°C (400°F, gas mark 6).

Sprinkle the buns with the crushed sugar and bake for 15 minutes until they are golden brown and sound hollow when tapped on the bottom. Dissolve the caster sugar in the milk, remove the buns from the oven and brush them immediately with the milk to glaze. Using a palette knife, transfer to a wire rack to cool.

Jumbles

For grown-up occasions it is traditional to serve jumbles, in which a crunchy crust encloses a soft cake, with Madeira or some other sweet wine

INGREDIENTS

- 150 G (5 OZ) BUTTER, SOFTENED
- 150 G (5 OZ) CASTER SUGAR
- 1 EGG, SIZE 2, BEATEN
- 275 G (10 OZ) PLAIN FLOUR
- FINELY GRATED RIND 1 LEMON
- 60 G (2 OZ) GROUND ALMONDS
- 115 G (4 OZ) GLACÉ CHERRIES, QUARTERED
- 85 G (3 OZ) ICING SUGAR, SIEVED
- 1 TABLESPOON LEMON JUICE

PREPARATION TIME: 1 HOUR
COOKING TIME: 20 MINUTES
MAKES 36 BISCUITS

PREHEAT the oven to 180°C (350°F, gas mark 4). Grease six baking sheets.

In a mixing bowl, beat the butter and sugar together until light and fluffy, then beat in the egg. Add the flour, lemon rind and ground almonds and mix together to form a soft dough.

Divide the dough into six equal pieces. Take one piece and, on a lightly floured surface, shape it into a roll about 61 cm (24 in) long. Cut the roll into six equal pieces and form each piece into an 'S' shape, about 3.8 cm (1½ in) long, on one of the baking sheets. Space the shapes well apart to allow for spreading while cooking. Decorate each biscuit with a piece of cherry placed in each curve.

Shape the remaining mixture into biscuits in the same way on the other baking sheets and decorate as before.

Bake the biscuits in the oven in batches for 10 minutes each until a light golden colour. Remove from the oven and leave to cool on the baking sheets for 2 minutes before transferring to a wire rack to cool completely.

Meanwhile, in a small bowl, mix the icing sugar with the lemon juice until thick enough to coat the back of the spoon. Using a teaspoon, drizzle the icing to and fro over each biscuit. Allow the icing to dry then store the jumbles, layered between sheets of waxed or nonstick baking paper, in an airtight container.

Glacé cherries decorate these unusual biscuits and lemon icing adds a tang to each bite.

CHERRY RIPE
Whatever damage they did to the small grocer in the early years of the century, David Greig's and the other chain stores did at least bring little luxuries like glacé cherries within the average household's reach.

Aunt Arabella's Lemon Iced Ginger Cake

Black treacle, lemon rind, stem ginger and almonds give great character to this tea-time favourite

INGREDIENTS

- 175G (6OZ) BUTTER, SOFTENED
- 175G (6OZ) SOFT LIGHT BROWN SUGAR
- FINELY GRATED RIND 1 LEMON
- 3 EGGS, SIZE 2, BEATEN
- 1 TABLESPOON BLACK TREACLE
- 115G (4OZ) PRESERVED STEM GINGER IN SYRUP, DRAINED AND CHOPPED, SYRUP RESERVED
- 225G (8OZ) SELF-RAISING FLOUR
- 2 LEVEL TEASPOONS GROUND GINGER
- 60G (2OZ) GROUND ALMONDS
- 3 TABLESPOONS MILK
- 115G (4OZ) ICING SUGAR, SIEVED
- 4 TEASPOONS LEMON JUICE
- 30G (1OZ) PRESERVED STEM GINGER IN SYRUP, DRAINED AND CUT INTO THIN SLICES

PREPARATION TIME: 35 MINUTES
COOKING TIME: APPROX 1¼ HOURS
MAKES 16 AVERAGE PIECES

PREHEAT the oven to 160°C (325°F, gas mark 3). Lightly grease an 18cm (7in) square, loose-based cake tin. Line the base and sides with nonstick baking paper or greaseproof paper, and grease lightly.

In a large mixing bowl, beat the butter, sugar and lemon rind together until light and fluffy. Adding a little at a time, beat about two-thirds of the egg into the creamed mixture, beating well after each addition. Gently mix in the black treacle, the chopped stem ginger and 3 tablespoons of the reserved ginger syrup.

Sift the flour and ground ginger into the creamed mixture, add the ground almonds and fold in gently, then mix in the remaining egg and the milk to make a soft dropping consistency. Spoon the mixture into the prepared tin, level the surface and bake in the centre of the oven for 1–1¼ hours until firm to the touch, or until a skewer inserted into the centre comes out clean. Leave to cool in the tin for 10 minutes, then remove and put onto a wire rack to cool completely. When cold, remove the baking paper.

In a small bowl, mix the icing sugar with the lemon juice to make a smooth icing, thick enough to coat the back of the spoon. Spread the lemon icing over the cake, allowing it to trickle down the sides. Scatter the thinly sliced ginger on top of the icing and leave to set.

Store in an airtight tin until ready to serve, then cut into squares or slices. The cake will keep for up to a week.

Tangy lemon icing mingled with stem ginger trickles deliciously over ginger sponge cake.

MASS CATERING
By Mrs Beeton's day, lemon juice was well established as 'an essential for culinary purposes'. Its extraction was a laborious business, carried out in restaurants and large houses by machines like these.

Thickly whipped cream and caster sugar provide a sumptuous finish to a traditional sponge.

To ensure both sponges are of equal thickness, put the tins on the scales and weigh in equal amounts of the mixture.

Victoria Sandwich

This classic sponge is made in an old, reliable way. The method of weighing the ingredients ensures the right quantities for perfection

Preheat the oven to 190°c (375°f, gas mark 5). Lightly grease two straight-sided 21.5 cm (8½ in) diameter sandwich tins. Line the bottom of each with greaseproof paper and grease the paper, then lightly dust the tins with flour.

If you have balance scales, put the eggs on the weight side and weigh out the butter, sugar and flour each to the same weight as the eggs. If you have spring or digital scales, weigh the four eggs in their shells, then measure out the same weight of the other ingredients.

Put the butter into a bowl and beat until soft. Add the sugar and continue beating until the mixture is light and fluffy. Gradually beat in the eggs one at a time, beating well after each addition, then beat in the vanilla extract or essence.

Sift the flour into the bowl and carefully fold it into the creamed mixture using a large metal spoon. Divide the mixture equally between the two prepared sandwich tins, spread evenly and bake in the oven for 30–40 minutes until well risen, springy to the touch and very slightly shrunk away from the sides of the tins. Allow to cool in the tins for 5 minutes, then turn out onto a wire rack and leave to cool completely.

When cold, place one of the cakes upside-down on a serving plate and spread evenly with the jam. Whisk the cream until it is just thick enough to hold its shape and spread it evenly over the jam, just up to the edge of the sponge. Place the second cake over the filling and sift the caster sugar evenly over the top.

Ingredients

- Approx 250 g (9 oz) butter, at room temperature
- Approx 250 g (9 oz) caster sugar
- 4 eggs, size 2, at room temperature
- ½ teaspoon natural vanilla extract or essence
- Approx 250 g (9 oz) self-raising flour
- 115 g (4 oz) strawberry jam, homemade (see p.389) or bought
- 285 ml (½ pint) double cream
- 2 tablespoons caster sugar for sprinkling

Preparation time: 25 minutes
Cooking time: 30–40 minutes
Serves eight

Currants sweetened with dark brown sugar burst through Eccles cakes and are fragrant with spice in flat currant cake.

Currant Cakes

'Raisins of Corinth,' or currants, have been a part of British celebratory cookery since time immemorial

With their rich currant fillings, these cakes keep well and both are splendid as stand-bys with mid-morning coffee or afternoon tea. The principal difference between the two is the type of pastry.

ECCLES CAKES

Sift the flour and salt into a large mixing bowl, then coarsely grate the frozen butter into the flour and mix lightly. Add the ice-cold water and mix to form a soft but not sticky dough.

Turn the dough onto a lightly floured surface and roll out to about 30 × 23 cm (12 × 9 in). With a short side facing you, fold down the top third of the dough over the middle third, then fold up the bottom third over the top third.

Give the dough a quarter turn and roll out again. Repeat the folding and rolling processes three times more, turning the dough each time, then wrap in cling film, put it into the refrigerator and leave to chill for 30 minutes.

To make the filling, while the dough is chilling, cream the softened butter with the soft brown sugar in a mixing bowl and stir in the currants and grated lemon rind. Unwrap the chilled dough and roll out thinly on a lightly floured surface. Using a 10 cm (4 in) plain cutter, stamp out as many rounds as possible. Lay the trimmings neatly on top of each other, reroll and cut out more rounds until you have 18 in all.

Place a heaped teaspoon of the filling in the centre of each round. Brush the edges lightly with cold water, gather together to enclose the filling and press down lightly. Turn the Eccles cakes over and roll them out gently, one at a time, into neat rounds until the currants just start to show through the dough. Make two or three cuts in the top of each cake and prick with a fork. Put the cakes, spaced a little apart, on baking sheets and chill for 15 minutes.

Meanwhile, preheat the oven to 230°C (450°F, gas mark 8). Brush the melted butter over the cakes, sprinkle with the caster sugar and bake for 15–20 minutes or until pale golden. Remove the cakes from the oven and transfer to wire racks to cool. Sprinkle with more caster sugar just before serving.

FLAT CURRANT CAKE

Preheat the oven to 190°C (375°F, gas mark 5) and lightly grease a baking sheet.

Sift the self-raising flour and the salt into a mixing bowl and rub in the margarine and the lard or white vegetable fat until the mixture resembles breadcrumbs. Add the milk and mix together to form a firm dough. Cover the bowl with cling film and stand aside to allow the dough to rest for 10 minutes.

While the dough is resting, make the filling. Put the currants, or the currants and sultanas, into a bowl and stir in the caster sugar and the mixed spice.

Turn the dough onto a lightly floured surface and knead for a few seconds until smooth. Cut off one-third and set aside. Roll out the remaining dough to a round 25 cm (10 in) in diameter and sprinkle the currant mixture over the centre, leaving a 2.5 cm (1 in) border all round the edge.

Roll out the reserved dough to a round 23 cm (9 in) in diameter and place it on top of the fruit. Brush the edge of the larger round with water, then fold it over the top round and press well to seal.

Carefully turn the currant cake over and put it onto the prepared baking sheet. Flatten it slightly with a rolling pin, prick all over with a fork and brush lightly with the milk. Bake in the oven for 25–30 minutes until golden brown and cooked through. Remove from the oven and transfer to a wire rack to cool.

Before serving, cut the cake into wedges and spread with the butter, if using. Serve warm or cold.

INGREDIENTS

Mrs Parkinson's Eccles cakes

For the dough

- 250 g (9 oz) plain flour
- Pinch of salt
- 175 g (6 oz) butter, frozen
- Approx 6 tablespoons ice-cold water

For the filling

- 45 g (1½ oz) butter, softened
- 60 g (2 oz) soft dark brown sugar
- 85 g (3 oz) currants
- Finely grated rind 1 small lemon
- 15 g (½ oz) butter, melted
- Caster sugar for sprinkling

Preparation time: 40 minutes
Chilling time: 45 minutes
Cooking time: 15–20 minutes
Makes 18 cakes

Flat currant cake

For the dough

- 225 g (8 oz) self-raising flour
- Pinch of salt
- 60 g (2 oz) margarine
- 60 g (2 oz) lard or white vegetable fat
- 3–4 tablespoons milk

For the filling

- 225 g (8 oz) currants, or 115 g (4 oz) each currants and sultanas
- 2 level tablespoons caster sugar
- 1–2 level teaspoons mixed spice
- Milk for brushing
- Butter for serving (optional)

Preparation time: 50 minutes
Resting time: 10 minutes
Cooking time: 25–30 minutes
Serves six to eight

Town & Country Buns

The temptation of Chelsea buns aglow with honey, or Cornish splits oozing cream and jam, is almost irresistible

INGREDIENTS

CHELSEA BUNS
FOR THE DOUGH
- 15G (½OZ) FRESH YEAST, OR 2 LEVEL TEASPOONS DRIED YEAST, PLUS 1 LEVEL TEASPOON CASTER SUGAR
- 225ML (8FL OZ) LUKEWARM MILK
- 450G (1LB) STRONG PLAIN WHITE FLOUR
- 1 LEVEL TEASPOON SALT
- 45G (1½OZ) CASTER SUGAR
- 60G (2OZ) BUTTER
- 1 EGG, SIZE 3, BEATEN

FOR THE FILLING
- 175G (6OZ) MIXED DRIED FRUIT
- 60G (2OZ) CHOPPED MIXED PEEL
- 115G (4OZ) SOFT DARK OR LIGHT BROWN SUGAR
- 2 LEVEL TEASPOONS GROUND CINNAMON OR MIXED SPICE
- 30G (1OZ) BUTTER, MELTED
- 2 TABLESPOONS CLEAR HONEY, MELTED
- GRANULATED SUGAR FOR SPRINKLING

PREPARATION TIME: 35 MINUTES
RISING TIME: 1 HOUR 20 MINUTES
COOKING TIME: 30–35 MINUTES
MAKES 15 BUNS

CORNISH SPLITS
- QUANTITY OF DOUGH, MADE AND RISEN AS FOR CHELSEA BUNS ABOVE
- ICING SUGAR FOR SIFTING

PREPARATION TIME: 30 MINUTES
RISING TIME: 1 HOUR 20 MINUTES
COOKING TIME: 10–15 MINUTES
MAKES 16 SPLITS

CHELSEA BUNS

To make the dough, dissolve the fresh yeast in the milk. If using dried yeast, see p.441, then stir in the rest of the milk.

Sift the flour, salt and sugar into a bowl and rub in the butter. Make a well in the centre, pour in the yeast liquid, add the beaten egg and mix to a soft dough. Knead the dough on a lightly floured surface for 5 minutes, put into a bowl, then cover and leave in a warm place for about an hour, or until doubled in size.

Mix the fruit, peel, sugar and spice together. Grease a baking or roasting tin, 30 × 23 cm (12 × 9 in). Turn the dough onto a floured surface and knead for 2–3 minutes, then roll out to about 51 × 25 cm (20 × 10 in). Brush with the melted butter, sprinkle evenly with the fruit mixture and roll up, like a swiss roll, from one long side. Cut into 15 equal pieces and space evenly, cut sides up, in the greased tin. Cover loosely with cling film and leave until doubled in size. Meanwhile, preheat the oven to 190°C (375°F, gas mark 5).

Bake for 30–35 minutes, until well risen, golden brown and firm. Remove from the oven, brush immediately with the melted honey and sprinkle with the granulated sugar. Cool in the tin.

CORNISH SPLITS

Divide the dough into 16 equal pieces, shape each piece into a smooth ball and place, spaced apart, on greased baking sheets. Leave to rise as for Chelsea buns while preheating the oven to 220°C (425°F, gas mark 7).

Bake in the centre of the oven for 10–15 minutes, until well risen, golden brown and hollow-sounding when tapped on the bottom. Cool on a wire rack, then sift lightly with the icing sugar. Serve split and filled with clotted cream and strawberry jam or black treacle.

Golden dough encircles plump fruit or is lightly dusted with icing sugar in a choice of buns.

Almonds and vanilla, walnuts and coffee are distinctive flavouring ingredients in these biscuits.

Jupiter's choice
From this cigarette card, one of a series of 50 produced in the interwar years, smokers learned that the walnut's botanical name *Juglans regia*, roughly translated, means 'Jupiter's nut'—an indication of its importance as a food in ancient times.

Rich Nutty Biscuits

Crisp macaroons and walnut butter biscuits make tempting nutty nibbles

MACAROONS

Preheat the oven to 180°C (350°F, gas mark 4). Put the ground almonds, caster sugar and cornflour into a mixing bowl and mix well. Add the egg whites and vanilla extract or essence and beat well to make a fairly stiff mixture.

Line two baking trays with rice paper and put teaspoons of the mixture, in round blobs, onto the paper, spacing them well apart. Alternatively, put the mixture into a piping bag fitted with a large, plain nozzle and pipe onto the paper. Lightly press a split almond into the centre of each macaroon and bake in the oven for 15–20 minutes or until pale golden brown. Remove from the oven and leave to cool on the trays.

When cold, remove the macaroons from the trays and tear away the excess rice paper from each biscuit. Store in an airtight container.

WALNUT BUTTER BISCUITS

Preheat the oven to 160°C (325°F, gas mark 3). Sift the flour and salt into a bowl and then add the butter. Reserve 15 g (½ oz) of the sugar and add the rest to the bowl with the coffee.

Rub all the ingredients together until the mixture resembles large breadcrumbs, then mould into small balls about the size of a walnut and roll each one in the chopped walnuts.

Space the balls well apart on lightly greased baking trays and flatten them with the bottom of a glass tumbler dipped in the reserved sugar.

Bake in the oven for 20–30 minutes or until the edges are lightly browned. Leave the biscuits to cool a little before lifting onto a wire rack to cool completely. Store in an airtight container.

A little icing sugar can be sifted over the biscuits just before serving, if wished.

INGREDIENTS

Macaroons

- 115 g (4 oz) ground almonds
- 175 g (6 oz) caster sugar
- 1 level teaspoon cornflour
- 2 egg whites, size 3, lightly beaten
- ¼ teaspoon natural vanilla extract or essence
- Rice paper
- 15 g (½ oz) split almonds

Preparation time: 15 minutes
Cooking time: 15–20 minutes
Makes 24 macaroons

Walnut butter biscuits

- 175 g (6 oz) plain flour
- ¼ level teaspoon salt
- 115 g (4 oz) butter, at room temperature, cut into small pieces
- 115 g (4 oz) granulated sugar
- 2 level teaspoons instant coffee powder or granules
- 30 g (1 oz) chopped walnuts

Preparation time: 30 minutes
Cooking time: 20–30 minutes
Makes 24 biscuits

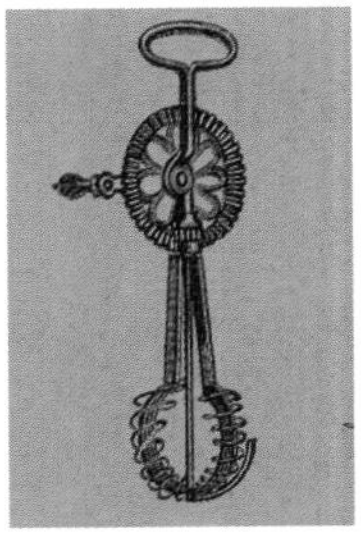

Beat that
The familiar rotary whisk was first patented in America in 1873 and its unique design has changed little since. Despite the popularity of electric beaters, hand-held whisks are still to be found among the utensils in most modern kitchens.

Create a sensation with this frivolous concoction of fluffy sponge layered with lemon curd and whipped cream and coated with cream and almonds.

Lemon Curd Sponge

Vigorous whisking of eggs and sugar ensures that this sponge rises perfectly

Ingredients

For the sponge cake
5 eggs, size 2
150 g (5 oz) caster sugar
150 g (5 oz) plain flour
30 g (1 oz) unsalted butter, melted and cooled

For the filling
570 ml (1 pint) double cream
1 level tablespoon caster sugar
½ teaspoon natural vanilla extract or essence
340 g (12 oz) lemon curd, homemade (see p.405) or bought
85 g (3 oz) flaked almonds, lightly toasted

Preparation time: 1 hour (if making lemon curd, allow extra time)
Cooking time: 20–25 minutes
Serves eight to ten

Preheat the oven to 190°c (375°f, gas mark 5). Grease and flour two sandwich tins, 21.5 cm (8½ in) in diameter and line the bottoms with nonstick baking paper.

Put the eggs and caster sugar into a large mixing bowl or a food mixer and whisk until they are very thick, pale and creamy and will hold a ribbon trail of the mixture almost indefinitely.

Sift the flour over the mixture and fold it in carefully with a large metal spoon then gently fold in the butter. Divide equally between the tins and tap gently to level the mixture, then bake in the oven for 20–25 minutes until well risen, firm and springy to the touch and slightly shrunk away from the sides of the tins.

Allow to cool in the tins for 1–2 minutes, then loosen with a knife and transfer to a wire rack to cool completely.

Whisk the cream with the sugar and vanilla until thick but not buttery. Using a very sharp knife, cut each sponge cake in half horizontally. Put 2 tablespoons of the lemon curd into a small paper piping bag and refrigerate.

Place one sponge layer on a flat serving dish and spread with a third of the remaining lemon curd followed by a layer of cream. Place another sponge layer on top and spread with more lemon curd and cream. Repeat with the third layer, then place the final layer on top and press together gently.

Spread cream round the side of the cake and coat with the flaked almonds, brushing away the excess nuts when the side is well covered.

Put 2 tablespoons of the remaining cream into a piping bag fitted with a small star nozzle, then spread the rest evenly over the top of the cake, marking it decoratively with a palette knife. Pipe small rings of cream round the top of the cake, then fill each ring with the reserved lemon curd. Chill until required.

Plain Cakes

Lemon and vanilla, coconut and orange, and nuts, spices and seeds flavour these elegant cakes

MADEIRA CAKE

Preheat the oven to 180°c (350°f, gas mark 4). Beat together the butter, sugar, lemon rind and vanilla until fluffy, then beat in the eggs, one at a time. Sift in the flour and baking powder and fold in with a metal spoon.

Spread evenly in a lined 18 cm (7 in) round cake tin and arrange the citron peel on top. Bake for 1–1¼ hours until lightly browned and a skewer inserted in the centre comes out clean. Sprinkle with the sugar and leave to cool on a wire rack.

COCONUT CAKE

Preheat the oven to 180°c (350°f, gas mark 4). Beat the butter, 175 g (6 oz) of the sugar and the orange rind until fluffy, then beat in the eggs, one at a time.

Fold in the coconut, flour and orange juice, spread the mixture evenly in a lined 23 × 12.5 × 7 cm (9 × 5 × 2¾ in) loaf tin, and bake for 30 minutes.

Whisk the egg whites until stiff, gradually whisk in the remaining sugar and fold in the coconut. Remove the cake from the oven, brush with the honey and then spread with the meringue mixture. Return to the oven for a further 30 minutes or until the topping is golden and the cake is cooked. Cool on a wire rack.

SEED CAKE

Preheat the oven to 180°c (350°f, gas mark 4). Cream the butter and sugar and add the eggs, one at a time. Mix in the ground almonds, sift in the flours and spices, add the caraway seeds and fold in with a metal spoon, then mix in the almond extract or essence and the milk.

Spread evenly in a lined 19 cm (7½ in) square cake tin and sprinkle with the demerara sugar and the slivered almonds. Bake for 1–1¼ hours or until cooked. Cool in the tin and cut into squares before serving.

Toppings of candied peel, coconut meringue and slivered almonds bring out each cake's individuality.

INGREDIENTS

Madeira cake

- 175 g (6 oz) butter, at room temperature
- 175 g (6 oz) caster sugar
- Finely grated rind 1 lemon
- ½ teaspoon natural vanilla extract or essence
- 4 eggs, size 2
- 225 g (8 oz) plain flour
- 1 level teaspoon baking powder
- 2–3 thin slices candied citron peel
- 1 teaspoon caster sugar for sprinkling

Coconut cake

- 175 g (6 oz) butter
- 200 g (7 oz) caster sugar
- Finely grated rind 1 orange
- 3 eggs, size 2
- 60 g (2 oz) shredded coconut
- 175 g (6 oz) self-raising flour
- 1 tablespoon orange juice
- 2 egg whites, size 2
- 60 g (2 oz) flaked coconut
- 1 tablespoon clear honey, warmed

Seed cake

- 175 g (6 oz) butter
- 175 g (6 oz) caster sugar
- 3 eggs, size 2
- 30 g (1 oz) ground almonds
- 175 g (6 oz) self-raising flour
- 30 g (1 oz) plain flour
- 1 level teaspoon each mixed spice and ground cinnamon
- ¼–½ level teaspoon freshly grated or ground nutmeg
- 1½ teaspoons caraway seeds
- ½ teaspoon natural almond extract or essence
- 1 tablespoon milk
- 45 g (1½ oz) demerara sugar
- 45 g (1½ oz) slivered almonds

Preparation time: 25 minutes

Cooking time: 45 minutes–1½ hours

Traditional Breads

Fill your kitchen with the irresistible aroma of freshly baked bread, reminiscent of an age when home baking was an essential part of everyday life

INGREDIENTS

- 425 ML (¾ PINT) LUKEWARM WATER OR HALF WATER AND HALF MILK FOR A SOFTER TEXTURE
- 15 G (½ OZ) FRESH YEAST OR 2 LEVEL TEASPOONS DRIED YEAST PLUS 1 LEVEL TEASPOON CASTER SUGAR
- 675 G (1½ LB) STRONG, PLAIN WHITE OR WHOLEMEAL FLOUR OR A MIXTURE OF BOTH
- 2 LEVEL TEASPOONS SALT
- 15 G (½ OZ) LARD, BUTTER OR MARGARINE

Preparation time: 30 MINUTES
Rising time: UP TO 2 HOURS DEPENDING ON ROOM TEMPERATURE
Cooking time: 20–40 MINUTES FOR LOAVES, 15–20 MINUTES FOR ROLLS

Women at war
The baker's round was one of the many jobs taken over by women in the First World War in order to release men to the trenches. This contribution to the war effort was a major factor in gaining women the vote in 1918.

If using fresh yeast, pour all the liquid into a bowl, add the yeast and stir with a fork until dissolved. If using dried yeast, stir the caster sugar into 150 ml (¼ pint) of the water and whisk in the yeast. Cover the bowl and leave to stand in a warm place for 15 minutes until frothy, then stir in the remaining water.

Sift the flour and salt into a large mixing bowl and rub in the butter or margarine. Make a well in the centre, pour in the yeast liquid and mix to a soft dough. Turn onto a lightly floured surface and knead well for 10 minutes until very smooth and elastic in texture and no longer sticky. Alternatively, using a dough hook, mix for 3 minutes at low speed in an electric mixer.

Put the dough into a lightly floured bowl, cover tightly with cling film and leave to stand in a warm place for 1–1½ hours or until doubled in size. Turn the risen dough onto a lightly floured surface and, with clenched fists, knock it back to its original size. Continue to knead for a further 2–3 minutes until smooth.

PREPARING LOAVES

Tin loaf Put the dough into a large, well greased loaf tin, or divide it equally between two smaller ones.
Cob loaf Shape the dough into a neat round. Place the round on a greased baking tray and mould in the bottom edge to plump up the shape of the loaf.
Coburg or scofa loaf Shape the dough as for a cob loaf but, halfway through the proving time, cut a deep cross in the top.
Cottage loaf Cut off one-third of the dough and shape it into a ball. Shape the other piece of dough into a larger ball. Place the larger ball on a greased baking tray and lay the smaller ball on top. Lightly flour the handle of a wooden spoon and push it down through the centres of both balls to join them together. Twist the handle slightly and pull it out.
Plaited loaf Cut the dough into three equal pieces and roll each one into a strand about 46 cm (18 in) long. Lay the strands side-by-side on the work surface and, working from the centre of each strand, plait them together, then pinch the ends to seal. Carefully turn the strands round, from top to bottom, and plait the other ends. Place on a greased baking sheet. If preferred, cut the dough in half and make two smaller plaits.

PREPARING ROLLS AND BAPS

Rolls Cut the dough into 60 g (2 oz) pieces and shape into smooth balls by rolling firmly with a cupped hand. Put the rolls onto greased baking sheets.
Baps Shape as for rolls, then flatten each with a rolling pin.

PROVING THE DOUGH

The dough must be proved—left to rise—after shaping. Loosely cover the tins or baking sheets with lightly oiled cling film and leave in a warm place for about 30 minutes, until the dough has doubled in size and will retain a small dent when pressed lightly with a fingertip. Meanwhile, heat the oven to 230°C (450°F, gas mark 8).

When doubled in size, leave the dough plain or, for a soft-topped bread, sprinkle it lightly with flour. For a crusty top, dissolve 1 level teaspoon of salt in 150 ml (¼ pint) of water and brush over the top of the dough. For a golden sheen, brush with milk.

Before baking, the dough can be sprinkled with cracked wheat, rolled oats, sesame seeds or poppy seeds.

Bake large loaves for 35–40 minutes, smaller ones for 20–25 minutes and rolls for 15–20 minutes. The bread is done when it sounds hollow if tapped on the bottom with your knuckles. When cooked, remove from the tin or baking sheet and cool on a wire rack.

Shape versatile dough into a cottage, plaited, cob, coburg or tin loaf, or into rolls or baps.

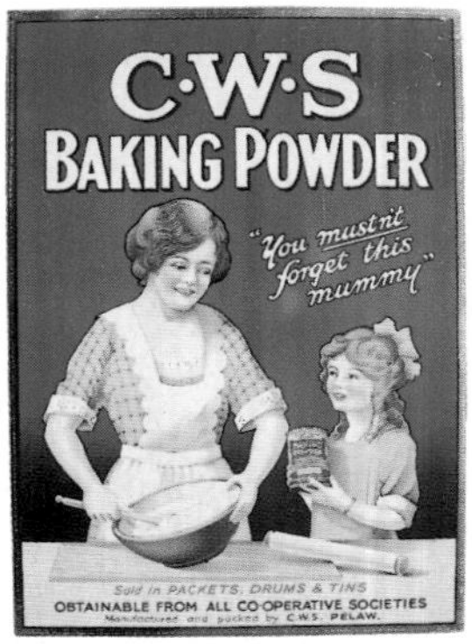

Baking powder
Baking powder was invented in 1843 by the Birmingham chemist Alfred Bird. The inspiration was his wife who found yeast-based products indigestible. But Bird's Fermenting Powder, as it was first called, was not a second-best for yeast. It actually resulted in cakes, bread and buns of a much lighter texture.

Tried, tested and delicious, this cake relies on a good, old-fashioned cake mixture to support the cherries, while the ground almonds contribute flavour and moisture.

Gran's Foolproof Cherry Cake

Evenly distributed glacé cherries are the secret of success in this delectable sponge

INGREDIENTS

- 225 G (8 OZ) PLAIN FLOUR
- ½ LEVEL TEASPOON BAKING POWDER
- 275 G (10 OZ) GLACÉ CHERRIES, QUARTERED
- 115 G (4 OZ) GROUND ALMONDS
- 225 G (8 OZ) BUTTER, AT ROOM TEMPERATURE
- 225 G (8 OZ) CASTER SUGAR
- 4 EGGS, SIZE 2
- FINELY GRATED RIND AND STRAINED JUICE 1 LEMON
- 12 SUGAR CUBES, COARSELY CRUSHED

PREPARATION TIME: 30 MINUTES
COOKING TIME: 1½ HOURS
SERVES SIX

Preheat the oven to 180°C (350°F, gas mark 4). Line the base and sides of a greased 20 cm (8 in) round cake tin with greaseproof paper, then grease the paper. Sift the flour and baking powder together into a bowl. In another bowl, toss the cherries with the ground almonds.

Beat the butter and sugar together in a mixing bowl until pale and fluffy. Beat in the eggs, one at a time, alternating with a tablespoon of the sifted flour and beating well between each addition. Fold in the remaining sifted flour. Carefully mix in the cherries and ground almonds and the lemon rind and juice.

Spoon the mixture into the prepared cake tin and level the top with the back of a spoon. Sprinkle with the crushed sugar cubes and bake in the centre of the oven for 1 hour, then rest a sheet of foil on top and continue to bake for a further 30 minutes or until the cake has shrunk away from the sides of the tin and is springy to the touch in the centre.

Leave it to cool in the tin for about 15 minutes before turning out onto a wire rack to cool completely. Store in an air-tight tin for one to two days before eating to let the cake mature and moisten—if you can bear to wait that long!

Ginger Biscuits

These old-time recipes, combining traditional ingredients, produced gifts for Mothering Sunday and a treat for a sweetheart at the fair

BRANDY SNAPS

Heat the butter, sugar, syrup, lemon juice and brandy gently together in a saucepan until the butter melts and the sugar has dissolved. Remove the pan from the heat, add the flour and ginger and leave to cool.

Preheat the oven to 190°c (375°f, gas mark 5). Line two baking sheets with nonstick baking paper and place 6 teaspoons of the mixture, spaced well apart, on each. Bake for 8–10 minutes until lightly browned. To ensure enough time to roll the brandy snaps, put one sheet into the oven 5 minutes before the other.

Remove the brandy snaps from the oven and cool on the baking sheet for a few seconds then lift with a palette knife and roll round wooden spoon handles. If they become too hard to roll, reheat for a few seconds. When firm, remove from the spoon handles and put onto a wire rack to cool. Repeat with the remainder of the mixture.

For filled brandy snaps, spoon the cream into a piping bag fitted with a small star nozzle and pipe into each end of the biscuits. Serve at once.

CORNISH FAIRINGS

Preheat the oven to 190°c (375°f, gas mark 5). Sift the flour, bicarbonate of soda, salt, ginger and spice into a bowl. Stir in the rice, rub in the butter and mix in the sugar. Warm the syrup and stir it in, then knead lightly in the bowl to form a smooth dough.

Shape into walnut-sized balls and space well apart on greased baking sheets. Bake in batches for 10–12 minutes each until they are golden. Cool the fairings on the baking sheets for 5 minutes, then transfer them to a wire rack and leave to cool completely.

Sweet, cream-filled brandy snaps and spicy Cornish fairings are equally tempting.

INGREDIENTS

Brandy Snaps

- 115g (4oz) butter
- 115g (4oz) caster sugar
- 115g (4oz) golden syrup
- 1 tablespoon lemon juice
- 1 tablespoon brandy
- 115g (4oz) plain flour, sieved
- 1 level teaspoon ground ginger
- 285ml (½ pint) double cream, whipped, if filling brandy snaps

Preparation time: 30 minutes
Cooking time: 8–10 minutes for each batch
Makes 36 biscuits

Cornish Fairings

- 115g (4oz) self-raising flour
- 1 level teaspoon bicarbonate of soda
- ¼ level teaspoon salt
- 1 level teaspoon ground ginger
- 1 level teaspoon mixed spice
- 45g (1½oz) ground rice
- 60g (2oz) butter
- 60g (2oz) caster sugar
- 115g (4oz) golden syrup

Preparation time: 20 minutes
Cooking time: 20–25 minutes
Makes 24 fairings

To allow time to roll the snaps while still soft, leave a 5 minute interval between putting the two baking sheets in the oven.

Spiced Sally Lunn

This famous old recipe from Bath yields a rich and satisfying teatime treat to serve warm and spread with clotted cream

INGREDIENTS

For the batter

- 85G (3OZ) STRONG PLAIN WHITE FLOUR
- 1 LEVEL TEASPOON CASTER SUGAR
- 2 TEASPOONS DRIED YEAST OR 15G (½OZ) FRESH YEAST
- 200ML (7FL OZ) WARM MILK

For the dough

- 175G (6OZ) STRONG PLAIN WHITE FLOUR
- 1 LEVEL TEASPOON SALT
- 1 LEVEL TEASPOON MIXED SPICE
- 30G (1OZ) CASTER SUGAR
- 30G (1OZ) BUTTER, MELTED
- 1 EGG, SIZE 4, BEATEN

For the glaze

- 1 TABLESPOON MILK
- 1 LEVEL TABLESPOON CASTER SUGAR

Preparation time: 30 MINUTES
Rising time: 1–1½ HOURS
Cooking time: 20–30 MINUTES
Serves eight

Grease a 15cm (6in) diameter cake tin, about 6cm (2½in) deep. Combine all the ingredients for the batter in a large mixing bowl and beat them until smooth. Cover the bowl and leave to stand in a warm place for 20–30 minutes until the mixture becomes frothy.

Add the ingredients for the dough to the batter, beating vigorously until it is smooth. Spoon into the prepared tin and cover with oiled polythene to prevent the surface from drying out. Leave in a warm place until the mixture has doubled in size and almost reaches the top of the tin (this will take from 30 minutes to an hour, depending on room temperature). Meanwhile, preheat the oven to 200°C (400°F, gas mark 6) and position the shelf on the rung below the centre.

Remove the polythene from the top of the tin and bake the cake in the oven for 20–30 minutes until well risen and pale golden on top and until a warm skewer inserted into the centre comes out clean. If the cake browns too quickly, cover it with foil or greaseproof paper.

Meanwhile, prepare the glaze. Bring the milk and sugar to boiling point in a very small saucepan, or heat in a small bowl in a microwave oven. Remove the cooked Sally Lunn from the oven and brush the top with the hot glaze. When cool enough to handle, remove from the tin and leave to cool on a wire rack.

Traditionally, a Sally Lunn is sliced into two or three layers, spread with butter or clotted cream, then reassembled and served while still warm.

The glazed Sally Lunn awaits layering with its traditional clotted cream filling.

The top of the cake can be given a shiny finish by brushing with hot, sieved apricot jam.

Candied peel, dried fruit, ground almonds and sherry result in a cake that improves with keeping.

Traditional Dundee Cake

Concentric circles of blanched whole almonds characterise the Dundee cake

PREHEAT the oven to 160°C (325°F, gas mark 3). Line the base and sides of a lightly greased 20 cm (8 in) diameter cake tin with nonstick baking paper or greaseproof paper and grease the paper lightly.

Sift the flour and baking powder together into a bowl. In another bowl, beat the butter with the sugar until light and fluffy. Gradually beat in the egg, a little at a time, beating well between each addition. Add a little of the flour if the mixture begins to curdle. Then add the remaining flour and fold in gently. Stir in enough sherry or milk to mix to a soft, dropping consistency. Fold in the fruit, peel, ground almonds and grated rinds.

Spoon the mixture into the prepared tin and level the top with the back of a spoon. Arrange the blanched whole almonds in concentric circles on top of the cake, dropping, not pressing them, lightly into place.

Bake in the centre of the oven for 2¼–2½ hours until the cake is firm to the touch and when a skewer inserted into the centre comes out clean. After 1 hour, cover the top with foil to prevent the almonds from overbrowning.

Leave to cool in the tin and then store in an airtight container. The cake will mature and develop in flavour if it is kept for two to three days before eating.

INGREDIENTS

340G (12OZ) PLAIN FLOUR
1 LEVEL TEASPOON BAKING POWDER
225G (8OZ) BUTTER, AT ROOM TEMPERATURE
225G (8OZ) CASTER SUGAR
4 EGGS, SIZE 2, BEATEN
4–5 TABLESPOONS SWEET SHERRY OR MILK
225G (8OZ) CURRANTS
225G (8OZ) SULTANAS
115G (4OZ) GLACÉ CHERRIES, HALVED
45G (1½OZ) EACH CANDIED ORANGE, LEMON AND LIME PEEL, CHOPPED, OR 130G (4½OZ) CHOPPED MIXED PEEL
85G (3OZ) GROUND ALMONDS
FINELY GRATED RIND 1 ORANGE
FINELY GRATED RIND 1 LEMON
130G (4½OZ) WHOLE ALMONDS, BLANCHED

PREPARATION TIME: 30 MINUTES
COOKING TIME: 2¼–2½ HOURS

Muffins

Toasting before a fire on a winter's afternoon, muffins recall the days of the lamplighters and muffin men who were once so much a part of town life

INGREDIENTS

340 ML (12 FL OZ) LUKEWARM WATER
½ LEVEL TEASPOON CASTER SUGAR
2 LEVEL TEASPOONS DRIED YEAST
450 G (1 LB) STRONG PLAIN FLOUR, WARMED
½ LEVEL TEASPOON SALT
30 G (1 OZ) BUTTER, MELTED

PREPARATION TIME: 35 MINUTES
RISING TIME: 1 HOUR 40 MINUTES
COOKING TIME: 25 MINUTES
MAKES 16 MUFFINS

Pour 150 ml (¼ pint) of the water into a bowl and stir in the sugar until it dissolves. Whisk in the yeast, cover and leave in a warm place for 10 minutes until the mixture is frothy.

Sift the flour and salt into a bowl and make a well in the centre. Add the yeast liquid, butter and remaining water and mix to a very soft dough, adding a little more water if necessary—the softer the dough, the more difficult it is to handle, but the better muffins it makes.

Knead the dough on a well-floured surface until even-textured and springy, then put it into a lightly oiled bowl. Cover with cling film and leave in a warm place to rise for about an hour, or until doubled in size.

Turn the dough onto a floured surface and knead for 2 minutes. Divide it into 16 equal pieces and shape each into a ball by rolling under the cupped palm of your hand. Heavily flour a board, place the dough balls on it and sift flour over them. Cover loosely with a clean tea towel and leave in a warm place to rise for about 40 minutes, until the dough keeps a slight dent if pressed lightly with a fingertip.

Heat a griddle or a heavy-based frying pan and oil it lightly. Lift in half the muffins and cook over a moderate heat for about 5 minutes until lightly browned. Turn the muffins over and cook the other side for 6–7 minutes. Remove from the griddle and wrap in a napkin to keep warm while cooking the remainder.

The Muffin man
With his basket or tray covered by a gleaming white cloth and his clanging handbell, the muffin man has been a feature of British streets since time immemorial. Nor is he yet extinct. This one was photographed in Liverpool in 1954, and a number still ply their trade on market days up and down the country.

Homemade muffins and strawberry jam are quite simply made for each other.

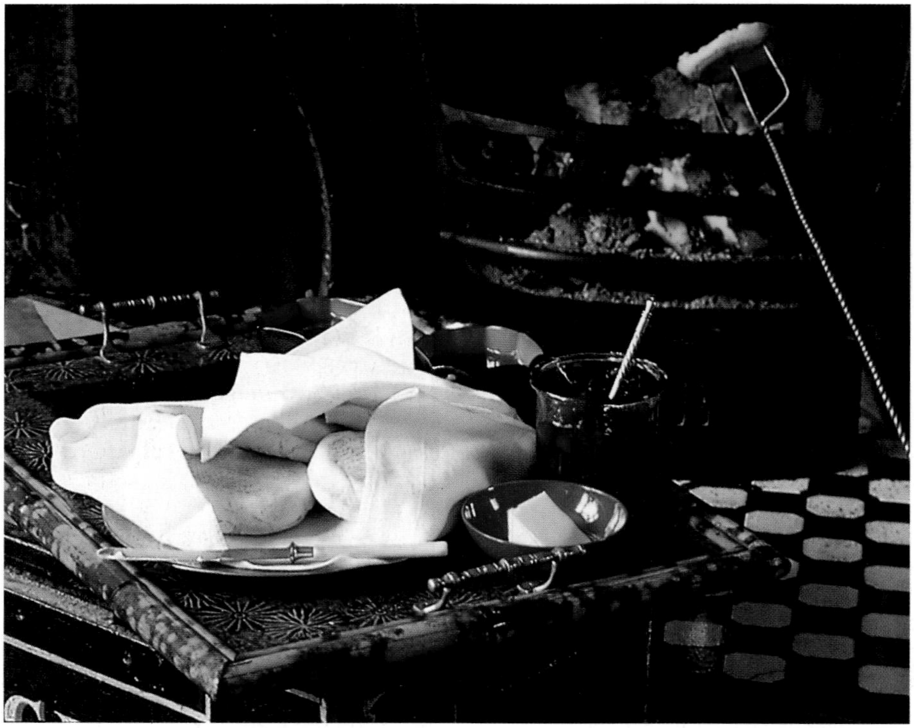

The mixture can also be shaped in a small mould to produce biscuit-sized shortbreads like these.

Never wash your shortbread mould; clean it by brushing with a dry pastry brush.

Shortbread Shapes

Whether as petticoat tails, fingers or moulded shapes, the crumbly buttery texture of shortbread guarantees its welcome on the tea table

SIFT the flour, caster sugar and the rice flour or semolina into a mixing bowl. Add the cubed butter and rub in with your fingertips until the mixture clings together in heavy lumps. Gather the dough into a ball and then knead it, on a lightly floured surface, until it is smooth. Proceed according to how you wish the finished shortbread to be shaped.

Moulded shortbread Lightly sprinkle an 18–20 cm (7–8 in) diameter shortbread mould with flour. Cut the dough in half, roll out each piece to a round a little smaller than the mould and press, smooth side down, into the mould to fit exactly, then carefully turn the dough onto a flat baking sheet.

Petticoat tails Cut the dough in half and roll out two rounds each 18–20 cm (7–8 in) in diameter. Flute the edges with your fingers, then prick all over with a fork. Alternatively, fit the rounds into two fluted flan tins and prick well.

Shortbread fingers Press the dough into a shallow, 28 × 18 cm (11 × 7 in) tin, smooth with a palette knife, then prick well with a fork.

Having prepared the dough according to the shape chosen, chill it in the refrigerator for 1 hour and preheat the oven to 160°C (325°F, gas mark 3). Bake moulded shortbread and petticoat tails for 20–25 minutes and fingers for 25–30 minutes until cooked through, but not browned.

Remove from the oven and leave to cool and firm up for 5 minutes. Loosen moulded shortbread and petticoat tails from the baking sheets with a palette knife. Mark petticoat tails into triangles. Cut fingers into 20 equal pieces while still in the tin. Dredge with caster sugar.

After 15 minutes, transfer petticoat tails and moulded shortbread onto wire racks to cool completely. Leave the shortbread fingers in the tin until cold, then store in an airtight container.

INGREDIENTS

275 G (10 OZ) PLAIN FLOUR
115 G (4 OZ) CASTER SUGAR
60 G (2 OZ) RICE FLOUR OR FINE SEMOLINA
225 G (8 OZ) SALTED BUTTER, CHILLED AND CUT INTO SMALL CUBES
CASTER SUGAR FOR DREDGING

PREPARATION TIME: 25 MINUTES
COOKING TIME: 20–30 MINUTES
MAKES TWO 18–20 CM (7–8 IN) MOULDED SHORTBREADS, 16 PETTICOAT TAILS OR 20 FINGERS

Cream-Filled Meringues

Ring the changes by flavouring the filling from a selection of ingredients—coffee or orange and Cointreau, for instance

INGREDIENTS

FOR THE MERINGUES
4 EGG WHITES, SIZE 2
225 G (8 OZ) CASTER SUGAR

FOR THE FILLING
150 ML (¼ PINT) DOUBLE CREAM

FOR THE FLAVOURING
FINELY GRATED RIND 1 LEMON
1 TABLESPOON LEMON JUICE
1 LEVEL TABLESPOON ICING SUGAR
OR
¼ TEASPOON NATURAL VANILLA EXTRACT OR ESSENCE
1 LEVEL TEASPOON ICING SUGAR
OR
1½ TABLESPOONS STRONG BLACK COFFEE
1 LEVEL TABLESPOON ICING SUGAR
OR
FINELY GRATED RIND 1 SMALL ORANGE
1 TABLESPOON COINTREAU OR GRAND MARNIER
1 LEVEL TEASPOON ICING SUGAR
A LITTLE ICING SUGAR FOR SIFTING

PREPARATION TIME: 15 MINUTES
COOKING TIME: 2–3 HOURS (TIME NEEDED TO DRY THE MERINGUES WILL VARY FROM OVEN TO OVEN)
MAKES EIGHT MERINGUES

Should a little of the yolk drop into the white when separating eggs, use a half eggshell to scoop it out.

PREHEAT the oven to 110°C (225°F, gas mark ¼). Line two flat baking sheets with nonstick baking paper. Make sure that the mixing bowl and whisk are perfectly clean and dry.

Whisk the egg whites until stiff but not dry. If using an electric whisk, add the sugar, a level tablespoon at a time, until it is all incorporated and the mixture is thick and glossy. If whisking by hand, add half the sugar, a level tablespoon at a time, then fold in the remainder.

Using two tablespoons, put 16 spoonfuls of the mixture onto the baking sheets. Make neat oval shapes and space them about 2.5 cm (1 in) apart. Bake in the oven for 2–3 hours until the meringues are lightly coloured on the outside but still slightly soft, like a marshmallow, in the centre.

Remove from the oven, allow to cool on the baking sheets, then store in an airtight container until ready to fill.

To make the filling, whisk the chosen flavouring into the cream until thick but not buttery. Sandwich the meringues together with the cream, place on a large serving dish and sift the icing sugar lightly over them. The meringues may be served in paper cake cases, if wished.

These cream-filled, fluffy meringues, sprinkled with icing sugar, are as light as a summer breeze.

Luscious chocolate sponge, filling and icing all add up to a delightfully decadent cake.

Wicked Chocolate Cake

This rich chocolate cake is best made a day ahead as it improves in flavour

To make the cake, preheat the oven to 190°C (375°F, gas mark 5). Grease and flour two 21.5 cm (8½ in) sandwich tins and line the bottom of each with a round of nonstick baking paper. Sift the flour, bicarbonate of soda and both sugars into a bowl and make a well in the centre.

Pour the water into a small saucepan, add the cocoa powder and butter and stir over a moderate heat until the butter melts and the mixture becomes smooth, but do not allow to boil. Remove from the heat and stir in the vanilla extract.

Stir the vinegar into the cream and pour it into the flour. Add the cocoa mixture and eggs and whisk together until smooth. Pour the mixture into the prepared tins, dividing it equally. Bake for 20–25 minutes or until the cakes have risen and are springy and firm to the touch. Remove from the oven, loosen the sides with a knife and turn onto wire racks to cool.

Meanwhile, to make the filling, put the chocolate and water into a small saucepan and stir over a low heat until melted and smooth, then set aside. Put the caster sugar, cream and butter into another saucepan and stir constantly over a moderate heat for 4–5 minutes until it becomes smooth and thick and will hold a trail, taking care not to let it burn. Remove from the heat and stir in the vanilla and chocolate. Allow to cool, stirring occasionally, then chill until cold.

Sandwich the two cakes together with the filling and leave on a rack over a tray.

To make the icing, put the chocolate into a small saucepan with the butter and water. Stir over a low heat until the chocolate melts and the mixture becomes smooth and will coat the back of the spoon thickly, but do not overheat.

Pour the icing over the top of the cake, allowing it to trickle randomly down the sides, then chill until set.

INGREDIENTS

For the cake

275 g (10 oz) plain flour
1½ level teaspoons bicarbonate of soda
175 g (6 oz) caster sugar
175 g (6 oz) light muscovado sugar
225 ml (8 fl oz) water
60 g (2 oz) cocoa powder
115 g (4 oz) unsalted butter
1 teaspoon natural vanilla extract or essence
1 teaspoon distilled malt vinegar
150 ml (¼ pint) single cream
2 eggs, size 2, beaten

For the filling

115 g (4 oz) dark plain chocolate, roughly chopped
3 tablespoons water
200 g (7 oz) caster sugar
6 tablespoons single cream
115 g (4 oz) unsalted butter
½ teaspoon natural vanilla extract or essence

For the icing

115 g (4 oz) dark plain chocolate, roughly chopped
30 g (1 oz) unsalted butter
3 tablespoons water

Preparation time: 1 hour
Cooking time: 30 minutes
Cooling time: 1–1½ hours
Serves twelve

Lost contentment
Bakers' shops like this, with a little tearoom attached, are now almost a vanished breed, but were once a feature of every high street. Seductive scents wafted from their doors, enticing shoppers to chatter among the teacups, sampling cakes dripping with melting butter.

Mouth-watering fruit tea cakes, fresh from the oven, glisten with sugar syrup.

Yorkshire Tea Cakes

Serve the tea cakes warm, split and buttered or cut in half and toasted, spread with butter and sprinkled with cinnamon sugar

INGREDIENTS

- 150 ML (¼ PINT) LUKEWARM MILK
- 150 ML (¼ PINT) LUKEWARM WATER
- 15 G (½ OZ) FRESH YEAST OR 2 LEVEL TEASPOONS DRIED YEAST PLUS 1 LEVEL TEASPOON CASTER SUGAR
- 450 G (1 LB) STRONG, PLAIN WHITE FLOUR
- ½ LEVEL TEASPOON SALT
- 60 G (2 OZ) BUTTER OR POLYUNSATURATED MARGARINE
- 85 G (3 OZ) CURRANTS
- 85 G (3 OZ) CASTER SUGAR
- 4 TABLESPOONS COLD WATER

For serving
- BUTTER FOR SPREADING
- 2 LEVEL TEASPOONS GROUND CINNAMON MIXED WITH 2 LEVEL TEASPOONS CASTER SUGAR (OPTIONAL)

Preparation time: 50 MINUTES
Rising time: 1–1½ HOURS
Proving time: 25–30 MINUTES
Cooking time: 25 MINUTES
Makes eight tea cakes

If using fresh yeast, mix the lukewarm milk and water together, add the fresh yeast and stir with a fork until dissolved. If using dried yeast see p.441, then stir in the milk.

Sift the flour and salt into a large, warmed mixing bowl and rub in the butter or margarine. Mix in the currants and 30 g (1 oz) of the caster sugar, make a well in the centre, pour in the yeast liquid and mix to form a soft dough. Turn onto a lightly floured surface and knead for 5–10 minutes until smooth and elastic. Put the dough into a clean, lightly floured bowl and cover with cling film. Leave in a warm place for 1–1½ hours until the dough has doubled in size.

Turn the risen dough onto a lightly floured surface and, with clenched fists, knock it back to its original size.

Divide the dough into eight equal pieces, shape each piece into a neat round and roll out to about 12.5 cm (5 in) in diameter. Put the dough rounds onto greased baking sheets, loosely cover the baking sheets with cling film and leave in a warm place until the dough has risen and doubled in size. Meanwhile, preheat the oven to 220°C (425°F, gas mark 7).

Bake the tea cakes for 20–25 minutes or until they are golden brown and sound hollow when tapped on the base. While they are cooking, put the remaining caster sugar into a small saucepan with the cold water, stir over a moderate heat until dissolved, then boil for 1 minute.

Remove the tea cakes from the oven and brush them immediately with the hot sugar syrup, then transfer them to a wire rack and leave to cool.

Fruit Malt Loaf

Wait—if you can—for this bread to mature. In just three days its malty moistness will be irresistible

INGREDIENTS

- 30G (1 OZ) FRESH YEAST OR 15G (½ OZ) DRIED YEAST PLUS 1 LEVEL TEASPOON CASTER SUGAR
- 150ML (¼ PINT) EACH LUKEWARM MILK AND WATER
- 60G (2 OZ) LARD
- 85G (3 OZ) MALT EXTRACT
- 85G (3 OZ) BLACK TREACLE
- 450G (1 LB) PLAIN FLOUR
- ½ LEVEL TEASPOON SALT
- 1 LEVEL TEASPOON SOFT DARK BROWN SUGAR
- 115G (4 OZ) SULTANAS
- 115G (4 OZ) RAISINS
- 60G (2 OZ) CURRANTS
- 1 EGG, SIZE 3, BEATEN
- 30G (1 OZ) PRESERVING OR GRANULATED SUGAR

PREPARATION TIME: 20 MINUTES
PROVING TIME: 1¾ HOURS
COOKING TIME: 40 MINUTES
MAKES TWO LOAVES

If using fresh yeast, mix the milk with the water, add the yeast and stir with a fork until dissolved. If using dried yeast see p.441, then stir in the rest of the milk.

Put the lard, malt extract and treacle into a small saucepan and stir over a moderate heat until melted. Remove from the heat and leave to cool until lukewarm, then stir in the yeast liquid.

Sift the flour and salt into a bowl, stir in the sugar and fruit and make a well in the centre. Add the egg and pour in the yeast mixture, but do not mix.

Cover the bowl and leave in a warm place for about 30 minutes or until the yeast mixture is frothy. Uncover and mix well for 5 minutes with your hand, until the dough becomes soft and sticky. Cover the bowl again and leave in a warm place for 45 minutes or until the dough has doubled in size.

Thoroughly grease two 20 × 10 × 6 cm (8 × 4 × 2½ in) loaf tins. Beat the dough for 8 minutes and then divide it equally between the tins. Cover the tins loosely with lightly oiled cling film and leave in a warm place for 30 minutes or until the dough has doubled in size.

Meanwhile, preheat the oven to 220°C (425°F, gas mark 7). Uncover and sprinkle each loaf with the sugar. Bake side-by-side in the centre of the oven for 10 minutes. If overbrowning, cover the tops of the loaves with greaseproof paper. Reduce the temperature to 190°C (375°F, gas mark 5) and cook for a further 30 minutes or until a skewer inserted into the centre comes out clean. Turn the loaves out of their tins and cool on a wire rack.

When cold, wrap them in greaseproof paper and foil and leave to mature for three days, until moist and slightly sticky.

Malt loaf brims with traditional ingredients, including treacle, sultanas, raisins and currants.

Put the saucepan on the scales and weigh the malt extract and treacle directly into it, allowing for the weight of the saucepan.

Supply lines
Local ladies dispensing tea and homemade cakes are an essential part of village activities, whether a fête or raising funds to restart the village clock. The occasion here was a flower and vegetable show in 1931.

This impressive tart contains a delicious filling of curd cheese, lemon rind and juice, and currants.

Ivy's Curd Cheese Tart

The currants sink during cooking, giving a surprise layer between the pastry and cheesecake-like topping

Ingredients

For the pastry
- 175g (6oz) plain flour
- 2 level tablespoons caster sugar
- 85g (3oz) butter
- 1 egg, size 2, beaten

For the filling
- 340g (12oz) curd cheese
- 60g (2oz) butter, softened
- 85g (3oz) caster sugar
- 3 eggs, size 2, beaten
- Finely grated rind 1 lemon
- 1 teaspoon lemon juice
- 60g (2oz) currants
- ¼ level teaspoon freshly grated nutmeg
- 1 level teaspoon icing sugar
- Single cream for serving (optional)

Preparation time: 25 minutes
Cooking time: 30 minutes
Serves six

Preheat the oven to 220°C (425°F, gas mark 7). To make the pastry, sift the flour and sugar into a mixing bowl and rub in the butter until the mixture resembles fine breadcrumbs. Add the egg and mix to form a soft but not sticky dough.

Turn the dough onto a lightly floured surface and knead for a few seconds until smooth, then roll out to a round a little larger than a 24 cm (9½ in) diameter pie plate. Line the pie plate with the dough, then trim the edge and decorate it. Prick the base and sides lightly with a fork and put into the refrigerator to chill while making the filling.

To make the filling, cream the curd cheese, butter and sugar together, then gradually beat in the eggs, lemon rind and juice. Stir in the currants and pour the mixture into the pastry case. Sprinkle the top with grated nutmeg.

Bake the tart in the centre of the oven for 15 minutes, then reduce the temperature to 190°C (375°F, gas mark 5). Then bake for a further 15 minutes or until the pastry has taken on a light golden colour and the filling has set.

Serve the curd cheese tart warm with icing sugar sifted over the top and, if wished, a little single cream.

Bara Brith

This rich Welsh bread is attractively speckled with mixed fruit

IF USING fresh yeast, add it to all of the milk and whisk with a fork until dissolved. If using dried yeast, see p.441, then stir in the rest of the milk.

Sift the flour and salt into a bowl and rub in the butter and lard. Mix in the spice, sugar and fruits. Make a well in the centre, add the egg and pour in the yeast liquid. Mix together, then beat well with your hand for 5 minutes. Cover the bowl with cling film and leave in a warm place for 1 hour or until doubled in size.

Grease two loaf tins, each measuring about 20 × 10 × 6 cm (8 × 4 × 2½ in). Turn the dough onto a well-floured work surface and knead for 5 minutes or until smooth and elastic. Cut in half, knead each piece for 5 minutes and shape into a roll. Place a roll in each tin. Cover loosely with oiled cling film and leave in a warm place for 30 minutes or until doubled in size and risen to the tops of the tins. While the dough is rising, preheat the oven to 200°C (400°F, gas mark 6).

Uncover the loaves and bake them side-by-side in the centre of the oven for 15 minutes. Reduce the temperature to 190°C (375°F, gas mark 5) and cook for 30 minutes more, covering with greaseproof paper if overbrowning. Cook for a further 30 minutes or until they are deep golden and, when removed from the tin, sound hollow when tapped on the underside.

Stir the milk, water and caster sugar in a saucepan over a moderate heat until the sugar has dissolved, then bring to the boil. Glaze the tops of the loaves straight away with the syrup and turn out onto a wire rack. Allow to cool completely, then serve sliced and buttered.

INGREDIENTS

- 30G (1 OZ) FRESH YEAST OR 15G (½ OZ) DRIED YEAST PLUS 1 LEVEL TEASPOON CASTER SUGAR
- 425ML (¾ PINT) LUKEWARM MILK
- 675G (1½ LB) STRONG PLAIN FLOUR
- 1 LEVEL TEASPOON SALT
- 115G (4 OZ) BUTTER
- 60G (2 OZ) LARD
- 1 TABLESPOON GROUND MIXED SPICE
- 175G (6 OZ) DARK MUSCOVADO SUGAR
- 115G (4 OZ) EACH RAISINS AND SULTANAS
- 60G (2 OZ) EACH CURRANTS AND CHOPPED CANDIED PEEL
- 1 EGG, SIZE 2, BEATEN

FOR THE GLAZE

- 2 TABLESPOONS EACH MILK AND WATER
- 3 TABLESPOONS CASTER SUGAR

PREPARATION TIME: 30 MINUTES
RISING TIME: 1½ HOURS
COOKING TIME: 1¼ HOURS
MAKES TWO LOAVES

Fruit-filled, lightly spiced bara brith glows with its topping of warm syrup.

Eat one loaf fresh and freeze the other for another day.

A thick batter of flour, egg and milk forms the base for quick and delicious drop scones.

INGREDIENTS

Farl oatcakes
115g (4oz) medium oatmeal
⅛ level teaspoon bicarbonate of soda
Pinch of salt
2 teaspoons melted lard or bacon fat
3–4 tablespoons very hot water
Fine oatmeal for kneading
Preparation time: 10 minutes
Cooking time: approx 8 minutes
Makes eight oatcakes

Drop scones
225g (8oz) plain flour
½ level teaspoon bicarbonate of soda
1 level teaspoon cream of tartar
¼ level teaspoon salt
1 level tablespoon caster sugar
30g (1oz) butter or margarine
1 egg, size 2
Approx 285ml (½ pint) milk
Preparation time: 5 minutes
Cooking time: 12 minutes
Makes approx 20 scones

Griddle Cakes

Although griddle cooking was once the only method of making breads and scones, happily the art was not lost with the advent of the oven

FARL OATCAKES

Mix the oatmeal, bicarbonate of soda and salt in a bowl. Make a well in the centre, add the lard or bacon fat and enough hot water to mix to a soft but not sticky dough. Cover and leave to stand for about a minute.

Meanwhile, heat a griddle or thick frying pan over a moderate heat and grease lightly with lard. Put a little dough onto the griddle—it should cook without burning when the temperature is right.

Lightly knead the dough, on a surface dredged with fine oatmeal, until smooth. Then roll out thinly to a round about 23cm (9in) in diameter. Cut into eight triangular segments (or farls), lift them carefully onto the heated griddle and cook for about 8 minutes or until the edges of the farls start to curl upwards. Remove from the heat and serve warm, spread with butter and jam.

DROP SCONES

Sift the flour, bicarbonate of soda, cream of tartar, salt and caster sugar into a mixing bowl and rub in the butter or margarine. Make a well in the centre, then add the egg and two-thirds of the milk and beat until smooth. Gradually beat in the remaining milk so as to make a thick batter.

Heat a griddle or thick frying pan as for the farl oatcakes, then drop tablespoons of the batter onto the griddle and cook for 1–2 minutes or until the top appears to be dry and is covered all over with bubbles. Turn the scones over with a palette knife and cook on the other side for 1 minute.

Remove the scones from the heat and wrap them in a clean napkin or tea towel to keep warm while cooking the remainder. Serve warm, spread with butter and jam or honey.

Herb Soda Bread

To appreciate fully the magnificent flavour of the bread, eat it freshly baked

Preheat the oven to 200°c (400°f, gas mark 6). Sift the flours, salt and bicarbonate of soda into a mixing bowl, adding any bran that remains in the sieve, and rub in the butter. Add the onion, celery and herbs, mix well with the fingertips and make a well in the centre. Stir the lemon juice into the milk, pour into the dry ingredients and mix to form a soft but not sticky dough. On a well-floured surface, knead lightly into a smooth ball, then flatten slightly into a 20 cm (8 in) round.

Place on a baking tray lightly dusted with flour and, with a sharp knife, cut a deep cross into the dough to indicate four equal portions.

Brush with the milk, sprinkle with the sesame seeds and bake in the centre of the oven for 35–40 minutes until the loaf is well risen and golden brown and sounds hollow when tapped on the bottom. Remove from the tray and cool on a wire rack or, if you prefer a soft crust, wrap in a clean tea towel and leave to cool. Spread the bread with butter and serve with cheese, meat or fish paté.

Alternatively, the herbs, onion and celery can be omitted and a plain soda bread made instead. White soda bread can be made by using all plain flour. Buttermilk soda bread can be made by substituting 285 ml (½ pint) buttermilk for the milk and lemon juice.

Ingredients

- 225 g (8 oz) wholemeal flour
- 225 g (8 oz) strong plain white flour
- 2 level teaspoons salt
- 1 level teaspoon bicarbonate of soda
- 60 g (2 oz) butter
- 1 small onion, peeled and very finely chopped or grated
- 60 g (2 oz) celery, very finely chopped or grated
- 2 level tablespoons chopped fresh parsley
- 1 level tablespoon chopped fresh mint
- 1 tablespoon lemon juice
- 250 ml (9 fl oz) milk
- A little milk for brushing
- Sesame seeds for sprinkling

Preparation time: 25 minutes
Cooking time: 35–40 minutes
Makes one loaf

Excellent bread merits excellent cheese—a mature farmhouse variety makes a perfect partner.

Churning and moiling
The farmer's wife is making butter in exactly the same way as the Romans did—by 'agitating the milk in long vessels with narrow openings'. Buttermilk, the sour residue at the end of the operation, is traditionally served chilled as a summer drink.

Rubbed-in Cakes

These cakes keep well and are ideal to have at hand for unexpected guests

INGREDIENTS

CORNISH SAFFRON ROCK CAKES
- Pinch of saffron threads, soaked in 2 tablespoons milk for 30 minutes or overnight
- 225 g (8 oz) plain flour
- 1 level teaspoon baking powder
- 45 g (1½ oz) butter, cut into small cubes
- 45 g (1½ oz) lard, cut into small cubes
- 90 g (3¼ oz) granulated sugar
- 60 g (2 oz) sultanas
- 30 g (1 oz) chopped mixed peel
- 1 egg, size 2, beaten

Preparation time: 45 minutes
Cooking time: 15 minutes
Makes 12 cakes

IRISH BUTTERMILK CAKE
- 450 g (1 lb) plain flour
- 1 level teaspoon bicarbonate of soda
- 1 level teaspoon mixed spice
- ¼ level teaspoon salt
- 225 g (8 oz) butter, at room temperature
- 225 g (8 oz) soft light brown sugar
- 115 g (4 oz) sultanas
- 115 g (4 oz) currants
- 115 g (4 oz) ready-to-use dried apricots, roughly chopped
- 115 g (4 oz) glacé cherries, roughly chopped
- 285 ml (½ pint) buttermilk
- 1 tablespoon black treacle
- 1 tablespoon demerara sugar

Preparation time: 20 minutes
Cooking time: 1½–2 hours

CORNISH SAFFRON ROCK CAKES

PREHEAT the oven to 200°C (400°F, gas mark 6). Sift the flour and baking powder into a large mixing bowl, add the cubed butter and lard and rub into the flour until the mixture resembles breadcrumbs. Reserve 1 tablespoon of the sugar, then mix the remainder, and the sultanas and chopped mixed peel, into the rubbed-in mixture in the bowl.

Make a well in the centre of the mixture, put the egg and the saffron milk into the well and mix to form a stiff dough. Spoon 12 rocky heaps of the dough onto a greased baking tray, spacing them well apart. Bake in the centre of the oven for 10–15 minutes until well risen and golden brown. Transfer the cakes from the baking tray to a wire rack, sprinkle with the remaining sugar and leave to cool. When cold, store the rock cakes in an airtight container.

IRISH BUTTERMILK CAKE

Preheat the oven to 180°C (350°F, gas mark 4). Sift the flour, bicarbonate of soda, spice and salt into a large mixing bowl and rub in the butter until the mixture resembles breadcrumbs. Mix in the soft brown sugar, dried fruits and the cherries. Make a well in the centre, add the buttermilk and treacle and mix well.

Spoon the mixture into a greased and lined 20 cm (8 in) round, deep cake tin. Smooth the surface and sprinkle with the demerara sugar. Bake on the shelf below the centre of the oven for 2–2¼ hours or until risen, lightly browned and firm to the touch and when a skewer inserted into the centre comes out clean. If the top browns too quickly, cover with foil halfway through cooking. Leave the cake to cool in the tin for 1 hour, then transfer to a wire rack to cool completely. When cold, store in an airtight container.

Saffron and sultana-studded rock cakes and buttermilk cake flavoured with apricots, cherries and treacle make scrumptious tea-time treats.

Plain, fruity, treacly or cheesy, scones are constant winners on the tea table.

Scones

To enjoy them at their very best, eat the scones on the day they are made

BASIC SCONES

To MAKE basic scones, preheat the oven to 220°C (425°F, gas mark 7) and lightly flour a baking sheet.

Sift the flour, salt, baking powder and sugar into a bowl and rub in the butter. Add the buttermilk, milk or yoghurt and mix with a round-bladed knife, adding some extra milk if necessary, to make a soft, slightly sticky dough. Turn onto a lightly floured surface and knead gently for a few seconds until smooth. Roll out to 1.9 cm (¾ in) thick then, using a 5 cm (2 in) plain, round pastry cutter, stamp out as many rounds as possible and lay them on the baking sheet. Reknead and reroll the trimmings and cut out more rounds, making nine or ten in all.

Bake for 12–15 minutes until they are well risen, golden brown and sound hollow when tapped on the bottom. Transfer to a wire rack and leave to cool slightly, then serve warm spread with butter or cream and strawberry jam.

SULTANA AND CANDIED PEEL SCONES

Make as for basic scones, mixing in the fruit before adding the liquid.

TREACLE SCONES

Make as for basic scones, omitting the baking powder and sifting the mixed spice in with the flour. Add the melted butter and the syrup or treacle with the buttermilk, milk or yoghurt.

CHEESE SCONES

Make as for basic scones, omitting the caster sugar, and adding the grated cheese before the liquid. Sprinkle with a little cheese before baking.

SCONE ROUNDS

Roll out the dough to an 18 cm (7 in) round, put onto the baking sheet and mark into eight wedges.

Brush with milk, sprinkle with granulated sugar and bake for 15–20 minutes or until cooked.

INGREDIENTS

BASIC SCONES

225 G (8 OZ) SELF-RAISING FLOUR
PINCH OF SALT
1 LEVEL TEASPOON BAKING POWDER
30 G (1 OZ) CASTER SUGAR
60 G (2 OZ) BUTTER
150 ML (¼ PINT) BUTTERMILK, MILK OR NATURAL YOGHURT
APPROX 1–2 EXTRA TABLESPOONS MILK

SULTANA AND CANDIED PEEL SCONES

AS FOR BASIC SCONES, PLUS
60 G (2 OZ) SULTANAS
30 G (1 OZ) CHOPPED MIXED PEEL

TREACLE SCONES

225 G (8 OZ) SELF-RAISING FLOUR
PINCH OF SALT
½ LEVEL TEASPOON MIXED SPICE
30 G (1 OZ) CASTER SUGAR
30 G (1 OZ) BUTTER, MELTED WITH 1 LEVEL TABLESPOON GOLDEN SYRUP OR BLACK TREACLE
150 ML (¼ PINT) BUTTERMILK, MILK OR NATURAL YOGHURT

CHEESE SCONES

225 G (8 OZ) SELF-RAISING FLOUR
¼ LEVEL TEASPOON SALT
1 LEVEL TEASPOON BAKING POWDER
1 LEVEL TEASPOON ENGLISH MUSTARD POWDER
PINCH OF CAYENNE PEPPER
60 G (2 OZ) BUTTER
85 G (3 OZ) MATURE CHEDDAR CHEESE, GRATED
150 ML (¼ PINT) BUTTERMILK, MILK OR NATURAL YOGHURT, PLUS 1–2 TABLESPOONS MILK

PREPARATION TIME: 20 MINUTES
COOKING TIME: 15 MINUTES
MAKES NINE TO TEN SCONES

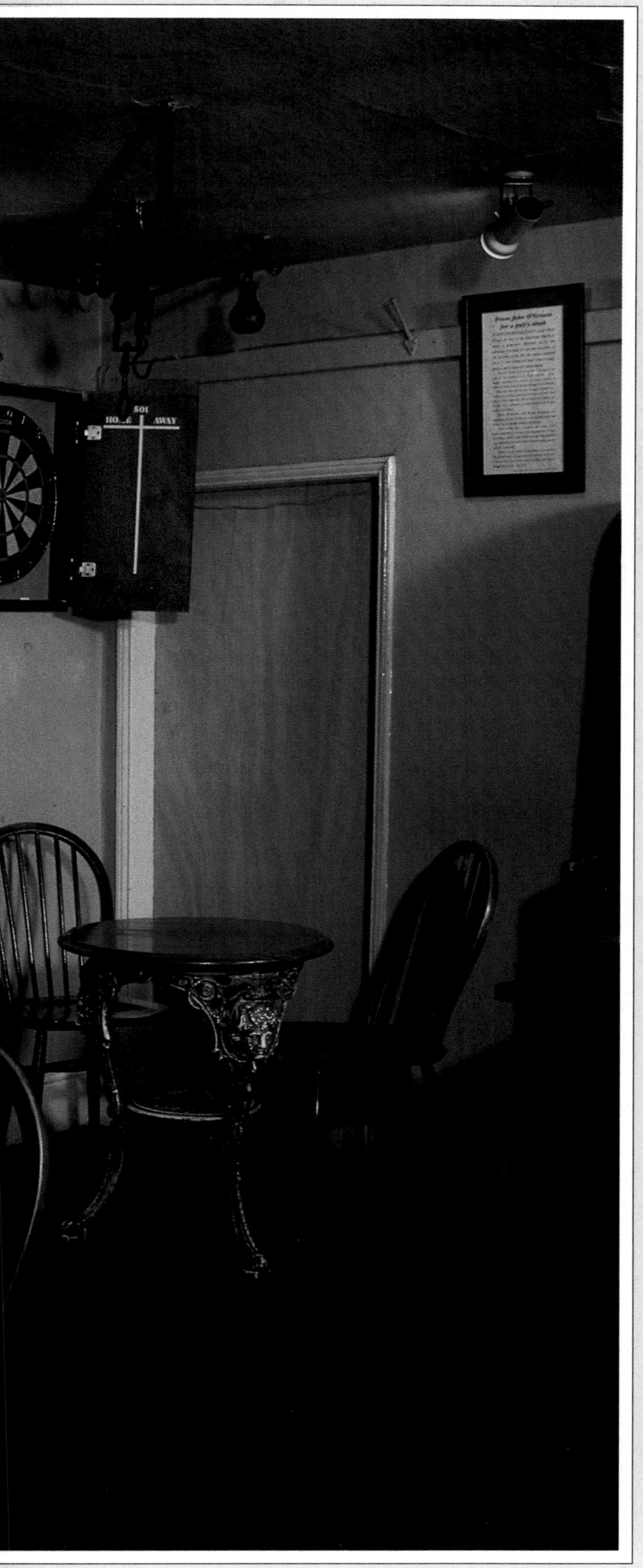

GOOD CHEER

Before the days of canned music and pressurised beer, there were pubs where the only sound was a cheerful buzz of conversation heard above the welcoming crackle of the fire. There, *Home-brewed Ale* was on tap and, if the landlord knew his business, favoured customers might be treated to *Country Wines*, made from *Rhubarb, Gooseberries* or *Parsnips*, and dispensed from china barrels. For the young there was *Ginger Beer* while for chilled wildfowlers there were always *Hot Toddies* and *Punches*, or a good pewter tankard of *Mulled Ale*.

Before starting to make the beer, ensure all the equipment to be used is thoroughly sterilised (see p. 439)

Traditional beer, brewed with hops, malt, sugar and yeast, is refreshing after hard physical slog.

Buckden Beer

This beer has few ingredients, is simple to brew and produces a 'hoppy' bitter with a reasonable strength

INGREDIENTS

60 G (2 OZ) GOLDING HOPS
900 G (2 LB) MALT EXTRACT
400 G (14 OZ) GRANULATED SUGAR
1 SACHET DRIED YEAST FOR BEER MAKING

PREPARATION TIME: 1 HOUR
STANDING AND MATURING TIME: 32 DAYS
MAKES 9 LITRES (2 GALLONS)

Boil 50 g (1¾ oz) of the hops in 1.15 litres (2 pints) of water for 15 minutes in a stainless steel or enamel saucepan.

Meanwhile, put the malt extract and 340 g (12 oz) of the sugar into a 13.5–18 litre (3–4 gallon) plastic brewing bin or clean, unused, white plastic dustbin. Strain the water from the hops into the bin and stir it until the sugar dissolves.

Return the hops to the saucepan, add another 1.15 litres (2 pints) of water and boil for 15 minutes. Strain the water into the bin. Repeat once more, then discard the hops. Top up to 9 litres (2 gallons) with cold water.

Allow the mixture (wort) to cool to 20°C (68°F), then add the yeast. Cover the brewing bin and leave to stand for two days, skimming the dirty froth from the wort on the second day. Stir and leave for another 24 hours, then skim and stir once again. Add the remaining hops, cover and leave for three days.

Siphon the wort equally into two sterilised demijohns, topping each demijohn up with cooled boiled water to make 4.5 litres (1 gallon). Fit the demijohns with corks and airlocks. Leave to stand for five days, during which time the wort will become clear and a heavy sediment will form on the bottom. The beer is now ready to be bottled.

Add 1 level teaspoon of the remaining sugar to each 570 ml (1 pint) sterilised beer bottle and siphon in the beer, taking care not to disturb the sediment in the bottom of the demijohns. Fill the bottles to within 2.5–5 cm (1–2 in) of the tops. Seal with crown corks or plastic seals and store in a warm place for one week, then move to a cooler place for two weeks.

Cool the beer to room temperature, 15°C (59°F), before serving. Open the bottles carefully and pour into glasses, taking care not to disturb any sediment which may lie at the bottom.

Ginger Beer

Made with pure, natural ingredients, this is the perfect pop for a children's party

Gently warm 1.15 litres (2 pints) of the water in a saucepan, remove from the heat and stir in the sugar until dissolved.

Blend the ginger, yeast and lemon juice with 1–2 tablespoons of water and stir into the sugar solution.

Pour into a sterilised demijohn, add the remaining water and shake gently. Fit with a sterilised cork and airlock, half fill the airlock chamber with cooled, boiled water and leave to ferment at room temperature for seven days.

Siphon the liquid into sterilised bottles (plastic or stone are best), taking care not to disturb the sediment. Add ½ level teaspoon of caster sugar to each 570 ml (1 pint), seal the bottles tightly and leave in a cold place for between 24 hours and seven days before drinking.

If using glass bottles, be sure to unscrew the tops or remove the corks daily to release any gases that may build up during fermentation and cause the bottles to explode.

INGREDIENTS

- 4.5 LITRES (1 GALLON) WATER
- 225 G (8 OZ) GRANULATED SUGAR
- 4 LEVEL TEASPOONS GROUND GINGER
- 1 LEVEL TABLESPOON DRIED YEAST OR 1 SACHET COLD WATER WINE YEAST
- STRAINED JUICE 1 LEMON
- 3½ LEVEL TEASPOONS CASTER SUGAR

PREPARATION TIME: 30 MINUTES
COOKING TIME: 5–10 MINUTES
FERMENTATION TIME: 8 DAYS
MAKES 4 LITRES (7 PINTS)

Fizzy and refreshing ginger beer tastes just like grandma used to make it.

Tuckshop days
William and the Outlaws, the creations of Richmal Crompton, were born at the age of 11 in 1922, and remained so for 47 years and through more than 350 adventures.

Country Wines

Whatever your preference—sweet or dry, red or white—these traditional country wines will transform an everyday meal into an occasion

INGREDIENTS

Elderberry & Blackberry Wine
- 450 g (1 lb) elderberries, stalks removed
- 900 g (2 lb) blackberries
- 250 g (9 oz) raisins, chopped
- 1 Campden tablet, crushed
- 900 g (2 lb) granulated sugar
- 1 level teaspoon pectic enzyme
- 1 level teaspoon citric acid
- 2 level teaspoons tartaric acid
- 2 level teaspoons yeast nutrient
- 1 sachet Burgundy wine yeast

Parsnip Wine
- 2.3 kg (5 lb) parsnips, scrubbed and diced
- 450 g (1 lb) sultanas, washed and chopped
- ½ level teaspoon tannin
- 1 level teaspoon pectic enzyme
- 2 level teaspoons citric acid
- 1 level teaspoon amylase
- 1 level teaspoon yeast nutrient
- Campden tablets
- 1 sachet dried yeast for wine making
- 675 g (1½ lb) granulated sugar

Tea Wine
- 3 level tablespoons scented tea leaves
- 1.4 kg (3 lb) granulated sugar
- 4 level teaspoons citric acid
- ½ level teaspoon ground ginger
- 340 g (12 oz) raisins or sultanas, chopped
- 1 tablespoon warm water
- 1 sachet dried yeast for wine making
- ½ level teaspoon yeast nutrient
- 1 slice white bread, toasted until well browned, but not burnt

Makes six 725 ml (1¼ pints) of each wine

ELDERBERRY & BLACKBERRY WINE

Wash the elderberries and blackberries and put them into a sterilised plastic bucket. Crush well, using a plastic potato masher, then add the raisins. Bring 2.8 litres (5 pints) of water to the boil, allow to cool for 2–3 minutes, then pour over the fruit and leave to cool. Stir in the Campden tablet, cover and leave to stand for 24 hours.

Bring 570 ml (1 pint) of water to the boil, remove from the heat, add the sugar and stir until dissolved, then add the pectic enzyme, citric acid, tartaric acid, yeast nutrient and yeast to the bucket. Stir well, cover and leave to ferment for five days, stirring daily.

Pour the fermented liquid into a nylon straining bag, drain thoroughly and discard the pulp. Pour the liquid into a demijohn, fit with a cork and airlock and leave to stand until 1.3 cm (½ in) of deposit appears in the bottom of the jar. Siphon into a clean, sterilised demijohn and make up to 4.5 litres (1 gallon) with cold water. Fit with a cork and airlock and allow to ferment out completely. When there are no more air bubbles in the airlock, bottle the wine.

PARSNIP WINE

Put the parsnips and sultanas into a sterilised plastic bucket and pour 3.4 litres (6 pints) of boiling water over them. Allow to cool, then stir in the tannin, pectic enzyme, citric acid, amylase, yeast nutrient and a crushed Campden tablet. Cover and leave to stand for 24 hours.

Add the yeast to the parsnip mixture, stir well and leave to ferment for two days, stirring occasionally.

Pour into a nylon straining bag and allow to drain thoroughly. Meanwhile, bring 570 ml (1 pint) of water to the boil, remove from the heat, add the sugar and stir until dissolved. Leave to cool.

Pour the parsnip liquid and sugar syrup into a demijohn and shake well. Fit with a cork and airlock and allow to ferment out completely until there are no more air bubbles in the airlock.

If a sediment forms on the bottom of the jar, siphon the wine off into another sterilised demijohn and add a crushed Campden tablet. Repeat this process, if necessary. Bottle the wine when it is clear and bright. Sweeten it if liked with non-fermentable (artificial) sugar.

TEA WINE

Put the tea leaves into a teapot or jug and add 1.15 litres (2 pints) of boiling water. Allow to cool, then strain into a sterilised plastic bucket. Add 2.3 litres (4 pints) of water with 900 g (2 lb) of the sugar and the citric acid. Stir until the sugar has dissolved, then add the ginger and the raisins or sultanas to the bucket.

In a small bowl, mix the warm water, yeast and yeast nutrient together to make a smooth cream, then spread over the slice of toast and float it on top of the tea, yeast side up. Cover the bucket with a clean cloth, tie it securely and leave to stand for 14 days without stirring.

Pour 285 ml (½ pint) of water into a saucepan and bring to the boil. Remove from the heat, add the remaining sugar, stirring until dissolved, then leave to cool.

Strain the tea mixture into a sterilised demijohn and add the sugar syrup. Fit the jar with a cork and airlock and allow to ferment out completely at room temperature until there are no more bubbles in the airlock. If a sediment forms on the bottom of the jar, siphon the wine off into another sterilised demijohn and refit with a cork and airlock. Should the cloudiness persist, add a wine-fining agent. Bottle when the wine is clear and bright. This is a sweet wine made in the traditional way.

Wine made with scented tea leaves, fruit from the hedgerows or parsnips from the garden tastes superb.

Mulled Drinks

Country folk have long held these warming, aromatic drinks in high regard as a means of warding off the colds and chills of winter

Ingredients

Wassail Bowl
- 6 red dessert apples, cored
- 12 cloves
- 225g (8oz) soft light brown sugar
- 570ml (1 pint) medium-dry sherry
- 15cm (6in) cinnamon stick, in 2 pieces
- 2.3 litres (4 pints) brown ale
- Thinly pared rind 2 lemons

Preparation time: 15 minutes
Cooking time: 30 minutes
Serves eight

Mulled Cider
- 1.15 litres (2 pints) pale, dry cider
- 1 level tablespoon caster sugar
- ¼ level teaspoon ground cinnamon
- 6 cloves
- 150ml (¼ pint) Calvados or brandy

Preparation time: 5 minutes
Cooking time: 5 minutes
Serves four

Mulled Ale
- 1.15 litres (2 pints) strong English ale
- 2 level tablespoons dark muscovado sugar
- Pinch of ground cloves
- Pinch of freshly grated nutmeg
- 1.3cm (½ in) piece fresh root ginger, peeled and cut into fine shreds
- 150ml (¼ pint) dark rum

Preparation time: 5 minutes
Cooking time: 7 minutes
Serves four

Wassail Bowl

Preheat the oven to 190°c (375°f, gas mark 5). Using a canelle, or other small, sharp knife, score each apple from top to bottom six times and stud with two cloves. Put the apples into a big casserole and spoon the sugar into the centre and over the top of each. Pour over the sherry, add the cinnamon stick and bake in the centre of the oven for 15–20 minutes until just beginning to soften and brown. Do not overcook, as the apples will break up.

Remove the casserole from the oven and then transfer the contents to a large saucepan; pour in the brown ale and add the lemon rind. Heat the ale on top of the cooker until it just begins to simmer, but do not allow it to boil. Serve immediately in heatproof glasses or punchcups.

Mulled Cider

Pour the cider into a large saucepan and add the caster sugar, ground cinnamon and the cloves. Stir over a low heat until the sugar has completely dissolved then bring almost to boiling point. Remove the pan from the heat, stir the Calvados or brandy into the spiced cider, and serve in heatproof glasses.

Mulled Ale

Pour the ale into a large saucepan and add the muscovado sugar, ground cloves, grated nutmeg and the shredded ginger. Heat gently until hot but not boiling, stirring occasionally until all the sugar has dissolved. Remove the saucepan from the heat and stir in the rum. Serve the mulled ale in heatproof glasses.

'Sugar and spice and all things nice' go into these hot, tempting drinks.

Between them, these two Celtic concoctions contain fruits and spices, oatmeal, honey and cream.

Waters of life
Most blended whiskies were evolved to capture the English market in the late 19th century. They are a mixture of patent still whisky with as many as 40 straight malts contributing to their individual characters.

Infused Whiskies

Each of these infusions has a special character and charm of its own

IRISH LIQUEUR

Pour the Irish whiskey into a large storage or preserving jar and add the raisins, sugar, cloves, cardamom pods, grated nutmeg, orange rind, and the saffron threads with their soaking water, if using.

Cover the jar tightly and store in a cool, dry, airy cupboard for two weeks, shaking daily.

Line a nylon sieve with a piece of scalded muslin, or a scalded tea towel, and strain the infused whiskey into a jug, then pour it into a clean bottle and seal well. Store the liqueur in a cool, dark cupboard until required.

ATHOLL BROSE

Put the oatmeal into a bowl, stir in the water and leave to stand for 1 hour. Place a nylon sieve over a small bowl, pour in the oatmeal mixture and leave to drain for 15 minutes, then press gently with the back of a spoon to extract the remaining liquid—but do not press the oatmeal through the sieve.

Stir the honey into the liquid until dissolved, then stir in the Scotch whisky and cream and whisk lightly with a fork until smooth. Serve immediately, or bottle and refrigerate. The brose will keep in the refrigerator for three or four days. Shake well before serving.

INGREDIENTS

IRISH LIQUEUR
725 ML (1¼ PINTS) IRISH WHISKEY
340 G (12 OZ) LARGE STONED RAISINS
100 G (3½ OZ) BROWN COFFEE-SUGAR CRYSTALS
½ LEVEL TEASPOON EACH CLOVES, CARDAMOM PODS AND FRESHLY GRATED NUTMEG
VERY THINLY PARED RIND OF 1 ORANGE (PREFERABLY SEVILLE)
LARGE PINCH SAFFRON THREADS (OPTIONAL), SOAKED IN 1 TABLESPOON BOILING WATER
PREPARATION TIME: 30 MINUTES
INFUSING TIME: 2 WEEKS
MAKES 725 ML (APPROX 1¼ PINTS)

ATHOLL BROSE
115 G (4 OZ) MEDIUM OATMEAL
285 ML (½ PINT) WATER
4 TABLESPOONS CLEAR HEATHER HONEY
285 ML (½ PINT) SCOTCH WHISKY
200 ML (7 FL OZ) SINGLE CREAM
PREPARATION TIME: 10 MINUTES
STANDING TIME: 1¼ HOURS
MAKES 725 ML (APPROX 1¼ PINTS)

Don't let the leaves for the tea punch infuse longer than 10 minutes, otherwise it will taste too strong.

Sip Irish coffee through whipped cream and tea punch with rum through orange and lemon slices.

Hot Toddies

These toddies are guaranteed to suffuse your guests with a warm glow at the end of a special meal

INGREDIENTS

Irish Coffee

- 3 level tablespoons ground coffee, freshly ground if possible
- 425 ml (3/4 pint) water
- 1 small orange
- 1 small lemon
- 3 whole cloves
- 2.5 cm (1 in) cinnamon stick
- 2 level teaspoons demerara sugar
- 150 ml (1/4 pint) Irish whiskey
- 1 level tablespoon caster sugar
- 115 ml (4 fl oz) double cream, whipped to soft peaks

Preparation time: 10 minutes
Cooking time: 10 minutes
Serves two

Hot Tea Punch

- 5 level teaspoons English breakfast tea leaves
- 570 ml (1 pint) boiling water
- 2 large oranges
- 1 large lemon
- 1 tablespoon clear honey
- 15 g (1/2 oz) preserved ginger in syrup, finely sliced, plus 2 teaspoons syrup from jar
- 285 ml (1/2 pint) dark rum
- 285 ml (1/2 pint) freshly squeezed orange juice
- 150 ml (1/4 pint) ginger wine

Preparation time: 15 minutes
Cooking time: 5 minutes
Serves four

IRISH COFFEE

Put the ground coffee into a large jug or cafetière. Bring the water to boil, allow to stand for 20 seconds, then pour onto the coffee. Cover the jug or cafetière and then leave it to infuse for 10 minutes. Meanwhile, peel the orange and lemon, taking care not to remove the white pith. Put the peel into a saucepan with the cloves, cinnamon and demerara sugar and cook over a very low heat, stirring occasionally, until the sugar has just melted.

Add the whiskey to the spice mixture, remove from the heat and ignite. Swirl the pan gently until the flames die out. Return the pan to the heat and strain the coffee into it. (If using a jug, strain the coffee through a fine coffee strainer or a sieve lined with kitchen paper.) Heat very gently in the pan for 5 minutes.

In the meantime, cut the lemon in half and rub a cut side carefully round the rims of two heatproof 250 ml (9 fl oz) serving glasses. Dip the rim of each glass into the caster sugar, and shake gently to remove the excess. Strain the coffee into the glasses, stir well and top with the whipped cream. Serve immediately.

HOT TEA PUNCH

Put the tea leaves into a warmed teapot, pour over the boiling water, cover and leave the tea to infuse for 10 minutes. Meanwhile, cut the oranges and lemon into thin slices, then cut each slice in half and remove the pips. Place the slices in four large, warmed, heatproof glasses. Put the honey, ginger, ginger syrup, rum, orange juice and ginger wine into a large, stainless steel or enamel saucepan and heat gently. Strain the tea through a fine strainer into the saucepan and heat until hot, but not boiling. Pour the mixture into the glasses and serve.

Hot Punches

Either of these brews will really pack a punch and put people in party mood

INGREDIENTS

Bishop's Punch

- 1 large lemon
- 2 large, unwaxed oranges, Seville when available
- 6 cloves
- 4 sugar cubes
- 2.5 cm (1 in) cinnamon stick
- 6 allspice berries
- 2.5 cm (1 in) fresh root ginger, peeled and coarsely grated
- 1.3 cm (½ in) mace blade
- 570 ml (1 pint) claret
- 75 cl bottle ruby port
- 1 whole nutmeg for grating

Preparation time: 25 minutes
Cooking time: 20 minutes
Serves four to six

Christmas Cup

- Thinly pared rinds 1 large lemon and 1 large orange, cut into very fine shreds
- 1½ level tablespoons caster sugar
- ½ level teaspoon ground cinnamon
- ¼ level teaspoon ground mace
- 285 ml (½ pint) each brandy and white rum
- 570 ml (1 pint) boiling water
- Strained juice 1 large lemon and 1 large orange
- 1 medium pineapple, peeled and cut into small pieces
- 725 ml (1¼ pints) bought country apricot wine

Preparation time: 10 minutes
Cooking time: 5 minutes
Serves eight

BISHOP'S PUNCH

Cut the lemon and one of the oranges into quarters, then stud the skins of three of the lemon quarters and three of the orange quarters each with a clove. Rub the sugar cubes over the remaining whole orange to extract the oil, then squeeze out and strain the juice. Set the sugar cubes and orange juice aside.

Preheat the grill to high. Line the grill pan with foil and cook the clove-studded fruit and the remaining pieces of orange and lemon for 10 minutes, turning occasionally, until soft and lightly browned.

Put the cinnamon stick, allspice, ginger and mace into a large saucepan with the claret, bring to the boil and boil until reduced by half.

Pour the port into a large, flameproof casserole, bring to the boil, then remove the pan from the heat. Ignite the port and allow it to burn for 1 minute, then cover the pan with a lid to extinguish the flames. Add the fruit, claret mixture, sugar cubes and orange juice to the port and heat gently, stirring until the sugar has dissolved. Do not allow the port to boil. Serve hot in punchcups or in heat-proof glasses.

CHRISTMAS CUP

Put the lemon and orange shreds, sugar, cinnamon, mace, brandy, rum and boiling water into a saucepan. Heat gently until the sugar has dissolved and the liquid is almost boiling.

Pour the lemon and orange juice into a warm, heatproof punchbowl and add the pineapple pieces. Strain the spiced liquid into the bowl and stir in the apricot wine. Put pineapple pieces into each punchcup before serving.

Hot wine or spirits, mingled with spices and fruit, are always irresistible.

Mead

This mead, with about 15 per cent alcohol content, can be drunk after six months, but will improve if kept for at least a year

INGREDIENTS

- 1.8 kg (4 lb) English honey, clear or set
- 4 litres (7 pints) water
- 3 level teaspoons citric acid
- 1 level teaspoon tannin
- 1 level teaspoon pectic enzyme
- 2 level teaspoons yeast nutrient
- 1 sachet dried yeast for wine making
- Campden tablets

Makes six 75 cl bottles

Pour the honey and water into a large saucepan, bring to the boil and boil gently for 20 minutes. Skim any scum as it appears on the surface.

Remove the pan from the heat and allow to cool, then pour the honeyed water into a demijohn. Add the citric acid, tannin, pectic enzyme, yeast nutrient and yeast to the demijohn, fit it with a cork and airlock and leave it to ferment out completely until there are no more air bubbles in the airlock.

If a sediment forms on the bottom of the jar during fermentation, siphon the mead into another demijohn, taking care not to disturb the sediment. Add a crushed Campden tablet and refit with a cork and airlock. Repeat if necessary.

Mature the mead in a demijohn fitted with a cork and airlock. Check the airlock frequently to make sure that it does not dry out and top up with cooled, boiled water as necessary. Bottle the mead when fully matured.

Pooh's first bow
When A.A. Milne introduces the reader to Winnie-the-Pooh, the bear is trying to steal honey from a bees' nest in the treetops. He rolls in mud and, attached to a blue balloon, sails up, hoping the bees see him as a small black cloud in a blue sky. To allay suspicion he hums, 'Every little cloud *always* sings aloud'. But the bees are unconvinced…

Honey and water are fermented to make a smooth alcoholic drink with a venerable history.

The fruits impart a delicious, mellow flavour and a rich, jewel-like colour to the brandies.

Infused Brandies

The brandies are ready to drink straightaway, but will keep well for several years

PINEAPPLE BRANDY

Put the pineapple slices into a bowl and sprinkle over 115g (4oz) of the caster sugar. Cover the bowl and leave it to macerate for 24 hours.

Remove and reserve three slices of the pineapple; then, using a potato masher, crush the remainder thoroughly. Strain the juice through a nylon sieve into a measuring jug.

Measure the pineapple juice—there should be about 285ml (½ pint)—and pour it into a clean storage or preserving jar. Add an equal amount of brandy and for every 285ml (½ pint) of brandy add 60g (2oz) sugar.

Cut the reserved pineapple slices in half and add them to the jar. Cover tightly and store in a cool, dark, airy cupboard for three weeks, shaking frequently.

Strain the brandy through a sieve lined with scalded muslin, then pour into a clean bottle and seal well.

CHERRY BRANDY

Put the cherries into a large, clean storage or preserving jar and add the sugar, fruit kernels or almonds, and the cinnamon stick and brandy. Cover tightly and leave to infuse in a cool, dark, airy cupboard for at least three months, shaking the bottle occasionally. Strain and bottle as for pineapple brandy.

ANGELICA RATAFIA

Put the sugar and water into a saucepan and stir over a gentle heat until the sugar has dissolved. Bring to the boil, remove the pan from the heat and stand aside until the syrup is cold.

Put the angelica into a clean storage or preserving jar, add the cloves and cinnamon stick and pour in the brandy and the cold syrup. Cover the jar tightly and leave the brandy to infuse in a cool, dark, airy cupboard for two months. Strain and bottle as for pineapple brandy.

INGREDIENTS

PINEAPPLE BRANDY

- 1 large pineapple, approx 1.1kg (2½lb), leaves, skin and brown 'eyes' removed, cut into slices, core removed
- Approx 175g (6oz) caster sugar
- Approx 285ml (½ pint) brandy

Preparation time: 30 minutes plus 24 hours macerating
Infusing time: 3 weeks
Makes 500ml (18fl oz)

CHERRY BRANDY

- 675g (1½lb) dark red cherries, washed and stoned
- 150g (5oz) brown coffee-sugar crystals
- 12 peach, plum, or apricot kernels, or blanched almonds split in half
- 15cm (6in) cinnamon stick
- 570ml (1 pint) brandy

Preparation time: 30 minutes
Infusing time: 3 months
Makes 725ml (1¼ pints)

ANGELICA RATAFIA

- 225g (8oz) sugar
- 150ml (¼ pint) water
- 60g (2oz) candied angelica
- ½ level teaspoon cloves
- 7.5cm (3in) cinnamon stick
- 570ml (1 pint) brandy

Preparation time: 30 minutes
Cooking time: 5 minutes
Infusing time: 2 months
Makes 725ml (1¼ pints)

Pleasing colours and excellent flavours characterise homemade rhubarb, gooseberry and cherry wines.

Fruit Wines

What better to accompany a good home-cooked meal than a fine wine made with fruits from your garden

INGREDIENTS

Rhubarb wine

- 2.7 kg (6 lb) frozen rhubarb
- 800 g (1¾ lb) granulated sugar
- 1 litre (1¾ pints) white grape juice
- 1 level teaspoon pectic enzyme
- 1 level teaspoon yeast nutrient
- 1 sachet dried yeast for wine making

Gooseberry wine

- 1 kg (2 lb 3 oz) frozen gooseberries
- 1 level teaspoon pectic enzyme
- 675 g (1½ lb) granulated sugar
- 1 litre (1¾ pints) white grape juice
- 1 level teaspoon yeast nutrient
- 1 sachet dried yeast for wine making
- 1 Campden tablet

Cherry wine

- 1.4 kg (3 lb) ripe cherries, stalks removed, washed
- 450 g (1 lb) sultanas, washed, dried and chopped
- 2 level teaspoons citric acid
- 1 level teaspoon grape tannin
- 1 level teaspoon pectic enzyme
- 1 level teaspoon yeast nutrient
- Campden tablets
- 1 sachet dried yeast for wine making
- 900 g (2 lb) granulated sugar

Makes six 725 ml (1¼ pints) of each wine

RHUBARB WINE

Thaw the rhubarb in a covered pan until it is very soft and the juice flows readily, then pour it into a bowl and crush it well with a potato masher to extract all the juice. Drain the juice from the crushed rhubarb through a nylon straining bag, then discard the pulp.

Meanwhile, bring 570 ml (1 pint) of water to the boil, add the sugar and stir until dissolved. Pour the rhubarb juice and sugar syrup into a demijohn, then add the grape juice, pectic enzyme, yeast nutrient and the dried yeast. Top up to the shoulder of the jar, leaving a 1.15 litre (2 pint) headspace.

Plug the neck of the jar with cotton wool and leave to ferment for three days, then top the jar up to the neck with more cold water. Fit with a cork and airlock and allow to ferment out. When there are no more air bubbles in the airlock, the wine can be bottled.

For a medium-dry wine, add 115 g (4 oz) nonfermentable (artificial) sugar before bottling. For a sweeter wine, add sugar, 15 g (½ oz) at a time, until the required sweetness is reached.

GOOSEBERRY WINE

Put the gooseberries into a sterilised plastic bucket or big bowl. Bring 1.15 litres (2 pints) of water to the boil, pour over the gooseberries and leave to stand until they soften. Using a potato masher, crush the gooseberries thoroughly. Add the pectic enzyme, cover the bucket or bowl and leave to stand for 4–6 hours.

Pour the gooseberry mixture into a nylon straining bag and press out the juice. Meanwhile, bring 285 ml (½ pint) of water to the boil, add the sugar and stir until dissolved.

Pour the gooseberry juice into a demijohn and add the sugar syrup, grape juice, yeast nutrient and the yeast. Pour in sufficient cold water to top the jar up to the shoulder, leaving a 1.15 litre (2 pint) headspace. Plug the top of the jar with cotton wool and leave it to ferment for three days, then top up the jar to the neck with cold water. Fit with a cork and airlock and leave to ferment out completely. Siphon the wine into a clean demijohn, add the crushed Campden tablet and top up to the neck with cold water. Cork and store for at least six weeks before bottling.

CHERRY WINE

Use black cherries, or a mixture of varieties, and buy them when they are plentiful and cheap.

Put the prepared cherries into a sterilised bucket and crush them well with a potato masher. Add the chopped sultanas and 3.4 litres (6 pints) of water, then stir in the citric acid, grape tannin, pectic enzyme, yeast nutrient and a crushed Campden tablet. Cover the bucket and leave to stand for 24 hours, stirring the mixture occasionally, then add the yeast to the bucket and leave to ferment for three or four days.

Pour the fermented cherry mixture into a nylon straining bag and leave it to drain thoroughly. In the meantime, bring 570 ml (1 pint) of water to the boil, add the sugar and stir until it has dissolved, then leave it to cool.

Pour the cherry liquid and the cooled sugar syrup into a demijohn. Fit with a cork and airlock and allow to ferment out completely, at a room temperature of about 18°C (65°F), until there are no more air bubbles in the airlock.

If a sediment forms on the bottom of the jar, siphon the wine off into another sterilised demijohn and add a crushed Campden tablet. Repeat this process, if necessary, until the wine appears clear and bright. It is then ready to be bottled.

This is a dry table wine. If a sweeter wine is preferred, sweeten when bottling with a nonfermentable (artificial) sugar.

Non-alcoholic Drinks

Less sweet and heavy than most shop-bought varieties, homemade lemon barley water and lemonade are free from artificial colours and flavours

INGREDIENTS

LEMON BARLEY WATER
115G (4OZ) PEARL BARLEY
60G (2OZ) SUGAR CUBES
2 LEMONS, WASHED
1.15 LITRES (2 PINTS) BOILING WATER
ICE CUBES AND SLICES OF LEMON FOR SERVING
PREPARATION TIME: 20 MINUTES
COOKING TIME: 5 MINUTES
COOLING AND CHILLING TIME: 4 HOURS
SERVES FOUR

OLD-FASHIONED LEMONADE
9 LARGE LEMONS, WASHED
115G (4OZ) CASTER SUGAR
1.4 LITRES (2½ PINTS) BOILING WATER
ICE CUBES AND MINT LEAVES FOR SERVING
PREPARATION TIME: 20 MINUTES
STANDING AND CHILLING TIME: 2½ HOURS
SERVES EIGHT

LEMON BARLEY WATER

PUT the pearl barley into a sieve, rinse under cold, running water and drain well. Tip the rinsed barley into a saucepan, cover with cold water and bring to the boil, then reduce the heat and cook gently for 5 minutes. Pour the barley back into the sieve and rinse again.

Put the cooked barley into a large jug or bowl. Rub each sugar cube over the skins of the lemons to extract the oils, then add the cubes to the jug or bowl.

Pour in the boiling water and stir until the sugar has dissolved. Cover the jug or bowl with a clean tea towel and leave to infuse for 3 hours or until cold.

Squeeze the juice from both lemons, add it to the barley water and strain through a nylon sieve into a serving jug. Cover the jug and chill for 1 hour. Put several ice cubes and one or two lemon slices into each of four tall glasses, pour in the lemon barley water and serve.

LEMONADE

Pare the rinds from the lemons, using a vegetable peeler. Take care to avoid the white pith. Squeeze out and strain the juice to make 425ml (¾ pint).

Put the lemon rind into a large, heat-proof bowl, add the sugar and the boiling water. Stir until the sugar dissolves, then cover and leave to stand for 30 minutes.

Strain the lemon liquid into a jug and stir in the lemon juice. Cover the jug and refrigerate for about 2 hours, until the lemonade is well chilled.

Put several ice cubes into tall glasses, pour in the lemonade and decorate with the mint leaves. Alternatively, put a large block of ice into a serving jug, add some lemon slices, pour in the lemonade and decorate with mint.

The lemonade will keep in the refrigerator for up to a week, but do not add ice to the jug before storing as this will dilute the flavour.

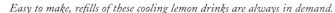

Easy to make, refills of these cooling lemon drinks are always in demand.

DISTANT SUMMERS
Prewar tennis parties were flavoured with lemonade, scented by lime trees and bright with laughter and romance. Spirit of the era was John Betjeman's dashing sportsgirl, Joan Hunter Dunn, 'furnish'd and burnish'd by Aldershot sun'.

Citrus, summer and exotic fruits flavour this trio of cool, alcoholic drinks.

Cold Cups

These fruity and refreshing cups will revive you on hot, sultry days

VICTORIAN SHERBET PUNCH

Dissolve the granulated sugar in 150 ml (¼ pint) of the water, stirring over a moderate heat, then boil for 2 minutes. Remove from the heat, stir in the remaining water and the lemon rind and juice and chill.

Strain the mixture into a bowl and freeze for 3–4 hours, whisking every 30 minutes until softly frozen. Whisk in the rum and refreeze, then whisk in the brandy and freeze until ready to serve.

Whisk the egg white until it will hold a soft peak, then whisk in the icing sugar. Blend the whisked mixture smoothly into the punch, pour into chilled glasses and serve immediately.

SHERRY COBBLER

Put the crushed ice cubes into a large serving jug and pour in the sherry. Add the icing sugar and mix well together. Pour in the soda water, add the orange slices, redcurrant sprigs and mint sprigs. Stir again, then pour into glasses and serve immediately.

STRAWBERRY CIDER CUP

Put 340 g (12 oz) of the strawberries into the bowl of a food processor. Add the Cointreau, caster sugar and orange juice and blend until smooth, then pass the purée through a nylon sieve into a bowl. Cover the bowl and chill in the refrigerator for 2 hours. Alternatively, mash the strawberries with the Cointreau, caster sugar and orange juice, chill for 2 hours, then pass the mixture through a nylon sieve into a bowl.

Add the passion fruit flesh and juice to the strawberry mixture and stir in the cider. Put crushed ice into a punchbowl or large serving jug and pour in the cider cup. Slice the remaining strawberries and add them to the jug. Decorate with the orange slices and mint before serving.

INGREDIENTS

VICTORIAN SHERBET PUNCH

225 G (8 OZ) GRANULATED SUGAR
285 ML (½ PINT) WATER
FINELY GRATED RIND 1 LEMON
STRAINED JUICE 3 LEMONS
115 ML (4 FL OZ) RUM, CHILLED
115 ML (4 FL OZ) BRANDY, CHILLED
1 EGG WHITE, SIZE 1
45 G (1½ OZ) ICING SUGAR, SIFTED

PREPARATION TIME: 10 MINUTES
COOKING TIME: 5 MINUTES
FREEZING TIME: 3–4 HOURS
SERVES FOUR TO SIX

SHERRY COBBLER

12 ICE CUBES, CRUSHED
570 ML (1 PINT) MEDIUM-DRY SHERRY
2 LEVEL TABLESPOONS ICING SUGAR
APPROX 285 ML (½ PINT) SODA WATER, CHILLED
4 SLICES ORANGE, HALVED
8 SMALL REDCURRANT SPRIGS, FROZEN (OPTIONAL)
4 MINT SPRIGS

PREPARATION TIME: 10 MINUTES
SERVES FOUR

STRAWBERRY CIDER CUP

450 G (1 LB) STRAWBERRIES, WASHED AND HULLED
30 G (1 OZ) CASTER SUGAR
150 ML (¼ PINT) COINTREAU
STRAINED JUICE 1 LARGE ORANGE
2 PASSION FRUITS, HALVED, FLESH AND JUICE SCOOPED OUT
1 LITRE (1¾ PINTS) VINTAGE CIDER, CHILLED
12 ICE CUBES, CRUSHED
3 SLICES ORANGE, HALVED
FRESH MINT SPRIGS

PREPARATION TIME: 15 MINUTES
CHILLING TIME: 2 HOURS
SERVES SIX

JAMS, PICKLES & PRESERVES

Yesteryear's country kitchens were armouries of vast iron pots and pans, measuring jugs and mixing bowls, kettles and ladles—all the equipment that was needed to make a large household independent of the outside world. From them, through the seasons, emerged the *Bottled Fruits* and the *Pickled Walnuts*, *Beetroot* and *Cabbage*, the sweet *Jams, Jellies* and *Syrups*, the *Pickled Eggs*... summer's plenty preserved to offset winter's shortage. But there were small, lovingly made luxuries too, such as *Relishes*, or the *Fruits Preserved in Brandy* or *Rum* for very special presents and occasions.

INGREDIENTS

- 1.1 kg (2½ lb) small carrots, peeled and thinly sliced
- 1.1 kg (2½ lb) caster sugar
- Finely grated rind and strained juice 2 lemons
- Finely grated rind and strained juice 1 small orange

Preparation time: 1 hour
Cooking time: 1 hour
Makes approx 1.4 kg (3 lb)

Carrot Jam

This unusual jam is delicious spread on scones or croissants, or as a sponge cake filling with whipped cream

Put the carrots into a large saucepan and add just enough water to cover. Bring to the boil and cook for 15–20 minutes, or until soft. Strain off and reserve the cooking water.

Purée the carrots with 150 ml (¼ pint) of the reserved cooking water in a food processor, then return to the pan. Pour a further 150 ml (¼ pint) of the reserved water into a separate pan and add the sugar. Stir over a low heat until dissolved, brushing down the sides of the pan with hot water to keep it free of sugar crystals.

Add the sugar syrup to the carrot purée and stir in the lemon and orange rinds and the juice. Bring to the boil over a low heat, stirring occasionally, then boil rapidly for 10 minutes. Remove the pan from the heat and test for a set (see p.438). If necessary, boil the jam for a further 5 minutes and test again until setting point is reached.

Pour the jam into clean, warm jars and cover immediately with waxed paper discs and cellophane covers. Label when cool and store in a cool, dry, airy cupboard.

Jammed with health
If soft and dried fruits were scarce during the war, carrots were not, and Dr Carrot, a creation of the Ministry of Food, was swift to point out their virtues. Not all his recipes were successful, but his carrot jam, even without citrus fruit, won at least a measure of approval.

A hint of orange and lemon in the jam makes it a tangy breakfast partner.

Pears, peaches or lemons can all be pickled perfectly in richly spiced vinegar.

Pickled Fruits

Serve these sharply flavoured pickled fruits with hot curries or cold meats

INGREDIENTS

PICKLED PEARS OR PEACHES

- THINLY PARED RIND AND JUICE OF 1 SMALL LEMON
- 2 LEVEL TEASPOONS CLOVES
- 2 LEVEL TEASPOONS ALLSPICE BERRIES
- 2 CINNAMON STICKS, EACH 5 CM (2 IN) LONG
- 1 SMALL PIECE DRIED ROOT GINGER, BRUISED
- 1 LITRE (1¾ PINTS) WHITE WINE VINEGAR OR DISTILLED MALT VINEGAR
- 150 ML (¼ PINT) WATER
- 1 KG (2 LB 3 OZ) CASTER SUGAR
- 2.3 KG (5 LB) FIRM WILLIAMS PEARS, PEELED, HALVED AND CORED, OR 1.8 KG (4 LB) RIPE BUT FIRM PEACHES, HALVED, SKINNED AND STONED

PREPARATION TIME: 1 HOUR
COOKING TIME: 45 MINUTES
STANDING TIME: 3 DAYS
FILLS APPROX 3 X 500 ML (18 FL OZ) OR 3 X 450 G (1 LB) JARS

PICKLED LEMONS

- 225 G (8 OZ) SALT
- 2.3 LITRES (4 PINTS) WATER
- 12 UNWAXED, THIN-SKINNED LEMONS, WELL WASHED, HALVED, PIPS REMOVED
- 1.7 LITRES (3 PINTS) DISTILLED MALT VINEGAR
- 30 G (1 OZ) WHITE MUSTARD SEEDS
- 30 G (1 OZ) DRIED ROOT GINGER, BRUISED
- 15 G (½ OZ) CLOVES
- 8 G (¼ OZ) MACE BLADES
- 8 G (¼ OZ) DRIED RED CHILLIES

PREPARATION TIME: 40 MINUTES
STANDING TIME: 6 DAYS
COOKING TIME: 20 MINUTES
FILLS APPROX 6 X 500 ML (18 FL OZ) OR 6 X 450 G (1 LB) JARS

PICKLED PEARS OR PEACHES

Tie the lemon rind and spices in a small square of muslin. Pour the vinegar and the water into a preserving pan, add the lemon juice, spices and sugar and stir over a moderate heat until the sugar has dissolved. Add the fruit to the syrup and simmer for 15 minutes or until just tender. Using a slotted spoon, transfer the fruit to a colander, set over a large bowl, to drain. Discard the bag of spices.

Boil the syrup for 15 minutes or until reduced by about a third and slightly thickened. Pack the fruit in warmed jars and cover with the syrup. Cover immediately with vinegarproof lids and seal tightly. Refrigerate any leftover syrup.

After three days, open the jars, pour the syrup into a saucepan and add any reserved syrup. Bring to the boil, boil for 3 minutes, then pour back over pears, cover and seal immediately. Label and store in a cool, dark, airy cupboard for at least a month before using.

PICKLED LEMONS

Dissolve the salt in the cold water in a large bowl, add the lemon halves and place a clean plate on top of them to keep them submerged in the salted water. Cover the bowl and leave to stand for six days, stirring daily.

On the seventh day, rinse and drain the lemons. Put them into a saucepan, add enough boiling water to cover, and boil for 15 minutes. Pour into a colander, rinse under cold water, and drain well.

Meanwhile, pour the vinegar into a saucepan, add the spices, bring to the boil and boil for 3 minutes. Remove the pan from the heat and strain the vinegar through a sieve lined with muslin or a clean tea towel, into a heatproof jug.

Pack the lemons into clean, warm jars and pour the hot vinegar over them. Cover the jars immediately with vinegar-proof lids. When the pickle is cold, label the jars and store in a cool, dry, airy cupboard for three months before using.

Many people really like beetroot better when it is transformed into choice chutney, and the same goes for marrow and green tomatoes.

Vegetable Chutneys

These appetising chutneys improve with keeping and make good use of unripe or misshapen garden vegetables

GREEN TOMATO CHUTNEY

Halve small or medium tomatoes, cut larger ones into quarters. Peel, core and slice the apples and chop the onions. Put all the vegetables into a large saucepan or preserving pan with the vinegar and bring to the boil, then reduce the heat and cook gently for 15 minutes.

Stir in the sultanas, demerara sugar, ground ginger, and the salt and cayenne pepper and continue simmering for a further 1½–2 hours or until the mixture is thick and leaves a clear trail when a wooden spoon is drawn slowly across the bottom of the pan.

Spoon the chutney into clean, warm jars and cover them immediately with vinegarproof covers. When the chutney is cold, label the jars and store them in a cool, dry, airy cupboard for two to three months to allow the chutney to mature and mellow before using.

To make the chutney with ripe tomatoes, use 1.4 kg (3 lb) ripe tomatoes. Put them into a large bowl, cover with boiling water, leave to stand for 1 minute, then drain and peel off the skins. Proceed as for green tomato chutney, including or omitting the sultanas as preferred.

MARROW AND TOMATO CHUTNEY

Peel the marrow, cut it in half and scoop out and discard the seeds. Cut the flesh into 1.3 cm (½ in) pieces and put them into a bowl in layers, sprinkling each layer with some of the salt. Cover the bowl and stand aside for 24 hours.

The next day, rinse the salted marrow under cold running water, drain well and set aside. Skin and chop the tomatoes, peel and chop the onions and peel, core and slice the apples. Put them into a large preserving pan with the malt vinegar, stir well, bring to the boil over a moderate heat, then reduce the heat and cook gently for 30 minutes.

Add the dates, brown sugar, mustard seeds, ginger, allspice, nutmeg and marrow to the pan. Stir well and bring to the boil over a moderate heat, then reduce the heat and simmer for 1½ hours, stirring frequently, until the chutney is thick and leaves a clear trail when a wooden spoon is drawn slowly across the bottom of the pan. Take care not to cook the chutney too quickly, as it will stick to the bottom of the pan.

Spoon into clean, warm jars and cover immediately with vinegarproof lids. When the chutney is cold, label the jars and store them in a cool, dark, airy cupboard for two to three months to allow the chutney to mature before eating.

This chutney can also be made with courgettes, pumpkin or squash. Peel and deseed the pumpkin or squash as for the marrow. Courgettes will need only to be trimmed before being cut into pieces.

BEETROOT CHUTNEY

Trim the beetroot, leaving 2.5 cm (1 in) of stalk and root attached. Put into a saucepan and simmer for 1½–2 hours or until tender, then drain and allow to cool. Remove the skin, stalks and roots, cut into 1.3 cm (½ in) dice and set aside.

Peel and chop the onions, peel, core and slice the apples, finely grate the rind from the lemon and squeeze out the juice. Put the onions, apples, lemon rind and juice, vinegar, ginger, salt, raisins and sugar into a large, heavy-based saucepan or preserving pan and bring to the boil. Reduce the heat and simmer for 30 minutes, then add the beetroot and simmer for 1 hour more or until the chutney is thick and all excess liquid has evaporated.

Spoon into clean, warm jars and cover them immediately with vinegarproof lids. When the chutney is cold, label the jars and store in a cool, dark cupboard for two to three months before using.

INGREDIENTS

Green Tomato Chutney
- 900 g (2 lb) green tomatoes
- 225 g (8 oz) cooking apples
- 675 g (1½ lb) onions, peeled
- 570 ml (1 pint) malt vinegar
- 225 g (8 oz) sultanas
- 450 g (1 lb) demerara sugar
- 2 level teaspoons ground ginger
- 1 level teaspoon salt
- ¼ level teaspoon cayenne pepper

Preparation time: 25 minutes
Cooking time: 1½–2 hours
Makes approx 1.1 kg (2½ lb)

Marrow and Tomato Chutney
- 1.4 kg (3 lb) marrow
- 85 g (3 oz) salt
- 900 g (2 lb) tomatoes
- 225 g (8 oz) onions
- 340 g (12 oz) cooking apples
- 570 ml (1 pint) distilled malt vinegar
- 225 g (8 oz) dates, stoned
- 450 g (1 lb) soft light brown sugar
- 1 level tablespoon mustard seeds
- 2 level teaspoons each ground ginger and ground allspice
- ¼ level teaspoon freshly grated nutmeg

Preparation time: 25 minutes
Cooking time: 2 hours
Standing time: 24 hours
Makes approx 1.1 kg (2½ lb)

Beetroot Chutney
- 900 g (2 lb) raw beetroot
- 450 g (1 lb) onions
- 450 g (1 lb) cooking apples
- 1 lemon
- 570 ml (1 pint) distilled malt vinegar
- 2 level teaspoons ground ginger
- ½ level teaspoon salt
- 225 g (8 oz) stoned raisins
- 225 g (8 oz) granulated sugar

Preparation time: 35 minutes
Cooking time: 3½ hours
Makes approx 1.4 kg (3 lb)

These piquant and decorative vinegars are concocted from spices, fruit, herbs and horseradish.

Spiced Vinegars

Vinegars like these can be made easily and cheaply at home

INGREDIENTS

Spiced vinegar
- 60G (2OZ) CASTER SUGAR
- 1 TABLESPOON CELERY SEEDS
- 1 TABLESPOON EACH MUSTARD SEEDS AND GREEN CARDAMOMS
- 2 TEASPOONS EACH CLOVES, CORIANDER SEEDS AND ALLSPICE BERRIES
- 10 DRIED RED CHILLIES
- 1 TABLESPOON BLACK PEPPERCORNS
- 30G (1OZ) FRESH ROOT GINGER
- 4 GARLIC CLOVES, PEELED
- 1.15 LITRES (2 PINTS) CIDER OR MALT VINEGAR

Fruit vinegar
- 450G (1LB) RASPBERRIES OR BLACKBERRIES, FRESH OR FROZEN
- 570ML (1 PINT) RED WINE VINEGAR

Herb vinegar
- 1.15 LITRES (2 PINTS) WHITE WINE VINEGAR
- 4 BAY LEAVES
- 6 GARLIC CLOVES, PEELED
- 45G (1½OZ) MIXED FRESH HERB SPRIGS

Horseradish vinegar
- 85G (3OZ) FRESH HORSERADISH, GRATED
- 1 SHALLOT OR SMALL ONION, PEELED AND CHOPPED
- 1 TABLESPOON MIXED WHOLE PEPPERCORNS
- ¼ TEASPOON CAYENNE PEPPER
- 1.15 LITRES (2 PINTS) DISTILLED MALT VINEGAR

Preparation time: 10 MINUTES
Infusing time: 1 WEEK–2 MONTHS
Cooking time: (FOR SPICED VINEGAR, SECOND METHOD) 2 HOURS

SPICED VINEGAR

There are two methods; the first gives the best results as it allows the full flavours of the spices to be absorbed by the vinegar, but the second method is useful if you need the vinegar quickly.

For the first method, put the sugar, celery seeds, mustard seeds, green cardamoms, cloves, coriander seeds, allspice berries and chillies into a bowl. Lightly crush the black peppercorns, peel and thinly slice the ginger and add them, with the garlic, to the bowl. Mix the spices together well, then put them into one or two clean, dry bottles and fill to the top with the vinegar. Seal and leave to stand for one to two months, shaking occasionally. Strain the vinegar before using.

For the second method, put all the ingredients into a bowl, cover with a plate and stand the bowl over a saucepan of water. Bring the water to the boil, remove the pan from the heat and leave the bowl over the pan for up to 2 hours to allow the spices to steep in the warm vinegar. Strain and use within a short time.

FRUIT VINEGAR

Put all the ingredients into a bowl or plastic container, cover and leave to stand for five to seven days, then strain into clean, dry bottles. Add a few whole berries, if desired, and seal well.

HERB OR HORSERADISH VINEGAR

Use the fruit vinegar method above, but allow the ingredients for the herb vinegar to stand for two weeks before straining, and for one week for the horseradish vinegar. For a decorative effect, add sprigs of fresh herbs and garlic cloves to the bottles of herb vinegar before sealing.

Fruit Syrups

Fruit syrups can be diluted to make jellies and drinks, or used to flavour sauces, cream and puddings

PICK over the chosen fruits and discard any that are damaged. (Remove currants or elderberries from their stalks and wash them.) Put the fruit and water into a large bowl and place over a saucepan of gently boiling water. Cook for 1 hour, pressing the fruit frequently with a wooden spoon to help to release the juice.

Meanwhile, prepare a jelly bag and stand or line a large, nylon sieve with several layers of scalded muslin or a scalded tea towel and place over a deep bowl. Pour the cooked fruit into the jelly bag or sieve and leave to drain overnight.

Measure the strained juice and pour it into a stainless steel or enamel saucepan. For every 570 ml (1 pint) of juice add 340 g (12 oz) of sugar. Stir over a low heat until the sugar has completely dissolved, then simmer for 15 minutes.

Pour the hot syrup into small, warm, clean screw-top bottles, filling them to within 3.8 cm (1½ in) of the top, then screw the tops on loosely.

Stand the filled bottles on a trivet or a piece of wood in a large, deep saucepan, spacing them well apart. Fill the saucepan with cold water until it comes to just above the level of the syrup in the bottles. Heat the water to 77°C (170°F) and maintain this temperature for at least 30 minutes to sterilise the syrup, regulating the heat as necessary.

Using kitchen tongs, carefully remove the bottles of syrup from the saucepan onto a wooden board. Screw the tops on tightly and wipe the bottles. When the syrup is cold, label the bottles and store in a cool, dark, airy cupboard. The syrup will keep well for up to two months.

The bright, clear colours of the syrups echo those of the fruits from which they are made.

INGREDIENTS

RED OR BLACKCURRANT SYRUP
900 G (2 LB) REDCURRANTS OR BLACKCURRANTS
285 ML (½ PINT) WATER
APPROX 450 G (1 LB) GRANULATED SUGAR
MAKES APPROX 850 ML (1½ PINTS)

RASPBERRY SYRUP
900 G (2 LB) RASPBERRIES, HULLED
150 ML (¼ PINT) WATER
APPROX 340 G (12 OZ) GRANULATED SUGAR
MAKES APPROX 725 ML (1¼ PINTS)

ELDERBERRY SYRUP
900 G (2 LB) ELDERBERRIES
150 ML (¼ PINT) WATER
APPROX 340 G (12 OZ) GRANULATED SUGAR
MAKES APPROX 725 ML (1¼ PINTS)

PREPARATION TIME: 30 MINUTES
STRAINING TIME: OVERNIGHT
COOKING TIME: 1¼ HOURS
STERILISING TIME: 30 MINUTES

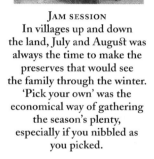

JAM SESSION
In villages up and down the land, July and August was always the time to make the preserves that would see the family through the winter. 'Pick your own' was the economical way of gathering the season's plenty, especially if you nibbled as you picked.

Bottled Fruits

Boiling with sugar, an excellent method of preserving fruit, was practised long before home freezing and remains popular today

INGREDIENTS

A 500 ML OR 1 LB JAR REQUIRES APPROX 340 G (12 OZ) PREPARED FRUIT AND 225 ML (8 FL OZ) OF SUGAR SYRUP TO COVER THE FRUIT

THE FOLLOWING ARE SUITABLE:

SOFT FRUIT
REDCURRANTS, WHITECURRANTS, BLACKCURRANTS, RASPBERRIES, LOGANBERRIES, TAYBERRIES, BLACKBERRIES, STRAWBERRIES, GOOSEBERRIES

STONE FRUIT
PLUMS, GREENGAGES, DAMSONS, CHERRIES, APRICOTS, PEACHES, NECTARINES

OTHER FRUIT
RHUBARB, PINEAPPLE, MANGO, KIWI FRUIT, APPLES, PEARS

SUGAR SYRUP
225 G (8 OZ) GRANULATED SUGAR
570 ML (1 PINT) WATER
MAKES 725 ML (1¼ PINTS)

PREPARATION AND COOKING TIME WILL VARY ACCORDING TO TYPE AND AMOUNT OF FRUIT BOTTLED

You can buy patent plastic discs which, inserted between the fruit and the jar lid keep the fruit submerged beneath the syrup.

THOROUGHLY wash and dry preserving jars and lids. Sterilise rubber bands and screw-on lids in boiling water.

PREPARING THE FRUIT

Currants. Using a fork, remove the berries from their strings, wash and drain well.

Raspberries, loganberries, tayberries, blackberries, strawberries. Hull, and wash only if necessary.

Gooseberries. Top and tail, then wash and drain well.

Plums, greengages, damsons, cherries. Remove stalks, wash and leave whole.

Apricots, peaches, nectarines. Remove skins, leave whole or halve and stone.

Rhubarb. Trim, wash and cut stalks into 2.5 cm (1 in) lengths.

Pineapple. Remove skin and all brown eyes. Cut into slices and remove centre core. Leave in slices or cut into pieces.

Mangoes. Remove peel, cut flesh from stone and slice flesh.

Kiwi fruit. Peel and slice.

Apples, pears. Core, peel, halve or slice. Place in cold water with a little lemon juice added to prevent discoloration.

SUGAR SYRUP

Preheat the oven to 150°C (300°F, gas mark 2), leaving only the centre shelf in place. Stir the sugar and water in a saucepan over a low heat until the sugar has dissolved completely. Bring to the boil, boil for 1 minute, then remove the pan from the heat.

Pack the fruit, as tightly as possible without damaging it, into clean, warm jars. Stand the jars in a heavy roasting tin, lined with several layers of newspaper, Space them at least 5 cm (2 in) apart. To ensure even heating, process only one tinful of jars at a time.

Bring the sugar syrup to the boil and pour into the filled jars to come within 2.5 cm (1 in) of the top. With the rubber rings attached, place the lids on the jars, but do not seal with their rings or clips. If using screw-on lids, screw on very lightly so that they are just in position.

PRESERVING THE FRUIT

Put the jars into the oven and cook for the recommended time according to the type of fruit. The cooking time is dependent on the number of jars and on how tightly the fruit is packed. For four jars of up to 1 litre of soft fruit, allow 35–40 minutes. Allow from 40 minutes to 1 hour for five to ten jars of up to 1.5 litres. Stone and other fruits need 40–50 minutes for up to four jars, and 50 minutes to 1 hour 10 minutes for five jars and over.

Once the minimum time has been reached, check the oven frequently. Wearing oven gloves, remove the jars as soon as bubbles are seen rising regularly. Stand them on a wooden board—not on a cold surface, as they will crack. Quickly wipe the tops of the jars with a clean, damp cloth to remove any syrup. Immediately tighten the clips, screw on the sealing rings or tighten the screw-on lids. Leave for 2–3 minutes, then retighten. Leave the jars on the board, preferably overnight, till cold.

TESTING THE SEAL

When cold, test the jars to make sure they are vacuum sealed. Undo the clip or ring and carefully lift each jar a little by its lid—if the lid holds, a seal has been formed. Metal lids on screwtop jars become concave when a vacuum has been formed. Use the contents of any unsealed jars immediately or reprocess them and test for a seal as before.

Wipe the outsides of the jars with a clean, damp cloth to remove any stickiness, then label and store in a cool, dark, airy cupboard. Properly sealed, the contents will keep indefinitely. Once opened, store them in the refrigerator.

During the cold winter months, you can still enjoy sun-ripened fruits, preserved in their prime.

Remember to wash the wax coating off the lemons before grating them.

Stem ginger and brandy add colour and gusto to the apples in this jam.

Apple, Ginger & Brandy Jam

This is an inspired way to use windfalls or imperfect apples from the orchard

INGREDIENTS

- 1.4 kg (3 lb) cooking apples, Bramley's Seedling or Grenadier
- Finely grated rind and strained juice 3 lemons
- 1.8 kg (4 lb) preserving or granulated sugar
- 725 ml (1¼ pints) cold water, plus 2 tablespoons
- 450 g (1 lb) dessert apples, preferably Cox or Russet
- 175 g (6 oz) preserved stem ginger, drained and chopped, 2 tablespoons of the syrup reserved
- 8 g (¼ oz) butter
- 3 tablespoons brandy, Calvados or rum

Preparation time: 1 hour
Cooking time: 50 minutes
Standing time: 15 minutes
Makes approx 2.7 kg (6 lb)

Preheat the oven to 180°c (350°f, gas mark 4). Peel, core and slice the cooking apples. Tie all the peelings and cores in a large square of scalded muslin.

Put the apples into a preserving pan and add the bag of peelings, a third of the lemon juice, 900 g (2 lb) of the sugar and 725 ml (1¼ pints) of the water. Put the pan on a low heat and stir until the sugar has dissolved. Bring to the boil, then reduce the heat and simmer gently for 30 minutes or until the apples are soft, stirring frequently during cooking.

Meanwhile peel, core and quarter the dessert apples. Cut each quarter into three slices, then cut each slice into three pieces. Put them into a heatproof casserole with the remaining water and 115 g (4 oz) of the remaining sugar. Cover and cook in the oven for 20 minutes, or until the apple pieces are tender but still intact. Remove from the oven and set aside.

Carefully remove the muslin bag from the preserving pan. Mash the apples in the preserving pan with a potato masher, until fairly smooth. Stir in the stem ginger, ginger syrup, lemon rind and remaining lemon juice and the remaining sugar. Stir over a low heat until the sugar has dissolved, then bring quickly to the boil, stirring constantly.

Add the cooked dessert apples and their juice to the pan and boil rapidly for 10 minutes, then remove from the heat and test for a set (see p.438). When setting point is reached, skim off any scum from the surface, then stir in the butter and the brandy, Calvados or rum. Let the jam stand for 15 minutes, then stir and pour into clean, warm jars. Cover the jars immediately with waxed paper discs and cellophane covers. When the jam is completely cold, label the jars and store in a cool, dark, airy cupboard.

Piccalilli

The recipe for this delicious, spicy piccalilli was taken from a Yorkshire cook's scrapbook, written in 1903

Put the water into a large stainless steel or enamel saucepan or preserving pan, add the salt and bring to the boil. Add the prepared vegetables and the red chillies and cook gently for 5 minutes. Pour into a colander, rinse well under cold water then drain very well on kitchen paper or a clean tea towel.

Meanwhile, to make the sauce, put the sugar, flour, allspice, ground ginger, curry powder, turmeric, mustard powder and cayenne pepper into a bowl. Add 3–4 tablespoons of the vinegar and mix to form a thick spicy paste.

Put the paste, the remaining vinegar and the peppercorns into a stainless steel or enamel saucepan and bring to the boil, stirring continuously. Reduce the heat and continue to cook, stirring continuously, for 3–5 minutes until the sauce thickens. Remove the pan from the heat and leave to cool, stirring occasionally to prevent a skin from forming.

Put the drained vegetables into a bowl, add the sauce and mix together. Cover the bowl and leave to stand for 24 hours.

The following day, stir the piccalilli again to coat the vegetables evenly, then spoon into clean, dry jars and cover with vinegarproof lids. Label the jars and store for two to three months in a cool, dark, airy cupboard, before eating.

The name 'piccalilli' probably comes from its chief components, vegetable pickle and red-hot chilli.

INGREDIENTS

- 1.15 LITRES (2 PINTS) WATER
- 85 G (3 OZ) SALT
- 450 G (1 LB) BUTTON ONIONS, PEELED
- 675 G (1½ LB) TRIMMED CAULIFLOWER, CUT INTO SMALL FLORETS
- 550 G (1¼ LB) MINI CUCUMBERS, OR STANDARD CUCUMBERS QUARTERED LENGTHWISE, THEN CUT INTO 1.3 CM (½ IN) PIECES
- 450 G (1 LB) FINE GREEN BEANS, TRIMMED AND CUT IN HALF
- 3 SMALL FRESH RED CHILLIES CUT INTO THIN STRIPS

For the sauce

- 225 G (8 OZ) GRANULATED SUGAR
- 85 G (3 OZ) PLAIN FLOUR
- 2 LEVEL TEASPOONS ALLSPICE
- 2 LEVEL TABLESPOONS GROUND GINGER
- 2 LEVEL TABLESPOONS MILD CURRY POWDER
- 2 LEVEL TEASPOONS TURMERIC
- 2 LEVEL TABLESPOONS MUSTARD POWDER
- ½ LEVEL TEASPOON CAYENNE PEPPER
- 1.15 LITRES (2 PINTS) DISTILLED MALT VINEGAR
- 2 LEVEL TABLESPOONS BLACK PEPPERCORNS

Preparation time: 30 MINUTES
Cooking time: 15 MINUTES
Standing time: 24 HOURS
Makes approx 1.4 KG (3 LB)

Three Pickles

These pickles are derived from traditional country recipes and are an excellent standby for quick and easy lunches and suppers

Ingredients

Bread and Butter Pickle

- 4 large cucumbers, washed
- 4 large onions, peeled
- 4 level tablespoons salt
- 850 ml (1½ pints) distilled malt vinegar
- 200 g (7 oz) granulated sugar
- 1½ level teaspoons fennel seeds
- 1½ level teaspoons black mustard seeds

Preparation time: 1 hour
Standing time: 1 hour
Fills approx 3 x 750 ml or 3 x 1¼ pint jars

Pickled Red Cabbage

- 1.4 kg (3 lb) firm red cabbage
- 4 level tablespoons salt
- 1.4 litres (2½ pints) malt vinegar
- 3 cinnamon sticks, each 7.5 cm (3 in) long
- 4 teaspoons allspice berries
- 4 teaspoons cloves
- 6 mace blades
- 1 teaspoon black peppercorns

Preparation time: 50 minutes
Standing time: 24 hours
Fills approx 3 x 750 ml or 3 x 1¼ pint jars

Pickled Walnuts

- 900 g (2 lb) fresh green walnuts
- 225 g (8 oz) cooking salt
- 2.3 litres (4 pints) water
- 1.15 litres (2 pints) malt vinegar
- 340 g (12 oz) soft light or dark brown sugar
- 1 level teaspoon salt
- 1 teaspoon pickling spice
- 1 teaspoon black peppercorns
- ½ teaspoon cloves

Preparation time: 1½ hours
Brining time: 14 days
Standing time: 1–2 days
Fills approx 4 x 750 ml or 4 x 1¼ pint jars

Bread and Butter Pickle

Slice the cucumbers and onions thinly, then layer them in a large bowl, sprinkling each layer with salt. Leave to stand for 1 hour, then pour into a colander and rinse under a cold tap. Drain well on kitchen paper.

Put the vinegar, sugar, fennel seeds and mustard seeds into a stainless steel or enamel saucepan and heat gently, stirring until the sugar dissolves. Bring the mixture to the boil and boil for 4 minutes.

Pack the cucumber and onion slices into clean, warm jars and cover with the hot vinegar. Cover with vinegarproof lids, label and store in a dark place—this is important as exposure to light will cause the cucumber to lose its colour. Store for two months before eating.

Pickled Red Cabbage

Remove any discoloured outer leaves and cut the cabbage into quarters. Remove the hard white core, shred the cabbage finely and put it, in layers, into one or two large bowls, sprinkling each layer with salt. Cover and leave for 24 hours.

Meanwhile, make the spiced vinegar. Pour the malt vinegar into a stainless steel or enamel saucepan and add the cinnamon sticks, allspice berries, cloves, mace blades and the peppercorns. Bring to the boil, then remove the pan from the heat, cover and leave until cold. Strain the cold vinegar through a muslin-lined sieve into a jug or bowl and discard the spices. Cover the bowl and reserve until needed.

The next day, transfer the cabbage to a colander and rinse under cold running water. Drain on several layers of kitchen paper, then pack loosely in clean jars. Pour the cold vinegar into the jars to come at least 1.3 cm (½ in) above the cabbage. Cover with vinegarproof lids, label and store in a cool, dark cupboard. Let it mature for one week before using, but use within two months as pickled cabbage loses its crispness after this time.

Pickled Walnuts

Use walnuts which have been gathered in the early summer while they are still green, and before the shells have begun to form. To protect your hands while preparing them, wear disposable polythene gloves as walnut stain is persistent and difficult to remove.

Test the walnuts by pricking them with a darning needle—they should be soft. Discard any that are firm and resist the needle as this means that the shell has started to form.

Prick the selected walnuts all over and put them into a large bowl. Dissolve 115 g (4 oz) of the salt in 2 pints of the water, then pour over the walnuts, making sure that they are covered with the brine. If necessary, place a clean plate on the surface to keep the walnuts submerged. Cover the bowl with a plate and leave to soak for seven days, stirring occasionally.

Drain, cover with brine made with the remaining salt and water, and leave for seven more days, stirring occasionally.

Drain the walnuts well and spread them, in single layers, on dishes. Leave them outside in the open air, preferably in the sunshine, for a couple of days until they are black. Take them in each night.

Meanwhile, to make the spiced vinegar, pour the malt vinegar into a stainless steel or enamel saucepan and add the soft brown sugar, salt, pickling spice, black peppercorns and the cloves. Stir over a moderate heat until the sugar has dissolved, then bring to the boil and boil gently for 5 minutes. Remove the pan from the heat, cover and allow to cool.

Pack the blackened walnuts into clean, dry jars. Strain the spiced vinegar into an enamel or stainless steel saucepan and bring to the boil. Remove the pan from the heat and pour the vinegar over the walnuts, making sure that they are well covered. Cover the jars with vinegarproof lids, label and store in a cool, dark cupboard for one month before eating.

Try this trio of flavourful pickles—bread and butter, red cabbage and walnut—with bread and cheese for a simple ploughman's lunch.

The various herb jellies are all made from the same basic stock of apple juice and white vinegar.

Herb Jellies

Piquant herb jellies are versatile accompaniments to roast meats, poultry and game, cold cuts, and raised pork or game pies

INGREDIENTS

For the basic apple juice stock
- 4.5 kg (10 lb) cooking apples, washed and roughly cut up (including the peel and cores)
- 2.3 litres (4 pints) water
- 2.3 litres (4 pints) distilled malt vinegar

Preparation time: 25 minutes
Cooking time: 50 minutes
Straining time: 2–3 hours or overnight
Makes approx 3.4–4 litres (6–7 pints), enough to make 1 batch each mint, sage, rosemary and thyme jelly

For mint or sage jelly
- 15 g (½ oz) fresh mint or sage leaves
- 850 ml (1½ pints) basic apple juice stock
- 675 g (1½ lb) preserving or granulated sugar
- Natural green food colouring (optional)

Cooking time: 25 minutes
Fills approx 4 x 225 g (8 oz) jars

For rosemary or thyme jelly
- 8–10 small fresh rosemary or thyme sprigs
- 850 ml (1½ pints) basic apple juice stock
- 675 g (1½ lb) preserving or granulated sugar
- 2 large fresh rosemary or thyme sprigs, washed

Cooking time: 25 minutes
Fills approx 4 x 225 g (8 oz) jars of each jelly

To make the basic apple juice stock, put the prepared apples and water into a preserving pan. Simmer for 45 minutes or until soft and pulpy. Add the vinegar and cook for a further 5 minutes.

Meanwhile, prepare a jelly bag and stand. Alternatively, line two large nylon sieves or colanders with several layers of scalded muslin or scalded tea towels and place them over two large bowls.

Pour the apples and all the liquid into the jelly bag or lined sieves and allow to drain for 2–3 hours or overnight.

MINT OR SAGE JELLY

Dip the mint or sage leaves into boiling water for 2–3 seconds, then rinse them under cold water. Pat the leaves dry with kitchen paper and chop them finely—there should be about a tablespoon.

Pour the apple juice stock into a large, heavy-based saucepan, add the sugar and stir over a gentle heat until all the sugar has dissolved. Bring to a full, rolling boil and boil for 5–10 minutes or until setting point is reached (see p.438).

Remove from the heat, quickly skim the scum from the surface, then stir in the chopped mint or sage and a few drops of green colouring, if using. Pour into clean, warm jars and cover immediately with waxed paper discs and vinegarproof screw tops or cellophane covers. When the jelly is cold, label the jars and store them in a cool, dark, airy cupboard.

ROSEMARY OR THYME JELLY

Dip the small rosemary or thyme sprigs into boiling water for 2–3 seconds, rinse under cold water, pat dry with kitchen paper and set aside.

Make the jelly as for mint or sage jelly, adding the larger herb sprigs while dissolving the sugar. Remove the herbs and boil until setting point is reached (see p.438). Put the small herb sprigs into clean, warm jars, then pour in the jelly. Cover, label and store as above.

Soft Fruit Jams

Stock the store cupboard with these juicy jams to spread liberally on toasted muffins, warm crusty bread or fresh, hot scones

BERRY JAMS

Put all the strawberries, raspberries or loganberries into a preserving pan or a large, heavy-based saucepan and crush them with a potato masher. Add the sugar and heat very slowly, stirring all the time until every granule of sugar has dissolved. Add the butter, increase the heat, bring to a full rolling boil and boil for exactly 4 minutes. Remove from the heat, cool for 1 minute, then pot and cover immediately (see p.438).

BLACKCURRANT AND RUM JAM

Put the blackcurrants and water into a preserving pan or a large, heavy-based saucepan and cook gently, stirring occasionally, for 20–30 minutes until the fruit is soft and the contents of the pan are considerably reduced. Add the sugar and stir over a low heat until completely dissolved. Bring to a full rolling boil and boil for 10 minutes until setting point is reached (see p.438). Remove from the heat and stir in the rum, then pot and cover immediately.

GOOSEBERRY AND REDCURRANT JAM

Put the fruit into a preserving pan or a large, heavy-based saucepan. Add the water and simmer gently for 30 minutes until the fruit has softened, mashing and stirring from time to time. Add the sugar and stir over a gentle heat until completely dissolved. Bring to a full rolling boil and boil for 20–30 minutes until setting point is reached (see p.438). Pot and cover immediately.

Soft fruits picked in high summer, make exquisite jams.

INGREDIENTS

Berry Jams

1.8 kg (4 lb) strawberries, raspberries or loganberries, hulled
2 kg (4½ lb) jam sugar with added pectin
15 g (½ oz) unsalted butter
Preparation time: 10 minutes
Cooking time: 25 minutes
Makes approx 3.6 kg (8 lb)

Blackcurrant and Rum Jam

900 g (2 lb) blackcurrants, stalks removed
850 ml (1½ pints) water
1.4 kg (3 lb) preserving or granulated sugar
4 tablespoons dark rum
Preparation time: 20 minutes
Cooking time: 45 minutes
Makes approx 1.8 kg (4 lb)

Gooseberry and Redcurrant Jam

900 g (2 lb) slightly under-ripe gooseberries, topped and tailed, washed
450 g (1 lb) redcurrants, stalks removed
570 ml (1 pint) water
1.4 kg (3 lb) preserving or granulated sugar
Preparation time: 20 minutes
Cooking time: 1 hour
Makes approx 2.3 kg (5 lb)

It may take longer to pick but the last of the crop is the best for making strawberry jam.

The fruity aroma of homemade marmalade permeating your kitchen is a foretaste of future delights.

Marmalades

Your own marmalade will supply the perfect finish to a traditional breakfast

OXFORD MARMALADE

Cut the oranges and lemons in half, squeeze the juice and strain it into a preserving pan. Using your fingers, remove all the flesh and pips from the squeezed fruit and tie them securely in a muslin square with the halves of lemon peel.

Cut the halves of orange peel in half, then widthways into strips about 6 mm (¼ in) thick. Add the strips and the muslin bag to the preserving pan, pour in the water and bring to the boil. Reduce the heat and simmer for about 2 hours, or until the peel is very soft and the liquid is reduced by half.

Remove the muslin bag from the pan, put it into a bowl and leave until cool enough to handle. Squeeze the bag to remove as much juice as possible, then pour the juice back into the pan.

Add the sugars and treacle to the pan and stir over a moderate heat until all the sugar has dissolved. Bring to a full rolling boil and boil for 15–20 minutes, or until setting point is reached (see p.438).

Remove the pan from the heat and skim any scum from the surface. Leave the marmalade to stand for 20 minutes to allow the peel to settle.

Stir the marmalade to disperse the peel evenly, then pour it into clean, warm jars and cover with waxed paper discs and cellophane covers. When the marmalade is cold, label the jars and store in a cool, dark, airy cupboard.

SEVILLE ORANGE MARMALADE

Put the oranges into a preserving pan and cover completely with cold water. Bring to the boil and boil gently for 15 minutes. Drain the oranges, return to the pan, cover with fresh water and bring to the boil once again, then reduce the heat and simmer gently for about 2 hours, or until the peel can be pierced easily with a fork. The oranges will float on the surface as they cook and should be stirred frequently to ensure even cooking.

Pour off the cooking water and reserve it. Allow the oranges to cool, then cut each into quarters and pull the flesh away from the skin, discarding any pips. Chop the flesh finely and put it into a measuring jug. Make up to 1.4 litres (2½ pints) with the reserved cooking water and, if necessary, a little more cold water, then pour the flesh and water into the preserving pan. Slice the orange peel thinly and put it into the pan. Add the preserving or granulated sugar and stir over a moderate heat until every granule has dissolved completely. Bring to a full rolling boil and boil for 10-15 minutes, or until setting point is reached (see p.438). Remove the pan from the heat and proceed as for Oxford marmalade.

FOUR FRUIT MARMALADE

Using a sharp knife, cut a thin slice from each end of each fruit and set aside.

Cut the grapefruit into eight wedges, the oranges into six and the lemons and lime into four. Cutting across each segment, thinly slice all the fruit, removing and reserving any pips.

Put the end slices and pips into a square of muslin, tie securely to form a bag and place in a large bowl with the sliced fruit. Cover with the water and leave to soak for 24 hours.

The next day, transfer the contents of the bowl to a preserving pan and bring to the boil. Reduce the heat and simmer for 2 hours, or until the peel is very soft—test by pressing a piece, after cooling, between your thumb and forefinger.

Remove and discard the muslin bag and add the preserving or granulated sugar to the pan. Stir over a moderate heat until every granule of the sugar has dissolved completely, then bring to a full rolling boil and continue boiling for about 20 minutes, or until setting point is reached (see p.438).

Remove the pan from the heat and proceed as for Oxford marmalade.

INGREDIENTS

OXFORD MARMALADE

- 900 G (2 LB) SEVILLE ORANGES, WELL WASHED
- 3 LEMONS, WELL WASHED
- 2.3 LITRES (4 PINTS) WATER
- 675 G (1½ LB) PRESERVING OR GRANULATED SUGAR
- 450 G (1 LB) DEMERARA SUGAR
- 60 G (2 OZ) BLACK TREACLE

PREPARATION TIME: 1 HOUR
COOKING TIME: APPROX 2 HOURS 20 MINUTES
MAKES APPROX 1.7 KG (3¾ LB)

SEVILLE ORANGE MARMALADE

- 900 G (2 LB) SEVILLE ORANGES, WELL WASHED
- 1.1 KG (2½ LB) PRESERVING OR GRANULATED SUGAR

PREPARATION TIME: 45 MINUTES
COOKING TIME: APPROX 2 HOURS 20 MINUTES
MAKES APPROX 1.6 KG (3½ LB)

FOUR FRUIT MARMALADE

- 1 LARGE GRAPEFRUIT, WELL WASHED
- 3 LARGE SEVILLE ORANGES, WELL WASHED
- 4 LARGE LEMONS, WELL WASHED
- 1 LIME, WELL WASHED
- 2.3 LITRES (4 PINTS) WATER
- 1.4 KG (3 LB) PRESERVING OR GRANULATED SUGAR

PREPARATION TIME: 1 HOUR
SOAKING TIME: 24 HOURS
COOKING TIME: APPROX 2 HOURS 20 MINUTES
MAKES APPROX 1.6 KG (3½ LB)

INGREDIENTS

NOTE THAT THE QUANTITY OF SUGAR GIVEN IS FOR CANDYING 450G (1 LB) OF ANY SINGLE FRUIT. CANDY FRUITS SEPARATELY.

CANDIED FRUIT

- 450G (1 LB) PREPARED, FRESH, RIPE BUT FIRM FRUIT SUCH AS PINEAPPLE, SKINNED, SLICED AND CORED; PEACHES, NECTARINES OR APRICOTS, HALVED, SKINNED AND STONED; PLUMS, HALVED AND STONED; OR STONED CHERRIES
- 570ML (1 PINT) BOILING WATER
- 750G (1 LB 11 OZ) GRANULATED SUGAR

PREPARATION TIME: 45 MINUTES, THEN 30 MINUTES EACH DAY FOR DAYS 2–8, 10 AND 14
SOAKING TIME: 13 DAYS
DRYING TIME: SEVERAL DAYS

CANDIED PEEL

- 4 LARGE LEMONS, WELL WASHED, OR 4 MEDIUM ORANGES, WELL WASHED
- 1.15 LITRES (2 PINTS) COLD WATER
- 675G (1½ LB) GRANULATED SUGAR

PREPARATION TIME: 45 MINUTES, THEN 30 MINUTES EACH DAY FOR 2 DAYS
SOAKING TIME: 6 DAYS
DRYING TIME: SEVERAL DAYS

CANDIED ANGELICA

- 225G (8 OZ) FRESH YOUNG ANGELICA STALKS, WASHED AND CUT INTO 7.5CM (3 IN) LENGTHS
- 1.7 LITRES (3 PINTS) WATER
- 2 LEVEL TEASPOONS SALT
- 675G (1½ LB) GRANULATED SUGAR

PREPARATION TIME: 45 MINUTES, THEN 30 MINUTES EACH DAY FOR 7 DAYS
SOAKING TIME: 7 DAYS
DRYING TIME: SEVERAL DAYS
MAKES APPROX 225G (8 OZ)

The perfumed flavours of fresh fruits are perfectly preserved in these sugary confections.

Candying

Candied fruit and peel are costly to buy, but can be made more cheaply at home

CANDIED FRUIT

PUT the fruit and boiling water into a pan and cook until just tender. Drain off the liquid, reserving 425 ml (¾ pint). Put the fruit into a heatproof bowl. Pour the liquid into a saucepan, add 250 g (9 oz) of sugar and stir over a gentle heat until dissolved. Bring to the boil and pour over the fruit. Cover and soak for 24 hours.

Day 2. Strain the syrup into a heavy-based saucepan and return the fruit to the bowl. Add 60 g (2 oz) of the sugar to the syrup and stir over a gentle heat until completely dissolved. Bring to the boil and pour over the fruit, submerging it fully. Cover and leave for 24 hours.

Days 3–7. Repeat Day 2.

Day 8. Strain the syrup into a saucepan, add 85 g (3 oz) of the sugar to the syrup and stir over a gentle heat until dissolved. Add the fruit, bring to the boil, then reduce the heat and simmer for 3 minutes. Return the fruit and syrup to the bowl, cover and leave for two days.

Day 10. Repeat Day 8, adding the remaining sugar, and leave for four days. By then the syrup should be very thick and heavy—if not, repeat the last process.

Day 14. Drain the fruit, place on a wire rack and leave in a dry, warm place for several days until no longer sticky.

CANDIED PEEL

Cut the fruit into quarters and remove the flesh. Weigh the peel—there should be about 225 g (8 oz).

Put the peel into a large, stainless steel or enamel saucepan, pour in the water and bring to the boil, then reduce the heat and simmer gently for about an hour or until the peel is very tender.

Reserve 570 ml (1 pint) of the cooking water and put the drained peel into a bowl. Pour the water into a saucepan and add 450 g (1 lb) of the sugar. Stir over a gentle heat until every granule of sugar has dissolved, then bring to the boil and boil for 1 minute. Pour over the peel, cover and leave to stand for 24 hours.

Day 2. Strain the syrup into a saucepan and add the remaining sugar. Stir over a gentle heat until dissolved, bring to the boil and boil for 1 minute. Pour back over the peel, cover and leave for 24 hours.

Day 3. Pour the peel and syrup into a heavy-based saucepan, bring to the boil, reduce the heat and simmer for 30 minutes, until the pith is transparent. Return to the bowl, cover and leave for four days.

Day 7. Drain the peel and store as for the candied fruit.

CANDIED ANGELICA

Soak the angelica in the water with the salt for 10 minutes, then bring to the boil. Rinse in a colander under cold water and return to the saucepan. Cover with fresh water and bring to the boil, then reduce the heat and simmer for about 10 minutes until tender. Reserve 425 ml (¾ pint) of the cooking water. Rinse the angelica in cold water and scrape off any tough outer skin from older stalks, drain well and put into a large bowl.

Pour the reserved cooking water into a saucepan and add 250 g (9 oz) of the sugar. Stir over a gentle heat until every granule has dissolved, then bring to the boil and boil for 2 minutes until slightly thickened. Pour the syrup over the angelica, cover and leave to stand for 24 hours.

Day 2. Strain the syrup into a saucepan, add 85 g (3 oz) of the remaining sugar and stir over a gentle heat until every granule of the sugar has dissolved. Bring to the boil and boil for 2 minutes to thicken the syrup a little more. Pour the syrup back over the angelica, cover the bowl and leave to stand for 24 hours.

Days 3–6. Repeat Day 2, adding 85 g (3 oz) sugar each day until the syrup has the consistency of clear honey—do not allow it to burn. On Day 6 add the angelica with the sugar, bring to the boil and boil for 2 minutes. Return to the bowl, cover and leave to stand for two days.

Day 8. Drain the angelica and store as for the candied fruit.

Keep the candies in a wooden or cardboard box lined with waxed paper or non-stick parchment. Mould may occur if you use airtight containers.

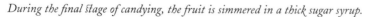

During the final stage of candying, the fruit is simmered in a thick sugar syrup.

Stone fruit jams—apricot, plum, greengage, lime and cherry, damson and marrow—are simple to make, scrumptious to eat.

Stone Fruit Jams

Find some time to prepare your own jams from quality fruit and relish their superior flavour, colour and texture

INGREDIENTS

Apricot Jam

- 1.4 kg (3 lb) apricots, washed, halved and stoned (half the stones reserved)
- Strained juice 1 large lemon
- 1.4 kg (3 lb) preserving sugar
- 15 g (½ oz) unsalted butter

Preparation time: 45 minutes
Cooking time: 30 minutes
Makes approx 2.3 kg (5 lb)

Lime and Cherry Jam

- 4 limes, washed
- 2.3 kg (5 lb) dark red cherries
- 1.4 kg (3 lb) preserving sugar

Preparation time: 1¾ hours
Cooking time: 1½ hours
Makes approx 2.7 kg (6 lb)

Greengage Jam

- 1.4 kg (3 lb) greengages, stalks removed, washed
- 1.4 kg (3 lb) preserving sugar
- 15 g (½ oz) unsalted butter

Preparation time: 35 minutes
Cooking time: 45 minutes
Makes approx 1.4 kg (3 lb)

Plum Jam

- 1.4 kg (3 lb) plums, washed
- 1.4 kg (3 lb) preserving sugar
- 15 g (½ oz) unsalted butter

Preparation time: 15 minutes
Cooking time: 1 hour 20 minutes
Makes approx 1.8 kg (4 lb)

Spicy Damson and Marrow Jam

- 1.4 kg (3 lb) damsons, washed
- 7.5 cm (3 in) cinnamon stick
- 60 g (2 oz) fresh root ginger, peeled and finely grated
- 1.4 kg (3 lb) marrow, peeled, deseeded and chopped
- Approx 1.4 kg (3 lb) preserving sugar

Preparation time: 1 hour 25 minutes
Cooking time: 1¼ hours
Makes approx 1.4 kg (3 lb)

APRICOT JAM

Using nutcrackers or a hammer, crack open the reserved apricot stones. Remove the kernels and blanch in boiling water for 1 minute, then drain and skin.

Put the apricot halves and kernels, the lemon juice and 285 ml (½ pint) of water into a large preserving pan and bring slowly to the boil, stirring occasionally. Then reduce the heat and simmer gently for 15 minutes or until the fruit is soft and the water has reduced.

Remove the pan from the heat, add the sugar and stir until completely dissolved. Return the pan to the heat, add the butter and stir until melted.

Bring the jam to a full rolling boil and boil rapidly for 15 minutes, then test for a set (see p.438). If setting point has not been reached, boil for 5 minutes more, then test again. Pour into clean, warm jars and cover immediately with waxed paper discs and cellophane covers.

LIME AND CHERRY JAM

Cut the limes in half and remove all the pips. Pass the fruit through a mincing machine or chop it finely in a food processor. Alternatively, the fruit may be chopped by hand.

Put the minced or chopped limes into a preserving pan with 570 ml (1 pint) of water and bring to the boil. Reduce the heat and simmer gently for 30 minutes stirring occasionally. Meanwhile, stone the cherries with a cherry stoner. Doing this with the cherries inside a polythene bag will prevent their juice from splashing. If you do not have a cherry stoner, make a deep cut with a knife into each cherry and pull out the stone. Tie the stones securely in a square of muslin. Add the cherries and stones to the pan and cook over a low heat for 30 minutes, stirring occasionally. Remove the stones, add the sugar and proceed as for apricot jam, boiling for 20 minutes.

GREENGAGE JAM

Put the greengages into a large preserving pan, add 150 ml (¼ pint) of water and cook over a moderate heat for 30 minutes, stirring occasionally, until the fruit is very soft and pulpy.

Reduce the heat, stir in the sugar until dissolved, then bring to the boil. Add the butter and boil rapidly for 15 minutes or until setting point is reached (see p.438).

Remove the pan from the heat and, using a slotted spoon, remove the stones and skim the froth from the surface. Pour the jam into clean, warm, dry jars and cover immediately. Label when cold.

PLUM JAM

Put the plums into a large preserving pan with 150 ml (¼ pint) of water and simmer gently for 1 hour or until the fruit is very soft and the liquid has reduced by about two-thirds. Then continue as for greengage jam above.

SPICY DAMSON AND MARROW JAM

Put the damsons into a preserving pan with the cinnamon stick and ginger. Add 150 ml (¼ pint) of water and simmer gently for 30 minutes or until the damsons are soft. Meanwhile, steam the marrow for 30 minutes until tender.

Add the marrow to the damsons and cook for 30 minutes or until very soft and pulpy. Cool slightly, then pass the mixture through a stainless steel or nylon sieve into a large bowl. Weigh the fruit pulp and allow 450 g (1 lb) of sugar for every 450 g (1 lb) of pulp. Pour the pulp into a preserving pan, add the sugar and stir over a moderate heat until the sugar has completely dissolved.

Increase the heat and boil rapidly for 15 minutes, then test for a set (see p.438). If necessary, continue to boil until setting point is reached.

Skim the froth from the surface, pot and cover immediately. Label when cold.

Fruit Chutneys

Every larder should stock a selection of sweet chutneys like these; for the components, use fruits that are perfect or only slightly blemished

INGREDIENTS

Date, apricot and walnut chutney
450g (1 lb) dried apricots
225g (8 oz) stoned dates
425 ml (3/4 pint) strong tea
450g (1 lb) onions
450g (1 lb) cooking apples
85g (3 oz) stoned raisins
85g (3 oz) walnuts
2 small, dried red chillies
2 teaspoons coriander seeds
85g (3 oz) sultanas
450g (1 lb) demerara sugar
Finely grated rind 1 orange
Finely grated rind 1 lemon
570 ml (1 pint) distilled malt vinegar
Preparation time: 1¼ hours
Standing time: 12 hours
Cooking time: 1¾–2 hours
Makes approx 2.7 kg (6 lb)

Mango and pear chutney
1.4 kg (3 lb) mangoes
450g (1 lb) pears
900g (2 lb) cooking apples
450g (1 lb) granulated sugar
570 ml (1 pint) cider vinegar
1 teaspoon allspice berries
2 mace blades
½ teaspoon cloves
1.9 cm (¾ in) cinnamon stick
¾ teaspoon black peppercorns
1 level teaspoon salt
Preparation time: 50 minutes
Cooking time: 2¼–2½ hours
Makes approx 1.6 kg (3½ lb)

Lemon chutney
4 large lemons
450g (1 lb) onions
30g (1 oz) salt
570 ml (1 pint) distilled malt vinegar
450g (1 lb) demerara sugar
175g (6 oz) seedless raisins
½ teaspoon cayenne pepper
1 teaspoon ground ginger
15g (½ oz) mustard seeds
Preparation time: 1 hour
Standing time: 24 hours
Cooking time: 1¾ hours
Makes approx 1.4 kg (3 lb)

DATE, APRICOT AND WALNUT CHUTNEY

This is a two day recipe. First chop the apricots and dates and put them into a large bowl. Pour over the hot, freshly made tea and stir well. Cover the bowl and leave to stand overnight.

The next day, peel and chop the onions; peel, core and finely chop the apples; chop the raisins and the walnuts then put all into a preserving pan. Add the soaked apricots and dates, including any soaking liquid from the bowl.

Using a mortar and pestle or an electric grinder, finely grind the chillies and the coriander seeds and add them to the preserving pan with the sultanas, demerara sugar, grated orange and lemon rinds and the vinegar.

Heat the mixture slowly, stirring occasionally, until the sugar has dissolved. Bring to the boil, then reduce the heat and simmer gently for 1½–1¾ hours until all the ingredients are soft and the mixture is thick, has reduced by about a quarter and there is no free liquid when a spoon is drawn across the bottom of the pan. Stir the mixture frequently during cooking to prevent it from sticking to the bottom of the pan.

Remove from the heat and spoon the chutney into clean, warm, dry jars. Cover immediately with vinegarproof lids. When cold, label the jars and store in a cool, dry, airy cupboard for two to three months before using.

MANGO AND PEAR CHUTNEY

Peel, slice and chop the mangoes. Peel, core and chop the pears and apples and put them into a preserving pan with the mangoes, sugar and vinegar. Using a mortar and pestle or an electric grinder, finely grind all the spices and add them to the pan with the salt. Heat the mixture gently, stirring occasionally, until the sugar has dissolved completely. Bring to the boil, then reduce the heat and simmer gently for 2–2¼ hours, or until the mixture is reduced by a quarter, the chutney is thick and pulpy and no excess liquid remains in the pan.

Remove the pan from the heat and spoon the chutney into clean, warm jars. Cover immediately with vinegarproof lids. When the chutney is cold, label the jars and store in a cool, dry, airy cupboard for two to three months before using.

LEMON CHUTNEY

This is a two day recipe. First wash and thinly slice the lemons and remove any pips. Peel and chop the onions. Layer the lemon slices and chopped onions in a large bowl, sprinkling each layer lightly with the salt. Cover the bowl and leave to stand for 24 hours.

The next day, pour the lemons and onions into a colander and rinse well under cold running water. Drain well, then put into a preserving pan with the vinegar, sugar, raisins, cayenne pepper and ground ginger. Wrap the mustard seeds in a small square of muslin and tie securely. Add the muslin bag to the preserving pan, making sure it is thoroughly immersed in the mixture.

Heat the mixture gently until the sugar has completely dissolved, stirring occasionally. Bring slowly to the boil, then reduce the heat and simmer gently for 1½ hours or until the chutney has reduced by a quarter and is thick and shiny and the lemons are tender.

Remove the pan from the heat, remove and discard the muslin bag of mustard seeds and spoon the chutney into clean, warm jars. Cover immediately with vinegarproof lids. When the chutney is cold, label the jars and store in a cool, dry, airy cupboard for two months.

The chutney is equally good made with sultanas instead of seedless raisins.

Dates, apricots, mangoes, pears, raisins, sultanas and lemons are blended with spices to produce richly aromatic chutneys.

Cook's motto
Before the advent of manufactured sauces, vinegar had an even wider range of roles than it does now. Among other concoctions, cooks used to make and bottle celery and cucumber vinegar for salads, cayenne vinegar for soups and chilli vinegar as a relish for fish.

Hard-boiled eggs, hens' and quails', are transformed into tangy treats when pickled.

Pickled Eggs

Use these tasty eggs for quick snacks and packed lunches or serve them as a side dish with curries and spicy rice dishes

INGREDIENTS

- 8 cloves
- 3 mace blades
- 10 allspice berries
- 6 peppercorns
- 7.5 cm (3 in) cinnamon stick
- 570 ml (1 pint) distilled malt vinegar
- 12 hens' eggs or 3 dozen quails' eggs

Preparation time: 15–30 minutes
Cooking time: 10 minutes for hens' eggs, 3 minutes for quails' eggs
Standing time: 6 weeks
Fills approx 3 x 500 ml (18 fl oz) jars or 3 x 450 g (1 lb) jars

Tie the spices in a small square of muslin and place in a saucepan with the vinegar. Cover the pan, bring to the boil and simmer for 3 minutes. Remove from the heat and leave to stand for 2 hours.

Meanwhile, to hard boil the eggs, put them into a saucepan, cover with cold water and bring to the boil. Reduce the heat slightly to maintain a steady boil. Boil hens' eggs for 10 minutes, quails' eggs for 3 minutes. When the cooking time is up, remove the saucepan of eggs from the heat and pour off the water.

Stand the saucepan in the sink and allow cold water to run onto the eggs for 2–3 minutes to cool them. Leave the eggs in the water until completely cold, then remove their shells.

Put the cold, hard-boiled eggs into clean, dry jars and pour the cold, spiced vinegar over to cover them completely. Add extra plain, cold vinegar if necessary.

Cover the jars with vinegarproof lids, label and store in a cool, dry, airy place for six weeks. The pickled eggs should be eaten within three months.

Summer Jellies

Crystal-clear jellies made from summer fruits can be used to glaze cakes, fruit flans and tartlets or served with meat, poultry and especially game

INGREDIENTS

Redcurrant Jelly
1.4 kg (3 lb) redcurrants, washed
570 ml (1 pint) water
Approx 900 g (2 lb) preserving or granulated sugar
Makes approx 900 g (2 lb)

Blackcurrant Jelly
900 g (2 lb) blackcurrants, washed
850 ml ($1\frac{1}{2}$ pints) water
Approx 900 g (2 lb) preserving or granulated sugar
Makes approx 900 g (2 lb)

Whitecurrant Jelly
1.4 kg (3 lb) whitecurrants, washed
570 ml (1 pint) water
Approx 900 g (2 lb) preserving or granulated sugar
Makes approx 675 g ($1\frac{1}{2}$ lb)

Raspberry Jelly
900 g (2 lb) raspberries, hulled
Approx 900 g (2 lb) jam sugar with added pectin
Makes approx 675 g ($1\frac{1}{2}$ lb)

Preparation time: 20–30 minutes
Cooking time: 35–40 minutes
Straining time: 3–4 hours or overnight

REDCURRANT, BLACKCURRANT AND WHITECURRANT JELLIES

This recipe can be used for any of the above fruits. Keep strictly to the quantities listed.

Put the currants, with their stalks still attached, and the water into a large, heavy-based stainless steel or enamel saucepan and simmer for 30–45 minutes or until very soft.

Meanwhile, prepare a jelly bag and stand, or place a large nylon sieve over a large deep bowl and line it with several layers of scalded muslin or a clean, scalded tea towel. Pour the fruit and all the juice into the jelly bag or sieve and allow it to drain for 3–4 hours or overnight. Do not squeeze the bag or press the fruit in the sieve, as this will make the jelly cloudy with fruit particles.

Measure the juice and pour it into a large, clean saucepan. Add 450 g (1 lb) of sugar for every 570 ml (1 pint) of juice and stir over a low heat until every granule of sugar has dissolved. Bring to a full rolling boil and boil until setting point is reached (see p.438). Start testing for a set after the jelly has boiled for 3–4 minutes.

Remove the pan from the heat, skim the scum from the surface of the jelly, then pot and cover immediately, working quickly before the jelly sets.

RASPBERRY JELLY

Simmer the raspberries, without water, for 20 minutes or until very soft and all the juice is extracted. Proceed as for redcurrant jelly, boiling for 4 minutes only.

Do not hasten the slow process of the jelly dripping into the bowl, as it is essential to ultimate success.

Fruits Preserved in Alcohol

Fruits preserved in this way make very acceptable presents, especially when packed in attractive airtight jars with decorative labels

INGREDIENTS

Peaches in rum
- 340g (12oz) granulated sugar
- 285ml (½ pint) water
- 2 cinnamon sticks, each 5cm (2in) long, broken in half
- 6 large ripe but firm peaches, washed
- 200ml (7fl oz) white or dark rum

Cherries in kirsch
- 550g (1¼lb) dark red cherries, washed, stalks left on
- 225g (8oz) granulated sugar
- 285ml (½ pint) water
- 150ml (¼ pint) kirsch

Pineapple in crème de menthe
- 2 medium pineapples, skin and 'eyes' removed
- 175g (6oz) granulated sugar
- 200ml (7fl oz) water
- 115ml (4fl oz) crème de menthe

Oranges in brandy
- 12 small oranges
- 340g (12oz) granulated sugar
- 285ml (½ pint) water
- 2 teaspoons allspice berries
- 200ml (7fl oz) brandy

Preparation time: 30 minutes, plus cooling time (for each fruit)

Cooking time: 15–20 minutes

Preserving fruit in alcohol is one of the oldest, simplest, and most delicious ways of preserving. These recipes use a syrup made with equal quantities of sugar syrup and alcohol. A different spirit is used with each kind of fruit, but you can, of course, use whichever spirit you prefer.

The amount of syrup required varies according to the type and quantity of the fruit and therefore it is best to prepare the fruits individually. Although the methods of preparing the fruits before cooking vary, the method of preserving is the same for each fruit.

BASIC METHOD

Put half the sugar and all the water specified in the recipe into a wide, shallow saucepan, adding any spices. Stir over a low heat until the sugar has dissolved, then add the prepared fruit and poach it gently for the time given.

Position a colander over a smaller saucepan and carefully spoon the fruit into it. Pour the poaching syrup into the saucepan. Leave the fruit to drain over the saucepan for 10 minutes, then transfer the colander to a plate and leave the fruit to become completely cold, covering the colander with muslin or a gauze cover to protect the fruit from dust or insects.

Add all the remaining sugar to the poaching syrup and stir over a low heat until every granule has dissolved. Then increase the heat, bring to the boil and boil rapidly until the temperature rises to 110°C (230°F) on a sugar thermometer. Remove the pan from the heat and pour the syrup into a measuring jug—the amount should be equal to the quantity of alcohol given in the recipe. If you have more syrup than is needed, reserve some for poaching other fruits or for using in a fruit salad; if less, make up the amount with alcohol. Cover the jug and stand aside until the syrup is completely cold, then stir in the alcohol.

Pack the poached and cooled fruits into clean, dry jars, filling them almost to the top. Pour enough syrup into the jars to cover the fruit completely. Cover the jars with airtight, acidproof screw tops. Label and store in a cool, dry, dark, airy cupboard for at least two months before using. Check the jars frequently. If the fruit rises to the top and is no longer covered by the syrup, stand the jars upside-down for a short while, but make sure that they do not leak.

SPECIAL INSTRUCTIONS

To make peaches in rum Cut the peaches in half and remove and discard the stones. When the syrup comes to the boil, poach the peaches in two batches for about 4 minutes each batch, turning them once. Drain as instructed above, leave until cold, then remove the skins.

To make cherries in kirsch Prick each cherry in two or three places with a clean darning needle, then poach for 4 minutes. The stalks can be left on the cherries if they are to be used to decorate cakes; otherwise, they may be removed before bottling if preferred.

To make pineapple in crème de menthe Cut each pineapple into slices, remove the woody core from the centre with a small, plain, round cutter and cut each slice in half. Poach for 4 minutes.

To make oranges in brandy With a potato peeler, peel the rind from three of the oranges very thinly, taking care not to cut off the white pith. Cut the rinds into fine strips and blanch in boiling water for 30 seconds, then drain and leave to cool. Using a very sharp knife, cut away all the peel and white pith from all 12 oranges. Poach for 5 minutes, turning once.

Add the blanched orange shreds to the syrup before pouring it over the fruit.

Take your pick from these mouth-watering cherries—preserved in kirsch over two months and matured to mellow perfection.

These jellies, with a country character, add piquancy to gammon and other hot or cold roast meats.

Autumn Jellies

Autumn fruits, such as crab apples, blackberries, japonicas and quinces, can be made into jellies with delightful mellow flavours to match the season

INGREDIENTS

Crab Apple Jelly
- 1.8 kg (4 lb) crab apples, washed and roughly chopped
- 1.7 litres (3 pints) water
- 1 lemon, washed and sliced
- Approx 800 g (1¾ lb) preserving or granulated sugar

Preparation time: 45 minutes plus straining
Cooking time: 1½ hours
Makes approx 1.1 kg (2½ lb)

Bramble Jelly
- 900 g (2 lb) blackberries, washed
- 900 g (2 lb) cooking apples, washed and chopped
- 1.15 litres (2 pints) water
- Finely grated rind and strained juice 1 lemon
- Approx 1.4 kg (3 lb) preserving or granulated sugar

Preparation time: 1 hour
Cooking time: 45 minutes
Straining time: Overnight
Makes approx 900 g (2 lb)

Quince or Japonica Jelly
- 2.7 kg (6 lb) quinces or japonicas, washed
- 3.4 litres (6 pints) water
- Thinly pared rind and strained juice 2 lemons
- Approx 1.1 kg (2½ lb) preserving or granulated sugar

Preparation time: 25 minutes plus straining
Cooking time: 2½ hours
Makes approx 1 kg (2 lb 3 oz)

CRAB APPLE JELLY

Remove any damaged parts from the apples and put them into a preserving pan with the water. Add the sliced lemon, bring to the boil, reduce the heat and cook very gently for about 35 minutes until the fruit is soft and pulpy.

Meanwhile, prepare a jelly bag and stand, or place a large nylon sieve over a large, deep bowl and line it with several layers of scalded muslin or a clean, scalded tea towel.

Drain the fruit through the bag or sieve for 3–4 hours, or overnight. Do not squeeze the bag or press the fruit as this will make the jelly cloudy.

Measure the strained juice, pour it into a clean preserving pan and add 450 g (1 lb) of sugar for every 570 ml (1 pint) of juice. Stir over a low heat until every granule of sugar has dissolved, then bring to a full, rolling boil and boil until setting point is reached (see p.438). Begin testing for setting point when the jelly has been boiling for 3–4 minutes. Once the setting point is reached, remove the pan from the heat, skim the scum from the surface and, working quickly before the jelly starts to set, pour it into clean, warm pots and cover immediately. When the jelly is cold, label the jars and store in a cool, dark airy cupboard.

BRAMBLE, QUINCE OR JAPONICA JELLY

Make in the same way as crab apple jelly, but use lemon rind and juice in place of sliced lemon. Cook blackberries for 35 minutes and quinces or japonicas for 1½–2 hours. Bramble jelly takes up to 15 minutes boiling to reach setting point.

Curds

Curds, consisting of fruit, butter and sugar, do not keep for long, but can be quickly made at any time of the year

Put the rind and juice of the fruit into a double boiler or heatproof bowl set over a saucepan of gently simmering water. Take care not to let the bottom of the bowl touch the water. Add the butter and sugar and strain in the eggs through a nylon sieve to remove the white threads.

Stir the mixture continuously over a moderate heat for 20–25 minutes or until thick enough to coat the back of the spoon and hold a light ribbon trail. Do not let it boil as it will curdle.

Remove the pan from the heat and immediately pour the curd through a fine nylon sieve into a clean, warm jar. Cover immediately with a waxed paper disc and leave until completely cold. When the curd is cold, cover the jar with cellophane, then label and store it in the refrigerator for up to six weeks.

Lemon, lime and orange curds can be spread on scones or used to fill sponge cakes and tartlets.

INGREDIENTS

Lemon curd
- Finely grated rind and strained juice 2 large lemons
- 85g (3oz) unsalted butter, cut into small pieces
- 225g (8oz) caster sugar
- 3 eggs, size 2, beaten

Lime curd
- Finely grated rind and strained juice 4 large limes
- 85g (3oz) unsalted butter, cut into small pieces
- 175g (6oz) caster sugar
- 3 eggs, size 2, beaten

Orange curd
- Finely grated rind and strained juice 2 large oranges, preferably Seville
- 85g (3oz) unsalted butter, cut into small pieces
- 85g (3oz) caster sugar—if using Seville oranges, add 30–60g (1–2oz) more
- 3 eggs, size 2, beaten

Preparation time: 30 minutes
Cooking time: 25 minutes
Makes approx 450g (1lb)

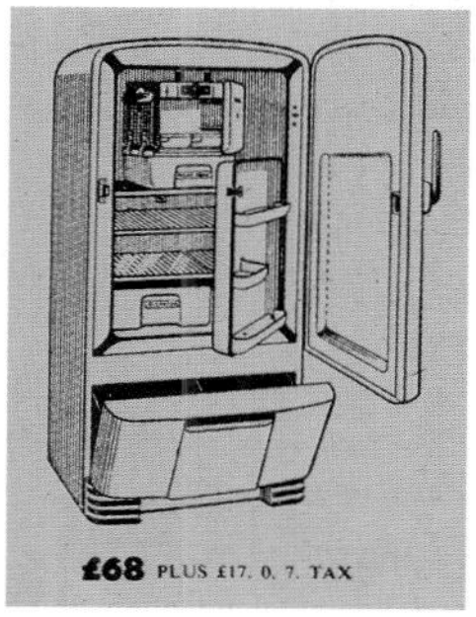

The revolutionary
In the years just after the war, big roomy refrigerators became more widely available, changing the lives of families that hitherto possessed only a larder or an icebox. But their full potential could not be explored until 1954, when rationing finally ended.

Vegetable Pickles

A truly memorable way of serving these pungent pickles is with rye bread and salt beef

Ingredients

Pickled beetroot with horseradish
- 570 ml (1 pint) distilled malt vinegar
- 2 level teaspoons allspice berries
- ½ level teaspoon salt
- 30 g (1 oz) demerara sugar
- 1.4 kg (3 lb) raw beetroot
- 175 g (6 oz) fresh horseradish

Preparation time: 50 minutes
Cooking time: 1½ hours
Makes approx 1.8 kg (4 lb)

Ma's pickled onions
- 1.8 kg (4 lb) silverskin onions
- 60 g (2 oz) white peppercorns
- 30 g (1 oz) allspice berries
- 6 cloves
- 2.3 litres (4 pints) white wine vinegar or distilled malt vinegar
- 1½ level tablespoons salt

Preparation time: 3–4 hours
Cooking time: 13–18 minutes
Makes approx 2 kg (4½ lb)

Mixed pickled vegetables
- 1 cucumber
- 2 large peppers, 1 red and 1 green
- 1 medium cauliflower
- 175 g (6 oz) fine green beans
- 175 g (6 oz) button onions
- 175 g (6 oz) baby carrots
- 150 g (5 oz) plus 1½ level teaspoons salt
- 1.7 litres (3 pints) distilled malt vinegar
- 450 g (1 lb) granulated sugar
- 1 teaspoon black peppercorns
- 1 teaspoon pickling spice

Preparation time: 50 minutes
Standing time: 48 hours
Makes approx 1.8 kg (4 lb)

Pickled beetroot with horseradish

Pour the vinegar into a stainless steel or enamel saucepan and add the allspice berries, salt and demerara sugar. Bring to the boil, then remove the pan from the heat, cover and leave to stand for 2 hours.

Meanwhile, wash the beetroot, taking care not to break the skin. Place it, unpeeled, in a saucepan and add enough water to cover. Bring to the boil, reduce the heat, cover and simmer for 1½ hours or until it is tender. While the beetroot is cooking, scrub, peel and coarsely grate the horseradish.

When the beetroot is cooked, remove the pan from the heat and leave the beetroot in the water to cool completely, then drain, remove the skin and dice the flesh.

Pack the beetroot and horseradish, in alternate layers, in clean, warm jars. Bring the spiced vinegar to the boil and pour it into the jars to cover the beetroot and horseradish completely. Cover the jars with vinegarproof lids and, when cold, label and store in a cool, dry, airy cupboard for one month before using. Use within three to four months.

Ma's pickled onions

Put the onions into a large bowl and cover them with cold water. Using a stainless steel knife, peel the onions under the water—to prevent tears! Once peeled, put them into a bowl of clean, cold water.

Tie up the peppercorns, allspice and cloves in a small square of muslin and put into a large, stainless steel or enamel saucepan with the vinegar and salt. Bring to the boil, reduce the heat and simmer for 3 minutes, then skim any scum from the surface and discard the spices.

Drain the onions and dry well with kitchen paper. Bring the vinegar to the boil, add the onions and cook for 5 minutes or until translucent.

Strain off the hot vinegar from the onions and reserve. Pack the hot onions tightly in clean, warm jars. Fill each jar with enough hot vinegar to cover the onions completely, then cover the jars with vinegarproof lids. When the onions are cold, label the jars and store in a cool, dry, airy cupboard for one month before eating. Use within six months.

Mixed pickled vegetables

To prepare the vegetables, wash the cucumber, cut it in half lengthways and scoop out the seeds with a teaspoon. Cut the flesh into small dice and put them into a very large bowl.

Deseed and wash the peppers, then cut each one in half lengthways. Cut up the halves into strips about 1.3 cm (½ in) wide, then cut the strips into squares and put them into the bowl.

Trim the cauliflower, cut it into small florets. Wash the florets well, then drain and add to the bowl.

Top and tail the beans, peel and halve the button onions and peel the carrots, then add to the bowl.

Sprinkle the vegetable mixture with 150 g (5 oz) of the salt and mix well together. Cover the bowl and chill in the refrigerator for 48 hours.

Meanwhile, make the sweet spiced vinegar. Pour the distilled malt vinegar into a stainless steel or enamel saucepan and add the sugar, peppercorns, pickling spice and remaining salt. Heat gently until the sugar has dissolved, stirring frequently. Strain the vinegar through a muslin-lined sieve into a heatproof bowl or jug, cover and leave until cold.

Pour the salted vegetables into a colander and rinse under cold running water. Drain, dry well on kitchen paper, then pack into clean jars. Pour in enough spiced vinegar to cover the vegetables completely. Cover with vinegarproof lids, label and store in a cool, dry, airy cupboard for at least two weeks before using. Use within two to three months.

As traditional as the cheeses they enhance are onion, beetroot and vegetable pickles.

Foods from the Wild

Left to its own devices, a hedgerow will, it is said, add to its complement of shrubs at the rate of one new species every 100 years. Looked at in this light, some of our hedges must date back to Saxon times, but whatever their age, there is no doubt about their bounty. Long ago our ancestors learned to harvest them and to produce such delicacies as *Hip and Haw Jelly, Nettle and Potato Soup* and *Whortleberry Tart*. Then, turning a feast into a celebration, they discovered the pleasures of *Sloe Gin, Hawthorn Liqueurs* and the sparkling delights of *Elderflower Champagne*.

Jam tomorrow
In wartime villages, not only sloes but many other wild fruits were called into service for jam-making. Each summer the Ministry of Food awarded an extra sugar ration for the purpose; the fruit was collected by schoolchildren and most of the work was carried out by the Women's Institutes.

The unusual rich, dark colour of the jam and its sharp flavour go well with buttered crumpets.

Sloe Jam

Sloes are the fruits of the blackthorn, whose flowers, on as yet leafless, spiky twigs, are among the first harbingers of spring

INGREDIENTS

1.8 kg (4 lb) sloes, washed
Approx 900 g (2 lb) preserving or granulated sugar
Preparation time: 25 minutes
Cooking time: approx 40 minutes
Makes approx 1.8 kg (4 lb)

Pick over the sloes and discard any damaged fruit, then put them into a saucepan with just enough cold water to cover. Bring to the boil, reduce the heat and simmer for 10 minutes or until very soft. Remove from the heat and cool slightly.

Rub the sloes through a nylon sieve. Discard the stones and measure the purée, then put it into an enamel or stainless steel, heavy-based saucepan. For every 570 ml (1 pint) of purée add 450 g (1 lb) of sugar, then heat slowly, stirring occasionally until the sugar has dissolved.

Increase the heat and boil gently until the jam reaches setting point (see p.438), then immediately remove the saucepan from the heat. Skim any scum from the surface of the jam, then pour it into clean, warm jars. Cover immediately with waxed paper discs and cellophane covers.

Rowan and Crab Apple Jelly

Rowan berries were once valued as a sure defence against witchcraft

INGREDIENTS

1.1 kg (2½ lb) rowan berries
1.4 kg (3 lb) crab apples or cooking apples, washed
1.7 litres (3 pints) water
Approx 1.4 kg (3 lb) preserving or granulated sugar

Preparation time: 30 minutes
Cooking time: 1½ hours
Straining time: 3–4 hours
Makes 1.6–1.8 kg (3½–4 lb)

Remove the rowan berries from their stalks, wash them well and put them into a large, heavy-based, stainless steel or enamel saucepan. Without peeling or coring, roughly cut up the crab apples and add them to the pan. Add the water, bring to the boil, then reduce the heat, cover and simmer for about 30–40 minutes until the fruit is extremely soft.

Meanwhile, prepare a jelly bag and stand or place a large, nylon sieve over a deep bowl and line it with several layers of scalded muslin or a clean, scalded tea towel. Pour the fruit and all the juice into the bag or sieve and leave to drain for 3–4 hours or overnight until it stops dripping.

Measure the juice and pour it into a clean saucepan. For every 570 ml (1 pint) of juice, add 450 g (1 lb) of sugar, then stir over a low heat until every granule of sugar has fully dissolved. Bring to a fast, rolling boil and boil for 10–15 minutes or until setting point is reached (see p.438).

Remove from the heat, skim the scum from the surface and quickly pour the jelly into clean, warm jam jars. Cover immediately with waxed paper discs and cellophane covers. Leave until cold and firmly set, without moving the jars. Store in a cool, dark, airy cupboard.

Cooking apples can be used instead of crab apples if preferred.

The bittersweet tang of this jelly makes it the classic accompaniment to game.

Take care not to move the jars while the jelly is setting. If moved, it will split.

Homemade bread with rhubarb jam and a compote of figs, honey and thyme turn a simple picnic into a celebration of summer's goodness.

Summer's Delight

Elderflower and thyme—traditional flavours of hedgerow and downland—are summoned to give flair to garden rhubarb and a luxurious combination of figs and honey

INGREDIENTS

Elderflower & rhubarb jam
1.4 kg (3 lb) trimmed rhubarb, washed and sliced
1.4 kg (3 lb) jam sugar with added pectin
85 g (3 oz) elderflower heads
15 g (½ oz) unsalted butter
Preparation time: 40 minutes
Standing time: 48 hours
Cooking time: 35 minutes
Makes 2.3 kg (5 lb) jam

Figs with wild thyme and honey
500 g (1 lb 2 oz) semi-dried honeyed figs or dried figs
4–6 small wild thyme sprigs, each about 5 cm (2 in) long
570 ml (1 pint) dry, fruity wine, such as a Semillon Chardonnay
Finely pared rind and strained juice 1 large lemon
60 g (2 oz) caster sugar
2 tablespoons clear or set honey
Thyme flowers to decorate
Preparation time: 15 minutes
Cooking time: 1 hour 20 minutes
Serves six

ELDERFLOWER AND RHUBARB JAM

Mix the prepared rhubarb and the sugar together well in a large bowl, preferably a plastic one with a lid.

Carefully trim the blossoms from the elderflower heads and discard the flower stalks. Lay the flowers in the centre of a small square of muslin and tie the corners together to enclose the flowers securely. Bury the muslin bag in the centre of the bowl of rhubarb. Cover the bowl and leave to stand in a cool place for 24 hours, stirring occasionally.

The next day, turn the rhubarb and the muslin bag into a large saucepan and heat gently until all the sugar has dissolved and the rhubarb is hot, but not boiling. Remove the pan from the heat and pour the rhubarb and the muslin bag back into the bowl. Cover and leave to stand for another 24 hours.

Remove the muslin bag from the rhubarb and squeeze it tightly over a preserving pan or a very large, heavy-based saucepan to extract all the juice. Add the rhubarb and syrup to the pan and discard the muslin bag. Put the jam jars into a warm oven to heat.

Stirring continuously over a moderate heat, bring the rhubarb to boiling point, then stir in the butter. Increase the heat, bring the jam to a full rolling boil and boil for 4 minutes. (Rhubarb is low in pectin and would normally need the addition of lemon juice plus lengthy boiling to reach setting point. By using jam sugar, which contains natural pectin, the boiling time is reduced, resulting in a jam with a better flavour and colour.)

Remove the pan from the heat and immediately pour the hot jam into the warm jam jars. Cover the jars with waxed paper discs and cellophane covers and leave to stand until cold.

When the jam is cold, label the jars and store in a cool, dry, airy cupboard.

Elderflower and gooseberry jam can be made by the same method but, as gooseberries are high in pectin, use ordinary preserving sugar in place of the jam sugar with pectin, and boil in the usual way until setting point is reached (see p.438).

FIGS WITH WILD THYME AND HONEY

The flavours of wild thyme, honey and lemon make this an unusual way of cooking dried figs, but when gathering any herbs or flowers from the wild, take care to take only as much as you need and never to damage or uproot the plants.

Using kitchen scissors, snip off the stalk end from each fig. Rinse and drain the sprigs of thyme. Pour the wine into a large, stainless steel or enamel saucepan and add the lemon rind, lemon juice, caster sugar and honey. Stir over a low heat until the sugar has dissolved, then bring to the boil.

Add the figs and thyme to the wine, reduce the heat, cover and simmer very gently for 1–1¼ hours, or until the figs are plump and soft. Remove the pan from the heat and pour the figs and wine into a heated serving dish—most of the wine will have been absorbed by the figs, the rest will have been reduced to a slightly syrupy consistency. Decorate with the thyme flowers and serve with whipped cream flavoured with vanilla.

Alternatively, pour the figs and wine into a bowl, allow to cool, then cover and refrigerate until cold. (They will keep in the refrigerator for seven to ten days.) Serve chilled with whipped cream.

These figs go particularly well with the flummery on p.261, making them a perfect punctuation in the long parade of summer fruits.

Reasonable force
In the kitchen gardens of the day before yesterday, early rhubarb was obtained by putting one of these crocks over the plant in late winter. This would force a fine crop along by February or March.

Bilberry Tart

INGREDIENTS

For the pastry case
175 g (6 oz) plain flour
30 g (1 oz) caster sugar
115 g (4 oz) butter
2 tablespoons beaten egg

For the filling
30 g (1 oz) ground almonds
175 g (6 oz) bilberries, washed and dried
30–60 g (1–2 oz) caster sugar
2 eggs, size 1
200 ml (7 fl oz) milk or single cream
½ level teaspoon ground cinnamon
Icing sugar for sprinkling
Preparation time: 40 minutes
Cooking time: 30 minutes
Serves four to six

Wild bilberries have a tangy flavour all their own; for a different but equally delicious tart, try blueberries, but use less sugar to sweeten the fruit

To make the pastry case, sift the flour and sugar into a mixing bowl and rub in the butter until the mixture resembles fine breadcrumbs. Add the beaten egg and mix to form a stiff dough. Knead gently on a lightly floured surface for a few seconds until smooth, then wrap and chill for 15 minutes.

Roll out the dough on a lightly floured surface and with it line a 21.5 cm (8½ in) diameter, 2.5 cm (1 in) deep flan tin. Chill the dough again, meanwhile preheating the oven to 190°C (375°F, gas mark 5).

Sprinkle the ground almonds evenly over the base of the unbaked pastry case, then add the bilberries and sprinkle with the sugar. Bake in the centre of the oven for 10 minutes until the berries are just beginning to soften.

Remove from the oven, lightly whisk the eggs with the milk or cream and the ground cinnamon, pour over the partly cooked berries and return to the oven for about 20 minutes until the custard is lightly set, risen and browned. Serve warm or cold, sprinkled with icing sugar.

Bilberries are generally harvested by means of a bilberry comb which, when raked through the low bushes, gathers berries and leaves together in its shovel-like scoop.

The sharpness of cranberries is mellowed by a blend of orange, brown sugar and Cointreau.

Lattice-topped Cranberry Pie

The delicious fruit filling lies encased in a crunchy, nutty pastry

Heat the cranberries, the orange rind and juice and the brown sugar gently in a saucepan until the sugar has dissolved. Cover and simmer for 5–8 minutes or until the cranberries are just softened. Drain in a nylon sieve placed over a bowl.

Return the juice to the pan and boil gently until reduced by half and syrupy. Remove from the heat and stir in the cranberries and the Cointreau, if using. Cover and allow to cool for 1 hour.

Preheat the oven to 200°C (400°F, gas mark 6). To make the pastry, mix the flour, ground hazelnuts, cinnamon and 30g (1oz) of the sugar in a bowl, then rub in the butter until the mixture resembles breadcrumbs. Bind with sufficient beaten egg to make a soft but not sticky dough. Reserve the remaining beaten egg for glazing. Wrap the dough in cling film and chill for 20 minutes.

Roll out two-thirds of the chilled dough to just over 6mm (¼in) thick, line a lightly buttered 23cm (9in) pie plate and fill with cranberry mixture. Roll out the remaining dough to an oblong and cut into long strips, each about 1.3cm (½in) wide, using a pastry wheel or knife. Brush the edges of the dough on the plate with a little cold water, then cover the pie with the strips, arranging them in a lattice pattern. Reroll the trimmings and cut more strips if necessary.

Press the edges gently to seal, then trim. Brush with the remaining beaten egg, scatter the chopped hazelnuts over the top and sprinkle with the remaining caster sugar.

Bake, on a baking tray, in the centre of the oven for 15 minutes, then reduce the oven temperature to 180°C (350°F, gas mark 4) and bake for a further 15 minutes or until crisp and golden. If the pie starts to overbrown, cover with foil or greaseproof paper. Serve warm or cold with whipped cream.

INGREDIENTS

- 900G (2LB) CRANBERRIES, TOPPED, TAILED AND WASHED
- FINELY GRATED RIND AND STRAINED JUICE ½ ORANGE
- 275G (10OZ) SOFT LIGHT BROWN SUGAR
- 2 TABLESPOONS COINTREAU (OPTIONAL)

For the pastry

- 225G (8OZ) PLAIN FLOUR, SIEVED
- 80G (2¾OZ) GROUND HAZELNUTS
- ½ LEVEL TEASPOON GROUND CINNAMON
- 60G (2OZ) CASTER SUGAR
- 150G (5OZ) BUTTER
- 2 EGGS, SIZE 2, BEATEN
- 30G (1OZ) HAZELNUTS, SKINNED AND COARSELY CHOPPED

Preparation time: 50 MINUTES
Cooking time: 30 MINUTES
Cooling time: 1 HOUR
Serves six

Sweet chestnuts collected on a country walk, plus sugar and patience, make elegant nibbles to round off a dinner party.

Instead of drying the chestnuts after candying, you can store them in their syrup for 3-4 weeks in a covered container in the refrigerator.

Candied Chestnuts

Prettily packed and labelled 'Marrons Glacés', your chestnuts would make impressive Christmas presents for your friends

INGREDIENTS

600G (1 LB 5 OZ) FRESH CHESTNUTS, PEELED (SEE P.440) OR 450G (1 LB) FROZEN PEELED CHESTNUTS

450G (1 LB) GRANULATED SUGAR

PREPARATION TIME: 1 HOUR (LESS FOR FROZEN CHESTNUTS) PLUS 15 MINUTES EACH DAY FOR 2 DAYS

DRYING TIME: 2–3 DAYS

PUT the prepared chestnuts into a large saucepan and add just enough cold water to cover them. Bring to the boil, then reduce the heat and simmer gently until they are just tender—fresh chestnuts will need about 20 minutes, frozen ones, about 5 minutes. Take care not to overcook them, as they may break up during the candying process. Drain well, reserving 150 ml (¼ pint) of the cooking water.

Pour the reserved water into a saucepan, add the sugar and stir over a gentle heat until dissolved. Add the chestnuts and bring to the boil, then remove from the heat, cover and leave to soak for 24 hours in a warm place.

Day 2: Uncover the saucepan and bring the chestnuts back to the boil. Remove the pan from the heat, cover and leave to soak for another 24 hours.

Day 3: Uncover the saucepan and bring the chestnuts back to the boil. Remove the pan from the heat and, using a slotted spoon, transfer the chestnuts to a wire rack placed over a tray. Leave to dry in a warm place for two to three days until no longer sticky.

Pack the candied chestnuts into wooden or cardboard boxes. Line the boxes and interleave the layers of nuts with waxed paper or nonstick parchment. Do not use airtight containers as the chestnuts may go mouldy.

Chestnut Flan

Despite its modest title, this is a pudding of seriously rich content

Sift the flour into a bowl and rub in the butter until the mixture resembles fine breadcrumbs. Stir in the sugar, then mix with the egg yolks to make a soft but not sticky dough. On a lightly floured surface, roll out the dough to a neat round about 30 cm (12 in) in diameter and line a 25 × 2.5 cm (10 × 1 in) fluted flan tin, pressing the dough well into the flutes. Trim the edge and prick the base and sides with a fork. Chill for 30 minutes.

Preheat the oven to 200°c (400°f, gas mark 6). Bake the flan case for 20 minutes or until crisp and lightly golden. Remove from the oven and allow to cool.

Meanwhile, to make the filling, put the chestnuts, single cream, 2 tablespoons of the brandy, the vanilla, orange flower water, caster sugar and butter into a heavy-based saucepan. Partially cover and cook gently, stirring frequently, for 40–45 minutes or until the chestnuts are soft and almost all the cream has been absorbed. Take care not to let the mixture burn or stick to the bottom of the pan.

Pass the mixture through a nylon sieve into a bowl and allow to cool. (At this stage it should be quite dry.) Stir in the cherry brandy and 2 tablespoons of the remaining brandy. Whisk 150 ml (¼ pint) of the double cream until it holds a soft peak, then fold into the chestnut mixture.

Transfer the flan case from the tin to a flat plate, fill with the chestnut mixture and level the surface. Whisk the remaining cream and brandy together until thick but not buttery. Spoon the brandy cream into a piping bag fitted with a star nozzle and pipe it decoratively round the edge of the flan. Alternatively, spread the brandy cream over the top of the flan and mark it into swirls. Decorate with candied chestnuts and the crystallised violets, if using, and chill before serving.

The pastry case can be made and filled with the luscious chestnut mixture, then chilled overnight, leaving the brandy and cream decoration as the final touch.

INGREDIENTS

For the flan case
- 150 g (5 oz) plain flour
- 85 g (3 oz) butter
- 30 g (1 oz) icing sugar
- 2 egg yolks, size 2

For the filling
- 600 g (1 lb 5 oz) fresh, peeled chestnuts, (see p.440) or 450 g (1 lb) frozen peeled chestnuts
- 285 ml (½ pint) single cream
- 6 tablespoons brandy
- ½ teaspoon natural vanilla extract or essence
- 2 tablespoons orange flower water
- 60 g (2 oz) caster sugar
- 60 g (2 oz) butter
- 2 tablespoons cherry brandy
- 425 ml (¾ pint) double cream
- Candied chestnuts, chopped or sliced, and crystallised violets (see p.286) to decorate (optional)

Preparation time: 1 hour (allow extra time to peel fresh chestnuts)
Cooking time: 50 minutes
Serves eight

Package deal
Between the wars, collecting cigarette cards became something of a national passion. One of a series was issued with every cigarette packet, and many different subjects, often beautifully illustrated, were covered. This depiction of a sweet chestnut was one of a British Trees series.

An Elderberry Trio

Most generous of shrubs, the elder lends its hollowed stems for small boys' peashooters—and its flowers and berries for food and wines

INGREDIENTS

Elderberry chutney

900g (2lb) elderberries
450g (1lb) cooking apples, peeled, cored and chopped
450g (1lb) onions, peeled and chopped
450g (1lb) seedless raisins
1 level teaspoon each ground cinnamon, paprika and ground ginger
¼ level teaspoon cayenne pepper
225g (8oz) granulated sugar
285ml (½ pint) distilled malt vinegar

Preparation time: 1½ hours
Cooking time: 1¾–2 hours
Makes 900g (2lb)

Elderberry port

2.3 litres (4 pints) fresh or frozen elderberries, measured without stalks
Approx 2.8 litres (5 pints) water
1.5kg (3¼lb) granulated sugar
115g (4oz) large seedless raisins
1 level teaspoon each yeast nutrient and pectic enzyme
1 sachet dried yeast for wine making
200ml (7fl oz) brandy (optional)

Makes 6 × 70cl (1¼ pint) bottles

Light elderberry wine

1kg (2lb 3oz) granulated sugar
2 level teaspoons citric acid
1 level teaspoon each yeast nutrient, tartaric acid, and pectic enzyme
1 vitamin B_1 tablet (3mg)
1 sachet dried yeast for wine making

Makes 6 × 70cl (1¼ pint) bottles

ELDERBERRY CHUTNEY

Wearing a pair of rubber gloves and using a fork, carefully strip the elderberries from their stalks. Wash the berries well, drain and put into a large, stainless steel or enamel saucepan. Cook gently for 10–15 minutes or until soft. Pass the berries and their juice through a nylon sieve into a bowl to remove the pips.

Pour the pulp into a large preserving pan and add the apples, onions, raisins, spices, sugar and vinegar. Cook gently for 1½–2 hours, stirring frequently, until the chutney is thick and leaves a clear trail that does not close up again quickly when a spoon is pulled across the bottom of the pan. Take care not to allow it to stick to the pan or burn.

Remove the pan from the heat and spoon the chutney immediately into clean, warm jars and cover with vinegar-proof lids. When cold, label the jars and store in a cool, dry, airy cupboard for at least a month before using.

ELDERBERRY PORT

Wash the elderberries in a large bowl of cold water, removing any that float as these are usually unripe. Drain the berries and put them into a large stainless steel or enamel saucepan and add the water, making sure that the berries are well covered (add more water if necessary). Bring to the boil, then reduce the heat and simmer gently for 15 minutes.

Strain the liquid through a nylon sieve into a sterilised bucket and discard the elderberries, or use them to make light elderberry wine. Add the sugar and raisins to the hot liquid and stir until the sugar is completely dissolved. Cover the bucket and allow the liquid to cool down to 35°–40°c (95°–104°f).

When cooled, add the yeast nutrient, pectic enzyme and the dried yeast, following the directions on the packets. Pour into a sterilised demijohn, filling only up to the shoulder of the jar to allow room for vigorous fermentation later. Fit the demijohn with a cork and airlock and allow to ferment out at a room temperature of about 19°–21°c (66°–70°f), shaking gently once each day for the first week. As fermentation subsides, top up with cooled, boiled water.

When the fermentation process is complete and there are no more bubbles in the airlock, strain the liquid into a sterilised demijohn and then discard the raisins. Alternatively, strain the wine first into a sterilised bucket, then clean and sterilise the demijohn and pour the wine back into it. Fit with a cork and airlock.

Allow the wine to mature for a minimum of six months, longer if possible. Check the airlock frequently to make sure that it does not dry out and top up with water as and when necessary. If a sediment forms in the bottom of the jar, siphon the wine off into a sterilised demijohn and fit with a cork and airlock.

When matured, bottle and cork the port. If wished, fortify it by adding about 7 teaspoons of brandy to each bottle.

LIGHT ELDERBERRY WINE

After draining the elderberries from the elderberry port, put them into a sterilised bucket and add 3.4 litres (6 pints) of cold water and the granulated sugar, citric acid, yeast nutrient, tartaric acid, pectic enzyme, vitamin B_1 tablet and the yeast. Cover the bucket and leave it in a warm place for four days, stirring daily.

Strain the liquid through a nylon straining bag, discarding the elderberries. Pour the liquid into a sterilised demijohn and top up to the shoulder with cooled, boiled water. Fit the demijohn with a cork and airlock and ferment out at 19°–21°c (66°–70°f), shaking the jar gently each day for the first week. Proceed as for elderberry port, but do not add the brandy when bottling.

Elderberry port—hardly distinguishable from the grape version—elderberry chutney and a bite of cheese round off a fine meal.

INGREDIENTS

900g (2lb) samphire
60g (2oz) salt
1.15 litres (2 pints) distilled malt vinegar
Preparation time: 30 minutes plus 24 hours for setting
Makes 900g (2lb)

Pickled Samphire

Samphire, over which the tide must flow twice a day, has something of the texture and flavour of salty asparagus

Cut the roots and any brown parts from the samphire stalks, leaving the fleshy green shoots, then wash and dry well. Put half the samphire into a glass or china bowl and sprinkle with half the salt, then cover with the remaining samphire and sprinkle with the rest of the salt. Cover and leave in a cool place for 24 hours.

Pour the samphire into a colander and rinse well under cold water. Drain, then dry thoroughly on a clean tea towel. Pack into clean, heatproof, preserving jars. Bring the vinegar to the boil and pour over the samphire, making sure it is completely covered. You may need more or less vinegar, depending on how tightly the samphire is packed, but do not pack too tightly. Seal with airtight, vinegar-proof covers and leave for at least a week before using.

Wind and water
Samphire comes from the strange world of mud flats, sandbanks and creeks that occurs where East Anglia meets the North Sea. It is a world of mists, whose voice is the plaintive cries of the marsh birds—which is why it is so often chosen as the setting for detective stories.

Salt and vinegar will turn a marsh plant into a sprightly companion for cheese or cold meats.

Make this Soup in Spring when nettles are young and tender - but wear rubber gloves when gathering them.

Chives, conveniently in flower at the time when young nettles are abundant, give a delicate garnish to the soup, while potatoes give body.

Nettle & Potato Soup

Once boiled, young nettles become stingless, whereupon they can be made the basis of a flavoursome soup

RINSE the nettle leaves under cold running water and pat them dry with kitchen paper. Melt a quarter of the butter in a large saucepan. When it is sizzling, add the nettle leaves and stir over a moderate heat for about 30 seconds until the leaves wilt. Transfer to a plate and set aside.

Heat the remaining butter in the saucepan, add the onion and potatoes and sauté over a moderate heat for 5–10 minutes until a very pale golden colour.

Pour the stock into the pan, season well with the salt and pepper and stir in the wilted nettle leaves. Bring the soup to the boil, stirring it continuously. Then reduce the heat, cover the pan and simmer, stirring occasionally, for 30 minutes, or until the potatoes are soft.

Using a slotted spoon, lift two spoonfuls of the potatoes from the soup and put them into a small bowl. Mash them with the spoon, then stir them back into the soup to thicken it slightly.

Pour the thickened soup into a heated tureen or ladle it directly into individual bowls. Just before serving, swirl the cream on top and garnish with the snipped chives and chive flower petals. Serve with slices of warm white or granary bread.

INGREDIENTS

- 15–30G (½–1 OZ) YOUNG NETTLE LEAVES
- 60G (2 OZ) BUTTER
- 1 LARGE ONION, PEELED AND FINELY CHOPPED
- 550G (1¼ LB) POTATOES, PEELED AND CUT INTO SMALL DICE
- 1 LITRE (1¾ PINTS) CHICKEN OR VEGETABLE STOCK (SEE PP.433, 434)
- SALT AND FRESHLY GROUND BLACK PEPPER
- 3–4 TABLESPOONS SINGLE CREAM
- 2 TABLESPOONS SNIPPED FRESH CHIVES
- 1–2 CHIVE FLOWER HEADS, SEPARATED INTO PETALS

PREPARATION TIME: 20 MINUTES
COOKING TIME: 40 MINUTES
SERVES FOUR

Rosehip Syrup

The lightly scented syrup makes an attractive base for a fresh fruit salad

INGREDIENTS

900 G (2 LB) RIPE ROSEHIPS, WASHED
2.6 LITRES (4½ PINTS) WATER
450 G (1 LB) GRANULATED SUGAR
PREPARATION TIME: 45 MINUTES
COOKING TIME: 1 HOUR
STERILISING TIME: 30 MINUTES
MAKES 850 ML (1½ PINTS)

TRIM the stalks from the rosehips, then mince them coarsely in a food processor or chop them roughly by hand.

Put 1.7 litres (3 pints) of the water into a large, stainless steel or enamel saucepan or preserving pan and bring to the boil. Add the prepared rosehips and boil gently for 15 minutes. Allow to cool for 15 minutes, then pour into a nylon sieve set over a bowl. Reserve the juice and the pulp. Return the pulp to the pan, add the remaining water, bring to the boil and cook gently for 15 minutes. Stir in the reserved juice, then strain the mixture through a scalded jelly bag or a large sieve lined with several layers of scalded muslin or a clean, scalded tea towel. Pour the strained juice into a stainless steel or enamel saucepan and boil gently until reduced to 850 ml (1½ pints). Add the sugar and stir until completely dissolved, then simmer for 10 minutes.

As quickly as possible, pour the hot syrup into small, warm, clean screw-top bottles, filling them to within 3.8 cm (1½ in) of the tops. Screw the tops loosely onto the bottles.

Stand the bottles, spaced well apart, on a trivet or piece of wood in a large, deep, heavy saucepan. Fill the saucepan with cold water to just above the level of the syrup. Heat the water to sterilising point, 77°C (170°F) on a thermometer, and maintain that temperature for 30 minutes, adjusting the heat as necessary. Using tongs, remove the bottles from the saucepan and screw the tops on tightly. Wipe and label the bottles when cold. Store in a cool, dark, airy cupboard. The syrup will keep for up to two months.

With its high vitamin content, this sweet, rosy-hued drink will help in warding off winter colds.

ROSY HEALTH
In 1941, the Ministry of Health discovered that rosehips contained five times more vitamin C than oranges. Vast quantities were gathered by the WI and the WVS and delivered to pharmaceutical processors to be made into National Rosehip Syrup. This was issued, free of charge, to all children over the age of five.

A few blanched almonds will mellow the flavour of the sloes, which will themselves be juicier if they are left on the blackthorn bush until after the first frosts.

Freezing and thawing the sloes before using them for the gin will make them softer and yield more juice.

Sloe Gin

A warming, very English tipple that has featured in sportsmen's flasks for centuries

Bruise the sloes by squeezing them between finger and thumb to split the skins, then put them into a large, clean jar (preferably one with a ground glass stopper). Add the sugar, gin and almonds to the fruit and stir well.

Cover the jar and leave the gin to infuse for about three months in a cool, dark cupboard, shaking twice weekly.

Strain through a nylon sieve lined with scalded muslin or a scalded tea towel, pour into a clean bottle and seal.

Sloe gin is usually drunk neat but can be turned into sloe gin fizz, a cocktail of one measure of sloe gin, a teaspoon of lemon juice and soda water to taste.

Damson gin may be made in the same way, using small damsons instead of sloes.

INGREDIENTS

450G (1 LB) SLOES, WASHED
200G (7 OZ) DEMERARA OR CASTER SUGAR
725ML (1¼ PINTS) GIN
30G (1 OZ) ALMONDS, BLANCHED

PREPARATION TIME: 30 MINUTES
STANDING TIME: 3 MONTHS
MAKES 725ML (1¼ PINTS)

It is the cherry kernels that add the final, distinctive fillip to this old-fashioned liqueur whose flavour departs entirely from the basic brandy.

Crack open the cherry stones with nutcrackers to extract the kernels, which will need to be skinned and blanched before use.

Victorian Wild Cherry Ratafia

There are ratafias—flavoured wines or spirits—all over the drinking world. This one could also be made with cultivated dark cherries

INGREDIENTS

675 G (1½ LB) WILD CHERRIES, STALKS REMOVED, WASHED AND DRIED
225 G (8 OZ) RASPBERRIES, HULLED AND CRUSHED
225 G (8 OZ) CASTER SUGAR
725 ML (1¼ PINTS) BRANDY, 40% VOL
1 LARGE FRESH CORIANDER SPRIG
1 CINNAMON STICK, APPROX 15 CM (6 IN) LONG

PREPARATION TIME: 30 MINUTES, PLUS STIRRING EVERY DAY FOR 4 DAYS.

MAKES 1 LITRE (1¾ PINTS)

WITH a cherry stoner, remove stones from some of the cherries until you have 45 g (1½ oz). Reserve the stones. Put the stoned and unstoned cherries into a bowl and stand a potato masher upright in the centre. Cover the bowl with a clean plastic bag to prevent splashes and make a hole to accommodate the handle of the potato masher. Mash the cherries and put the pulp and juice into a jar. Stir in the raspberries, cover and leave for four days, stirring two or three times daily.

On the fourth day, crack open the reserved cherry stones, remove the kernels and blanch and skin them. Add the sugar to the fruit and stir until completely dissolved. Stir in the kernels with the brandy, coriander and cinnamon. Cover and leave in a cool, dark, airy cupboard to infuse for one month.

Sterilise a large bowl, a square of muslin and a nylon sieve with boiling water. Drain well and squeeze the muslin dry. Line the sieve with the sterilised muslin and place it over the bowl. Pour the infused brandy and all the fruit pulp into the sieve, discarding the coriander and cinnamon.

Allow the liquid to drain through the muslin into the bowl, then squeeze the pulp in the muslin until every drop of remaining liquid is extracted. To do this, bring the sides of the muslin up over the pulp and fold it over several times, then twist the ends of the muslin in opposite directions—this is easier if someone helps with the twisting. Discard the pulp and pour the ratafia into a clean bottle. Seal tightly with a cork or screw cap and store in a cool place.

Wild Strawberry Tartlets

If these tiny strawberries elude you in the wild, try growing them in earthenware pots in a warm corner of your garden

Ingredients

For the tartlet cases
115 g (4 oz) plain flour
60 g (2 oz) caster sugar
85 g (3 oz) butter
1 tablespoon beaten egg

For the filling
115 g (4 oz) granulated sugar
150 ml (¼ pint) water
200 g (7 oz) wild strawberries
150 ml (¼ pint) double cream

Preparation time: 40 minutes
Cooking time: 15 minutes
Makes 12 tartlets

To make the tartlet cases, sift the flour and half the sugar into a bowl and rub in the butter until the mixture resembles fine breadcrumbs. Add the egg and mix to form a dough. Knead gently on a lightly floured surface until smooth, then wrap and chill for 15 minutes.

Roll out on a lightly floured surface, stamp out 12 rounds, using a 7.5 cm (3 in) fluted cutter, and line a dozen 6 cm (2½ in) bun tins. Prick lightly all over with a fork, then chill while preheating the oven to 200°C (400°F, gas mark 6).

Bake the cases blind for 10 minutes, then remove from the oven and sprinkle the inside of each with ½ teaspoon of the remaining caster sugar. Return the bun tins to the oven for 5 minutes, then remove and leave to cool.

Stir the granulated sugar in the water, over a moderate heat, until the sugar dissolves. Bring to the boil, add 15 g (½ oz) of the strawberries and boil for 1 minute. Discard the strawberries and boil the syrup until it is reduced by a third, then remove from the heat and leave to cool.

Whisk the cream until it will hold a soft peak, then fold in 2 tablespoons of the strawberry syrup. Divide the remaining strawberries among the tartlets and spoon the rest of the syrup over them. Top each tartlet with a piped or spooned whirl of cream. Serve the remaining cream separately in a jug.

The slightly sharp flavour of the wild strawberries is nicely balanced by the cream.

All on a summer's day
The Knave of Hearts prepares to steal the tarts lovingly prepared by the Queen in her bower. This version comes from an Alphabet designed by Walter Crane (1845–1915), which he based upon traditional nursery rhymes.

Bulgur wheat, a staple cereal of the Middle East, is the vehicle for a piquant filling.

Stuffed Field Mushrooms

Serve as a light lunch or supper dish or as a partner for a mixed grill

INGREDIENTS

- 4 LARGE FIELD MUSHROOMS, EACH APPROX 9 CM (3½ IN) IN DIAMETER AND 85 G (3 OZ) IN WEIGHT, WIPED
- 115 G (4 OZ) BUTTER
- 60 G (2 OZ) SHALLOTS, PEELED AND FINELY CHOPPED
- 1 GARLIC CLOVE, PEELED AND CRUSHED
- 1 MILD GREEN CHILLI, DESEEDED AND FINELY CHOPPED
- 60 G (2 OZ) BULGUR WHEAT
- 150 ML (¼ PINT) DRY WHITE WINE
- ½ LEVEL TEASPOON SALT
- FRESHLY GROUND BLACK PEPPER
- 1 LEVEL TEASPOON GROUND CORIANDER
- 1 TABLESPOON LEMON JUICE
- 115 G (4 OZ) TOMATOES, SKINNED, DESEEDED AND FINELY CHOPPED
- 4 TABLESPOONS CHOPPED FRESH PARSLEY
- 60 G (2 OZ) CHEDDAR CHEESE, CUT INTO 4 SLICES
- 4 THICK SLICES GRANARY BREAD
- FLAT-LEAF PARSLEY SPRIGS AND CAYENNE PEPPER OR PAPRIKA TO GARNISH

PREPARATION TIME: 20 MINUTES
COOKING TIME: 35 MINUTES
SERVES FOUR

PREHEAT the oven to 200°C (400°F, gas mark 6). Remove the mushroom stalks, chop them finely and set the caps aside.

Heat a quarter of the butter in a saucepan, add the shallots and chopped mushroom stalks and cook gently until softened. Add the garlic and chilli and cook for 1 minute. Stir in the bulgur wheat, wine, seasoning, coriander and lemon juice and cover and simmer for 15–20 minutes until all the liquid is absorbed and the wheat is just tender. Add 1–2 tablespoons of water if the liquid is absorbed too quickly. Remove from the heat, stir in the tomatoes and parsley, and add a little more seasoning if necessary.

Melt the remaining butter and brush it over both sides of each mushroom cap. Place the caps in a roasting tin. Spoon the bulgur wheat mixture evenly over them, drizzle over the remaining butter and top each cap with a slice of cheese. Bake in the centre of the oven for 10–15 minutes until the mushrooms are just tender and the cheese has melted and is lightly browned.

Toast the slices of granary bread on both sides, then cut off the crusts. Put the stuffed mushrooms onto the toast and garnish with the parsley sprigs. Sprinkle with the cayenne pepper or paprika, and serve immediately.

Hedgerow Pie

A sound and solid apple pie with a satisfying element of food for free

To make the pastry, sift the plain and self-raising flours, ground cinnamon and 30 g (1 oz) of the caster sugar into a bowl, then rub in the butter until the mixture resembles breadcrumbs. Add the egg yolk and about 2 tablespoons of cold water and mix to form a soft but not sticky dough. Wrap the dough in cling film and chill for 15 minutes. Preheat the oven to 200°C (400°F, gas mark 6).

To make the filling, put the prepared, ripe elderberries and blackberries into a small, stainless steel or enamel saucepan. Without adding water, cook over a low heat for 5 minutes to release some of the juices. Strain off and reserve the juice. In a large bowl, mix together the sliced apples, flour, sugar and the drained elderberries and blackberries. Fill a 24 cm (9½ in) diameter pie plate with the fruit.

Roll out the chilled dough, on a lightly floured surface, to a 30 cm (12 in) round and cut off a 1.3 cm (½ in) wide strip from round the edge. Brush the edge of the pie plate with water and press the strip onto it. Dampen the strip, then cover the pie with the remaining piece of dough, pressing the edges together well to seal. Trim and decorate the edge.

Reroll the trimmings and use them to make decorations, such as apples and leaves, for the top of the pie. Lightly beat the egg white and brush a little of it over the pie. Arrange the decorations on top and make a small hole in the centre to allow the steam to escape. Glaze the pie with more egg white and sprinkle with the remaining sugar.

Put the pie onto a baking tray and bake in the centre of the oven for 30 minutes or until the pastry is crisp and light golden. If it starts to brown too much, cover it loosely with foil.

Serve the hedgerow pie warm or hot with the reserved juice, sweetened with sugar, and whipped cream or ice cream. If liked, the cream can be flavoured with some of the fruit juice.

Ingredients

For the pastry
- 85 g (3 oz) plain flour
- 85 g (3 oz) self-raising flour
- ½ level teaspoon ground cinnamon
- 60 g (2 oz) caster sugar
- 85 g (3 oz) butter
- 1 egg, size 2, separated
- Approx 2 tablespoons water

For the filling
- 115 g (4 oz) ripe elderberries, stalks removed, washed and drained
- 115 g (4 oz) blackberries, hulled, washed and drained
- 675 g (1½ lb) cooking apples, peeled, quartered, cored and thickly sliced
- 30 g (1 oz) plain flour
- 150 g (5 oz) caster sugar

Preparation time: 45 minutes
Cooking time: 35 minutes
Serves six

The apple filling has been stained to a luscious crimson by the elderberries and blackberries.

The hedger
A hedge is made by cutting part way through growing stems, 'pleachers', then bending them over and weaving them through stakes driven into the ground. A skilled hedger can lay 100 yd of hedge in a week; a smallish, 40 acre field has a mile of hedging.

Apple & Wild Mushroom Soup

This soup is easy to prepare but special enough to launch a dinner party

INGREDIENTS

- 450G (1 LB) COOKING APPLES, WASHED, QUARTERED AND CORED
- 1.15 LITRES (2 PINTS) CHICKEN STOCK (SEE P.433)
- 30G (1 OZ) DRIED MIXED FOREST MUSHROOMS OR CEPS, SOAKED IN 175ML (6 FL OZ) WARM WATER FOR 1 HOUR, OR 115G (4 OZ) FRESH CEPS OR CHANTERELLES, CLEANED AND CHOPPED
- 60G (2 OZ) BUTTER
- 1 TABLESPOON FINELY CHOPPED FRESH GINGER
- 2 SHALLOTS, PEELED AND FINELY CHOPPED
- 3 LEVEL TABLESPOONS PLAIN FLOUR
- 2 TABLESPOONS FINELY SNIPPED FRESH CHIVES
- SALT AND FRESHLY GROUND BLACK PEPPER
- 150ML (1/4 PINT) SINGLE CREAM

PREPARATION TIME: 30 MINUTES
COOKING TIME: 40 MINUTES
SERVES SIX

THE MUSHROOM PICKERS
No small part of rural families' income depended upon what could be gathered from woods and fields. Just after dawn in summer and autumn was the time to pick mushrooms, which were borne to market with the dew still fresh upon them.

PUT the apples and chicken stock into a large saucepan and bring to the boil. Reduce the heat, cover and simmer for about 20 minutes until the apples are very soft and fluffy. Strain the liquid through a nylon sieve into a bowl, pressing the apple pulp through the sieve with the back of a spoon. Discard the skins and put the stock to one side.

Meanwhile, if using dried mushrooms, strain the water in which they have been soaking through a sieve lined with muslin or kitchen paper. Reserve the water and rinse and chop the mushrooms.

Heat the butter in a large saucepan, add the chopped ginger and shallots and cook gently for about 5 minutes until soft. Stir in the chopped mushrooms, add the flour and cook for 1 minute, then gradually stir in the apple stock and the reserved soaking water from the dried mushrooms, if using. Bring to the boil, stirring all the time, then add half the chives, season with salt and pepper to taste and cook for 10 minutes.

Serve the soup from a heated tureen or in individual bowls, topped with the cream and the remaining chives.

It is the mingling of shallots and ginger with the apple and mushrooms that gives this soup its distinctive savour.

Plastic mineral water or lemonade bottles are ideal for elderflower champagne. They are less likely to explode should the drink become too effervescent.

These drinks are as refreshing to the palate as the blossom-laden elder is to the eyes.

Elderflower Cordial and Champagne

The sparkle of early summer is subtly captured by this duet of drinks

INGREDIENTS

ELDERFLOWER CORDIAL

- 1 KG (2 LB 3 OZ) CASTER SUGAR
- 850 ML (1½ PINTS) BOILING WATER
- 45 G (1½ OZ) CITRIC ACID
- 15 LARGE ELDERFLOWER HEADS, FLOWERS SNIPPED FROM STEMS
- 2 LEMONS, SLICED

PREPARATION TIME: 20 MINUTES
STANDING TIME: 5 DAYS
MAKES APPROX 1.7 LITRES (3 PINTS)

ELDERFLOWER CHAMPAGNE

- 675 G (1½ LB) CASTER SUGAR
- 4.5 LITRES (1 GALLON) WATER
- 2 TABLESPOONS WHITE WINE VINEGAR
- FINELY PARED RIND AND STRAINED JUICE 1 LARGE LEMON
- 4 LARGE ELDERFLOWER HEADS, FLOWERS SNIPPED FROM STEMS

PREPARATION TIME: 20 MINUTES
STANDING TIME: 48 HOURS
MAKES 4.5 LITRES (1 GALLON)

ELDERFLOWER CORDIAL

PUT the caster sugar into a large bowl, add the boiling water and stir until all the sugar has dissolved. Stir in the citric acid, then add the elderflowers and sliced lemons. Cover the bowl and leave to stand for five days, stirring daily.

Put a sieve, lined with a piece of double-thickness muslin, into a large bowl, scald the sieve and bowl with boiling water and drain well.

Strain the cordial through the muslin-lined sieve into the bowl, then pour it into clean bottles. Cork the bottles and store in the refrigerator. It will keep for up to a year.

Dilute one part cordial with two to three parts soda, tonic or mineral water, add ice and lemon slices and serve.

ELDERFLOWER CHAMPAGNE

Put the caster sugar into a large bowl, add the water and stir until the sugar has dissolved, then stir in the vinegar, lemon rind and juice and the elderflowers. Cover and leave to stand for 48 hours.

Strain through scalded muslin and pour into clean screw-top bottles. Screw the tops on the bottles and leave the champagne to stand for three weeks or longer, by which time it will be very effervescent. Chill well before serving.

Hawthorn Liqueurs

Hawthorn flowers and fruit turn a humble brandy into fine liqueurs

INGREDIENTS

Hawthorn flower liqueur
- 115g (4oz) hawthorn flowers, petals only
- 725ml (1¼ pints) brandy, 40% vol
- 175g (6oz) caster sugar
- 4 tablespoons water

Preparation time: 1 hour (includes picking flowers)
Standing time: 2–3 months
Cooking time: 5 minutes
Makes 725 ml (1¼ pints)

Hawthorn berry liqueur
- 450g (1lb) hawthorn berries, stalks and leaves removed, well washed, dried and lightly crushed
- 175g (6oz) caster sugar
- 725ml (1¼ pints) brandy, 40% vol

Preparation time: 1 hour
Standing time: 3 months
Makes 725 ml (1¼ pints)

HAWTHORN FLOWER LIQUEUR

Ensure that the flowers are free of insects. Put them into a large, clean jar and cover with the brandy. Cover with a tightly fitting lid and store in a cool, dark cupboard for two to three months.

When ready to strain the brandy, stir the caster sugar and water in a saucepan, over a moderate heat, until the sugar has dissolved, then bring to the boil and boil for 1 minute. Strain through muslin into a small bowl and leave until cold.

Strain the brandy through a muslin-lined sieve into a large jug, then stir in sugar syrup to sweeten to taste. Pour into a clean bottle, and cork tightly. Store in a cool, dry, airy cupboard.

HAWTHORN BERRY LIQUEUR

Put the clean berries, the sugar and the brandy into a large, clean jar and stir well. Cover the jar with a tightly fitting lid and store in a cool, dry, airy cupboard for at least three months, shaking the jar daily during the first week to ensure that the sugar dissolves completely.

Strain the brandy through a nylon sieve, lined with double thickness muslin, into a clean jug, leaving it until every drop of brandy has dripped through the sieve. Do not be tempted to squeeze the muslin, as this may cause the sediment to go through. Pour the liqueur into a clean bottle, cork tightly and store in a cool, dry, airy cupboard.

The pale flower liqueur has a delicate almond flavour, while the darker version, made with the hawthorn berries, is more reminiscent of rich plum brandy.

The flowers appear in May and should be gathered on a dry day. The bright red berries can be picked from early September.

Countryside fruits are transformed into perfect companions for poultry or game.

HEDGEROW HARVEST
One of the perennial joys of childhood is that of obtaining food for free. These boys were photographed blackberrying on Wimbledon Common in 1904; no doubt their descendants plunder the same hedge today.

Jellies from the Hedgerow

The rich reds and purples of autumn are preserved in these tangy jellies

BLACK JACK JELLY

PUT the fruits into three saucepans. Add 285 ml (½ pint) water to the blackberries, 570 ml (1 pint) to the elderberries and 1.15 litres (2 pints) to the crab apples.

Bring each pan to the boil, reduce the heat and simmer gently for about 45 minutes until the fruits are very soft, stirring occasionally with a wooden spoon.

Meanwhile, prepare a jelly bag and stand, or put a large nylon sieve, lined with scalded muslin or a scalded tea towel, over a deep bowl. Pour the fruits and their juices into the bag or sieve and leave for at least 2 hours or overnight.

Measure the juice, pour it into a preserving pan and bring to the boil. For every 570 ml (1 pint) of juice, add 450 g (1 lb) of sugar and heat gently, stirring until the sugar is dissolved. Return to the boil, and boil rapidly for 10–15 minutes until setting point is reached (see p.438). Remove from the heat, skim off the scum and immediately pour the jelly into clean, warm jars. Cover with waxed paper discs and cellophane covers. When cold, label and store in a cool, dry, airy cupboard.

HIP AND HAW JELLY

In a large preserving pan, bring the fruits to the boil in 2.3 litres (4 pints) of water, reduce the heat and simmer gently for about 30 minutes. Mash the fruits with a potato masher to release the seeds from the hips and cook for another 15 minutes until the fruits are very soft, stirring occasionally with a wooden spoon. Strain and proceed as for the black jack jelly.

INGREDIENTS

BLACK JACK JELLY

- 900 G (2 LB) BLACKBERRIES, HULLED AND WASHED
- 900 G (2 LB) ELDERBERRIES, WEIGHED WITHOUT STALKS, WASHED
- 900 G (2 LB) CRAB APPLES, WASHED
- APPROX 900 G (2 LB) PRESERVING OR GRANULATED SUGAR

PREPARATION TIME: 1 HOUR
COOKING TIME: 1½ HOURS
STRAINING TIME: 2 HOURS OR OVERNIGHT
MAKES 1.4 KG (3 LB)

HIP AND HAW JELLY

- 900 G (2 LB) WILD ROSEHIPS, WASHED
- 450 G (1 LB) HAWTHORN BERRIES, WASHED
- 450 G (1 LB) COOKING APPLES, WASHED AND ROUGHLY CHOPPED
- APPROX 675 G (1½ LB) PRESERVING OR GRANULATED SUGAR

PREPARATION TIME: 1 HOUR
COOKING TIME: 1½ HOURS
STRAINING TIME: 2 HOURS OR OVERNIGHT
MAKES 1.1 KG (2½ LB)

TECHNIQUES

Explained below are methods of preparation and cooking used throughout this book and which have been referred to in individual recipes.

Making Basic Stocks

A good stock will add richness and depth of flavour to soups, stews, casseroles and sauces. Fresh stock can be bought from some supermarkets, but although this can be very good, it is not as good as any you will make yourself. Stock cubes can be used, but remember that they contain a lot of monosodium glutamate and other synthetic flavourings.

Stock is made by the long, slow cooking in water of meat and bones with aromatic vegetables and spices; or for vegetable stock, just vegetables alone. Fish stock is made in a similar way, but has a much shorter cooking time.

Rich stocks are made with meat and bones and when cartilaginous cuts of veal and beef, such as knuckle and shin, are used, the stock will set to a rich jelly. Simple stocks can be made from bones alone.

Stock should have a good flavour and be almost crystal clear. To achieve this, the scum must be constantly skimmed from the surface.

The following recipes for stock include salt, but this can be left out if you prefer your stock to be salt free, especially if you are on a low-salt diet.

Also, the quantities of the ingredients may be reduced to suit the size of your stockpot or saucepan.

A place for everything
Storing the vast array of ingredients and utensils needed for this 1928 Christmas pudding was easy for the housewife with the Quicksey kitchen cabinet. Glass drawers and containers allowed her to see everything at a glance and, with a lifetime's guarantee, it was a snip at £9.

-BEEF STOCK-

- 60G (2OZ) BEEF DRIPPING OR 3 TABLESPOONS OLIVE OIL
- 2.3KG (5LB) BEEF BONES, INCLUDING A MARROW BONE AND A VEAL KNUCKLE, IF AVAILABLE—CHOPPED BY YOUR BUTCHER
- 450G (1LB) ONIONS, PEELED AND QUARTERED
- 1.4KG (3LB) SHIN OF BEEF OR STEWING STEAK, DICED
- 900G (2LB) MIXTURE OF CHICKEN BACKBONES, WING TIPS, LEGS AND FEET AND GIBLETS (EXCLUDING LIVER), WASHED OR THE SAME WEIGHT IN CHICKEN PIECES
- 6.75 LITRES (12 PINTS) WATER
- 225G (8OZ) CARROTS, PEELED AND SLICED
- 225G (8OZ) TURNIP, PEELED AND SLICED
- 2 CELERY STICKS, TRIMMED AND CHOPPED
- LARGE PARSLEY SPRIG, WASHED
- 1 THYME SPRIG
- 2 BAY LEAVES
- 1 MEDIUM LEEK, TRIMMED, SLICED AND WASHED
- 1 TABLESPOON BLACK PEPPERCORNS
- 4 CLOVES
- 1 TEASPOON ALLSPICE BERRIES
- 1 LEVEL TABLESPOON SALT

Preparation time: 40 minutes
Cooking time: 6–7 hours
Chilling time: overnight
Makes 4–4.5 litres (7–8 pints)

Heat the beef dripping or olive oil in a stockpot or very large saucepan. Add as many bones as will fit in a single layer in the bottom of the stockpot or pan and cook them gently in batches until they are a rich brown all over. Take care not to let the fat or oil burn. Remove each batch from the stockpot or pan and set aside.

Add the onions to the stockpot or pan and cook them slowly until they are a rich brown, then return the bones and add the meat, chicken and water. Heat very slowly until the water comes close to the boil, then add a teacupful of cold water and reduce the heat.

Skim any scum from the surface, then add the prepared vegetables, herbs, spices and salt. Partially cover the stockpot or pan with a lid and simmer over a gentle heat for 5–6 hours, skimming the scum frequently from the surface of the stock.

Remove the stockpot or pan carefully from the heat and strain the stock through a large colander, lined with a piece of muslin or a clean tea towel, into a very large bowl. Discard all the bones, meat and vegetables.

Cover the bowl with a piece of muslin or a net cover to protect it from dust and allow the stock to cool. Once cold, refrigerate overnight. Next day, carefully remove the solidified fat from the surface, then freeze in measured quantities of either 285 or 570 ml (½ or 1 pint).

-VEAL STOCK-

- 2.3 kg (5 lb) veal bones, including a knuckle, chopped by your butcher
- 900 g (2 lb) British stewing veal, diced
- 900 g (2 lb) mixture of chicken backbones, wing tips, legs and feet and giblets (excluding liver), washed or the same weight in chicken pieces
- 5 litres (9 pints) water
- 2 large carrots, peeled and sliced
- 1 medium leek, sliced and washed
- 2 large onions, peeled and quartered
- Large parsley sprig
- 1 thyme sprig
- 2 bay leaves
- 2 mace blades
- 2 teaspoons white peppercorns
- 1 level tablespoon salt

Preparation time: 30 minutes
Cooking time: 6 hours
Chilling time: Overnight
Makes 4–4.5 litres (7–8 pints)

Put the bones, meat and chicken pieces into a stockpot or large saucepan. Add the water and bring slowly to the boil, then proceed as for beef stock (opposite).

-CHICKEN STOCK-

- 1 boiling fowl, approx 2.7 kg (6 lb), washed and chopped or same weight drumsticks and wing tips
- 900 g (2 lb) chicken giblets (excluding livers), washed
- 5.7 litres (10 pints) water
- 450 g (1 lb) onions, peeled and quartered
- 450 g (1 lb) carrots, peeled and sliced
- 3 celery sticks, trimmed and chopped
- 1 leek, sliced and washed
- Large sprig each parsley, marjoram, oregano and basil
- 2 bay leaves
- Small sprig each thyme and rosemary
- 3 mace blades
- 3 cloves
- 1 tablespoon black peppercorns
- 2 level teaspoons salt

Preparation time: 30 minutes
Cooking time: 6 hours
Chilling time: Overnight
Makes 4–4.5 litres (7–8 pints)

Put the chicken, giblets and water into a stockpot or large saucepan and bring slowly to the boil. Proceed as for beef stock (opposite), simmering for 5 hours.

-GAME STOCK-

- 1.4 kg (3 lb) game carcasses, cooked or uncooked, roughly chopped or use up older birds from the freezer
- 900 g (2 lb) beef or veal bones, chopped by your butcher
- 900 g (2 lb) shin of beef, or stewing veal, diced
- 225 g (8 oz) ham bone
- 4.5 litres (1 gallon) veal stock or water
- 1 large onion, peeled and roughly chopped
- 2 large carrots, peeled and sliced
- 1 small turnip, peeled and sliced
- 2 celery sticks, trimmed and sliced
- 2 small leeks, trimmed, sliced and washed
- Sprig each thyme, marjoram, basil and parsley
- 2 tablespoons black peppercorns
- 1 mace blade
- 8 allspice berries
- 4 cloves

Preparation time: 30 minutes
Cooking time: 5 hours
Chilling time: Overnight
Makes 3.4 litres (6 pints)

Put all the carcasses, bones and meat into a stockpot or large saucepan. Add the water and bring slowly to the boil, then proceed as for beef stock (opposite).

-FISH STOCK-

- 1.4 kg (3 lb) white fish trimmings (bones and heads with gills removed), washed
- 1 medium onion, peeled and thinly sliced
- 1 small carrot, peeled and thinly sliced
- 1 small lemon, thinly sliced
- Sprig each parsley and thyme
- 1 bay leaf
- 12 black peppercorns
- ½ level teaspoon salt
- 285 ml (½ pint) dry white wine
- 1.7 litres (3 pints) water

Preparation time: 20 minutes
Cooking time: 40 minutes
Cooling time: 2–3 hours
Makes 1.7 litres (3 pints)

Put all the fish trimmings into a large stainless steel or enamel saucepan. Add the sliced vegetables and lemon, the herbs, peppercorns, salt and wine. Pour in the water and bring slowly to the boil.

Immediately turn down the heat and skim the scum from the surface of the liquid, then partially cover the pan and simmer for 30 minutes.

Strain as for beef stock (opposite), then use at once or cover and leave to cool for 2–3 hours. When cold, store in the refrigerator and use within one day. Alternatively, freeze when cold and use as required.

Under pressure
Papin's Digester, the very first pressure cooker, made its introductory bow in 1679. But it was working housewives who gave this version their accolade in the late 1940s, both for its economical use of fuel and its time-saving qualities.

Saved by a whisker
Few later, and much more sophisticated, mixers would claim the versatility of the 1950 Cheeto model. This 'handy mains mixer' could not only attend to the blending of the pastry but also, when the party was over, assume the role of the butler and polish the silver too.

-VEGETABLE STOCK-

85 G (3 OZ) BUTTER
225 G (8 OZ) CARROTS, PEELED AND SLICED
2 LARGE ONIONS, PEELED AND SLICED
225 G (8 OZ) TURNIP, PEELED AND SLICED
450 G (1 LB) RIPE TOMATOES, CHOPPED
3 CELERY STICKS, TRIMMED AND CHOPPED
1 MEDIUM LEEK, TRIMMED, SLICED AND WASHED
1 SOFT ROUND LETTUCE, WASHED
SPRIG EACH PARSLEY, THYME, BASIL AND MARJORAM
1 BAY LEAF
12 BLACK PEPPERCORNS
2 CLOVES
1 MACE BLADE
½ LEVEL TEASPOON SALT
3.4 LITRES (6 PINTS) WATER
PREPARATION TIME: 30 MINUTES
COOKING TIME: 4 HOURS
CHILLING TIME: OVERNIGHT
MAKES 2.3 LITRES (4 PINTS)

Melt the butter in a large stainless steel or enamel saucepan. Add all the vegetables, except the lettuce, and stir until they glisten with the butter, then cook over a very low heat for about 15 minutes or until the vegetables just begin to soften. Do not allow them to brown.

Add the lettuce, herbs, peppercorns, spices and salt to the saucepan and bring slowly to the boil. Reduce the heat, skim any scum from the surface, partially cover the saucepan and cook gently for 2–3 hours.

Strain the stock as for beef stock (p.432). Stand aside until cold, then chill in the refrigerator overnight. Next day, remove any solidified fat from the surface of the stock and store in the refrigerator or freeze until required.

-GIBLET STOCK-

450 G (1 LB) CHICKEN, TURKEY OR DUCK GIBLETS (EXCLUDING LIVER)
1.15 LITRES (2 PINTS) WATER
1 SMALL ONION, PEELED AND STUDDED WITH 2 CLOVES
1 MEDIUM CARROT, PEELED AND SLICED
1 CELERY STICK, TRIMMED AND SLICED
SPRIG EACH THYME, ROSEMARY AND PARSLEY
1 BAY LEAF
8 BLACK PEPPERCORNS
½ LEVEL TEASPOON SALT
PREPARATION TIME: 20 MINUTES
COOKING TIME: 1¼ HOURS
MAKES 850 ML (1¼ PINTS)

Put the giblets into a large saucepan, add the water and bring slowly to the boil. Reduce the heat, skim the scum from the surface of the water, then add the vegetables, herbs, peppercorns and salt.

Partially cover the pan and cook gently for 1 hour, then strain through a fine sieve. Use immediately or allow to cool, then store in the refrigerator or freeze and use as required.

-HAM-BONE STOCK-

Proceed as for giblet stock (above), but using a roughly chopped ham bone. Add a little more water if necessary and omit the salt.

-ASPIC JELLY-

570 ML (1 PINT) COLD, GOOD STOCK (FISH, MEAT, CHICKEN, GAME OR VEGETABLE)
3 TABLESPOONS DRY WHITE WINE
3 TABLESPOONS DRY SHERRY
2 TABLESPOONS RED WINE VINEGAR
30 G (1 OZ) GELATINE
2 EGG WHITES, SIZE 2
SHELLS FROM THE EGGS, WASHED
PREPARATION TIME: 5 MINUTES
COOKING TIME: 15 MINUTES
COOLING TIME: 2–3 HOURS OR OVERNIGHT
MAKES 570 ML (1 PINT)

Put all the ingredients into a large, clean saucepan and whisk over a gentle heat until the mixture forms a thick froth on the top and starts to come to the boil. Stop whisking immediately and let the mixture rise to the top of the saucepan, taking care not to let it boil over.

As soon as it reaches the top, remove the saucepan from the heat and allow the mixture to subside, then return the pan to the heat and allow the mixture to rise and subside once more in the same way. Repeat the process once more, then stand aside for 5 minutes.

Meanwhile, scald a large bowl, a sieve and a large piece of muslin or a clean tea towel with boiling water. Drain both bowl and sieve well and wring out the muslin or tea towel. Line the sieve with the piece of muslin, folded double, or the tea towel, and place it over the bowl.

Taking care not to break up the froth, pour the aspic jelly carefully into the sieve and leave undisturbed to strain into the bowl. Cool the aspic and use immediately. Alternatively, you can refrigerate for up to 24 hours.

If you do not feel sufficiently confident to make your own aspic jelly, you can buy packets of aspic jelly powder from grocers or supermarkets. Simply dissolve the powder in boiling water according to the instructions. It is quite acceptable to use this in recipes that require aspic jelly.

Making Sauces and Dressings

-Tomato Sauce-

30g (1oz) butter or 2 tablespoons olive oil
1 large onion, peeled and finely chopped
1 garlic clove, peeled and crushed
Sprig each fresh rosemary, thyme, oregano and parsley
450g (1lb) fresh tomatoes, roughly chopped
400g (14oz) tinned tomatoes
½ level teaspoon sugar
½ level teaspoon salt
Freshly ground black pepper
Preparation time: 15 minutes
Cooking time: 1 hour 10 minutes
Makes approx 570ml (1 pint)

This sauce can be made and used immediately, stored in the refrigerator for two to three days or frozen.

Melt the butter or heat the oil in a stainless steel or enamel saucepan. Add the onion and cook gently until softened but not browned.

Put all the remaining ingredients into the saucepan and bring to the boil. Reduce the heat, partially cover and simmer, stirring frequently, for about an hour or until the sauce has thickened and reduced by about a third.

Remove the saucepan from the heat and discard the herbs. Strain the sauce through a nylon sieve into a clean saucepan, season to taste and reheat.

-Curry Sauce-

30g (1oz) butter or 2 tablespoons olive oil
1 large onion, peeled and finely chopped
1 large dessert apple, peeled, cored and chopped
1 level tablespoon curry powder
1 level tablespoon plain flour
570ml (1 pint) beef, chicken or vegetable stock (see pp.432–434)
2 level teaspoons desiccated coconut
1 teaspoon curry paste
1 tablespoon mango chutney
Salt and freshly ground black pepper
1 tablespoon lemon juice
Preparation time: 10 minutes
Cooking time: 1 hour
Makes 425ml (¾ pint)

Melt the butter or heat the oil in a saucepan. Add the onion and apple and cook gently until softened but not browned. Stir in the curry powder and flour and cook for 1 minute, then stir in the stock, coconut, curry paste and chutney. Bring the sauce to the boil, stirring, then reduce the heat, cover and simmer for 1 hour.

Pass the sauce through a sieve into a clean saucepan, season with salt and pepper and add lemon juice to taste. Reheat and use the sauce as required.

-Custard Sauce-

570ml (1 pint) full cream milk
1 vanilla pod, halved lengthways
2 eggs, size 2
4 egg yolks, size 2
30 g (1oz) caster sugar
Preparation Time: 5 minutes, plus 1 hour standing
Cooking Time: 2–4 minutes
Makes 725ml (1¼ pints)

Pour the milk into a saucepan, add the vanilla pod and bring to the boil, then remove the saucepan from the heat, cover and leave to infuse for 1 hour.

Put the eggs, egg yolks and sugar into a bowl and whisk lightly. Reheat the milk until it comes to the boil, then quickly stir it into the egg mixture. Pour the mixture back into the saucepan and stir constantly over a low heat until the custard thickens enough to thinly coat the back of the spoon.

If preferred, the custard can be cooked in the bowl over a saucepan of gently boiling water, but this will take longer.

Immediately the custard thickens, strain it into a heated serving jug. Serve immediately, or keep warm until required.

If serving cold, strain the custard into a bowl and cover the surface with cling film to prevent a skin from forming. Allow to cool, then chill.

-Vinaigrette Dressing-

½ level teaspoon salt
Freshly ground black pepper
½ level teaspoon English mustard powder or 1 level teaspoon Dijon mustard
¼ level teaspoon caster sugar
1 tablespoon vinegar (red or white wine, malt or distilled malt)
2–5 tablespoons virgin or extra virgin olive oil
Preparation time: 5 minutes

Put the salt, pepper, mustard and sugar into a small bowl, add the vinegar and stir until the salt and sugar have dissolved. Gradually whisk in

Fitted kitchen
By the mid 1950s, flat-dwelling had become commonplace and kitchen furnishings and equipment were scaled down accordingly. Food, crockery, knives, forks, spoons and saucepans, plus a pull-down work surface, could be accommodated in this Cresta kitchen cabinet which occupied a floor area of rather less than 5 sq ft—about 0.5 m².

the olive oil, according to taste: for a smooth, mild dressing add 4–5 tablespoons, for a sharper dressing, add just 2 tablespoons.

Freshly chopped herbs such as parsley, chives, basil, chervil or tarragon may be stirred into the dressing after adding the oil.

-MAYONNAISE-

1 EGG YOLK, SIZE 2
¼ LEVEL TEASPOON SALT
½ LEVEL TEASPOON ENGLISH MUSTARD POWDER OR 1 LEVEL TEASPOON DIJON MUSTARD
FRESHLY GROUND BLACK PEPPER
2 TEASPOONS LEMON JUICE
175 ML (6 FL OZ) LIGHT OLIVE OIL OR CORN OIL
1–2 TABLESPOONS WARM WATER

PREPARATION TIME: 10 MINUTES
MAKES 225 ML (8 FL OZ)

The golden rule for making mayonnaise is to add the oil very slowly at first. Because mayonnaise is made with raw egg yolk, it must be kept chilled in the refrigerator and used on the day it is made.

Put the egg yolk, salt, mustard and some pepper into a small mixing bowl. Stand the bowl on a clean, damp cloth to prevent it from slipping, then whisk the yolk with a stainless steel wire whisk, or a hand-held electric mixer, until it becomes lighter in colour. Gradually whisk in the lemon juice, then, whisking continuously, add the oil, a few drops at a time, until the mayonnaise begins to thicken. The oil can now be whisked in a little more quickly and can be poured into the mayonnaise in a fine, steady stream. If, midway through mixing, the mayonnaise becomes very thick, add another teaspoon of lemon juice. When all the oil has been added, stir in enough of the warm water to bring the mayonnaise to the required consistency.

To make tartare sauce
Roughly chop two small gherkins, 2 teaspoons of capers and six stuffed green olives and mix them into the mayonnaise.

PREPARING SHELLFISH

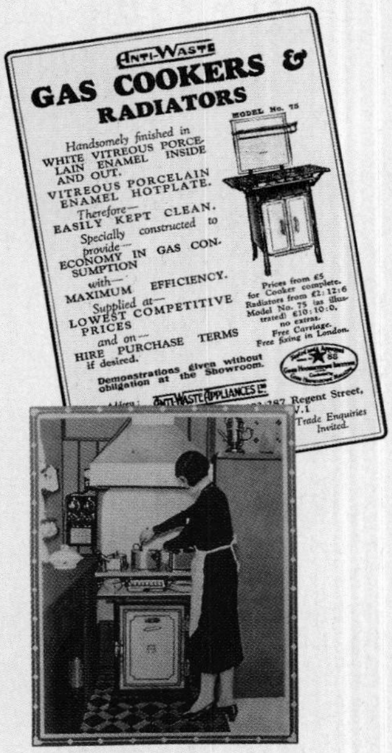

THE ROARING '20S
Energy saving was the chief selling point of these cookers. Both claimed maximum economy in fuel consumption and minimum effort on the part of the cook.

-PRAWNS-

Hold the body of the prawn firmly and twist off the head, then hold it with the legs uppermost and, using your thumbs, break the shell away from the body, peel it off and discard it.

-SHRIMPS-

Hold the tail of the shrimp with one hand, the head with the other, and gently open it out flat. Push the head and tail gently towards each other to break the shell free, then slide out the flesh.

-MUSSELS-

Fill a large bowl or sink with cold water, add the mussels and sort through them, discarding any that have damaged shells and those that are open and do not close up when their shells are tapped gently.

Using a small knife, scrape off any barnacles from the shells, then pull away the 'beards' (the thread-like strands on the shells by which the mussels attach themselves to rocks). Scrub the shells under cold running water until clean, then rinse well in several changes of clean water.

-OYSTERS-

Hold the oyster firmly, flat side up, in a thick cloth to prevent it from slipping and to protect your hands.

Insert an oyster knife into the join between the halves of the shell, approximately in the middle of the straight edge. Slide the knife from end to end along the inside of the top shell to sever the muscle, then twist the knife to separate the shell.

Run the knife gently under the oyster to loosen it from the bottom shell, keeping the shell in a horizontal position to retain the juice.

-SCALLOPS-

Hold the scallop with the flat shell uppermost. Insert a thin, sharp knife between the shells, opposite to the hinge. Carefully run the knife across the inside of the top shell to sever the muscle, then remove the shell.

Rinse out any grit from the scallop with cold water, then slide the knife under the membrane that attaches the scallop to the curved shell and cut the scallop free.

Trim off the membranes, black stomach sac and black intestinal vein, leaving only the white flesh and orange 'coral', or roe.

-CRAB-

Carefully twist off the claws and legs and set them aside, then pull off and discard the pointed tail flap.

Hold the crab upright with the top of the shell pointing towards you and the tail end uppermost. Holding the shell with both hands, use your thumbs to push the body free from the shell. Pull the two sections apart carefully.

Remove the greyish-white bulbous gills, known as dead men's fingers, and the feathery wisps attached to them. Most are attached to the edge of the body, but some may have fallen into the shell. Be sure that all are removed and discarded.

Spoon the brown meat out of the shell, scrape off any that may be sticking to the body and set aside.

With a fine skewer, prise out the white flesh from the leg and claw sockets in the body and from all the other crevices, cutting the body in half to get all the meat out.

With a kitchen weight or hammer, crack open all the joints in the claws and legs, taking care not to hit them too hard as fragments of shell may get into the meat. Remove the meat from the joints with the skewer.

If serving the crabmeat in the shell, clean out the inside of the shell thoroughly, discarding both the transparent membrane that lines it and the stomach sac. Scrub the shell vigorously and break the irregular inner back edge as far as the dark line that runs round near the outer edge.

-LOBSTER-

Twist off the claws and legs and set them aside. If the lobster is a berried female (female with eggs), open out the tail carefully and scrape out and reserve the roe from the underside.

Lay the lobster, back uppermost, on a board. With a large, sharp knife, split the tail in half, starting where it meets the head and cutting down along the back. If necessary, hit the back of the knife with a heavy kitchen weight to help the blade to penetrate the shell.

Split the head down the centre in the same way, starting where it meets the tail. Separate the halves.

Remove and discard the transparent stomach sac, then remove and discard the gills which lie in the head near the tip. There may be parts of the stomach sac and gills in both halves of the lobster.

With the tip of the knife, remove the beige or grey intestinal vein that runs down the tail, which may also be in both halves.

Remove the flesh from the claws and legs as instructed for crab (opposite). Slice the claw and leg meat and arrange it neatly on top of the meat in the shell.

Preparing Poultry and Game

If asked to do so, a butcher will always joint or bone poultry or game for you if you do not feel sufficiently confident to do it yourself.

The following methods for jointing or boning chicken also apply for duck, turkey, goose and all game birds.

-JOINTING A CHICKEN-

Place the chicken, breast side up, on a large chopping board and cut off the wing tips at the last joint.

Pull one leg away from the body to stretch out the skin then, using a large, sharp knife, cut through the skin and flesh between the body and the thigh until the knife comes into contact with the ball and socket joint.

Holding the leg firmly, twist and bend it outwards until the ball of the thigh bone pops from its socket. Continue cutting through the flesh to free the leg completely from the body. Repeat with the other leg.

Separate the drumstick from the thigh by cutting in half where the thigh bone joins the leg bone. Neaten the drumstick by removing any remaining piece of leg.

Next, hold the chicken firmly upright with the neck end on the board and cut halfway down through the ribs to separate the breast and wings from the back part of the carcass.

Pull the breast away from the remaining part of the back and cut through the skin at the neck. (The back can be reserved for making stock.)

Lay the breast on the board, skin side up, and cut it in half lengthways. Tap the back of the knife with a heavy kitchen weight to make cutting through the bone easier. Cut each breast in half widthways through the flesh just behind the wing.

-BONING-

Cut off the parson's nose and then trim the wing tips at the last joint.

Lay the chicken, breast side down, on a board. Using a small, sharp knife, carefully make a deep cut along the centre of the back to expose the backbone.

Cutting comments
This 'modern cutlery for the modern kitchen' brought with it the dilemma of which knife to employ for particular tasks. Enlightenment, however, was at hand. Readers of *Good Housekeeping* in the 1930s could reply to this advertisement and receive a free booklet entitled 'What knife shall we use?'

Starting at the tail end of the bird, cut the meat away from one side of the the rib cage, taking care to keep the knife close to the bone at all times and using small cutting strokes only.

At the point where the thigh bone joins the body, carefully work the knife round the joint to remove the flesh and expose the joint. Cut through all the tough white ligaments that hold the ball and socket together and then twist the ball free from the socket.

Continue to cut the meat away from the rib cage until you reach the wing joint. Work the knife round the joint, cutting through the white ligaments and twisting the wing to free it from the socket. Continue cutting until all the flesh is removed from the rib cage as far as the tip of the breastbone, but do not attempt to free the rib cage at this point.

Repeat the process on the other side of the chicken until you come to the tip of the breastbone. Lift the rib cage and, with great care, scrape along the top of the breastbone to free it.

To bone the leg and wing joints, take hold of the exposed end of each bone, then scrape the meat down and away from the bone, working over the joints, until the bone can be cut free at the other end.

PRESERVATION ORDER
Purchase of 'The Magic' marmalade machine in 1930 promised a new era of savings in time and energy for the housewife. Eleven years later she could further relax in the knowledge that 'healthful' snap closures were protecting the fruits of her labours from bacterial invasion.

MAKING JAMS AND PRESERVES

Any clean, glass jar can be used for storing homemade jam, provided that it is free from cracks, chips or any other flaws.

Wash the jars thoroughly in very hot water and drain well. Dry them in the oven, heated to 140°C (275°F, gas mark 1) and leave them there until you are ready to pot the jam. The jars must be warmed before filling, otherwise the boiling-hot jam will cause them to crack.

-TESTING FOR A SET-

When the sugar has dissolved completely, bring the jam to a full, rolling boil (one that cannot be broken down when the jam is stirred with a wooden spoon). Boil the jam for the minimum time given in the recipe, then test for a set as follows.

Turn the heat off under the pan, or carefully remove it from the source of heat, and put about 2 teaspoons of the jam onto a cold saucer. Allow it to cool, then push your fingertip across the centre of the jam. If the surface wrinkles well, and the two halves remain separate, the jam has reached setting point. If, however, it forms only a thin skin or remains runny, return the pan to the heat and bring the jam back to the boil. Boil for 5 minutes and test again in the same way.

It is important to turn the heat off, or to remove the pan from the heat, to prevent the jam from overcooking each time you test for a set.

-POTTING AND COVERING-

Once setting point has been reached, the jam must be potted immediately. The exceptions to this rule are strawberry or raspberry jam and all marmalades. These should be left to stand for 10–15 minutes to let the fruit settle, in order to prevent it from rising in the jar.

Carefully lift the preserving pan off the heat and put it onto a wooden board. Remove the heated jars from the oven and stand them on another board—if they are put onto a cold surface, they could crack.

Pour the jam into the jars, using a ladle or a small jug. Fill them almost to the very top in order to leave no space in which bacteria could grow. A jam funnel makes filling easier and helps to prevent jam from dripping down the outside of the jars.

Immediately the jars are filled they must be covered to make them airtight. You can do this using the metal lids with nonreactive linings that are used on jars of commercially produced jam, but they must be washed, rinsed and dried thoroughly. Alternatively, you can make the jars airtight with traditional waxed paper discs and cellophane covers. Place the waxed discs, wax side down, on the hot jam, then cover the tops of the jars with dampened cellophane covers and secure with rubber bands.

-STORING-

Stand the jars of jam aside until completely cold, then label the jars, stating clearly the type of jam and the date on which it was made.

Stored in a cool, dark, dry and airy cupboard, homemade jam will keep well for up to a year, but may deteriorate in colour and flavour if kept for longer.

Making Wine and Beer

-STERILISING-

Sterilising is an essential part of winemaking, if the end results are to be successful.

All vessels, bottles and equipment must not only be visibly clean, but chemically clean too. These can all be sterilised easily by using boiling water and one of the proprietary sterilising agents, such as Campden tablets, which contain sodium metabisulphite.

-STRAINING-

In the recipes, a nylon straining bag is recommended for straining fermented mixtures because it is extremely fine and allows only the juice or liquid to pass through. These bags are obtainable from any shop or store that specialises in home-winemaking or brewing equipment. Alternatively, a piece of very fine net curtain can be used.

-RACKING-

This is the technical name for siphoning off wine from the lees or sediment that forms in the bottom of a demijohn during fermentation—a process that should be carried out regularly in order to clear and stabilise the wine.

When racking the wine, you will need a length of polythene tubing and an empty, sterilised demijohn.

Place the empty demijohn at a lower level than the base of the full jar. Insert the tubing into the wine and start to siphon it by sucking the end of the tube. As soon as the wine begins to flow, pinch the end of the tube with your finger and thumb to prevent it from spilling. Put the tube straight into the empty jar and leave it until all the wine has siphoned off.

This ensures that the wine is transferred to the clean demijohn without the sediment being disturbed.

-AIR LOCK-

An air lock is a device, normally made of glass or plastic, which fits into the cork in the neck of a demijohn. When partly filled with water, the air lock allows the fermentation gases to pass out through it, but prevents anything else from entering the demijohn and contaminating the wine.

-DEMIJOHN-

A demijohn is a narrow-necked glass jar, usually with a capacity of about 4.5 litres (1 gallon) in which wine is left to ferment and mature.

-FERMENTING OUT-

The length of time needed by a wine to ferment out will vary according to the type of wine, the conditions under which it is stored, and the weather—a change, such as a sudden drop in temperature, can cause the fermentation process to cease temporarily.

When the wine is fermented out completely, the fermentation process will cease. This occurs when all the sugar has been used up by the yeast or when the yeast has reached its maximum alcohol tolerance and died. It is easy to tell when the wine has fermented out because bubbles cease to pass through the air lock and the wine gradually begins to clear.

-SWEETENING-

Nonfermentable sugar, known as lactose (a milk sugar), is a type of sugar which cannot be converted into alcohol and carbon dioxide gas when in contact with brewer's yeast. Consequently, it can be used safely to sweeten wines after the fermentation process is completed. The possibility is eliminated of the fermentation process being reactivated when the sugar is added to the wine. Thus, there is no risk that the bottles might become over-pressurised and explode.

Lactose can be obtained from all winemaking shops or stores that sell winemaking equipment. Artificial sweeteners are also nonfermentable and can be used instead of lactose. These are easily obtainable from any pharmacy or supermarket.

-FINING-

Most wines will normally clear of their own accord but, occasionally, a wine may fail to clear and will obstinately remain cloudy. Should this happen, visit your local home-winemaking shop or a store that sells winemaking equipment, and ask for a fining agent that is suitable for the type of wine that you wish to clear.

Fining agents can contain either chemical or natural substances. These react with the particles which cause the cloudiness in the wine and allow them to settle at the bottom of the bottle. The manufacturer's instructions are printed on the packet and should be followed carefully.

The test of time
Once a kitchen gadget gains wide acceptance, it is very difficult to expunge. The bean cutter dates from 1930 and the mincer from 1952, yet they can still be bought today in essentially the same forms. Little has altered in either but the price.

Making Miscellaneous Items

Scouring around
Ever since the discovery of the cleaning properties of the horsetail plant in the Middle Ages, the quest for the ultimate in scourers has continued to vex industrial chemists. Over the years, a succession of soaps, powders and pads has polished our pots and pans. Some, such as Monkey Brand, have faded; others, like Vim and Brillo, have become, literally, household words.

-Bouquet Garni-

A bouquet garni can be made from the traditional combination of a sprig each of fresh parsley and thyme with a bay leaf—or else it can consist of a wider selection of herbs along with a few aromatic vegetables, such as the white part of a leek and a celery stick. A strip of orange or lemon rind can be added for extra flavour. The combination of herbs used will vary according to the recipe, or can be selected to suit your personal preference.

Arrange the herbs in a neat bunch and tie them together tightly with clean, fine string. For easy removal during or after cooking, simply insert a fork through the string and lift the bouquet garni out of the saucepan or casserole.

-Clarified Butter-

Put butter into a saucepan and heat gently until melted, skimming off any surface scum that may form. Remove the butter from the heat and pour it through a muslin-lined sieve into a bowl.

Allow the butter to cool, but not to set. Pour off the clear liquid into a clean bowl, leaving the white solids behind. Use immediately or store in the refrigerator for two or three days.

-Peeled Chestnuts-

Using a small, sharp knife or, preferably, a curved chestnut knife (obtainable at good cooks' shops), cut a deep cross through the shell on the rounded side of each nut. Put the nuts into a saucepan and cover them with cold water. Bring the water to the boil and boil the chestnuts gently for 5 minutes.

Remove the saucepan from the heat and, using a slotted spoon, remove the nuts, three or four at a time, from the water. Peel off the shells—the fine inner brown skin should come away easily with the outer shell. Any stubborn pieces of inner skin that remain within the crevices of the nuts can be removed with tweezers. If, towards the end, the nuts become harder to peel, simply bring the water back up to the boil.

-Fresh Fruit Puree-

Soft fruits and cooked fruits can be made into a purée by pressing them through a fine nylon sieve with the back of a wooden spoon, or by using a food processor.

After puréeing in a food processor, seeded fruits such as raspberries and blackberries should be passed through a nylon sieve to remove their seeds.

Always use a nylon sieve when puréeing fruit—metal, other than stainless steel, will react with the acid in the fruit and taint its flavour.

Soft fruits do not need to be cooked before puréeing. They can be puréed as they are or macerated first with a little sugar if preferred.

Firmer fruits, such as apples, gooseberries, apricots, plums and peaches, must be softened first by being cooked in a little water (just enough to prevent them from sticking) and a little sugar.

Fruits such as rhubarb and apples produce a lot of juice as they cook. This is best drained off before puréeing as it may make the purée too thin. Reserve the juice and use it, if necessary, to dilute the finished purée to the desired consistency.

As a guide, 450g (1lb) of soft fruit will yield 425 ml (¾ pint) purée, and 450g (1lb) of cooked fruit will yield 285ml (½ pint) purée.

-Melba Toast-

Melba toast, traditionally served as an accompaniment to soups, terrines and patés, is very simple to make. It can be made well in advance and stored for up to a month in an airtight container in a cool, dry, airy cupboard.

A traditional white sandwich loaf or tin loaf is best for making Melba toast. Slicing is easier if the bread is two or three days old.

Remove the crusts and cut the bread into as many almost paper-thin slices as required. Cut each slice in half diagonally. Arrange the triangles in a single layer on a baking tray and put them into the oven, heated to 150°C (300°F, gas mark 2), for about 1–1¼ hours, or until crisp and a pale golden yellow. As they dry out, the toasted triangles will curl attractively.

Remove the Melba toast from the oven, allow to cool, then store in an airtight tin. Warm through just before serving, or serve cold.

-Raspings-

These are fine breadcrumbs made from oven-dried bread—an ideal way to use up stale bread. Raspings can be used for coating boiled gammon or ham, croquettes and fish for frying; sprinkling over gratins; or adding a crispy finish to roast chicken.

Stale, traditional white bread is best for raspings. Cut the bread, with or without the crusts, into thin slices and arrange them in a single layer on one or two large baking trays. Put the bread into a cool oven, heated to about 140°C (275°F, gas mark 1) and leave for about 2½ hours or until it becomes very crisp and pale fawn in colour—it should not be allowed to become any darker.

Remove the bread from the oven and allow to cool, then put it into a strong polythene bag and crush it finely with a rolling pin. Alternatively, grind it finely in a food processor. Sift the crumbs through a wire sieve to remove any coarser pieces.

When stored in an airtight container, such as a jar with a screw-on lid or ground glass stopper, the crumbs will keep in a cool, dark, airy cupboard for three to four months.

-RECONSTITUTING YEAST-

Pour 150 ml (¼ pint) of lukewarm water (or milk, if specified in the recipe) into a small bowl. Add 1 level teaspoon caster sugar and stir until the sugar has dissolved.

Sprinkle the dried yeast into the sugared water and whisk well with a fork. Cover the bowl with cling film and stand aside in a warm place for 10–15 minutes until the yeast has become very frothy. Whisk and use as instructed in the recipe.

-STRAW POTATOES-

Straw potatoes, as their name implies, resemble stalks of straw. The easiest way to make them is with a mandolin cutter, adjusting the blade to cut peeled potatoes into the thinnest, narrowest strips possible. Alternatively, slice peeled potatoes into the thinnest slices you can cut with a sharp knife. Another method is to slice them on the wide cutting blade of a grater or in a food processor.

Taking a few slices at a time, pile them on top of each other and cut them into very fine strips about 3 mm (⅛ in) wide.

Rinse the potato strips in cold water, drain very well and dry in a clean tea towel. Deep fry in batches, in oil heated to 190°C (375°F), until golden brown and crisp, stirring with a slotted spoon to prevent them from sticking together. Using the slotted spoon, remove the straws from the hot oil and drain well on kitchen paper. Season lightly with salt and serve immediately.

-PUFF PASTRY-

225 G (8 OZ) PLAIN FLOUR
¼ LEVEL TEASPOON SALT
225 G (8 OZ) ENGLISH BUTTER
8 TABLESPOONS ICED WATER
1 TABLESPOON LEMON JUICE
PREPARATION TIME: 4 HOURS (MOSTLY UNATTENDED)
MAKES 600 G (1 LB 5 OZ)

Sift the flour and salt into a mixing bowl and rub in 30 g (1 oz) of the butter.

Place the remaining butter between two sheets of nonstick baking paper or greaseproof paper and beat into a 15 cm (6 in) square with a rolling pin.

Make a well in the centre of the flour, add the iced water and lemon juice and mix with a round-bladed knife to form a soft dough.

Turn the dough onto a lightly floured surface—a marble slab, if possible. Without kneading it, roll out the dough to a 25 cm (10 in) square using short, sharp strokes with the rolling pin to avoid squashing out the air which is trapped between the layers of dough.

Position the butter to look like a diamond in the centre of the square of dough. Bring the corners of the dough to the centre of the butter to enclose it, then turn the dough to square it up.

Roll out to an oblong about 46 cm (18 in) long. Fold the bottom third of the dough over the centre third, then bring the top third down over the bottom third, trapping as much air as possible between each layer. Seal the open edges with the rolling pin, then wrap in cling film and chill for 30 minutes. Do not chill for longer, as the butter will become too hard and will break through the dough when it is rolled out.

Unwrap the chilled dough and place it on the floured surface with the short, sealed ends to the top and bottom. Roll out and fold as before, then wrap and chill for another 30 minutes. Repeat this process six times more. (Keep note of how many times the dough has been folded by making a small indentation on a scrap of dough with your fingertip each time.)

When folded for the last time, wrap the dough in nonstick baking paper, put it into a polythene bag and refrigerate until required. It will keep well in the refrigerator for two or three days, or can be frozen for up to three months.

TWINKLE, TWINKLE ... Long before self-cleaning ovens were so much as a twinkle in their inventor's eye, products were available for removing burnt-on grease from household ovens to leave them sparkling like new. Most of these products, however, had to be augmented with a considerable amount of elbow grease.

FOODS IN SEASON

There is nothing quite like food eaten in season at its freshest and best. Once, the availability of British produce was strictly governed by the seasons but today's technology enables us to enjoy home-produced food for much longer

-FRUIT-

Apples *August to May*
Bilberries, Blackberries, Blackcurrants, Blueberries, Redcurrants *May to October*
Cherries *June to August*
Damsons *August to October*
Gooseberries *June to August*
Loganberries *May to October*
Pears *September to June*
Plums *August to October*
Raspberries *May to October*
Rhubarb *November to April,* outdoor *April to September*
Strawberries *May to October*

-VEGETABLES-

Artichokes, globe *January to June*
Artichokes, Jerusalem *October to March*
Asparagus *May to June*
Beans, broad *June to July*
Beans, fine green *March to May*
Beans, runner *June to October*
Beetroot *All year*
Brussels sprouts *August to April*
Cabbages 'Celtic' *October to February*; 'January King', 'Drumhead' *November to March*; 'Hispi' *May to June*; 'Primo' *May to August*; red *October to June*; green, white *All year*
Calabrese *May to November*
Carrots *July to May*
Cauliflower *All year*
Celeriac *August to January*
Celery *July to November* hothouse *May to July*
Courgettes *May to October*
Cress, salad *All year*
Cucumbers *January to November*
Curly kale *October to April*
Fennel *August to October*
Garlic *July to January*
Horseradish *June to September*
Kohlrabi *July to February*
Leeks *July to May*
Lettuce Flat *All year*; 'Webb's', 'Cos' *May to October*
Marrow *May to October*
Mushrooms *All year*
Onions *All year*
Parsley *March to November*
Parsnips *July to April*
Peas *May to October*
Potatoes 'Home Guard', *May to June,* boiling, steaming, salads; 'Arran Comet', 'Maris Bard', 'Ulster Sceptre' *May to July,* boiling, steaming, salads; 'Estima', 'Wilja' *July onwards,* boiling, baking, chipping; 'Cara', 'Romano' *August onwards,* boiling, baking, roasting, 'King Edward' *August onwards,* roasting, chipping, baking, mashing; 'Desirée' *August onwards,* boiling, roasting, chipping, mashing, baking; 'Pentland Crown' *August onwards,* baking, mashing, roasting; 'Pentland Dell' *August onwards,* baking, chipping; 'Pentland Squire' *August onwards,* boiling, baking, chipping, roasting; 'Maris Piper' *August onwards,* boiling
Radishes *All year*
Rocket *April to December*
Salsify *October to April*
Spinach *April to October*
Spring onions *All year*
Swedes *July to May*
Sweetcorn *July to November*
Tomatoes *All year*
Turnips *August to May*
Watercress *All year*

-FISH-

Most fish can be bought all year round but there are times when they are better and more plentiful—these are the times shown here. Availability can vary depending on region and weather conditions.

Most supermarkets sell a range of whole, small fish, such as trout, herring and mackerel, but most of the larger fish are sold ready filleted or cut into steaks. A supermarket may neither stock nor be able to order what you need, whereas a traditional fishmonger should always be able to help.

Ask your fishmonger for advice well in advance when you need something a little out of the ordinary, or fish for a special occasion which he may need to order specially.

-FLAT WHITE FISH-

Brill *June to February*
Dab *September to May*
Flounder *March to November*
Halibut *June to March*
Megrim *May to March*
Plaice *May to February*
Skate *May to February*
Sole, Dover *May to February*
Sole, lemon *May to March*
Turbot *April to February*
Witch *May to February*

-ROUND WHITE FISH-

Bass *August to March*
Bream, sea, black *July to December*
Bream, sea, red *June to February*
Catfish (Rockfish) *February to July*
Cod *June to February*
Conger eel *March to October*
Coley (Coalfish, Saithe) *August to February*
Gurnard, red *July to February*
Haddock *May to February*
Hake *June to March*
Huss (Dogfish, Flake, Rigg) *All year*
John Dory *All year*
Ling *September to July*
Monkfish (Angel fish) *All year*
Mullet, grey *September to February*
Mullet, red *May to November*
Pollack *May to September*
Redfish (Ocean perch, Norway haddock) *All year*
Whiting *June to February*

-OILY FISH-

Anchovy *June to December*
Herring *May to December*
Mackerel *All year*
Pilchards *January, February, April, November, December*
Sardines *January, February, April, November, December*
Sprats *October to March*
Tuna *All year*
Whitebait *February to July*

-SHELLFISH-

Cockles *May to December*
Clams *All year*
Crab, brown *April to December*
Crab, spider *April to October*
Crawfish (Spiny lobster) *April to October*
Lobsters *April to November*
Mussels *September to March*
Oysters *September to April*
Prawns *All year*
Prawns, Dublin Bay (Norway lobsters, Langoustines, Nephrops, Scampi) *April to November*
Scallops *September to March*
Shrimps *February to October*
Whelks *February to August*
Winkles *September to April*

-FRESHWATER FISH-

Carp farmed *All year*
Char, Arctic farmed *All year,* wild (from Coniston Water or Lake Windermere) *March 15 to September 30*
Eel farmed *All year*
Pike *All year*
Salmon farmed *All year,* wild *February to October*
Trout, brown England and Wales *available only in the open season which varies from area to area—ask your fishmonger.* Scotland *April 1 to September 30*
Trout, rainbow *All year*

-FEATHERED GAME-

Duck (teal, wigeon, mallard) inland *September 1 to January 31,* foreshore *September 1 to February 20* (teal and wigeon best *October to November,* mallard best *November to December*)
Grouse, black Devon and Somerset *August 20 to December 10,* New Forest *September 1 to December 10* (best *August to September*)
Grouse, red *August 12 to December 10* (best *August to October*)
Partridge *September 1 to February 1* (best *October to November*)
Pheasant *October 1 to February 1* (best *October to January*)
Quail *All year*
Snipe *August 12 to January 31* (best *December to January*)
Woodcock England and Wales *October 1 to January 31,* Scotland *September 1 to January 31* (best *November to December*)
Wood pigeon *All year*

-VENISON-

Deer, fallow Bucks in England, Wales and Scotland *August 1 to April 30;* does in England and Wales *November 1 to February 28/29,* Scotland *October 21 to February 15* (bucks best *October to November,* does best *December to February*)
Deer, red Stags in England and Wales *August 1 to April 30,* Scotland *July 1 to October 20*; hinds in England and Wales *November 1 to February 28/29,* Scotland *October 21 to February 15*
Deer, roe Bucks in England and Wales *April 1 to October 30,* Scotland *May 1 to October 20*; does in England and Wales *November 1 to February 28/29,* Scotland *October 21 to February 28/29* (bucks best *October,* does best *December to February*)

-FURRED GAME-

Hare *August to February* (best *October to January*)
Wild rabbit *All year* (best *September to November*)

Index

Index

Acknowledgments

The publishers wish to thank the following individuals and companies for their help during the preparation of THE COOK'S SCRAPBOOK.

Antiques & Things. Ernest Chance. Joss Graham Oriental Textiles. Nigel Harrison, Clarke & Carter Boatyard. Old Town. Stitches & Daughters.

The photographs of the recipes in this book are Reader's Digest copyright; the photographer for each is listed below.

Martin Brigdale, 1, 2-3, 4, 12, 14, 18, 24, 25, 29, 42, 46, 52, 57, 59, 61, 66, 67, 69, 88, 89, 96, 100, 107, 111, 114, 115, 129, 132, 134, 135, 137, 148, 149, 150, 153, 154, 155, 160, 172, 173, 174, 196, 202, 203, 205, 208, 210, 222, 235, 251, 254, 255, 256, 265, 300-5, 312-325, 331, 337, 343, 349, 355, 364, 367, 373, 379, 389, 391, 401, 406, 410, 414, 415, 423, 425.

Laurie Evans, 15, 20, 26, 28, 32, 33, 35, 36, 41, 47, 50, 53, 60, 79, 80, 81, 83, 84, 85, 91, 93, 102, 103, 117, 122, 123, 126, 128, 130, 131, 140, 143, 152, 163, 164, 175, 176, 177, 178, 179, 191, 195, 197, 198, 211, 212, 213, 218, 230, 232, 238, 239, 240, 242, 243, 257, 258, 296-9, 306-311, 328, 340, 342, 342, 347, 353, 354, 365, 369, 372, 376, 377, 382, 388, 411, 416, 420, 421, 422, 426, 430.

Vernon Morgan, *Home economist,* Kathy Man, 78, 125, 146, 147, 188, 216, 217, 250.

Pia Tryde, 16, 17, 27, 30, 31, 40, 43, 49, 56, 63, 68, 70, 72, 73, 75, 76, 77, 92, 94, 97, 105, 110, 112, 116, 118, 121, 124, 127, 141, 156, 162, 165, 166, 167, 182, 183, 189, 194, 199, 204, 206, 223, 224, 225, 229, 241, 244, 247, 248, 252, 253, 260, 261, 276-281, 288-295, 329, 330, 341, 346, 348, 356, 357, 362, 366, 371, 380, 381, 395, 396, 398, 400, 402, 408-9, 413, 424, 429.

Peter Williams, 13, 19, 21, 22, 23, 34, 37, 48, 51, 54, 55, 58, 62, 71, 74, 82, 86, 87, 90, 101, 104, 106, 113, 120, 133, 136, 138, 139, 142, 157, 161, 168, 170, 171, 180, 181, 184, 185, 186, 190, 200, 209, 214, 219, 226, 228, 231, 234, 245, 246, 259, 262, 263, 264, 266, 267, 270-275, 282-287, 333, 335, 336, 338, 350, 351, 352, 360, 361, 368, 384, 385, 386, 392, 397, 404, 405, 417, 418, 428, 431.

Cover potograph Vernon Morgan *Home economist,* Bridget Sargeson; *stylist* Fanny Ward.

Picture credits, T=top B=bottom. **1** Edwin Smith, **2-4** private collection, **10-11** Tim Woodcock, **13** Robert Opie, **15** Topham Picture Library, **17** Mary Evans Picture Library, **19** Hulton Deutsch, **20** Mary Evans Picture Library, **25** Hulton Deutsch, **26** Robert Opie, **30** The National Railway Museum, York, **32** Hulton Deutsch, **35** Topham Picture Library, **38-39** Images Colour Library, **41** Robert Opie, **44** The Mansell Collection, **45** (milkman) The Mansell Collection, (golden syrup) Robert Opie, (doorstep milk), (baker's boy) The Mansell Collection (fish and chip van) Topham Picture Library, (Co-op token), (hot chestnuts) The Mansell Collection, (handbell) courtesy of Tobias & The Angel, (ice-cream vendor) Barnabys Picture Library, (Wall's) Robert Opie, **47, 49, 51, 53** Robert Opie, **55** Science & Society Picture Library NRM, **57** Robert Opie, **59** Jennifer Davies, **60** The Mansell Collection, **64-65** Andrew Lawson, **67** Robert Opie, **68** The Mansell Collection, **70** Robert Opie, **74** Beamish North of England Open Air Museum, **76** Robert Opie, **79** The Ronald Grant Archive, **83-84** Robert Opie, **87** Imperial War Museum, **88** Robert Opie, **93** Imperial War Museum, **98** Hulton Deutsch, **98-99** private collection, **99** (Let your shopping) Robert Opie, (shop front) Hulton Deutsch, (horse flesh) Popperfoto, (spam), (Gert & Daisy), (dried egg) Robert Opie, (Grow your own), (National Wheatmeal) Imperial War Museum, (fish paste), private collection, **101** Punch Picture Library, **103** Hulton Deutsch, **104** Bill Doyle, **107** Billie Love Collection, **108-9** Images Colour Library, **110** Mary Evans Picture Library, **112** The Mansell Collection, **115** Robert Opie, **117** Mary Evans Picture Library, **120** Hulton Deutsch, **122** Topham Picture Library, **127** Angelo Hornak, **129, 131** Robert Opie, **132** Mary Evans Picture Library, **135** The Mansell Collection, **136** Beamish North of England Open Air Museum, **139** Robert Opie, **142** Barnabys Picture Library, **144-5** Andrew Lawson, **146** John Heseltine, **152** Mary Evans Picture Library, **155** Lilian Ross, **158** The National Trust, **158-9** The Mansell Collection, **159** (menu) The Mansell Collection, (tea table) The Bridgeman Art Library, (servants) Hulton Deutsch, (newspaper) John Frost Historical Newspaper Service, (Freeman's), (Leetham's) Robert Opie, (lighting fire) Popperfoto, (Zebo) Robert Opie, **161** Mary Evans Picture Library, **163** Public Record Office, **164** Mary Evans Picture Library, **166** Rex Features Ltd, **171** Mary Evans Picture Library, **173** Westminster City Archives/photo by Geremy Butler from 'The Book of London' by Ian Macmillan, courtesy of Michael Joseph Ltd, **177** Jennifer Davies, **181** The Bridgeman Art Library, **184** Retrograph Archive, **190** Robert Opie, **192-3** Robert Harding Picture Library/Adam Woolfitt, **194** Retrograph Archive, **196** Hulton Deutsch, **205, 209** Robert Opie, **210** Mary Evans Picture Library, **213** Hulton Deutsch, **219** Mary Evans Picture Library, **220** Robert Opie, **220-1** Robert Opie, **221** (bacon slicer) J. Sainsbury plc, (Oxo), (Toyland biscuits), (Swift's Cheddar) Robert Opie, (Waitrose coffee), (grocery counter) John Lewis Partnership Archives Collection, (Lewisham News) J. Sainsbury plc, **223** By kind permission of Imperial Publishing Limited, sole licensees of the copyright holders, Imperial Tobacco Limited, **224** Collections, **229** Robert Opie, **236-7** Sheila & Oliver Mathews, **239** Denis Gifford Collection, D.C Thomson & Co. Ltd, 'The Beano', **240** Gordon Coupe, **243** Robert Opie, **244** Mary Evans Picture Library/Henry Grant, **246, 251** Robert Opie, **252** Hulton Deutsch/Bert Hardy, **255** Mary Evans Picture Library, **258** From 'When We Were Very Young' by A.A. Milne; illustrated by E.H. Shepard, published by Methuen Children's Books, reproduced by permission of Reed Books, **262** B.T. Batsford Ltd, **265** Hulton Deutsch, **267** Denis Gifford Collection, **268-9** Holt Studios Ltd, **274** Beamish North of England Open Air Museum, **277** Robert Opie, **285** The Bridgeman Art Library, **290** Punch Picture Library, **295, 297** Robert Opie, **301** Topham Picture Library/Line illustration by E.H. Shepard, copyright under the Berne Convention, permission of Curtis Brown, **305** Hulton Deutsch, **309** Robert Opie, **310** Hulton Deutsch, **326-7** Patrick Eagar, **329** Robert Opie, **330** Mary Evans Picture Library, **335** By kind permission of Imperial Publishing Limited, sole licensees of the copyright holders, Imperial Tobacco Limited, **336** Mary Evans Picture Library, **338** The Royal Photographic Society, **340** Robert Opie, **344** National Museums & Galleries on Merseyside, **344-5** Retrograph Archive, **345** (family tea), The Mansell Collection, (ABC) Mary Evans Picture Library, (Willow tearoom), (counter hand) Hulton Deutsch, (shortbread) Retrograph Archive, (Sally), (swiss rolls), (Lyons nippy) Robert Opie, (Kardomah tea) Bramah Tea & Coffee Museum, **346** Hulton Deutsch, **350** Beamish North of England Open Air Museum, **352** Gill Corbishley, **355** The Mansell Collection, **358-9** Homer Sykes, photo from 'The Village Pub', Weidenfeld & Nicolson, **361** Retrograph Archive/Illustration © Thomas Henry Fisher, reproduced with permission of Macmillan Children's Books, taken from 'William the Explorer' by Richmal Crompton, published by Macmillan Children's Books, **365** Mary Evans Picture Library, **368** Line illustration by E.H. Shepard, copyright under the Berne Convention, permission of Curtis Brown, **372** Punch Picture Library, **374-5** The National Trust/Andreas von Einsiedel, **376** ET Archive, **381** Rural History Centre, University of Reading, **396, 400** Robert Opie, **405** Retrograph Archive, **408-9** Pia Tryde, **410** Hulton Deutsch/Bert Hardy, **413** Jennifer Davies, **417** By kind permission of Imperial Publishing Limited, sole licensees of the copyright holders, Imperial Tobacco Limited, **420** Edwin Smith, **422** Imperial War Museum, **425** The Bridgeman Art Library/Anthony Crane Collection, **427-8, 431-2** Mary Evans Picture Library, **433** Retrograph Archive, **434** T Retrograph Archive, B Hulton Deutsch, **435** Hulton Deutsch, **436** Beamish North of England Open Air Museum, **437** Reprinted from Good Housekeeping Magazine, **438** Retrograph Archive, **439** T Reprinted from Good Housekeeping Magazine, B Retrograph Archive, **440** Robert Opie, **441** T Reprinted from Good Housekeeping Magazine, B Robert Opie.

SEPARATIONS Saxon Photo Litho Ltd., Norwich.
PRINTING AND BINDING Grafica Editoriale Srl., Bologna